Thomas Nugent, Charles-Jean-François Hénault

A New Chronological Abridgement of the History of France

containing the publick transactions of that kingdom from Clovis to Lewis XIV, their wars, battles, sieges - their laws, manners, customs. Vol. 2

Thomas Nugent, Charles-Jean-François Hénault

A New Chronological Abridgement of the History of France
containing the publick transactions of that kingdom from Clovis to Lewis XIV, their wars, battles, sieges - their laws, manners, customs. Vol. 2

ISBN/EAN: 9783337270391

Printed in Europe, USA, Canada, Australia, Japan

Cover: Foto ©ninafisch / pixelio.de

More available books at **www.hansebooks.com**

Thomas Nugent, Charles-Jean-François Hénault

A New Chronological Abridgement of the History of France
containing the publick transactions of that kingdom from Clovis to Lewis XIV, their wars, battles, sieges - their laws, manners, customs. Vol. 2

ISBN/EAN: 9783337270391

Printed in Europe, USA, Canada, Australia, Japan

Cover: Foto ©ninafisch / pixelio.de

More available books at **www.hansebooks.com**

A NEW
CHRONOLOGICAL
ABRIDGMENT
OF THE
HISTORY
OF
FRANCE,

CONTAINING

The Publick Tranſactions of that kingdom, from Clovis to Lewis XIV. their wars, battles, ſieges, &c. their laws, manners, cuſtoms, &c.

Written in FRENCH by

M. HENAULT,

PRESIDENT of the Court of Inqueſts and Requeſts in the Parliament of Paris;

AND

Tranſlated into ENGLISH, with additional Notes, relative chiefly to the Hiſtory of England,

By Mr. NUGENT.

From the FIFTH EDITION, corrected and improved by the Author.

VOL. II.

Content, if hence th' unlearn'd their wants may view,
The learn'd reflect on what before they knew.
Pope's Eſſay on Criticiſm.

LONDON,
Printed for J. NOURSE, oppoſite *Catharine-Street* in the *Strand*.
MDCCLXII.

A Chronological Abridgment

OF THE

HISTORY of FRANCE.

PART THE SECOND.

The HISTORY of FRANCE.

1589.
Accession to the crown.

REMARKABLE EVENTS.

HENRY IV, *king of Navarre, born at Pau, Dec. the 13th 1553, the rightful heir to the crown, being the descendant of Robert count of Clermont, son of St. Lewis, which Robert married the heiress of Bourbon: he succeeds Henry III. in 1589, at the age of thirty-six. He was crowned at Chartres on Sunday the 27th of Feb. 1594, by Nicholas de Thou, bishop of Chartres. With him began the branch of Bourbon. He was king of Navarre, in right of his mother Jane d'Albret, the daughter of Henry king of Navarre, who was married to Antony of Bourbon, duke de Vendome. He was surnamed the Great.*

1589.

HENRY IV. is acknowledged king by most of the lords, whether catholics or protestants, who happened to be then at court, such as the prince of Conty, the duke de Montpensier, (called the dauphin prince in his father's life time, from his being possessed of the dauphiné of Auvergne) the marshals de Biron and d'Aumont, Sancy, who prevailed on the Swiss to stay, the duke de Longueville, la Force, Givry, Humieres, &c. Vitry withdrew, as likewise the duke d'Epernon, of whom the king was not fond, and who had taken it amiss that he should be obliged to yield the precedency to the marshals d'Aumont and de Biron: with him went off a considerable number of troops. The marshal de Matignon, by his prudent conduct, preserves Bourdeaux in the king's interest. An arret of the parliament of Toulouse against the king. His majesty finding his army diminished, raises the siege of Paris, begun by Henry III, and retires to Normandy, in order to be near the succours which he expected from the queen of England. The duke de Mayenne got himself declared lieutenant general of the kingdom, after he had caused the old cardinal of Bourbon, who was still a prisoner, to be proclaimed king in Paris: he then marched towards Dieppe, which city had been delivered up to Henry IV. by Aimar de Chattes, and was defeated at the battle of Arques, though his army was three times more numerous than the king's. After this victory, Henry having received a reinforcement of troops from England, advances towards Paris, and forces his way into five suburbs, but is obliged to retire upon the approach of the dukes de Mayenne and Nemours. He is acknowledged king of France by the Venetians.

1590.

The THIRD RACE. 3

WIVES.	CHILDREN.	1610. DEATH.	Cotemporary PRINCES.
Margaret of Valois, daughter of Henry II. Henry IV. was divorced from her by the authority of the Pope, in 1599, after a marriage of eight and twenty years. She died in 1625.		HENRY IV. is assassinated in the rue de la Feronnerie, on Friday the 14th of May 1610, at the age of fifty-seven, after having reigned one and twenty years. He was interred at St. Denis. His heart was sent to the college of Jesuits at la Fleche, in pursuance of his promise.	*Popes.* Sixtus V. 1590. Urban VII. 1590. Gregory XIV. 1591. Innocent IX. 1591. Clement VIII. 1605. Leo XI. 1605. Paul V. 1611. *Turkish Emperors.* Amurath III. 1595. Mahomet III. 1604. Achmet. 1617. *Emperor of Germany.* Rodolphus. 1612. *Kings of Spain and Portugal.* Philip II. 1598. Philip III. 1621. *Kings of England and Scotland.* Elizabeth 1603. James VI. 1625. *King of Denmark.* Christian IV. 1648.
Henry duke de Guise had been in love with this princess, before she became queen; and among his chimerical notions of grandeur, he had formed a design to marry her.		His funeral oration was pronounced at Rome in the chapel of the Vatican, before the pope and cardinals, an honour	*Kings of Sweden.* John. 1592. Sigismund, banished. 1599. Charles. 1611. *King of Poland.*
Mary of Medicis, daughter of Francis, great duke of Tuscany; married in 1600, died in 1642.	LEWIS XIII. N. duke of Orleans. 1611. John Baptist Gaston. 1660. Elizabeth, married to Philip IV. king of Spain. 1644 Christina, married to Victor Amadeus, prince of Piedmont, afterwards duke of Savoy. 1663. Henrietta Maria, wife of Charles I. king of Great Britain. 1669. *Natural Children:* Henry IV. had by Gabrielle d'Estrées, dutchess of Beaufort, who died in 1599. Cæsar, duke de Vendome. 1665. Alex-	which had never been done except to Charles V. and Philip II. The author of this detestable parricide, was Francis Ravillac, a native of Angouleme; about one or two and thirty years of age. He was executed in the PLACE DE GREVE the 27th of the same month. This monster had entered himself as a lay-brother among the Feuillans, of the rue St. Honore; who dismissed him, before he had made his monastic vows,	Sigismund III. king of Sweden. 1632. *Czars of Muscovy.* Fœdor Joannowitz. 1597. Boris Godenow. 1605. Fœdor Borissowitz. 1605. Demetrius, surnamed the Impostor. 1606. Basil Zuski. 1610. Demetrius, the second impostor. 1610.

B 2   be-

REMARKABLE EVENTS under HENRY IV.

1590.

The duke de Luxemburg, being sent to Rome by the catholics of the royal party, meets with a bad reception from the pope. The king lays siege to Dreux, and the duke de Mayenne marches to its relief. The battle of Yvry, fought on the 14th of March, where Henry IV. gained a second victory over the duke de Mayenne, though the duke's army was superior in numbers to the king's by one third: Henry does not make a right use of his victory, but shews himself tardy in laying siege to Paris. The cardinal de Bourbon, stiled Charles X, dies of the gravel the 9th of May, in his confinement at Fontenay in Poitou, aged sixty-seven: he was the younger brother of Antony de Bourbon, king of Navarre, and uncle to Henry IV. A cotemporary writer has observed, that much about the time when this cardinal was declared king, he sent one of the gentlemen of his bed chamber to Henry IV. with a letter, wherein he acknowledged that prince as his lawful sovereign. *(Journal of Henry IV. vol. 4. p. 310.)* And he is said to have unbosomed himself in these words to one of his confidents. "Do not think but I have my reasons for siding with "these people (the leaguers): do you imagine me to be igno- "rant that their designs are against the house of Bourbon, and "that they would have carried on the war, even if I had "never joined them? At least this may be said, that so long as I "am with them, they acknowledge one of the Bourbon family. "The king of Navarre will make his way; what I do, is only "to maintain the right of my nephews; both the king and the "queen-mother are well satisfied in regard to my intention." *(Chron. Noven.)* Cardinal Cajetan the legate, and Mendoza the Spanish ambassador, agreed to settle the crown of France on the infanta of Spain; the duke of Lorrain wanted it for his son; and the duke de Mayenne having lost all hopes of getting himself to be declared king, thought only to protract his authority, by traversing the election of a sovereign. Henry IV. takes Corbeil, Melun, and Lagny, and lays siege to Paris, where the spirit of fanaticism enabled the citizens to endure a most cruel famine with unshaken constancy. D'Andelot, son to the admiral de Coligny, finding that he was not of sufficient consequence in

the

The THIRD RACE.

CHILDREN.	1610. DEATH.
Alexander, *called the chevalier de Vendome, grand prior of France.* 1629. Catharine Henrietta, *married to Charles of Lorrain, duke d'Elbœuf.* 1663. By Henrietta de Balzac d'Entragues, *marchioness of Verneuil, who died in* 1633. Henry bishop of Metz, afterwards duke de Verneuil. 1682. Gabrielle Angelica, *married to the duke d'Espernon.* 1627. By Joan de Beuil, *countess de Moret.* Antony of Bourbon, count de Moret, *slain at the battle of Castelnaudary.* 1632. By Charlotte des Essarts, *countess de Romorantin.* Jane Baptist of Bourbon, *abbess of Fontevrault.* 1670. Mary Henrietta of Bourbon, *abbess of Chelles.* 1629. Charlotte des Essarts, *deceased in* 1651, *married to the marshal de l'Hopital, after having had children by Lewis of Lorrain, the last cardinal of Guise, and son of the scarred duke.* (Genealogical history of the house of France.)	*because they discovered that he was* a lunatic, and even a demoniac. *(Capitularies of the Feuillans.)* *There are letters patent of king Henry II. dated from Compiegne, on the 14th of May 1554, fifty-six years before the assassination of Henry IV. in the same month and on the same day, directing the rue de la Feronnerie to be widened, in order to open an easier passage for the king, from his palace of the Louvre to his house Des Tournelles.*

REMARKABLE EVENTS under HENRY IV.

the king's army, deserts to the league. A ridiculous procession of the leaguers, among whom were several monks in arms.

The death of Sixtus Quintus, who began to be disgusted with the Spanish faction. Montholon, upon the decease of Henry III, delivered the seals to the cardinal de Vendome, president of the council, who sealed in full council; the king afterwards caused the seals to be fixed in his presence, signing with his own hand, or appointing the sieur de Lomenie, who had the custody of the key of the great seal, to sign. The warrants, which used to be directed to the chancellor or the lord keeper, were now made to the council of state, having the custody of the seals, where marshal de Biron the father was president. At length the seals were restored to the chancellor de Cheverny, who had been deprived of them by Henry III. The leaguers had also their lords keepers; the duke de Mayenne gave the seals to Peter d'Espinac, archbishop of Lyons, and afterwards to Charles Boucher d'Orsay, master of requests, and first president of the grand council. The king of Spain sends the duke of Parma, with the flower of his troops, to the relief of Paris: the duke would have been too late, if Henry IV. had thought proper, as he had it in his power, to take the town by assault; but he never would consent to expose this city to the calamities, which generally attend the storming of a town. " I am, said he, the father of my " people; and like the good mother in Solomon, I had rather " be without the city of Paris, than have it ruined and destroyed " by the death of such a multitude of inhabitants." He raises the siege to give battle to the duke of Parma, who chuses to run no risk, but satisfied with relieving the capital, takes Lagny, and Corbeil, and after throwing a fresh supply of provisions into Paris, retires to the Netherlands. A decree of the Sorbonne against Henry IV. The war between the king's party and the leaguers is not confined to the neighbourhood of Paris, but extends itself with great fury over all the kingdom. The duke de Mercœur recovers Hennebon in Britany, which had been seized by the royalists: this prince had got to be the head of

the

The THIRD RACE.

MINISTERS.	WARRIORS.	MAGISTRATES.	EMINENT and LEARNED MEN.
Phil. Hurault de Cheverny. 1599. Franc. d'O, superintendant of the finances. 1594. He was likewise governor of Paris; at his decease, the king reserved the government of Paris for himself. Maximilian de Bethune de Rosny. 1641. Nic. de Harlay de Sancy, superintendant of the finances. 1629. J. Bochart, superintendant of the finances. 1630. *Secretaries of state.* Nic. de Neuville de Villeroy. 1617. Peter Brulart. 1608. Claude Pinart. 1605. Lewis Revol. 1594. Martin Ruzé. 1613. Lewis Potier de Gevres. 1630. P. Forget de Frenc. 1610. Ant. de Lomenie. 1638. Peter Brulart de Puifieux. 1640. Antony Potier. 1621. Paul Phelypeaux de Pontchartrain. 1621.	*Constable.* Henry de Montmorency. 1614. *Marshals of France.* Albert de Gondy de Retz. 1602. Armand de Gontaut de Biron. 1592. James Goyon de Matignon. 1597. John d'Aumont. 1595. William de Joyeuse. 1592. H. de la Tour de Bouillon. 1623. Charles de Gontaut de Biron. 1602. Cl. de la Chastre. 1614. Ch. de Cossé de Brissac. 1621. John de Montluc de Balagny. 1603. John de Beaumanoir de Lavardin. 1614. Henry de Joyeuse de Bouchage. 1608. Alphonsus Corse d'Ornano. 1610. Urban de Laval de Bois-dauphin. 1629. Will. de Hautemer de Grancey. 1613. Fr. de Bonne de Lesdiguieres. 1626.	*Chancellors.* Phil. Hurault de Cheverny. 1599. Fr. de Monthoulon. 1590. Charles de Bourbon, cardinal de Vendome, lord keeper. 1594. Pompone de Bellievre. 1607. He had served under five kings. Nic. Brulart de Sillery. 1624. *First president.* Achilles de Harlay. 1616. *Attorneys general.* James de la Guesle 1612. P. Pithou, nominated at the reduction of Paris, to exercise that office, till la Guesle returned from Tours. Eust. de Megrigny, practises at Chalons. *Advocates general.* Hugh de Lestre, nominated the 16th of August 1589, to practise at Chalens. Lewis Duret. 1616. Antony Hotman. 1596. Lewis Servin. 1626. Ant. Loisel, nominated upon the reduction of Paris, to practise	James Amiot. 1593. John d'Angennes. 1593. Ant. de Baif. 1592. Will. Barclay. 1605. Cæsar Baronius. 1607. Will. Salufte du Bartas. 1590. Theodore Beza. 1605. Johan. Bodinus. 1596. Soffroy Colignon, chancellor of Navarre: *a cross answer from the king, cost him his life.* 1606. Hannibal Caracci, painter. 1609. Michael de Castelnau. 1592. Peter Charron. 1603. Flor. Chretien, preceptor to Henry IV. 1596. Guy Goquille. 1603. James Cujas. 1590. Steph. Duranty. 1589. James Fayed'Espesses. 1590. Henry Stephen. 1598. Cl. Fauchet. 1603. Robert Garnier. 1595. La Gaucherie, preceptor to Henry IV. Gilbert Genebrard. 1597. Bernard de Girard du Haillan. 1610. Fr. Hofman. 1590. Card. de Lenoncourt. 1592. Justus Lipsius. 1606. Aldus Manutius. 1597. Phil. Melancthon. 1597. H. de Mesmes. 1596. Francis Miron. 1608. Lewis Molina. 1600. Michael de Montagne. 1592.

B 4

REMARKABLE EVENTS under HENRY IV.

the league in that province, independent on the duke de Mayenne; and had entered into a treaty with the king of Spain: but though Philip II. and he were united againſt Henry IV, it was from different views; both of them wanted to become maſters of Britany; the duke de Mercœur, in right of his wife, the heireſs of Penthievre; and Philip the ſecond, for his daughter by Elizabeth of France. Monſieur de Leſdiguieres beats the duke of Savoy, and after taking Grenoble, is made governor of that city. The parliament of Aix declare the duke of Savoy governor and lieutenant general of Provence, *under the crown of France*. Gregory XIV. excommunicates Henry IV. The prophecies of St. Malachy concerning the pontifical elections, are forged during the conclave in which Gregory XIV. was choſen.

Prince Maurice ſurprizes Breda by the ſtratagem of a boat laden with turf, in which ſome ſoldiers were concealed.

1591.

Gregory XIV. publiſhes monitory letters in France againſt Henry IV; which were condemned to the flames by the parliaments ſitting at Tours and Chalons. The king on his part renews the edicts of pacification in favour of the proteſtants. The chevalier d'Aumale undertakes to ſurprize St. Denis in behalf of the league, but is ſlain in the attempt. The duke de Mercœur, at the head of the leaguers and the Spaniſh troops, defeats the duke de Montpenſier before the town of Craon in Anjou. Henry IV. makes an unſucceſsful attempt againſt the gate of St. Honoré: the French ſtile it *la journée des farines**. The king takes Chartres the 12th of April. The leaguers make themſelves maſters of Chateau-Thierry.

The brave la Noue, fighting for his ſovereign, is ſlain before the caſtle of Lambale. The young duke de Guiſe, ſon of the *ſcarred* duke, eſcapes from his confinement at Tours. The king was not at all ſorry for this event, as it was likely to create new diviſions among the leaguers, by giving them another pretender to the crown. The young cardinal de Bourbon, ſon of Lewis I. prince

---

* Or *the day of corn:* he ſent ſeveral waggons laden with corn, attended by ſixty determined officers, in the diſguiſe of peaſants, to ſeize the above gate, not knowing that the leaguers had cauſed it to be walled up.

of

The Third Race.

		Magistrates.	Eminent and Learned Men.
		Advocates general.	S. Philip de Neri. 1595.
		tife till the return of the parliament from Tours. It was he that proposed the general proceſſion, which is performed every year on the 22d of March. He wrote the life of M. Pithou, and is the author of the cuſtomary inſtitutes, which the firſt preſident de Harlay ſaid to be worth its weight in gold. Simon Marion. 1605. Cardin le Bret. 1654.	Lewis of Gonzaga, duke de Nevers. 1595. John Nicot. 1600. *It was he that introduced the uſe of tobacco into France.* Gilles de Noailles. 1606. Arnaud d'Oſſat, cardinal. 1604. John Paſſerat. 1602. Nic de Pellevé, cardinal. 1594. Peter Pithou. 1596. Chriſtopher Plantin, printer. 1598. Lancelot Voiſin de la Popeliniere. 1608. Ph. des Portes. 1606. Nic. Rapin. 1607. John Riolan. 1605. Fr. d'Epinay de St. Luc. 1597. Joſ. Scaliger. 1609. John de Serres. 1598. FauſtusSocinus.1604. Orlando Taſſo, muſician 1594. Torquato Taſſo. 1595. *It is owing to Virgil, ſays Balzac, that Taſſo is not the prince of poets; and to Taſſo, that Virgil is not the only poet.* Fr. Tolet, *the firſt Jeſuit that was made cardinal.* 1596. Henry IV. acknowledged the ſervices, which this cardinal had done him, by ordering magnificent obſequies for him in the churches of Notre Dame, at Paris and Rouen : the great uſe he

REMARKABLE EVENTS under HENRY IV.

of Condé, and nephew to cardinal Charles de Bourbon, forms a third party to get himself declared king, to which he was advised by Touchard his preceptor, by d'Elbenne, and by du Perron, afterwards cardinal, who betrayed him: he died in 1594, lamented by Henry IV, to whom he had been reconciled.

The marriage between Henry de la Tour, viscount de Turenne, and Charlotte de la Marck, heiress of Bouillon. The viscount de Turenne, having had only one child, who died in 1594, the very day of his birth, eight days before his mother, kept his wife's portion, in consequence of a will, which she was said to have made in her last illness. This same nobleman surprised Stenay on the day of his nuptials, was made marshal of France the year following, and after his marriage was stiled duke de Bouillon. The king had contrived the match, to hinder this heiress from being carried off by the duke of Lorrain, or by the duke de Nevers, the one his declared enemy, the other a suspected ally, each of whom wanted her for his son. This duke de Bouillon took to his second wife the daughter of William prince of Orange, who preserved her husband's life, by her courage and resolution, at the time when marshal Biron was condemned to death; for she retired to Sedan, and threatened to deliver that town up to the enemy, if a prosecution were carried on against the duke: by this lady he had the duke de Bouillon, so famous in the civil wars of Paris, and marshal de Turenne. The king lays siege to Rouen, which is valiantly defended by Andrew-Baptist (afterwards admiral) de Villars Brancas. The council of sixteen, in their great presumption, pretend to dictate to the duke de Mayenne; and propose to Philip II. a match between his daughter and the young duke de Guise, in order to put them in possession of the crown. They likewise take advantage of the duke de Mayenne's absence, to hang Brisson the first president, Larchet a counsellor of Parliament, and Tardif a counsellor of the Chatelet, all three suspected by that junto. The duke de Mayenne, at his return, caused four of their members to be hanged; which put an end to the tyranny of the council of sixteen.

The

				EMINENT and LEARNED MEN.
				he was of to this prince, contributed to the recalling of the Jesuits. Horace Turselíin. 1599. Tycho Brahe. 1601. Blaise de Vigenere. 1596. Nic. Vignier. 1596. Ger. Vossius. 1609.

The HISTORY *of* FRANCE.

REMARKABLE EVENTS *under* HENRY IV.

The prefident Jeannin, and Villeroy, notwithftanding they had acceded to the league, are fufpected by the council of *fixteen*, from their having a real regard for religion, and for their country.

1592.

The king advancing to reconnoitre the army under the duke of Parma, who was marched from Flanders a fecond time, to the relief of Rouen, at that time clofely befieged, is in great danger at Aumale, by expofing his perfon, and receives a wound in the reins, the only one he ever received in his life. He is obliged to raife the fiege of Rouen, as he had raifed that of Paris: to diminifh the difgrace, he gave out in excufe, that he defigned to meet the duke of Parma, who indeed was marching towards him, but wanted only to fuccour Rouen: as foon as this general gained his point, he thought of retiring, yet not till he had made himfelf mafter of Caudebec, on which fide the city of Rouen was too much ftreightened. The duke had his arm fhattered at the taking of this town, and his army was juft furrounded by the French, when he luckily extricated himfelf by his military fkill, and by the connivance of the marfhal de Biron, who intended, it is faid, to protract the war: he paffes the Seine, before his fcheme is in the leaft fufpected; and the king finding it impoffible to purfue him, for want of being properly fupported by the chiefs of his army, the duke makes his retreat to the Netherlands. The war continues in Britany, between the prince of Conty, and the duke de Mercœur: the French fends marfhal d'Aumont thither to fupply the place of the prince de Dombes, who was gone to take poffeffion of the government of Normandy, vacant by the death of his father the duke de Montpenfier. The taking of Epernay was purchafed very dear, by the death of Armand marfhal de Biron: he was father of Charles, afterwards marfhal of France, and beheaded in 1602. Armand wrote fome commentaries, the lofs of which is greatly lamented by M. de Thou: he had given his Chriftian name to cardinal Richelieu, to whom he ftood god-father; he was alfo a zealous catholic; and it is faid that he afked the king to grant him the fovereignty of the county of Perigord.

Anthony

REMARKABLE EVENTS under HENRY IV.

Anthony Scipio, duke de Joyeuse, is routed by the royalists at the battle of Villemur, and drowned in the river Tarn. Father Angel de Joyeuse, his brother, having after a life of great dissipation turned Capuchin friar, throws off the religious habit with the pope's permission, and takes his place among the factious leaguers. William, their father, marshal of France, died in the beginning of the year, and though he had seven male children, yet none of his posterity are left. The duke d'Epernon returns to the king's service. Lesdiguieres obtains some advantages in Piedmont. The duke of Parma dies on the 3d of December, at the age of forty seven, just as he was preparing to march into France the third time. This prince by his valour and good conduct shewed himself worthy of being the son of the celebrated dutchess of Parma, governess of the Netherlands. At Paris the divisions increase between the royalists, who where stiled the *politicians*, and the council of sixteen. The cardinal de Gondy, and the marquis of Pisani, repair to Rome on the behalf of the king; but are very ill received. Seraphin, auditor of the *Rota*, a man of spirit and abilities, finding that pope Clement VIII. started new difficulties every day against granting absolution to Henry IV, said to him plainly: *Holy father, permit me to tell you, that Clement VII. lost the kingdom of England, by being over complaisant to Charles V; and Clement VIII. will lose the kingdom of France, if he persists in his partiality to Philip II.*

The institution of the fathers of the christian doctrine.

1593.

The assembly of the pretended states convened at Paris, by the duke de Mayenne. An absurd proposal of the Spaniards, for abolishing the Salic law, and not acknowledging the king as lawful sovereign, even if he were to become a catholic, and for declaring the Spanish infanta queen of France. The parliament of Paris published a solemn arret, agreeable to the fundamental laws of the kingdom: M. le Maitre, who officiated there as first president, shewed an extraordinary firmness on this occasion. The duke de Mayenne, despising the chimerical notions of the Spaniards, and vexed to see himself slighted by that nation, prevails on the states to consent to a conference between the catholics of both parties: and this was all the success attending this assembly,

REMARKABLE EVENTS under HENRY IV.

assembly, from which the Spaniards had promised themselves such mighty advantages. The conference of Surene, begun the 29th of April, in spite of the duke de Feria, of the cardinal legate, and of cardinal Pellevé. Renaud de Beaune, archbishop of Bourges, acquired great honour on this occasion. The king makes his abjuration in the church of St. Denis, on Sunday the 25th of July, and notifies it to all the parliaments. A truce for three months with the leaguers, during which the king sent the duke de Nevers, Claud d'Angennes bishop of Mans, and Lewis Seguier dean of Notre Dame, to pope Clement VIII. In the mean time Arnaud d'Offat, afterwards cardinal, was negotiating with cardinal Tolet a Jesuit, who, although a Spaniard, did great service to Henry IV.

Peter Barriere is executed for having formed a design to murder the king; he was detected by a Dominican friar of Florence, whose name was Seraphin Baucher *.

The duke de Mayenne, suspecting that the duke de Nemours intended to render himself independent in Lyons, causes him to be arrested: he was his half brother, being born of his mother Anne of Este, by a second marriage. Corisande de Guiche, widow of the count de Grammont, desirous of being revenged of the infidelity of Henry IV, who had been once her lover, encourages the count de Soissons, and Catharine, sister of Henry IV, in their scheme of marrying against the king's will: but this marriage did not take place. The count de Soissons died in 1612, in very little esteem, on account of his levity, having changed religion and party several times: he was father to Lewis, killed at Marfée.

This year was published the *Spanish Catholicon*. The year following the *Abridgment of the states of the league* was added to it, and the whole was intitled the *Menippean Satyr*. M. le Roy, almoner to the young cardinal de Bourbon, and afterwards canon of Rheims, was the sole author of the Catholicon. As for the *Abridgment of the states*, there were several hands concerned in it: Passerat and Rapin, two famous poets, composed the verses. M. Gillot, counsellor of the parliament of Paris, by whom we have Calvin's elogium in Latin, wrote the harangue of the cardinal

* Others say his name was *Bianchi.*

legate.

REMARKABLE EVENTS under HENRY IV.

legate. Florent Chretien, a man of wit, compofed the fpeech of cardinal Pellevé: we are indebted to the learned Peter Pithou for that of M. d'Aubray, which is the beft of the whole; and to Rapin, for the difcourfe of the archbifhop of Lyons, as alfo for that of doctor Rofe, head of the college of Navarre, and bifhop of Senlis. In all probability the Menippean Satyr did as much fervice to Henry IV. as the battle of Ivry: for the force of ridicule is greater than people imagine.

1594.

The king's abjuration gives the finifhing ftroke to the league, in fpite of the oppofition of Rome.

Vitry, governor of Meaux, had fhewn his fubmiffion to the royal authority the preceding year, and delivered the keys of that town to the principal inhabitants, who furrendered themfelves to the king. This year d'Alincourt puts his majefty in poffeffion of Pontoife; the marfhal de la Chaftre furrenders. Orleans and Bourges; and Ornano, the city of Lyons. Paris at length opens her gates, by the prudent management of the count de Briffac, affifted by the Sieurs de Vic, de Belin, the prefident le Maitre, de Molé, and other members of the parliament, by l'Huilliers, provoft of the merchants, and by the fheriffs. The king confirmed la Chaftre in his poft of marfhal of France, which had been conferred upon him by the duke de Mayenne. The fame thing happened to the marfhal de Bois-dauphin, (Laval): Chanvalon forefaw this, when he told the duke, *that he was making baftards, who would one day or other be legitimated at his expence.*

The duke de Feria retires from Paris with the Spanifh troops; and the moft obftinate leaguers are expelled the city. The four faculties of the univerfity, affembled by James d'Amboife the rector, make their fubmiffion to the king. Peter Pithou and Antony Loifel, are commiffioned to cancel every thing in the parliament rolls that might be injurious to the memory of the late fovereign, or to Henry IV. The parliament of Tours, with Achilles de Harlay at their head, return to Paris.

Admiral de Villars reftores the city of Rouen to the king, who confirms him in his feveral dignities and governments. The duke de Guife makes his peace with his majefty. All the cities throughout the kingdom exprefs their eagernefs to acknowledge

Henry

REMARKABLE EVENTS under HENRY IV.

Henry IV, who was crowned at Rheims in the month of February.

Balagny, the baftard fon of John de Montluc, bifhop of Valence, is confirmed in the fovereignty of Cambray, which he puts under the king's protection. A famous procefs of the univerfity againft the Jefuits, in which the rectors of the feveral parifhes of the city of Paris were a party: Antony Arnauld was council for the univerfity, Dolé for the rectors, and Duret for the fociety of Jefuits. The Spaniards take la Capelle, and Henry IV. the town of Laon.

John Chatel attempts to affaffinate the king, who fortunately comes off with only a wound in the lip. The parricide is publickly executed. The Jefuits are banifhed out of France by an arret of the parliament of Paris, which was not executed within the jurifdiction of the parliaments of Bourdeaux, and Touloufe; but the king recalled thofe fathers a few years after.

The firft edition of Pithou's work on *the liberties of the Gallican church,* comprized in eighty three articles; and printed at Paris with a privilege: the maxims here contained, have in fome meafure the force, though not the authenticity of laws. The prefent king acknowledged the importance of them by his edict in 1719, in which the fiftieth article is quoted. The clerks of the difpatches at the court of Rome quote the articles of our liberties in their certificates.

1595.

France declares war againft Spain. The king reduces the remainder of his kingdom, and Charles marfhal de Biron has a confiderable fhare in thefe fucceffes. The Spaniards retake Cambray, and drive Balagny from that city, who does not appear to be much affected with the lofs of his principality: but the uneafinefs it gave his wife, who was fifter to the brave Buffy, coft that lady her life. The duke de Nevers affronted by an angry expreffion of Henry IV, dies of chagrin. Admiral Villars is killed in cold blood before Dourlens, by order of Contreras, the commiffary general of the Spaniards. Marfhal d'Aumont receives a mortal wound before the town of Comper; and d'Humieres dies before Ham, an event which draws tears from Henry IV. The duke d'Epernon aimed to be mafter of Provence,

though

REMARKABLE EVENTS under HENRY IV.

though he had been reconciled to the king; he continues to bid defiance to this prince. The king confers the government of Provence upon Charles duke de Guife, the fon of him who was killed at Blois, in order to fet him in oppofition againft the duke d'Epernon: but was it not imprudent in him to beftow this government on a prince, whofe family had *an old rufty pretenfion*, as the cardinal d'Offat expreffes it, to this province? This was the reafon that the chancellor de Cheverny protefted openly in council againft the patent granted by his majefty, and infifted on having his proteft regiftered in the parliaments of Paris and Aix, before he would fign it. A peace is concluded with Lorrain.

The fight or *fkirmifh* of *Fontaine Francoife* on the 5th of June, when Henry IV, having rafhly expofed himfelf with a very fmall body of horfe, gave chafe to eighteen thoufand men, commanded by Ferdinand de Velafco and the duke de Mayenne. The king wrote to his fifter, after this affair: *you was very near inheriting my eftate.* His majefty concludes a truce with the duke de Mayenne, and with the duke de Mercœur, who perfifted in their revolt, notwithftanding the former had loft feveral towns in Burgundy, and the latter in Britany. The pope grants abfolution to the king the 17th of September, and the cardinals du Perron and d'Offat receive it in his name. It was upon this occafion, according to a MS. of M. de Salo, that the king, defirous of keeping fair with the court of Rome, " gave the title of *coufin* indifferently " to all the cardinals; whereas before that time they were ftiled " only *dear friend*, unlefs they happened to be princes or favou- " rites." Don Antonio, the prior of Crato, dies at Paris, and appoints the king his heir to the crown of Portugal.

The dutchy of Thouars created a peerage: the letters patent were not regiftered till 1599.

1596.

The duke de Mayenne makes his peace with the king: it would have been more to his advantage, had he done it fooner; but though he is allowed to have been a great man, yet it is faid of him, that he was not very expert in making either war or peace. The new duke de Nemours and the duke de Joyeufe are reconciled to the king: the latter, who afterwards returned to the order of Capuchins, from whence he had been taken by the

REMARKABLE EVENTS under HENRY IV.

leaguers, and who had so long and so furiously supported the rebellion in Languedoc, is created marshal of France: on the other hand the marshal de Montmorency, for the services done the king in the same war, is made constable. Thus was Henry IV. obliged, during his whole life, to share his favours between his enemies and his servants. The duke de Guise recovers Marseilles for the king, by the bravery of a person named Libertat; though the Spaniards were in possession of the harbour. The duke d'Epernon is reconciled to his majesty, in consequence of the advantages which the duke de Guise had obtained over the duke of Savoy and himself. Francis de la Ramée is hanged at the Greve in Paris: this was a young man, about three or four and twenty years of age, who pretended to be the son of Charles the IXth, and in that quality had been at Rheims, to get himself crowned king.

The archduke Albert having entered upon the government of the Netherlands, of which the count de Fuentes had only a temporary administration, makes himself master of Calais and Ardres: (they were restored at the peace of Vervins.) Henry IV. carries the town of la Fere, after a long and difficult siege.

A treaty of offensive and defensive alliance signed by France, England, and Holland. The earl of Essex having surprized and plundered the town of Cadiz, sets fire to all the ships in the harbour: the damage was computed by the Spaniards at upwards of twenty millions of ducats.

Alexander of Medicis is sent legate into France, and received in a most honourable manner. Henry IV. sends the duke de Piney to Rome. The duke de Mercœur perseveres in his revolt in Britany, which, together with the troubles in Picardy, emboldens the Huguenots to make more exorbitant demands: the marshal de Bouillon and the duke de la Trimouille encourage them under hand.

A declaration annulling the privileged seat, which the dukes de Joyeuse and d'Epernon had in parliament.

An assembly of the notables held at Rouen, the plague being then at Paris. In this assembly there happened to be a dispute of precedency between messieurs de Joyeuse and de Luxemburg, for which reason neither of them was present. At Rouen the

king

REMARKABLE EVENTS under HENRY IV.

king received the order of the garter from queen Elizabeth by the hands of the earl of Shrewfbury.

An arret of parliament on the 24th of July, declaring Charlotte de la Trimouille innocent of the charge, of having been an accomplice, in the poifoning of her hufband the prince of Condé.

1597.

The Spaniards furprize the city of Amiens; an event which fpreads a terror throughout the kingdom, and ftrengthens the prefumption of the Huguenots. *Let us go,* fays Henry IV, hearing of this news, *we have acted the king of France long enough, it is now time to act the king of Navarre:* upon which he befieged the town, and took it, in fpite of the archduke Albert. The duke of Savoy is beaten on every fide by M. de Lefdiguieres.

Spain begins to long for peace, and the pope is defirous of promoting a reconciliation between the two crowns.

A confpiracy of one Peter Ouin, to affaffinate the king.

1598.

At length the duke de Mercœur fubmits to Henry IV, and gives his only daughter, and heirefs, to Cæfar-Monfieur, duke de Vendome, the king's legitimated fon. Philip Emmanuel duke de Mercœur, was grandfon of Antony duke of Lorrain, the elder brother of Claude, who had attempted to deprive him of that dutchy. (See the year 1550.) Therefore Philip was not of the branch of Lorrain, which came and fettled in France under king Francis I. Nicholas his father, whofe daughter had been married to Henry III, was made duke de Mercœur in 1576, and by this marriage Philip was become the brother-in-law of the late king. After the accommodation concluded this year with Henry IV, he went to affift the emperor Rodolphus in Hungary againft the Turks, where he acquired great honour, and died of a purple fever in 1602. The king grants confiderable advantages in fupport of this match; and from thence came the great eftate of the family of Vendome. Among other fignal favours which he did to Cæfar-Monfieur, we are to obferve that he erected the county of Beaufort into a dutchy and peerage fo early as the year 1597, upon condition that this dutchy fhould go firft to his mother the marchionefs of Monceaux,

REMARKABLE EVENTS under HENRY IV.

and with the privilege *that the said dutchy of Beaufort should, in the person of the said lady, her heirs and representatives, take rank and precedency in all places and public meetings, where dukes and peers are present, as if it had been created immediately after the dutchy and peerage of Montmorency.* The king further conferred upon him this year (1598) the dutchy and peerage of Vendome, to have and to enjoy it from the day of its ancient erection in 1514; and made him take the oath in parliament on the 9th of March 1606, at the age of eleven years and nine months. At length his majesty published a declaration in 1610, granting rank and precedency to Cæsar-Monsieur, immediately after the princes of the blood. Upon the decease of Henry IV, this rank was disputed with his son; and on the 31st of December 1619, the duke de Vendome received the order of the Holy Ghost after the dukes de Guise, de Mayenne, and de Joyeuse. True it is that this same duke de Vendome took his seat in the beds of justice of 1619 and 1622, after the princes of the blood, and before the duke d'Uzès; but this was as duke de Penthievre, a more ancient peerage than those of Beaufort and Vendome. Francis de Vendome, the son of Cæsar, took his seat in parliament in 1649 and 1663, only from the day of registering the peerage of Beaufort. And lastly, Lewis XIV. having, by his declaration of the fifth of May 1694, granted a precedency over all the peers, to the duke de Maine and to the count de Touloufe, Lewis de Vendome, the grandson of Cæsar, recovered the rank assigned him by the declaration of 1610, took his oath in parliament on the 8th of June 1694, and seated himself next to the duke de Maine.

Britany makes its submission. The edict of Nantes in favour of the protestants : the president de Thou, and Calignon chancellor of Navarre, had the drawing of the memoirs, upon which this edict was framed. The memoirs of the duke de Sully mention also messieurs de Schomberg and Jeannin; on the contrary Varillas says it was Daniel Chamier, the most learned of the protestant clergy, that drew the edict.

The treaty of Vervins, concluded the 2d of May betwixt the kings of France and Spain: the ministers on the part of France were the sieurs de Bellievre and de Sillery; on the part of Spain, messieurs

REMARKABLE EVENTS under HENRY IV.

messieurs Richardot, Taxis, and Verreikens: the mediators in the pope's name were the cardinal of Florence, and Francis Gonzaga, bishop of Mantua; the ambassadors of the duke of Savoy were also admitted. By this treaty the king of Spain was left in possession of the county of Charolois; but in every other respect it proved favourable to France, and indeed gave the first blow to the power of the house of Austria. This county of Charolois, which had been in possession of that house, with the right of sovereignty reserved to France, devolved at last to the house of Condé; Lewis II, prince of Condé, having seized it for the moneys due to him by Philip IV, king of Spain, and likewise obtained a decree of the parliament of Burgundy in his favour, against which Charles II, the son of that king, never lodged an appeal.

A treaty of accommodation between Henry IV. and the grand duke of Tuscany, in regard to the restitution of some islands on the coast of Provence, which that prince had seized during the civil war. D'Ossat, who concluded this treaty, was made a cardinal the same year. The death of Philip II, the 12th of September. Christopher de Mora, one of that prince's officers, shewed a great mark of fidelity to his dying sovereign; for Philip III, his successor, having applied to Mora for a particular key which was in his custody, the honest servant chose to incur the displeasure of his master's son, who was just upon the point of becoming his sovereign, rather than commit a breach of trust. The infanta Clara Eugenia, daughter of Philip II. by his third wife Elizabeth of France, is married to Albert the archduke; and Philip III. confirms the renunciation of the sovereignty of the Netherlands, which the king his father had made in favour of the infanta. An arret of parliament against William Rose, bishop of Senlis, a famous leaguer, forbidding him to set foot within his diocese, for a twelvemonth.

1599.

Catherine, the king's sister, is married to the duke of Bar, the son of Charles duke of Lorrain. The marshal de Joyeuse returns to the order of Capuchins. The king's marriage with Margaret of Valois, is declared null and void by the pope's commissioners, with consent of parties. The death of Gabrielle d'Estrée, whom it was said the king intended to marry. *She had been married in the beginning of her amours with Henry IV. to M.*

REMARKABLE EVENTS under HENRY IV.

de Liancourt of Picardy, and afterwards divorced from him, with his confent, by the bifhop of Amiens, to whom they both declared upon oath, that they had never been joined in wedlock with mutual agreement, and that there was no relation at all between them. (Mem. de Cheverny.) The king makes a promife of marriage to mademoifelle d'Antragues. A negotiation is entered into with the duke of Savoy, for reftoring the marquifate of Saluzzo, which had been invaded in full peace by Charles Emmanuel duke of Savoy, in the reign of Henry III, during the troubles of the league: the duke himfelf undertakes a journey to France, hoping to evade the king's demand.

1600.

Henry IV. being inflexible with regard to the marquifate of Saluzzo, declares war againft the duke, who lofes Breffe and Savoy in three months. The conference of Fontainebleau, concerning du Pleffis Mornay's book, intitled, *The inftitution of the Eucharift:* cardinal Perron had intirely the advantage in this difpute. They had both of them, as M. Huet obferves, more reputation than learning; and in vain do we now endeavour to find in their writings, on what that reputation was founded.

The king marries Mary of Medicis at Lyons; and appoints madame de Guercheville, whom he had made love to without fuccefs, to be one of her ladies of honour, faying, *that fince fhe was a lady of real honour, fhe fhould be in that poft with the queen his wife.* He was not more fortunate in his addreffes to the dutchefs of Mantua, and to the princefs of Condé. The battle of Newport gained by prince Maurice of Naffau, againft Albert archduke of Auftria.

An edict concerning the regulation of the *tailles*, by which the king declares that the military profeffion fhall no longer ennoble his fubjects, and that it fhall not even be fuppofed to have completely ennobled thofe, who followed it only fince the year 1563, viz. fince the æra of the religious wars in France. This article requires fome explication. All *men at arms* were gentlemen at the time of Lewis XII, that is, all thofe who compofed the companies under particular orders*; but by the gentlemen of thofe

* The ordinary men at arms were firft reduced into certain companies, and under particular orders, by Charles VII. in 1444.

REMARKABLE EVENTS under *HENRY IV.*

days, we are not to underſtand ſuch as were deſcended from a noble ſtock ; it was ſufficient for this purpoſe that a member of the third eſtate only followed the profeſſion of arms, without bearing any other employment: by a much ſtronger reaſon was it ſufficient, that this man, who was member of the third eſtate, had acquired a *noble fief, and paid competent ſervice*, that is, had followed his lord to war, to be reckoned a gentleman: conſequently at that time a perſon might ennoble himſelf; ſo that he ſtood in no need of letters patent, or of public employments to acquire nobility: a man of noble extraction, and a perſon lately ennobled, were equally ſtiled gentlemen of name and arms. Things continued thus in France till the reign of Henry III, and then the nobility acquired by the poſſeſſion of fiefs, as well as that obtained by the profeſſion of arms, was no longer conſidered. The hundred and fifty-eighth article of the ordinance of Blois, in the year 1599, ſuppreſſed the nobility obtained by fiefs, and the edict of Henry IV. aboliſhed that acquired by arms. Thus the gentleman is no longer he who has been in the army, or has acquired lordſhips or noble fiefs, but he who is deſcended from a noble lineage, or has had letters of ennoblement, or laſtly, is poſſeſſed of an office to which nobility is annexed. It is ſurprizing that Henry IV, who owed ſo much to his gallant officers, ſhould have requited their long ſervices ſo ill. Lewis XV, by his edict of nobility in 1750, ſhews his great regard for thoſe gentlemen; and has immortalized his reign as much by this new law, as by the foundation of a military ſchool.

The marquis de Roſny is made maſter of the ordnance upon the reſignation of M. d'Eſtrées. This was for a long time a poſt of no conſequence, from its being divided into ſo many branches: Lewis XI. rendered it more conſiderable, and it became afterwards of greater importance, by the ſuppreſſion of the office of grand maſter of the croſs-bow men, which expired with Aymar de Prie towards the year 1534; at length it was made one of the great offices of the crown in favour of the duke de Sully.

1601.

The treaty of Lyons, by which the king relinquiſhes the marquiſate of Saluzzo to the duke of Savoy, in lieu of the diſtricts

REMARKABLE EVENTS under HENRY IV.

of la Breſſe, le Bugey, &c. which are ceded to him by that prince. Bonaventure of Caltagirone, general of the order of St. Francis, negotiated this peace; and the duke of Savoy had the whole honour of it. Lewis XIII. is born. The earl of Eſſex is beheaded at London. The death of the impoſtor don Sebaſtian, who pretended to be the king of Portugal, ſlain in Africa.

The inſtitution of the order of religious penitents, called Picpuſſes.

1602.

The conſpiracy of marſhal de Biron, the count d'Auvergne, and marſhal de Bouillon, in conjunction with the duke of Savoy, is diſcovered by Laffin, a perſon in whom the marſhal confided. The firſt advice was given by Roſcieux, formerly mayor of Orleans, and afterwards ſecretary of ſtate to the duke de Mayenne's council, a famous leaguer, who after the reduction of Paris retired to the Netherlands. The marſhal was beheaded in the Baſtile the thirty-firſt of July, by an arret of parliament, the king having ſent them a commiſſion to try him. His majeſty granted a pardon to the count d'Auvergne, the natural ſon of Charles IX, afterwards duke d'Angoulemé, and to marſhal de Bouillon; but the latter not caring to truſt to it, quitted the kingdom. " The marſhal de Biron was a proud, haughty " man, almoſt ungovernable in his temper ; he took a delight " in nothing but what was arduous and next to impoſſible; he " envied every body's greatneſs; the jealouſy he bore to the " duke de Montmorency, on account of the office of conſtable, " extended even to Louiſa de Budos, his wife; for he made a " propoſal of marriage to her even in her huſband's life time, as " one that expected to ſucceed him; and the match was ſettled " betwixt them ; but the conſtable ſurvived them both." (*Le Laboureur on Caſtelnau.*) Biron having been erected into a dutchy and peerage four years before, became a barony once more after the death of the marſhal without iſſue. It was again created a dutchy and peerage in 1723.

The embaſſy of the Swiſs, who renew their alliance with France. An edict againſt duels. The office of ſuper-intendant of the mines, created in favour of Roger de Bellegarde, maſter of the horſe: Beringhen was made comptroller general of the mines.

An

REMARKABLE EVENTS under HENRY IV.

An arret of parliament againſt the biſhop of Angers, for attempting to introduce a new breviary, without having previouſly obtained the king's permiſſion, or conſulted with his metropolitan.

Letters of legitimation for the king's ſon by Henrietta de Balzac, authorized by the like letters in favour of the duke de Vendome, which were the firſt of the kind. The duke of Savoy miſcarries in his attempt againſt Geneva; an enterprize of the ſame nature proved as unſucceſsful in 1534. The order of the Charitable Brethren, founded by St. John of God, and approved by pope Pius V, in 1572, was introduced into France in 1601, and ſettled at Paris in 1602, by queen Mary of Medicis.

Remonſtrances of the parliament againſt an ediƈt for raiſing the ſpecie: they were not pronounced in public, according to the uſual cuſtom; but the king was ſatisfied with cauſing them to be read in private, and not in the preſence of the deputies, contrary to the eſtabliſhed praƈtice, as M. de Thou obſerves.

1603.

The death of queen Elizabeth, aged ſixty-nine: her ſucceſſor was James VI, king of Scotland, and ſtiled James the firſt. She was a princeſs of great learning. One day converſing with Calignon, afterwards chancellor of Navarre, ſhe ſhewed him a Latin tranſlation of ſome of Sophocles's tragedies, and of two of Demoſthenes's orations, which ſhe had made herſelf: ſhe likewiſe permitted him to take a copy of a Greek epigram of her own compoſing, and aſked his opinion in regard to a few paſſages of Lycophron, which ſhe had then in her hand, in order to tranſlate them. But her chief knowledge was that of government; and England ranks her among its greateſt princes. James VI. was the firſt that poſſeſſed the kingdoms of England, Scotland, and Ireland; the firſt who took the title of king of Great Britain. From the reign of Henry VIII, to that of queen Elizabeth, the Engliſh changed their religion four times. Is it poſſible to conceive that a free people ſhould alter their opinion ſo often? And could a deſpotic government do more?

A negotiation is entered upon by the marquis de Roſny in England, who renews the treaties already concluded with James VI, when only king of Scotland, and with queen Elizabeth: by the ſame treaty the two princes promiſed to ſupport the Dutch againſt Spain.

REMARKABLE EVENTS under HENRY IV.

Spain. The Jesuits are recalled into France; and the next year the king chose father Cotton, one of that society, for his confessor. The princes of Courtenay produce their title deeds, in order to be acknowledged of the blood royal; but are disappointed. The regulation of the finances, and of the different branches of the administration, by the marquis de Rhony, who had been made superintendant of the revenue in 1599. The government proved to be in debt to the amount of three hundred and thirty millions of livres. The establishment of silk manufactures, the direction of which is committed to Saintot. Other manufacturies of tapestry, earthen ware, glass, &c. The king erects new buildings, makes new parks, and gardens, &c. and is fond of being compared to Francis I. The viscount de Rohan is created duke and peer; Bouthillier, his advocate, presented his letters to parliament. It was Catherine, sister of this nobleman, that gave the following answer to a declaration of gallantry from Henry IV, *that she was too poor to be his wife, and of too good a family to be his mistress.*

1604.

The death of the dutchess of Bar: she was a Huguenot; and Cayet, a protestant minister, had been placed near her person, to instruct and confirm her in the new religion. This same Cayet afterwards turned catholic, and was made doctor of divinity: he is the author of the *Chronologie Novenaire et Septenaire.* Marshal de Bouillon continues his intrigues. Four seditious persons in Britany are put to death. The establishment of the French colony in Canada. The introduction of the Paulette *.

Pont-neuf † is finished. Ostend is taken from the Dutch by the Spaniards: this siege lasted thirty-nine months, by the gallant resistance of prince Maurice, with the loss of a hundred and forty thousand men on both sides. And what is worthy of observation, notwithstanding a most obstinate and expensive war, the Dutch commerce rose to a very surprizing height. The canal of Briare ‡ begun.

Charles of Sudermania, son of Gustavus Vasa, being declared regent of the kingdom of Sweden, upon the death of

---

* A kind of yearly tax paid to the king.   † A bridge over the Seine at Paris.   ‡ For uniting the Loire with the Seine.

John

REMARKABLE EVENTS under HENRY IV.

John his elder brother, seizes the crown during the absence of his nephew Sigismund, the lawful heir, who had been elected king of Poland after the decease of Battori. The death of Clement VIII, *a pacific pope*, says l'Etoile, *and well affected to the French nation*.

This year the parliament regiftered the edict for establishing the Capuchins in France, who had been already invited into this kingdom by Charles IX, in the year 1573, with the consent of Gregory XII.

1605.

A conspiracy of the count d'Auvergne, of the marchioness de Verneuil, and M. d'Antragues her father: the king takes back from them the promise of marriage*, which they intended to put in force: the criminals are convicted, and the king grants them a pardon. This conspiracy had been conducted by father Archangel, a Capuchin friar, natural son of queen Margaret, and of Chanvallon, father confessor of the marchioness de Verneuil. The said lady was not at all fortunate in promises of marriage, for she had obtained one of the duke de Guise, with no better success. The impostor Demetrius, grand duke of Muscovy, is murdered. The Spaniards exclude Baronius from the papal dignity, for his treatise on the *Sicilian monarchy*. The foundation of the royal hospital called the *Christian Charity*, in favour of the officers and soldiers lamed in the king's service. A foolish fellow, named John de Lisle, attempts to kill the king; but is arrested and confined. The discovery of the gunpowder treason in England.

1606.

The duke de Bouillon makes his peace, by resigning Sedan to the king, who is so well satisfied with his submission as to restore that town to him again in the space of a month. Sully erected into a dutchy and peerage in favour of the marquis de Rhony. The interdict of Venice.

1607.

The interdict is taken off at the sollicitation of Henry IV, and by the care of the cardinal de Joyeuse. The king reunites

* He had given a promise of marriage to mademoifelle d'Antrague, afterwards marchioness de Verneuil, in order to obtain that lady.

REMARKABLE EVENTS under HENRY IV.

Navarre, and his other patrimonial eftates, to the crown, fo as to render them inalienable. (See the particular remarks.) The duke d'Epernon enters into the court-yard of the Louvre in his coach, under pretence of illnefs: the king granted the fame diftinction to the duke de Sully in 1609; and under the regency of Mary of Medicis this honour was extended to all dukes and crown officers, who have preferved it ever fince.

1608.

The negotiation of the prefident Jeannin, for putting an end to the war betwixt the archduke and the ftates of Holland. The inundation of the Loire, attended with a vaft deal of damage: this was ftiled the year of the hard winter.

The inftitution of the military order of Mount Carmel, to which that of St. Lazare was united. The king made the captain of his guards, M. de Nereftang, grand mafter of the order.

1609.

A truce of twelve years between the Spaniards, and the United Provinces, by which the fovereignty of the Dutch republic is acknowledged. John William duke of Cleves dies without iffue; which occafions the pretenfions of the marquis of Brandenburg, of the duke of Newburg, of the duke of Deux Ponts, of the elector of Saxony, and of the marquis of Burgau, in confequence of their alliances by marriage to the family of the duke of Cleves.

The prince of Condé retires to Bruffels, and from thence to Milan, with Margaret de Montmorency his wife, for whom the king had difcovered fome affection. A regulation of the police of the 12th of November, determining that the comedians of the theatres of the *hotel de Bourgogne*, and of the *Marais*, fhall open their doors at half an hour after twelve, and begin their reprefentations precifely at two, whether there be fpectators fufficient to make a houfe or not, fo that the play fhall be over before half an hour after four. This regulation took place from the feaft of St. Martin to the 15th of February. Paris at that time was very different from what it is at prefent: the town was not lighted; the ftreets were exceffively dirty; there were very few coaches; and there was a great number of robbers: all which was a vaft hindrance to the frequenting of play houfes, efpecially in the winter;

REMARKABLE EVENTS under HENRY IV.

winter; and this was the cause of the present determination of the police.

1610.

Henry IV. forms a project in regard to Germany, occasioned by the succession of Cleves and Juliers. The project was, according to several writers, to establish a body called the *Christian republic*, which would have divided Europe into 15 parts: but this has the appearance of a chimera. In all probability Henry IV. had no other scheme than to execute, on the one hand, the treaty of Brusol between him and the duke of Savoy, whereby he was to furnish that prince with sixteen thousand men, in order to seize the dutchy of Milan, as an indemnity for the smallness of the portion he had received with the daughter of king Philip II; and on the other, the treaty of Hall, by which he bound himself to assist the heirs of the duke of Juliers with ten thousand men, with a view of enabling them to take possession of the duke's dominions. The remainder of his troops, which might amount to eighty thousand men, were probably intended to take advantage of the critical situation of the Spaniards on the side of the Pyrenees, as he had many reasons to hate that nation.

Henry IV. is assassinated in his coach, in which he had with him messieurs d'Epernon, de Montbason, de Lavardin, de Roquelaure, de la Force, de Liencourt, and de Mirebeau.

Philip III. expels the Moors out of Spain, to the number of very near nine hundred thousand souls: the duke d'Ossuna was against this measure. *They could not*, says a Spanish commentator on Commines, *do a better action, nor follow worse counsel.*

France never had a better, nor a greater king than Henry IV. He was his own general, and minister: in him were united great frankness, and profound policy; sublimity of sentiments, and a most engaging simplicity of manners; the bravery of a soldier, and an inexhaustible fund of humanity. And what forms the characteristic of great men, he was obliged to surmount many obstacles, to expose himself to danger, and especially to encounter with adversaries worthy of himself. In short, to make use of the expression of one of our greatest poets, *he was the conqueror and the father of his subjects.*

The HISTORY of FRANCE.

1610.
Accession to the crown.

LEWIS XIII, *born at Fontainebleau the 27th of September 1601, succeeds to the crown the 14th of May, 1610. He received the regal unction at Rheims, by the hands of the cardinal de Joyeuse, archbishop of Rouen, the 17th day of October following, because the archbishop of Rheims, of the house of Lorrain, was not yet consecrated; and he was declared of age in the year 1614. He was surnamed the Just.*

REMARKABLE EVENTS.

1610.

AN arret of parliament, declaring queen Mary of Medicis regent of the kingdom. This princess is jointly possessed of the tutelage and the regency.

Marshal de la Chastre marches a body of troops into Germany, where joining prince Maurice of Nassau, the youngest son of prince William, founder of the Dutch republic, he retakes the city of Juliers, and restores it to the claimants, the marquis of Brandenburg and the duke of Newburg, from whom the archduke Leopold had wrested it.

This quarrel about the succession of Juliers, lasted very near twenty years, and ended in a provisional treaty, which still subsists between the houses of Brandenburg and Palatine.

1611.

The duke de Sully retires from court, with a present of a hundred thousand crowns. Chasteauvieu, gentleman to the queen, had the government of the Bastile. " *Three directors,*" says Bassompierre, " *were appointed to manage the* " *finances; these were messieurs de Chateauneuf,* " *the president de Thou (the historian), and Jean-* " *nin; but the latter had moreover the office of* " *comptroller general of the revenue, which gave* " *him the intire management thereof, and excluded* " *the rest who only assisted in the direction.*" The queen changes the system of politics, and courts the alliance of Spain, to the great concern of the protestants, who were headed by the marshal de Bouillon, and the duke de Sully. The death of the famous duke de Mayenne, on the third of October. A war breaks out betwixt Sweden and Russia, occasioned by Gustavus Adolphus's aiming to be elected *Czar*, upon the death of

the

The THIRD RACE. 31

WIVES.	CHILDREN.	1643. DEATH.	Cotemporary PRINCES.
Anne of Auftria, daughter of Philip III, married in 1615, died in 1666.	LEWIS XIV. Philip of France. His firft wife, princefs Henrietta of England, the daughter of Charles I, died at St. Cloud in 1670. He had by her Philip-Charles of Orleans, who died foon after he was born: Mary Louifa, married to Charles II. king of Spain, died in 1689. N. died juft after fhe was born: Anna Maria of Orleans, married to Victor Amadeus duke of Savoy, died in 1728. His fecond wife, Charlotte Elizabeth of Bavaria, daughter of the elector Palatine, died in 1722, by whom he had Alexander-Lewis of Orleans, who died young: Philip of Orleans, regent of France, died the 2d of December 1723, and Elizabeth-Charlotte, married to the duke of Lorrain, died in 1745.	LEWIS XIII. died at St. Germain the 14th of May 1643, in the forty-fecond year of his age, on the fame day as his father Henry IV. after a reign of thirty years. He was interred at St. Denis.	*Popes.* Paul V. 1621. Gregory XII. 1623. Urban VIII. 1644. *Turkifh Emperors.* Achmet. 1617. Muftapha depofed 1617. Ofman. 1622. Amurath IV. 1640. Ibrahim. 1655. *Emperors of Germany.* Rodolphus. 1612. Matthias. 1619. Ferdinand II. 1637. Ferdinand III. 1657. *Kings of Spain.* Philip III. 1621. Philip IV. 1665. *Kings of Portugal.* Philip III. 1621. Philip IV. 1665. John duke of Braganza, elected king in 1640, died in 1656. *Kings of Great Britain.* James I. 1625. Charles I. 1649. *King of Denmark.* Chriftian IV. 1648. *Kings of Sweden.* Charles IX. 1611. Guftavus Adolphus. 1632. Chriftina abdicated in 1654. Died in 1689. *King of Poland.* Sigifmund III. king of Sweden. 1632. Ladiflaus Sigifmund. 1648. *Czars of Mufcovy.* Demetrius, the third impoftor. 1610. Ladiflaus of Poland, till 1613. Demetrius, the fourth impoftor. 1613. Michael Foederowitz. 1645.

REMARKABLE EVENTS under LEWIS XIII.

the impoftor Demetrius. The Ruffians chofe Michael Federowitz, who was only a private *Boyar*, or gentleman.

The county of Briffac is erected into a dutchy and peerage: the letters patent were not regiftered till the year 1620.

The lordfhip of Lefdiguieres created a dutchy and peerage, in favour of Francis de Bonne (afterwards conftable Lefdiguieres), and of his fon-in-law Charles de Crequy.

The fettlement of the Urfelline nuns in France, who were founded in 1537.

1612.

The publication of the double marriage between the king and Anne of Auftria infanta of Spain, and between Elizabeth the king's fifter and the prince of Spain, who was afterwards Philip IV. The beginning of the difturbances of the Huguenots. The duke de Rohan feizes the town of *St. John de Angeli*. Foundation of the oratory by father de Berulle, afterwards cardinal. Concini, marquis d'Ancre, and Eleanor Galiguai, his wife, having an intire afcendant over the queen, fow divifions amongft the princes and the minifters, in order to augment their own authority. The marquis d'Ancre had procured one of the two offices of mafter of the wardrobe for M. de la Rochefoucaut; and now he purchafes the place of firft gentleman of the bed-chamber for M. de Bouillon: at that time there were only two, M. de Bellegarde had the other. Charles of Bourbon, count of Soiffons, dies the firft of November; he was fon by a fecond venter of Lewis I. prince of Condé, and of Frances de Longueville: his fon, who was killed at Marfée, left no iffue. The treatife of *Ecclefiaftic and civil power*, written by doctor Richer, fyndic of Sorbonne, is condemned by the provincial affembly of Sens held at Paris, with a refervation of the king's rights and the liberties of the Gallican church. Richer fubmitted in 1629, and died in 1631.

1613.

The marfhal de Bouillon, uncle of Frederic elector Palatine, by Ifabella of Naffau his wife, who was Frederic's aunt, concludes a match between that prince and Elizabeth the daughter of James I. king of England. This marriage encouraged him to feize the crown of Bohemia, and proved the fource of all his misfortunes, by placing an ill judged confidence in his father-

in-

The THIRD RACE. 33

MINISTERS.	WARRIORS.	MAGISTRATES.	EMINENT and LEARNED MEN.
Henry de Schomberg, superintendant of the finances. 1632. Concino Concini d'Ancre. 1617. Charl. d'Albert de Luines. 1621. Armand John du Plessis, cardinal de Richelieu, prime minister. 1642. J. Bochart. 1630. Charles duke de la Vieuville, superintendant of the finances. 1653. Michael de Marillac, superintendant of the finances, keeper of the seals. 1632. Barbin, comptroller general of the finances. P. Jeannin, comptroller-general of the finances. 1622. Maupeou, comptroller-general of the finances. Claud Bullion, superintendant of the finances. 1640. *Secretaries of state.* Nic. de Neuville de Villeroy. 1627. Martin Ruzé. 1613. Lewis Potier de Gevres. 1630. Ant. de Lomenie. 1638. P. Brulart de Puisieux. 1640. Antony Potier. 1621. Paul Phelypeaux de Pontchartrain. 1621. Vol. II. Henry	*Constable.* Henry de Montmorency. 1614. Charles d'Albert, duke de Luines. 1621. Francis de Bonne, duke de Lesdiguieres. 1626. *The office of constable was suppressed by an edict dated in the month of February, 1627.* *Marshals of France.* Henry de la Tour de Bouillon. 1623. Cl. de la Chastre. 1614. Charles de Cossé de Brissac. 1621. John de Beaumanoir de Lavardin. 1614. Urban de Laval. 1629. Will. Hautemer de Grancey. 1613. Concino Concini d'Ancre. 1617. Gilles de Souvrê. 1625. Ant. de Roquelaure. 1626. L. de la Chastre. 1630. Pons de Cardaillac de Themines. 1627. Fr. de la Grange de Montigny. 1617. Nic. de l'Hopital de Vitry. 1644. Ch. de Choiseul. 1626. John Fr. de la Guiche. 1632. Honoré	*Chancellors.* Nicholas Brulart de Sileri. 1624. Will. du Vair, keeper of the seals. 1621. Cl. Mangot, keeper of the seals in 1617. Ch. Albert de Luines, keeper of the seals. 1621. Meri de Vie d'Ermenonville, keeper of the seals. 1622. L. le Fevre de Caumartin, keeper of the seals. 1623. Stephen d'Aligre. 1635. Michael de Marillac, keeper of the seals. 1632. Ch. de l'Aubespine de Chateauneuf, keeper of the seals. 1653. Peter Seguier, keeper of the seals, afterwards chancellor. 1672. *First presidents.* Achilles de Harlay. 1616. Nicholas de Verdun. 1627. *It was he that gave the first presidents the hotel in which they now reside.* Jer. de Hacqueville. 1628. J. Bochart. 1630. D Nic.	Theodore Agrippa d'Aubigne. 1630. Lord Bacon. 1626. John Barclay. 1621. Robert Bellarmin. 1621. Peter de Berulle, cardinal. 1629. Antony de la Boderie. 1615. James Bongars. 1612. Peter de Bourdeille de Brantome. 1614. John Busee. 1611. James Callot. 1634. Will. Cambden. 1622. Thomas Campanella. 1639. Is. Casaubon. 1614. Will. Catel. 1626. P. Victor Palma Cayet. 1610. Michael Cervantes. 1620. Herc. de Charnacé. 1637. Andrew du Chesne. 1640. Nicholas Coeffeteau. 1623. Father Cotton. 1616. Peter Daviti. 1635. Henry Davila, living in 1638. Guichard Deageant. 1639. Domenichini the painter. 1641. Nicholas le Fevre, preceptor of Lewis XIII. 1612. S. Francis of Sales. 1622. Phil. Canaie de Fresne. 1610. Fronton du Duc. 1625. Galileo. 1642. Dionysius Godefredus. 1623. J. B.

REMARKABLE EVENTS under LEWIS XIII.

in-law, a weak inconstant prince, who gave him no manner of assistance. From this match sprung the princess Sophia, who was married into the house of Hanover, and through her the crown of England was transferred to this family, upon the exclusion of the catholic branches.

The beginning of the factions and intrigues in the king's minority.

The king publishes an edict against duels, protesting he will never pardon any: this was on account of the baron de Luz, who had been killed by the chevalier de Guise. And what is very extraordinary, not long after, the same chevalier de Guise slew the baron de Luz's son, and was not at all prosecuted; the queen wanting to keep fair with the family of the Guises, in order to detach them from the prince of Condés party. This chevalier de Guise was killed the year following by the bursting of a cannon. Mary of Medicis begins the aqueduct of Arcueil.

The duke of Savoy wants to seize the dutchy of Montferrat, during the minority of Mary his grandchild, daughter of Francis, the late duke of Mantua; but is prevented by the Venetians, the Spaniards, and the French.

1614.

The princes dissatisfied with the government, retire from court. These were Henry II, prince of Condé, Cæsar duke de Vendome, and Alexander, grand prior of France (both of them natural sons of Henry IV.) Henry duke de Mayenne, son of the chief of the league, the dukes de Longueville, Guise, Nevers, Rohan, Luxemburg, la Trimouille, &c. The marshal de Bouillon was at the head of this whole cabal, without being suspected by the queen.

The death of Henry, constable of Montmorency. "Henry IV.
" would often rally him for his ignorance, but admired his good
" sense; and in regard to the grand project, which miscarried by
" his death, he had been observed to say, that there was nothing
" but he could accomplish by means of a constable who knew
" not how to write, and a chancellor who did not understand
" a word of Latin; this was his opinion of the chancellor de
" Sil-

The THIRD RACE. 35

MINISTERS.	WARRIORS.	MAGISTRATES.	EMINENT and LEARNED MEN.
Secretaries of state. Henry Aug. de Lomenie de Brienne. 1666. Cl. Mangot, who was keeper of the seals. Rem. Phelypeaux d'Herbault. 1629. Nic. Potier de Ocquerre. 1628. Ch. le Beauclerc. 1630. Cl. Bouthillier, superintendant of the finances. 1651. Lewis Phelypeaux de la Vrilliere. 1681. Abel Servien, superintendant of the finances. 1659. Leo Bouthillier de Chavigny. 1652. Fr. Sublet des Noyers, surveyor of the royal buildings. 1645. H. de Guenegaud de Plancy. 1676. Michael le Tellier. 1685.	*Marshals of France.* Honoré d'Albert de Chaulnes. 1647. Fr. de Aubeterre. 1628. Charl. de Creques. 1638. Gaspard de Coligny, called the marshal de Chatillon, grandson to the admiral. 1646. James Nompar de Caumont, duke de la Force. 1652. Fr. de Baffompierre. 1646. Henry de Schomberg. 1632. Francis Hannibal d'Estrees. 1670. John Baptist d'Ornano. 1626. Thimoleon d'Epinay de St. Luc. 1644. Lewis de Marillac. 1632. H. de Montmorency d'Anville. 1632. J. de S. Bonnet de Toyras. 1636. Antony Coeffier d'Effiat. 1632. Urb. de Maillé de Breze. 1650. Maxim. de Bethune de Sully. 1641. Ch. de Schomberg. 1656. Ch. de la Porte de la Meilleraie. 1664. Antony	*First presidents.* Nic. le Jai. 1640. Matthew Molé. 1656. *Proctors general.* James de la Guesle. 1612. Nic. de Bellievre. 1650. Matthew Molé. 1656. Bl. Meliand. 1661. *Advocates general.* Lewis Servin. 1626. Cardin le Bret. 1654. James Talon. 1648. Jerome Bignon practises till 1640. Omer Talon. 1652. Stephen Briquet practises in the place of Jerome Bignon, his father-in-law. 1645.	J. B. Guarini. 1613. Guido the painter. 1642. Cornelius Janfenius. 1638. P. Jeannin. 1622. Father Joseph the Capuchin. 1638. Fr. de Joyeuse, cardinal. 1615. John Kepler. 1630. Ch. Loifeau. 1628. Ant. Loifel. 1617. Fr. de Malherbe. 1628. J. Mariana. 1624. Cavalier Marini. 1625. Papir. Maffon. 1611. Peter Mathieu. 1621. Cl. Bachet de Meziriac. 1638. Phil. de Mornay, du Pleffis. 1623. Steph. Pafquier. 1615. Cl. Fabr. de Peirefc. 1637. J. Davi du Perron, cardinal. 1618. Francis Pithou. 1621. Matt. Regnier. 1613. P. de Gondy de Retz, cardinal. 1616. Edm. Richer. 1631. Dav. Rivault, preceptor of Lewis XIII. 1618. Alf. Roderiquez. 1616. Henry duke of Rohan. 1638. P. Paul Rubens. 1640. John de Hauranne de St. Cyran. 1643. Scev. de Sainte Marthe. 1623. Nic. de Harlai de Sanci. 1629. Paolo

D 2

REMARKABLE EVENTS under LEWIS XIII.

"Sillery." *(Le Laboureur on Caſtelneau.)* Henry of Montmorency was the laſt conſtable of his family. He had a ſon by a ſecond wife, who ſucceeded him in his dutchy and in the government of Languedoc: but the ſon was afterwards beheaded, and marſhal Schomberg obtained that government.

The treaty of S. Menehoud of the 15th of May, by which every thing is granted to the malecontents: they all ſubmit, except the duke of Vendome, who refuſed to ſign the treaty, though he was reſtored to his government of Britany; but he was forced to comply, upon the king's approach with an army.

The marquis of Spinola, general of the Spaniſh forces, wages war in the country of Juliers, on account of the ſucceſſion of Cleves. The Dutch on the other hand diſmembered as much as they could of that ſame ſucceſſion, whilſt the marquis of Brandenburg, and the duke of Newburg, who were called the *poſſeſ-ſing princes*, preſerved thoſe towns, which they had ſeized in the beginning. The treaty of Santen, concluded at this time, did not determine the diſpute among the ſeveral claimants.

The king is declared of age in the bed, or throne, of juſtice, held in the parliament of Paris the 2d of October, where it was decided that the cardinals ſhould take place of the eccleſiaſtical peers, upon which the latter retired.

An aſſembly of the ſtates is convened by the queen the 27th of October, as ſhe had promiſed by the treaty of St. Menehoud: this is the laſt that was held in this kingdom. On which occaſion I muſt obſerve, that in France we acknowledge no other ſovereign but the king; it is his authority that conſtitutes the law; *whatever the king wills, the law wills:* therefore the ſtates of the kingdom have only the privilege of remonſtrating or of making humble ſupplications; and the king complies with their addreſſes or petitions, according to the rules of his royal juſtice and prudence. For were he obliged to grant all their demands, ſays one of our moſt celebrated authors, he would ceaſe to be their ſovereign. And hence it is, that during the ſitting of the ſtates, the authority of the parliament, which indeed is no other than that of the king, receives no diminution, as may be eaſily proved by the proceedings in this laſt aſſembly of the ſtates. *(Plea of M. de la Moignon de Blancmenil of the 14th of February 1719.)*

The

The THIRD RACE.

WARRIORS.	EMINENT and LEARNED MEN.
Marſhals of France. Antony de Grammont. 1678. John Baptiſt Budes de Gueſbriant. 1643. Ph. de la Mothe Houdancourt. 1657. Fr. de l'Hoſpital. 1660.	Paolo Sarpi. 1623. John Savaron. 1622. Will. de Saulx de Tavannes, towards 1633. Will. Shakſpear. 1616. Henry Sponde. 1643. Fr. Suarez. 1617. Theophilus. 1626. James Aug. de Thou. 1617. Lewis de Nogaret de la Valette, cardinal. 1639. Antony Vandyke, painter. 1640. Lucilio Vanini. 1619. Lopez de Vega. 1635. Dominic de Vic. 1630. Honoré d'Urfé. 1624. Zamet. 1614.

REMARKABLE EVENTS under LEWIS XIII.

The equestrian statue of Henry the great, sent by Cosmo III. grand duke of Tuscany, was erected this year on Pont neuf the 23d of August. This is the first monument of the kind at Paris, in honour of our kings. The death of Francis of Bourbon, prince of Conti, without issue, the 3d of August; he was the younger son of Lewis I. prince of Condé.

1615.

Disturbances in parliament, excited by the marshal de Bouillon. Remonstrances of that body, which prove ineffectual. The treaty of Asti the 21st of June, to determine the differences in Italy about the dutchy of Montferrat.

The prince of Condé, dissatisfied at not having the chief direction of affairs, and complaining of the non-performance of the treaty of St. Menehoud, retires again from court, and publishes a bitter manifesto against the government. The king issues a declaration the 10th of September, depriving the prince of Condé and his adherents of all their honours and estates, as guilty of high treason.

Lewis XIII, in spite of the malecontents who might have incommoded him in his march, sets out for Bourdeaux, where the double marriage was consummated. He returns from Bourdeaux to Chatelleraut, in order of battle, having nominated the duke de Guise lieutenant general of the army, which covered his march from the insults of the malecontents and of the Huguenots, with whom the prince of Condé was connected, notwithstanding the aversion he bore to those people all his life.

Mary of Medicis employs James de Brosse her architect, to build the palace of Luxemburg; it was likewise by her order that the walk called the *Cours* was planted with trees.

1616.

The treaty of Loudun, between the queen and the prince of Condé, the head of the malecontents; it was equally in favour of this prince and of the Huguenots. The queen, by the advice of the marshal d'Ancre, imprisoned the prince of Condé, who had forced her to this treaty, and, although a peace was concluded, still continued his intrigues. Themines, who arrested him, was that very same day made marshal of France.

Condé

The THIRD RACE.

REMARKABLE EVENTS under LEWIS XIII.

Condé was sent to the Baftile, and afterwards conducted to Vincennes. Upon the news of this imprifonment, the princes, and feveral of the chief nobility, retired from court, in order to prepare for war. The queen mother fet three armies on foot, under the command of the duke de Guife, the marfhal de Montigny, and the count d'Auvergne: marfhal d'Ancre procured the latter his liberty (he had been confined to the Baftile by Henry IV.) with the government of Paris and that of the ifle of France. Out of the different corps of the Swifs nation, the king makes a draught of a particular number of companies, in order to form a regiment of Swifs guards, and Gafpar Gallati of Glaris was the firft colonel.

Richelieu, bifhop of Luçon, is made fecretary, by the patronage of marfhal d'Ancre.

James I, at the perfuafion of Barnewelt, the penfionary of Holland, reftores to the Dutch the cautionary towns, viz. Flufhing, Brille, and Ramekins, by which that republic had been held in a dependance on England. This prince was foon made fenfible of his miftake; and it is thought that his refentment againft Barnewelt, contributed to the death of that great man. Marfhal d'Ancre difplaces all the minifters, and haftens his own deftruction.

1617.

The war is carried on fuccefsfully againft the malecontents, and fuddenly concludes with the death of marfhal d'Ancre. The king guided intirely by the advice of M. de Luines, his favourite, ordered him to be arrefted; Vitry, who had been intrufted with the commiffion, attempted to put it in execution; and the marfhal, making refiftance, was killed upon the bridge of the Louvre. His wife was beheaded by an arret of parliament: meffieurs de la Porte and de Bouthillier owed their fortune to this woman. The death of marfhal d'Ancre, who had governed the kingdom the fpace of feven years in the name of the queen, put an end to the civil war. Mary of Medicis is exiled to Blois. Thither fhe was followed by the bifhop of Luçon, who had met with fome difficulties about his feat in council; being afterwards fufpected by the duke de Luines, he received orders to retire to his priory of Couffay in Anjou, from thence to Luçon, and at length to Avignon.

REMARKABLE EVENTS under LEWIS XIII.

An aſſembly of the Notables held at Rouen, at which Gaſton, the king's brother, then only nine years of age, preſided: he was aſſiſted by the cardinals du Perron and de la Rochefoucaud, the duke de Montbazon, and marſhal de Briſſac: this aſſembly was productive of nothing.

The treaty of Pavia, concluded by the mediation of France, between the king of Spain and the duke of Savoy: the duke de Leſdiguieres had ſerved the latter to ſome purpoſe in the war between thoſe two powers; and the French aſſiſted him ſtill more effectually againſt Spain, as ſoon as the duke de Luines recovered the reins of government out of the hands of the queen.

The kingdoms of Bohemia, and Hungary, devolved to the houſe of Auſtria in the ſixteenth century, by the marriage of the emperor Ferdinand I. to Anne, the ſiſter of Lewis the laſt king, who poſſeſſed both thoſe crowns, but left no iſſue. The emperor Matthias, having no children, cauſed his couſin Ferdinand, the grandſon of Ferdinand I, to be crowned king of Bohemia, from an apprehenſion of the diſturbances which broke out the next year. Philip III. laid claim to Bohemia and Hungary, as being deſcended by his mother from Anne Jagellon, who brought theſe kingdoms for her portion to Ferdinand I. This diſpute concluded with an agreement, by which Ferdinand II. was ſuffered to enjoy both thoſe kingdoms, on condition that for want of male iſſue in the German line, they ſhould go to the Spaniſh branch. The houſe of Bavaria had likewiſe pretenſions to thoſe countries, in right of a prior ſubſtitution or intail, ſettled by the will of Ferdinand I, and by the marriage contract between his eldeſt daughter and the duke of Bavaria. A ball, at which the king, and M. de Luines, &c. danced.

The count du Lude is made governor of Gaſton the king's brother, and Contade is appointed under-governor.

1618.

The archduke Ferdinand, who was already king of Bohemia, is crowned king of Hungary.

The beginning of the troubles in Bohemia, where the proteſtants take up arms againſt the emperor Matthias, for invading their privileges. The count de Buquoy commanded the Imperial troops; and Erneſt, the natural ſon of count Mansfeld, the Bohemians. This is called the thirty years war. The

The THIRD RACE. 41

REMARKABLE EVENTS under LEWIS XIII.

The Jesuits open the college of Clermont, where they begin to teach in public.

The *Palais* is set on fire. The foundation of the Madelonnettes. The conspiracy of Venice.

1619.

The queen mother escapes from Blois, and retires to Angouleme, with the assistance of the duke d'Epernon, who had quitted the court. The duke de Luines sends for the bishop of Luçon to Avignon, who persuades the queen to come to an accommodation with the king. The agreement is settled by the treaty of Angouleme.

An interview in Touraine between Lewis XIII. and Mary of Medicis: she retired afterwards to Angers. The duke de Luines sets the prince of Condé at liberty; who from that time proved a most faithful subject to the king. The constable of Montmorency's lady, mother-in-law to prince Condé, resigned her place of lady of honour to the queen, when madam de Luines was made superintendant of the houshold: madam de Lanoy, by the interest of Puisieux, obtained the place of lady of honour: this was a person of merit. (*Mem. of Brienne.*)

The manor of Maillé in Touraine is erected into a dutchy and peerage, under the name of Luines.

Ferdinand II. is elected emperor after the decease of Matthias. The Bohemians, instead of acknowledging him, chuse Frederic V, the elector palatine, for their king. The synod of Dordrecht, where prince Maurice, at the head of the Gomarists, procured the condemnation of the Arminians, who were the party that opposed him: this brought on the sentence and public execution of Barnewelt. Thus did Maurice reward that statesman for the care he had taken of him in his youth, and for causing him to be nominated to the command of the armies upon the death of William his father. The sage republican thought only of guarding against the ambition of the prince of Orange; who had invaded the liberties of his country. His zeal cost him his life, for he was beheaded at the age of seventy two: by the same arret, Grotius, an adherent of Barnewelt, and of the Arminians, was condemned to perpetual imprisonment; but he made his escape in 1621, from the castle of Louvestein (where

REMARKABLE EVENTS under LEWIS XIII.

he had been confined) by a stratagem of Mary Regesberg his wife, who conveyed him away in a trunk. He retired to Paris, where he wrote his book *Of the rights of war and peace*, which was published in 1625. Sir William Temple, who was attached to the house of Orange, speaking of the Arminians, says, *that they were rather a state party, than a sect*. The absolute power usurped by the synod of Dordrecht, has greatly puzzled the protestants, who have since opposed the lawful authority of the church in the council of Trent. The town of Batavia founded by the Dutch in the isle of Java in Asia.

1620.

A promotion of fifty nine knights of the order of the Holy Ghost. M. de Luines apprehending left this promotion should make all those his enemies at court, that were not included in it, suggested an expedient to the king, which had been practised before; this was to leave the chapter at liberty to chuse those, who had been nominated to the vacant ribbons. (*Mem. of Brienne.*)

Proctors made officers of the court, and their number limited.

The pacification of Ulm. This was a treaty between the catholics and protestants, to procure the peace of Germany, and to grant no assistance either to the emperor or to the king of Bohemia: which was the sure way to render Ferdinand II. triumphant. The king mediated this treaty with the advice of the president Jeannin; by which means he strengthened the house of Austria, which at that time he might have easily crushed. The queen dissatisfied with the non-performance of the treaty of Angouleme, and advised by the bishop of Luçon, who wanted to render himself necessary at court, and to make them purchase his mediation, revives the war, in hopes she should be supported by the grandees. This war was of very short duration: orders are issued out to all the provinces, to guard against the enterprizes of the rebels; and the king, after marching into Normandy, went to Angers, where his troops forced the bridge of Cé, and the queen submitted. A secret article of this treaty, was the promise of a cardinal's hat from M. de Luines to the bishop of Luçon; and the marriage of mademoiselle de Vigneron to M. de Combalet, the favourite's nephew: thus the bishop of Luçon, having begun to make his fortune by means of the mar-

shal

REMARKABLE EVENTS under LEWIS XIII.

fhal d'Ancre, continued to improve it under the patronage of the duke de Luines. The king iſſues out an edict for annexing the country of Bearn to the crown, for erecting the council of that province into a parliament, and for reſtoring the church lands, of which the Huguenots had been in poſſeſſion near ſixty years. The religioniſts had oppoſed this project ſome years ago; but the king having marched in perſon to Bearn, his preſence completed the work. This is the æra of the diſturbances under this reign, raiſed by the Huguenots only, without any aſſiſtance from the catholics.

Anne d'Halluin having been married to Henry count de Candale, got him to be declared duke and peer of Halluin: this match was annulled, and in 1620, ſhe was joined in wedlock to Charles de Schomberg, for whom ſhe likewiſe obtained the dutchy and peerage of Halluin, by virtue of new letters of creation the ſame year. A diſpute ariſes between M. de Candale and M. de Schomberg concerning the peerage. It was determined that both ſhould enjoy this honour; and that when one of them took his ſeat in parliament, the other ſhould keep away.

The battle of Prague on the 8th of November, in which the elector Palatine is defeated by Maximilian duke of Bavaria, brother-in-law to Ferdinand, and chief of the catholic league. To reward him for this victory, the emperor transferred the electoral dignity from Frederic to Maximilian, together with the upper Palatinate, in exchange for the lower Auſtria, which that prince held as a ſecurity for ſums lent to Ferdinand. While Frederic was loſing a crown, Spinola ravaged his hereditary dominions, and James I. his father-in-law ſuffered himſelf to be amuſed with Spaniſh negotiations, and with the hopes of marrying the prince of Wales his ſon, to the infanta of Spain. Frederic was obliged to take ſhelter in Holland, where the ſtates allowed him a penſion of ten thouſand florins a month. Luſatia is detached from Bohemia by the emperor, and given to the elector of Saxony, for the ſervices done him during the war. Prince Maurice and the marſhal de Bouillon, at whoſe inſtigation the princeſs Elizabeth, daughter of James I, had perſuaded her huſband to accept of the crown of Bohemia, differed in opinion about the manner of doing it; for Maurice

wanted

wanted the elector Palatine to assume the regal title and dignity, in compliance with the Bohemians; whereas the marshal de Bouillon judged it more advisable for him to be satisfied with the title of captain general, till affairs were perfectly settled. *(Mem. of Brienne.)*

1621.

The first war with the Huguenots, whose leaders were Rohan and Soubise: this flame raged two years, broke out again at three different times, and was not extinguished till 1629, a year after the taking of Rochelle. The design of the Huguenots was to model France into a republic: they had already divided it into eight circles, the government of which was to be settled on the lords of their party. The duke de Luines is made constable, and the duke de Lesdiguieres marshal general of the king's camps and armies. The royal forces, victorious in every other part, are baffled at the siege of Montauban, which was defended by the marquis de la Force. The king took six marshals of France with him upon this expedition, besides all the great lords and able captains in the realm; but the multitude of chiefs only prejudiced the enterprize, for want of due subordination. Lewis is obliged to raise the siege; and the duke de Mayenne was killed. The Calvinists make themselves masters of Montpellier.

The constable de Luines dies the 17th of December at Longueville, either of chagrin or poison: the seals which the king had kept ever since the death of M. du Vair, were given to M. de Vic. Cardinal de Retz, and the count de Schomberg, are placed at the head of the administration. The congregation of S. Maur, of the order of S. Benedict, established in France.

The death of Philip III, who is succeeded by his son Philip IV: the latter had the duke d'Olivares for his minister, as his father had had the duke de Lerma. The treaty of Madrid in regard to the Valteline, a province subject to the Grisons, where the protestants of that nation wanted to maintain their religion. The Spaniards, under pretence of establishing the true faith in that country, had made themselves masters of the passes, which preserve the communication between the dutchy of Milan and Germany. Lewis XIII, finding it his interest to check the Spaniards in their career, acts in conjunction with the pope, and engages the king of

REMARKABLE EVENTS under LEWIS XIII.

of Spain to defift: it is therefore fettled by treaty, that the Grifons fhall give no difturbance to their fubjects, and that the Spaniards fhall withdraw their troops from the valley. Baffompierre, then ambaffador extraordinary at Madrid, and who concluded this treaty, forewarns the king, that the Spaniards will obferve it no longer than fuits their conveniency; which was actually the cafe. The truce of 1609 being expired, the war is renewed in the Netherlands; Spinola commanding the Spaniards, and prince Maurice the Dutch. Mansfeld carries on the war in Germany for Frederic.

1622.

Creation of the firft company of mufketeers: it was broke in 1646, and reftored in 1657. The fecond was created 1660: this was the company of cardinal Mazarine's guards, which that minifter gave to the king.

The county of Rochefoucaud erected into a dutchy and peerage; the king's letters patent were not regiftered till 1681, and Francis de la Rochefoucaud, in whofe favour they were granted, was not admitted till 1637: he had married the heirefs of Rocheguyon and Liancourt. His fon, the author of the maxims, was a friend of madam de Longueville. The grandfon had the honour of being called the *king's friend*; his majefty having given him the place of great mafter of the wardrobe, the government of Berry, and the office of great huntfman: and yet thefe favours were not attributed to madam de Fontange, whofe confidence he enjoyed. His fon married the daughter of M. de Louvois.

The war continues, with alternate advantage, between the king and the proteftants. His majefty gave a fignal mark of courage in Poictou, when at the head of his guards he croffed over to the ifle of Riés at midnight, and drove M. de Soubife from thence, after defeating the troops, which defended that poft.

The king vifits the trenches at the fiege of Royan in Saintonge, and mounts the banquette three or four times to reconnoitre the place, at the hazard of his life. The proteftants grow tired of the war. The marquis de la Force fubmits, and is made marfhal of France. The Rochellers are defeated at fea by the duke de Guife,

REMARKABLE EVENTS under LEWIS XIII.

Guife, while the duke de Rohan makes his peace. The war ends in a confirmation of the edict of Nantes. The blockade of Rochelle is raifed, but fort Lewis is left ftanding. The duke de Lefdiguieres receives the conftable's fword, after having made his abjuration of Calvinifm: he had promifed cardinal Ludovifio to turn catholic, whenever that ecclefiaftic became pope; both cafes happened; Ludovifio (Gregory XV.) changed his ftation, and Lefdiguieres his religion. The fee of Paris, which before had been fubject to the jurifdiction of the metropolitan of Sens, is created an archbifhopric on the 20th of October; and has for its fuffragans, the bifhoprics of Chartres, Meaux, and Orleans, to which was afterwards added the bifhopric of Blois, created under Lewis XIV. The queen mother takes her feat in council, on condition that the bifhop of Luçon fhall not appear in that affembly. The prefident Jeannin, the chancellor de Sillery, and Puifieux his fon, fecretary of ftate, have the principal direction of affairs. The Spaniards amufe king James I. with the hopes of marrying the infanta to the prince of Wales, who fet out the next year for Madrid, in order to haften the nuptials; but they did not take place, neither did James I. grant any affiftance to Frederic his fon-in-law. The emperor continues the war againft this prince with great fuccefs; having made himfelf mafter of Heidelberg, he removes the famous library of that city to Rome, and gives it to pope Urban VIII.

1623.

A league is entered into by France, the duke of Savoy, and the republic of Venice, to procure the execution of the treaty of Madrid. The commander de Sillery, who fucceeded the marquis de Cœuvres as ambaffador to the court of Rome, concludes a treaty, on this head, with the Spaniards, which being difadvantageous to the king, was difavowed as foon as cardinal Richelieu came to the miniftry. The Dutch undertake an expedition to America, from whence they carry off an immenfe booty. Count Tilly obtains great advantages over the Dutch in Weftphalia. The death of the marfhal de Bouillon.

The THIRD RACE. 47
REMARKABLE EVENTS under LEWIS XIII.

1624.

The difgrace of the chancellor de Sillery, and of Puifieux his fon, who had oppofed the promotion of Richelieu to the cardinalate. The privy council is compofed of the duke de Vieuville, who fucceeded Schomberg in the office of fuperintendant of the finances, cardinal Rochefoucaud, the conftable Lefdiguieres, Aligre, keeper of the feals, and Bullion.

Richelieu, having received the cardinal's hat, is made member of the council, at the queen's recommendation, and takes his feat oppofite to cardinal Rochefoucaud, but below the conftable. Vieuville, who was fucceeded by Marillac, is confined in the caftle of Amboife; whence he made his efcape, and was appointed fuperintendant a fecond time in the next reign. Cardinal Rochefoucaud was difgufted, and the feals were taken from Aligre in 1626. The king grants a writ, or warrant, figned by two fecretaries of ftate, and dated the 9th of May; by which, without making it a precedent, his majefty declares that one of the cardinals only, affifting in council, fhall take place of the conftable. Vieuville, fuperintendant of the finances, and du Hallier, who was afterwards called the marfhal de l'Hopital, captain of the guards, figned as witneffes to this warrant, and we find in the memoirs of the count de Brienne, that it was afterwards *deftroyed*. The commander de Sillery, being involved in the difgrace of his family, is recalled from his embaffy at Rome, and M. de Bethune fucceeds him. The war of the Valteline, in which Cœuvres commands the king's army: the defign of it was to oblige the Spaniards to abandon the forts in their poffeffion; and to induce the pope to deliver up to France the places fequeftered into his hands. The treaty of Compiegne concluded with the Dutch.

The expedition of the Dutch againft Brafil and Peru, under the command of the admirals l'Hermite and Willekens. They make themfelves mafters of Lima and San-Salvador, but are not able to keep poffeffion of thofe places.

The Spaniards mifcarry in feveral expeditions againft the Hollanders. Spinola lays fiege to Breda.

The duke of Buckingham, a favourite of the prince of Wales (afterwards Charles I.) prevails on James I. to declare war againft the

REMARKABLE EVENTS under LEWIS XIII.

the king of Spain, with whom he had been at variance, since the marriage of the prince of Wales with the infanta had been set aside. Charles of Lorrain, who espoused Nicole, the eldest daughter of Henry II, surnamed the *Good*, duke of Lorrain, succeeds him in that dukedom: he was stiled Charles IV.

The monks of St. Genevieve reformed by cardinal de la Rochefoucaud, abbot of that monastery.

1625.

The Huguenots renew the war, under pretence of the non-execution of some promises; but the real motive was their taking umbrage at fort Lewis. M. de Soubise seizes Blavet or port Lewis. The Spaniards abandon the remainder of the Valteline, and Chiavene surrenders to the sieur de Longueval d'Haraucourt. The treaty of Monçon in Arragon, the following year, put an end to this contest: it was less favourable to the Grisons than that of Madrid; but cardinal Richelieu being engaged in the war with the French protestants, did not think it yet a right time to quarrel with Spain.

The king's troops, joined by those of the duke of Savoy, make incursions upon the territories of Genoa; but are soon dispossessed of their conquests. The death of James I. on the 6th of April, prevented that prince from assisting, on the 11th of May, at the solemnization of the marriage between Henrietta, the sister of Lewis XIII, and his son Charles I. The court conducted the young queen as far as Amiens; on which occasion the duke of Buckingham behaved with that imprudence, which laid the foundation of his aversion to France and the cardinal. James I. was just entering upon a war with Spain when he died; "But it was the fate of that pacific king to end " his days in peace; and he ceased to live, as soon as he became " desirous of war." (*Revol. of England.*) What is very extraordinary, this prince, the weakest of mortals, was strangely possessed with the notions of his *royal prerogative*, and absolute power. Buckingham had the same ascendant over Charles I, as he had enjoyed over the king his father. Instances of favourites to two succeeding princes are very rare. The constable de Montmorency had the same good fortune, of being in favour with Francis I, and Henry II; but upon close observation, we shall find there was a similarity of circumstances in regard to

those

REMARKABLE EVENTS under LEWIS XIII.

thofe two men, by which we might account for the continuance of their power; that is, they had quarrelled with their firſt maſter juſt before he died. Cardinal Barberini is ſent legate to France, where he ſerves his uncle, pope Urban VIII, but very indifferently; and miſcarries in his negotiation, by reaſon of his partiality to the Spaniards.

The civil war between the Huguenots and Catholics continues. A ſea fight near the iſle of Rhé, in which the royaliſts commanded by the duke de Montmorency, are victorious, and retake the iſland from the rebels. The duke of Feria raiſes the ſiege of Verue, defended by the prince of Piedmont, and is defeated in his retreat by the conſtable Leſdiguieres, and his ſon-in-law the marſhal de Crequy.

Spinola, after a ſiege of ten months, makes himſelf maſter of Breda, which had been taken from the Spaniards in 1590 by Maurice prince of Orange. Maurice died of chagrin, at not being able to raiſe the ſiege: his father was William, founder of the republic; and he was ſucceeded by Frederic Henry, his brother.

It was the misfortune of Europe, ſays Nani, to have, at this time, three young kings, on whom her fate depended; princes reſpectable for their power, remarkable for their ambition, and claſhing in their intereſts: but conformable in this only, that they committed the whole management of their affairs to their miniſters; Lewis to Richelieu, Philip to Olivarez, and Charles to Buckingham.

1626.

The beginning of the jealouſy between the king and Gaſton his brother, which interrupted the tranquillity of the kingdom. Gaſton marries mademoiſelle de Montpenſier at Nantes: ſhe died the year following, and left an only daughter her heireſs. This marriage had been productive of great agitations at court, where the cardinal's enemies were deſirous that Gaſton ſhould marry a foreign princeſs, in order to render him independent on the miniſter. A ſcheme is formed to aſſaſſinate the cardinal in his houſe at Fleury. The conſpiracy is detected; Chalais, maſter of the wardrobe, who owed his fortune to this miniſter, was ſaid to have joined in the deſign againſt his perſon, and had obſtructed this marriage, in order to

REMARKABLE EVENTS under LEWIS XIII.

pleafe madam de Chevreufe, the favourite of the young queen, who was afraid that Gafton would not marry. Chalaïs was beheaded. Marfhal d'Ornano, Gafton's confident, died in confinement at Vincennes; madam de Chevreufe efcaped to Lorrain; meffieurs de Vendome were arrefted; and the count of Soiffons withdrew to Rome, where, notwithftanding the cardinal's orders, M. de Bethune paid him the honours due to his birth: but this unfortunate prince loft his life afterwards at the battle of Marfée; as if it had been decreed, that deftruction was to attend every one who dared to oppofe the firft minifter. The cardinal who knew how to avail himfelf of every circumftance, even that of his late danger, had a company of life guards allowed him, for the fecurity of his perfon. Baradas, who fucceeded Chalais as the king's favourite, being fufpected by the cardinal, young Saint Simon was introduced in his room.

The remainder of this reign abounded in cabals and intrigues, but the cardinal triumphed over them all. The proteftant powers, Holland, Sweden, and the circle of Lower-Saxony, with the king of Denmark at their head, enter into a league againft the emperor. The emperor's generals were Tilly and Walftein; on the oppofite fide were Mansfeld, Chriftian of Brunfwick, ftiled the adminiftrator of Halberftadt, and the duke of Saxe Weimar. Mansfeld loft the battle of Deffau againft Walftein, and died foon after; the adminiftrator met with the fame fate. Tilly defeated the king of Denmark at the battle of Lutter.

The beginning of the quarrels between Charles I. and the parliament of England: the former was influenced by Buckingham; the latter perceived that the king was defirous of extending the *royal prerogative*, and rendering himfelf independent.

A fruitlefs expedition of the Englifh againft Cadiz. Charles I. difmiffes all the queen's fervants of the Roman Catholic perfuafion.

Poufin in Dauphiné, which had been feized by the rebels, is reftored to the king. An affembly of the *Notables* at the Thuilleries, which ended in ftrengthening the cardinal's intereft.

An arret of parliament, condemning a treatife written by Santarel, wherein this writer extends the authority of the pope

REMARKABLE EVENTS under LEWIS XIII.

beyond its due bounds. A declaration forbidding the impreſſion of all ſorts of books, without the name of their author: Henry II. made an order of the ſame nature in 1555.

1627.

The king aboliſhes the office of admiral, and grants an equivalent for it to the duke de Montmorency: he likewiſe ſuppreſſes the poſt of conſtable, vacant by the death of Leſdiguieres. "This general, in the early part of his life, applied himſelf to "letters; and if he had continued his ſtudies, would have been "as great a ſcholar as he proved afterwards a ſoldier." *(Brantome.)* The cardinal is created grand maſter and ſuperintendant general of the navigation and commerce of France, by an edict regiſtered the 10th of March: he likewiſe took his ſeat in parliament, in virtue of the king's letters patent, and had the ſame rank as he enjoyed in council.

The renewal of our alliance with the Dutch. The cardinal, having two principal objects in view, the reduction of the houſe of Auſtria, and the deſtruction of the Huguenots, begins with the latter, and undertakes to deprives them of the city of Rochelle, the bulwark of their religion.

A new war with the proteſtants. The duke of Buckingham jealous of the glory of cardinal Richelieu, and deſirous of regaining the affection of the Engliſh nation, prevails on Charles I. to aſſiſt the Rochellers. The fleet under his command appears off of the iſle of Rhé, at the requeſt of the Rochellers, and of the duke of Rohan, the avowed leader of that party. The Engliſh having been defeated by Toiras upon their landing in the iſland, and compelled by Schomberg to raiſe the ſiege of St. Martin, where they had made a fruitleſs aſſault, reimbarked with the loſs of eight thouſand men. On the 10th of Auguſt, the duke of Angouleme begins the ſiege of Rochelle. The king, attended by the chief nobility of the kingdom, arrives before the town. Francis Montmorency de Boutteville, and Romadec des Chanelles, are executed for the crime of duelling: this ſeverity had a greater effect upon the minds of the people, than all the edicts publiſhed on that account.

A diſpute, in regard to the command of the army, between M. l'Angouleme, and M. de Baſſompierre: to ſettle this difference,

REMARKABLE EVENTS under LEWIS XIII.

Baſſompierre was appointed to command a ſeparate body of forces; and M. d'Angouleme ſerved under the king. Lewis XIII. returned to Paris the 17th of February the enſuing year, and the cardinal ſtaid behind to direct the ſiege. On the 20th of November this year was begun the famous dyke, by Lewis Metezeau and John Tiriot. The king of Denmark abandoned by the princes of his party, and purſued on every ſide by Tilly and Walſtein, grows uneaſy about his own dominions, and makes propoſals of peace. The war continues between Guſtavus Adolphus, king of Sweden, and Siſgiſmund, king of Poland, who maintained his right to the crown of Sweden, which had been uſurped by Charles of Sudermania, the father of Guſtavus.

1628.

The duke de Rohan miſcarries in his attempt upon the citadel of Montpellier: the prince of Condé takes Palmier and Realmont, and after waſting the country about Caſtres, marches to the relief of Creſſels, in the neighbourhood of Milhau, attacked by M. de Rohan.

Pouſin, Mirabels, Chemeras, Bays and Garlangues, ſurrender to the king's troops commanded by the duke de Montmorency.

A treaty between the king of England and the Rochellers: Buckingham ſends a fleet to their aſſiſtance, which, being inſufficient for the purpoſe, returns to England the 18th of May. Some attribute this miſcarriage to a letter, which the queen is ſaid to have written at the cardinal's requeſt to the duke of Buckingham; but there does not ſeem to be a ſufficient proof of any ſuch letter. Buckingham is aſſaſſinated at Portſmouth the 2d of September. My lord Clarendon mentions a very extraordinary circumſtance relating to this murder. Sir George Villiers, the father of Buckingham, who died a great many years before, appeared to an old officer of his acquaintance, deſiring him to tell his ſon from him, that unleſs he ſtudied to render himſelf more agreeable to the nation, he would meet with an untimely end. The officer, as might naturally be expected, looked upon this as a dream: the ſpectre however was not diſcouraged, but returned a ſecond and a third time; and to give a further ſanction to this commiſſion, he informed the perſon of many particulars known only to the duke, which would convince that nobleman

REMARKABLE EVENTS under LEWIS XIII.

man of his not being a visionary. At length the person complied, and waited on the duke of Buckingham, who seemed to be very much disturbed at his discourse. Clarendon finishes this story with affirming, that it was founded in greater probability, than is usually met with in such predictions. I thought this anecdote worthy of being related, not in order to give much weight to it; but only to shew the high opinion the English had of the duke of Buckingham, since they imagined his death to have been attended with such wonderful circumstances; as if it were impossible for extraordinary men to die otherwise than as they lived. The fleet fitted out by the duke of Buckingham, which was much stronger than the former, makes a third, and last, effort in favour of Rochelle; the commander de Valançay engaged it, as he had done before. The king returned to the siege the 29th of March, and posted himself at the battery of *chef de bois*, or *Baye*, where upwards of three hundred cannon balls went over his head. The English attempt in vain to force the dyke, which was finished by Pompey Targon: their fleet returns to England; and Rochelle submits to the king the 28th of October. His majesty made his entry into the town, the first of November: the fortifications were demolished; the ditches filled up, the inhabitants disarmed, and rendered liable to the tailles, the privileges of the city abolished, and the catholic religion restored. This was a mortal blow to Calvinism, and may be reckoned the most glorious and most useful event, during the administration of cardinal Richelieu.

Thus was this rebellious town subdued; a town that had bid defiance to her sovereigns near two hundred years, and according to the usual policy of rebels, always chose to erect the standard of revolt, when our kings were most embarrassed. Such was the rebellion against Lewis XI, during the disturbances under his brother the duke of Guyenne; such that against Charles VII, when all the powers of Italy were combined against him at Fornova: that against Lewis XII, during the contest about the dutchy of Milan: that against Francis I, when he was at war with Charles V: that against Francis II, and Charles IX, under their minority: that against Henry III, by setting him at variance with his brother: that against Henry IV, when he was just ready to engage the duke of Savoy: and lastly, this against Lewis XIII, with whom the Rochellers had thrice waged open war, and who had expended forty millions in carrying on this siege.

As the king of Spain, and the dukes of Savoy and Lorrain, only waited for the issue of this enterprize to declare themselves; they continued very quiet upon hearing of its success. The cardinal said, he had taken Rochelle in spite of three kings; the king of Spain, the king of England, and especially the king of France: what rendered this strictly true, in regard to Lewis XIII, was the inquietude of this prince, from the suggestions of the minister's enemies who envied his glory.

Charles I. dissolves a third parliament, which would not submit to his will: *this made the power of parliaments,* says my lord Clarendon, *more formidable, since the sovereign seemed to be reduced to that rough cure of laying them aside, because he could not limit their jurisdiction.*

The Dutch continue successful by sea. Peter Adrian sets sail for the West-Indies, and falling in with the Spanish galleons, sets fire to the ships after plundering the cargo. Peter Hein attacks another fleet bound from Peru to Mexico, and becomes master of upwards of sixteen millions of livres in specie and in merchandize. Captain Carpentier and Peter de Nuits make new discoveries in the East-Indies, and give their names to those countries. This establishment of the Dutch in various parts of the globe, affords room for a general reflection, on the present commerce of the eastern and western world: and we find that the difference between the trade to America, and that to the East-Indies, is, that the former supports the European manufactures, while the latter maintains those of the East-Indies; this draws the specie from America to Europe, and from hence to the East.

1629.

Francis IV, duke of Mantua, died in 1612: he was succeeded by his brother Ferdinand, who died in 1626. Vincent, the youngest of the three, reaped the succession, and deceased in 1627. The legitimate heir was Charles Gonzaga, great uncle to the three last dukes: his son, the duke de Rhetelois, had espoused Mary the daughter of Francis IV, and therefore the several rights centered in him. The emperor, the king of Spain, the duke of Savoy and all Italy declared against the duke de Nevers, who had

REMARKABLE EVENTS under LEWIS XIII.

had no other support than France, where he was settled; each of those princes wanting to seize either the whole, or a part of that dutchy.

Cardinal Richelieu, zealous for his master's glory, and desirous to prevent his being led away by the intrigues of the queen and council, prevails on his majesty to march in person to the assistance of the duke of Mantua.

The queen mother is declared regent.

The Code Marillac, commonly called *Code Michaut*, published in the form of edict: this was a collection of our most famous ordinances, to which had been joined the edicts, relative to the remonstrances of the last assembly of the states, and to the demands of the assembly of the *Notables* at the Thuilleries. The king, notwithstanding the opposition of the parliament, ordered it to be published in his bed of justice, for it is not said to have been verified there; hence this edict was not afterwards observed, neither do our advocates quote it as law. It consists of four hundred and sixty one articles, of which there are a hundred and thirty-two relating to war, and thirty-one to the marine. We may take notice of some of the principal articles: the XXXIXth relative to clandestine marriages, declares them to be invalid; and lays an injunction on the ecclesiastic judges to determine concerning the said marriages, in pursuance of this article: the LVIIIth touching the masters of requests, who ought to be sent by the chancellor every year into the provinces, and there to perform nearly the same functions, as were anciently exercised by our king's commissaries, stiled *missi dominici*; so that by this edict, the masters of requests seem to be designed intirely for supplying the place of the intendants: the CCXIth, by which all gentlemen are commanded to sign the name of their families, and not of their lands or estates, in order to distinguish them from the *roturiers*, or plebeians, who were permitted to bear the name of the fiefs in their possession, &c.

The king in person forces the three barricades of the pass of Susa the 6th of March, having under him the marshals de Crequi and de Bassompierre. The treaty of Susa, by which the duke of Savoy delivers up this town into the hands of Lewis XIII. as

REMARKABLE EVENTS under LEWIS XIII.

a security for his assisting to raise the siege of Casal. The siege of Casal raised by the Spaniards. The king, at his return, finding that the Huguenots were still creating disturbances, notwithstanding the order he had sent them before his departure from Italy, to lay down their arms, marches towards Privas, which was taken and plundered the 27th of May: Alais capitulates the 8th of June; the cardinal enters Montauban the 20th of August; and a treaty is signed with the Calvinists by the last edict of pacification. The duke of Rohan, perceiving the inutility of the convention which he had lately signed with Spain, retired to Venice, till the circumstances of affairs, and the esteem due to his abilities, procured him the command of our troops in the Valteline. Cardinal Richelieu is made prime minister, by letters patent of the 21st of November.

The king, intending to suppress the states of the province of Languedoc, issues out an edict, creating twenty-two elections in that province; which was putting it on the same footing with the rest of the kingdom. This edict obtained only for two years, at the end of which it was repealed: the privileges of the province of Languedoc were restored, together with the custom of assembling the states.

Lewis XIII. had signed a treaty the 24th of April with the king of England, whereby this prince engaged not to assist the rebels during the other's absence.

A peace signed at Lubec the 27th of May, between the king of Denmark and the emperor: the arms of the latter had struck a terror into all Germany.

1630.

A decree of the consistory on the 1st of January, conferring the title of eminence on the cardinals, the ecclesiastic electors, and the grand masters of the order of Malta.

The duke of Savoy refuses to execute the treaty of Susa; and Spinola, in concert with that prince, persists in the design of stripping the duke of Mantua. The war breaks out again in Savoy, Piedmont, the dutchy of Montferrat, and the rest of Italy. The king and the Venetians continue to support the duke of Mantua. The emperor makes himself master of some towns belonging to the Grisons. Marshal Crequy take Pignerol

REMARKABLE EVENTS under LEWIS XIII.

in two days. Marshal Schomberg seizes Briqueras. Spinola, who died not long after, lays siege once more to Casal. The king returns to the army. Julius Mazarine, afterwards cardinal, makes his first appearance, and treats with the king in behalf of the duke of Savoy. His majesty is taken ill, and returns to Lyons, where he was expected by the two queens. The battle of Veillane on the 10th of July, in which the duke de Montmorency, after exposing himself rashly, defeats general Doria. The Imperialists taking advantage of the king's absence, surprize and plunder Mantua. The town of Saluzzo is carried by the marshals de la Force and Montmorency. Charles Emmanuel, duke of Savoy, dies of chagrin, to see his country a prey, through his own imprudence, to the French and to his allies. A suspension of arms between the French and Spaniards negotiated by Mazarine. The king of Sweden, aged five and thirty, having been invited last year by the inhabitants of Stralsund, a Hanse town of Germany, to defend them against Walstein, had the honour of stemming a torrent, which had hitherto carried every thing before it: and now this prince in resentment of the emperor's contemptuous behaviour, and under colour of defending the protestant religion oppressed by Ferdinand (who had lately published an edict for restoring the church-lands usurped by the protestant princes, since the reign of Charles V.) begins his German expedition with making himself master of the isle of Rugen.

The treaty of Ratisbon the 13th of October, between the king and the emperor. The duke of Mantua is maintained in the possession of his dominions, which were evacuated by the enemy the 27th of November. The king's stay at Lyons had like to have proved fatal, not only to the cardinal, by the forming of cabals against him, but also to France, by the dangerous malady which seized that prince. The queen mother conducts her son back to Paris, after obtaining a promise from him, that he would dismiss the cardinal as soon as the affair of Italy was settled. Richelieu seemed to be undone, and was preparing to retire; when the cardinal de la Valette advised him to wait upon the king at Versailles, whither the queen, too confident of her influence, had neglected to follow her son. The cardinal

dinal saw the king, and made him change his mind. From that moment he became more powerful than ever: the seals were taken from Marillac, who was imprisoned: the marshal, his brother, was arrested in Piedmont, and executed in 1632, (his memory was afterwards restored) and all the cardinal's enemies underwent the same punishment, which they were said to have intended for that minister. This was called *la journée des dupes*, or *all fools day.*

1631.

Gustavus Adolphus had in vain exhorted the emperor to abandon the king of Poland, and to do him justice in regard to some other grievances: Ferdinand did not give himself much uneasiness about the northern crowns; but little did he know Gustavus. This prince possesses himself of Stettin, which had been deposited in his hands by the duke of Pomerania, a secret enemy of the Imperial family; when cardinal Richelieu and Gustavus finding it their interest to unite, in order to oppose the exorbitant power of the house of Austria, a treaty was concluded by Charnacé, on the 23d of January, between France and Sweden: the conditions of it were to carry the war into the heart of Germany; to obtain full restitution to those princes, who had been deprived of their estates, without prejudicing however the Roman Catholic religion; and to live upon good terms with the duke of Bavaria. Gustavus found troops, the king money; and this diversion intirely changed the face of affairs in Germany.

A league between France and the catholic branch of Bavaria. A congress of the protestants at Leipsick, to declare war against the emperor. The treaty of Querasque: there were properly three treaties, the first on the 31st of March, the second on the 6th of April, and the third on the 30th of May. These put an end to the war of Italy. The duke of Mantua received the investiture of his dominions from the emperor, who relinquished the passes in the country of the Grisons; and the town of Pignerol, having been ceded to the king for six months, by a treaty signed at Millefleurs the 17th of October, was confirmed to his majesty by another treaty at St. Germains, the 5th of May, 1652, and was not recovered by the duke of Savoy till 1696. Gustavus Adolphus makes himself

REMARKABLE EVENTS under LEWIS XIII.

master of the town of Demin upon the Pene the 15th of February; takes Frankfort on the Oder by storm; restores the dukes of Mecklenburg to part of their dominions, of which they had been stripped by Walstein; and gains the battle of Leipsick the 7th of September, against Tilly and Papenheim. Gassion distinguished himself in the Swedish army. Gustavus takes Wurtzburg; and Rostock is surrendered to the dukes of Mecklenburg. The city of Prague is carried by storm, the 28th of November, by John George I, elector of Saxony. It is worth while to observe that this very town was taken by escalade, on the same day of the month in 1741, by marshal Saxe, that prince's great grandson, who afterwards rose to be marshal general of our armies. This elector having quarrelled with the emperor, in consequence of an edict of that prince concerning the restitution of church lands, commanded the left wing of Gustavus's army at the battle of Leipsick. The elector of Treves puts himself under the king's protection, against the arms of Gustavus. Wismar and Mentz surrender to the Swedes.

During these transactions, the court of France was in the utmost agitation. Gaston retired to Lorrain, and the queen to Brussels, both of them extremely dissatisfied with the cardinal. The former marries the princess Margaret, sister of Charles duke of Lorrain, at the instigation, as it is said, of his favourite Puilaurens, who was in love with the princess of Phalsburg, Margaret's sister: for it was ever the fate of both the brothers, Lewis XIII. and Gaston, to act intirely by the impression of their ministers, or their favourites. The king punished every person concerned in this marriage. The princess of Conti, the dutchesses of Elbœuf and Lesdiguieres, and madam d'Ornano were exiled; the marshal de Bassompierre, the abbe de Foix, and Vautier, the queen's physician, were sent to the Bastile. The princess of Conti, who had been privately married to Bassompierre, dies of grief; (she was daughter to the duke de Guise, killed at Blois, and had for her first husband the prince of Conti, who was deaf and dumb.) The count de Moret, the dukes d'Elbœuf, de Bellegarde, and de Rouanés, the president le Coigneux, the counsellor Payen, the sieur de Puilaurens, Monsigot, master of the accompts, and father Chanteloube, were declared

REMARKABLE EVENTS under LEWIS XIII.

guilty of high treason. The two offices of le Coigneux and Payen were suppressed, and the king published a declaration, bearing that those employments should be extinct, without waiting five years for the proof of contumacy, as usual in cases of high treason.

Moyenvic is wrested from the duke of Lorrain, who makes his peace with the king, by the treaty of Vic, on the 31st of December: to this treaty an article was added the 6th of January following, by which Gaston, having engaged to quit Lorrain, retires to Flanders, where he joins his mother, Mary of Medicis. The court of aids, having scrupled to register some edicts, is suspended; and justice is administered by a committee of masters of requests, and members of the grand council. The gazette was begun by Theophrastus Renaudot, a physician.

The town of Richelieu is erected into a dutchy and peerage, in favour of the cardinal, his heirs, successors, and assigns, male, and female.

The old gate of St. Honoré, near the hospital of the *Quinze-vingts* * is pulled down, and a new one erected; it was demolished again in 1733, that there might be no longer any separation between the city and this suburb, which was considerably enlarged.

1632.

The duke of Lorrain delivers up Marsal to the king, by virtue of the treaty of Vic. The marshal de Marillac is tried by commissaries, and beheaded. The arret of parliament, concerning this affair, is reversed by a decree of council; Molé, the attorney-general, is summoned to appear in person, and suspended from his office; "But his presence, and natural gra-
"vity, which he firmly supported, soon procured an order for
"his discharge." (*Mem. de Talon.*) The duke of Orleans, assisted by the Spaniards, penetrates into the kingdom by the way of Burgundy.

The king having just reason of complaint against the duke of Lorrain, on account of the disturbances raised by Gaston, seizes Pont-a-Mousson, Bar-le-duc, and St. Michel. The duke has

---

* *Quinze-vingts* signifies three hundred; it is so called, because three hundred blind people are relieved here with bread, lodging, and about four-pence a day.

REMARKABLE EVENTS under LEWIS XIII.

recourse a second time to the king's clemency; and concludes the treaty of Liverdun the 26th of June, in confirmation of the treaty of Vic, whereby he not only deposits Jametz and Stenay into the hands of the king, but surrenders the fortress of Clermont in full property, and yields homage for the dutchy of Bar: could this experience have rendered him more steady, he might have avoided the calamities, in which he was afterwards involved. The duke of Orleans, finding no resource from that quarter, carried his evil genius with him into Languedoc. The duke de Montmorency having joined in the revolt, was wounded and taken prisoner in the battle, or rather skirmish, of Castlenaudary, on the first of September, where the king's troops were commanded by marshal Schomberg. M. de Montmorency fell into an ambuscade, and this determined the fate of the day, though Gaston was stronger by one half than the marshal. "A report being instantly spread through "the army, says Pointis, that M. de Montmorency is slain; "Gaston lays down his arms, says he will fight no more, and "then orders a retreat." The count de Moret, son of Henry IV. and of mademoiselle de Beuil, countess of Moret, was killed on the same occasion: some pretend this count was not slain, but turned hermit; but there is no foundation for such a story. Gaston is reconciled once more to the king, by the advice of M. de Bullion, in hopes of saving the life of M. de Montmorency.

Henry de Montmorency, duke and peer, and marshal of France, is tried by commissioners; the president was l'Aubespine de Chateauneuf, keeper of the seals, an ecclesiastic, who had been obliged to obtain a dispensation from the pope to sit in judgment upon the marshal de Marillac, and now he obtained another for the trial of the duke de Montmorency; but he should have considered, that he had been page to this duke's father.

The duke de Montmorency is beheaded at Toulouse the 30th of October, at the age of thirty-seven. If it be true, that he gave the cardinal the first intelligence of the cabal of Lyons, he had reason to repent this good office, which proved his ruin. Gaston quits the kingdom the third time, imagining himself actuated by resentment for the death of Montmorency, but in reality only yielding to the impulses of Puilaurens: he retires to the queen his mother in Flanders. The

REMARKABLE EVENTS under LEWIS XIII.

The duke of Bavaria having refused to join the Swedes, who would have obliged him to restore the Upper-Palatinate, Gustavus makes himself master of Augsburg, and ravages Bavaria. At length this hero, and head of the protestants in Germany, after defeating the Danes and Imperialists, and subduing Pomerania, Lower-Saxony, Franconia, Bavaria, the Palatinate, and the electorate of Mentz, is slain at the age of eight and thirty, on the 16th of November, at the battle of Lutzen, where Walstein nevertheless is defeated by SaxeWeimar, the Swedish general. Gustavus delighted in Grotius's treatise of the rights of war and peace, which was found in his tent. He would allow of no rank or precedency among kings, but such as arises from merit. This prince was succeeded by the celebrated Christina, his daughter: he began to be suspected by the French, who did not invite him into Germany with a view of rendering him formidable to that country, but to reduce the power of the house of Austria. There is no reason to believe that cardinal Richelieu hired a person to kill him: Puffendorff thinks he was shot by Francis Albert, duke of Saxe-Lawenburg, at the instigation of the Imperialists: others pretend that this same Albert did it out of revenge for a box on the ear, which he received from Gustavus, for living in too great a familiarly with the queen his mother. Frederic V, king of Bohemia, dies of despair, his hopes being blasted by the death of Gustavus.

Letters patent establishing the missionary priests, known by the name of St. Lazare.

1633.

An edict creating the parliament of Metz: the inhabitants of that district used to carry their appeals to the Imperial chamber at Spire. The alliance, betwixt France and Sweden, renewed by M. de Feuquieres and the chancellor Oxenstiern; in consequence of which, the league concluded by Gustavus Adolphus, was likewise renewed by Sweden, England, Holland, and part of the princes of Germany, against the house of Austria: this confederacy proved the more serviceable to the king, as without coming to an open rupture with the emperor, he ravaged Germany, and cut out too much work for the house of Austria to afford any assistance to the rebels in France. This year abounds

The THIRD RACE. 63

REMARKABLE EVENTS under LEWIS XIII.

abounds with skirmishes and engagements betwixt the two parties. A few bishops, who had been concerned in Gaston's revolt, are tried at Paris by the Pope's delegates; but the clergy protested in 1650, against this delegation. A creation of knights of the order of the Holy Ghost. The duke of Lorrain goes to war the third time with France: this prince refused to yield homage for the dutchy of Bar, either because he would not absolutely make his submission, or he scrupled only, as some pretend, to make it in the name of the princess Nicole, since this would be acknowledging that he held the dukedom of Lorrain in right of his wife; whereas he claimed it in his own right, according to the Salic law, which had been established in Lorrain by René II. Be that as it may, Lewis XIII. reunites the dutchy of Bar to the crown; seizes St. Mihel and Luneville; lays siege to Nancy, and obliges the duke to sign a treaty at Charmes, by which the town of Nancy is surrendered as a deposit; on the other hand the king is not to restore it, but upon condition that the duke shall deliver up the princess Margaret his sister, whose marriage with the duke of Orleans was void, according to the customs of France, for want of the king's consent.

Lewis XIII. takes possession of the town of Nancy, because the duke of Lorrain had not performed his engagement, his sister having followed Gaston, her husband, to Brussels. The elector of Treves is restored to his capital by the French.

This year the title of lieutenant-general was first heard of in the French armies: the principal officers before that time were the marshals de-camp, of whom there was but a very small number, under the marshals of France. The first commission of lieutenant-general is to Melchior Mitte de Chevrieres, marquis de S. Chamond, dated the 6th of February, this year 1633: (this has escaped father Daniel) their number was augmented under Lewis XIV, in the war of 1667, and greatly enlarged after that of 1672. This institution was of use: 1. It made a degree between the marshals de-camp, and a marshal of France; as another was also created viz. that of a brigadier, between the colonel and the marshal de-camp, in order to excite and maintain an emulation among the officers, by establishing a greater proximity between the different steps of military honour. 2. Each of those ranks increases the

duty

duty of the officer, and of courſe qualifies him the better for command. 3. The armies, becoming more numerous, required a greater number of general officers for their ſeveral diviſions.

The court of Inquiſition at Rome condemns Galileo for maintaining the Copernican ſyſtem of the motion of the earth; he was obliged to retract this opinion, in order to obtain his liberty.

The chapel of St. Roch at Paris erected into a pariſh.

1634.

Charles IV, duke of Lorrain, to evade his engagements with the king, reſigns his dominions to cardinal Francis, his brother, who marries the princeſs Claude, ſiſter of Nicole, by whom he had Charles Leopold, the ſucceſſor of Charles IV. Upon receiving this news, marſhal de la Force inveſts Luneville; and the two princes quit their dominions, which are ſeized by the king. Charles IV. joins the Imperial army. Nicole, dutcheſs of Lorrain, having quarrelled with her huſband, repairs to Paris, where the king gives her a kind reception. Marſhal de la Force takes la Mothe which was deemed impregnable: at this ſiege the French made uſe of bombs for the firſt time, though invented in 1588.

Walſtein, who from a private gentleman of Bohemia, was become all-powerful in the empire, the emperor ſtanding in need of ſo great a commander, forgets he was born a ſubject, and, upon ſome diſguſt, forms a project to make himſelf ſovereign of Bohemia. Cardinal Richelieu encouraged his ſcheme, but Oxenſtiern and the reſt of the league were tardy in ſupporting him. The emperor having been appriſed of his deſign, Walſtein was aſſaſſinated in Egra, by the treachery of Gordon his intimate friend. A treaty betwixt France and Holland, for continuing the Dutch war againſt Spain.

A general and extraordinary ſeſſion * held at Poitiers. M. Talon obſerves, that it is proper to hold this court every eight or ten years; "Becauſe the very apprehenſion of it, he ſays, is "ſufficient to reſtrain the nobility and officers within their duty." But the royal authority ſtands no longer in need of ſuch precautions.

* The French call this court the *grands jours*.

Urban

REMARKABLE EVENTS under LEWIS XIII.

Urban Grandier, convicted of the crime of forcery by a particular commiffion, is burnt alive. La Peyrere, the author of the Preadamites, but who has alfo written a hiftory of Greenland, very much efteemed, was once afked the reafon, why there were fo many wizards in the north; it is becaufe, faid he, the effects of thofe pretended wizards are, upon conviction, confifcated in part to the profit of the judges.

An arret of parliament dated the 5th of September, upon the determination of Bignon, the firft advocate-general, declaring the marriage of the king's brother with the princefs of Lorrain null and void. (*See Mem. de Talon.*) The general affembly of the clergy paffed the fame judgment the next year. The war was ftill carried on in Germany with t' ? fame vigour; but the battle of Nordlingen gave a great turn in favour of the emperor: it was fought the 6th of December; when Ferdinand king of Hungary, the cardinal infant, and Charles duke of Lorrain, gained a complete victory over the Swedifh army, commanded by the duke of Weimar and marfhal Horn, who were marching to the relief of Nordlingen. The war continued likewife in Flanders, between the marquis of Ayetone, governor of the Netherlands, and the prince of Orange.

The king's brother, who had concluded a treaty with Spain, which came to the cardinal's ear, and gave him great uneafinefs, is ftrongly preffed to make his peace with the king: this negotiation was managed with the abbe d'Elbene; and Puilaurens, as a reward for difpofing his mafter to the treaty, had the dutchy of Aiguillon, and married mademoifelle du Pont-du-Chateau, a relation of the cardinal. But this profperity was of fhort duration; for Puilaurens, ftill continuing to encourage the duke of Orleans in his refolution of maintaining the validity of his marriage, contrary to the king's will, was fent the next year to the Baftile, where he died the 1ft of July.

The queen mother follicited the cardinal in the ftrongeft manner for leave to return to France, but in vain, becaufe he had nothing to fear from that quarter. The king's brother arrives at St. Germains the 21ft of October.

The defeat before Nordlingen obliged the Swedes to abandon feveral towns in Alface, which received French garrifons. The

French likewise became masters of Philipsburg and Spire, in consequence of a treaty signed by the king, the crown of Sweden, and the rest of the princes of Germany; this baffled the design the Imperialists had formed of marching into Lorrain. The king causes several strong places in Alsace to be dismantled.

The garden of plants established at Paris, by the care of Bouvard, the king's chief physician, and of Guy de la Brosse, physician in ordinary; it is called the *king's garden*. The first meridian fixed at the isle of *Fer*.

1635.

The manor of St. Simon erected into a dutchy and peerage.

Letters patent of the month of January, instituting the French academy: they were not registered till the 10th of July, 1637. The academicians had begun to assemble in 1634. The first officers were M. de Serizay, director, M. Desmarets, chancellor, and M. Conrart, secretary.

Philipsburg surprized by the Imperialists. The famous treaty signed at Paris the 8th of Feb. between Lewis XIII. and the States-General; whereby the king engages to declare war against Philip IV, if this prince does not give full satisfaction for several grievances and subjects of complaint. This treaty contained also a partition of the Spanish Netherlands between the two contracting powers. Not to mention the absurdity of such a negotiation, Richelieu let the Dutch see, they were going to be next neighbours to France, without a barrier; for this reason they acted with great reserve in assisting the king, and the common cause was greatly hurt, tho' they seemed very desirous at first of our alliance.

The Spaniards being informed of this treaty, surprize the city of Treves the 26th of March, and take the elector prisoner. The king declares war against Spain. The war lasted thirteen years against the emperor, and five and twenty against Spain: the successes this year were various. The marshals de Chatillon and de Brezé gained the battle of Avein the 20th of May, over the Spaniards commanded by prince Thomas of Savoy, who endeavoured to hinder the junction of our troops with those of the States-General. Folard attributes the whole honour of it to marshal Chatillon's arriving in time to the assistance of M. de Brezé, whose imprudence and vanity had prompted him to engage

REMARKABLE EVENTS under LEWIS XIII.

a superior enemy, only to prevent his being obliged to share the honour of a victory with M. de Chatillon. The sack of Tillemont the 6th of June. The siege of Lovain raised; this was owing to the jealousy of the prince of Orange, who hated cardinal Richelieu. A league offensive and defensive signed at Rivoli, the 6th of July, by France, Savoy, and the duke of Parma. Victor Amadeus is made captain general of the league. The marshal de Crequy marches ten thousand men into Italy. This war proved unsuccessful, through the misunderstanding of the chiefs. Galas, the Imperial general, takes Keiserloutre from the Swedes. The Spaniards make themselves masters of fort Schenck.

The cardinal de la Valette obliges the Imperialists to raise the siege of Mentz, and general Galas the siege of Deux-Ponts.

The Spaniards make a descent in Provence, and marshal de Vitry flies to its assistance. The duke de Weimar, and cardinal de la Valette, defeat five thousand men commanded by Galas, in the neighbourhood of Vaudrevange. Saint Mihel in Lorrain surrenders at discretion to marshal de la Force. The emperor had lately gained the elector of Saxony, whose example was followed by several other princes; and as there was reason to fear left the duke of Saxe-Weimar should be carried away with the stream, the king concluded a treaty with that prince at St. Germains the 26th of October, by which he entered into closer connections with France.

The duke de Rohan beats Serbelloni's troops twice in the Valteline. Gassion, with five hundred horse, repels six thousand under John de Wert, and takes fifteen hundred prisoners. The Imperialists make themselves masters of Saverne. The count of Sufa defends Porentru against Colloredo. Chalard concluded a treaty of commerce the first of September, in the behalf of the king with the emperor of Morocco. The taking of Guadalupe. The death of Thomas Parr, aged a hundred and fifty-two years; he had seen ten kings of England.

1636.

The war is carried on with greater vigour than ever in Germany, Italy, and France. Cardinal de la Valette obliges the Imperialists to raise the siege of Colmar the 25th of January.

REMARKABLE EVENTS under LEWIS XIII.

The marquis de la Force beats Colloredo, and takes him prisoner, the 17th of March. The Swedes surrender Mentz to the Imperialists for want of provisions. The treaty of Wismar between the king and queen Christina, signed the 20th of March: the celebrated Grotius was her ambassador in France. The duke de Rohan defeats the Spaniards on the borders of the lake of Como the 18th of April. Fort Schenck is recovered from the Spaniards by count William of Nassau the 30th. The Dutch after this remain inactive; which enables the cardinal Infant to penetrate into France. The Imperialists raise the siege of Hanau, upon the approach of the Swedes, the 22d of June. The duke of Savoy, and marshal de Crequy, defeat the marquis of Leganes at the battle of Tesin: marshal Toiras was killed a few days before. The count of Susa makes himself master of Befort the 29th. The Spaniards take la Capelle the 9th of July, and Catelet soon after. Saverne surrenders to the duke of Weimar, and cardinal de la Valette, July 11th. Viscount Turenne, who acted as marshal de-camp on this occasion, was wounded. The prince of Condé raises the siege of Dole the 15th of August, part of his army having been recalled for the defence of Picardy. Corbie is taken by the Spaniards the same day: this misfortune throws the city of Paris into a panic; an army of twenty thousand men is raised, chiefly among the lackeys and apprentices, discharged by their masters, in consequence of an arret of council the 13th of August. The Parisians imagining John de Wert to be just at their gates, contributed generously towards the support of the troops. The king advances into Picardy, and invests the duke of Orleans with the command of an army of fifty thousand men, which obliged the Spaniards to repass the Somme. Cardinal Richelieu was so greatly dejected as to think of retiring, *and would have taken this foolish step,* says Siri, *had it not been for father Joseph, who raised his spirits; in which he was seconded by the superintendant de Bullion.* The admiral of Arragon surprizes St. John de Luz, and sets fire to that town in the month of October. Duke Charles of Lorrain, and general Galas, penetrate into Burgundy, spreading terror through the whole dutchy: they lay siege to St. John de Lone; but M. de Rantzau obliges them to raise it the 3d of November. Cardinal de la Valette, and the duke of

REMARKABLE EVENTS under LEWIS XIII.

Weimar drive them back to the Rhine; and the Imperialists lose very near eight thousand men. The count of Soissons and marshal Chatillon retake Corbie, under the command of the duke of Orleans, the 10th of November: the cardinal was at Amiens; and the king between Amiens and Corbie, from whence he went every day to examine the works.

General Banier, who three months before could not hinder the elector of Saxony from taking Magdeburg, defeats this same prince at Wistoc, the 14th of October, possesses himself of Erfurt, and ravages all Misnia.

A treaty signed the 21st of October, between the king and William Landgrave of Hesse. The disgrace of M. le Premier (this was M. de St. Simon); he wanted to support his uncle St. Leger, who was said to have behaved very ill in the defence of Catelet.

The count of Soisson had determined to get rid of cardinal Richelieu during the siege of Corbie; the blow was to be struck at Amiens; and Montresor and St. Ibal had undertaken the base office. The duke of Orleans embarked in the scheme; but either through weakness or religion, hindered it from being put in execution; yet the apprehension of its having taken wind, caused both the duke and the count suddenly to withdraw from court, the former to Blois, and the latter to Sedan. The duke's fears were soon quieted; the king offered to confirm his marriage: and endeavours were used to gain the count of Soissons, to whom M. de Bouillon had granted a retreat at Sedan.

Ferdinand Ernestus, king of Hungary, son of Ferdinand II, was crowned king of the Romans; and succeeded his father the year following, on the 8th of February.

1637.

This year, which seemed to open very inauspiciously, proved more favourable than any of the preceding to the king's arms. The duke of Parma, hard pressed by the Spaniards, and menaced with papal excommunications, renounces his alliance with France.

The Grisons, reconciled to Spain, oblige the duke de Rohan to withdraw his troops from the Valteline. The duke apprehensive of the cardinal's partiality, and of being condemned for an event, which was owing entirely to that minifter's neglect, in not fending the promifed fubfidies, remained in Swifferland, and ferved the next year under the duke of Saxe-Weimar. The rambling foldierly life of Charles IV, duke of Lorrain, did not hinder him from falling in love with Margaret, princefs of Cantecroix, whom he married at Befançon, pretending, that his marriage with Nicole was void, from the plea of force or reftraint. The count d'Harcourt takes the town of Oriftan in Sardinia; and recovers the iflands of St. Margaret and St. Honorat, on the coaft of Provence, which had been poffeffed by the Spaniards fince the year 1635. This general was founder of the branch of Armagnac in France, and died in 1666. Experience fhews us, fays this great captain, that as there are unforefeen misfortunes in war, fo there are profperous turns, which exceed our moft fanguine expectations. The duke de Longueville takes the caftle of St. Amour, and Lyon le Saunier in Franche Comté. The Lorrainers are twice defeated by the duke de Weimar. The cardinal de la Valette carries Landrecy and la Capelle: the towns of Yvoy and Damvilliers, in the dutchy of Luxemburg, furrender to marfhal Chatillon. The duke of Savoy and marfhal Crequy gain a complete victory in Italy, over the Spanifh army under the duke of Modena. The duke d'Halluin, known afterwards by the name of marfhal Schomberg, and fon of the marfhal of the fame name, obliges Serbelloni, the Spanifh general, to raife the fiege of Leucate. The elector of Treves obtains his enlargement of the emperor the 25th of Auguft, upon quitting his alliance with France: Buffy-Lamet had furrendered Hermenftein to the elector of Cologn, fo early as the 20th of July, after a defence of two years. Breda taken by the prince of Orange.

Charles I. following the footfteps of James I, who had reftored epifcopacy in Scotland, and excited by William Laud, archbifhop of Canterbury, attempts to introduce the liturgy of the church of England into North Britain. This proved the fource of the misfortunes of that reign, and the principal caufe of the king's cataftrophe; to which cardinal Richelieu might likewife have contributed, by the intrigues of the marquis of Senneterre, ambaffador from France to the court of London.

The

The THIRD RACE. 71

REMARKABLE EVENTS under LEWIS XIII.

The death of Victor Amadeus, duke of Savoy, who leaves the tutelage of his children to his wife, the sister of Lewis XIV. Prince Thomas, and his brother the cardinal, gave great uneasiness to that princess during her regency.

The marquisate of la Force erected into a dutchy and peerage.

1638.

Lewis XIII. puts his kingdom under the protection of the virgin Mary.

France begins to feel the effects of a long war; the troops, and the annuitants on the public revenue, being ill paid. Two battles in the neighbourhood of Rheinfeld, one on the 28th of February, the other on the 3d of March. In the former the duke of Weimar, who had laid siege to Rheinfeld, was beaten by John de Wert; the duke de Rohan was mortally wounded, and died the 13th of April, at the abbey of Kunisfeld, in the canton of Bern: his corpse was interred in the great church of Geneva. The Venetians received with extraordinary respect the present of his suit of armour, which he bequeathed to that republic. In the latter, the duke of Weimar obtained a complete victory over the Imperialists, and made their four generals prisoners: John de Wert was led in triumph to Paris. This victory struck the whole empire with terror. The duke of Weimar having made himself master of Friburg, Rheinfeld, and several other towns, invested Brisac.

Bremen surrenders to the marquis of Leganes, the 27th of March; here the marshal de Crequy was killed by a cannon ball on the 17th. William of Nassau is defeated by the cardinal Infant in the country of Waes *. The duke de Longueville obtains a complete victory over Charles, duke of Lorrain, and makes himself master of Poligny. The prince of Conde having penetrated by *Iron* in Navarre, takes fort Figuiro, and port Passage, with twelve ships belonging to the enemy. Marshal Chatillon raises the siege of St. Omer the 15th of July. Marshal de la Force, who was come to join him, had been defeated the 8th by prince Thomas of Savoy.

Weimar gains the battle of Wittenweyer against Gœutz and Savelli the 9th of August; and the same day the king makes him-

* The north-east division of Flanders.

The HISTORY of FRANCE.

REMARKABLE EVENTS under LEWIS XIII.

self master of Renty. The archbishop of Bourdeaux burns the Spanish fleet, near the Mole of Gatary in Biscay, the 22d of August. The prince of Orange raises the siege of Gueldres the 31st. Pontcourlay puts fifteen Spanish gallies to flight in the neighbourhood of Genoa. The birth of the dauphin (afterwards Lewis XIV.) on the 5th of September, at St. Germains in Laye, in the 23d year of the king's marriage with Anne of Austria: according to Bassompierre this princess had hurt herself in 1622, and miscarried. The 7th of September the prince of Condé raises the siege of Fontarabia. Cardinal Richelieu, who did not love the duke de la Valette, laid the blame upon this general, and appointed commissaries to try him, who condemned him to lose his head, which was executed in effigy *.

Du Hallier retakes Catelet, September the 14th. M. de Bellefond obliges duke Charles to raise the siege of Luneville the 20th. The duke of Weimar defeats the duke of Lorrain, near Thann the 15th of October. The generals Gœutz and Savelli are repulsed with loss by the count de Guebriant, at the attack of the lines before Brisac the 24th. This same Savelli is beaten near Blamont the 7th of November by the duke de Longueville. Brisac surrenders to the duke of Weimar, December the 19th, Messieurs de Turenne and de Guebriant were at this siege.

Aiguillon created a dutchy and peerage in favour of Magdalen de Vignerot, widow of M. de Combalet, with this extraordinary clause, *for the said lady to hold, and for her heirs, and successors, as well males as females, as she shall think proper to appoint:* in virtue of this clause, by her will in 1674 she called to the succession her niece Maria Theresa, and, at the same time, substituted her grand nephew Lewis, marquis of Richelieu, whose son the count d'Agenois was declared duke d'Aiguillon, by an arret of parliament in 1731, contrary to the opinion of all the peers of France.

1639.

The king had six armies on foot, the first commanded by M. de la Meilleraie, in the Netherlands; the second by M. de Feuquieres towards Luxemburg; the third by marshal Chatillon, on the frontiers of Champagne; the fourth in Languedoc, un-

* He withdrew to England after the battle, to avoid the cardinal's resentment.

REMARKABLE EVENTS under LEWIS XIII.

der the prince of Condé; the fifth in Italy, commanded by the duke de Longueville; and the sixth in Piedmont, subject to the orders of cardinal de la Valette. The duke of Weimar marches into Franche Comté, with the count de Guebriant after defeating the troops commanded by the prince of Lorrain, they take Pontarlier the 29th of January, the town and castle of Noseray the 4th of February, and the fort of Joux the 14th. The marshal de Chaulnes obliges the Spaniards to raise the siege of Cateau Cambresis the first of March. The Swedes under general Banier obtain a victory over the Imperialists the 2d of March, in the neighbourhood of Ulnitz; and another on the 24th of April not far from Kemnitz. Demin taken by the Swedes the 20th.

Chivas was surprized by prince Thomas March the 26th, and retaken by cardinal de la Valette the 28th of June. Quiers, Montcalier, and Yvrée, declare in favour of this prince, who makes himself master of Trin the 4th of May, after the marquis of Leganes and himself had been forced, by cardinal de la Valette, the 12th of April, to raise the siege of Turin. The king came as far as Grenoble, attended by cardinal Richelieu, to have an interview with the dutchess of Savoy; where he agreed with this princess, to garrison the towns of Carmagnola, Saviliano, and Cherasco. This was the surest way of detaching the princes of Savoy from their alliance with Spain, lest the French should keep possession of the fortresses deposited in their hands. June the 7th Piccolomini defeats the marquis de Feuquieres, who had laid siege to Thionville: we lost in this action upwards of six thousand men killed or taken prisoners. M. de Feuquieres died soon after of his wounds. Cardinal Richelieu laid the whole blame of this defeat on the count de Grancey, afterwards marshal of France, and on the marquis of Praslin, who were both sent to the Bastile.

Piccolomini raises the siege of Mouson, defended by Refuge, upon the approach of marshal Chatillon.

Charles I, having assembled an army at York against the rebels of Scotland, is obliged to come to an agreement with them at Berwick, on the 28th of June, promising that all matters ecclesiastical shall be determined in a general assembly, and

confirmed

confirmed by parliament. This affembly obliged the whole nation to fign an affociation called the *covenant*; whereby they engaged themfelves to defend their religion againft the king himfelf. The Englifh prefbyterians join with thofe of Scotland. Hefdin is furrendered to Lewis XIII, and la Meilleraye receives the ftaff of marfhal of France upon the breach. The prince of Condé makes himfelf mafter of Salces, July the 19th, and marfhal Chatillon takes Yvoy, the 2d of Auguft. The princes of Savoy furprize the city of Turin, Auguft the 27th. The dutchefs of Savoy retires to Sufa, where the princes, her children, refided, and from thence to Grenoble, where fhe had an interview with the king. The citadel remained in the hands of the French. The duke of Saxe-Weimar died, at Newburg upon the Rhine, the 18th of July, not without fufpicion of poifon, aged only fix and thirty. The death of this prince would have been a very great lofs to France, if he had not given fome reafon to fufpect his defign, of rendering himfelf independent of this crown, in order to form a principality of Brifac and fome other places. The king concluded a treaty with major general Erlac, by virtue of which the Weimar troops remained in our fervice, and the ftrong places in their poffeffion were given up to France. By this treaty the alliance with Sweden was renewed. The duke de Longueville, who had the command of thofe troops, makes himfelf mafter of feveral towns in the Palatinate. Charles Lewis, the fon of Frederic, who had been ftripped of that electorate, though protected by England, the prince of Orange, and the Dutch, laid claim to the fucceffion of the duke of Weimar: but paffing through France incognito, in his way to the Rhine, he was arrefted by order of his majefty, and conducted to Vincennes, from whence he was not releafed, till he relinquifhed his pretenfions.

The equeftrian ftatue of Lewis XIII. erected in the *place royale*, September the 27th, at the expence of cardinal Richelieu.

Admiral Tromp, after taking two Spanifh galeons, laden with treafure, near Dunkirk, on the 16th of September, defeats the fleet of that nation on the coaft of England the 18th of October.

REMARKABLE EVENTS under LEWIS XIII.

The count d'Harcourt, having succeeded cardinal de la Valette, who died the 28th of September, detaches la Mothe Houdancourt, who takes Quiers, and re-victuals Casal. The battle of Quiers the 20th of November, in which the count d'Harcourt is victorious over prince Thomas. Binghen surrendered to the duke de Longueville.

Mademoiselle de la Fayette, a favourite of the king, had been obliged to retire from court in 1637, by a contrivance of the cardinal, who grew jealous of her influence: father Cauffin, the king's confessor, as well as that lady's, had encouraged her to intrigue against this minister, even after she took the veil among the nuns of the order of the Visitation: the cardinal got him banished to Lower-Britany. Madam d'Hautefort and mademoiselle de Chemeraut, being in high favour both with the king and queen, occasioned great uneasiness this year to the minister: he procured their disgrace, and substituted young Cinqmars, son of the marshal d'Effiat, in their stead.

The king's declaration, suspending the parliament of Rouen, for having neglected to exert themselves against an insurrection in that city. The chancellor Seguier was sent the next year to Rouen, to declare the suspension, and to fine several towns concerned in the revolt: he had the command of the troops, and the white standard was carried every night into his apartment, *(The History of Cardinal Richelieu by Aubery, p. 423. The History of Lewis XIII, by Vassor, tom. 16. p. 391. See also Duchesne)* and monf. de Gassion was under his command. The king's council attended him in this expedition; M. Vrilliere, secretary of state, had orders to be near his person, and to sign the dispatches necessary on that occasion: we must observe further, that the arrets of the council of the finances, which must pass through the great seal, were dated from those places where the chancellor then happened to reside.

The king sends a letter of cachet to the parliament, directing them to signify, in his name, to the bishops and other prelates then in Paris, that his majesty forbids them to have any communication with M. Scoti, the pope's extraordinary nuncio. His holiness had disobliged the king on several occasions, as well by

the

the treatment of marſhal d'Etrees, his ambaſſador at Rome, as by violating the privileges of the French nation.

1640.

The king's declaration of the 26th of November, in regard to clandeſtine marriages and rapes, confirming the edict of 1556, and the articles 40. 41. 42. 43. and 44. of the edict of Blois: it contains among other points, *that the puniſhment due to rapes ſhall be incurred, notwithſtanding the conſent of parents, guardians, &c. afterwards obtained; and it aboliſhes the cuſtoms, by which children are permitted to marry after the age of twenty without the conſent of parents.*

Since the beginning of the Spaniſh war, France never had greater ſucceſs than this campaign, when her enemies experienced ſurprizing revolutions, in which the French nation however had no concern.

The Spaniards make themſelves maſters of the town of Salces, the 6th of January. The magiſtrates of Saverne take the oath of allegiance to the king. The count de Guebriant obliges the enemy to raiſe the ſiege of Binghen. The duke of Luneburg, who had quitted the northern league through fear of the Imperial arms, embraced it again as ſoon as he found that the Landgravine of Heſſe had renewed the treaties betwixt France and the late Landgrave her huſband. The count d'Harcourt, after forcing Leganes, in his lines before Caſal, on the 29th of April, and thereby enabling himſelf to lay ſiege to Turin, obtains a ſecond victory the 11th of July, over that ſame general, who advanced to attack him in his entrenchments. The ſiege of Turin undertaken by the count d'Harcourt: there was a concurrence of extraordinary circumſtances; for the citadel was beſieged by prince Thomas, then in poſſeſſion of the town; count d'Harcourt beſieged prince Thomas; and was beſieged himſelf ſoon after in his camp by the marquis of Leganes. The town ſurrendered the 24th of September. M. de Turenne acquired great honour at this ſiege, having ſhewed his ſuperior ſkill in conducting convoys to the camp. The Spaniards received two great defeats at ſea; the firſt was on the 12th, the 14th, and the 18th of January, from the Dutch; and the ſecond on the 22d of July, from the duke de Brezé. Arras beſieged by three marſhals

of

REMARKABLE EVENTS under LEWIS XIII.

of France, de Chatillon, de Chaulnes, and Meilleraye. This siege was famous for the attempts the enemy made to relieve the town, and the besiegers to disappoint them. Chatillon was a pupil of Maurice and Frederic Henry, princes of Orange: the duke d'Anghien, the dukes de Nemours and de Luines, messieurs des Gevres, de Coaslin, de Guiche, de Grancey, de Breauté, and de Gassion, served on this occasion. The cardinal infant, duke Charles of Lorrain, Lamboy, and others, endeavoured to raise the siege; but the town surrendered at length the 20th of August.

This year concluded with two very surprizing events in the same kingdom; the revolt of Catalonia, and the revolution of Portugal. The count duke d'Olivarez was the Richelieu of Madrid, but had not the same success as the Richelieu of France. Philip IV. imputing all misfortunes to that minister, whom he had employed two and twenty years, discarded him six weeks after the death of cardinal Richelieu, that is, just at the very time when, having no longer any rival in Europe, he might have retrieved the affairs of Spain. This was a great blunder of Philip IV, who was upon the point of rectifying it, " if the duke had not hindered him, by publishing an apology " for his conduct, wherein he offended several persons of interest " and power. And so great was their resentment, that the king " thought proper to remove him still to a greater distance, by " confining him to Toro, where he died of chagrin, which ge- " nerally happens to great geniuses, unaccustomed to repose." (*Bapt. Nani.*) It is the opinion of several that the affair of Catalonia, as well as the revolution of Portugal, were owing to the cardinal's contrivance; he might possibly have had a hand in the former; but he had no manner of concern in the latter: the revolution of Portugal happened the first of December.

Philip, duke of Anjou, brother of Lewis XIV, is born the 21st of September.

Charles I. summons, what an English author calls, the *bloody parliament*, from the murder of their prince; and the unparralleled revolution which subverted the English monarchy.

1641.

The king's edict concerning the functions of the parliament, is registered in a bed of justice.

REMARKABLE EVENTS under LEWIS XIII.

The Catalans lay aside the scheme of forming a republic: finding themselves unable to resist the king of Spain, they surrender their country to Lewis XIII, stipulating only the preservation of their privileges, and sign a treaty to that effect the 20th of February. Le Vassor says, that this affair was not ultimately settled till the 2d of September. The count de la Mothe is sent to their assistance with five thousand men. Sourdis, archbishop of Bourdeaux, takes five Spanish men of war in the bay of Roses, the 27th of March; but was surprized the 20th of August by the Spaniards, who threw a large supply into Tarragona; upon which de la Mothe was obliged to raise the blockade of that place, and the archbishop was banished to Carpentras.

The cardinal, apprehending left Charles IV. should join the count of Soissons, had gained him over once more by means of the countess of Cantecroix, whom he is said to have amused with the hopes of establishing the legitimacy of her marriage. The duke comes to Paris, and signs a treaty at St. Germains, the 2d of April, which he intended to break the first opportunity: he does homage for the dutchy of Bar the 10th of April, and is restored to his dominions upon very hard terms. Charles I, yielding to the violence of the house of commons, is so weak as to pass the bill of attainder against the earl of Strafford, one of the greatest men in England, and the most strongly attached to his service: this nobleman himself advised the king to give him up, and was executed the 22d of May. Charles likewise passed another bill, importing, that the parliament should not be dissolved without the consent of both houses: these were the steps by which this unhappy prince was led to the scaffold. A treaty of alliance on the first of June, between France and John IV, king of Portugal: the Dutch, who were invited as contracting parties, signed a truce with that crown for ten years. Honoré, prince of Monaco, tired of the uncontrouled power of the Spaniards, who had caused his father to be assassinated in 1605, and ever since had deprived him of all authority in his dominions, puts himself under the protection of France by a treaty concluded with Lewis XIII, July the 8th; in consequence of which he admits a French garrison into Monaco the 18th of November. In
virtue

REMARKABLE EVENTS under LEWIS XIII.

virtue of this same treaty the king engaged to indemnify him for the territories he possessed in the kingdom of Naples, by granting him an estate of the same value in France, part of which should be erected for him into the dutchy and peerage of Valentinois, and the other part for his son, with the titles of marquisate and county. Antony of Monaco, the great grandson of Honoré, having no issue male, married his daughter Louisa Hippolyta of Monaco, in 1715, to M. de Matignon. Before the concluding of this match, M. de Monaco had obtained the king's warrant, bearing promise of a new creation in favour of M. de Matignon upon the consummation of the nuptials. By this warrant the dutchy of Valentinois was reserved with the title of peerage for his son-in-law: but as the marriage did not take place till after the king's decease, the new patent of erection was not made out till the reign of Lewis XV, in the month of December the same year, and verified in 1716. The archbishop of Braga conspiring against the new king of Portugal, is confined, and his accomplices are put to death. This conspiracy was conducted with the same secrecy as the revolution, and had like to have met with the same success. Let us return to the military operations.

In Germany, general Banier and the count de Guebriant cannonaded Ratisbon the 28th of January. Banier died not long after: he was a Swede, and greatly resembled Gustavus Adolphus. The troops of France, Hesse, and Luneburg, under the command of the count de Guebriant, gained the battle of Wolfembuttle, the 29th of June, against the archduke Leopold and Piccolomini. Dorstein surrenders to the Imperialists the 10th of September, the troops of Sweden and Luneburg having refused to attack Piccolomini in his entrenchments at the desire of M. de Guebriant. The duke of Luneburg makes his peace with the emperor. The Swedes restore Gorlitz to the elector of Saxony the 3d of October. The war, which seemed to be over in Piedmont and Italy by the taking of Turin, is revived with greater vigour than ever. The count d'Harcourt beats the cardinal of Savoy before Yvrée the 24th of April; obliges prince Thomas to raise the siege of Chivas the 25th of May; and the 15th of September makes himself master of Coni, which he delivers up to the dutchess dowager. The pope's troops

take

take Castro from the duke of Parma the 12th of October. In Catalonia, la Mothe Houdancourt possesses himself of the town and castle of Constantine the 14th of May, and obtains a victory the 10th of June over the Spaniards, who wanted to throw a supply of provisions into Taragona. The prince of Conde takes the town of Elne in Roussillon the 29th of June.

But far more important was the scene on the side of Flanders. The count of Soissons, no longer able to bear the cardinal's ill treatment, had joined the dukes of Guise and Bullion, and signed a treaty with Spain. The king sends two armies against him: the one, under the command of the marshal de la Meilleraye, penetrates into the heart of Flanders, to prevent the cardinal Infant from sending any succours to Sedan; the other drew near to this town, and was commanded by marshal Chatillon. General Lamboy brought succours to the princes, who marched out of Sedan, and engaged the king's troops: this was the battle of Marfée, which happened on the 6th of July; marshal Chatillon was routed, but the count of Soissons perished in an unaccountable manner. The loss of this battle might have proved fatal to the cardinal; but the death of the count of Soissons prevented the malecontents from reaping any advantage by it. This young prince was very agreeable in his person, but of a slender capacity; grave in his deportment, suspicious and haughty; a declared enemy of the cardinal, whose niece he had refused to marry, and more considerable at court on that account, the malecontents being hearty in his interest, than for his other qualifications. The duke de Bouillon soon after entered into an accommodation with the king, and preserved Sedan. As for the duke de Guise, named Henry II, the grandson of him who was killed at Blois, he was not at the battle, having quarrelled with the count of Soissons a little before, and retired to Brussels, where he fell in love with the countess of Bossut. This prince was as fickle in his marriages, as others are in their amours: he had procured a divorce from his first wife, Anne of Gonzaga, of whom he had been desperately fond, to marry the countess Bossut, of whom he was enamoured; yet he spent the remainder of his days in endeavouring to be divorced from this lady, in order to marry mademoiselle de Pons, who had also engaged his affection. The

The THIRD RACE.

REMARKABLE EVENTS *under* LEWIS XIII.

The town of Aire, taken by marſhal de la Meilleraye the 27th of July, was retaken by the Spaniards, who made uſe of our lines, which we had neglected to demoliſh; and Donchery, having ſurrendered to Lamboy after the battle of Marſée, was recovered by the king the 6th of Auguſt. The count de Grancey and du Hallier invade Lorrain, and difpoſſeſs Charles IV, who had revolted again, of Bar-le-duc, Epinal, and ſeveral other towns. Lens ſurrenders to marſhal Brezé; and la Baſſée to marſhal de Meilleraye, who likewiſe makes himſelf maſter of Bapaume the 18th of September. St. Preuil happening to meet the garriſon, accompanied only by a trumpet belonging to marſhal de Meilleraye, attacked and beat them, without ſeeing the trumpet. Cardinal Richelieu made uſe of this pretext to cauſe him to be beheaded: he likewiſe charged him with having laid duties by his own private authority (of which he pretended to have received complaints) on goods imported into Arras; and with raiſing contributions all over the country: but it was ſaid then, that St. Preuil was guilty of no other crime, than that of having incurred the difpleaſure of marſhal de Meilleraye, and of des Noyers, who had reaſon to be diſſatisfied with his conduct. Mazarin is made cardinal the 16th of December.

1642.

The death of the duke d'Epernon, at the age of eighty-eight. This man ſhared the favour of Henry III. with the duke de Joyeuſe. He was haughty and violent; and the only nobleman in the kingdom, who never truckled to cardinal Richelieu: but this miniſter was amply revenged of him by the unlimited ſubmiſſion of his ſon, the cardinal de la Valette.

The war continues in Germany. The Imperialiſts raiſe the ſiege of Hothenwiel the 7th of January, upon the approach of the French and Swedes. The count de Guebriant defeats the generals Lamboy and Mercy at Kempen the 17th of the ſame month, and takes them both priſoners: for which ſervice he was created a marſhal of France. This victory made him maſter of the electorate of Cologne. February the 14th Lemberg is ſurrendered to the Imperialiſts; who raiſe the ſiege of the caſtle of Mansfeld the 3d of March, upon the approach of the Swedes.

VOL. II. G Tortenſon,

REMARKABLE EVENTS under LEWIS XIII.

Tortenson, the Swedish general, takes Great Glogau the 10th of May, and beats the Imperialists in the neighbourhood of Schweidnitz the 30th. Neifs surrenders to the Swedes the 9th of June; and soon after they take Olmutz by storm. The 5th of December, Tortenson compels the archduke Leopold to raise the siege of Great Glogau; and makes himself master of the castle of Leipsic the 4th of December.

On the side of France, the grand object of this campaign, was the conquest of Rouffillon. In the Netherlands it was thought sufficient to act upon the offensive. The count d'Harcourt and marshal de Guiche were charged with the defence of that frontier; one on the side of Picardy and Artois; the other towards Champagne. Guebriant had the command of the king's forces on the Rhine; and the duke of Bouillon, whom the cardinal wanted to remove from Sedan, commanded in Italy: marshal de Meilleraye was at the head of the army in Rouffillon, where the principal scene was to be acted. Marshal Brezé, with the splendid title of viceroy of Catalonia, was to join la Mothe Houdancourt, to prevent the Spaniards from penetrating into Catalonia, and succouring Rouffillon.

The apparent motive of these mighty preparations was the king's glory; but the real cause was the cardinal's suspicion of Cinqmars, his majesty's favourite. This suspicion was sufficiently justified by the discovery of the treaty concluded at Madrid, the 13th of March, and signed by Olivarez in the name of the king of Spain, and by Fontrailles for the duke of Orleans. Mess. de Bouillon and Cinqmars were mentioned in this treaty; the intent of which was to subvert the government, and to destroy the cardinal. Cinqmars was arrested at Narbonne the 13th of June; the duke of Bouillion was seized in the midst of his army the 23d; and the duke of Orleans asked forgiveness according to custom, accusing and abandoning his accomplices. The dutchefs of Bouillon having threatened to deliver up Sedan into the hands of the Spaniards, the duke was pardoned upon resigning that town and principality to the king, for which he obtained an equivalent in 1651; when by a contract of exchange he received the dutchy and peerage of Albret, the dutchy and peerage of Chateau Thierry, the county of Auvergne,

REMARKABLE EVENTS under LEWIS XIII.

the county of Evreux, &c. for the dutchy of Bouillon, and for Sedan and Raucourt. Cinqmars fell a victim to his own ambition: he loft his head at Lyons, September the 12th. De Thou fuffered the fame punifhment, for having been privy to the treaty, and not revealing it. The arret was founded on an edict of Lewis XI, the 22d of December 1477, produced by Laubardemont*. The father of the unfortunate de Thou, who mentions feveral inftances of fuch condemnations in his hiftory, did not forefee that his fon would meet with the like treatment. The memoirs of Chouppes make him more criminal, but without any proof. Fontrailles efcaped to England. Fabert feized Trevoux, which was a town of fome confequence, as it belonged to mademoifelle de Montpenfier, and her father Gafton was guardian of the young nobleffe of that place, during their minority.

In the midft of thefe intrigues, Lewis XIII. and his minifter were in a languifhing condition; the king in his camp before Perpignan, and the cardinal at Narbonne: the latter having removed to Tarafcon, received a copy of the treaty with Spain, and fent it to his majefty, who was beginning to recover. The king came to Tarafcon, and concerted with his minifter (who from that moment refumed his full authority) the proper means for bringing the offenders to juftice. Let us return to the operations of the campaign: the war was concluded in Savoy, by a treaty figned the 14th of June, between the dutchefs dowager and the princes of Savoy, who renounced their alliance with Spain.

La Mothe Houdancourt defeats five thoufand Spaniards the 19th of January, at the affair of Vals. The battle of Villafranca gained againft the Spaniards the 31ft of March. Colioure furrendered to marfhal de Meilleraye the 13th of April. The fortune of war was very different in the Netherlands: the Spaniards took Lens the 19th of April; la Baflée the 13th of May; and marfhal de Guiche was beaten at Honnecourt the 26th of the fame month, exactly at the very time when the treaty of Madrid was difcovered: yet meafures were, fo wifely concerted, that thefe difappointments did not produce any bad confequences; neither did they ftop the progrefs of the French army in Rouffillon.

* One of the judges.

Rouſſillon. Marſhal de la Mothe made himſelf maſter of Monçon the 4th of June; and Perpignan ſurrendered at length the 9th of September to marſhals Schomberg and Meilleraye, after a three months ſiege. The town of Salces was alſo reduced; and thus the king took poſſeſſion of the whole province of Rouſſillon, which has been ever ſince united to the crown. The French marched afterwards into Catalonia; where the marſhal de la Mothe gained the battle of Lerida the 7th of October, while the duke of Longueville attacked Tortona in the Milaneſe, and took it the 26th of November. Nothing of importance was tranſacted on the ſide of Lorrain; but marſhal de Brezé obtained ſome advantages in the Mediterranean on the coaſt of Catalonia.

Charles I, compelled by the inſolence of the commons, had withdrawn himſelf from London the 20th of January: he miſcarried in his attempt upon Hull, where the famous Cromwell *, who began then to be known, arrived before his majeſty: the 2d of November was fought the battle of Keynton †, which proved no way deciſive, between the king and the rebels under the command of the earl of Eſſex: if the king had marched directly from thence to London, as he was inclined to do, there would have been an end of the war. Is it poſſible, that what father Orleans ſays on this ſubject ſhould be true? viz. That the generals of this unfortunate prince diſſuaded him from this meaſure, apprehending left if he entered London ſword in hand, he might pretend to a right of conqueſt over the nation, and become too abſolute.

Mary of Medicis died at Cologne the 3d of July, in the greateſt diſtreſs, at the age of ſixty-eight; a princeſs whoſe end deſerves our pity, but whoſe capacity was far inferior to her ambition: and perhaps ſhe was neither ſurprized, nor afflicted ſo much as ſhe ought to have been, at the fatal cataſtrophe of one of our greateſt kings. Cardinal Richelieu died in his palace at Paris, aged fifty-eight years, on the 4th of December, and was interred at Sorbonne. The government by his death ſaved an annual revenue

---

* This is a miſtake; the king was denied admittance into Hull by ſir John Hotham, who held it for the parliament.

† This is the battle of Edge-hill, near Keynton in Warwickſhire, which was fought on Sunday the 23d of October.

REMARKABLE EVENTS under LEWIS XIII.

of four millions of livres, which he expended in his houshold; but France was deprived of a great minister.

Upon this subject, which seems to have been exhausted, I shall confine myself to a single consideration. Cardinal Richelieu having steadily pursued the scheme of enlarging his master's authority, which was now become his own, spent his life under a continual apprehension of his enemies; whereas he stood in need of the utmost serenity of mind, to form those projects of so vast and complicate a nature, by which he signalized his administration. The same man who exposed himself to the hatred and revenge of the grandees, by endeavouring to render his master's government more absolute, had as much to fear from the king, for whom he run every risk, as from the resentment of those whom he compelled to obey. That under these circumstances he should act with such resolution, form so compact a system, and engage in enterprizes so useful as well as glorious to the nation; that he should be possessed of such magnanimity and disinterestedness, as to employ his whole time in the administration of a kingdom, where he was equally feared by the prince whom he served, and by the subjects whom he enslaved; must have been owing either to an unbounded ambition, or to a public spirit superior to humanity; which of the two is hard to determine. What would add, if possible, to the glory of this minister, is the following anecdote, which though well known, cannot be too often repeated in honour of two great men. When the Czar Peter paid a visit to Paris, he was conducted to the Sorbonne, where they shewed him the famous mausoleum of this minister: he asked whose statue it was, and they told him, cardinal Richelieu's: the view of this grand object threw him into an enthusiastic rapture, which he always felt on the like occasions, so that he immediately ran to embrace the statue, saying, " Oh! " that thou wert but still living; I would give thee one half of my " empire to govern the other."

Cardinal Richelieu founded the king's printing-house: the expences came to three hundred and sixty thousand livres. Trichet du Frene had the care of correcting, Cramoisy was the printer, and Sablet Desnoyfers the superintendant.

REMARKABLE EVENTS under LEWIS XIII.

The *palais royal*, which still exists, was built by cardinal Richelieu, by the name of *palais cardinal*; and he made a present of it to the king. Even in his sepulchral monument he shewed a taste of grandeur and magnificence. The college of Sorbonne, which according to Mezeray is become the *perpetual council of Gaul, the areopagus of the church, and the luminary of faith*, was at first only a community of poor scholars, called the *poor masters*, founded by Robert Sorbonne, confessor to St. Lewis. As this prince had contributed to that establishment, and had even laid the first stone, Robert would not take the title of founder, but contented himself with that of *provider*. Cardinal Richelieu, in the same office, chose this for his burying place, after he had rebuilt it in a most magnificent manner. The mausoleum in the church is the master-piece of the celebrated Girardon.

1643.

Lewis XIII. had published an edict the 1st of Dec. the preceding year, declaring his brother for ever incapable of the regency; at the same time he deprived him of his government, and suppressed his companies of gendarmes and light horse. He revoked this edict three weeks before his death. The very same day on which Richelieu died, the king made cardinal Mazarin a member of the privy council: he continued messieurs de Chavigny and des Noyers in their offices, as well as the chancellor, Bouthillier, superintendant of the revenue, Brienne, and la Vrilliere. He wrote to the superior courts of his kingdom, and to his ambassadors, that he meant to make no change in the administration. *In a word*, says M. de Rochfoucaud, *the court continued to pay the same submission to the cardinal after his decease, as it had done in his life time.*

The king's brother returned to St. Germains, the 12th of January, and was followed by some exiles and prisoners, such as the duke de St. Simon, Vitry, Bassompierre, &c. The latter had been compelled, when he was sent to the Bastile, to sell his post of colonel-general of the Swiss to the marquis de Coaflin, who was succeeded by the marquis de la Chastre; but this marquis having afterwards incurred the displeasure of cardinal Mazarin, the place was restored to Bassompierre. The duke of Beaufort returned from England, whither he had voluntarily exiled himself towards the end of Richelieu's administration. The

REMARKABLE EVENTS under LEWIS XIII.

The expectation of the regency, which from the king's ill state of health seemed to be at hand, occasioned two factions at court, one for the queen, the other for the duke of Orleans. The king liked neither of them; but as he believed, from past experience, that the government could not be in worse hands than in his brother's, he dismissed his confessor, the learned father Sirmond, for solliciting him to associate the duke of Orleans in the regency. Des Noyers, who was firmly attached to the queen, obtained leave to resign; by which step he either presumed, that the king would think it necessary to retain him in his service; or he expected to be recalled by the queen regent, and to have the merit with that princess, of not being concerned in any scheme to limit her authority. The queen had placed her chief confidence in Poitier, bishop of Beauvais. The duke of Beaufort attached himself to her majesty; the duke de Rochefoucaud undertook to secure the duke of Anguien in her interest: Mazarin and Chavigny, finding they could not prevail on the king to make any concessions in favour of his brother, joined with the queen's party, so that des Noyers was intirely forgot. The latter had orders to dispose of his office of secretary to monsieur le Tellier, with whom cardinal Mazarin had been acquainted in Italy, where he acted as intendant of the army. Le Tellier had a clear head, a quick conception, and a capacity for business; nobody knew better than he how to maintain his ground, under the colour of moderation, amidst the tempestuous motions of the court; and he never pretended to the first place in the ministry, thinking this the safer way to preserve the second.

The royal declaration of the 19th of April concerning the regency, which is settled on Anne of Austria. The duke of Orleans is appointed lieutenant-general, during the minority of his nephew, under the authority of the queen mother; and the king nominates a council of regency. This declaration was registered the next day in parliament. His majesty, eight days before his death, consents to the marriage of his brother with Margaret princess of Lorrain, on condition, that the nuptials shall be solemnized again in France, which was accordingly performed the 26th of May, twelve days after the king's decease. The bans

REMARKABLE EVENTS under LEWIS XIII.

were published the 25th, and the archbishop of Paris (John Francis de Gondy) performed the ceremony at Meudon, where Gaston declared, "that he was come to ratify his marriage; that there was no necessity for renewing it, since it had been lawfully contracted; but that what he did now, was in obedience to the king's will and pleasure." In consequence of which declaration the archbishop pronounced this form: *Ego vos conjungo in matrimonium, in quantum opus est,* &c. Lewis XIII. dies the 14th of May, on Ascension-day.

Lewis XIII. was somewhat unsociable in his disposition: he seemed to be afraid of being seen, except on public ceremonies, of which he was extremely fond.

Henry IV, being greatly distressed for money, paid his officers with good words; but this was not the temper of Lewis XIII. He had a reservedness, as he himself acknowledges, which he imbibed from the queen his mother. (Test. Polit.) His inclination for retirement was the cause of his being attached to his favourites, in whom he reposed an intire confidence, till they were dismissed: but his attachment to them did not proceed so much from judgment and choice, as from a necessity of having some body to converse with in his solitude; so that it was easy to supplant them, and to substitute others in their stead; in short, he could not live without a favourite, and this was in some measure a crown office.

He never was fond of cardinal Richelieu, who had always an absolute sway over him: he was jealous of his power, yet submitted to be governed by this minister; and he could not forgive him, for being so necessary to the state. He had mistresses as well as favourites: he had fits of jealousy, and that was the *non plus ultra* of his passions. His views were upright, his understanding was sound; he had not a sprightly imagination, but he judged well; and his minister governed him, only by convincing him of the rectitude of his measures.

He was as brave as Henry IV, but his bravery was without heat or eclat, and no way proper for the conquest of a kingdom. Providence placed him on the throne at a proper time: earlier he would have been too weak; later too circumspect: son and father of two of our greatest kings, he fixed the throne, yet tottering,

REMARKABLE EVENTS under LEWIS XIII.

tering, of Henry IV, and prepared the way for the wonders of the reign of Lewis the fourteenth.

Gomberville, in his treatise of the *Doctrine of Manners*, says, that Lewis XIII. did not love reading; and the motive of this prince's taking a dislike to it, was that the first book he began with, had been the *history of France by Fauchet.*

It is not well known for what reason Lewis XIII. obtained the surname of *Just*: it is certain however, that he had this title in the beginning of his reign. Neither are writers agreed as to the æra, in which the surname of Great was conferred upon Henry IV; for Barclay, in his dedicatory epistle to the Argenis, affirms that this appellation was not given him till after his death, although the father of this very Barclay, dedicating his book *de Regno* to Henry IV, had already stiled him the *Great, Henricus Magnus*. But posterity will not be under the same uncertainty with respect to the surname of *Beloved*, bestowed on Lewis XV. This prince marching with the utmost expedition, in 1755, from one extremity of his kingdom to the other, and discontinuing his conquests in Flanders, to fly to the assistance of Alsace, was stopt at Metz by a fit of a violent illness, which endangered his life. The news threw the whole city of Paris into as great a consternation, as if it had been taken by storm; the churches resounded with vows for his recovery, and with heart-felt groans; the prayers of the clergy and the people were every moment interrupted with their sobbings; and from so dear, so tender an affection, was derived the surname of *Beloved*, a title superior to any other which this great prince has merited.

The HISTORY of FRANCE.

*1643.
Accession to the crown.*

LEWIS XIV, *born at St. Germains in Laye the 5th of September 1638, comes to the crown the 14th of May, 1643. His godfather was cardinal Mazarin, and the princess of Conde his godmother. He was baptized by Dominic Seguier, bishop of Meaux, in the chapel of the old castle of St. Germains, the 21st of April, 1643.*

• REMARKABLE EVENTS.

1643.

AN arret of parliament of the 18th of May, pronounced in the bed of justice by the chancellor, conferring the regency and tutelage of the king without any restriction on the queen mother. Cardinal Mazarin had the direction of the king's education; so that the declaration of Lewis XIII. did not take place. The queen soon grew sensible of the incapacity of the old bishop of Beauvais; for which reason he was dismissed, and she placed her whole confidence in Mazarin. Queen Blanche behaved in the same manner upon the death of Lewis VIII, when the young cardinal Romain was substituted in the room of Guerin, the old bishop of Senlis. There is a great resemblance between these two princesses.

Mademoiselle de Montpensier says in her memoirs, that she stood godmother to the king, and that Gaston, duke of Orleans, stood godfather; but this was only when this prince was confirmed.

The marquis de Villeroy was his governor; and the abbe de Beaumont, known by the name of Perefixe, afterwards archbishop of Paris, was his preceptor.

Bouthillier was removed from the superintendancy of the finances, and Chavigny his son continued in council; but his place of secretary of state was given to the count de Brienne: Brienne's family name was Lomerie; but he had married Louisa of Luxemburg-Brienne. Chateau-neuf, who had been deprived of the seals so long ago as 1633, had leave to return to his house at Montrouge, where he created a great deal

The THIRD RACE.   91

WIVES.	CHILDREN.	1715. DEATH.	Cotemporary PRINCES.
MaryTherefa of Auſtria, only daughter of Philip IV. by his firſt marriage with Elizabeth of France, and ſiſter of Charles II. and Margaret Thereſa, whom Philip IV. had by his ſecond marriage with Mary Anne of Auſtria. MaryThereſa of Auſtria was born the 20th of September, 1638. She was married to Lewis XIV. by proxy at Fontarabia, the 3d of June, 1666, and the marriage was ſolemnized at St. John de Luz the 9th. She made her public entry into Paris the 26th of Auguſt following, and died at Verſailles on Friday the 30th of July, 1683, at the age of forty-five. Her body was carried to St. Denis, her heart to Val de Grace. The king, who honoured her virtue, made uſe of theſe words upon hearing of her death, *This is the firſt uneaſineſs ſhe ever gave me.*	Lewis the Dauphin, called *Monſeigneur*, died at Meudon the 14th of April, 1711. He had by Mary Anne Chriſtina Victoria of Bavaria, who died the 20th of April, 1690, 1. Lewis duke of Burgundy, who died the 18th of February 1712. He had by Mary Adelaïd of Savoy, who died the 12th of Feb. 1712, N. duke of Britany, who died in 1705. Lewis duke of Britany, who died the 8th of March 1712. And LEWIS XV. born Feb. the 15th, 1710. 2. Philip duke of Anjou, king of Spain, who died the 9th of July, 1746. 3. Charles duke of Berry, who died the 4th of May, 1714. Lewis XIV. had alſo two ſons and three daughters, who died young.	LEWIS XIV. dies at Verſailles on Sunday the 1ſt of September, 1715, at a quarter of an hour after eight in the morning, aged ſeventy ſeven years wanting four days. His body was carried to St. Denis, his heart to the Jeſuits of the rue St. Antoine, and his bowels to Notre Dame. His funeral oration was pronounced at St. Denis by M. Quinqueran de Beaujeu, biſhop of Caſtres; at Notre Dame, by M. Maboul, biſhop of Alet; at the holy chapel by father Maſſillon; at the Jeſuits by father Porée, in Latin; and by other orators in different parts of the kingdom.	*Popes.* Urban VIII. 1644. *It was he that gave the title of Eminence to cardinals.* Innocent X. 1655. Alexander VIII. 1667. Clement IX. 1669. Clement X. 1676. Innocent XI. 1689. Alexander VIII. 1691. Innocent XII. 1700. Clement XI. 1721. *Turkiſh emperors.* Ibrahim. 1649. Mahomet IV. 1687. Solyman III. 1691. Achmet II. 1695. Muſtapha II. 1703. Achmet III. depoſed. 1730. *Emperors of Germany.* Ferdinand III. 1657. Leopold I. 1705. Joſeph I. 1711. Charles VI. 1740. *Kings of Spain.* Philip IV. 1665. Charles II. 1700. Philip V. 1746. *Kings of Portugal.* John duke of Braganza. 1656. Alphonſus Henry dethroned in 1667. died in 1683. Peter II. 1706. John V. 1750. *Kings of G. Britain.* Charles I. 1649. Charles II. 1685. James II. dethroned in 1688. died in 1701. William III. 1702. Anne Stuart. 1714. George I. 1727. *Kings of Denmark.* Chriſtian IV. 1648. Frederic III. 1670. Chriſtian V. 1699. Frederic IV. 1730.

REMARKABLE EVENTS under LEWIS XIV.

deal of trouble to cardinal Mazarin. Chancellor Seguier, whom neither the queen nor the cardinal could bear, continued in possession of the seals, only because they wanted to set him against Chateau-neuf, who insisted upon being restored to his office, as he found himself supported by madam de Chevreuse, in respect to whom, as the queen expressed herself, he was both a martyr and idolater.

The duke of Beaufort being accused of having formed a design against the cardinal's life, is sent to the castle of Vincennes. He was naturally formed to be a favourite of the populace; and indeed he bore the title of *the king of the butchers*, with whose cant he was well acquainted: he was tall, well-shaped, adroit in his exercises, indefatigable, presumptuous, and rude in his behaviour, which was looked upon as frankness; but withal as artful and cunning, as it is possible for a man of no great understanding to be. He believed, and persuaded the whole court, that he was going to act a part in the beginning of the regency: he made his escape out of prison, and became afterwards the hero of the Parisian war. This duke was the second son of Cæsar of Vendome, natural son of Henry IV. His elder brother, Lewis duke of Vendome and Mercœur, was made cardinal after the decease of Laura Mancini his wife, by whom he had the duke of Vendome and the grand prior. Madam de Chevreuse, widow of the constable de Luines, an old favourite of the queen, being returned from her exile, after an absence of eighteen years, would judge of the court from her own experience, and from her former knowledge, by which means she was involved in the disgrace of M. de Beaufort. The queen was a good deal embarrassed on the occasion; but made no scruple at length to sacrifice her to the resentment of cardinal Mazarin, whose addresses madam de Chevreuse had received too coldly; so that she was banished to Tours: she had been married a second time to the prince of Chevreuse of the house of Lorrain, by whom the dutchy of Chevreuse came to the children by her former husband. She afterwards acted a considerable part in the troubles of the *Fronde*. Madam de Hautefort was also recalled, and the queen, mindful of the services she had received of that lady, who had been a favourite of Lewis XIII, placed an entire confidence in her: but madam de Hautefort forgot herself,

and

The THIRD RACE. 93

CHILDREN.	Cotemporary PRINCES.
Natural and legitimated children. Lewis XIV. had by the dutchefs of Valiere, *who entered herself among the Carmelite nuns the 2d of June 1674, made her religious vows the 4th of June 1675, and died the 6th of June 1710, at the age of 65,* Lewis of Bourbon, count of Vermandois. 1683. Mary Anne, *ftiled* mademoifelle de Blois, princefs of Conty. 1739 *Other natural and legitimated children.* Lewis Auguftus of Bourbon, duke of Maine. 1736. Lewis-Cæfar, count of Vexin, abbot of St. Denis, and of *St.Germain-desprez.* 1683. Lewis Alexander of Bourbon, count of Touloufe.1737. Louifa Frances of Bourbon, *ftiled* mademoifelle de Nantes, dutchefs of Bourbon, *married to Lewis III. duke of Bourbon,* died 1743. Louifa Maria of Bourbon, *ftiled* mademoifelle de Tours. 1681. Frances Maria of Bourbon, *ftiled* mademoifelle de Blois, *married to Philip II. duke of Orleans, and regent of France.* Two other fons, who died young.	*Kings of Sweden.* Chriftina abdicates in 1654. dies in 1689. Charles Guftavus. 1660. Charles XI. 1697. Charles XII. 1718. *Kings of Poland.* Ladiflaus Sigifmund. 1648. John Cafimir abdicates. 1667. Michael Wiefno Weisky. 1673. John Sobiefky. 1696. FredericAuguftus elector of Saxony.1733. Staniflaus. *Kings of Pruffia.* Frederic III. 1713. Frederic William. 1740. *Czars.* Michael Fœderowitz. 1645. Alexis Michaelowitz. 1676. Fœdor Alexiowitz. 1682. Iwan Alexiowitz. 1696. Peter Alexiowitz. 1725.

REMARKABLE EVENTS under LEWIS XIV.

and treated the queen so very ill, as to deserve a second banishment; from which she soon returned, to be married to M. de Schomberg. Messieurs de Vendome, who were at the head of a party called the *Importants*, in opposition to the duke of Orleans and to the prince of Condé, underwent the same fate, and were also banished. A duel between the duke of Guise and Coligny. D'Estrades, afterwards marshal of France, was Coligny's second against Bridieu. Coligny was disarmed, and died a few months after. This duel was occasioned by a quarrel between madam de Montbason and madam de Longueville, which set the whole court in an uproar.

The Spaniards intending to avail themselves of the trouble and confusion, which generally attend the beginning of a minority, lay siege to Rocroy. The duke d'Anguien, then only two and twenty years of age, having under him the marshal de l'Hopital, Gassion, and la Ferté, who were afterwards marshals of France, marches to the relief of this town, and gains the battle of Rocroy the 19th of May, five days after the death of Lewis XIII. The count de Fontaine, a Spanish general, being ill of the gout, was obliged to be carried in a chair, in which he was slain: the Spanish infantry never recovered itself since that defeat. This battle was fought contrary to the opinion and advice of the marshal de l'Hopital, who was afraid of hazarding a decisive action at the beginning of a regency. On this occasion, I cannot help taking notice of one of the most beautiful passages of the life of Lewis XV. Prince Charles of Lorrain having passed the Rhine (in 1744) threatened to seize Alsace: the king, attended by marshal Noailles, marches a detachment of his army from Flanders to the assistance of that province, and is taken ill at Metz. Noailles conducts the troops to Alsace, where he finds marshal Coigny, who was general of the king's forces on the Rhine: it became now a question, to whom the command of this army properly belonged; and the decision was referred to the king, who lay at the point of death: his majesty gathering all the strength he had left, determines in favour of marshal Noailles, and, surviving himself in some measure, orders his minister (M. d'Argenson) to write to the marshal, desiring he would remember, that the prince of

The Third Race.

Ministers.	Warriors.	Magistrates.	Eminent and Learned Men.
Julius Mazarin, cardinal and first minister. 1661.	*Marshals of France.* Nic. de l'Hopital de Vitry. 1644.	*Chancellors.* Charles de l'Aubespine de Chateauneuf, keeper of the seals. 1653.	James Abbadie. 1727. Nich. Perrot d'Ablancourt. 1664. Luke d'Achery. 1685. Joseph Addison. 1719. John d'Aillé. 1670.
Superintendants of the finances. Cl. Bouthillier. 1651.	Honoré d'Albert de Chaulnes. 1649. Gaspard de Coligny, stiled *marshal Chatillon*, grandson of the admiral. 1646.	Peter Seguier. 1672. Matthew Molé, keeper of the seals. 1656.	N. Abr. Amelot de la Houssaye. 1706 Francis Annat. 1670. Father Anselm. 1694. Ant. Arnaud. 1694.
Abel Servien. 1659. Cl. de Mesmes, count d'Avaux. 1650. Nicholas Bailleul. 1652.	James Nompar de Caumont, duke de la Force. 1652.	Stephen d'Aligre. 1677. Michael le Tellier. 1685. Lewis Boucherat. 1699.	Rob. Arnaud d'Andilly. 1674. George d'Aubusson, archbishop of Embrun. 1697.
Charles de la Vieuville. 1653. Emery (his name was Michael Perticelli) René de Longueil de Maisons. 1677.	Fr. de Bassompierre. 1646. Francis Hannibal d'Etrees. 1670. Timoleon d'Epinay de St. Luc. 1644.	LewisPhelypeaux de Pontchartrain continues in office till 1714. died in 1727.	Jerome Audran. 1703. Hyacinth. Robillard d'Avrigny. 1719. Adr. Baillet. 1706. Ch. Barbeyrac. 1699. Stephen Baluze. 1718.
NicholasFouquet. 1680. *The office of superintendant of the finances was suppressed, upon the arresting of M. Fouquet.*	Urb. de Maillé de Brezé. 1650. Ch. de Schomberg. 1656. Ch. de la Porte de la Meilleraye. 1664.	Den. Fr. Voisin. 1717. *First Presidents.* Matthew Molé. 1656. Pompone de Bellievere. 1657. William de La-	J. Lewis Guez de Balzac. 1654. Michael Baron, comedian. 1729. John Bart. 1702. James Basnage. 1723. Mich. Antony Baudrand. 1700.
Secretaries of State. Henry Aug. de Lomenie de Brienne. 1666. *He left some memoirs behind him.*	Antony de Gramont. 1678. John Baptist Budes de Guebriant. 1646. Ph. de la Mothe Houdancourt. 1657.	moignon. 1677. Nicholas Potier de Novion. 1693. Achilles de Harlay. 1712. Lewis le Pelletier	Peter Bayle. 1706. Isaac de Benserade. 1691. Fr. Bernier. 1688. Cavalier Bernini, painter, sculptor, and architect. 1680.
Cl. Bouthillier, superintendant. 1651. LewisPhelypeaux de la Vrilliere. 1681.	Fr. de l'Hopital. 1660. H. de la Tour de Turenne. 1675.	resigns in 1712. John Antony de Mesmes. 1723. *Attorneys General.* Blaise Meliard.	James Bernouilly, 1705. John Bernouilly. 1748. Nicholas Bernouilly. 1726. Sam. Bochart. 1667.
Abel Servien, superintendant. 1659. Leon Bouthillier de Chavigny. 1652.	John de Gassion. 1647. Cæsar de Choiseul. 1675. Jos. de Rantzau. 1650.	1661. NicholasFouquet. 1680.	Herm. Boerhave. 1738. Nich. Boileau Despreaux. 1711. Johannes Bollandus. 1665. J. C. du Bos. 1742

REMARKABLE EVENTS under LEWIS XIV.

Condé gained the battle of Rocroy five days after the death of Lewis XIII.

The duke d'Anguien took Thionville the 10th of August, and Sirk the 2d of September; from whence he returned to court, but marched soon after to the assistance of marshal Guebriant. The latter takes Rothweil, November the 19th, where he was mortally wounded. The queen caused him to be interred in the church of Notre Dame at Paris, and would have all the supreme courts of judicature assist at the ceremony. The death of this general having occasioned a division between the French and Germans; duke Charles of Lorrain, Mercy, and John de Wert, obtained a complete victory over Rantzau at Tudelingen, the 25th of November. This defeat was the cause of our losing Rothweil again. On the side of Spain, marshal Brezé defeated the Spanish fleet the 3d of September within sight of Carthagena, and marshal de la Mothe gained several advantages in Catalonia. The king of Spain in person reduced Monçon, which la Mothe had it not in his power to relieve. Prince Thomas, unable to prevent the Spaniards from taking the town of Tortona in the Milanese the 27th of May, made himself master of Asti, as likewise of Trino the 24th of September, where the viscount de Turenne merited the batoon of marshal of France at the age of thirty two. The count du Plessis Praslin (afterwards marshal de Choiseuil) possessed himself of the bridge of Stures the 28th of October. The queen reduced the several pensions by one third. An edict against duels: there were several upon this subject during this reign.

Advocates in council created in the way of office, by the edict of the month of September.

In England, the battle of Newbury was fought the 29th of September, between Charles I. and the parliamentarians, which proved no way decisive, no more than that of Edge-hill. Anne of Austria sends the count d'Harcourt into England, to offer the mediation of France between the king and parliament; but this step was ineffectual.

1644.

The Third Race. 97

Ministers.	Warriors.	Magistrates.	Eminent and Learned Men.
Secretaries of state. Fr. Sublet des Noyers, surveyor of the king's buildings. 1645. H. de Gunegaud de Plancy. 1676. Mich. le Tellier, chancellor. 1685. Lewis Phelipeaux de la Vrilliere resigns in 1669. Hugh de Lionne. 1671. Henry L. de Lomenie de Brienne. 1698. J. B. Colbert, comptroller general. 1683. J. B. Colbert de Seignelay. 1690. Fr. Mich. le Tellier de Louvois. 1691. Ch. Colbert de Croissy. 1696. Sim. Arnaud de Pompone. 1699. Balth. Phelypeaux de Chateauneuf. 1700. Lewis Francis Mary le Tellier de Barbesieux. 1701. Lewis Phelypeaux de Pontchartrain, chancellor. 1727. Denis Francis Voisin, chancellor. 1717. Lewis Phelipeaux de la Vrilliere. 1725. Vol. II.	*Marshals of France.* Nic. de Neuville de Villeroy, governor of Lewis XIV. 1685. Ant. d'Aumont. 1669. James d'Estampes. 1668. Charles de Monchy d'Hocquincourt. 1658. Henry de Senneterre de la Ferté. 1681. James Rouxel de Grancey. 1680. Armand Nompar de Caumont de la Force. 1675. Lewis Foucault. 1659. Cæsar Phœbus d'Albret. 1676. Phil. de Clairambault. 1665. James de Castelnau. 1658. John de Sculemberg de Montdejeu. 1671. Abraham de Fabert. 1662. Francis de Crequy. 1687. Bernard Gigault de Bellefonds. 1694. Lewis de Crevant Humieres. 1694. Godfrey d'Estrades. 1686. Phil. de Montault Benac de Navailles. 1684. Lewis Armand de Schomberg. 1690.	*Attornies general.* Basil Fouquet, admitted by a grant of the reversion of his brother's office, he did not practise, but died in 1680. Achilles de Harlay. 1671. Achilles de Harlay. 1712. John Arnauld de la Briffe. 1700. Henry Franc. Daguesseau, afterwards chancellor. 1750. *Advocates general.* Omer Talon. 1652. Stephen Briquet. 1645. Jerome Brignon practises a second time, upon the death of his son-in-law; but then he held only the rank of second advocate-general. 1656. Jerome Bignon, son of the preceding. 1697. Den. Talon. 1698. Christian Francis de Lamoignon. 1709. Achilles de Harlay. 1717. Henry Franc. Daguesseau, afterwards chancellor. 1750. Joseph Omer Joly de Fleury. 1704.	René le Bossu. 1680. James Benig. Bossuet. 1704. John Boucher, a leaguer. 1644. The president Bouhier. 1746. Dominic Bouhours. 1702. Em. Theodore de la Tour de Bouillon, cardinal. 1715. Nich. Bourbon. 1644. Lewis Bourdaloue. 1704. Antoinette Bourignon. 1680. Edm. Boursault. 1708. Will. de Brebeuf. 1661. Ch. le Brun, painter. 1690. J. de la Bruyere. 1696. Roger de Rabutin de Bussy. 1693. Gautier de la Calprenede. 1663. John Galbert Campistron. 1723. And. Campra. 1744. Ch. du Cange. 1688. John Dom. Cassini. 1712. Nic. Caussin, confessor to Lewis XIII. 1651. F. de la Chaize, confessor to the king. 1709. Martin Cureau de la Chambre. 1669. Peter Cureau de la Chambre. 1693. Claude-Em-Luillier Chapelle. 1686. William Amfrye de Chaulieu. 1720. Thim. Cheminais. 1689.

REMARKABLE EVENTS under LEWIS XIV.

1644.

Messieurs d'Avaux and Servien set out the preceding year for Munster, with the necessary instructions to conclude a peace, of which all Europe stood greatly in need, and the preliminaries of which had been signed at Hamburg on the 25th of December, 1641, by the ambassadors of the emperor, France, Spain, and Sweden: but there was too great a complication of interests for a speedy accommodation; and our plenipotentiaries, having stopped at the Hague, signed a treaty this year, the first of March, before their departure for Munster, between the king and the States-General, confirming that of 1635: in consequence whereof the war was continued. The king likewise grants them the title of *high and mighty lords*; as seven years before Lewis XIII. had granted the title of *highness* to the princes of Orange, who till then had only that of excellency. The renewal of the treaty of 1641 between France and Portugal.

The defeat of Rantzau at Tudelingen, had obliged the remains of our army in Germany to take shelter on this side of the Rhine; and towards the close of the preceding year, the viscount de Turenne had been ordered from Italy, to take upon him the command of those shattered forces.

Turenne begins with recruiting this army at his own expence, and passes the Rhine with a view to oblige general Mercy to raise the siege of Friburg; but the town was taken the 28th of July. The duke d'Anguien, who had been sent to the assistance of Turenne, could not arrive time enough to save the place; but crossing the Rhine, he joined the viscount, having under him the marshal de Grammont. On this occasion were fought the three famous battles of Friburg, one the third of August, the other the 5th, and the third the 9th, if we can look upon that of the third day as an engagement, since it was only a pursuit of the enemy's army, with the taking of their cannon and baggage. General Mercy, though obliged to decamp with the loss of near nine thousand Bavarians, still preserved the reputation of a great general, by his masterly retreat; while the duke d'Anguien and Turenne acquired the honour of being esteemed the best commanders in Europe. Without losing time to retake Friburg,

The Third Race. 99

Ministers.	Warriors.	Magistrates.	Eminent and Learned Men.
Secretaries of state. Michael Chamillard, comptroller-general of the finances. 1721. Jerome Phelypeaux de Pontchartrain resigns in 1715, dies in 1747. J. B. Colbert de Torcy. 1746. Lewis Phelypeaux, count of St. Florentin. John Frederic Phelypeaux, count of Maurepas, resigned in 1749. His place was given to M. Rouillé. *Comptrollers-general of the finances.* J. B. Colbert. 1683. *He is the first, who without being superintendant, had the chief administration of the revenue.* Cl. le Pelletier. 1711. Lewis Phelypeaux de Pontchartrain, chancellor. 1727. Michael Chamillard. 1721. Nicol. Desmaretz. 1721.	*Marshals of France.* J. Henry de Durfort de Duras. 1704. Lewis Victor de Rochechouart, stiled the duke of Vivonne. 1688. Francis d'Aubusson de la Feuillade. 1691. Francis Henry de Montmorency, de Luxembourg. 1695. H. Lewis d'Aloigny de Rochefort. 1676. Guy d'Aldonce de Durfort de Lorges. 1702. John d'Estrées. 1707. *He is the first that introduced the dignity of marshal of France on board the navy.* Cl. de Choiseiul. 1711. Francis de Neuville de Villeroy, governor of Lewis XV. 1730. J. Arm. de Joyeuse. 1710. L. Fr. de Boufflers. 1711. Anne Hilarion de Constantin de Tourville. 1701. Anne Julius de Noailles. 1708. Nicholas de Catinat. 1712.	*Advocates general.* Antony Portail, afterwards first president. 1736. John le Nain. 1709. William Francis Joly de Fleury, now attorney-general. William de Lamoignon de Blanc menil, afterwards president of the parliament, first president of the court of aids, and at length chancellor. Lewis Chauvelin. 1715. Germain Lewis Chauvelin, afterwards president of the parliament, secretary of state, and at length keeper of the seals.	Urb. Chevreau. 1700. Peter Chirac. 1732. Fr. Thim. de Choisy. 1724. John Claude. 1689. John le Clerc, protestant minister. 1736. Seb. le Clerc, engraver. 1714. Memnon Cohorn. 1704. Charles le Cointe. 1681. Pasc. Colasse, musician. 1709. Paul Colomiez. 1692. J. Commire. 1702. Gerard de Cordemoy. 1684. P. Corneille. 1684. Th. Corneille. 1709. Peter Coste. 1747. Lewis Cousin. 1707. Ant. Coysevox, sculptor. 1720. Andrew Dacier. 1722. Madam Dacier. 1720. Ant. Dauchet. 1748. Peter Danet. 1709. Gabr. Daniel. 1728. Renatus Descartes. 1650. Andrew Destouches, musician. 1749. J. Domat. 1689. John Doujat. 1689. Cæsar d'Estrées, cardinal. 1714. Guy Crescent Fagi, first physician. 1718. Ch. Aug. de la Fare. 1713. Magdalen de la Vergne de la Fayette. 1693. And. Felibien. 1695. Fr. de Salignac de la Mothe Fenelon, archbishop of Cambray, preceptor to the duke of Burgundy. 1715.

burg, the generals determined to make themselves masters of the whole course of the Rhine. Spire did not wait for the summons of the marquis d'Aumont, but sent her keys to the duke d'Anguien the 25th of August. This prince possesses himself of Philipsburg the 9th of September; and the city of Mentz opens her gates to him the 17th, after the surrender of Worms and Oppenheim. Marshal Turenne carries Benghen, Creutznac, and Landau.

On the side of Flanders, the duke of Orleans, having under him the marshals de Meilleraye and de Gassion, took Graveline the 28th of July, after it had been valiantly defended for the space of two months by Don Fernando Solis. At this siege, where most of the nobility of the kingdom distinguished themselves, a dispute arose betwixt the marshals de Meilleraye and de Gassion, about taking possession of the town: they were going to blows, when Lambert, a marshal-de-camp, rode up and forbad the troops in the name of the duke of Orleans to obey either of those generals: this gave the duke time to decide according to rule, that the right of entering the first into conquered towns, belongs to the regiment of guards, which was commanded by marshal de Meilleraye. The prince of Orange on his side took Sas von Gand, the 7th of September. In Italy, prince Thomas, general of the French troops, made himself master of the town of Santia.

Beyond the Pyrenees our arms met with different success: Don Philip de Selva obtained a victory over marshal de la Mothe, who wanted to prevent the taking of Lerida. The king of Spain having made himself master of this place and of Balaguier, obliged the marshal to raise the siege of Tarragona: the marshal was recalled, and sent to *Pierre-Encise*. Le Tellier, secretary at war in the room of des Noyers, is said to have greatly contributed to this general's disgrace; for he hated the marshal because of his connexions with des Noyers, who had not as yet resigned his employments. The cardinal wanted to bring him to his trial; but after he had been dragged before several tribunals, he was fully acquitted by the parliament of Grenoble, and obtained his discharge, in 1648, from the castle of Pierre-Encise.

WARRIORS.	EMINENT and LEARNED MEN.
Marshals of France. Lewis Hector de Villars. 1734. Noel Bouton de Chamilly. 1715. Victor Maria d'Estrées. 1737. Francis Lewis Rousselet de Chateau-Renaud. 1716. Seb. le Pretre de Vauban. 1707. Conrad de Rosen. 1715. Nic. du Blé d'Huxelles. 1730. René Froullay de Tessé. 1725. Nic. Aug. de la Baume de Montrevel. 1716. Camille d'Hostein de Talard. 1728. Henry d'Harcourt. 1718. Ferdinand de Marsin. 1706. James Fitz-James duke of Berwick. 1734. Charles Augustus Goyon de Matignon. 1729. James Bazin de Bezons. 1733. Peter de Montesquiou. 1725.	Tanaquil le Fevre. 1671. Ch. Fevret. 1661. Ant. de Pas de Feuquieres. 1711. Esprit Flechier. 1710. And. Hen. cardinal de Fleury, prime minister, and preceptor to Lewis XV. 1743. Claude Fleury. 1723. J. de la Fontaine. 1695. Charles Riviere du Fresny. 1724. Ant. Furetiere. 1688. John Gallois. 1707. Peter Gassendi. 1655. Th. Germain, goldsmith. 1748. Peter Giannone. 1748. Fr. Girardon. 1715. Ant. Godeau. 1672. Dionys. Godofredus. 1649. James Godefroy, 1652. Peter Goudelin. 1649. Hugo Grotius. 1645. Du-Gue-Trouin. 1736. John Baptist du Hamel. 1698. John Hardouin. 1729. William Harvey. 1657. Daniel Heinsius. 1655. Bartholomew d'Herbelot. 1675. Th. Hobbes. 1679. William Fr. Antony de l'Hopital. 1704. Peter d'Hosier. 1660. Daniel Huetius. 1721. Touss. de Forbin de Janson. card. 1713. John Jouvenet, painter. 1717. Athanasius Kirker. 1680. Phil. Labbe. 1667. John le Laboureur. 1675.

REMARKABLE EVENTS under LEWIS XIV.

The civil war continues in England with various succefs, Oliver Cromwell defeats prince Rupert, at the battle of Marston-Moor the 12th of July. The earl of Effex preparing to lay fiege to Exeter, the queen of England retires from that city, where fhe had been lately delivered of a daughter *. Her majefty arrives at Paris, and has apartments affigned her in the Louvre: fhe likewife receives the compliments of the fupreme courts of judicature. The war betwixt the pope and the duke of Parma, was terminated this year by cardinal Bichi: the preceding year Lyonne had fet this accommodation on foot by the king's order. Caftro was furrendered to the duke, who yielded homage for it to the holy fee.

Cardinal Pamphilio, notwithftanding the oppofition of the French, fucceeds Urban VIII, under the name of Innocent X, by the intrigues of the Barberins: the latter had occafion to repent it, and withdrew afterwards to France for fhelter againft that very pontif, who was indebted to them for his election.

The Theatins, whofe order was founded in 1594, are eftablifhed at Paris.

1645.

Marfhal Turenne, hearing of the victory obtained at Tabor over the Imperialifts by Tortenfon, on the 6th of March, refolved to take advantage of it, in order to penetrate into Germany, and to hinder Mercy from entering into Franconia. His march was attended with great difficulties: Rofen, being fent to reconnoitre, imagined the Imperialifts were at a great diftance; the marfhal, yielding to the importunity of the German cavalry, who demanded quarters of refrefhment, gave them leave to feparate, and took his own ftation at Mariendal: Mercy availing himfelf of this miftake, the only one that Turenne had ever reafon to charge himfelf with, fell upon him all of a fudden, before he could affemble his troops, and beat him at Mariendal the 5th of May. The duke d'Anguien quitted the army under his command in Champagne, and haftened to fuccour M. de Turenne, after affifting the marquis de Villeroy by the way, to take the fortrefs of la Mothe in Lorrain, which was razed to the ground. This prince having joined M. de Turenne and marfhal Grammont, advanced towards Bavaria, took Wimphen, which

* The princefs Henrietta.

opened

The THIRD RACE. 103

EMINENT and LEARNED MEN.	EMINENT and LEARNED MEN.	EMINENT and LEARNED MEN.
Mich. Lambert, musician. 1696.	Charles de SainteMaure, duke de Montausier, governor to the Dauphin. 1690.	Nich. Poussin, painter. 1665.
Madam de Lambert. 1733.		Sam. Puffendorf. 1694.
		Peter Puget, sculptor. 1695.
Bern Lamy. 1715.	De Montesquieu. 1755.	
Mich. Richard de la Lande, musician. 1726.	Charles de Montchal. 1651.	Peter du Puis. 1652.
		Pasquier Quesnel. 1719.
	Bernard de Montfaucon. 1741.	Phil. Quinault. 1688.
Cl. Lancelot. 1695.		John de la Quintinie. 1686.
John de Launoy. 1678.	Lewis Morery. 1680.	
Godf. Will. Leibnitz. 1716.	John Morin. 1654.	Hon. de Beuil de Racan. 1670.
	Francis de la Mothe le Vayer. 1672.	
Cl. de Lisle. 1720.		John Racine. 1699.
John Locke. 1704.	Antony Houdart de la Motte. 1731.	John Armand le Bouthillier de Rancé. 1700.
Lewis de Longuerue. 1733.	Frances Bertaud de Motteville. 1689.	
J. Bapt. Lully. 1687.		Prince Ragotsky. 1732.
J. Mabillon. 1707.	Muratori. 1750.	René Rapin. 1687.
Lewis Maimburg. 1686.	Baptist Nani. 1678.	Rapin de Thoiras. 1725.
Lewis Isaac le Maitre de Sacy. 1684.	Robert Nanteuil. 1678.	Franc. Regnier Desmaretz. 1713.
	Gabriel Naudé. 1653.	
Nicholas Malebranche. 1715.	Sir Isaac Newton. 1727.	Silv. Regis. 1707.
	Peter Nicole. 1695.	John Francis Renard. 1709.
Fr. Mansard. 1666.	Ant. card. de Noailles. 1729.	
Hardouin Mansard. 1709.		Eus. Renaudot. 1720.
	Andrew le Notre. 1700.	John Francis Paul de Gondy de Retz, cardinal. 1679.
Peter de Marca. 1662.	Peter Joseph d'Orleans. 1698.	
Nic. de la Marc. 1723.		
James Marsollier. 1724.	Ant. Pagi. 1699.	Hyacinth Rigaud, painter. 1744.
Julius Mascaron. 1703.	Daniel Pappebrock. 1714.	
J.Bapt. Massillon. 1743.		Francis de la Rochefoucaud, cardinal. 1645.
Cl. Melan, engraver. 1688.	John Parocel, painter. 1704.	
Gilles Menage. 1692.	Blaise Pascal. 1662.	Fr. duke de la Rochefoucaud. 1680.
Cl. Francis Menestrier. 1705.	Guy Patin. 1672.	Ch. Rollin. 1741.
	Stephen Pavillon. 1705.	John de Rotrou. 1650.
Marin Mersenne. 1648.	John Pecquet, physician. 1674.	John Bapt. Rousseau. 1741.
John Ant. de Mesmes count d'Avaux. 1709.	Paul Fontanier Pellisson. 1693.	Charles de la Rue. 1725.
Fr. Eudes de Mezeray. 1683.	Charles Perrault. 1703.	D. Thierry Ruinart. 1709.
Peter Mignard. 1695.	Claude Perrault. 1688.	Peter du Ryer. 1656.
John Milton. 1674.	Dionysius Petavius. 1652.	Ch. de St. Denis de St. Evremond. 1703.
John Bapt. Poquelin de Moliere. 1673.	Paul Pezron. 1706.	Cæsar Vichard de St. Real. 1692.
Mich. Molinos. 1692.	Bern. Picard, engraver. 1733.	Abel Lewis de Sainte Marthe, general of the fathers of the oratory. 1697.
Nicholas Hub. Mongault. 1747.	Melchior de Polignac, cardinal. 1741.	
Bernard de la Monnoie. 1728.	Alexander Pope. 1744.	
		Lewis

H 4

REMARKABLE EVENTS under LEWIS XIV.

opened to him a paſſage on the Neckar, notwithſtanding the defection of Konigſmark; attacked general Mercy the 3d of Auguſt, contrary to the opinion of M. de Turenne, near Nortlingen, an imperial city in Swabia, and obtained a complete victory: Mercy was killed, and marſhal Grammont, having been taken priſoner, was exchanged for general Gleſne. The duke d'Anguien falling ill in conſequence of the fatigues of this campaign, the marſhals Turenne and Grammont continued the ſiege of Hailbrun, which had been inveſted by that prince. The archduke Leopold, the emperor's brother, and general Galas, aſſumed the command of the imperial army, raiſed the ſiege, and recovered all they had loſt between the Neckar and the Danube. Marſhal Turenne finiſhed the campaign on this ſide with taking Treves the 16th of November, and reſtoring the elector: this prince had recovered his liberty by the king's mediation, who declared, that otherwiſe he would liſten to no propoſals of peace.

On the ſide of Flanders, the duke of Orleans, having under him the marſhal de Gaſſion, and Rantzau, took the fort of Mardyke the 10th of July; for which Rantzau obtained the ſtaff of marſhal of France. The fortreſs of Link ſurrenders to Gaſſion on the 23d. Bourbourg is taken the 9th of Auguſt, Bethune the 30th, as alſo Caſſel, Etaire, Merville, and St. Venant. The duke of Orleans returned to Paris; but the marſhals de Gaſſion and Rantzau made themſelves maſters of Liliers, la Mothe aux fois, Armentieres, Warneton, Comines, Marchiennes, le Pont à Vendin, Lens, Orchies, l'Ecluſe, and Arleux. The prince of Orange confined himſelf to the taking of Hulſt, and was even engaged in this ſiege, in ſome meaſure, againſt his will by Gaſſion, who facilitated the operations. The jealouſy, which the province of Holland conceived againſt that of Zealand, prevented the ſiege of Antwerp, left the conveniency of this harbour ſhould prejudice the trade of Amſterdam. The enemy retake Caſſel and the fort of Mardyke.

The count d'Harcourt having ſucceeded to marſhal de la Mothe in Catalonia, kept the field, while the count du Pleſſis-Praſlin was employed in the ſiege of Roſes, which ſurrendered the laſt of May, after forty-nine days open trenches: he was made

EMINENT and LEARNED MEN.	EMINENT and LEARNED MEN.	EMINENT and LEARNED MEN.
Cl. de St. Marthe. 1690.	John Francis Senault. 1670.	Jof. Pitton de Tournefort. 1708.
Lewis ⎫	Mary de Rabutin de Sevigné. 1696.	René Jof. de Tournemine. 1739.
Scevola ⎬ de St. Marthe.	Rich. Simon. 1712.	John Foi-Vaillant. 1706.
twins ⎭ 1650.	Vittorio Siri. 1685.	Adrian de Valois. 1692.
Denis de Salo. 1669.	James Sirmond. 1651.	Henry de Valois. 1676.
Denis Salvaing. 1688.	Benedict Spinoza. 1677.	Ant. Varillas. 1696.
Nicholas Samfon. 1667.	Euft. le Sueur, painter. 1655.	Lewis le Vau, architect. 1670.
John Bapt. de Santeuil. 1697.	Michael le Tellier, the king's confeffor. 1719.	Fr. Vavaffeur. 1681.
John Francis Sarafin. 1654.	L. Thomaffin. 1695.	Cl. Faure de Vaugelas. 1649.
Claude Saumaife. 1653.	Seb. le Nain de Tillemont. 1698.	René Aubert de Vertot. 1735.
Paul Scaron. 1660.	Nich. Toinard. 1707.	Vincent Voiture. 1648.
Mad. de Scudery. 1701.		John Warin. 1672.
J. Renaud de Segrais. 1701.		
John Selden. 1654.		

REMARKABLE EVENTS under LEWIS XIV.

made a marſhal of France. The taking of this town opened a communication between Catalonia and Rouſſillon. The count d'Harcourt, after making himſelf maſter of Agrammont and St. Aunais, croſſed the Segne, and won the battle of Liorens the 23d of June, againſt Don Andrew Canteleme; after which he took Balaguier.

The conſpiracy of the Catalans, managed by the baroneſs d'Albi, the abbé Gallicans, and Onuphrius Aquilles, to reſtore the Spaniſh government. It is diſcovered and quaſhed by the count d'Harcourt.

On the ſide of Portugal, the Spaniards, under the command of the marquis de Terracuſe, were routed and obliged to raiſe the ſiege of Elvas. The young duke of Savoy is reſtored to the poſſeſſion of Turin, and of other places which had French garriſons, by virtue of the treaty concluded the 3d of April. Prince Thomas, in order to drive the Spaniards intirely out of his country, poſſeſſed himſelf of Rocca-di-Vigevano: then advancing to join marſhal du Pleſſis-Praſlin, who was upon his march with ſuccours from France, he forced the Spaniſh quarters, and paſſed the river Mora.

Cardinal Mazarin having oppoſed the exaltation of Innocent X. to the pontificate, endeavoured afterwards to make him forget it; but finding he could not ſucceed, he was reconciled to the Barberins, who were ill uſed by that pontif, although he had been indebted to them for the triple crown. Mazarin receives them at Paris; and upon the eldeſt, named Antony, he confers the archbiſhopric of Rheims, with the poſt of high-almoner of France. The duke de St. Simon reſigns his place of maſter of the horſe, in favour of Beringhen. Anne of Auſtria begins to build the church of Val de Grace; the architect of which was Francis Manſard.

November the 6th the princeſs Mary of Gonzaga, daughter of the late duke of Mantua, was married to Ladiſlaus IV. king of Poland, in the chapel of the *palais royal.* She was eſpouſed afterwards to Caſimir that prince's ſucceſſor. The duke of Orleans made love to her once; but the queen oppoſing this match, and the duke himſelf proving inconſtant, ſhe comforted herſelf with his favourite Chalais. The marſhal de

Guebriant's

REMARKABLE EVENTS under LEWIS XIV.

Guebriant's wife attended her to Poland, with the title of ambaſſadreſs. To the honour of this lady we muſt not omit to mention, that Ladiſlaus, in proof of his great eſteem for her perſon, would have the ſame compliments paid to her, as had been ſhewn in 1637 to Claude de Medicis, archdutcheſs of Inſpruc, upon coming to Warſaw with queen Cecilia, daughter of the emperor Ferdinand II, and firſt wife to Ladiſlaus. The wife of marſhal Guebriant died in 1659: it is ſaid that ſhe was to have been lady of honour to Mary Thereſa: the title of *marechale de France*, ſays Laboureur, belonged to her as well as to her huſband. In England the rebels beheaded William Laud, archbiſhop of Canterbury*. The war was carried on in that kingdom with as much vivacity as ever; but the battle of Naſeby, in which the king was defeated by the rebel army under ſir Thomas Fairfax and Oliver Cromwell, proved deciſive againſt his majeſty.

1646.

In Germany the viſcount de Turenne could enter upon no important expedition for want of ſuccours: having joined the Swedes and Heſſians, he laid ſiege to Augſburg, which he was obliged to raiſe; and a ſtop was ſuddenly put to his operations, by the treaty of neutrality between France and the duke of Bavaria. The queen regent began to grow jealous of the Swedes, which, together with the advantage ſhe found in detaching that elector from the emperor, was the cauſe of the abovementioned treaty.

Chriſtina, queen of Sweden, being of age, ſent her favourite the count de la Gardie into France, to keep up her alliance with the king.

In Flanders, the duke of Orleans, having under his command the marſhal de Meilleray, maſter of the ordnance, with the marſhals de Grammont and de Gaſſions, laid ſiege to Courtray, and took it the 20th of June, notwithſtanding the alarms he received at different times from the enemy's army, under the command of the duke of Lorrain and Piccolomini, with the generals Bec and Lamboy. It was thought this conqueſt would facilitate that of Gaunt or Antwerp, which was then in agitation: but whether

---

* He was beheaded on Tower-hill, Jan. the 10th 1644-5. O. S.

REMARKABLE EVENTS under LEWIS XIV.

it was owing to the great age of the prince of Orange, who died the year following; or to the clashing of interests betwixt the provinces of Holland and Zealand; or, in short, to the jealousy of the Dutch, who were already meditating to break off their alliance with France; these schemes did not take place. The duke of Orleans marched towards Bergues St. Venox, and took it the 1st of August. From thence he went and laid siege to Mardyke, which the Spaniards had retaken during the winter: the siege was very bloody, and lasted seventeen days; the place received fresh supplies from Lamboy and Caracena, who were encamped in the neighbourhood of Dunkirk; but the Dutch fleet appearing before the town, the siege was greatly forwarded, so that Mardyke was obliged to capitulate the 24th. The duke of Orleans returned to court, and the duke d'Anguien prepared to make himself master of Dunkirk by the taking of Furnes. The latter surrendered the 7th of September, and the former the 7th of October. The young king made his first tour this year, and came to Amiens in the spring, where the army was assembling.

Nothing of consequence was transacted in Savoy, where the Spaniards still preserved some towns; but cardinal Mazarin, desirous of punishing the pope's ingratitude to the Barberins, and still more so of revenging the affront he had received from Innocent X, in being refused the cardinal's cap for his brother the archbishop of Aix, laid siege to Orbitello in Tuscany, a town then belonging to the Spaniards, with a view of drawing near to Rome. Prince Thomas had the command of the land army, and the duke de Brezé of the fleet. The prince having opened the trenches, the Spanish fleet, under the command of Pimentel, came to relieve the town, and was met by admiral Brezé the 14th of June: the conflict proved bloody, and the Spaniards were discomfited; but the French admiral was killed at the age of twenty-seven, and prince Thomas was obliged to raise the siege. We give the title of admiral to M. de Brezé for no other reason, but because he acted in that capacity; for the post itself had been suppressed in 1627, and did not revive till 1669; so that M. de Brezé was stiled only *superintendant of the seas:* the duke d'Anguien would fain have succeeded him in this employ,

but

REMARKABLE EVENTS under LEWIS XIV.

but the queen, to evade his importunity, procured it for herself.

The check before Orbitello was repaired by the taking of Urbino, which surrendered October the 8th to the marshals de Meilleraye and du Plessis; and by the conquest of Portolongone, the 29th of the same month. The pope was more sensibly affected with the taking of this place, than he would have been with that of Orbitello, or than he was with the conquest of Piombino, because this estate belonged to his nephew Ludovisio. These expeditions were soon followed by a reconciliation between the pontif and the Barberins; and the cardinal's cap being sent to the archbishop of Aix, brother of Mazarin, he assumed the title of St. Cecilia.

The duke of Modena declares in favour of France. In Catalonia the count d'Harcourt was beaten by Leganez, November the 21st, and obliged to raise the siege of Lerida. Charles I. having thrown himself into the arms of the Scotch, the two houses at Westminster declare he had forfeited all his right to the crown. Henry II, prince of Conde, departs this life the 26th of December.

1647.

This year did not prove fortunate to France. The plenipotentiaries for concluding a peace continued their conferences, to which they had invited the different states and princes of the empire: this was very disagreeable to the emperor, who made great difficulty to treat upon equal terms with those powers, but was willing they should accustom themselves to consider him as their sovereign. The catholic princes assembled at Munster, the protestants at Osnabrug. The duke de Longueville had been sent to Munster with the title of plenipotentiary; the other two ministers did not agree: Servien, an able statesman, had the intire confidence of the cardinal; but d'Avaux was a superior genius. It is observable that there was the same disunion between Salvius, a creature of the queen, and Oxenstiern, the chancellor's son, both of them plenipotentiaries of Christina.

A suspension of arms betwixt Spain and the Dutch, which was followed the next year by a treaty of peace between those two powers. Antony Brun, a native of Franche Compté, and plenipotentiary

nipotentiary of Philip IV, served his master extremely well on this occasion, while Servien suffered himself to be imposed upon. The town of Tubingen in the dutchy of Wirtemberg is taken by marshal d'Hocquincourt.

Marshal Turenne, having received orders, in consequence of the treaty of neutrality between France and Bavaria, to repass the Rhine, and to march into the dutchy of Luxemburg, could not prevail on the German cavalry to follow him; they chose to be commanded by Wrangel, the Swedish general. The elector being freed from the proximity of our army, renewed his alliance with the emperor.

In Flanders, the archduke Leopold, the emperor's brother, being apprized of the disposition of the Dutch, and that he had nothing to fear from that quarter, took Armentieres the 31st of May, in fourteen days open trenches, notwithstanding the vigorous resistance of du Plessis-Belliere, and afterwards made himself master of Comines: then laying siege to Landrecy, which was prevented from receiving succours, by a misunderstanding between Gassion and Rantzau, he obliged it to surrender the 18th of July. Rantzau, after taking fort Knock, became master of Dixmude July the 13th; and Gassion signed a capitulation with la Bassée the 19th, upon hearing that the archduke was marching to its assistance. Rantzau carried the fort of Neudam and the town of Sluys, but was attacked in his return by the marquis of Caracena: it proved a drawn battle.

Marshal Gassion lays siege to Lens, where he was mortally wounded the 28th of September, and departed this life October the 2d. Lens was taken the 3d. *France,* says Monglat, *gained a paltry town, and lost a great captain.* He used to answer those who proposed to him to marry, *that he did not set so great a value upon life, as to want to share it with any body.* He was upon ill terms with the cardinal when he died, and was interred at Charenton. His government of Courtray, where he had erected a kind of empire of his own, was given to Paluau, and marshal Rantzau succeeded him in the command of the army. The campaign concluded with the siege of Dixmude, which the Spaniards retook the 14th of November.

The THIRD RACE.

REMARKABLE EVENTS *under* LEWIS XIV.

In Italy, the conſtable of Caſtile recovered Nice de la Paille the 23d of May; but the duke of Modena's junction with France, and the inſurrection of the Neapolitans, prevented this general from making any further progreſs.

The Neapolitans, finding themſelves overloaded with taxes, riſe up in arms, with a man of the dregs of the people at their head, named Maſſaniello: this firſt commotion was pacified by the duke d'Arcos, viceroy of Naples, who cauſed Maſſaniello to be aſſaſſinated. About two months after, Don John of Auſtria, a natural ſon of Philip IV, having entered the city, in order to puniſh the delinquents, a freſh inſurrection enſued, which was headed by one Gennaro; yet having more prudence than his predeceſſor Maſſaniello, he adviſed the people to put themſelves under the protection of France: in conſequence of which, the duke of Guiſe, who was then at Rome, ſolliciting for a divorce from the counteſs of Boſſu, was invited to put himſelf at the head of the rebels: accordingly he went to Naples, where he was declared generaliſſimo. France reaped no advantage from this event: the duke de Richelieu contented himſelf with inſulting the Spaniſh fleet; and M. de Guiſe received neither the proviſions nor money promiſed him: ſome pretend he had a deſign to make himſelf king of Naples; but was that a reaſon for abandoning him?

In Catalonia, the duke d'Anguien, now ſtiled the prince of Condé after the death of his father, which happened December the 26th, 1646, was obliged to raiſe the ſiege of Lerida, the 17th of June. The parliament of Scotland * deliver up Charles I. to the Engliſh parliamentarians: this prince makes his eſcape to the iſle of Wight, where he believed he ſhould be ſafe; but found he had only changed his priſon. Lewis XIV. was ſeized with the ſmall-pox the 10th of November, and had like to have died of it.

Marſhal Schomberg obtained the office of colonel of the Swiſs, vacant by the deceaſe of Baſſompierre, after it had been refuſed to the duke de Longueville. Towards this year the diſputes about Janſeniſm began.

* Not the parliament of Scotland, but the Scotch army, who delivered him to the Engliſh rebels in conſideration of 40,000 l. of their arrears.

REMARKABLE EVENTS under LEWIS XIV.

1648.

The peace of Munſter, and the war of Paris, conſtitute the two grand objects of this year, after we have taken a curſory view of the operations of the campaign. The war continued with as much vigour in Germany, as if the peace was not ſo near at hand. Marſhal Turenne rejoined the Swedes, under the command of Wrangel and Konigſmark, from whom he had withdrawn himſelf the preceding year by order of the court; and fell upon Bavaria, to puniſh the duke for infringing the late treaty of neutrality. General Melander and Montecuculli were beaten at Summerhauſen, in the neighbourhood of Augſburg, the 17th of May; and the duke of Bavaria, who was ſeventy-eight years old, (he died in 1651) was obliged to retire from his dominions, which fell a prey to the enemy: on the 26th of July the Swedes plundered the caſtle of Prague and the little town, where Konigſmark took an immenſe booty: but the news of the ſigning of the peace put an end to this devaſtation.

The treaty of peace was ſigned at Munſter the 30th of January betwixt Spain and Holland; in conſequence of which the king of Spain renounced for himſelf, and for his ſucceſſors, all right whatever to the United Provinces, and acknowledged them to be a free and independent ſtate.

By this peace France was deprived of the alliance of Holland, notwithſtanding the aſſurance this republic had given of never entering into a ſeparate treaty; and Spain was encouraged to make new efforts againſt France, whoſe power was weakened by the civil wars.

The archduke Leopold makes himſelf maſter of Courtray the 19th of May: the count de Paluau had weakened the garriſon of that place, to reinforce the army under the prince of Condé, who was beſieging Ipres, which ſurrendered the 28th: he had under him the marſhals de Grammont and Rantzau. The archduke carries the town of Furnes Auguſt the 3d, and Lens the 19th of the ſame month. The prince of Condé, though he could not prevent the taking of this place, attacked the archduke in the plain of Lens, and obtained a complete victory the 20th of Auguſt: marſhal Grammont commanded the left wing, and the duke de

Chatillon

REMARKABLE EVENTS under LEWIS XIV.

Chatillon the center. This victory was followed by the siege of Furnes, which the prince of Condé retook the 10th of September, having the marshal de Rantzau under him: but the *barricades* of Paris recalled him to court, where his presence was wanting to oppose the *Frondeurs* *.

In Catalonia marshal Schomberg made himself master of Tortosa the 10th of July. The revolt of Naples concluded with the taking of the duke of Guise, who had left that capital to lay siege to the little town of Nisitra: he could not get back again, but was made prisoner the 6th of April, and carried into Spain, where he continued in confinement till the year 1652. The Spaniards were afraid lest this prince should foment the Neapolitan rebellion, and assert his claim to that crown, by Joland of Anjou, dutchess of Lorrain, and daughter of René king of Sicily: the prince of Condé, who afterwards went over to the Spaniards, procured him his liberty. He died in 1664.

The duke of Modena, having been drawn into the alliance of France, by his brother the cardinal d'Este, protector of that crown at the court of Rome, joined the marshal du Plessis-Praslin, and forced the entrenchments of the marquis of Caracena, near Cremona, on the 30th of June; but was obliged, the 6th of October, to raise the siege of Cremona, the garrison having received continual supplies from the Spaniards.

The treaties of Munster and Osnabrug signed, the former at Munster on the 24th of October with the Catholics; and the latter at Osnabrug, the 6th of the preceding August, with the Protestants. The king of Spain, having concluded a peace on the 30th of January with the Dutch, resolved, as we have before mentioned, to prosecute the war against France, which was not terminated till the Pyrenean treaty. The principal articles of the treaty of Munster were, that an eighth electorate should be created in favour of the Palatine line of Bavaria, called the Rodolphine; and that in case, either the Wilhelmine line, or the other, should happen to fail, then the eighth electorate should be suppressed; that nothing should be transacted in the empire with-

* *Frondeurs* or *slingers*, a name given to the malecontents in France, during Mazarine's ministry, because they flattered themselves with the hopes of pulling down the minister, with the same success as David brought Goliah upon his face to the earth with his sling.

out the advice and consent of a free assembly of the states; that each of those states should have a perpetual right of concluding such alliances among themselves, and with foreign princes, as might be necessary for their security and preservation, provided they were not designed against the emperor and the empire: in regard to France, that the sovereignty of the bishoprics of Metz, Toul, and Verdun, and the territory of Moyenvic, should belong to that crown; that the emperor and the empire should resign in favour of the king of France, all their rights to Pignerol, as also to Brisac, to the landgraviate of the Upper and Lower Alsace, to the Sundgaw, and to the provincial prefecture of the ten imperial towns situated in Alsace; that the king should have a right to maintain a garrison in Philipsburg, &c. It was likewise mentioned in this treaty, that those of the confession of Augsburg, who had seized the lands or estates of catholic churches, should be maintained in the possession of them; and that it should be lawful for the princes of the empire to conform to the Protestant religion, if they thought proper. The duke of Lorrain was not included in this treaty; the discussion of his interests having been deferred till the peace with Spain.

By the treaty of Osnabrug, all hither Pomerania, the isle of Rugen, Stettin, and some other places in further Pomerania, the mouths of the Oder, the town of Wismar, the archbishopric of Bremen, and the bishopric of Verden, &c. were ceded for ever to the crown of Sweden. These treaties may be considered as the political codex of part of Europe; and are the basis of all the negotiations, which since that time have been set on foot by those same powers. The pope and the Venetians were the mediators of this peace; Fabio Chigi (afterwards Alexander VII.) for the pope, and Contarini for the Venetians.

The civil war broke out in France, on the following occasion. The salaries of some of the officers of parliament had been withheld: the people oppressed with taxes, encouraged those magistrates to make loud complaints: among other pecuniary edicts, that for creating twelve new places of masters of requests, which had been opposed by this body the 17th of January, gave rise to the first commotions. The parliament of Paris published two arrets of union with the parliaments and other courts of

judi-

REMARKABLE EVENTS under LEWIS XIV.

judicature of the kingdom, one the 13th of May, the other the 15th of June. (The reader will find these transactions in the memoirs of the times, which are curious and interesting.) The presidents, Gayan and Barillon, having been put under arrest in the beginning of the year without any ill effect, the cardinal imagined that the day of commemorating the victory obtained at Lens, which was the 26th of August, would be a favourable opportunity for confining two more members of parliament. He therefore caused the president Poitier de Blancmenil and Brouffel to be arrested: the former, who was nephew to the bishop of Beavais, could not forgive the queen for taking such a dislike to her uncle in the beginning of her regency: the latter, who had no other merit but his poverty and presumption, was dissatisfied with the regent for refusing a company in the guards to his son. This imprisonment made more noise than was expected. The populace insisted upon their being set at liberty: the streets were soon barricaded with iron chains (which is the reason of its being called the day of the *barricades*), and the queen was compelled to deliver up the prisoners. The public good (as is generally the case in all revolts) was only a pretext for these troubles, while the coals of sedition were blown by the enemies of the government, who being unable to make an open attack upon the crown, directed their artillery against the ministry: hence the two parties had the name, the one of the *Frondeurs* or slingers, and the other of *Mazarins*. At the head of the Frondeurs were the duke of Beaufort, who had made his escape from the castle of Vincennes, where he had been confined five years; de Retz, coadjutor of the bishop of Paris, and afterwards cardinal; the dutchess of Longueville; the prince of Marsillac, who was in love with that lady; the prince of Conty; the duke of Vendome; his brother-in-law the duke de Nemours; the duke of Bouillon, who was the soul of the confederacy; his brother marshal Turenne; marshal de la Mothe, &c. The court party were the prince of Condé, marshal Grammont, the duke de Chatillon, &c. And what is very extraordinary, in less than three years there was a total revolution of interests: the prince of Conty, who had headed the rebels against the cardinal, married that minister's niece; the prince of Condé, who had laid siege to Paris, at the head of the king's army, defended this capital againſt the king; this very prince of Condé, who had reconducted the cardinal in triumph to Paris, was confined by that miniſter; and laſtly, marſhal Turenne having withdrawn himſelf from the prince of Condé, commanded the king's forces at the battle of St. Antoine. The duke of Orleans fluctuating between the two parties, often changed ſides, according as his humour, or the abbé de la Riviere directed him. Chavigny, being ſuſpected by the cardinal, is ſent to Vincennes, and from thence to Havre de Grace; but the parliament coming to an accommodation with the court, after the declaration of the 4th of October, he obtained his liberty, yet was never reſtored, neither did he long ſurvive his diſgrace.

Margaret of Rohan, daughter of Henry duke de Rohan, (whoſe dutchy having been created in 1603, was extinct by his deceaſe in 1638, for want of male iſſue, according to the clauſe of the patent) obtains new letters of creation from the king in favour of herſelf and her huſband Henry de Chabot, and their male deſcendants; but they were not verified till 1652.

Erection of the land of Cœuvres into a dutchy and peerage, under the name of Eſtrées; the letters were not verified till 1663.

The county of Guiche erected into a dutchy and peerage by the name of Grammont; the letters patent were not verified till 1663.

The county of Treſmes created a dukedom and peerage in favour of Renè Poitier, ſon of Lewis baron of Gevres, ſecretary of ſtate: he was deſcended from James Poitier, counſellor of parliament, who had two ſons; the eldeſt was *preſident a mortier*, and from the youngeſt came the dukes of Treſmes; the letters patent were not regiſtered till 1663.

In England, after divers encounters between the royaliſts and the rebels, Cromwell hearing that a treaty was ſet on foot by the king and parliament, excludes the greateſt part of the members *, and cauſes king Charles I. to be removed from the iſle of

---

* Lord Clarendon ſays, near one hundred were denied entrance; and forty-one members were put under cuſtody.

REMARKABLE EVENTS under LEWIS XIV.

Wight to Hurst castle *, the 28th of September. It seems as if the spirit of rebellion had spread itself at this time over all Europe: the English bring their king to his trial as a criminal; the allegiance of the parliament of Paris is shaken by a few turbulent members; and sultan Ibrahim is strangled by the Janissaries.

1649.

The declaration of the preceding year had been productive only of an apparent calm; the parliament assembled again, under pretence that the declaration had been violated.

The king is compelled by the *Frondeurs* to quit his capital, at the very time when the treaty of Munster rendered his power respectable over all Europe: he withdraws to St. Germains, the 6th of January in the night; and on the 7th the prince of Condé, accompanied by the duke of Orleans, forms the blockade of Paris. On the 8th of February he takes Charenton, where the duke de Chatillon was slain. Tancred, who pretended to be the son of the duke de Rohan, had been killed a few days before; and his death put an end to the suit, which he had commenced against Margaret de Rohan Chabot. Spain, sollicited by the princes of the blood, interferes in the civil broils, in order to distress France; and the archduke Leopold, governor of the Netherlands, prepares to invade the kingdom at the head of fifteen thousand men. The queen, being justly alarmed, listens to the proposals of the parliament: on the other hand those magistrates had exhausted their finances, their troops were mouldering away, and they had little or no confidence in their generals. The disturbances are appeased, and the terms of accommodation signed the 11th of March, without giving satisfaction to either party. The parliament continued to have liberty to assemble, which the court was desirous to prevent, at least for the remainder of the year; and the minister was continued in his office, when both the parliament and people had demanded his dismission. There was a general act of indemnity, in which all the chiefs of the rebel party were included; the

---

* Hurst castle is in Hampshire, situated on a neck of land, opposite to the isle of Wight: it was built by king Henry VIII.

REMARKABLE EVENTS under LEWIS XIV.

cardinal however willing to mortify the coadjutor, did not name him perfonally, but confounded him in the crowd.

The queen mother would not fuffer the king to return immediately to Paris, but conducted him to Compiegne, under pretence of being near the army in Picardy; fo that their majefties did not make their entry into Paris till the 18th of Auguft, when the prince of Condé and cardinal Mazarin, againft whom the parliament had publifhed fuch fanguinary arrets, appeared in the fame coach with the king. This treaty did not put a ftop to the difturbances of the kingdom, efpecially in Provence and Guyenne, where the parliaments, following the example of that of Paris, declared againft their governors, the count d'Alais and the duke d'Epernon.

The Spaniards profiting by the civil broils in France, retook Ipres the 8th of May, and St. Venant the 10th. The count d'Harcourt defeats a body of the troops of Lorrain, in the neighbourhood of Valenciennes, on the 10th of June; and cuts eight hundred horfe in pieces on the 23d, between Doway and St. Amand. He had invefted Cambray, but was obliged to raife the fiege of that town the 3d of July; and concluded this campaign with the taking of Condé the 25th of Auguft in two days open trenches; yet he abandoned it afterwards, not thinking the place tenable in winter.

In Italy, the duke of Modena concluded a peace with the Spaniards, with the confent of cardinal Mazarin, who was unable to fupport him.

In Catalonia, Don John de Garay, after obtaining fome advantages, was obliged to lay afide his defign of befieging Barcelona, Marfini having thrown a French garrifon into the town.

Charles I. was beheaded at Whitehall the 9th of February, N. S. in his fifty-firft year. The houfe of lords was fuppreffed, the oath of allegiance and fupremacy abolifhed, and the whole power fell into the hands of the people. Cromwell was declared captain-general of the troops of the ftate, and afterwards rofe to the fovereign power with the title of protector. The nation, that fuffered this parricide, fhewed their deteftation of it as foon as it was committed: even the very enemies of Charles I. could not help admiring his conftancy of mind: they faid, that he

died

REMARKABLE EVENTS under LEWIS XIV.

died with more fortitude than he had lived, so as to verify an old observation on the Stuart family, *that they bear adversity better than prosperity*. The new republic was first acknowledged by the king of Spain, afterwards by Sweden, Holland, the republic of Venice, and at length by the regency of France. Charles II, after being proclaimed in Ireland by the loyal marquis of Ormond, is defeated in England [*], and obliged to retire to the queen his mother in France.

1650.

The prince of Condé, to whom the state and the cardinal were indebted, the one for its glory, the other for his security, set too high a value upon his services, and by raising his pretensions became a rebel: besides he opposed the match between the cardinal's niece and the duke de Mercœur. It was resolved in council to arrest him: and there appeared now a favourable opportunity of doing it, as he had openly quarrelled with the *Frondeurs*. The prince accused that party, particularly the duke of Beaufort, and the coadjutor, of having formed a design to murder him; while his case was making ready, both parties appeared in parliament, and had like to have come to blows in the great hall. The queen, availing herself of this conjuncture, was reconciled to the Frondeurs. The dutchess of Chevreuse gained the duke of Orleans, after detaching him from the abbé de la Riviere, who was disgraced: she made him so jealous of the prince of Condé, as to desire him to be arrested; which was accordingly executed the 18th of January by Guitaut, captain of the queen's guards, Comminges his nephew, and Miossants, lieutenant of the king's gendarmes (the marshal d'Albret). The prince of Condé, the prince of Conty, and the duke of Longueville, were conducted at first to Vincennes, from thence to Marcoussy, and at length to Havre de Grace: but what is very surprising, the people made bonfires on this occasion. The dutchess of Longueville made her escape to Normandy, whither she was followed by Marsillac; M. de Bouillon went to Turenne; and M. de Turenne to Stenay: Marsin, being attached to the prince, was arrested in Catalonia, amidst the army under his command. The queen, with a few troops conducted by the count d'Harcourt, sets out the first of February, and takes the

[*] At the battle of Worcester, on the 3d of Sept. 1657.

REMARKABLE EVENTS under LEWIS XIV.

king with her to Normandy, in order to secure that province against the enterprizes of madam de Longueville: this lady had escaped to Holland, and from thence returned to Stenay, where, in conjunction with marshal Turenne, she concluded a treaty with the Spaniards. The seals are taken from the chancellor de Seguier, and given to Chateauneuf, who was recommended by the *Fronde*.

In Lorrain, the towns of Clermont, Stenay, and Jametz, which had been surrendered to the prince of Condé, are obliged to submit to the king. The marquis de la Ferté beats the count de Ligneville the 9th of October. The adherents of the prince of Condé are unable to maintain him in the possession of Bourges, or of Dijon and Seurre in Burgundy: the latter surrendered to the king the 21st of April; and their majesties having advanced as far as Dijon, arrived at Paris the 3d of May: from thence they repaired to Guienne, where their presence restored the tranquillity of Bourdeaux. The queen resigns the post of superintendant of the seas in favour of the duke of Vendome, with the reversion to the duke of Beaufort.

Marshal Turenne having assumed the title of lieutenant general of the king's army, in order to set the princes at liberty, joins the archduke in pursuance of the treaty concluded by madam de Longueville; and after making himself master of Aubenton and Irson, he took Catelet the 15th of June. Marshal du Plessis-Praslin obliges the archduke to raise the siege of Guise the 1st of July. M. Turenne takes Capelle the 3d of August, and advances towards the castle of Vincennes to release the princes, but they had been removed to Marcoussy. November the 6th, Monzon surrenders to the Spaniards, after a vigorous defence. Marshal du Plessis possessed himself of Rethel, December the 13th; and marshal Turenne, having made a fruitless attempt to relieve the town, resolved upon a battle, but was defeated by marshal du Plessis the 15th of December: this is the battle of Rethel. M. de Puysegur, in his memoirs, claims the whole merit of that action.

The marquisate of Mortemart erected into a dutchy and peerage; the letters patent were not verified till 1663.

The barony of Villemor erected into a dutchy in favour of the chancellor Seguier and his heirs, as well male as female; the letters patent were not registered. In

REMARKABLE EVENTS under LEWIS XIV.

In Italy, the Spaniards retook Portolongone the 15th of August: in Catalonia they recovered Flix on the Segre, Tortofa, Balaguier, and the whole plain of Urgel. Cromwell gains the battle of Dunbar on the 15th of September, againſt the Scots of king Charles II's party. The unfortunate marquis of Montrofe, a loyal fubject and great captain, being taken prifoner by the rebels, was hanged the 30th of May.

Defcartes departs this life at Stockholm the 11th of February. It has been faid of this great man, that he was the leading philofopher of the age: and it might have been further added, that he banifhed a particular tafte of literature, which had prevailed till his time, namely, that of erudition unaffifted by philofophy; and as the preceding age could be only diftinguifhed by the title of learned, his might be truly deemed enlightened; for this is the judgment that Bayle paſſes on the fixteenth and feventeenth centuries. "I believe, fays he, that the fixteenth century "produced a greater number of literati than the feventeenth, "and yet the former was far from being fo enlightened as the latter. "The prefent age is lefs learned, and more knowing." Hobbes improves upon Bayle: this Englifh philofopher, being a perfon of greater meditation than reading, fet no manner of value upon learning; nay, he would fay by way of raillery, that if he had applied as much of his time to reading, as other men of letters, he fhould have been as ignorant as they. It is obvious that Hobbes has carried the point too far: but we muft confider that he was finding fault with the ill ufe, which men of letters but too frequently made of their erudition; and that his defign was to decry fuch perfons, as knew not how to reafon but by quotations and authorities. To thefe a third age has fucceeded, which inftead of adopting the opinions of others, has perhaps too much affected to draw from its own fpring; and by aiming at wit, has fometimes fallen into a deviation from good fenfe. Let us take heed that the eighteenth century does not complain of too great an affectation of *wit*, as the fixteenth did of too great a ftore of erudition.

1651.

Cardinal Mazarin had quarrelled with the Frondeurs upon too flight an occafion, imagining that he no longer ſtood in need of their

their assistance. He charged the duke of Orleans with having treated with a Spanish envoy in the king's absence; which indeed was a high misdemeanor, but this was not a time to call him to an account: he likewise laid the blame of the duke's behaviour on the coadjutor, who had succeeded the abbé de la Riviere as that prince's favourite; and he deprived him of all hopes of being nominated to the purple. The *Frondeurs* on the other hand were reinforced by the duke de Nemours, who was drawn into the confederacy by the dutchess of Chatillon, being in love with this lady, who compelled him to serve under his rival the prince of Condé: the princess Palatine, who was very intimate with that prince, added further strength to the party. In fine, the parliament being spirited up by the *Frondeurs*, insisted that the princes should be set at liberty; and the court was not in a condition to refuse their demand: but those magistrates went further, for after they had intimidated cardinal Mazarin to such a degree, as to oblige him to quit the kingdom, they published a perpetual arret of banishment against him. The queen issues an order for releasing the princes from their confinement; and the cardinal, without waiting for the order, goes and discharges them himself, expecting to conciliate their favour; but they gave him a very cool reception, and he was obliged to retire to Liege. The princes return to Paris, as it were in triumph, on the 16th of February, accompanied by the duke of Orleans.

Marshal Turenne having received an invitation from the king, quits the Spanish service, and returns to Tours, where he obtains the final conclusion of the contract of exchange for Sedan, which had been entered into so early as the year 1642. In this instrument it is mentioned, that the lands of Albret and Chateau-Thierry, which had been exchanged for the sovereignty of Sedan, *shall be transferred to the lord of Bouillon, and to his descendants male and female, with all the titles, dignities, and ancient pre-eminences, ... to take effect from the day of their first creations*, which referred to the year 1556, when the dutchy of Albret was erected in favour of the king and queen of Navarre; this contract was registered in parliament in the month of February 1652, but with this proviso, *that the said peerages of*
Albret

REMARKABLE EVENTS under LEWIS XIV.

Albret and Chateau-Thierry should not be capable of having their effect and rank, but from the day of the present arret, the said de la Tour d'Auvergne obtaining letters patent of our lord the king. Accordingly the duke of Bouillon obtained letters of erection of the dutchies of Albret and Chateau-Thierry in the same month of February, 1652; but as he died that very year, before he had caused them to be verified, his son the duke of Bouillon obtained new letters patent in 1662, in which marshal Turenne, his uncle, was also included. The duke of Bouillon was not admitted till 1665.

The parliament register the declaration extorted from the queen, by which all foreigners, and even French cardinals are excluded from being members of the council: they likewise publish several arrets against Mazarin. The queen pretends to be reconciled to the prince of Condé, by granting such demands as would have destroyed her whole authority; but at the same time she endeavours to render him obnoxious to the *Frondeurs*, who were his chief support; by which means she prepares to violate her late engagements with impunity. The nobility demanded an assembly of the states; she persuades the prince of Condé that this assembly is contrary to his interest; and he prevents its being held. The *Frondeurs* wanted the prince of Conty to marry mademoiselle de Chevreuse; but the prince being made sensible of the influence, which this match would give to the coadjutor, by whom that lady was governed, abruptly breaks it off. Thus the court was divided into three parties; that of the queen, with whom were the duke of Bouillon and marshal Turenne, &c. that of the prince of Condé, supported by messieurs de Nemours, de la Rochefoucaud, &c. and that of the *Frondeurs*, headed by the duke of Orleans, the coadjutor, madam de Chevreuse, &c.

The prince of Condé, distrustful of all parties, refused to appear at the bed of justice, where the king declared his majority the 7th of September. The cardinal, who was at Cologne, continued to govern the queen. The prince of Condé retires to his government of Guyenne, and prepares for war. The count d'Harcourt obliges the prince of Condé to raise the siege of Cognac. The marshal de la Ferté, having laid siege to

Chatté

Chatté in Lorrain, takes it the 13th of September, after forty-three days open trenches. Bergues St. Venox surrenders to the Spaniards.

In Catalonia, the Spaniards retook Cervers, and laid siege to Barcelona.

Nicholas de Neufville, secretary of state, having obtained letters patent in 1610, bearing creation of the seignory of Villeroy into a chatellany, his son Charles, marquis of Alincourt, obtained another patent in 1615, for erecting it into a marquisate; and marshal Villeroy, the son of Charles, and governor of Lewis XIV, was made duke and peer by letters patent of the month of September, which were not verified till 1663.

1652.

Villars-Brancas created a dutchy and peerage. George de Brancas, the admiral's elder brother, had obtained letters patent for this creation in 1627: and now he obtains a new patent of erection; but as he had it registered only in the parliament of Aix, his great grandson Lewis Antony of Brancas obtained letters of *surannation* * in 1716, which were verified in the parliament of Paris.

The cardinal, having been met upon the frontier by marshal d'Hocquincourt, waits upon the king, who was advanced as far as Poitiers, in order to watch the male-contents of Guyenne: and from thence he attends his majesty back to Angers.

The duke of Orleans, whom the queen had gained over once more, and afterwards lost, and who fluctuated between the two parties, enters into an agreement with the counts de Fiesque and Gaucourt, agents of the prince of Condé, to oblige the queen to dismiss the cardinal. Gaston sends his daughter to Orleans, to preserve that place in his interest; the dukes of Nemours and Beaufort, notwithstanding they were brothers-in-law, and connected with the same party, had a quarrel in that city, which ended in a duel; and the duke of Nemours lost his life.

The prince of Condé falls upon marshal d'Hocquincourt's quarters at Blenau on the 6th of April, and puts him to flight;

---

* *Surannation* in France signifies a sentence or commission not executed within the year and a day.

REMARKABLE EVENTS under LEWIS XIV.

but marshal Turenne saved the remainder of the army, and perhaps the king himself, who was at Gien, where the prince intended to seize his person.

The battle of Etampes: the marshals Turenne and Hocquincourt having forced the suburbs, slew upwards of a thousand of the prince's best troops, and took several prisoners: they were the third day before this town, when the duke of Lorrain appeared in the neighbourhood of Paris, at the head of nine thousand men; which produced an alteration of measures: the court entered into a treaty with the duke, who agreed to retire for a sum of money. The prince of Condé, who had reason to mistrust the wavering disposition of Gaston, undertakes a painful and dangerous march to Paris, with a view of keeping him steady to his interest. There he began to negotiate with the court of St. Germains, by the interposition of the duke of Rohan, Chavigny, and Goulas, who had orders not to see the cardinal. The negotiation proving fruitless, the prince resolved to renew the war: he was posted at St. Cloud, with the river before him, and marshal Turenne on this side; which appeared to the prince a good situation, so long as he had no occasion to be afraid of his rear; but upon the arrival of marshal de la Ferté, he grew apprehensive of being surrounded; and therefore thought proper to occupy the post of Charenton, where he passed the river, having Paris on his right, consequently nothing that could separate him from marshal Turenne. Finding himself hard pressed upon his march by the king's army, he had but just time to throw himself into the suburb of St. Antony, where, on the 2d of July, was fought the famous battle of that name. This day, on which the prince and M. de Turenne gained equal glory, would have been decisive against the former, in consequence of the reinforcement of marshal de la Ferté, if the citizens of Paris, who beheld this engagement from their walls with an eye of unconcern, had not opened the town gates, at the persuasion of mademoiselle de Montpensier, who directed the cannon of the Bastile to be fired against the king's troops: for this she had obtained an order from Gaston her father, the original whereof is still preserved in the king's library. The presence of the prince of Condé, joined with that of the duke of Orleans, revived the aversion of the parliament against the cardinal. The duke was declared lieutenant general of the kingdom. The king being at Pontoise, removes the parliament to that place, by a declaration of the 6th of August; but the assembly was not numerous.

The cardinal consents once more to retire from court, and repairs to Bouillon the 19th of August. The troubles subside: the king publishes an act of grace the 21st of October, forgiving all that had passed since the year 1648, and returns to Paris the same day; the prince of Condé had withdrawn from thence five days before, to throw himself into the hands of the Spaniards; the duke of Orleans retires to Blois, and mademoiselle de Montpensier to her estate: the cardinal de Retz was justly confined to the castle of Vincennes, and afterwards sent to the citadel of Nantes, from whence he made his escape in 1654. Chateauneuf received orders to retire to his house at Montrouge. Montrond, which held out for the prince of Condé, surrendered to Paluau the 1st of September.

The civil commotions gave great advantage to the Spaniards: they retook Barcelona, in spite of marshal de la Mothe, the 13th of October, after a fifteen months siege, by the treachery of Marsin, who had quitted the army, to join the prince of Condé. Casal is taken by the Spaniards from the duke of Savoy, and restored to the duke of Mantua. Graveline surrenders also to the Spaniards on the 18th of May, after a siege of sixty-nine days; and Dunkirk the 16th of September, after a defence of thirty-nine days, under the count d'Estrades. Rethel is obliged to surrender the 30th of October to the prince of Condé, who possesses himself of St. Menehoud the 14th of November. Marshal Turenne sets out for the frontier to stop the progress of the Spaniards, and makes good his promise to the king, that he should hinder the enemy from taking up their winter-quarters in France.

1653.

Cardinal Mazarin returns to Paris the 3d of February. The storm was now blown over, and the public began to respect a man, who had been able to withstand such a torrent of opposition. The princes, the ambassadors, the parliament, the people, all

crowded

REMARKABLE EVENTS under LEWIS XIV.

crowded to pay their court to this minister: he lodged in the Louvre, and the king gave orders that the *porte de la Conference* * should be watched by a company of the regiment of guards. (*Memoirs de Brienne.*)

Queen Christina would fain interpose in the disturbances of France: she offered her mediation, which no body wanted; she wrote to her hero the prince of Condé, as also to the parliament, to the duke of Orleans, to mademoiselle de Montpensier, &c. The cardinal did not thank her; the queen was still less satisfied; and the public opinion was, that by intermeddling in an affair, which no way concerned her, she had acted contrary to decorum, and to her dignity: hence she met with so indifferent a reception at the court of France, when she passed through this country after her abdication.

This year the intendants of the provinces began to exercise their authority: there had been some of those officers appointed in 1634, but they only concerned themselves with the revenue: they were recalled in 1648, at the representation of several parliaments, to whom their power was obnoxious; though, considering the calamity of the times, those magistrates were possessed of too much power themselves. But in 1653 they were commissioned with the title of intendants for the administration of justice, for the police, and the revenue: this is their present state.

A war breaks out betwixt England and Holland; the pretext was the striking of the flag, but the real cause seemed to be of a more ancient date. The English accused the Dutch of fraudulent practices in their commerce, and of having dispossessed them of one of their Molucca islands in 1623, for which they could not obtain satisfaction during the reigns of James I. and Charles I, when these princes were busier in asserting the prerogatives of their crown, than in defending the commerce of the nation. The English fleet was commanded by admiral Blake; the Dutch by Van Tromp; and they fought with alternate advantage. Cromwell afterwards appointed general Monk in the room of Blake.

* One of the gates of Paris.

REMARKABLE EVENTS under LEWIS XIV.

The domestic disturbances still infested some provinces of France, while the war with Spain continued on the frontiers. The cardinal sends succours to the duke of Savoy, in order to keep him steady to his alliance with France; the duke of Candale takes upon him the command of the army in Guienne, which the count d'Harcourt had lately resigned: this general was son of the duke d'Epernon, and colonel-general of the infantry; he had been very near marrying the cardinal's niece, who was afterwards espoused to the prince of Conty; and he died at Lyons in 1658. Sauvebeuf makes himself master of Sarlat the 23d of March; Bourg in Guyenne surrenders to the duke of Vendome the 3d of July; Bellegarde to the duke d'Epernon the 8th; Rethel to marshal Turenne on the 9th; and Mouzon the 28th of September. The prince of Condé takes Roye, August the 7th. Bourdeaux, having in vain implored the assistance of Cromwell, submits to the king the 31st of July. M. de Vendome locked up the harbour, to prevent its receiving any succours from Spain. The king insists that the inhabitants shall rebuild Chateau-Trompette and Ha, in order to awe that city. The count de Doignon, one of the prince's adherents, having been gained by the court, surrendered his governments of the country of Aunix, of the islands of Oleron and Rhé, and of Brouage: in return for this piece of service he received a considerable sum of money, and was made a marshal of France, by the name of marshal Foucault. An engagement the 23d of September, between marshal Grancey and the marquis of Caracena, near Roqueta on the Tanaro, where the advantage on each side was equal. Rocroy surrenders to the Spaniards the 30th of September. St. Menehoud, defended by Montal, is taken the 26th of November by marshal du Plessis-Praslin: messieurs de Turenne and de la Ferté covered the siege. The king was here in person; and had been at the siege of Mouzon.

1654.

The count de Grandpré takes Virton, in the dutchy of Luxemburg, by storm, on the 25th of February.

The king is crowned at Rheims on the 7th of June by the bishop of Soissons: Henry of Savoy, duke de Nemours, who had been nominated to the archbishopric of Rheims, was not as

REMARKABLE EVENTS under LEWIS XIV.

yet in prieſt's orders. The count d'Harcourt being in open rebellion, had made himſelf maſter of ſome towns in Alſace; when marſhal de la Ferté was ordered to march to the relief of that province: the court had already retaken Philipſburg by ſurprize. Marſhal de la Ferté poſſeſſes himſelf of Beffort on February the 23d, and ſoon after of the little town of Tannes; and he had begun the ſiege of Briſac, when the count d'Harcourt made his peace. The prince of Condé, having with him the archduke and the count of Fuenſaldagna, laid ſiege to Arras, where the marquis de Montdejeu, afterwards marſhal of France, commanded. Viſcount Turenne left the marquis de Fabert at the ſiege of Stenay, and advanced towards Arras, with the marſhals de la Ferté and d'Hocquincourt. His view at firſt was only to ſtraiten the enemy, ſo as to prevent them from receiving any further ſupply of proviſions; but the count de Boutteville, afterwards known by the name of marſhal Luxemburg, and who happened then to be of the prince of Condé's party, having reached the beſiegers camp with a convoy, marſhal Turenne was determined to force the enemies lines: upon which a battle enſued; the Spaniards were beaten, and the ſiege was raiſed. This memorable exploit, which happened on the 25th of Auguſt, quieted the fears of France and of the cardinal, whoſe fortune almoſt depended on the ſucceſs of that day. The retreat of the prince of Condé was much admired. It is obſervable, that the taking of this town in 1640 had been as ſerviceable to cardinal Richelieu, as the raiſing of the ſiege proved advantageous this year to cardinal Mazarin.

The king makes his firſt campaign at the ſiege of Stenay, which he took the 6th of Auguſt, having under him M. de Fabert, afterwards marſhal of France. M. de Turenne makes himſelf maſter of Queſnoy the 6th of September. Marſhal de la Ferté obliges Clermont in Argonne to capitulate on the 24th of November. The prince of Conty, having ſhaken off the yoke of madam de Longueville, and married Anna Maria Martinozzi, the cardinal's niece, ſoon after quitting the prince of Condé's party, made himſelf maſter of Villafranca the 5th of July, and of Puicerda the 17th of October.

REMARKABLE EVENTS under LEWIS XIV.

Charles IV, duke of Lorrain, being fufpected by the Spaniards, becaufe he had juft reafons to complain of their conduct, is arrefted at Bruffels the 15th of February, by count Fuenfaldagna, and fent prifoner to Toledo, where he continued till the Pyrenean treaty. Cromwell figns a peace with Holland on the 15th of April, which contains three important articles. The firft, that the Dutch fhall acknowledge the fovereignty of the Englifh flag in the channel. The fecond, that they fhall never chufe a prince of Orange for their ftadtholder, or admiral: this article was confented to only by the province of Holland. And the third, that they fhall abfolutely renounce all connexion with Charles Stuart.

The above treaty is the only wrong policy the Englifh lay to Cromwell's charge: they pretend that he had it in his power to render Holland tributary to England. This ftate had been upon the decline fince the death of William of Naffau, prince of Orange, and father of king William. The jealoufy which thofe republicans had conceived againft the houfe of Orange, was the caufe of their making a confiderable reduction in their forces by fea and land, upon prince William's deceafe, with a view of diminifhing the power of the general who commanded them; fo that depending on the continuance of peace, they had neglected to maintain themfelves in a pofture of defence: in this fituation were they attacked by Cromwell; but he had particular reafons for altering his policy. The connexions of the houfe of Orange with the royal family of England, rendered the princes of that houfe as obnoxious to him as to the Dutch; feeing thofe princes were likely to protect the Stuarts: his fcheme was therefore to deftroy the houfe of Orange, and to enter into a clofe alliance with the United Provinces, in order to render them the irreconcileable enemies of the fon of Charles I; and thus preferring his private intereft to that of his country, he gave the States time to fee the error, into which they had been drawn by their jealoufy.

Charles II, purfued on every fide by Cromwell, is obliged to quit the kingdom of France, and retires to Cologne.

Chriftina, queen of Sweden, abdicates the crown the 16th of June, in favour of her coufin german Charles Guftavus, duke

of

of Deux-Ponts, of the Palatine family, and son of the great Gustavus's sister. In vain did the literati, whom this princess protected, endeavour to defend her reputation; they have not been able to hinder the public from judging unfavourably of her character and her manners. She passed through France, where she met with a very indifferent reception.

Cardinal de Retz, having succeeded his uncle in the archbishopric of Paris, continued, though in confinement, to disturb the court, attempting to govern his diocese by his grand vicars: at length he made his escape out of prison.

1655.

Marshal Turenne, having reinforced the garrison of Quesnoy, makes himself master of Landrecy on the 14th of July, with the assistance of the marshal de la Ferté: the taking of this place, and of Quesnoy, opened a passage into the Spanish Netherlands, and paved the way for all the advantages which France obtained to the end of the war. Condé is taken by M. de Turenne the 18th of August, and Saint Guillain the 25th. The king was with the army the whole campaign, and assisted at the latter siege, where marshal de la Ferté also commanded. The cardinal causes the dutchess de Chatillon to be arrested, for endeavouring to draw the marshal d'Hocquincourt into the prince's party. This marshal had been dissatisfied with the cardinal for neglecting him: the court is obliged to treat with him; in consequence of which he receives two hundred thousand crowns, and resigns his governments of Peronne and Ham to his son. Catelet is taken the 29th of August by the marquis de Castelnau.

Duke Francis of Lorrain, brother of the reigning duke, goes over with his army into the French service.

The duke of Modena, who had married Laura Martinozzi, a sister of the princess of Conty, obliges the Spaniards to raise the siege of Reggio. Prince Thomas is forced by the marquis of Caracena to raise the siege of Pavia.

The prince of Conty takes Cap de Quiers the 27th of May, and Castillon the 10th of July. The marquis de Merenville compels the Spaniards to raise the siege of Solsonne. The duke de Vendome defeats the Spanish fleet before Barcelona on the 29th of September. Bordeaux, the king's ambaſſador extraordinary in England, concluded a treaty on the 2d of November with Cromwell, in which it was ſtipulated that France ſhould intirely abandon the intereſts of Charles II. On the other hand, Cromwell declared againſt the Spaniards, and difpoſſeſſed them of Jamaica, which has ever ſince remained in the hands of the Engliſh.

An edict for eſtabliſhing ſtamped paper.

The tomb of Childeric diſcovered at Tournay: beſides that prince's gold ring and ſeveral medals of the ſame metal, there are bees, of a natural ſize, made of maſſive gold; which has afforded room for conjecture, that by the wretched imitation of ignorant painters, the bees were transformed into flower de luces in the twelfth century, when France and other chriſtian ſtates began to make uſe of coats of arms. The reader may ſee the diſſertation of M. Chifflet upon the diſcovery of this monument, which the elector of Cologne, who had it of the emperor Leopold, preſented to Lewis XIV; and it is ſtill preſerved in the king's library.

1656.

The cardinal reſumes the propoſals of peace, which he had made ſeveral times.

Lionne repairs to Madrid, to propoſe the match between the king and the infanta Maria Thereſa. This match was the favourite point of the cardinal's adminiſtration; but Ferdinand III. likewiſe wanted this princeſs for his ſon Leopold, who ſucceeded him in the imperial dignity, and whoſe mother was the younger ſiſter of Anne of Auſtria, mother of Lewis XIV. The king of Spain having no male iſſue, was more inclined to leave his ſucceſſion to one of his own family, than to a foreign prince, and a rival of the houſe of Auſtria: beſides, the cardinal would not liſten to the demands in favour of the prince of Condé, ſo that the negotiation proved abortive.

M. de Turenne and marſhal de la Ferté lay ſiege to Valenciennes: the dyke, by which the quarters of thoſe generals were made to communicate, having been broke, that of marſhal de la Ferté was attacked and forced by the prince of Condé and Don John of Auſtria. Marſhal Turenne, finding himſelf conſtrained

constrained to raise the siege the 16th of July, made a gallant retreat, and came and encamped under the walls of Quesnoy; but marshal de la Ferté was taken prisoner. The governor of Valenciennes was named Don Francisco de Menesses. Marshal Grammont, having been sent to Madrid in order to demand the infanta, was greatly surprized that the above governor, who happened to be in that city at the same time, was not known to the admiral of Castile; and that this same admiral had not so much as heard of raising the siege of Valenciennes. The prince takes Condé the 19th of August. Don John raises the siege of St. Guillain, valiantly defended by the count de Schomberg, to march to the relief of Capelle; but M. de Turenne made himself master of this place the 27th of September.

The dukes of Modena and Mercœur take Valentia on the Po the 16th of September. The latter was come to supply the place of prince Thomas, who died a few months before.

1657.

The king makes a reform in the council; and reduces the counsellors of state to the number of twenty-four, not including the three ecclesiastic counsellors, and the three sword-men.

A bull of Alexander VII. condemning the five propositions of Jansenius, and confirming the bull of Innocent X. The same pontif sent the formulary in 1665, which was received in France by a declaration verified in parliament; four bishops, at the head of whom was Henry Arnaud bishop of Angers, had refused to sign it in 1664. The prince of Condé makes himself master of St. Guillain the 22d of March. Marshal Turenne undertakes the siege of Cambray: he invested the town, which was garrisoned only by a small number of invalids and fifty troopers; but the prince having thrown himself into that place with eighteen squadrons on the 1st of June, M. de Turenne raised the siege. The king prevails on the senate of Venice to recal the Jesuits.

The death of the emperor Ferdinand III. on the 2d of April, at the age of forty-nine, of which he had reigned twenty. The power of the German branch of the house of Austria was very much declined, especially since the treaty of Westphalia, by which Lewis XIV. became guarantee of the liberties of Germany against the emperor. The king sends the marshal de Grammont and Lionne to the diet of Frankfort, with a design of hindering the election of Leopold the son of Ferdinand; and advances in person as far as Metz, in order to support the negotiation. Neither the duke of Bavaria, nor the archduke Leopold, brother of Ferdinand, would appear as candidates for the imperial dignity; though France used all her endeavours to persuade them: yet the election met with some difficulty, and Leopold was not chosen till the 18th of July the year following.

The marquis de St. Abre obliges the Spaniards to raise the siege of Urgel, the 13th of May. They take Olivença the 20th. The king makes himself master of Montmedy the 6th of August; it was besieged by marshal de la Ferté, and M. de Turenne covered the siege. The prince of Conty and the duke of Modena raise the siege of Alexandria *della Paglia* on the 10th of August. Marshal Turenne carries St. Venant the 27th, and compels the prince of Condé to raise the siege of Ardres. On the 3d of October he makes himself master of Mardyke, and delivers this place up to the English, in pursuance of an agreement with Cromwell's ambassadors. The discovery of a plot against Cromwell, who was to be assassinated in the road to Hampton-Court. The Spaniards possess themselves of Hesdin, by the treachery of Riviere, the king's lieutenant.

The Dutch declare war against the Portuguese, who had lately driven them out of Brasil. Foundation of the general hospital at Paris. The dutchess Nicole, wife of the duke of Lorrain, departs this life at Paris, and is interred at St. Paul's: she had obtained a decree from the court of Rome, declaring her marriage with duke Charles IV. good and valid, without any mention of the princess of Cantecroix, whom the duke had espoused after his marriage with Nicole. This prince had dropped his suit for the dissolution of his first marriage, being offended with the conduct of the princess of Cantecroix, who was suspected of incontinency: besides, he was affected with the pains, which the dutchess Nicole had taken to procure his liberty; he even resigned his whole authority to her in the year 1665.

The THIRD RACE.

REMARKABLE EVENTS under LEWIS XIV.

The death of Bellievere the first president, who was not much regretted by the cardinal: he was the only man in the kingdom, whom this minister thought proper to treat with caution, from an apprehension of his abilities.

Queen Christina causes Monaldeschi, her master of the horse, to be assassinated, on the 10th of November, in the stag gallery at Fontainbleau: this was her second visit to France, whence she departed soon after to return to Rome. The death of Charles X. recalled her to Sweden in 1660, but finding the nation very ill affected to her, she returned the third time to Rome, and died in that capital in 1689, at the age of sixty-three.

1658.

This year was productive of a series of victories, which paved the way to a peace. The Spaniards had made an agreement with Cromwell in 1656 to besiege Calais with their joint forces, and to let this town remain in the possession of the English; in the mean time Dunkirk was to be delivered up to them as a security: this treaty having never been carried into execution, the cardinal availed himself of the conjuncture, and entered into a convention with Cromwell upon the same plan as that of the Spaniards, to dispossess them of Dunkirk. Marshal Turenne gains the battle of the Downs on the 4th of June, against the prince of Condé and Don John, who had marched to the relief of Dunkirk. This town having been blocked up towards the sea by the English, was obliged to surrender the 23d of June: the king made his entry on the 26th, and ordered the place to be delivered up to the English, pursuant to the treaty concluded with Cromwell. It was at this battle, that the great Condé said to the young duke of Gloucester; *If you have never seen a battle lost, you will see one presently.* Marshal Turenne, pursuing his conquests, took Bergues-Saint-Vinox the 2d of July; Furnes the 3d; Dixmude the 7th, (Bussy says the 3d); Oudenarde, September the 9th; and Menin the 17th: he beats the prince of Ligne on the 19th; and makes himself master of Ipres the 24th. Marshal de la Ferté carries Graveline the 30th of August.

The HISTORY of FRANCE.

REMARKABLE EVENTS under LEWIS XIV.

The king was taken dangerously ill at Calais. A physician of Abbeville, named du Saufoy, being called in, had a long consultation with Vallot the first physician, and cured his majesty with an emetic wine of singular virtue. The league of the Rhine, between the king and several electors and princes of the empire, signed in the presence of marshal Grammont and Lionne, after the emperor's election, to maintain the peace of Germany. The electors make the emperor sign a perpetual capitulation, by which, among other engagements, he binds himself not to grant any succours, either directly or indirectly, to the enemies of France, either as emperor, or as archduke of Austria, and submits himself in every respect to the treaty of Munster.

In Italy, the duke of Modena took winter quarters in the territories of the duke of Mantua, who had declared in favour of the Spaniards, notwithstanding his obligations to France: yet upon demanding a neutrality, it was granted him. The marquis de Ville takes the town of Trin on the 21st of July; and Mortare is obliged to surrender to the dukes of Modena and Navailles on the 25th of August. The death of the duke of Modena, October the 14th.

The dutchess of Savoy, sister to Lewis XIII, takes advantage of the proposals she had received from Spain, to negotiate a match between the princess Margaret her daughter and the king of France, to whom the Spaniards refused to grant the infanta in marriage. Cardinal Mazarin on the other hand encouraged the expectations of the dutchess, with a design of giving umbrage to Spain: the king sets out for Lyons, where he arrived the 28th of November, in order to have an interview with the princess Margaret, whom the dutchess had conducted to that city, along with the duke her son. This artifice of the cardinal succeeded; for Pimentel arrived immediately from Spain with proposals of marriage on the part of that crown: the queen made no secret of it to the dutchess, but dismissed her with a promise, that if the Spanish match broke off, she would certainly conclude that with the princess her daughter. Margaret was afterwards married to Rainuccio Farnese II, duke of Parma. The Portuguese miscarry in their attempt against Badajos; and Don Lewis de Haro is obliged to raise the siege of Elvas, after losing the battle of Villaviciosa

REMARKABLE EVENTS under LEWIS XIV.

viciofa againſt the Portugueſe, who forced him in his lines, with the aſſiſtance of the count of Schomberg. The death of Oliver Cromwell, a man, ſays Pope, damned to everlaſting fame; he departed this life on the 13th of September, at the age of fifty five, and had enjoyed the ſupreme power but nine years [*]: was it worth while for this to murder his king, and to ſubvert the laws of his country! He was interred in the burying place of the kings of England: his ſon Richard, a man of no abilities, ſucceeded him in the protectorſhip; but reſigned in a few months, and lived upwards of fifty years as a private perſon. The body of Cromwell was afterwards dug out of the grave; and Charles II. was reſtored to the crown in 1660.

1659.

A treaty of peace concluded on the 7th of November, between the king of France and the king of Spain, by cardinal Mazarin and Don Lewis de Haro, plenipotentiaries of thoſe two powers, in the iſland of Pheaſants, upon the river of Bidaſſoa, after four and twenty conferences, the firſt of which was on the 13th of Auguſt: ſo that in leſs than three months, two men only eſtabliſhed a peace, which all the miniſters in Europe had not been able to conclude at Munſter in a number of years; and cardinal Mazarin was heard to ſay, that this treaty would have been ſooner determined, had it not been for the delays of Don Lewis, unacquainted with foreign affairs. The Pyrenean treaty contains a hundred and twenty-four articles; the principal of which was the king's marriage with Maria Thereſa, the infanta, who had five hundred thouſand crowns for her dower, upon condition of her renouncing the Spaniſh ſucceſſion; a condition which even then was allowed to be of no ſignification, both by Lewis de Haro and by Philip IV. himſelf, who ſaid upon the occaſion, *eſto es una patarata*. The reſtoration of the prince of Condé created very great difficulty, and the cardinal agreed to it at laſt, upon receiving a hint from Don Lewis, that if the king would not reinſtate this prince, Spain would procure a ſettlement for him in the Netherlands, which might occaſion no ſmall uneaſineſs. The cardinal likewiſe obtained

---

[*] He had not been protector quite five years; but the author dates his uſurped power from the murder of king Charles.

another advantage, which was the ceding of the town of Avennes to France; and the restitution of Juliers to the elector Palatine. By another article, this minister promised not to grant any succours to the king of Portugal, which article was not properly executed; he likewise agreed to the restoration of the duke of Lorrain. There were several fortresses and towns delivered up on both sides. Towards the Pyrenees, the king kept nothing but Perpignan, Roussillon, and Conflans; but on the side of the Netherlands his majesty was a great gainer. The king of Spain quitted his pretensions to Alsace, and ceded a considerable part of the county of Artois. Charles II. went as far as Fontarabia, in hopes of prevailing on the two monarchs to procure his restoration; but they were still frightened at Cromwell's shadow: cardinal Mazarin begged of this prince not to pay him a visit, and there was no notice taken of him in the treaty. St. Evremond, writing to M. de Crequy, took it into his head to turn the cardinal and this treaty into ridicule. But if St. Evremond was a man of wit, as some pretend, all the world must allow he was a very bad politician. This letter was the cause of his disgrace, and obliged him to retire to England, where he ended his days. Had he been better informed, he would have known, that the match, between the king and the infanta, was not the work of a single day, nor a sudden resolution, but the fruit of cardinal Mazarin's reflexions, who gave sufficient proofs, that foresight in politicks is not a chimera. This able minister had been contriving this alliance fourteen years, that is, since 1645, with a view not only of procuring a formal resignation from Spain, of whatever the king had obtained by the treaty of Munster; but likewise of acquiring other rights of much greater importance, such as those of the succession to the crown of Spain; for thus he explains himself in his letters to the king's ministers at Munster. " If the most Christian king could obtain the Ne-
" therlands and Franche Comté, as a portion for marrying the
" infanta of Spain, then we should be solid gainers; for we
" might aspire to the Spanish succession, notwithstanding any
" renunciation the infanta might be persuaded to make; and it
" would not be a very distant expectation, since there is only
" one

REMARKABLE EVENTS under LEWIS XIV.

" one life, that of the prince her brother, to exclude her?"
Was not this a ſtrong inſtance of foreſight?

A national ſynod of the proteſtants at Loudun: the cuſtom was to hold this aſſembly every year, for which the king allowed them ſixteen thouſand livres; but when they wanted to meet again three years afterwards, cardinal Mazarin gave them to underſtand, that they muſt content themſelves with their provincial ſynods; ſo that there never was another national ſynod ſince that of Loudun.

Charles Guſtavus, after ſeveral diſadvantages, finds himſelf under a neceſſity of concluding a peace with the Dutch; who likewiſe oblige him to be reconciled to the king of Denmark: he died of chagrin the year following.

1660.

The death of Gaſton, duke of Orleans, at Blois, on the 2d of February, at the age of fifty-two: by his firſt wife, the dutcheſs of Montpenſier, he had a daughter, ſtiled *mademoiſelle*, the ſame who was ſo often diſappointed of a huſband, and who wrote the memoirs known by her name. By his ſecond wife, Margaret of Lorrain, ſiſter of Charles IV, he had three princeſſes who were married; the firſt to Coſmo III, grand duke of Tuſcany; the ſecond to Lewis Joſeph, duke de Guiſe; and the third to Charles Emmanuel II, duke of Savoy. *This prince,* ſays the cardinal de Retz, *intermeddled in all affairs whatever, becauſe he had not the reſolution to withſtand thoſe who dragged him on; and he always came off with ſhame, becauſe he had not courage enough to ſupport them.* M. de Chavigny wrote to cardinal Richelieu, that fear was an excellent orator to perſuade the duke to whatever they had a mind. "Indeed, ſays Montreſor, Gaſton was afraid
" only for his own perſon; this is the only fear I obſerved him
" to have, during the time I ſerved him; for I never found he
" was uneaſy about any body belonging to him, let the dan-
" gers to which they expoſed themſelves, for his ſake, be ever
" ſo great." Voiture and Vaugelas had employments in his family. While the king of Spain was conducting the infanta to the frontier, the king made a tour through Provence, and ordered a citadel to be built at Marſeilles, to puniſh that town for diſobeying the duke of Mercœur its governor. His majeſty likewiſe cauſed

REMARKABLE EVENTS under LEWIS XIV.

caufed the fortifications of Orange to be demolifhed, having wrefted that place from its prince, at that time a minor; and it was not reftored till the treaty of Nimeguen.

M. de Turenne was created marfhal-general the 6th of April, in order to diftinguifh him from the other marfhals of France: the fame honour had been conferred on marfhal Biron and M. de Lefdiguieres; but the count d'Harcourt could never obtain it. It is obfervable, that in the patent of marfhal-general, there is no mention made of any command over the other marfhals of France. We have feen marfhal Villars honoured with the fame poft in 1733, and marfhal Saxe in 1747.

King Charles II. is reftored to the Britifh throne, by means of general Monk; and makes his entry into London on the 8th of June. In his way through Holland he obtains the repeal of the declaration againft the prince of Orange, which had been made at the inftigation of Cromwell. The perils and adventures which this prince went through, after the battle of Worcefter, are well known; efpecially the ftory of the famous oak, in which he lay concealed. Doctor Halley, profeffor of aftronomy in the univerfity of Oxford, has immortalized this tree, by giving its name to a conftellation, which he had obferved in the fouthern hemifphere, and which, by its fituation in the heavens, had efcaped the eye of Tycho.

This fame year Charles II. founded the Royal Society by letters patent: the works with which this fociety favours the public, are ftiled the *Philofophical Tranfactions*. He likewife revived a law relative to commerce, called *the act of navigation*; it had been the work of Cromwell, but was repealed at his death, out of hatred to his perfon. Charles II, upon coming to the crown, took very little notice of thofe who had contributed to his reftoration; and not knowing how to make them all amends, he refolved to forget them all. His miftreffes, fays the duke of Buckingham, had their gallants; but this never gave him any uneafinefs; and the time he fpent in their company, was as much devoted to lazinefs as to love. In a word, thinking to imitate the gallantry of Lewis XIV, he fell into ribaldry and debauch. His character is equivocal; and his indifference with regard to religion was carried fo far, as to render it dubious in the laft mo- ment

REMARKABLE EVENTS under LEWIS XIV.

ment of his life, whether he died a Catholic, or a Protestant.

The king marries the infanta, at St. John de Luz, on the 9th of June. Their majesties made their public entry into Paris on the 26th of August, with the greatest pomp and magnificence that had been ever seen in that capital. On this occasion the gate of St. Antony was erected. The foreign ministers were not present at this entry of the king and queen, M. Fabert having procured a decision, that the marshals of France should take the precedency of them.

The treaty of Oliva, on the 23d of May, between Charles XI, then only four years old, and the crown of Poland. Casimir at length renounces his just pretensions to Sweden, who ceded the remainder of her conquests to Poland. Denmark was declared an hereditary monarchy, in favour of the brave king Frederic. This was owing to the divisions between the nobility on one side, and the clergy, in conjunction with the people, on the other. The latter being tired of the continual encroachments of the nobility, invested their king with an absolute power, renouncing their privileges, and signing a charter, which rendered the crown hereditary.

The king sends succours to the Venetians in the isle of Candia.

1661.

A treaty concluded at Vincennes the last of February, nine days before the cardinal's decease, between this minister, in the king's name, and duke Charles of Lorrain. This treaty was somewhat more favourable to the duke, than that of the Pyrenees: it was agreed, that the fortifications of Nancy should be demolished; that the king should keep possession of Moyenvic, with the county of Clermont, Stenay, and Jamitz; that the duke should be restored to the dutchy of Bar, and yield homage for it, excepting Sirk, and a few other villages; that the king should be put in possession of Sarbourg and Phalsbourg; and that he should be master of the several posts necessary for the communication between Metz and Alsace.

Cardinal Mazarin dies at Vincennes the ninth of March, at the age of fifty-nine, leaving his name and his estate to the marquis de la Meilleraye, who had married his niece Hortensia Mancini,

Mancini, and taken the title of duke of Mazarin. He had four other nieces, and a nephew of the name of Mancini: the latter was duke de Nevers. Olympia Mancini was married to the count of Soiſſons, colonel-general of the Swiſs, who died in 1673; ſhe was ſuperintendant of the queen's houſhold, and mother of prince Eugene, who deceaſed in 1736. Laura Mancini was married to the duke de Vendome, afterwards cardinal. Maria, of whom the king had been fond, eſpouſed the conſtable Colonna; and Mary Anne the duke of Bouillon. We have already taken notice of the marriage of his other two nieces, of the name of Martinozzi.

With regard to the duke de Nevers we are to obſerve, that cardinal Mazarin, after acquiring the dutchy of Nivernois, died before the letters patent of erection into a dutchy and peerage were verified; that his nephew the duke de Nevers obtained a patent, confirming this dutchy and peerage, in 1676; upon which there were letters of renewal in 1692; and laſtly, that his ſon the duke de Nevers obtained in 1720 not new letters patent of erection, as father Simplician pretends, but a confirmation of thoſe iſſued out in 1676, upon which there was a *ſoit montré*, or *be it ſhewn*, which hindered the renewal. Indeed this *ſoit montré* had been miſlaid, but a minute thereof was found in the office of la Vrilliere, and it was through ignorance of this fact, that the father of the duke de Nevers took out letters of renewal in 1672, for which he had no occaſion: yet the duke de Nevers did not take his rank in parliament, but from the day of his reception, purſuant to the diſpoſition of the edict in 1711.

Cardinal Mazarin was as moderate, as Richelieu had been violent. One of his greateſt accompliſhments was a perfect knowledge of mankind. His politicks were characterized rather by ſubtlety and patience, than by force or violence. He was oppoſed by Don Lewis de Haro, as Richelieu had been by the duke d'Olivarez. In the midſt of the civil diſturbances in France, he determined all Germany to make a voluntary ceſſion of what his predeceſſor had taken by the right of war: but the advantage he derived from the obſtinacy of the Spaniards on that occaſion, was of a much higher nature; for after having given them full leiſure

to

REMARKABLE EVENTS under LEWIS XIV.

to exhaust themselves, at length he obtained that celebrated match, by which the king acquired a legitimate, and vainly contested, right, to one of the most powerful monarchies in the world. This minister was of opinion, that force should never be employed but for want of other means; and his good sense supplied him with a courage adapted to time and place: he was intrepid at Casal; tranquil yet active in his retreat at Cologne: he shewed himself a man of enterprize, when it became necessary to put the princes under arrest; but expressed an equal contempt for the raillery of the *Frondeurs*, and the tauntings of the coadjutor: and as to the murmuring of the populace, it went through his ear like the lashing of the surges on the sea-shore. There was something in cardinal Richelieu that shewed him to be the greater genius, more comprehensive in his schemes, but less composed: cardinal Mazarin was master of more subtlety and address, of more moderation and less extravagance: one was hated, the other despised, but they were both masters of the state.

There was no public library in the university, except that of St. Victor, which had been opened in 1652, when cardinal Mazarin made a present of his to the college known by his name.

Don Lewis followed cardinal Mazarin very soon, and died on the 17th of November the same year. He was successor in the administration to the Conde-duke d'Olivares under Philip IV: the duke de Lerma the same place under Philip III; cardinal Espinosa, cardinal Granvelle, and the duke of Alva, enjoyed it under Philip II; and the same duke of Alva, as well as the father of Granvelle, were possessed of it under Charles the fifth.

On the first of April the king's brother marries Henrietta of England, sister of Charles II.

The king causes M. Fouquet, superintendant of the finances, to be arrested at Nantes the 5th of September: he had very imprudently, sometime before, resigned his office of attorney-general. Out of such a number of friends in his prosperity, Pelisson was the only man that proved true to him: he was condemned by commissioners the 20th of December, 1664, to perpetual banishment, which, for reasons of state, was changed into perpetual imprisonment: they confined him to

the

the citadel of Pignerol, where he died in 1680. M. d'Ormeſſon vigorouſly oppoſed the miniſters, who were for putting him to death. M. Fouquet, the father of the ſuperintendant, had behaved with the ſame honour under the like circumſtances. M. Colbert, a friend of madam de Chevreuſe, and who was greatly inſtrumental in perſuading the queen mother to abandon M. Fouquet, ſucceeded the ſuperintendant only as comptroller-general; and the poſt of ſuperintendant was ſuppreſſed: he had the direction of the buildings at the *place de Ratabon*, and was made member of the council. He likewiſe purchaſed the office of ſtate-ſecretary, of M. Dupleſſis Guenegaud, who having been included in the proſecution, at that time ſet on foot againſt the perſons concerned in the management of the finances, was deprived of the beſt part of his fortune, and obliged to ſell out. The great connexions of this M. Dupleſſis did not hinder his diſgrace: he was the ſon of the king's treaſurer, and had been in that poſt himſelf, before he was made ſecretary of ſtate; he married the daughter of marſhal de Praſlin, and his mother was of the family of Courtenay. M. de Colbert's fortune was not a ſudden elevation: we ought to reckon it among the ſervices done this nation by cardinal Mazarin, his having introduced M. de Colbert to court towards the latter end of his days, and paved the way for that confidence, which his majeſty repoſed in this miniſter immediately upon the cardinal's deceaſe. Le Tellier and Lionne likewiſe ſhared the king's favour: the latter was nephew to M. Servien, and became known to cardinal Mazarin, when this miniſter was employed by his majeſty in the negotiations at Parma; he had been ſecretary to the queen, but enjoyed no poſt at that time; he was afterwards made miniſter of ſtate, and had the commiſſion of the marine, which he ſold to M. Colbert; he had moreover the whole department of foreign affairs, for M. de Brienne only ſigned the diſpatches. The latter reſigned his place in 1663, and M. de Lionne died in 1671, poſſeſſed of the office of ſecretary of ſtate, which M. de Brienne ſold him upon retiring from court, through grief for the loſs of his wife, daughter of M. de Chavigny. M. de Louvois had the reverſion of M. le Tellier his father, who reſigned in 1666, but ſtill kept his ſeat in council, and, in 1667, ſucceeded M. d'Aligre in the office of chancellor.

From

The THIRD RACE. 145

REMARKABLE EVENTS under LEWIS XIV.

From this period begins a new reign, under the same prince. Lewis XIV, by his close attention to business after the decease of cardinal Mazarin, plainly shewed that good nature alone had hindered him from taking the administration into his own hands, lest he should mortify a minister to whom he thought himself greatly indebted. He had promised him the government of Britany in favour of the duke of Mazarin: but the queen being possessed of that post, refused to resign it; and her resistance disengaged his majesty from a promise, which he was not inclined to keep.

The baron de Batteville*, ambassador from Spain, under a chimerical notion of precedency, insults the count d'Estrades, his majesty's ambassador at London, on the 10th of October, at the public entry of Brahe, ambassador extraordinary from Sweden; and the reparation was equal to the affront. Batteville, who had shewn some evil dispositions in regard to France, at the time of exchanging the ratifications of the Pyrenean treaty, was recalled from his embassy; and on the 24th of March the following year, the marquis de la Fuentes, ambassador extraordinary from Spain, made a declaration to the king in the presence of the foreign ministers, *that the king his master had ordered all his ambassadors, to desist from entering into any further competition with those of his majesty:* immediately after this declaration, the king, addressing himself to the foreign ministers, said, *you have heard the declaration of the Spanish ambassador; I beg you will signify to your masters, that his Catholic majesty has given orders to his ambassadors, to yield the precedency to mine, upon all occasions.* (Leonard's Treaties.) In consequence hereof, la Fuentes happening to be at Venice in 1669, in the Jesuits church, along with the French ambassador, took his seat below that minister. It was likewise owing to this declaration of the marquis de la Fuentes, that the Dutch ambassador, then residing at Paris, said, " I knew that " Roman Catholic princes paid their obeisance to the pope by " embassies; but I never heard that any prince sent such an em- " bassy to another." (Leonard's Treaties.) M. de Brienne, in his

* Others call him baron Watteville.

VOL. II. L memoirs,

memoirs, surmises, that Charles II, king of England, connived at the insulting behaviour of the baron de Batteville, imagining, as he had a design to marry the infanta of Portugal, that it was his interest to see France and Spain at variance.

The birth of the dauphin (stiled *monseigneur*) at Fontainebleau the first of November. His governor was the duke de Montausier; his preceptor the president de Perigny, who died in 1670, and was succeeded by M. Bossuet, bishop of Meaux, of whom la Bruyere has said, *Let us anticipate the language of posterity, and stile him a father of the church*; his tutor was M. de Cordemoy, the celebrated historiographer. Madam de Montausier has the place of governess to the children of France, which she resigned to the lady of marshal de la Mothe, upon her being appointed lady of honour to the queen in 1664. Madam de Ventadour, daughter of madam de la Mothe, was governess to Lewis XV. The chamber of justice established the 28th of December. Public entertainments at Fontainebleau, where the court endeavour to imitate the gallantry of the sovereign. Lully is made superintendant of the king's musicians. The office of colonel-general of the infantry is suppressed, upon the decease of the duke d'Epernon; in consequence of which the *masters de camp*, belonging to the regiments of foot, take the title of colonels: the duke of Orleans, when regent of the kingdom, revived this post in favour of the duke of Chartres, who resigned it to the king after the death of his father. Marshal Grammont takes the title of colonel of the guards, pursuant to an ordinance of the 28th of July, and quarters the white ensign in his arms, as the colonel-general had done before.

The Dutch had possessed themselves of Brasil and of the Portuguese settlements in the East-Indies, at the time when Portugal was subject to the king of Spain. But upon the revolution in 1640, the new king of Portugal courted the friendship of the States General, who, in spite of treaties, continued the war under hand. The court of Lisbon began to think seriously of making a defence, and recovered Brasil in 1657. The war ended in a treaty at the Hague, the 6th of August this same year, by which the republic relinquished all her pretensions to Brasil.

REMARKABLE EVENTS under LEWIS XIV.

1662.

A promotion of knights of the order of the Holy Ghost. Marshal Fabert refused the honour of being admitted, saying, that he did not chuse to produce false proofs of nobility: for he was the son of a bookseller of Metz. This is he, whom cardinal Mazarin wanted to act as his spy in the army; but Fabert made answer: "A great minister, like you, ought to have all "sorts of people at your command; some to serve you with "their swords, and others with their pens; permit me, my lord, "to be ranked in the former class." The treaty of Montmartre on the 6th of February, by which Charles IV, duke of Lorrain, makes the king his heir to his whole estate; and promises, as a security for the execution of the treaty, to put him in possession of the town of Marsal, upon condition that the heirs of duke Charles shall be declared princes of the blood royal of France. The parliament verified this treaty, with a proviso, that it should not take place, till signed by all the parties concerned: and it was owing to this clause, that the treaty remained unexecuted. Who could have foretold that the donation which Charles IV. was then making of Lorrain, under illusory conditions, should take effect in the reign of Lewis XV, and that this monarch should become sovereign of that country with the consent of all Europe?

The king concludes a new treaty of defensive alliance with Holland, preparatory to the designs he had formed against the Spanish Netherlands. The duke de Crequy, his majesty's ambassador, is insulted at Rome, the 20th of August, by the Corsic soldiery, whose chief employment was to assist the *sbirri*, or civil officers, in the execution of justice: the pope refusing to grant satisfaction, the king ordered the nuncio to quit the French territories, possessed himself of Avignon the year following, and made preparations for marching an army into Italy. Alexander VII. is under the necessity of imploring his clemency; and by virtue of a treaty, signed at Pisa in 1664, cardinal Chigi, the pope's nephew, came in person to make an apology to the king. The criminals were punished; the Corsic soldiery were banished for ever from the ecclesiastic state, and a pyramid was erected over against their ancient *corps de garde*, with an inscription specifying the particulars of this submission: the pyramid stood during the pontificate of Alexander VII. The king however consented to its being pulled down in 1667, upon the accession of Clement IX. to the papal throne. Avignon was restored to Alexander VII. immediately upon the execution of the treaty of Pisa. His majesty seized that town once more, under pope Innocent XI, and restored it to Alexander VIII.

The count d'Estrades negotiates the restitution of Dunkirk at the court of London: it was restored to France by king Charles II, for the sum of five millions of livres; the French took possession of it the 27th of November, and the king made his entry the 2d of December. By the same treaty, Mardyke, and all the other posts which the English possessed on the coast of Flanders, were delivered up to the French. The parliament of England were greatly displeased with this treaty, and laid the whole blame on lord Clarendon, who had a considerable hand in it, and would have been in danger of losing his head, if he had not made his escape. A Scotchman, named Lockhart, who had been Cromwell's ambassador in France, had married that protector's niece, and was afterwards appointed ambassador to that same court by Charles II, says, that he was not so much respected in France, when he represented the king, as he had been in Cromwell's time: this was very natural, for there was a prodigious difference between him, who obliged the French to take Dunkirk, in order to put the English in possession of it; and the prince, who sold this place again to the French, after he mounted the throne.

The king exhibits a magnificent carousal the 5th of June, in the square before the Tuilleries, which ever since hath retained this name. The triple alliance concluded by France, England, and Holland.

The court withdraws from Paris, and goes to reside at St. Germains.

1663.

The king marches into Lorrain, and sends marshal de la Ferté to invest Marsal, either for failure of executing of the treaty of Montmartre, which however was now out of the question,

question, or to make sure of duke Charles, whose inconstancy was too well known. This prince signed a treaty at Nomeny the first of September, by virtue of which the king was put in possession of Marsal, and the duke was restored to the remainder of his territories.

Marshal Turenne, who was related to the queen of Portugal, had never ceased, since the Pyrenean treaty, to represent to his majesty, the great importance of supporting that kingdom against the crown of Spain: the king continues to assist the Portuguese with money, and likewise supplies them with a body of troops, under the command of the count de Schomberg, who acted in such a manner, as if France had no concern in the affair. M. de Schomberg wrote to marshal Turenne, that the Spaniards were only jealous of the title of king of Portugal, and that if his Portuguese majesty would be satisfied with that of king of Brasil, they would agree to a peace, and leave him in possession of the full sovereignty of Portugal. The alliance with the Swiss renewed at Paris, the 20th of November. Foundation of the academy of Inscriptions and Belles Letters, as also of that of Painting and Sculpture.

The following letter reflects as much glory on the king and M. Colbert, as on Isaac Vossius.

Although the king is not your sovereign, yet he chuses to be your benefactor, and for this reason has commanded me to send you the inclosed bill of exchange, as a token of his esteem, and a pledge of his protection: the public knows that you are a worthy imitator of the example of the celebrated Vossius your father; and that having received from him a name, which he has rendered illustrious by his writings, you take the same method to perpetuate its glory. His majesty apprized of these matters, takes a pleasure in rewarding your merit, and I have the greater satisfaction in being honoured with his commands of acquainting you with his gracious disposition, as it affords me an opportunity of assuring you, that I am,

SIR,

Your most humble, and most affectionate servant,

Paris, June 21, 1663.

COLBERT.

There

REMARKABLE EVENTS under LEWIS XIV.

There were several presents of this kind sent to the literati in different parts of Europe. One may easily judge that the arts and sciences were not less encouraged in France. Who could imagine that Lewis XIV. maintained a greater number of learned men, than all the princes of Europe put together. The founding of nineteen professorships in the *royal college*; the erecting of five academies; the gratuitous instructing of youth in the university; the committing the king's library to the care of men of parts and learning; the instituting of journalists and censors; the providing of lodgings in the Louvre for celebrated artists, &c. these were the encouragements given by the king and his minister to the arts and sciences.

The glorious age of Lewis XIV. begins to unclose: we might apply to it what Velleius Paterculus says of the Augustan age: *Eminentia cujusque operis, arctissimis temporum claustris circumdata*: the master pieces in every kind are confined within the narrow circle of a few years.

The erection of the manor of Meilleraye into a dutchy and peerage, in favour of Charles de la Porte, lord of Meilleraye, marshal and grand master of the ordnance, grandson of Francis de la Porte, advocate in parliament. The same day his son Armand Charles de la Porte Mazarin, husband to Hortensia Mancini, obtained letters patent of erection of the manor of Rethelois into a dutchy and peerage, by the name of Mazarin. The father and son were received the same day, the father to the dutchy of Meilleraye, and the son to that of Mazarin.

The barony of St. Aignan, which came by marriage to the house of Beauvilliers in 1496, was erected this year into a dutchy and peerage in favour of Francis de Beauvilliers. His son was governor of the dukes of Burgundy, Anjou, and Berry.

The county of Noailles created a dutchy and peerage.

The marquisate of Coislin created a dutchy and peerage, extinct by the decease of the bishop of Metz in 1733.

The verification of all these letters patent was made in a bed of justice; at the same time those, which had been granted since the year 1648, were verified also: the latter had not taken effect, because of the difficulties the parliament made to register them, as they had been granted under a minority. The king likewise

The THIRD RACE. 151

REMARKABLE EVENTS under LEWIS XIV.

wife confirms the erection of the manor of Randan into a dutchy and peerage, made in 1661, in favour of the marchioness of Senecey, who had been his governante, and lady of honour to the queen mother (of the house of Rochefoucaud) for her daughter, widow of Gaston de Foix, count of Flex, and her issue. Gaston de Foix, her son, was admitted duke and peer in 1664, and this peerage became extinct by his death in 1714.

A famous duel between la Frette, St. Aignan, and Argenlieu on the one side, and Chalais, Noirmontier, d'Antin, and Flamarens, on the other.

1664.

An expedition against Gigeri in Africa: the king desirous of punishing those corsairs, gave this commission to the duke of Beaufort. Gigeri was taken the 22d of July, after defeating the corsairs; but a misunderstanding among the chief officers obliged the French to retreat, so that they reimbarked the 30th of October. The battle of St. Godart on the 1st of August, in which the Turks were defeated by the Germans under the command of Montecuculli, who was seconded by six thousand French, and by prince Charles Leopold, nephew of the duke of Lorrain. Coligny, who commanded the French, was not in the engagement; but la Feuillade distinguished himself on that occasion. Notwithstanding the above victory, the emperor concluded a truce of twenty years with Mahomet IV, on the 17th of September, at Temeswar, in order to oppose the designs of France. The canal of Languedoc, for opening a communication between the two seas, is undertaken this year by Riquet; but was not perfected till 1680. This project had been formed under Francis I, and resumed under Henry IV; but the execution thereof was reserved for the reign of Lewis XIV. Le Brun has the title of first painter to the king.

The possession of the coast of Guinea creates a war between England and Holland.

1665.

Denis de Salo, counsellor of the parliament of Paris, published the *Journal des savans*, which has been the model of all the literary journals since that time. The king causes the observatory of Paris to be built under the care and direction of

REMARKABLE EVENTS under LEWIS XIV.

M. Colbert. The battle of Villaviciosa on the 17th of June, where the Portuguese gained the advantage over the Spaniards. The duke of Beaufort defeats the Algerine corsairs twice at sea.

Notwithstanding the king's good offices, a war breaks out between England and Holland. Charles II. could not forget the behaviour of that republic, during the usurpation of Cromwell. The duke of York and prince Rupert obtained a victory on the 13th of June over admiral Opdam, who was slain in the engagement: the Dutch commander would willingly have avoided this action; but the repeated orders of the pensionary de Witt, who wanted to ruin that officer, obliged him to fight, though he foresaw the consequence. Vice-admiral Tromp saved the remainder of the fleet. It was said, that the English knew not how to make a right use of their victory. The bishop of Munster, instigated by the English, and still more so by his own military ardour, declared against the Dutch: Lewis XIV. assisted this republic, in consequence of the treaty of 1662; and ordered a fleet to be fitted out under the command of the duke of Beaufort. The death of Philip IV, king of Spain, on the 17th of September.

A general and extraordinary sessions held in Auvergne against the lords possessed of judiciary power, who oppressed the vassals subject to their jurisdiction. The establishment of a West-India company, and of divers manufactures of glass, French lace, linen, tapestry, &c. The front of the Louvre was begun this year, after the designs of Charles Perrault; though the friends of le Veau, first architect to the king, would make the public believe that they were his drawing. M. Colbert likewise associated the famous le Brun in this undertaking.

A counterfeit letter in the Spanish language had been delivered to the queen in 1662; wherein endeavours were used to make that young princess jealous of the king, with a view of prejudicing a person, for whom his majesty had a personal regard. The authors of this intrigue were detected: the king pardoned the dutchess of Orleans; the count de Guiche was banished; de Vardes was sent to prison, where he continued a long time; and the countess of Soissons was ordered away to Champagne, where her husband was governor. De Vardes was the most guilty of

them

REMARKABLE EVENTS under LEWIS XIV.

them all; for he had not only composed the letter, which the count de Guiche translated into Spanish, but he threw the suspicion on the dutchess of Noailles, lady of honour to the queen; and this calumny was the cause that both the husband and wife were divested of their employments. The duke was obliged to sell his post of lieutenant of the light horse to the duke of Chaulnes for five hundred thousand livres, and his government of Havre de Grace to the duke de St. Aignan for three hundred thousand livres. The dutchess was also forced to resign her employment of lady of honour, in favour of madam de Montausier, for a hundred and fifty thousand livres: they were the worthiest persons belonging to the court.

The erection of the dutchy and peerage of Choiseul in favour of the marshal du Plessis Praslin: this dutchy became extinct by the death of the duke de Choiseul in 1705, who left no issue behind him.

The marquisate of Isles created a dutchy and peerage, under the title of Aumont.

Bussy is sent to the Bastile for his *Amours of the Gauls*. Tardieu, lieutenant criminal, and his wife, are murdered in their house by two robbers.

A professorship of French law was founded this year in the university of Bourges.

1666.

The death of Anne of Austria, at the age of sixty-four, on the 20th of January. She was daughter of Philip III, sister of Philip IV, wife of Lewis XIII, and mother of Lewis XIV. The death of Armand prince of Conty.

The troops are reviewed at Compiegne, to prepare for the expeditions of the ensuing year. D'Artagnan is made captain-lieutenant of the first company of musketeers, by the resignation of the duke de Nevers. The king causes the harbour of Cette to be built.

Two bloody engagements were fought at sea this year between the English and the Dutch; the first on the 11th of June lasted four hours; and in this the Dutch had the advantage; the second was on the 4th of August, when they were defeated. The duke of Albemarle, known before by the name of general Monk,

REMARKABLE EVENTS under LEWIS XIV.

Monk, and prince Rupert (of the Palatine family, son of Frederic, king of Bohemia) commanded the English fleet; Ruyter and Trump had the command of the Dutch. The king had declared war against the English, in favour of Holland. A misunderstanding between the Dutch admirals, each of whom had a strong party in the republic, proved extremely prejudicial to that nation. Ruyter was supported by the pensionary deWitt, and Tromp by the prince of Orange. In the sequel of this history, we shall see in what manner these two factions had like to have ruined the commonwealth, and how the pensionary lost his life in the contest. The fleet, under the command of the duke of Beaufort, could not join the Dutch. Bernard Van Galen, bishop of Munster, makes his peace with Holland.

The French beat the English on the 20th of April, and drive them out of the island of St. Christopher.

War declared between England and Denmark. The fire of London broke out on the 13th of September, and lasted four days. The first establishment of the academy of sciences.

1667.

This year is famous for many wise institutions of Lewis XIV. M. de Colbert, after settling the finances, extended his views to other objects. The courts of justice, commerce, the navy, and the police, were all put upon a new footing, and felt the good effects of the spirit of order, which formed the characteristic of that minister; and of those superior lights, in which he viewed every part of the administration: he established a council, where those several matters were to be discussed, from whence resulted such a number of regulations and excellent ordinances, as constitute the basis of our present government. The names of those who composed this council, deserve to be transmitted to posterity: they were M. Seguier the chancellor, the marshal de Villeroy, in favour of whom the post of president of the council was erected, messieurs Colbert, d'Aligre, de Lezeau, de Machault, de Seve, Menardean, de Morangis, Poncet, Boucherat, de la Marguerie, Pussort, uncle to M. Colbert, Voisin, Hotman, and Marin. Their sittings began on Thursday the 28th of October, 1666, and continued every week, sometimes for several days, to the 10th of February this year.

The

REMARKABLE EVENTS under LEWIS XIV.

The civil ordinance of the month of April: for the digesting of so important a law, the king thought proper to join to the abovementioned ministers some commissioners from the parliament, among others messieurs de Lamoignon, Talon, and Bignon, who set the last hand to this work.

While Colbert was endeavouring to promote the internal prosperity of the kingdom, M. de Louvois determined to extend the glory of his majesty's arms, and to assert the rights accruing from the death of Philip IV. to the queen Mary Theresa, that king's daughter by the first venter, exclusive of Charles II, his son by a second wife. The rights of this princess were founded on the law of devolution, which obtains in some provinces of the Netherlands, whereby even the females of the first venter inherit before the males of the second. The king marches into Flanders, having under him the marshal de Turenne. In this expedition he was followed by the queen and his whole court. There were two flying camps, besides the one commanded by the marshal d'Aumont, the other by M. de Crequy. This was called the campaign of Lille. Charleroy is taken by M. Turenne on the 2d of June. Marshal d'Aumont possesses himself of Armentieres the 28th of May, of St. Vinox the 6th of June, and of Furnes the 12th. His majesty takes Ath the 16th; Tournay the 24th; Doway and Fort de l'Escarpe the 6th of July. Courtray surrenders to marshal d'Aumont the 18th, and Oudenard the 31st. The king makes himself master of Lille, in nine days, on the 27th of August: at this siege he exposed himself in such a manner, that M. de Turenne threatened to resign his command, if his majesty would not take more care of his person. The count de Marsin, and the prince de Ligne, having marched to the relief of that town, are beaten by messieurs de Crequy and de Bellefons, on the 31st. At this siege the marshal de Grammont mounted the trenches at the head of the regiment of guards, though the marshal de Turenne, his junior, commanded the army. M. de Turenne carries Alost the 12th of September. This year the king created the rank of brigadier for the cavalry, and the year following for the infantry and the dragoons.

REMARKABLE EVENTS under LEWIS XIV.

The feignory of Vaujour erected into a dutchy and peerage, by the title of la Valliere, in favour of Louifa-Frances de la Valliere, and of Mary Anne (afterwards princefs of Conty) the king's natural daughter. The princefs of Conty made a prefent of this dutchy, with the king's confent, in 1668, to the marquis de la Valliere, her coufin-german, who obtained new letters patent of erection into a dutchy and peerage in 1723, verified the fame year.

M. de la Feuillade marries the heirefs of the dutchy of Rouannois, and is made a duke and peer. Rouannois had been created a dutchy and peerage fo long ago as 1579, in favour of Arthur de Gouffier, but the letters patent were not regiftered, no more than thofe afterwards obtained by Claude and Lewis de Gouffier.

The peace of Breda, by the mediation of the king of Sweden, is figned in that city the 31ft of July: there were three feparate treaties, or inftruments; the firft between France and England, in which the count d'Eftrades and Courtin agreed, that the conquefts on both fides fhould be reftored; the fecond between England and Denmark; and the third between England and Holland: in the latter it is obfervable, that the fuperiority of the Englifh flag was preferved. During the conferences for a peace, the Dutch failed up the river Thames *, and burnt feveral Englifh men of war. Alfonfo VI, king of Portugal, equally unworthy of his crown and of his wife, is obliged to refign both to his brother Don Pedro. This princefs, named mademoifelle d'Aumale, was daughter to the duke de Nemours, who had been killed in a duel in 1652, by the duke de Beaufort his brother-in-law: her fifter had much the fame fate as herfelf; for her marriage with the prince of Lorrain was diffolved, and fhe efpoufed the duke of Savoy. Don Pedro took only the title of regent, during the life of his brother. Charles II, king of Spain, tired of a war, which had lafted eight and twenty years, concluded a peace with this prince on the 13th of February the year following; by

* They failed up the Medway, as far as Chatham, and there it was they burnt the Englifh men of war.

which

REMARKABLE EVENTS under LEWIS XIV.

which he acknowledged the crown of Portugal to be free and independent of that of Castile.

1668.

The conquest of Franche Comté, accomplished in less than a month, and in the depth of winter, by the king in person: he had under him the prince of Condé, whom he is said to have preferred, on this occasion, to M. de Turenne, by the advice of M. de Louvois. The prince made himself master of Besançon in two days, on the 7th of February, while M. de Luxemburg took Salins. Dole surrenders to the king the 14th, and Gray the 19th. The French academy had the honour, for the first time, of complimenting the king upon his conquest.

The treaty of triple alliance signed by England, Sweden, and Holland, on the 28th of January. This alliance was owing to the umbrage, which Lewis XIV. had given to Europe. Sir William Temple, ambassador from Charles II, king of England, persuaded John de Witt, the pensionary of Holland, to quit his connexions with France; but he had reason afterwards to repent this resolution. Count Dona was minister for Sweden. A peace is signed at Aix la Chapelle, the second of May, between France and Spain. The king preserved his conquests in the Netherlands, viz. Charleroy, Binch, Ath, Doway, Fort de l'Escarpe, Lisle, Oudenarde, Armentieres, Courtray, Bergues, Furnes, together with their bailiwicks, &c. Franche Comté was restored, contrary to the opinion of marshal de Turenne: M. de Croissy, brother of Colbert, was minister at the concluding of this peace on the part of the king. M. de Montausier is made governor to the dauphin.

The king orders the several transactions, from the year 1647 to 1657, to be struck out of the parliamentary registers. M. de Turenne makes his abjuration on the 23d of October. He had long had a glimmering idea of the true religion; but was still retained in his errors by the prejudice of education, as well as by an extraordinary fondness for his wife, daughter of the duke de la Force, and a zealous Calvinist. The death of this lady in 1666, together with the instructions of the bishop of Meaux, at length completed the conversion of the marshal de Turenne. It was for the use of this great captain, that the abovementioned pre-

REMARKABLE EVENTS under LEWIS XIV.

late wrote his treatife intitled, the *Expofition of the Faith*, a rational and folid performance, to which the proteftants have publifhed no anfwer, and which clears the church of Rome of the ridiculous fuperftitions laid to her charge. This year there were three marfhals of France; M. de Crequy, M. de Bellefonds, and M. d'Humieres.

A fupreme court of judicature eftablifhed at Tournay, and erected afterwards into a parliament in 1686. Upon the furrender of this town in 1713, the parliament was transferred to Doway.

1669.

The edict of the 21ft of January, fuppreffing the chambers eftablifhed in favour of the proteftants, by the edict of Nantes, in all the parliaments of the kingdom. Thefe chambers being diftributed throughout the realm, were bipartite; but in the parliament of Paris, where the chamber of the edict of Nantes was to confift of fix proteftant counfellors, and ten catholics, only one proteftant was fuffered to remain; and the other five were diftributed among the chambers of inquefts, without being permitted to afcend to the grand chamber: yet this court ftill preferved the name of the chamber of the edict, though there was only one proteftant member, to fhew that it had been created in favour of thofe of the reformed religion.

Difturbances concerning the formulary, occafioned by the diftinction of fact and right in the affair of Janfenius; they were quieted by pope Clement IX.

The taking of Candia by the Turks on the 16th of September: the French fuccours, under the command of meffieurs de Beaufort and Navailles, retarded the furrender of that place, the fpace of three months. M. de Beaufort was killed in a fally the 25th of June, but his body was never found. We muft not omit mentioning, that the duke de Rouannois, afterwards marfhal de la Fuillade, had landed in that ifland the preceding year, with a reinforcement of four or five hundred men, and two hundred gentlemen of the beft families of the kingdom. Michael Koributt Wiefnowifki, of the blood of the Jagellons, but of no perfonal merit, is elected king of Poland, the 19th of June, after Cafimir's abdication, notwith-

ftanding

REMARKABLE EVENTS under LEWIS XIV.

standing the competition of the duke of Neuburg, of prince Charles of Lorrain, and of the prince of Condé. Casimir, upon the death of the queen his wife, retired to France; the king gave him the abbey of St. Germain des Près, where he died in 1672: with him ended the Swedish branch, which had reigned in Poland ever since Sigismund his grand-father. Another Casimir, also king of Poland, acted quite the contrary of this prince; by quitting the monastic habit in the order of Cluny, to ascend the throne.

M. de Guise is allowed the privilege of having a cushion in the king's presence at mass, as had been enjoyed by his father. The king revives the post of admiral, and confers it on the duke de Vermandois, his natural son. A great change of places at court. The count du Lude obtains the office of master of the ordnance, upon the duke de Mazarin's quitting; the duke de Tresmes is made first lord of the bedchamber, upon the resignation of the count du Lude; and the duke of Tresmes having laid down his post of captain of the guards, M. de Lausun is appointed to succeed him.

The office of grand master of the wardrobe, created in favour of the marquis de Guitry. The marquis de Soyecourt is made great huntsman, upon the resignation of the chevalier de Rohan: the duke d'Aumont becomes first lord of the bedchamber, in the room of the duke de Mortemart, who succeeds him in the government of Paris; and the duke d'Aumont having given up his post of captain of the guards, is succeeded by the marquis de Rochefort.

1670.

The marquis de Martel compels the Algerines to conclude a peace on the 26th of January.

The duke of Lorrain, having entered into new intrigues, is stripped of all his strong holds by the marshal de Crequy, who leaves him only an open and defenceless country. Epinay is taken the 24th of September, Chatté and Longwy the 26th of October, upon which that prince retires to Cologne. M. de Pomponne, who succeeded the count d'Estrades in the embassy to Holland, gives the king notice of the alliance, which the

Dutch

REMARKABLE EVENTS under LEWIS XIV.

Dutch had concluded with the emperor and the king of Spain; and his majesty intending to chastise that republic, thinks of securing the king of England in his interest. The dutchess of Orleans, sister to that monarch, was employed in this negotiation, which had been kept a secret from the duke her husband; and she would willingly have concealed it even from M. de Louvois. To the end that her voyage to England might create less suspicion, the king made a feint as if he only designed to visit his conquests in the Netherlands, and the whole court attended him upon this journey. M. de Lausun, in whose favour the post of colonel-general of dragoons had been erected two years before, commanded the king's escort, consisting of his houshold troops and the gendarmery. The dutchess of Orleans, under pretence of paying a visit to her brother, took an opportunity to cross the sea, and disengaged him from the triple league. There were several reasons to make the king of England enter into this new alliance: such as the burning of his ships in the Thames, during the negotiations of peace at Breda; the perpetual edict against the election of a stadtholder; but above all, the view of rendering himself more absolute at home, by his connexion with France. The dutchess of Orleans left the dutchess of Portsmouth * in England, where she did great service to Lewis XIV, and was afterwards mother to the duke of Richmond. The above princess repassed the sea, the 12th of June; but did not long enjoy the fruits of her voyage, for she was taken ill, and died in less than eight hours at St. Cloud, the 30th of the same month, at the age of twenty-six: she came into the world amidst a camp, and all the horrors of civil war; and she was suddenly snatched out of it, amidst a brilliant court, of which she herself was the principal ornament.

"The dutchess of Orleans had a solid and delicate wit; she
"was possessed of good sense, and well acquainted with the
"nicest circumstances of things; she had a great and just mind,
"that made her perfectly sensible of what ought to be done, and
"yet she did not always do it; which proceeded either from
"natural indolence, or a certain elevation of mind springing

* Than only madame de Querouaille.

" from

REMARKABLE EVENTS under LEWIS XIV.

"from the confciousness of her birth, that made her con-
"sider her duty as beneath her. She transfused into her
"whole conversation, a sweetness not to be found in that
"of other royal personages; and might be said to usurp
"an empire over all hearts, instead of leaving them in com-
"mon. She had an inexpressible something, by which she
"had always the power to please; and even the delicacy of
"behaviour, which in others appeared copied, was generally
"allowed to belong originally to this princess." (*Mem. de Cosn.*)

M. de Turenne, having been intrusted with the secret of the English negotiation, was so weak as to disclose it; but as his fault was considerable, the frankness with which he acknowledged it to the king, was truly heroic. This able general took part with the princes in 1650, out of complaisance to the dutchess of Longueville, with whom he was in love: great men, under the influence of this passion, are apt to commit great mistakes.

The ordinance relating to criminal matters, published in the month of August.

The king's edict, enjoining, that the profession of a merchant should not derogate from the honour of the nobility. If it be true, that commerce is the most certain means of augmenting the number of inhabitants in any kingdom; if it be true, that commerce supplies the place of the mines of gold and silver, which nature has refused us; if it be true, that war is at present carried on, rather by making use of the riches of one nation against another, than by opposing man to man; if it be true, in short, that we cannot too much honour a profession, which has continually the universe for the field of its operations, and which supposes in the persons who exercise it, those sudden resources of genius, by which one nation suddenly augments its credit at the expence of its neighbours; how greatly ought we to be astonished, that our nation has been so long without such a law, and still more, that this law has not hitherto been able to overcome the prejudices of vanity! We shall see, that the author of the Spirit of Laws, who has not sufficiently explained himself on this subject (book xx. chap. xix.) has more fully given his thoughts in the new edition he is going to publish, which he has shewn me. I was at this part of my work, when death snatched him from us: the loss of this great man gives concern to every true citizen, and grief to those who knew him; how then must it affect his intimate friends!

1671.

Lewis XIV. prevails on Charles XI, king of Sweden, to quit the triple league, in which he had been engaged by the Swedish regency, during his minority; and to break off his alliance with Spain. He likewise gains over the emperor, who was then employed in quelling the disturbances in Hungary, and, not foreseeing the rapid success of Lewis XIV, seemed to be not at all offended at the humbling of Dutch arrogance. M. de Furstemberg, bishop of Strasburg, entered into a negotiation with the elector of Cologne, over whom he had an ascendant; and flattering him with the hopes of recovering Rhimberg, of which he had been dispossessed by the Dutch, he made him sign a treaty to deliver up Nuitz and Keyserwert, which the king wanted for his magazines on the Lower Rhine. The bishop of Munster espoused the same cause. There remained no other power than Spain, at that time governed by the queen regent: but the marquis de Villars, our ambassador, could never prevail upon her to break off her engagements with the Dutch, notwithstanding the great disputes betwixt her and Don John, which weakened her authority; and the methods that had been used to intimidate her, by threatening to seize the remainder of the Spanish Netherlands. The emperor acts with great severity in Hungary, where the nobility were impatient under the Austrian yoke; and the court of Vienna wanted to render that kingdom hereditary. This war proved of great service to the king, during the whole course of his reign, as it made a considerable diversion in his favour.

The duke of Orleans marries a second wife at Chalons, on the 16th of November, namely, the princess Charlotte Isabella, daughter of Charles Lewis, elector Palatine, the same who had been restored to that electorate by the treaty of Munster, and whose father, Frederic, was dispossessed of his dominions

upon

REMARKABLE EVENTS under LEWIS XIV.

upon accepting of the crown of Bohemia. This princefs died in 1722, and left two children; the one Philip, regent of France under Lewis XV, and who died in 1723; the other, the dutchefs of Lorrain, who breathed her laft in 1745.

The inftitution of the academy of Architecture. The hofpital of Invalids, founded by the care of M. de Louvois. The king publifhed an edict in the year 1674, for annexing to this houfe, the penfions granted to the *Oblats*, a kind of lay monks of great antiquity in the church, who were placed by the king in every abbey of his nomination, and maintained at the expence of the houfe: they were for the moft part difabled foldiers. This maintenance was afterwards changed into out-penfions, which were paid by the abbies; and the penfions, as we have obferved, were applied to the fupport of the hofpital of Invalids.

The departure of the princefs of Montpenfier to Chateauroux, on Afh-Wednefday, the 11th of February, where fhe died in 1694.

M. de Laufun is imprifoned at Pignerol, from whence he was not releafed till 1681. This is the very fame perfon, who was upon the point of marrying mademoifelle de Montpenfier the year before, and to whom the king, upon breaking off the match, had offered to make him marfhal of France; an honour which he refufed, under pretence that he had done nothing as yet to deferve it. His commiffion of captain of the guards was given to M. de Luxemburg. The death of M. de Lionne. M. de Pomponne, ambaffador in Sweden, was recalled from thence to fupply his place. M. de Berny, the fon of Lionne, purchafes the office of mafter of the wardrobe, for four hundred and fifty thoufand livres.

This is a curious æra with regard to the Swifs troops, and affords us an opportunity to diftinguifh two periods of their eftablifhment in France: the firft from 1477, when they ferved only during the war in which they were actually employed: the fecond from the year 1671 to the prefent time, when their fervice became permanent in peace, as well as in war.

1672.

War is declared againft the Dutch, by France and England on the fame day, viz. on the 7th of April.

REMARKABLE EVENTS under LEWIS XIV.

The conquest of Holland. This republic was the cause of her own misfortunes, by the imprudent behaviour of her ambassadors in all the courts of Europe, and especially of Van Beuninghen in France; by the insolence of her news-writers; and by the striking of particular medals. The marshals de Bellefons, de Crequy and d'Humieres, retired from court, to avoid serving under M. de Turenne, whom the king had nominated marshal-general, so early as the year 1660. His majesty had three different armies; one commanded by himself, and M. de Turenne; the second by the prince of Condé; and the third by the count de Chamilly. The latter seized Maseick the 15th of May: Orsey surrendered to the king, the 3d of June, while M. de Turenne made himself master of Burich. The prince takes Wesel the 4th: Rhimberg surrenders to the king the 6th; Emmeric to the prince the 7th; and Rees the same day to the marshal de Turenne. The pensionary John de Witt, who understood the interests of his republic the best of any man living, made no scruple to declare, upon hearing of the reduction of Rhimberg, that the king of France might boast of having one moiety of Holland in his power. M. de Beauviré possesses himself of Doetekum, the 8th; the duke of Luxemburg, general of the troops of Munster, takes Grool on the 9th. The famous passage of the Rhine, in the neighbourhood of Tolhuys on the 12th: the first who swam over it, was the count de Guiches, at the head of the cuirassiers, commanded by the count de Revel: the young duke de Longueville, having passed the Rhine, fell by his own indiscretion, and was the cause of the prince of Condé's being wounded in the hand; with him ended the house of Longueville, when he was just upon the point of being elected to the crown of Poland. M. de Turenne having taken upon him the command of the prince of Condé's army, makes himself master of Arnheim the 15th, and of Fort Schenck the 19th, which the Dutch did not wrest from the Spaniards in 1636, till after a siege of nine months. Utrecht submits to the king the 20th, and Dœsburg the 21st. The bishop of Munster makes himself master of Deventer the same day, and of Swoll the 22d. The duke of Orleans takes Zutphen the 25th. Nimeguen surrenders to M. de Turenne on the 9th of July, and Coeverden

REMARKABLE EVENTS under LEWIS XIV.

to the bishop of Munster on the 12th. Naerden was carried the same day by the marquis de Rochefort; it is said, that if he had not neglected to make himself master of Muyden, we must have taken Amsterdam, and consequently all Holland. Grave surrenders on the 14th to the count de Chamilly. M. de Turenne takes the fort of Crevecœur the 19th of July, and the island of Bomel the 26th of September. This great captain suddenly retires from the Dutch territories into Germany, where, with an army of twelve thousand men only, he awes the elector of Brandenburg, who had acceded to the alliance against France, and marched into Westphalia at the head of five and twenty thousand men. The duke of Luxemburg obliges the prince of Orange to raise the siege of Voerden, the 12th of October: this action was admired even by the Dutch themselves. M. de Montal compels the prince of Orange to raise the siege of Charleroy the 22d of December. The duke of Luxemburg, under favour of the ice, makes himself master of Bodegrave and Swammerdam on the 28th. To be brief, the king's armies, in the space of three months, crossed three rivers, took three provinces, Guelderland, Utrecht, and Overissel, and upwards of forty strong towns. This campaign was admired by all Europe, and would hardly gain credit at present, if the campaign of 1745 had not demonstrated, that no undertaking is too arduous for the French, when headed by their sovereign.

The war would have been at an end in three months, if M. de Pomponne's advice had been taken, which was to be contented with the advantages proposed by the Dutch, and to fall suddenly on the Spanish Netherlands, in order to punish that crown for the violation of the late treaty of Aix-la-Chapelle, in assisting the republic. But M. de Louvois's opinion was followed preferably to any other, even to that of marshal de Turenne, who counselled the king to dismantle the strong towns, as fast as he took them, knowing the difficulty of finding garrisons for them all. The marshal du Plessis was hindered by his age from making this campaign: he told the king that he envied his children, who had the honour of serving his majesty; but for his own part he desired to die, since he was

REMARKABLE EVENTS under LEWIS XIV.

no longer fit for action: the king, embracing him, said; *monsieur le marshal, they who expose themselves to the perils and fatigues of war, do it only with a view of attaining some part of your reputation: there is a pleasure in reposing under the shade of so many laurels.* On the 7th of June happened a sea fight in Southwold bay*, between the combined fleet of France and England, commanded by the duke of York and the count d'Etrées, and that of the Dutch under de Ruyter. This admiral said it was the most obstinate engagement he ever saw; and both sides claimed the advantage. In this dangerous situation, the Dutch declared the prince of Orange stadtholder, and repealed the perpetual edict for the suppression of that office, which edict Cornelius and John de Witt, enemies of that family, had procured, upon the decease of William II. The reputation of the young prince of Orange proved fatal to the two brothers, who were charged with all the misfortunes of the state, and massacred by the populace the 22d of August. The aversion of the pensionary and his brother, against the house of Orange, proceeded from a cause of a higher date. William II, father of William III, would fain persuade the republic, after the treaty of Munster, to keep a body of troops on foot, with a view no doubt of rendering them subservient to his own private purposes; and in this he acted in concert with cardinal Mazarin, who flattered the ambition of that young prince. The States General would not consent to it: and William was hardy enough, to cause six of the deputies to be arrested in their way to the Hague, among whom was the father of the two de Witts. Further, as the chief opposition came from Amsterdam, which suspected this prince of hav-

---

* Or Solbay in Suffolk. The French fleet consisted of forty, and the English of a hundred men of war. The Dutch had seventy-two large ships and forty frigates, and fire-ships. The admiral ship of the English being disabled, the duke of York was obliged to hoist his flag in the London. The Royal James, commanded by the earl of Sandwich, not being able to disengage from a fire-ship, after she had sunk two, was blown up with the earl, and her whole crew. There were two English ships burnt, three sunk, and one taken; of the French one was burnt, another sunk. The Dutch lost three ships, and Van Ghent was killed. Bonfires were equally made at London and the Hague. The English complain the French did not discharge their duty, which is ascribed to secret orders given to count d'Etrées.

ing

REMARKABLE EVENTS under LEWIS XIV.

ing a defign to fubvert the liberty of Holland, he endeavoured to make himfelf mafter of that city in 1650, but mifcarried in his attempt: he died foon after, as it was faid, of the fmall-pox; yet cardinal Mazarin gave broad hints, that this event was too lucky to be natural. The averfion of the parents defcended to the children, and the deWitts fell a facrifice in the conteft. William III, fon of the above William II, was made ftadtholder on this occafion; and being afterwards raifed to the throne of England, he ftill retained this dignity, which was fuppreffed at his death, but revived again in 1747.

The death of the chancellor Seguier. This place was vacant two years; and the king held the feal three months: his majefty afterwards appointed M. d'Aligre, keeper of the feals, who was not made chancellor till the year 1674: his father had alfo enjoyed this dignity. It was no new thing for the king to hold the great feal himfelf: Lewis XIII. held it in the camp before Montauban, after the deceafe of the conftable de Luines. Henry IV. held the feal in 1590, upon the refignation of Montholon, till Chiverny was recalled. Henry III. fealed fome letters patent himfelf, to which the chancellor de Biragne had refufed to fix the feal.

The king grants an apartment in the Louvre to the French academy; their meetings had been at the chancellor Seguier's houfe, till the time of his deceafe, which happened the 20th of January.

The dutchefs dowager of Orleans (Margaret of Lorrain) Gafton's fecond wife, departed this life the 3d of April. The duke de la Feuillade is created colonel of the regiment of guards, upon the refignation of the marfhal de Grammont. The duke de Duras is made captain of the guards, in the room of the duke de Charoft.

1673.

The feignory of Charoft erected into a dukedom and peerage, by the title of Bethune Charoft.

The fuccefs of the French arms was too great not to alarm the reft of Europe: the emperor and the crown of Spain renewed a treaty with the Dutch the 3d of Auguft. Who could have dreamt in 1609, that Spain fhould undertake to defend Holland againft the French and Englifh! The

REMARKABLE EVENTS under LEWIS XIV.

The elector of Brandenburg and Montecuculli had been endeavouring, upwards of three months, to pass the Rhine in the neighbourhood of Mentz, Coblentz, Strasburg, and other strong towns; but wherever they moved, they were sure to meet with M. de Turenne, who hindered them, on the one hand, from succouring the Dutch, and, on the other, from making a diversion in Alsace. The elector finding himself stripped of all his possessions in Westphalia, at length concluded a treaty of neutrality with France, in the month of May. The king makes himself master of Maestricht on the 29th of June, after a siege of thirteen days, with a view to establish the communication with his conquests in Holland; from thence marching into Alsace, in order to secure the neutrality of the city of Strasburg, and to maintain a good understanding with the Swiss, he resigns the command to his generals. Though the siege of Maestricht lasted no more than thirteen days, yet it is memorable for the gallant behaviour of the besiegers and the besieged. This town having been restored at the peace of Nimeguen, was taken again under Lewis XV, in the month of May, 1748, by the marshal-general count Saxe, who had under him the marshal de Lowendahl. And here we cannot help mentioning, for the instruction of posterity, the secrecy with which this enterprize was planned and conducted, as also the means that were used to the very last moment for putting the enemy upon a wrong scent. It was a masterly stroke to conceal from the enemy a most important design, the taking of Maestricht, by means of the revictualling of Bergen-op-zoom, which had been reduced the preceding campaign; to march towards the Scheld, in order to secure the conquest of the Maese; and thus by a vigorous effort to put an end to a war, which our enemies, from their great animosity, seemed desirous to perpetuate. The plan of this campaign will be read one day with as much curiosity, as the instruction of M. de Louvois to the marshal d'Humieres for the taking of Gaunt.

A declaration of war by Spain against France on the 15th of October, and by France against Spain on the 20th.

The Dutch and Spaniards, on the 14th of September, retake Narden, which was ill defended by du Pas, an officer, however esteemed

REMARKABLE EVENTS under LEWIS XIV.

esteemed by M. de Turenne: he was degraded, and recovered his reputation, by the loss of his life, at the siege of Grave, where he was killed the next year. Bonne surrenders to Montecuculli the 12th of November: M. de Louvois imputes these advantages of the enemy to M. de Turenne, notwithstanding that this general had done all he could to prevent the junction of the Imperialists and the Dutch. M. de Rochefort possesses himself of Treves the 15th of November. The king is obliged to evacuate several of the conquered towns. This year there were three sea fights: the first on the 7th of June, the second on the 14th, and the third on the 22d of August, which proved no way decisive. Prince Rupert commanded the English fleet in the place of the duke of York, whose religion began now to be suspected. The count d'Estrees had still the command of that of France; and the Dutch had joined Tromp in command with Ruyter. (Madam de Sevigné used to say, that engagements at sea had never been decisive, since the battle of Actium.) So early as the 28th of March, plenipotentiaries had been appointed to meet at Cologne. The duke of York had buried his consort *, daughter of the earl of Clarendon, and mother of the princess Mary, afterwards princess of Orange, and of the princess Anne, afterwards queen of England: on the 30th of September this year he married his second wife, viz. Mary d'Este, daughter of the duke of Modena and of Laura Martinozzi: (she was mother of the chevalier de St. George born in 1688.) The edict of the 10th of February, by which the king declares, that the *regale* extends to all the dioceses of his kingdom, except such as were exempt on account of some other acknowledgments. Only two bishops in the kingdom refused to submit to this edict, viz. those of Alet and Pamiers; and what is very observable, after refusing to sign the formulary, they appealed to the pope against whatever was done by the king with respect to the regale. The chamber of the queen's maids reformed; she was afterwards attended by the *ladies of the palace*.

The death of Moliere: he had opened his play-house in 1659, at the *petit Bourbon*, with a company of comedians, who were said to belong to the duke of Orleans. At that time there were three

* March 31, 1671.

theatres, the *hotel de Bourgogne*, that of the *Marais*, and that of the *petit Bourbon*. The king having demolished the hall of the *petit Bourbon* in 1660, to build the great portal of the Louvre, gave the hall of the *palais royal* to Moliere; and, in 1665, the players under his direction took the name of his majesty's company of comedians. It is not at all surpizing, that Moliere should occasion a revolution in the theatres: after his decease, which happened the 17th of February, the king granted the hall of the *palais royal* to Lulli. Moliére's company, now without a manager, were divided between the two theatres, that of the *hotel de Bourgogne*, and that of the *Marais*; the company of the *Marais* came and settled in the tennis court *rue de Seine*, having an inlet into that of the *fossés de Nesle* (now *Mazarine*) over against *rue Guenegaud*, with the title of his majesty's company; and at length the two companies of the *hotel de Bourgogne*, and of the *Marais* were united in 1680. The *hotel de Bourgogne* remaining vacant, was occupied by the Italian comedians. The opening of the Mazarin college in 1668, was the cause of the French comedians being removed; and by an arret of council the same year, they were settled in the hall they occupy at present, which was the tennis court *de l'Etoile*.

1674.

France is upon the point of being abandoned: the two last campaigns had raised enemies against her; and the present deprived her of allies. The king of England makes a peace with Holland, on the 19th of February; but refuses to comply with his parliament in declaring war against France. Marshal de Turenne, by his skilful manœuvres in the last campaign, had kept the elector of Cologne and the bishop of Munster in our alliance: this year those princes made some attempts in the country of Groningen, but were soon recalled from thence by the incursions of the enemy in their own dominions; and at length they came to an accommodation with the Dutch, who restored Rhimberg to the elector of Cologne.

The emperor causes prince William of Furstemberg, brother of the bishop of Strasburg, and afterwards bishop of that city, to be arrested the 14th of February; the committing of this outrage, in a place where the congress was held, broke off the negotiations. The

REMARKABLE EVENTS *under* LEWIS XIV.

The elector Palatine, notwithstanding his obligations to France, signs an offensive alliance with the emperor, on the 10th of March. The king seized Franche Comté a second time, and kept possession of it after the peace. If the duke of Lorrain's opinion had been followed, he would have prevented us on that side; but the emperor chose to carry his arms into Alsace, expecting to make a conquest of that country for himself. The duke de Navailles takes Gray the 28th of February, and Vesoul the 11th of March. Besançon surrenders to the king the 15th of May, and Dole the 6th of June. The dauphin was present at this siege. The parliament of Besançon is erected. M. de la Feuillade possesses himself of Salins the 22d. The parliament coming to compliment the king, at his return from this conquest, M. de Talon, advocate-general, introduced a new custom: after the harangue of the first president, instead of barely saluting the king as he passed along, he made a speech to his majesty; and ever since the king's council have retained this privilege.

The king had three armies, the first in Germany, the second in Flanders, and the third in Roussillon.

In Germany, the viscount de Turenne passed the Rhine at Philipsburg the 12th of June: eager to fight the duke of Lorrain and the count of Caprara, before they were joined by the duke de Bournonville, he attacked them at Sintzheim, a small town of the Palatinate, between Philipsburg and Hailbrun, and obtained a victory over them the 16th of June: his army consisted of about twelve thousand men, that of the enemy of as many; but they had the advantage of the ground, and our troops were fatigued with a long march of five and thirty leagues in four days. The retreat of the Imperialists beyond the Neckar and the Maine, left the Palatinate at the mercy of the victors, who receiving a reinforcement of troops, defeated the rear guard of the enemy at Lademburg, on the 5th of July, notwithstanding the junction of the duke de Bournonville: the country was laid waste with fire and sword, in revenge for the cruelties practised on some of our soldiers, who had strayed from the army. The elector Palatine, provoked at the calamity of his subjects, for which he ought to have blamed his own infidelity, sent a challenge
to

to M. de Turenne; but this general answered that prince with such moderation, as made him ashamed of his bravado.

The elector of Brandenburg having nothing farther to apprehend on the side of Westphalia, broke the treaty which he had concluded the preceding year with the marshal de Turenne, and endeavoured to join the Imperial army.

The duke of Lorrain's plan was to drive the viscount de Turenne out of Alsace, and to penetrate into Lorrain, after joining the elector of Brandenburg: in consequence hereof he passed the Rhine at Spire and Strasburg, the last of which towns broke the neutrality it promised the king. M. de Turenne, though one third inferior to the enemy, judged nevertheless that it behoved him to run every risk; otherwise, France would be open to their incursions. He therefore marched his army, consisting only of two and twenty thousand men, to attack the enemy, who were forty thousand: he fought them at Entzheim in the neighbourhood of Strasburg, the 4th of October, and defeated them a second time: M. de Boufflers had a great share in the honour of this day. Still the work was imperfect: the junction of the elector of Brandenburg would have made any other general than M. de Turenne lose all hopes of preserving Alsace. The enemy's commanders were under a necessity of extending their quarters in upper Alsace, in order to subsist an army of sixty thousand men: M. de Turenne avails himself of this conjuncture, and, pretending to march into Lorrain, he turns short and falls of a sudden upon Mulhausem, where he routed a body of six thousand horse the 29th of December: this misfortune disconcerted the enemy, and obliged them to act upon the defensive. The successes of marshal de Turenne were solid, and void of ostentation; they were not pitched battles, which oftentimes are only attended with eclat, without producing any real advantage: they were useful conflicts, which saved his country; and the conduct of the general left nothing to chance. We may apply to him, what was said of Cæsar, that he made war, just as he pleased himself, and not according to the caprice of fortune.

In Flanders, on the 11th of August was fought the battle of Senef, a village betwixt Marimont and Nivelle: there were two actions

actions the same day: the prince of Condé headed an army of fifty thousand men, against very near fourscore thousand commanded by the prince of Orange, who had under him the young duke of Lorrain, the count de Souche, Monterey, the prince of Vaudemont, and count Waldeck. The prince of Condé's aim being to prevent the siege of Charleroy, he defeated the rear-guard of the enemy at Senef, an advantage sufficient for any other general: but, not content with this success, he fell upon the remainder of the prince of Orange's army, who committed a mistake in exposing his flank as he decamped. The conflict was bloody; or rather it was an assemblage of several great conflicts: according to the relation of people of credit in that neighbourhood, about seven and twenty thousand dead bodies were buried within the circumference of two leagues. The generals did prodigies of valour on both sides, and we remained in possession of the field of battle. The prince of Orange wanted to claim the honour of this victory, by laying siege to Oudenarde, which he was obliged to raise on the 21st of September, upon the approach of the prince of Condé. General Rawenhaup obliges Grave to surrender the 28th of October: the prince of Orange was there in person to forward the siege; the marquis de Chamilly distinguished himself in the defence of that place, which did not capitulate till after a siege of ninety-three days. Dinan is carried by general Spork, the 18th of November. The Spaniards and Dutch possess themselves of Huy, the 2d of December. In Roussillon, the count de Schomberg, celebrated for his exploits in Portugal, prevented the attempts of the Spaniards against Perpignan.

By sea, admiral Tromp, having made a descent upon Belleisle near the coast of Britany, is forced to reimbark the 28th of June, upon the arrival of M. de Cœtlogon: and admiral Ruyter, after landing a body of men near Port Royal in Martinico, was obliged to desist from that enterprize; he lost twelve hundred men by the cannonading of one of the king's ships, commanded by M. d'Amblimont. The inhabitants of Messina, tired with the severity of the Spanish government, rise up in arms; and the chevalier de Valbelle, sails with some troops to their assistance:

this

this proved a serviceable diversion; as the Spaniards were obliged to make detachments from Roussillon for their army in Sicily.

A conspiracy of the chevalier de Rohan, to deliver up Quillebeuf to the Dutch, and to raise an insurrection in Normandy; he was beheaded the 28th of November, and madam de Villiers underwent the same fate: one of the accomplices, who suffered death, was a school-master, named Vanden Ende; and the famous Spinosa had been his disciple. A few days before the execution, the tragedy of Cinna was acted in the presence of the king, to excite his royal clemency; but the ministers made him sensible of the necessity of a public example, and the chevalier de Rohan was consigned to the punishment, which he had deserved for his temerity. The archbishopric of Paris is erected into a dukedom and peerage; the letters patent were not verified till the year 1690, in favour of M. de Harlay and his successors, archbishops of Paris. It is surprizing, that the bishop of Paris was not one of the peers of France; and that, even at present, since the erection of the dutchy of St. Cloud into a dukedom and peerage, he ranks only in the order of his creation, but does not make one of the ancient peers; this is because originally he held no seignory of the king.

An academy erected at Soissons. Quebec is made a bishopric.

1675.

The campaign still continued in Alsace: the mistake which the enemy had committed, in dividing their forces, made them resolve to contract their quarters. The elector of Brandenburg assembled the army in the neighbourhood of Colmar, a post that seemed to be inaccessible; M. de Turenne advanced towards the Germans, and having made a feint, as if he intended to fall upon them by the way of Colmar, where their left wing was extended, he took post near Turkheim, over against their right, and attacked them the 5th of January: after a bloody engagement, he obliged them not only to abandon their camp, but to repass the Rhine with twenty thousand men; for no more were left out of sixty thousand, of which their army consisted at the opening of the campaign. The elector of Brandenburg, the duke

of

REMARKABLE EVENTS under LEWIS XIV.

of Lorrain, and the duke de Bournonville, laid the disgrace of this campaign upon one another.

The advantages obtained by the marshal de Turenne, in the four last engagements, seem to have been owing to the blunders of the enemy, of which he made a proper advantage; and this would have been a high encomium for any other captain: but what raises him above all competition, is, that he had not only foreseen, but gradually led them into those mistakes, by real stratagem: this is sufficiently proved by a letter of his to the king, dated so early as the 30th of October of the preceding year, wherein he explained the method by which he intended to oblige the enemy to repass the Rhine. M. de Turenne returned to court, being sent for by the king, after the battle of Turkheim; he left the command of his army to the marquis de Vaubrun, who, by making himself master of Dachstein the 29th of January, as also of Molseim and Mutzig, the only places that had been left in possession of the confederates; and by taking several other places in the Brisgaw, which communicated with both sides of the Rhine, drove the enemy intirely out of Alsace, while the French garrison of Philipsburg compleated the ruin of the Palatinate.

M. de Turenne's only desire, in the midst of his glory, was to retire: the king would not consent to it, but obliged him to return to the army the 11th of May, in order to oppose the attempts of Montecuculli, whom the jealousy of the allies had excluded last year from the command of their army. *The present campaign*, says the chevalier de Folard, *was the master-piece of the viscount de Turenne, and of the count de Montecuculli: there is not so curious a manœuvre in all antiquity; and none but those who are expert in the art of war, can be judges of its beauty.* The marshal de Turenne musters his army at Schelestad, advances towards Benfeld, and encamps the 27th of May, at the village of Achenheim, a league from Strasburg, with a view of obliging that city to observe a neutrality, and of defeating the enemy's scheme of entering Alsace. Their motions determined him to pass the Rhine, the 7th of June, and after having exhausted, for the space of two months, every resource in the art of war, relative to encampments, marches and coun-
termarches,

termarches, this great captain fancied at length he had hit on the lucky minute for attacking Montecuculli to an advantage, when he was fnatched away by a cannon ball on the 27th of July, in the neighbourhood of Saverne, at the age of fixty-four: he was interred at St. Denis, the 29th of Auguft. With him perifhed the fecret of that day, which had all the appearance of being crowned with fuccefs: inftead of attacking the enemy, the French thought only of retiring: the difpute about the command of the army, between the count de Lorges and the marquis de Vaubrun, added ftill to our misfortune; and at length the mafterly retreat of the count de Lorges had the appearance of a victory, confidering the great confternation of the army. Montecuculli purfued him, and, on the firft of Auguft was fought the battle of Altenheim, in which the marquis de Vaubrun was killed: the advantage was equal on both fides, owing intirely to the bravery of our troops, who drew up in a line of themfelves. M. de Vendome was wounded in this engagement. The French army repaffed the Rhine at Altenheim, and the enemy at Strafburg. The prince of Condé having taken upon him the command of M. de Turenne's army, obliges Montecuculli to raife the fiege of Haguenau, the 22d of Auguft; as alfo that of Saverne, the 14th of September; and at length to repafs the Rhine: this was the laft exploit of the prince of Condé; the gout compelled him to retire. It is worthy of obfervation that this year three of the greateft generals in Europe ended their career; M. de Turenne was flain; the prince of Condé retired; and Montecuculli followed his example, faying, that a man like him, who had had the honour of entering the lifts with Mahomet Coprogli, the prince of Condé, and marfhal de Turenne, ought not to put his glory in competition with perfons, who only juft began to have the command of armies.

In the Netherlands, the count d'Eftrades had thrown a French garrifon, the 27th of March, into the citadel of Liege, which the Imperialifts wanted to feize, with a view of facilitating the fiege of Maeftricht. The king made himfelf mafter of Dinan, the 29th of May; he had under him the marfhal de Crequy, who, at length, confented, as well as the marfhals d'Humieres

and

REMARKABLE EVENTS under LEWIS XIV.

and de Bellefons, to yield the preference to M. de Turenne. . The marquis de Rochefort carried Huy, the 6th of June; and the duke d'Anguien made himfelf mafter of Limburg the 21ft, before the prince of Orange, who was taken ill of the fmall-pox, could march to its relief. The marfhal de Crequy attempting to throw fuccours into the city of Treves, befieged by the prince of Luneburg, is defeated at Confarbrick, the 11th of Auguft. It is not true, what feveral have written, that the duke of Lorrain commanded the enemy; fo far from it, he was not prefent in the engagement: the honour of this victory was owing to duke George William of Brunfwick, as alfo to the duke of Zell, the duke of Holftein, and general Chauvel. The prince of Condé faid, that the marfhal de Crequy wanted that difgrace, to make him one of the greateft generals in Europe: and indeed the two campaigns of 1677 and 1678, fhewed the fuperior abilities of this commander; fo as to wipe off the ftain of the affair of Confarbrick. The lofs of this battle proceeded from his having too great a contempt for the enemy, whofe army was fuperior in numbers; and from his being unacquainted with the fords on both fides of the bridge, by which the enemy attacked him: true it is, that he was deferted by his cavalry. After this defeat, M. de Crequy threw himfelf into Treves with three more, and was taken prifoner when that place capitulated the 6th of September, by the treachery of one Boisjourdan, who concluded the capitulation unknown to the marfhal. Boisjourdan made his efcape, but was afterwards taken, and loft his head: this wretch had been condemned to death for a murder committed in the foreft of Senlis, yet was pardoned at the interceffion of the bifhop of Munfter; and his grandfather betrayed the town of Mons, in the reign of Charles IX.

The prince of Orange laid fiege to Binch, the laft day of Auguft, and made himfelf mafter of that place in a few days. This year the king of Sweden took the part of France againft the elector of Brandenburg: upon which the Dutch, Spaniards, and Danes, declared againft Sweden. The war did not turn out to the advantage of that crown; general Wrangel behaved very ill, fo that the Swedes were difpoffeffed of Pomerania; but

The HISTORY of FRANCE.

REMARKABLE EVENTS under LEWIS XIV.

the king procured it for them again at the treaty of Nimeguen. Bremerfurt in Germany is taken the 29th of October, by the troops of Luneburg; and Wolgaft by the elector of Brandenburg, the 10th of November. Wifmar furrenders to the king of Denmark, the 22d of December. In Sicily, the marquis de Valavoir had thrown fuccours into Meffina the 3d of January: on the 9th of February the duke de Vivonne, and the fieur du Quefne, defeated the Spanifh fleet before Meffina. The 17th of Auguft M. de Vivonne made himfelf mafter of Augufta, but mifcarried in his attempt againft Syracufe and Catania: the inactivity of the French general, and the irregularities among his troops, contributed to reftore the Spanifh affairs.

In Catalonia, the count de Schomberg, having made himfelf mafter of Figuieres, Bafchara, and fome other fmall places, retook Bellegarde the 27th of July, which the Spaniards had feized the preceding year: he was created a marfhal of France, and the marfhal de Navailles was appointed to fucceed him toward the end of the campaign.

The congrefs of Nimeguen, to which the king fends his plenipotentiaries, viz. the marfhal d'Eftrades, M. de Croiffy, and the count d'Avaux, nephew of him who acted as plenipotentiary at Munfter. The king creates eight marfhals of France, the 30th of July, namely, meffieurs d'Eftrades, the duke de Navailles, the count de Schomberg, the duke de Duras, the duke de Vivonne, the duke de la Feuillade, the duke de Luxemburg, and the marquis de Rochefort. It was fettled that they fhould no longer rank alternately, but the fenior marfhal fhould command the reft; madam de Cornuel obferved in regard to this promotion, *that it was marfhal de Turenne's coin.*

The death of the old duke of Lorrain, the 18th of September, at the age of feventy-two. This prince was poffeffed of natural courage, and great abilities for war: he had an enterprizing fpirit, which would have made his fortune, if he had been born to no paternal eftate; yet he knew not how to preferve his own dominions. It fared with him in his amours as in war: though he was hufband to the dutchefs Nicole, he married the

princefs

REMARKABLE EVENTS under LEWIS XIV.

princefs de Cantecroix, under colour that his former nuptials were void; but the court of Rome paffed a different decifion. He afterwards fell in love with Mariamne Pajot at Paris, whom he intended to marry, although the princefs de Cantecroix was living: the contract was figned the 18th of April, 1662; but the king, being unwilling that even his enemy fhould demean himfelf, caufed Mariamne to be confined to a convent, as well as mademoifelle de Saint Remi, whom Charles wanted alfo to make his wife. In 1663 he became amorous of madam de Ludres, a canonefs of Pouffay, whom he would have efpoufed, had it not been for the oppofition of the princefs de Cantecroix. This lady died in 1663, and he confirmed his marriage with her before her deceafe: he had iffue by her, M. de Vaudemont, and the princefs de Lillebonne. At length, at the age of fixty-three, he was joined in wedlock to Mary Louifa d'Apremont in 1665, in fpite of madam de Ludres.

Charles V, his nephew, fucceeded him in his dominions, or rather in the expectation of recovering them. The emperor never had a greater general, nor a more faithful ally than this prince: he made him marry his fifter Eleonora Maria, daughter of the emperor Ferdinand III, and queen dowager of Poland. From this marriage fprung duke Leopold I, who was reftored to his dominions by the treaty of Ryfwick, and whofe wife was the princefs of Orleans, niece of Lewis XIV. Duke Leopold was father to the prefent emperor (1748), on whom, the treaty of Vienna in 1735, for the general conveniency of Europe, fettled the great dukedom of Tufcany, the patrimony of the houfe of Medicis, in exchange for Lorrain: the latter has been ceded to Lewis XV, and annexed to the crown, referving the ufufruct to Staniflaus king of Poland, father of the prefent queen of France.

1676.

The congrefs of Nimeguen did not hinder the profecution of the war; it was carried on with vigour by fea, where we had three confiderable advantages. Admiral Ruyter, having failed from the coaft of Holland the 18th of Auguft, 1675, in order to affift the Spanifh fleet, attempted to oppofe the fuccours which du Quefne was carrying to Meffina: this was the firft engagement;

it lasted a long time; the French had the advantage, and Messina was relieved. The Dutch fleet had been so severely handled, that Ruyter thought of returning to Holland, when he received contrary orders, and a second engagement ensued, the 22d of April, between the same commanders. Ruyter lost his life in this action, and the siege of Augusta was raised. The Dutch, by the death of Ruyter, were as great losers, as the French had been by that of M. de Turenne: Lewis XIV. was so generous as to lament that admiral's fate. Lastly, in the action of the 2d of June, the marshal de Vivonne, who had defeated seven thousand Spaniards, in the neighbourhood of Messina, so early as the 25th of March, intirely demolished the combined fleets of Spain and Holland, in the Mediterranean, and made himself master of la Scalette the 20th of November. The fortune of war was different in the Baltic. Admiral Tromp, having joined the Danes, defeated the Swedish fleet, the 11th of June. There had been two other engagements between the Danes only and the Swedes, on the coast of Schonen, the 4th and 5th of the same month, with dubious success.

The king of Denmark penetrates into Sweden, where he obtains great advantages. Lewis XIV. had four land armies; the first commanded by himself in Flanders, having under him the duke of Orleans, with the marshals d'Humieres, de Schomberg, de la Feuillade, and des Lorges. (The latter was, at that time, made captain of the guards, upon the decease of the marshal de Rochefort.) M. de Crequy had the command of a flying camp. There was a second army under M. de Luxemburg; another between the Sambre and the Meuse, under the conduct of the marshal de Rochefort; and a fourth in Roussillon, commanded by the marshal de Navailles. The king causes the citadel of Liege to be demolished the 31st of March, and carries Condé in person the 26th of April. The duke of Orleans makes himself master of Bouchain the 11th of May: at this siege it was that we missed the opportunity of fighting the prince of Orange in the neighbourhood of Valenciennes; the king ever recollected this critical moment with regret; he had made a disposition for the engagement, and seemed to be very desirous of

gathering

REMARKABLE EVENTS under LEWIS XIV.

gathering new laurels, but was prevented by the irresolution of his generals and his minister.

Aire is taken the 31st of July, by the marshal d'Humieres, while the prince of Orange lays siege to Maestricht; the gallant Calvo, a Catalan by birth, commanded in this town, during the absence of the marshal d'Estrades, who was at the conferences of Nimeguen. We should not forget a saying of Calvo, to the engineers in garrison: *Gentlemen, I do not understand the defending of a town; all I know is, that I will not capitulate.* After a hard contest between the besiegers and the garrison, during the space of forty days, the prince of Orange was obliged to raise the siege the 27th of August, upon the approach of marshal de Schomberg. His miscarriage was complete; for the transports on board of which the prince had loaded his artillery, provisions, and all the implements of the siege, were attacked by the count de Montal and the duke de Villeroy, who caused those vessels to be brought up the Maese to Maestricht.

The young duke of Lorrain made himself master of Philipsburg the 17th of September, after a blockade of six months, and a siege of seventy days, the town being gallantly defended by du Fay. This misfortune was owing to the marshal de Rochefort, who commanded in Lorrain and the three bishopricks during the winter, and had been so imprudent as to suffer the enemy to fortify the post of Lauterburg, which rendered it impossible to succour Philipsburg. Marshal de Turenne looked upon this, as a place of the utmost importance to France; but, at that time, we were not in possession of Strasburg. It was in regard to the defence of Philipsburg by du Fay, that the king said, there were four men, whom the enemy respected in his garrisoned towns, Montal, Chamilly, Calvo, and du Fay.

A treaty concluded the 15th of October, between Sobieski, king of Poland, and the Turks, in virtue of which all that had been yielded to the Porte, by the late king Michael, was restored again, except the town of Caminiek. The marshal de Crequy makes himself master of Bouillon, the 30th of October. M. de Luxemburg detaches a body of men, who seize Montbelliard the 14th of December: he lay encamped under the walls

REMARKABLE EVENTS under LEWIS XIV.

of Brisac; this good posture of defence, together with the fidelity of the inhabitants of Basil, who refused to grant a passage to the duke of Lorrain, hindered that prince from passing the Rhine, and executing the projects he had formed against Lorrain and Franche Comté.

The king of Sweden defeats the king of Denmark at the battle of Lunden the 12th of December, and compels him to evacuate Sweden.

The count d'Estrées retakes the fort of Cayenne in America, from the Dutch, who had made themselves masters of it six months before; and he seizes the island, which has continued in our possession ever since. In Roussillon, nothing of moment was transacted.

Alby erected into an archbishopric: its metropolitan, the archbishop of Bourges, preserved his jurisdiction, as primate.

Mary Margaret d'Aubrai de Brinvilliers is beheaded and burnt for the crime of poisoning.

1677.

The king sincerely wished for peace; finding however he could not oblige the enemy to consent to it, but by his successes, and that these depended on the celerity of his operations; he made himself master of three of the strongest towns in the Netherlands, and the duke of Orleans gained a victory over the prince of Orange, before the usual time of taking the field.

His majesty sets out from St. Germains the 28th of February, while M. de Luxemburg invests the town of Valenciennes: the trenches are opened in the night between the 9th and 10th of March; and on the 17th by the valour of the musqueteers, who possess themselves of the counterscarp, the works are carried in the open day, so that the town capitulated, when least it was expected.

Cambray surrenders to the king the 5th of April, after nine days open trenches, and the citadel the 17th; though his majesty had weakened his army by sending succours to the duke of Orleans, who was employed in the siege of St. Omer.

The prince of Orange marches to the relief of St. Omer, and on the 11th was fought the battle of Mount Cassel, where

REMARKABLE EVENTS under LEWIS XIV.

where the duke of Orleans, feconded by the marfhals d'Humieres and de Luxemburg, obtained a complete victory over the prince of Orange, and gave fignal proofs of his valour, having a horfe killed under him, and a mufket fhot in his armour; the chevalier de Lorrain, fpeaking to him, received a mufket-ball in his hat, which grazed his forehead; the chevalier de Nantouillet was wounded in the thigh clofe by his fide; and fome of his attendants were flain behind him. The town of St. Omer having furrendered the 20th of the fame month, the king and his brother returned to Verfailles. It was on this occafion, that the king faid to Racine and Defpreaux, who were appointed to write his hiftory; *I am forry you was not with us the laft campaign, you would have feen fome warlike fcenes, and your journey would not have lafted long:* Racine made anfwer, *your majefty did not give us time to get our clothes ready.*

The prince of Orange, apprehenfive of being attacked by the marfhal de Luxemburg, raifes the fiege of Charleroy the 14th of Auguft, which was defended by Montal: this prince had not been more fuccefsful in 1672, before the fame town, where the fame governor commanded. The taking of Treves in 1675, and of Philipfburg in 1676, gave hopes to the young duke of Lorrain, named Charles V, that he fhould be able to reconquer his dominions: he reckoned that Treves and Luxemburg would open a paffage for him to the Saarre and the Maefe, while the prince of Saxe-Eifenach penetrated into Alface, by the way of Philipfburg. The baron de Montclar defended Alface againft the latter, and marfhal de Crequy oppofed duke Charles with a very inferior army. This prince paffed the Saarre, and advanced as far as Metz; but was hindered from undertaking any further operation, by the fuperior fkill of the marquis de Crequy, who fkirted along his army from day to day, and cut off his provifion on every fide. Neither had he more fuccefs on the Maefe, the paffage of which was defended by the marfhal de Crequy, fo that he found himfelf under the neceffity of returning to Alface, where M. de Crequy had got the ftart of him. M. de Montclar had fo ftreightened the troops under the prince of Saxony, that they

they were obliged to capitulate in the neighbourhood of Strasburg, the 24th of September, in consequence of which they retired to Rastat with a passport from the marshal. The same marshal defeated a body of troops under the command of duke Charles, on the 7th of October, at the battle of Cokesberg, in the neighbourhood of Strasburg, where the marshal de Villars, then a young man, distinguished himself: at length he concluded that glorious campaign with the taking of Friburg, the 14th of November, in five days open trenches. This place, from a mean hamlet, had the honour of being made a walled town in 1120, and became the property of the house of Austria in 1386: it was taken by Gustavus Adolphus in 1632, and returned under the dominion of the emperor in 1648, in whose possession it continued afterwards, (notwithstanding the three famous battles, in which the prince of Condé and M. de Turenne defeated Montecuculli) till it surrendered this year to the marshal de Crequy: it was ceded to the king by the treaty of Nimeguen, and restored to the house of Austria by that of Ryswick. The marshal de Villars wrested it again from the emperor in 1713; but the house of Austria recovered it by the treaty of Rastat. Lastly, Lewis XV, having taken this place in 1744, caused the fortifications, both of the town and citadel, which had been so often an annoyance to France, to be entirely demolished: the trenches were opened the 22d of September, the town surrendered the 7th of November, and the citadel the 26th of the same month, the garrison being made prisoners of war: the prince de Soubise had his arm broke at this siege. Friburg was restored to the emperor by the treaty of Aix-la-Chapelle, (1748.)

The king grants a pension of a thousand crowns to Racine and Despreaux, to encourage them to write the history of his reign.

The marshal d'Humieres makes himself master of Saint Guillain the 11th of December. The count d'Estrées, having obtained an advantage over admiral Binck at Tabago the 23d of February, seizes that place the 12th of December. The count de Monterey is defeated in the Lampourdan the 4th of July by marshal de Navailles; he was son of Don Lewis de Haro.

The prince of Orange marries the princess Mary, daughter of the duke of York (afterwards James II.): little was it then imagined,

The THIRD RACE. 185

REMARKABLE EVENTS *under* LEWIS XIV.

imagined, that this alliance would one day cause the dethroning his father-in-law. With regard to this match there are two things worthy of notice; one, that the ceremony was performed in London on the day appointed for celebrating the anniversary feast of gunpowder treason; the other, that the prince of Orange, as stadtholder, asked the consent of the States General, and that this step was considered not as a matter of ceremony, but a positive duty; in consequence of which the States General passed a decree the 11th of April, declaring, that the republic agreed to, and approved of, the stadtholder's choice; and ordained that his marriage with the princess Mary of England, should be notified on the part of the government, to the ambassadors of the emperor and of other foreign princes, residing at the Hague. The marshal d'Estrades formed this early judgment of the prince of Orange, *that William the Silent, prince Maurice, and Frederick Henry, would one day revive in that young man.* The duke of York (afterwards James II.) was of the same opinion as the marshal d'Estrades; and the haughtiness with which the abovementioned prince behaved in London, when he came to demand the princess Mary in marriage, ought to have opened the eyes of Charles II; but the misfortune was, that he mistook this haughtiness for frankness and honesty.

The king of Sweden takes the castle of Elsimburg, the 9th of January; his fleet is defeated by the Danes, the 11th of June and the 12th of July: he gains a victory over the king of Denmark at Lendskroon, the 24th of July. The elector of Brandenburg makes himself master of Stettin, the 26th of December. The parliament of Paris suppress the congress by an arret of the 18th of February.

1678.

Lewis XIV, in order to deceive the enemy, marched into Lorrain early in the month of February, with the queen and all his court, and caused Charlemont, Namur, and Luxemburg, to be invested; then turning short of a sudden, and passing from the banks of the Maese to the Scheld, he sat down before Ghent, which had been invested by the marshal d'Humieres; the town was taken the 9th of March, after a siege of only four days; and the citadel capitulated the 12th. This conquest proved of great importance,

portance, for Ghent was to have been the general magazine of the allied army, till they were in a condition to take the field. Ipres surrenders to the king after seven days open trenches, in spite of the inundations, and the gallant resistance made by the marquis de Conflans, who commanded the Spanish garrison: there were two assaults given at the same time, under the direction of the marshal de Luxemburg, one to the counterscarp of the town, and the other to that of the citadel, which hastened the surrender of the place: the duke d'Elbœuf, the king's aid-de-camp, had his leg broke. This town continued in the possession of the French by virtue of the treaty of Nimeguen, but was ceded to the emperor at the peace of Utrecht, and at length retaken again by Lewis XV, in person, in 1744.

The rapidity of these successes occasioned so great a ferment in England, that Charles II. was empowered by the parliament to borrow such sums of money as he should judge proper, at the rate of seven per cent. to maintain his armies. This looked like a preparation for succouring the enemies of France, which, with the prohibition of commerce between the two kingdoms, was absolutely inconsistent with the character of mediator, assumed by Charles II; but he was not his own master. The parliament likewise obliged him to recal the English troops, which had been in the service of France since the commencement of the war; they accordingly were sent back, but in a very indifferent plight.

His majesty having executed his design, quitted the army the 2d of June, and returned to St. Germains. Upon his departure from Paris, he told the deputies of the parliament, that he had committed his power intirely into the hands of the chancellor, to dispose of every thing in his absence according as he should judge proper. It is observable, that the king performed all these expeditions on horseback.

M. de Bretesche, colonel of dragoons, surprizes the town and castle of Leuve within four leagues of Lovain on the fourth of May. The marshal de Noailles makes himself master of Puicerda the 28th.

This campaign proved as glorious to the marshal de Crequy as the preceding, and both afford excellent instructions in
the

the art of war. The object of the duke of Lorrain was to recover Friburg, and to penetrate into Lorrain by the upper Alsace. The marshal de Crequy, after beating a detachment under the prince of Baden, marches towards the bridge of Rhinsfeld, where he defeats the Imperialists the 6th of July: he then attacks the duke of Lorrain in the neighbourhood of Gegembak, overthrows the rear guard of his army the 23d, carries Fort Kell the 27th, burns a part of the bridge of Strasburg on the same side, and at length makes himself master of Lectemberg the 15th of October.

The licentiousness with which the French troops behaved in Sicily, had prejudiced the minds of the people against them: every day there were new conspiracies, which the supineness of M. de Vivonne neither prevented nor punished. The English being ready to declare in favour of Holland, it might have been very difficult for our troops to get back to France: a resolution was therefore taken to quit that kingdom; and M. de la Feuillade, having the command of this expedition, embarked the forces on board his fleet the 8th of April, with as many of the inhabitants of Messina in the interest of France, as he could conveniently take along with him. Count Konigsmark vanquishes the Danes the 18th of January in the isle of Rugen, but is obliged to abandon this island the 22d of September. The castle of Elsimburg surrendered to the Danes the 7th of July: they raise the siege of Bahus the 21st. The king of Sweden retakes Christianstadt the 14th of August. The elector of Brandenburg makes himself master of Stralsund the 18th of October, and of Gripswald the 25th.

The peace of Nimeguen, the conditions of which were dictated by the king. There were three treaties; the first between France and Holland, signed the 10th of August; the second with Spain, signed the 17th of September; and the third with the emperor and the empire, exclusive of the elector of Brandenburg, and some other princes. But what is very remarkable in the treaty with the Dutch; though they had been the only object of the war of 1672, they were the only power to whom full restitution was made. By the treaty with Spain it was agreed, that the king should keep possession of Franche Comté, as also of the towns of Valenciennes, Condé, Bouchain, Cambray, Aire, St. Omers, Ipres, Warneton, Poperingue, Bailleul, Cassel, Menin, Bavay, Maubeuge, and Charlemont. The treaty with the emperor was not signed till the 5th of February, 1679; and the basis thereof was that of Munster: by one of the articles, the king resigns to his imperial majesty his right to Philipsburg, and the emperor cedes his pretensions to Friburg in favour of the king; Huninghen, then no more than a simple redoubt, was relinquished to the French, and is since become a fortress, that commands the whole head of the Rhine. The duke of Lorrain, dissatisfied with the conditions of this treaty, was not included therein, and therefore did not recover his dominions till the peace of Ryswick. But what does honour to his majesty, he obtained a full restitution to his ally the king of Sweden, of the several possessions wrested from that prince by the king of Denmark, and the elector of Brandenburg. Yet this did not hinder Sir William Temple from saying, that the French ambassadors had treated the affairs of Sweden with great indifference; nor Puffendorff from mentioning the speech of the chancellor Oxenstiern, " That for a subsidy of three millions from France, " it had cost the crown of Sweden fifty, besides the loss of the " reputation of her arms." The king of Sweden, as it generally happens in time of war, had also increased his prerogative at home. After the first treaty signed with Holland, on the 10th of August, the prince of Orange, feigning ignorance, attacked the duke of Luxemburg at St. Denis, near Mons, the 14th of August: the French had blockaded that city, to obtain satisfaction for the king of Sweden; the prince's pretence was to oblige them to raise the blockade; but in truth he only wanted to protract the war, and to surprize the duke of Luxemburg: this insincerity contributed to give a new lustre to the French arms; the battle was bloody, and the advantage on our side.

Buffy Lamet, being informed of the intrigues of his wife with the marquis d'Albret, obliges that lady to make an assignation to her gallant, in which M. d'Albret is murdered: he was

half

REMARKABLE EVENTS under LEWIS XIV.

half brother to the marshal d'Albret, both bastards of the house of Albret: Stephen, from whom they were descended, had been legitimated by Francis I. The marquis d'Albret having on this occasion absented himself from the army, with leave of the marshal de Schomberg, M. de Louvois wrote word to the latter, that the king had been greatly surprized, at his granting a furlough to a general officer without his majesty's orders.

1679.

The death of the cardinal de Retz. It is difficult to comprehend how a man that spent his whole life in cabals, should have had no fixed object in view. He loved to intrigue, merely for intriguing sake; he was a vast genius, enterprizing, artful, and somewhat romantic; making an ill use of the authority which his station of life gave him over the people, to render religion subservient to politicks; and often ascribing to his own sagacity, effects that were only owing to chance. He waged war against the king, merely from a spirit of rebellion; he loved magnificence, and had a fund of wit, but was of a restless temper, having more sallies of imagination than connexion of thought, and more chimeras than real designs: he was unfit to live under a monarchy, yet void of the qualities necessary for a republican, being neither a loyal subject, nor a good citizen: he was as vain as Cicero, but more daring, and not so honest: to be short, he had more sense, but less ambition and less villany than Catiline. His memoirs are very agreeable; but it is surprizing, that a man should have the courage, or rather the folly, to say worse things of himself, than could have been advanced by his greatest enemy. And yet this very person, towards the decline of life, was intirely changed; being grown meek and peaceable, an enemy to intrigue, and beloved by all honest men; as if his former ambition had not been a real passion, but an effervescency of youth, which naturally subsided with age. After having lived with vast magnificence, and contracted debts to the sum of upwards of four millions of livres, the whole was paid, either in his life time, or after his decease.

As the peace with the emperor was not concluded till the beginning of this year, Nuitz was taken in the month of January, and

and restored to the elector of Cologne, as soon as the emperor signed the treaty.

The elector of Brandenburg at length accedes to the peace the 29th of June: which was owing to the losses he had sustained in the course of this campaign. Calvo dispossessed him of the town and dutchy of Cleves on the 25th of March. The marquis de Sourdis took Lipstadt the 14th of May, and the marshal de Crequy beat him twice in the neighbourhood of Minden. The whole empire agreed to the treaty of Nimeguen in the course of this year.

Mary Louisa, daughter of the duke of Orleans, and of Henrietta of England, is married at Burgos to Charles II, king of Spain, the 18th of November.

The death of madam de Longueville, the 15th of April. Every body knows the part she acted in the civil war. Being the sister of the great Condé, she espoused his cause, as much from a love of intrigue, as from friendship to her brother. Cardinal de Retz says of her, *that from the heroine of a great party, she became their female Quixote.* The prince of Marsillac, afterwards duke de la Rochefoucaud (author of the Maxims) had been extremely fond of this princess. The chambers of the edict of Nantes in the parliaments of Toulouse and Bourdeaux are suppressed. The death of Don John of Austria, natural son of Philip IV, on the 17th of September, a prince of merit, and persecuted by the queen dowager of Spain.

The disgrace of M. de Pomponne, secretary of state for foreign affairs, who had succeeded M. de Lionne in 1671: his place was given to M. Colbert de Croissy, brother of the comptroller-general, who at that time was in Bavaria, negotiating the marriage of the dauphin. Among other things laid to M. de Pomponne's charge, was his not having included the villages between Friburg and Brisac in the treaty of Nimeguen: and indeed when the king had made his entry into Strasburg, and wanted to pay a visit to Friburg, he was obliged to dine in this town without stopping by the way, because the intermediate lands belonged to the empire. This mistake would not perhaps have been taken notice of, no more than some other inadvertencies imputed to M. de Pomponne, if M. de Louvois and M. Colbert

bert had not longed for his place: they both concurred, contrary to their usual custom, to the same end; but M. de Louvois, who acted for M. Courtin, was very much surprized to see the preference given to the president Colbert.

1680.

The first settlement of the French in the East-Indies, by confirming the acquisition of Pondichery in 1674.

The declaration of the 11th of January against poisoners and fortune-tellers. La Voisin is burnt the 22d of February, having been convicted of administering poison; several, whom an idle curiosity led to her house, were involved in this affair. The dutchess of Bouillon appeared before the judges; the countess of Soissons made her escape to Flanders; and the marshal de Luxemburg was sent to the Bastile, but soon recovered his liberty. Antonietta Bourignon dies at Franecker; she was an enthusiastic preacher, and had many disciples.

Madam de Montespan secures to herself a more independent rank at court, by giving two hundred thousand crowns for the place of superintendant of the queen's household, which the countess of Soissons was obliged to sell her.

Lewis the Great (for now this title was given him, even with the consent of foreign nations) causes Sar Louis to be fortified, in order to cover Lorrain, and gives directions for building the fort of Huningen in upper Alsace. The council of Brisac, by an arret of the 22d of March, reunites the lands dismembered from Alsace; and the chambers of Metz, by a like decree of the 22d of April, reunites all the dismembered fiefs of the three bishoprics to the crown. The king publishes an edict the 24th of July for putting these arrets in execution. The princes interested in those reunions, pretended they were a contravention of the peace. These disputes gave rise to a congress at Courtray the next year, and were the first seeds of that animosity, which revived against France, and broke out at length in 1689.

The marriage of the dauphin, on the 7th of March, to Mary Anne Victoria of Bavaria. This princess was so fond of retirement, that it prevented her from being happy in France, where

REMARKABLE EVENTS under LEWIS XIV.

she might have had great influence and authority, had she studied to please the king: but she liked to spend her days in her apartment, with a German waiting woman, named Beſſola: after many ineffectual endeavours, his majesty resigned her to her favourite ſolitude; and the natural consequence was, that no body took any further notice of her. The dutcheſs of Richelieu was appointed her lady of honour, which poſt she had held under the queen ever ſince the death of madam de Montauſier; and to make her amends, her husband was made knight of honour or chief gentleman-uſher to the dauphineſs. This princeſs had two tiring ladies, madam *la marechale* de Rochefort, and madam de Maintenon: the former was afterwards lady of honour to the dutcheſs of Chartres; the latter, through modeſty, refuſed the place of lady of honour, upon the death of the dutcheſs of Richelieu, and procured it for the dutcheſs of Arpajon. The king appoints eight perſons of quality, who were called Minions, with a penſion of ſix thouſand livres, to attend the dauphin.

Lewis XIV. gives orders for making the Spaniards lower their flag to the French; and viſits the ports of Flanders with the queen and all his court.

The 26th of December appeared the largeſt comet that had ever been ſeen. On this occaſion M. Caſſini publiſhed his ſyſtem concerning the periodical return of comets, of which our deſcendants will be able to form a judgment. The ſame comet procured us the treatiſe of Mr. Bayle, intitled, *Various thoughts upon a comet*. This phænomenon ſtruck a great terror into the minds of the people: but *we are too much aſtoniſhed at uncommon events, and not enough at thoſe which happen every day*. Foundation of a profeſſorſhip for the French law. The preceding year there had been an edict for the re-eſtabliſhment of *lectures on the civil inſtitutes, in conjunction with thoſe of the canon law*. We are ſurprized at finding a decretal of pope Honorius III, in 1255, whereby this pontif prohibited the teaching of the civil law in the univerſity of Paris; and ſtill greater is our ſurprize to ſee that Philip the Fair, in purſuance of this decretal, removed that ſchool to Orleans; and that the ordinance of Blois, in 1579, perſiſts in depriving the city of Paris of this aſſiſtance.

This

REMARKABLE EVENTS under LEWIS XIV.

This may be accounted for, by saying that the decretal of pope Honorius was made only with a view to the clergy, left they should be diverted by the study of the civil law, from that of the canon-law and divinity; and our kings had not yet discovered the utility of the civil law. Be that as it may, Lewis XIV. restored things to their right footing, just a hundred years after the ordinance of Blois.

1681.

The king causes the harbours of Brest and Toulon to be completed, and increases his marine with upwards of sixty thousand sailors. On the 23d of July M. du Quesne sinks several vessels belonging to Tripoli, which had taken shelter in the port of Chio; and on the 4th of December, he concluded a peace with that state.

The 19th of May, the canal of Languedoc was made navigable.

The county of Chiney in the Netherlands, is ceded to the Spaniards, the 31st of July. Strasburg surrenders to the king the 20th of September; the capitulation was signed by M. de Louvois, and by M. de Monclar, commandant of Alsace, in the room of the duke de Mazarin, governor of the province: the king makes his entry into that city on the 23d of October, accompanied by the queen, the dauphin, and the whole court. The marquis de Chamilly, famous for the defence of Grave, was made governor of Strasburg: Francis Egon, of Furstem berg, was bishop of that city, and his brother William succeeded him the next year.

At Ensisheim his majesty receives a general deputation of compliment, from the thirteen cantons and their allies.

While Strasburg was capitulating, the marquis de Boufflers, on the 30th of September, took possession of Casal, the capital of Montferrat, subject to the duke of Mantua, who agreed to admit a French garrison into the town, under the command of M. de Catinat. The death of the dutchess de Fontange: the son she had by the king, died soon after he was born.

REMARKABLE EVENTS under LEWIS XIV.

1682.

The edict of 1673, with regard to the *regale*, having been received by the bishops of the assembly of the clergy in 1682, Pope Innocent XI. wrote some briefs to those prelates, containing maxims contrary to the edict. This gave occasion to examine into the propositions presented by the Sorbonne in 1663; and the result of the assembly was the four propositions comprized in the declaration of the deputies of the clergy, concerning ecclesiastic power; the first, that the pope has no authority over the temporalties of kings; the second, that a general council is superior to the pope, pursuant to the declarations in the fourth and fifth sessions of the council of Constance; the third, that the exercise of the apostolic power ought to be regulated by the canons, without infringing the liberties of the Gallican church; the fourth, that it chiefly belongs to the pope to decide in matters of faith, that his decrees bind all churches, but that his decisions are not *infallible*, till they have had the approbation of the church. This declaration was confirmed by the king's edict, verified in parliament the 23d of March.

The king establishes companies of cadets for the land service, and *guard marines* for the navy.

Lewis XIV. fixes his residence at Versailles the 6th of May, and banishes several young people of the first quality from court on account of their morals. Du Bois-Baillet is sent as intendant into the province of Bearn, which never had an officer of that sort before, the whole authority having been engrossed by the parliament of Pau: his business was likewise to preside at the assembly of the states of the province, an office hitherto exercised by the intendant of Guienne, who had each time a particular commission.

In the month of March, a declaration was brought to the parliament, in favour of the duke du Maine, concerning the sovereignty of Dombes, conferred upon him by the princess de Montpensier. The king declares, that he acknowledges the seignory of Dombes, as a sovereignty under his protection, reserving to himself, as his predecessors had done, *homage and fealty*, which is to be yielded as from a lesser sovereign to his protector, and not as from a subject to his king, or from a vas-

REMARKABLE EVENTS under LEWIS XIV.

fal to his lord; that he grants to the lords of Dombes the judicial power in the laft refort, and forbids the parliament of Paris to include the country of Dombes any longer in the rolls of the province of Lyonnois, and others, fubject to their jurifdiction. This declaration only reftored the princes of Dombes to the rights, which they had enjoyed before the confifcation of that feignory, under the conftable of Bourbon. The principality of Dombes came to the branch of Bourbon by Lewis II, duke of Bourbon, to whom Edward de Beaujeu made a prefent of it in 1400.

The king fends M. de Menars, intendant of Paris, and brother-in-law to M. Colbert, to the Huguenot meeting-houfe at Charenton, to afk them what profeffion of faith they followed, none but that of Calvin being tolerated in France: this was done very wifely to difunite thofe people, for indeed there were hardly any two of them of the fame belief. M. Juftel, a Calvinift, at the age of fifty-fix, having efpoufed mademoifelle de Lorme, his near relation, with a difpenfation from the chancellor, caufed the ceremony to be performed in the Englifh ambaffador's chapel, out of contempt to the minifters of Charenton, whom he would not confult: but as he immediately imparted his marriage to M. Simon, this gentleman told him it was void, and that he was as much obliged as thofe of the Catholic religion, to be married *coram proprio parocho* *. The confequence was, that he prefented a petition to the civil lieutenant, in order to confirm his nuptials: and it was ordained, that purfuant to the laws of the kingdom, he fhould be married in the parifh of Charenton. (*Simon's Letters.*)

The birth of the duke of Burgundy on the 6th of Auguft.

The bombardment of Algiers by M. du Quefne, the 30th of the fame month. The machine of Marli is conftructed.

The inftitution of a royal academy at Nifmes.

The dauphin is admitted into the council of difpatches: this council, at firft, was fomewhat different from what it is at prefent; the members, even the chancellor himfelf, were obliged to ftand all the time; none were permitted to fit, except the fecretary of

---

* In his own parifh church.

state, when he wrote; but then they were not a court of judicature.

1683.

The death of the queen Maria Therefa, aged forty-five years, on the 30th of July, upon her return from a journey with the king to Burgundy and Alface. We cannot give a jufter idea of the virtue of this princefs, and, at the fame time, of the elevation of her fentiments, than by recording her anfwer to a Carmelite nun, whofe affiftance fhe had defired in examining her confcience for a general confeffion: the nun afked her, whether before her marriage, fhe had never defired to render herfelf agreeable to fome of the young nobility of the court of Madrid: *O no, mother*, replied fhe, *there were no kings among them.*

The death of M. Colbert, at the age of fixty-four, on the 6th of September. France muft ever lament the lofs of this her greateft minifter; to whom the fplendor and profperity of the prefent reign, the grandeur of the fovereign, and the felicity of the people, muft be abfolutely attributed: it was by his means the arts and manufactures were carried to that degree of perfection, which has rendered the reign of Lewis XIV. the moft brilliant of our whole monarchy. And what is very remarkable, perhaps this fignal encouragement of the polite arts, did not entirely proceed from his own tafte and knowledge: it was as a ftatefman that he took the artifts and men of learning under his protection, knowing that they alone are capable of perpetuating the glory of empires. He was no more than eight days ill; and it is faid that he died in difgrace; an inftructing leffon to minifters! M. Pelletier fucceeds him in the place of comptroller-general.

Algiers is again bombarded by M. du Quefne, the 26th and the 27th of June. M. de Tourville obliges the Algerines the year following to fue for peace. The fiege of Vienna, undertaken by the grand vizir, Cara Muftapha, with an army of two hundred thoufand men. The emperor and emprefs withdraw from Vienna. Sobiefky, king of Poland, feconded by the duke of Lorrain, obliges the Turks to raife the fiege the 12th of September: this engagement, in which the infidels were
put

REMARKABLE EVENTS under LEWIS XIV.

put to flight, did not coſt the Chriſtian army above ſix hundred men; and the Turks loſt no more than eight hundred. The emperor, at his return, received the king of Poland very cooly, doubtleſs, becauſe his obligation to him was too great. There happened two actions afterwards between the Poles and the Turks, one the 7th, and the other the 9th, of October: in the former, the Turks were victorious, and Sobieſky was in imminent danger of his life; in the latter, where the duke of Lorrain was preſent, the Turks were diſcomfited. This prince and Sobieſky make themſelves maſters of the town of Gran, the 26th of October. Theſe ſucceſſes of the Chriſtian army coſt Cara Muſtapha his life, for he was ſtrangled by order of the grand ſignior. This miniſter having ſucceeded Croprogli, was bribed by Dutch money in the year 1677, to hinder M. de Nointel, the French ambaſſador at the Porte, from continuing to enjoy the honours of the ſopha; he likewiſe did every thing in his power to mortify that ambaſſador, ſo as to find fault with his rejoicings for the ſucceſſes of Lewis XIV. But M. de Guilleragues, his ſucceſſor, having refuſed to receive audience, till this honour was granted him, at length obtained it in 1682. By the execution of the vizir the year following, France was revenged of his inſolence.

The king has once more recourſe to arms, to enforce the execution of the treaty of Nimeguen. The marſhal d'Humieres lays ſiege to Courtray, and carries it the 6th of November. The count de Vermandois, the king's natural ſon, who was preſent at this ſiege, died a few days after. Dixmude ſurrenders the 10th. The marſhal de Crequy bombards Luxemburg. The birth of the duke of Anjou (Philip V.) on the 19th of December. The king appoints the marſhal de Noailles governor to the duke de Chartres; but Noailles dying the ſame year, marſhal d'Eſtrades ſucceeded him, and deceaſed in 1686; which made Benſerade ſay, that there was no poſſibility of keeping a governor for the duke de Chartres. The marſhal d'Eſtrades had the viceroyalty of America, which, at his deceaſe, was given to the marſhal d'Etrées. The duke de la Vieuville is appointed governor to the duke de Chartres.

REMARKABLE EVENTS under LEWIS XIV.

The king of Poland in vain attempts to effectuate an accommodation between the emperor and Tekely.

1684.

The marshal de Bellefons beats the duke de Bournonville, on the 12th of May, at Pontmayor in Catalonia, and lays siege to Gironne, which he was obliged to raise on the 23d, for want of the necessary reinforcements. The duke of Savoy, on the 8th of May, espouses Anna Maria, the second daughter of the duke of Orleans; the eldest had been married to Charles II, king of Spain. From this match sprung the dutchess of Burgundy, mother of the present king, as also the first wife of Philip V.

The Genoese, contrary to their alliance with France, maintained a correspondence with the Spaniards, and even with the Algerines, so as to favour the depredations of those corsairs: M. de St. Olon demanded satisfaction of that state, and they refused it: upon which the king causes Genoa to be bombarded, in the month of May, by the marquis du Quesne. M. de Seignelay was on board the fleet.

Luxemburg surrendered the 4th of June to the marshal de Crequy, after four and twenty days open trenches. The king took some ladies with him to the army, and covered the siege. M. de Belingue maintains an engagement in the Mediterranean, the 10th of July, against five and twenty Spanish gallies.

An ambassador from Algiers makes a submission to the king, the 4th of July. The Algerines had released a great number of Christian slaves of all nations, out of respect to the king, and consigned them into the hands of M. d'Amfreville: some Englishmen among them would have it, that they had been set at liberty merely through fear of their sovereign; d'Amfreville proved the contrary, by delivering them back to the Algerines, who bound them once more in chains.

The truce of Ratisbon for twenty years, signed the 10th of August, between France and Spain, and the 16th, between France and the empire: the pensionary Fagel, intirely devoted to the prince of Orange, used all his endeavours to oppose it: the king keeps possession of Luxemburg. The envoys of Siam had an audience of M. de Seignelay and of M. de Croissy at Versailles;

The THIRD RACE.

REMARKABLE EVENTS under LEWIS XIV.

failles; they faw the king in the gallery the 27th of November, as he went to mafs, but were not admitted to an audience. The king of Siam had fent another embaffy in 1680, but thofe appointed to that office were loft at fea. The chevalier de Chaumont was nominated ambaffador to the king of Siam, the beginning of the next year; and the abbé de Choify accompanied him thither in a public character. The relation he gave of that voyage, is well known.

The duke of Lorrain, after obtaining feveral advantages over the Turks in the courfe of this campaign, is obliged to raife the fiege of Buda, the 1ft of November; which he had begun the 1ft of July.

The king having, in the year 1674, reunited the bailiwick of the *palais*, and all the judicial courts of the feignories in the city and fuburbs of Paris; having reunited them, I fay, to the Chatelet, created a new prefidial feat by the fame edict, with the fame number of officers, as thofe of the ancient Chatelet. But the two courts of judicature being continually at variance about the limits of their jurifdiction, and thefe difputes difturbing the order of the civil polity, his majefty fuppreffed the new Chatelet, ten years after its erection: thofe who had not been incorporated in the ancient Chatelet, were reimburfed their expences; and the king reftored the bailiwick of the *palais*, and part of the feignorial jurifdictions, which had been fuppreffed.

The death of the princefs Palatine, the 6th of July; fhe was daughter to the duke of Mantua, and younger fifter of the queen of Poland: fhe married prince Edward, fon of the elector Palatine, king of Bohemia, after the duke of Guife (known by his adventures at Naples) had broke his word to her: fhe was mother of the princefs of Condé, of the dutchefs of Hanover, and of the prince of Solmes. It is well known what part fhe acted at court.

1685.

The death of Charles II, king of England, on the 16th of February. *He had great vices, but fcarce any virtues to correct them: he had in him fome vices, that were lefs hurtful, which corrected his more hurtful ones.* (Burnet's hift. of his own time, vol. I. p. 612.) Hamilton alfo faid of this prince, that he was capable of any atchievement whatever in cases of emergency, but at other times quite indolent, and utterly averse to application. He was succeeded by his brother king James II. The public is indebted to this prince, when only duke of York, (and that was the most brilliant part of his life) for the contrivance of signals on board a fleet, by the means of flags and streamers: this invention was afterwards perfected by the marshal de Tourville. The pope intercedes in behalf of the Genoese; the king promises his holiness, he will not possess himself of their city, or territory, provided they make him proper satisfaction: in consequence hereof, the doge, Francesco Maria Imperiali, attended by four senators, pays his submission in person to the king the 15th of May: he was covered at the audience in the gallery, where his majesty received him with great ceremony. By the laws of Genoa, the doge loses his dignity, whenever he quits the precincts of that city: but the king insisted, that this law should not take effect on the present occasion, otherwise it would have been no more than giving audience to a private gentleman.

As the Genoese, at that time, felt the effects of the king's clemency, so they experienced, in a more distinguished manner, the protection of Lewis XV. in 1746, when the queen of Hungary, by an unjust, but most vigorous attempt, possessed herself of Genoa, and plundered that capital. In vain did those brave republicans expel the German forces; they would have been overpowered at last by an exasperated enemy, if Lewis XV. had not stood up in their defence, and ordered the duke of Boufflers, who died in that expedition, and afterwards the marshal duke de Richelieu, to fly to their assistance: further, this prince suspending the course of his victories, to promote the advantage and welfare of his allies, gave peace to his enemies at Aix-la-Chapelle, reinstated Genoa in her ancient possessions, and considered himself as a sufficient gainer, by convincing all Europe, that his equity and moderation were not inferior to his valour, and to the terror of his arms.

The feast of Sceau, with which the king was entertained the 16th of July, by M. de Seignelay. The preceding month there
had

REMARKABLE EVENTS under LEWIS XIV.

had been a carousal at Versailles. The duke of Orleans espouses mademoiselle de Nantes, the king's legitimated daughter, the 24th of July.

The marshal d'Etrées bombards Tripoly the 22d of June: from thence he sails to Tunis; and this city concludes a peace with the king the 30th of August.

The rebellion of the duke of Monmouth, a natural son of Charles II, who is taken in arms, and beheaded the 25th of July.

The duke of Bavaria marries the daughter of the emperor Leopold: by this princess he had a son, whom Charles II, king of Spain, appointed his heir by his first will; but whose violent death (as it is reported,) gave occasion to a second will, which placed Philip V. on the throne of Spain.

The battle of Gran, in which the duke of Lorrain and the elector of Bavaria defeated the Turks the 16th of August: this victory was followed by the taking of Neuhausel, which after a gallant defence was carried by assault the 19th of the same month. The princes of Conty, the prince of Turenne, and other French volunteers, who served this campaign in Hungary, distinguished themselves on that occasion.

The revocation of the edict of Nantes, by an edict of the 22d of October. Tekely, being suspected by the Turks, is arrested: his imprisonment was the cause of the loss of Cassovia, of which the Imperialists made themselves masters the 25th of October. The death of the prince of Conty at Fontainebleau the 12th of November, of the small-pox, which he catched from his wife, the king's daughter: he had no issue by that princess. His brother, the prince of Roche-fur-you, continued this branch, by marrying the eldest daughter of the prince of Condé.

The death of the chancellor Tellier at Paris, the 31st of October; he was succeeded by M. Boucherat. M. de Guilleragues, the king's ambassador, dies at Constantinople: he procured the restoration of the honours of the sopha, which M. de Nointel had imprudently lost.

1686.

REMARKABLE EVENTS under LEWIS XIV.

1686.

The foundation of St. Cyr *; the king had already reunited the *menfa abbatialis* of St. Denis to this houfe, but that reunion was not confirmed by the pope till the year 1690. This community was before at Noify: madam de Maintenon affumed the title of fuperior of the houfe, with all the privileges of a founder of that eftablifhment: hither fhe retired upon the death of the king; and here fhe died, at the age of eighty-three, the 15th of April 1719. M. de Chaumont returns to France with the ambaffadors of the king of Siam, who had an audience in the gallery the 1ft of September.

The marfhal d'Eftrées appears before Cadiz with the king's fleet, and compels the Spaniards to fatisfy the French merchants in regard to fifteen hundred thoufand livres, which were withheld from them on frivolous pretences. The taking of Buda by the duke of Lorrain, the 18th of September; this prince committed a confiderable miftake in not marching immediately againft the Ottoman army, when their confternation was fo great, that they might have been eafily deftroyed.

The ftatue of the *place des victoires*, erected by the marfhal de Feuillade, in honour of the king, the 28th of March.

The birth of the duke of Berry the 31ft of Auguft.

The much lamented death of M. de Nicolay, firft prefident of the chamber of accounts; his fon fucceeded him in this office at the age of twenty-eight; he was the eighth firft prefident of his family. One of their anceftors, named John de Nicolay, was chancellor to Lewis XII, in the kingdom of Naples. M. de Vendome receives the dauphin at Anet, where Acis and Galatea, the laft opera of Lully, was reprefented.

Ranuzzi, the nuncio, had the honour of dining with the king, the 6th of November, after receiving the cardinal's cap from the hands of his majefty.

The operation of cutting for the fiftula performed on the king the 18th of November.

---

* A community for three hundred young gentlewomen, who are carefully educated here, from the age of feven till twenty, when they are either provided with fome advantageous match, or, if their inclination fo leads them, are fent to a nunnery.

REMARKABLE EVENTS under LEWIS XIV.

had been a carousal at Versailles. The duke of Orleans espouses mademoiselle de Nantes, the king's legitimated daughter, the 24th of July.

The marshal d'Etrées bombards Tripoly the 22d of June: from thence he sails to Tunis; and this city concludes a peace with the king the 30th of August.

The rebellion of the duke of Monmouth, a natural son of Charles II, who is taken in arms, and beheaded the 25th of July.

The duke of Bavaria marries the daughter of the emperor Leopold: by this princess he had a son, whom Charles II, king of Spain, appointed his heir by his first will; but whose violent death (as it is reported,) gave occasion to a second will, which placed Philip V. on the throne of Spain.

The battle of Gran, in which the duke of Lorrain and the elector of Bavaria defeated the Turks the 16th of August: this victory was followed by the taking of Neuhausel, which after a gallant defence was carried by assault the 19th of the same month. The princes of Conty, the prince of Turenne, and other French volunteers, who served this campaign in Hungary, distinguished themselves on that occasion.

The revocation of the edict of Nantes, by an edict of the 22d of October. Tekely, being suspected by the Turks, is arrested: his imprisonment was the cause of the loss of Cassovia, of which the Imperialists made themselves masters the 25th of October. The death of the prince of Conty at Fontainebleau the 12th of November, of the small-pox, which he catched from his wife, the king's daughter: he had no issue by that princess. His brother, the prince of Roche-sur-you, continued this branch, by marrying the eldest daughter of the prince of Condé.

The death of the chancellor Tellier at Paris, the 31st of October; he was succeeded by M. Boucherat. M. de Guilleragues, the king's ambassador, dies at Constantinople: he procured the restoration of the honours of the sopha, which M. de Nointel had imprudently lost.

1686.

REMARKABLE EVENTS under LEWIS XIV.

1686.

The foundation of St. Cyr *; the king had already reunited the *menſa abbatialis* of St. Denis to this houſe, but that reunion was not confirmed by the pope till the year 1690. This community was before at Noiſy: madam de Maintenon aſſumed the title of ſuperior of the houſe, with all the privileges of a founder of that eſtabliſhment: hither ſhe retired upon the death of the king; and here ſhe died, at the age of eighty-three, the 15th of April 1719. M. de Chaumont returns to France with the ambaſſadors of the king of Siam, who had an audience in the gallery the 1ſt of September.

The marſhal d'Eſtrées appears before Cadiz with the king's fleet, and compels the Spaniards to ſatisfy the French merchants in regard to fifteen hundred thouſand livres, which were withheld from them on frivolous pretences. The taking of Buda by the duke of Lorrain, the 18th of September; this prince committed a conſiderable miſtake in not marching immediately againſt the Ottoman army, when their conſternation was ſo great, that they might have been eaſily deſtroyed.

The ſtatue of the *place des victoires*, erected by the marſhal de Feuillade, in honour of the king, the 28th of March.

The birth of the duke of Berry the 31ſt of Auguſt.

The much lamented death of M. de Nicolay, firſt preſident of the chamber of accounts; his ſon ſucceeded him in this office at the age of twenty-eight; he was the eighth firſt preſident of his family. One of their anceſtors, named John de Nicolay, was chancellor to Lewis XII, in the kingdom of Naples. M. de Vendome receives the dauphin at Anet, where Acis and Galatea, the laſt opera of Lully, was repreſented.

Ranuzzi, the nuncio, had the honour of dining with the king, the 6th of November, after receiving the cardinal's cap from the hands of his majeſty.

The operation of cutting for the fiſtula performed on the king the 18th of November.

* A community for three hundred young gentlewomen, who are carefully educated here, from the age of ſeven till twenty, when they are either provided with ſome advantageous match, or, if their inclination ſo leads them, are ſent to a nunnery.

REMARKABLE EVENTS under LEWIS XIV.

The death of the great Condé, at Fontainebleau, at the age of sixty-six, on the 11th of December: the title of *great*, which was given to this hero by the whole nation, has perpetuated his glory; and the most celebrated orators have exhausted themselves in his praises. He had resided at Chantilly ever since his retreat, from whence he went to see his granddaughter, the dutchess of Orleans, at Fontainebleau, where she was ill of the small-pox: perhaps the desire of paying his court to the king might have occasioned this journey, as much as his regard for that princess's health; no body would have imagined this in 1652; it was his intention without doubt, after having committed the same faults as his father, to give the same example of repentance, and submission. He was greatly afflicted with the gout, which made him refuse the command of the army in 1676: struck with the example of general Wrangel, who by means of the gout and gravel had lost all his former reputation, and at the same time done immense prejudice to Sweden, he told the king, that every man, if he were wise, ought to dread the same misfortune.

The camp of Maintenon for the construction of the aqueduct: the marquis d'Huxelles commanded the troops; and Caillavel, captain of the guards, acted as aid-major.

Foundation of the academy of Angers.

1687.

The famous league of Augsburg, projected the preceding year, is concluded during the carnival at Venice, at which the duke of Savoy and the elector of Bavaria were present. The promoter of this league was the prince of Orange, whose aim was only to embroil matters: the new elector Palatine, duke of Newburg, entered into the alliance with great warmth; he looked upon it as his interest to raise all the enemies he could against the king, in order to prevent him from supporting the pretensions of the dutchess of Orleans, to the inheritance of the late elector her brother. The emperor, the king of Spain, the elector of Brandenburg, &c. in a word, all the confederates in the last war joined in this alliance.

REMARKABLE EVENTS under LEWIS XIV.

By a separate article of the treaty between England and Holland, it was stipulated, that those two powers should engage to assist the house of Austria, "upon the demise of Charles II. without lawful heirs, in seizing and keeping possession of the Spanish monarchy;" so early did that event employ the attention of Europe.

The affair of the franchises contributed not a little to strengthen the league of Augsburg. Pope Innocent XI. had taken the resolution to abolish the privileges enjoyed by ambassadors at Rome, not only in their own palaces, but in the whole ward, or quarter, in which they resided: all the foreign ministers had consented to this regulation; but the king having just reasons to be dissatisfied with the pope, would maintain his rights. The death of the duke d'Estrées, his ambassador at Rome, appeared to that court a very proper opportunity for suppressing this privilege, which no other foreign minister enjoyed: accordingly his holiness issues out a bull the 12th of May, abolishing the franchises of the quarter of the ambassadors at Rome, and excommunicating such, as should pretend to maintain this privilege. Under these circumstance, M. de Lavardin, being nominated by the king in the place of the duke d'Estrées, arrived at Rome on the 16th of November, with a numerous retinue: the pope being convinced of the king's intention, interdicted the church of St. Lewis, where M. de Lavardin had performed his devotions on Christmas night.

The states of Hungary are compelled to declare their crown hereditary in favour of the house of Austria: and the archduke Joseph is crowned king of that realm the 19th of December.

The palace of Versailles was finished this year; the king had resided here some time.

The death of the duke, and of the marshal de Crequy. The duke de Gesvres succeeds the former in the government of Paris.

1688.

M. de Lavardin had published his protests in the city of Rome, so early as the 27th of December, against the pontifical excommunications on account of the franchises: the attor-

REMARKABLE EVENTS under LEWIS XIV.

...ey general appeals to a general council from the bull of the 2th of May, and from the sentence of the interdict pronounced ...he 26th of December: the parliament received his appeal; the ...uncio at Paris was arrested; and the king seized Avignon, in ...he same manner, as in 1663.

The causes which rekindled the war, were as follow. The ...mbrage, which France continued to give, by asserting her ...ights derived from the treaty of Nimeguen; the king's preten-...ons in behalf of his sister-in-law, the dutchess of Orleans, to ...he succession of Charles the late elector Palatine; the affair of ...he franchises; the election to the archbishopric and electorate ...f Cologne, which was conferred on the prince of Bavaria at ...he sollicitation of pope Innocent XI, notwithstanding the instances ...ade by the king in favour of the cardinal de Furstenberg; ...stly, the invasion of England by the prince of Orange, and ...ie discovery of the league of Augsburg: all these considerations ...duced the king to have recourse again to arms.

The marquis de Boufflers, after taking Keiserlauter, the 20th of ...eptember, makes himself master of Creutznach and Oppenheim. ...M. d'Huxelles possesses himself of Neustat. The French seized ...eilbrun, the 15th of October, Heidelberg and Mentz the ...5th: Montclar invested Philipsburg, and the dauphin laid siege ...o it in person, having under him the marshal de Duras to com-...and the army, and M. de Vauban to direct the siege; this town ...zing ill defended by M. de Staremberg, surrendered on the 29th; ...ie next day the chevalier de Longueville was killed by an acci-...ent. This same town was besieged in 1734 by the duke of ...erwick, (who was killed by a cannon-ball) and taken by ...arshal d'Asfeld, but restored to the empire by the treaty ...f Vienna in 1738. The dauphin makes himself master of Man-...eim, the 11th of November, and of Frankendal the 18th. ...oblentz is bombarded, to punish the elector of Triers for ad-...itting the troops of the elector of Saxony into that town; the ...rench also possess themselves of Triers, Spire, Worms, &c. ...he duke of Orleans, and the prince of Conty, served in this ...ampaign, as well as the duke du Maine.

Belgrade is stormed the 6th of September, by the elector of ...avaria: prince Lewis of Baden had defeated fifteen thousand ...urks the 6th of August. The

REMARKABLE EVENTS under LEWIS XIV.

The revolution in England. The prince of Orange, attended by the marſhal de Schomberg, ſet ſail for that kingdom, the 30th of Oct. but contrary winds obliging him to put back into Holland, he did not depart from thence till the 11th of Nov. The 15th he landed at Torbay. King James had received early intelligence of this deſign from the king of France, but was too late convinced of the truth of it; he advanced however at the head of his army as far as Saliſbury, where finding himſelf abandoned by all the world, and even by his favourite Churchill, (afterwards duke of Marlborough) he returned to his capital: being obliged to withdraw from thence, he embarked for France the 22d, and was invited back to London, where his ſtay was very ſhort; for upon receiving an order from his ſon-in-law, the prince of Orange, he quitted that capital the 27th, never to ſee it more, and retired to Rocheſter *. M. de Seignelay propoſed to the king, to fit out a fleet of forty men of war, which ſhould be ready to intercept the Dutch ſquadron; but M. de Louvois oppoſed this ſcheme, and was for making a diverſion; this would have been right, if we had laid ſiege to Maeſtricht, which would have employed the republic; but the ſiege of Philipſburg alarming all Germany, the Dutch were at liberty to act where they thought proper.

The king declares war againſt Holland, on the 3d of December. Marſhal d'Eſtrées had bombarded Algiers the 1ſt of July.

The arret of the 15th of February, condemning Langlade to the gallies, for a robbery committed on M. de Montgomery; the real robber, who was taken in 1690 for other crimes, acknowledged this fact. The death of mademoiſelle de Guiſe the

* The king, upon his arrival at Saliſbury found he could not depend on the army, and therefore returned to London, where he convened the few lords who were then in that city, and declared he would call a free parliament, which was accordingly appointed to meet the 15th of January. The prince ſends propoſals to the king, which he was going to accept, when his fears induced him to retire to France, whither he had ſent the queen and the young prince before him. He left London in the night between the 10th and 11th of December; but was ſeized at Feverſham by ſome people, who not knowing his perſon, uſed him with great rudeneſs. The lords in London invited the king back to Whitehall, where he was received with great reſpect, on the 26th of December. The prince of Orange, in the mean time, ſent ſome forces to London, who ſecured Whitehall, and ordered his majeſty to retire to Ham; but upon his deſiring to withdrew to Rocheſter, he obtained his requeſt, and the ſame day, viz. the 28th, the prince of Orange came to London. The king withdrew privately from Rocheſter the 22d, and embarked on board a frigate, which landed him at Ambleteuſe.

13th

REMARKABLE EVENTS under LEWIS XIV.

13th of March; she was the grand-daughter of Henry, killed at Blois a hundred years before.

The revolution in Siam: Opra Pitracha, the king's favourite, usurps the throne, and causes M. Constance, minister of the late king, to be put to death, on the 5th of June: France, by this event, lost her settlements in that kingdom. The emperor possesses himself of Alba Regalis, the 19th of May. The chevalier de Tourville, accompanied by the count d'Estrées, and the count de Chateau Renard, obliges Papachin, vice-admiral of Spain, on the 2d of June, after an engagement, which lasted three hours, to salute the king's flag with nine cannon shot. A new tax on the gentlemen of the law. The queen of England, conducted by the count de Lausun, lands at Calais the 21st of December, with the young prince of Wales, born at London, the 20th of June.

The Beaufort estate erected into a simple dutchy, in favour of Charles-Francis-Frederic de Montmorency-Luxemburg, eldest son of the marshal de Luxemburg, who died in 1695, and father of the present duke of Luxemburg. The name of Beaufort was changed the next year for that of Montmorency: eight years afterwards (in 1696) the estate of Chatillon-sur-Loing was made a dukedom, in favour of Paul Sigismund de Montmorency-Luxemburg, the marshal's third son, by letters patent of the month of February.

The dauphin is allowed to vote in the council of finances.

1689.

A grand promotion of the knights of the order of the Holy Ghost; this was the 8th made by the king, and the 28th since the original institution. The death of the queen of Spain, for whom her husband had a very great affection; she was said to have been poisoned by the Spanish ministers; but I should rather think it was done by the ministers of Vienna, who were all powerful at Madrid, and disliked the ascendant which the young queen had over the king her husband. The power of the Imperial ministers at the court of Spain was so notorious, that so early as the year 1680, the marchioness de Villars, whose husband was ambassador at Madrid, wrote to madam de Coulanges, " Shall I tell you news, neither the king, nor the two queens, " nor

REMARKABLE EVENTS under LEWIS XIV.

" nor the prime minifter, have any credit here." King James, having retired to Rochefter with the duke of Berwick, his natural fon, arrives on the 7th of January at St. Germains, which the queen had reached the preceding day. M. de Laufun, who attended this princefs in her efcape from London, was at length permitted to come to court.

The throne of England being declared vacant, the eftates affembled under the name of *convention*, fettled the crown, the 17th of February, on the prince and princefs of Orange: they are proclaimed the 24th of the fame month, and crowned the 21ft of April: the fame is done in Scotland.

The diet of Ratifbon proclaims France and the cardinal de Furftemberg enemies of the empire. The prince of Orange declares war againft France the 17th of May: the king makes the fame declaration againft England, and againft the prince of Orange, the 25th of June. There is a vaft difference between this war and that of 1672, when the king of England was neuter, and the king of Sweden made a ftrong diverfion in favour of France. What a difference is there alfo between the year 1648 and 1689. The king then acted as a guarantee of the Germanic liberty; but in 1689 he was become the terror of Germany. This was owing to the prince of Orange, who conftantly exaggerated the ambition of Lewis XIV, in order to conceal his own. The king of Sweden was alfo engaged in the general league, the allies having procured an accommodation betwixt him and Denmark, by the treaty of Altena, to the end that thofe two princes fhould be intirely at leifure to promote the common caufe.

Lewis XIV. makes king James II. embark for Ireland on board a fleet, commanded by Gabaret: he landed in that ifland the 17th of March, and was received by Tyrconnel, the lord lieutenant, who continued to efpoufe his caufe. The count de Chateau Renaud brings him a reinforcement of troops the 12th, and returns to Breft the 28th, after defeating * admiral Herbert, and taking feven Dutch veffels richly laden. The Irifh royalifts

---

* Admiral Herbert, having been prevented by ftrefs of weather, from meeting the enemy at fea, fteered directly for *Bantry bay*, and there was fought this battle, which lafted two hours, when fortune declared in favour of the French.

REMARKABLE EVENTS under LEWIS XIV.

raife the fiege of Londonderry the 13th of July. Lewis XIV. declares war againft the king of Spain, after endeavouring in vain to engage him in the fupport of James II, which was the common caufe of all kings.

Campredon is taken the 23d of May, by the duke de Noailles; he caufed it to be difmantled in the prefence of the enemy, who wanted to retake it.

The king fees himfelf under a neceffity of ravaging the Palatinate, in order to make a barrier between France and his enemies.

The marfhal d'Humieres is beaten at Walcourt the 27th of Auguft by the prince of Waldeck. The elector of Brandenburg makes himfelf mafter of Keyferwert the 28th of June: and the marquis de Boufflers carries Kocheim on the Mofelle the 26th of Auguft.

The enemy lay fiege to Mentz and Bonn: the former, defended by the marquis d'Huxelles, furrenders to duke Charles of Lorrain the 8th of September, after feven weeks open trenches. The marquis d'Huxelles would have held out much longer, if the town had been better ftocked with provifions; but, as this was the province of M. de Louvois, he was fo prudent as not to complain, and that minifter acknowledged the obligation. The marquis began to make his fortune, by afking the place of mufter-mafter-general, at a time when there were hardly any but lieutenant-colonels, who would accept of it: the marfhal d'Harcourt purfued the fame plan. The baron d'Asfeld furrenders the town of Bonn the 12th of October, after a gallant defence: the elector of Brandenburg had formed the fiege; but he was afterwards joined by duke Charles with the Imperial army. M. d'Asfeld died at Aix-la-Chapelle of the wounds he had received at this fiege.

The Algerines are once more obliged to fue for peace, which his majefty granted them on the 25th of September.

M. de Pontchartrain fucceeds as comptroller-general to M. Pelletier, who voluntarily refigned that office, but ftill kept his place as minifter, and the fame feat in council. The king made M. de Seignelay a member of the privy-council; which is what we call being minifter, for fince the year 1659,

REMARKABLE EVENTS under LEWIS XIV.

his majesty never granted any letters-patent of minister of state. The first president de Novion resigns his employment in favour of M. de Harlay, attorney-general; who pays him a hundred thousand crowns upon a *warrant of reserve* *, and sells his place of attorney-general for seven hundred thousand livres to M. de la Briffe, son-in-law of the first president de Novion. M. de Novion, grandson of the first president, purchases the place of president *a mortier* of M. de Croissy, to whom the king grants, in favour of his son M. de Tourcy, the post of secretary of state in reversion. M. de Pomereu is appointed intendant in Britany, where there never had been any such officer. The embassy to Constantinople, is conferred on M. de Chateauneuf, upon the death of M. de Girardin. M. de Beauvilliers, first lord of the bed-chamber, and president of the council of finances, is appointed governor to the duke of Burgundy; and the abbé de Fenelon his preceptor: the abbé de Fleury, who wrote the *ecclesiastic history*, and had been preceptor to the princes of Conty, and to the count de Vermandois, was made sub-preceptor. The king publishes an order for carrying all the plate to the mint, and sets the example himself: the establishment of the *Tontine*, or annuities on survivorship, projected upwards of thirty years before, by a person of the name of Tonti.

A duel between M. de Brionne and M. de Hautefort.

1690.

The death of pope Innocent XI, an avowed enemy of France, (which happened on the 12th of August, the preceding year) and the election of Ottoboni, by the name of Alexander VIII, on the 6th of October, put an end to the disputes between Rome and France. The duke de Chaulnes succeeded M. de Lavardin: the latter had behaved himself very ill in his embassy, by opposing the cardinal d'Estrées in every thing, though he had been directed

---

* The French call it *Brevet de retenue, diploma reservativum*. It is a warrant, which the king grants a person at his entering upon an office, to transmit it to his children after his decease, or to have a part of the purchase money repaid him by his successor. The king seldom grants this warrant, but when the officer has been possessed of his employment a number of years, and his majesty has had reason to be pleased with his conduct.

REMARKABLE EVENTS under LEWIS XIV.

to act in concert with his eminence. The king restored Avignon to the pope, who wrote a brief, full of confidence and esteem, to a person at court in the highest consideration. The death of the dauphiness the 20th of April: a little before she expired, the bishop of Meaux said to the king, who was in her apartment; *it would be proper for your majesty to withdraw: no, no,* answered the king, *it is fit I should see, in what manner my equals depart this life.* Charles V. duke of Lorrain dies, on the 17th of April, at Velz near Lintz, aged about forty-eight. It is said, that he wrote the following letter to the emperor before his decease. " Sacred majesty, pursuant to your orders, I set out from In-
' spruck, in my way to Vienna, but was stopped in this place
' by a higher master; I am going to give an account of a life
' entirely devoted to your service: remember, that I leave be-
' hind me a wife nearly related to you; children to whom I
' have nothing to give but my sword; and subjects groaning
' under oppression." There happened no transaction of any moment on the Rhine, where the dauphin commanded, with the marshal de Lorges under him.

The elector of Bavaria durst not attack Philipsburg.

The battle of Fleurus in the neighbourhood of Charleroy, gained the 1st of July, by the marshal de Luxemburg, against the prince of Waldeck: the marshal was joined by M. de Boufflers, who had the command of a separate corps on the lower Maese, before the prince of Waldeck was apprized of it. M. de Luxemburg caused his cavalry to make a bold movement, which determined the victory in his favour, but was unperceived by the prince of Waldeck, because of the inequality of the ground: by this manœuvre the right wing of the enemy was taken in flank, while the prince of Waldeck imagined we were marching up to him, with a front equal to that of the army under his command. The Dutch cavalry behaved very ill, but their infantry displayed great bravery. The preceding day an attack had been made by order of the duke de Luxemburg, with a view to cover the junction of M. de Boufflers: the duke du Maine commanded in this action, and defeated near two thousand of the enemy's cavalry.

P 2 A battle

REMARKABLE EVENTS under LEWIS XIV.

A battle was fought at sea * the 10th of July, off of Dieppe, in the Channel, in which M. de Tourville, vice-admiral of France, and M. de Chateau-Renaud, defeated the English and Dutch fleets. This victory was complete: the enemy were pursued; and the count d'Estrées, son of the marshal, made a descent at Tinmouth the 5th of August, where he burnt four ships of war belonging to the enemy, and several merchant vessels.

The battle of the Boyne the 11th of July, in which the prince of Orange defeated king James: this victory determined the fate of England; the marshal de Schomberg was killed in the action, and the prince of Orange received a slight hurt from a cannon-ball, which had like to have decided that famous contest. A report of his death being spread at Paris, the inhabitants of this capital gave demonstrations of joy, which did honour to that prince: notwithstanding his victory, he was obliged to raise the siege of Limerick, defended by Boiseleau, a captain of the French guards, and by the Irish troops. May I be permitted to make a reflexion, upon seeing M. de Schomberg in arms against king James, and to revive the memory of a fact, which perhaps cannot be too well known; viz. that this same Schomberg had been lieutenant in the company of Scotch gendarmes commanded by James duke of York. This likewise obliges me to make another remark (*milice Francoise*) viz. that since this company had been created by Charles VII, it was generally commanded by lords or princes of the house of Stuart; and that Mary queen of Scots, after her return to Scotland, desired it should thenceforward be given to a son of the king of Scotland; accordingly Charles I. enjoyed it after the decease of Henry his elder-brother, as also James II. after his father; but it is not certain that Charles II. ever had this commission.

---

* This was the battle of *Beachy-Head*: the French fleet consisted of seventy-eight ships of war, and twenty-two fire ships. The combined fleet did not exceed fifty-five ships of war. Lord Torrington, who led the center, was committed for this misconduct to the Tower. Six Dutch and two English ships of the line were destroyed. Night prevented the total ruin of the Dutch. As to the descent on Tinmouth, the English writers assert, that only a few small craft fell in the hands of the enemy.

The THIRD RACE.

REMARKABLE EVENTS under LEWIS XIV.

The duke of Savoy acting underhand, and in concert with the emperor, reckoned he should be able to surprize us: the king, after fruitless negotiations, being informed of his connexions, declared war against him the 13th of June; and M. de Catinat attacked him the 18th of August at Stafard, where he obtained a complete victory. This advantage was attended with the taking of Saluzzo, and with the surrender of Suza, the 12th of November. While this was transacting, M. de St. Ruth made the conquest of Savoy.

The death of M. de Seignelay the 3d of November; his post of secretary of state for the department of the marine, was given to M. de Pontchartrain, comptroller-general, who was made member of the council. The king created two new offices of presidents *a mortier*, sixteen of counsellors, and a third of advocate-general, with which the late M. Daguesseau, afterwards chancellor, was invested: he likewise instituted the employ of first president of the grand council, which was purchased by M. Bignon, and has since been held by M. de Vertamon his son-in-law; and eight places of presidents: to M. Racine he gave the post of gentleman in ordinary, vacant by the decease of Torf.

The English retake the isle of St. Christopher from the French in the month of December. Mignard succeeds le Brun, as first painter to the king.

1691.

The war against the duke of Savoy continued. M. de Feuquieres, who commanded in Pignerol, attacks the Barbets * on all sides; and keeps the road, through the vallies, free and unmolested, as far as Briançon. M. de Catinat takes Villafranca the 21st of March; Nice the 2d of April; Veillana the 30th of May; Carmagnola the 9th of June, (which was retaken by the enemy) and Montmelian the 21st of December. Bulonde had raised the siege of Coni the 29th of June, upon receiving the news that prince Eugene (who afterwards made so great a figure) was marching to its relief: he was sent prisoner to the citadel of Pignerol.

* The Vaudois in the mountains of Piedmont; they take this name from their ministers, whom they call *Barbes*, which in their language signifies uncle; most of them follow the doctrine of Calvin.

REMARKABLE EVENTS under LEWIS XIV.

On the 9th of April, the king makes himself master of Mons, defended by the prince of Bergue, after a siege of sixteen days; he was attended by all the princes of the blood, and had under him the marshals de Luxemburg and de la Feuillade: it had been invested by M. de Boufflers. The prince of Orange gave some alarm during the siege, by approaching towards our lady of Hall. It was at this siege that the king granted the rank of colonels to the captains of the French and Swifs guards. Lewis XV. ordered the prince of Conty to lay siege to this same town, which was obliged to surrender the 10th of July, 1746, after fifteen days open trenches. M. de Boufflers bombards Liege the 4th of June, to punish the inhabitants for giving admittance to the allies.

The king having left the command of his army to the marshal de Luxemburg, this general encamped under Tournay towards the end of the campaign, waiting till the enemy went into winter-quarters. The prince of Orange, supposing the campaign finished, was returned to Holland, and had resigned the command of the army to the prince of Waldeck, who was encamped at Leuze. The distance from Tournay to Leuze, made the prince of Waldeck imagine he might decamp without using much precaution. The marshal de Luxemburg, having intelligence of this motion, sets out from Tournay with a detachment of cavalry, and defeats his rear-guard at Leuze the 18th of September. The king's houshold and the gendarmes distinguished themselves on this occasion. M. de Luxemburg had no more than twenty-eight squadrons against seventy-five.

The battle of Kilconnel * in Ireland on the 22d of July, won by the English: M. de St. Ruth, who had quitted Savoy, and taken upon him the command of the French troops in Ireland, was slain in the engagement. The surrender of Limerick, and the loss of the whole island, were the consequence of this defeat; yet, in pursuance of the capitulation of Limerick, M. de Chateau-Renaud brought off all the French and 15000 Irish. In Germany, the marshal de Lorges acted upon the defensive.

The duke de Noailles carries la Seu d'Urgel the 11th of July;

* Commonly called the battle of Aghrim.

REMARKABLE EVENTS under LEWIS XIV.

this was an important place, as it opened a paſſage into the kingdom of Arragon.

The death of M. de Louvois, the 16th of July: it is ſaid, that he did not die of a natural cauſe; others imagined that he broke his heart: and indeed towards the latter end of his life, he greatly declined in the king's favour. Though the ſiege of Mons was well conducted, yet his majeſty thought it laſted too long, becauſe the prince of Orange had time to attempt to raiſe it: Bulonde, to juſtify himſelf for his miſcarriage in the ſiege of Coni, was ſaid to have ſhewn a letter from M. de Louvois: the duke of Savoy made uſe of the conduct of that miniſter in reſpect to himſelf, as a pretence for his averſion againſt France: Mentz would have held out much longer, if it had been better provided: the devaſtation of the Palatinate, and laſtly, the bombardment of Liege, all together, are ſaid to have alienated the mind of the king, who was naturally juſt and merciful. M. de Louvois perceived this change in the tranſacting of buſineſs with his majeſty; upon which he drank the waters, and was ſuddenly ſeized with the diſorder that put an end to his life. Be this as it may, for we do not warrant the truth of thoſe facts, M. de Louvois was a perſon of great abilities, eſpecially in the department of war: he eſtabliſhed order and diſcipline in the king's armies, as M. Colbert had done in the finances. He had frequently better information than the general himſelf; he was equally attentive to reward as to puniſh; he was ſparing and generous according to circumſtances; he foreſaw every thing and neglected nothing; joining to the quickeſt and moſt extenſive views, the knowledge of the minuteſt particulars; he obſerved the profoundeſt ſecrecy, and formed enterprizes, which appeared like prodigies, from the ſuddenneſs with which they were executed, and from the ſucceſs, which, in ſpite of the many combinations neceſſary to produce it, was never uncertain: thus the inſtruction to the marſhal d'Humieres for the ſiege of Ghent, was conſidered as a maſter-piece. But we could have wiſhed that he had not carried his zeal for the glory of his maſter too far, and that contented with ſeeing the king the object of the reſpect of Europe, he had not wanted to render him its terror. Villacerf ſucceeded him, as

REMARKABLE EVENTS under LEWIS XIV.

the superintendant of the king's buildings; and Mansard was made intendant. M. de Louvois enjoyed the revenue of the foreign post-office, that is, of the postage of letters from all the offices of the frontiers and conquered towns; upon his decease, the king wanted to know the neat amount. M. de Rouillé (grandfather to the minister of that name) had the management of the foreign post-office, for which he accounted to his majesty himself every three months, having had a dispensation by letters patent, from being answerable either to the council, or to the chamber of accounts. This administration lasted from the month of July, 1691, to the month of January, 1695.

The dauphin takes his place in the council of state: at the same time, the king gave orders for admitting M. de Beauvilliers and M. de Pomponne, who had been dismissed in 1679; to the latter he granted a pension of sixty thousand livres, over and above the twenty, which had been settled on him already.

The count d'Estrées bombards Barcelona the 10th of August, and Alicant the 22d. The first president obtains the gratuities given to the king by the first lords of the bed-chamber, upon taking possession of their places.

The prince of Baden defeats the Turks at Salankamen the 19th of August.

The death of Alexander VIII: in his last hours he distributed all the money he had amassed, among his nephews; which made Pasquin say, that it would have been better for the church to have been his niece than his daughter.

1692.

M. de Boufflers obtains the regiment of guards, vacant by the death of M. de la Feuillade: and sells his post of general of the dragoons to the count de Tessé. The king was three months before he nominated to the regiment of guards, being willing to be acquainted with the particulars of that corps himself.

Lewis XIV. had not dropped his scheme of restoring king James II. This prince advanced to the coast of Normandy, with the marshal de Bellefons : the French imagining they had good intelligence on board the enemy's fleet, M. de Tourville received orders to attack them at all hazards: he obeyed,

REMARKABLE EVENTS under LEWIS XIV.

obeyed, and an engagement enfued, which lafted from morning till night, on the 29th of May; our men behaved with diftinguifhed valour, and it ended at length in favour of the enemy by our retreat; it is true, they had eighty-eight fhips againft fifty. But what rendered this an unfortunate affair to France, was that our fleet having been difperfed on the coaft of Britany and Normandy, the Englifh admiral burnt thirteen of our men of war * at the Hogue, and at Cherburg. In regard to this fea fight, it has been obferved, that we might have waited for the arrival of the count d'Eftrées, who was on his way from Toulon to Breft.

The king commanding his army in perfon, takes the town of Namur the 5th of June, in feven days open trenches, and the citadel the 30th. In vain did the prince of Orange and the elector of Bavaria endeavour to relieve it: they were prevented by the marfhal de Luxemburg, who covered the fiege; and by the fituation of the country, which rendered his camp of moft difficult accefs. This fiege was remarkable for the fkill fhewn in the attack and defence; M. de Vauban carried on the approaches againft fort Cohorn, defended by Cohorn himfelf, who was Vauban's rival, but not his equal. This fame town was retaken by the prince of Orange in 1695, and fubdued again by Lewis XV, in 1746, when the count de Clermont carried it after a fiege of eight days. The battle of Steinkerk on the 3d of Auguft; this was the bloodieft action in the whole war: it is well known that the marfhal de Luxemburg had been deceived by falfe intelligence; he did not believe the enemy were approaching, till he heard that the brigade of Bourbonnois was attacked; but he recovered this furprize, and after two unfuccefsful charges, putting himfelf at the head of the king's guards, together with the duke of Chartres, the duke of Orleans, the prince of Conty, meffieurs de Vendome, &c. he obliged the prince of Orange to repafs the defiles. This prince having endea-

---

* The Royal Sun carrying 104 guns, the Admirable 102, the Conquerant 80, with three more of a leffer rate, were driven afhore near Cherburg, and burnt by admiral Delaval. Eighteen fhips more run into La Hogue, where they were deftroyed by Sir George Rooke. This was the firft fignal blow given to the marine of France in the laft century.

voured

REMARKABLE EVENTS under LEWIS XIV.

voured, during the whole campaign, to come to an engagement where the horfe had not room to act, muft have been convinced at Steinkirk, of the bravery of the French infantry, as he had felt at Leuze the fuperior weight of our cavalry.

The duke of Savoy in revenge for the affronts of the two laſt campaigns, ravages Dauphiné, as we had laid waſte the Palatinate, carries Embrun the 17th of Auguſt, and becomes maſter of Gap. M. de Catinat had not an army sufficient to oppoſe this invaſion, which perhaps would have been attended with more fatal conſequences, had it not been for the ſudden illneſs of the duke of Savoy.

The marſhal de Lorges beats the prince of Wirtemberg on the 17th of September, at the battle of Phortzeim; and obliges the landgrave of Heſſe Caſſel to raiſe the ſiege of Ebernburg the 18th of October. The marquis de Feuquieres had routed ſome of the enemy's detachments, the firſt day of the month: and the marquis d'Harcourt, on the 8th of September, defeated a corps of upwards of four thouſand Germans, in the county of Chiney. M. de Boufflers bombarded Charleroy the 19th of October.

The dukedom of Hanover is erected into an electorate, the 19th of December: but the college of princes oppoſing this ſtep; the duke of Hanover was not admitted till the year 1711, though the ſtates of the empire had acknowledged him in that quality in 1708.

The duke de Chartres, on the 18th of February, is married to mademoiſelle de Blois, the legitimated daughter of Lewis XIV; and the duke du Maine, on the 19th of March, to Anna Louiſa Benedicta of Bourbon, daughter of the prince of Condé.

In conſequence of the duke of Chartres's marriage, the king confirms the donation of *palais royal* to the duke of Orleans, and grants it to him as an appanage; it had been bequeathed to the crown by cardinal Richelieu. The academy of painting and ſculpture, which had been eſtabliſhed at the *palais royal*, is removed to the Louvre.

The king declares, that henceforward the ſurvivorſhips ſhall not annul the prior *warrants of reſerve* *: this regulation was

* See page 210.

REMARKABLE EVENTS under LEWIS XIV.

made on account of the place of the marquis de Tilladet, captain of the guard of hundred Swifs, when it fell to the marquis de Courtanvaux.

The Imperialists take great Waradin on the 5th of June: and the Turks, over whom the Venetians had obtained great advantages in the latter campaigns, raise the siege of Lepanto the 19th of December.

The pope continuing to refuse the bulls, the king by an arret of the month of January, puts the persons whom he had nominated, into possession of the revenue of their bishoprics.

1693.

Pope Innocent XII, who had succeeded Alexander VIII, in 1691, at length grants bulls to the bishops, named by the king since the disputes between France and the court of Rome: this accommodation was managed by the cardinals d'Estrées and de Janson. The new bishops wrote letters of submission to the pontif, expressing their concern for what had passed: yet we continue to adhere to the maxims in the declaration of the clergy.

The institution of the order of St. Lewis.

On the 6th of January, Furnes is taken by M. de Boufflers, who makes 4000 English prisoners. M. de Taillards raises the siege of Rhinfelds the 8th.

Seven marshals of France created the 27th of March, namely, messieurs de Choiseuil, de Villeroy, de Joyeuse, de Boufflers, de Tourville, de Noailles, and de Catinat.

The death of mademoiselle de Montpensier, on the 5th of April: this princess was haughty, courageous, and of a frank disposition; but she had mean abilities, and was disappointed in as many treaties of marriage, as queen Elizabeth had broken; still flattering herself that the nuptial knot was going to be tied; and never imagining that she was beloved with any other view. At length her indignation rendering her wife, and having finished by loving M. de Lauzun, to whom she was said to be married, she wrote her memoirs, which she begins from her birth, that is, from the 7th of May, 1627, to the year 1688. They are written ill enough, to render it certain that she was the author;

REMARKABLE EVENTS under LEWIS XIV.

and yet they have a simplicity which pleases those, who love to employ themselves in the perusal of genuine facts.

The marshal de Lorges makes himself master of Heidelberg, the 21st of May, and of the citadel two days after: many cruelties were committed on this occasion, nor were even the tombs of the electors Palatine respected.

The king sets out for his army in Flanders, but is taken ill at Quesnoy, and returns to Versailles, after detaching the dauphin into Germany: the dauphin advances against the prince of Baden, who was encamped under Hailbrun; but judging it impracticable to attack him in his camp, and not being able to bring him to an engagement, he returned to Versailles towards the end of the month of August. M. de Luxemburg orders a body of troops to fall upon a detachment under the command of count Tilly, in the neighbourhood of Maestricht; and the enemy is put to flight. The marshal de Villeroy makes himself master of Huy the 24th of July.

After the king's departure the marshal de Luxemburg sought for an opportunity to bring the prince of Orange to an engagement: with this view, he attempted to dislodge him from his entrenchments at Mount St. Andrew, and at length he obtained his end, by making as if he intended to attack the town of Liege. The prince of Orange and the duke of Bavaria drew near this place to defend it, and the marshal finding they had quitted their camp, prepared to give them battle.

The battle of Nerwinde * on the 29th, gained by the duke of Luxemburg over the prince of Orange, where we lost seven or eight thousand men, and kept the field; the enemy's loss was far more considerable. We took from them seventy-four pieces of cannon, eight mortars, nine pontons, the greatest part of their artillery, sixty standards, and twenty-two colours †: we made two thousand prisoners, and killed twelve thousand men; our princes of the blood behaved with their usual valour. The consequence of this victory was the taking of Charleroy, by the marshal de Villeroy, the 11th of October. M. de Vauban

---

* Or Landen.   † The prince of Conty used to call Luxemburg the upholsterer of Notre Dame, the church in which those trophies were displayed.

REMARKABLE EVENTS under LEWIS XIV.

conducted the approaches, and M. de Luxemburg covered the siege.

The duke of Savoy, having undertaken the siege of Pignerol, is attacked and defeated at Marsaglia, by the marshal de Catinat, the 4th of October. Messieurs de Vendome, who had had some difference with the duke de Luxemburg, were at this action, where they distinguished themselves: the gendarmes, who came from Germany but the day before, had a great share in the victory. The consequence of this advantage was the devastation of the whole country about Turin, which had been preceded by setting fire to the palace of *la Venerie*, in revenge for the ravage committed in Dauphiné. The duke was not able to keep St. Bridget, which he had taken in the beginning of the campaign; nor Pignerol, which he had bombarded; nor to make himself master of Casal, which he had blockaded.

On the side of the Pyrenees, the marshal de Noailles possesses himself of Roses the 9th of June; the count d'Estrées had laid siege to it by sea.

The English made a descent upon Martinico, but were repulsed with loss the 5th of April. On the 27th of June, the marshal de Tourville discovering sir George Rooke between Lagos and Cadiz, with the Smyrna fleet under convoy, attacked the English squadron, burnt four men of war, and took, burnt, or sunk eighty ships richly laden. It was said, that M. de Tourville did not make a proper use of his advantage; and he laid the blame upon M. Gabaret. On the 5th of October, the Dutch dispossessed us of Pondichery: we recovered it again in 1699, by the treaty of Ryswick. The English bombarded St. Maloes, on the 29th of November: the vessel called the *infernal machine*, only made a great noise and damaged a few houses.

A new regiment of carabineers created in favour of the duke du Maine. The procession of the shrine of St. Genevieve; to put a stop to the calamities occasioned by the scarcity of this year.

1694.

The marshal de Noailles obtains advantages in Catalonia; having passed the Ter within sight of the Spanish army, he defeats them

them on the 27th of May, and carries Palamos by assault the 7th of June; the citadel and garrison surrender at discretion the 10th. M. de Tourville battered the citadel by sea. M. de Noailles makes himself master of the strong town of Gironne, the 25th of June, and from thence marches to Ostalric, the citadel of which was taken the 20th of July, in spite of the seven retrenchments, which the Spaniards had raised in the only part accessible. At length he took Castel Follit the 8th of September, and concluded the campaign with obliging the duke d'Escalona to raise the siege of Ostalric. The king of Spain, alarmed at these reverses, is desirous of peace, but meets with opposition from the emperor, and the prince of Orange. The queen-mother, an Austrian princess, controls the whole council, and gains over the young queen, by supporting the baron de Perlis, of whom the king had taken it into his head to be jealous. The duke d'Ossuna, continuing faithful to his master, is poisoned; and the court of Madrid is divided between a weak king, and a ministry devoted to the court of Vienna.

The famous march of the dauphin, and of the marshal de Luxemburg, from Vignamont to *Pont d'Espierres:* from the 22d of August to the 25th, the army marched forty leagues in four days, and by this expedition, the dauphin, though inferior in numbers by one half to the prince of Orange, guarded the frontiers from the Schelde and the Lis to the sea side, and prevented that prince from attacking the maritime towns, menaced by the enemy's fleet.

The prince of Orange retakes Huy the 28th of September.

By sea the enemy made unsuccessful attempts upon our coast: they landed at Brest the 18th of June, but were repulsed with loss *: the 22d of July they bombarded Dieppe, where the houses were reduced to ashes, through the fault of the inhabitants who neglected to quench the fire: Havre de Grace was also bombarded the 26th of the same month, without any great damage: at length upon their drawing near to Dunkirk on the 21st of September with two such machines as they had used the

---

* General Talmash commanded the forces on this expedition; most of those that landed, were killed or wounded, among the rest the general himself was mortally wounded, and died at his return to Portsmouth.

REMARKABLE EVENTS under LEWIS XIV.

preceding year against St. Maloes, one of them went off without doing any mischief; and the explosion of the other, only destroyed the people on board. On our side captain John Bart was more succesful: the Dutch had made themselves masters of a convoy of ships laden with corn, which the king had sent for from the Baltic, on account of the present scarcity; Bart attacked them with only six frigates, on the 19th of June, off the Texel; out of eight ships, belonging to the enemy, he took three, put the other five to flight, and brought our vessels safe to France. For this exploit John Bart was ennobled.

There happened nothing considerable in Germany or in Italy.

The Poles obtain a complete victory over the Turks on the banks of the Niester the 6th of October. The Venetians possessed themselves of the isle of Chio the 14th of October; but they lost it four months after.

The king's declaration granting precedency to the duke du Maine and the count de Toulouse over all the peers. There had been a previous arret for restoring messieurs de Vendome to the rank allowed them in 1610: but the duke de Vendome took his seat in parliament below the duke du Maine.

The death of the abbé de Longueville, in whom that illustrious house became extinct. This event occasioned a great contest about the succession of Neufchatel. The said abbé had made two wills, the first in favour of the prince of Conty, the second to the advantage of his sister the dutchess of Nemours. Madam de Nemours made a donation in her life-time of the whole succession of M. de Longueville, (out of which she afterwards excepted the estates in Swisserland) to the chevalier de Soissons, a natural son of the count de Soissons killed at the battle of Marfée; he was cousin-german to this princess, (for her mother was sister to the count de Soissons) and he had been legitimated in 1643: she made him take the name of the prince of Neufchatel, upon his marrying the daughter of the duke of Luxemburg. The cause relating to Neufchatel was determined by the states of the country, in favour of madam de Nemours.

REMARKABLE EVENTS under LEWIS XIV.

The king purchases of madam de Guise the palace of Orleans, at present known by the name of Luxemburg. To the duke du Maine, who had been ten years colonel-general of the Swiss, his majesty grants the place of master of the ordnance, vacant by the decease of the marshal d'Humieres, who obtained it in 1685, upon the death of the duke du Lude. The Floral games of Toulouse erected into an academy.

1695.

The death of the marshal de Luxemburg at Versailles, on the 4th of January, at the age of sixty seven; he was a posthumous son of the count de Boutteville, who had been beheaded in 1627 for fighting a duel: his place of captain of the guards was given to M. de Villeroy. The consequences plainly shewed the just concern of his majesty and of all France for the loss of this great general.

The princess Mary, wife of the prince of Orange, departs this life the 7th of January, at the age of thirty-three.

Creation of a poll-tax, which was to terminate, and did actually terminate, at the next peace.

M. de Crenan surrenders Casal to the duke of Savoy the 11th of July, on condition that the fortifications shall be demolished, and the town restored to the duke of Mantua.

The admired retreat of the prince de Vaudemont on the 14th of July before the marshal de Villeroy and the duke du Maine, who missed the opportunity of attacking him.

M. de Montal carries Dixmude in six and twenty hours the 28th of June, and Deinse the 29th. The marshal de Villeroy, upon the enemy's refusing to promise they would no longer insult our maritime towns, bombards Brussels the 13th, 14th, and 15th of August. But this did not hinder the prince of Orange from investing Namur the 1st of July: he carried the town the 4th of August, and the citadel the 2d of September: the marshal de Villeroy had advanced as far as the banks of the Mehaigne, but could attempt nothing. M. de Boufflers, having thrown himself into the town, in order to defend it in conjunction with the count de Guiscard the governor, was detained prisoner upon the surrender of the citadel, under colour that we

had

REMARKABLE EVENTS under LEWIS XIV.

had violated the capitulations of Dixmude and Deinfe; but he was foon fet at liberty: this is the moft fignal exploit of the prince of Orange.

In Catalonia, the marfhal de Noailles falling fick, M. de Vendome fucceeded in his ftead, and obliged M. de Caftanaga to raife the fiege of Palamos, the 25th of Auguft: we were afterwards under a neceffity of difmantling this place, as well as feveral others, taken from the enemy, which we could not hold for want of provifions.

In Germany, the indifpofition of the two generals, the marfhal de Lorges, and the prince of Baden, rendered the campaign inactive. Neither did there happen any thing at fea; except a few captures, and among others that by M. de Nefmond, with fome infults upon the coaft: both parties feemed tired and defirous of peace. The edict concerning ecclefiaftical jurifdiction.

M. de Noailles fucceeds M. de Harlay in the archbifhopric of Paris. The abbé de Fenelon, preceptor to the king's grandchildren, is appointed to the archbifhopric of Cambray: the pope grants the king an indult for life, to nominate to that fee. There had been already a concordate in the year 1602 between the chapter and the king, whereby the former refigned their right of election, and the latter his prerogative of the *regale*.

The king grants the government of Britany to the count de Touloufe, with a view to unite both the admiralties under that prince. In former times the governors of the maritime parts were admirals of their provinces; but Britany alone has retained this privilege. The princefs of Montpenfier having bequeathed the houfe of Choify to the dauphin, upon her deceafe; this prince exchanges it for Meudon, giving four hundred thoufand livres over and above to madam de Louvois. Meudon formerly belonged to M. Servien, who laid out a vaft deal of money upon it: he purchafed it of the duke de Guife. Choify having been fince difpofed of to the princefs of Conty, by the duke de Villeroy, fon-in-law to madam de Louvois; the duke de la Valliere, her next heir, fold it to the king, in 1739.

The death of madam de Guife, daughter of Gafton duke of Orleans.

Vol. II.   Q   1696.

REMARKABLE EVENTS under LEWIS XIV.

1696.

A treaty negotiated by the count de Teffé, between the king and the duke of Savoy, and concluded the 4th of July: it came abroad at firft under the name of the neutrality of Italy. His majefty promifed to reftore all, that had been taken from the duke, and among the reft the town of Pignerol, which was in fome meafure the key of his dominions, and ever fince the year 1630, had ferved for a paffage to the French from Dauphiné into Piedmont. A marriage was alfo agreed to, between the princefs Mary Adelaid his daughter, and the duke of Burgundy: in confideration of this match, the fame honours were granted to the duke of Savoy, as to crowned heads. The duke on the other hand promifed to ufe all his good offices with the allies, in hopes of engaging them in the neutrality: he accordingly made them come into his meafures, by undertaking the fiege of Valentia the 24th of September, in conjunction with M. de Catinat. The peace with Savoy, proclaimed at Paris the 10th of September. The contract of marriage was figned the 15th.

Our land armies were inactive as well as thofe of the enemy; only M. de Vendome defeated a body of cavalry under the duke of Darmftat at Oftalric in Catalonia the 1ft of June.

By fea, the allies bombarded Calais the 13th of April, and the fort in the ifle of Rhé, with the *fands of Olone* * the 15th and 16th of July; but all to no purpofe. On the 18th of June, Bart took five Dutch men of war coming from the Baltic, and fifty fail of merchant men. M. de Nefmond took another prize the 31ft of March. King James II. went as far as Calais, with the marquis d'Harcourt, the firft of this fame month, in hopes of making another attempt upon the coaft of England, but did not fucceed.

M. de Frontenac, governor of new France, undertakes an expedition againft the Iroquois in the month of July, by means of which he fecures Quebec and all Canada againft the incurfions of thofe barbarians.

The death of Sobiefky, king of Poland, the 17th of June.

His majefty makes the new cardinal Cavallerini dine with him, after prefenting him with the cardinal's cap.

---

* Olone is a town of Poitou, on the fea coaft, with a good harbour: it has a large fuburb, called the *fables d'Olone* or the *fands of Olone*, in Latin *Arenæ Olonenfes*

REMARKABLE EVENTS under LEWIS XIV.

The death of M. de Croiſſy: M. de Torcy, his ſon, at that time very young, ſucceeds him in his office, wherein he is aſſiſted by M. de Pomponne, whoſe daughter he married, and who had been again admitted into the privy-council in the year 1691.

1697.

This year is famous for the peace eſtabliſhed over all Europe, by the treaty of Ryſwick. The king appoints meſſieurs de Harlay, de Crecy, and de Callieres, his plenipotentiaries at the congreſs: they had been negotiating already upwards of three months; yet, as the emperor and the king of Spain ſtill expreſſed ſome averſion to a peace, the military operations were not ſuſpended.

In Flanders the marſhal de Catinat makes himſelf maſter of Ath the 5th of June. The prince of Orange defeats the deſign of the marſhal de Villeroy upon Bruſſels and the fortreſs *des trois trous*.

The count d'Harrach had been ſent to Spain, in order to make ſome inſinuations concerning that important ſucceſſion, in favour of the archduke Charles, with expectation that if he could prevail upon the king of Spain, to declare the archduke his ſucceſſor, this ſhould be made one of the chief articles of the treaty of Ryſwick. But how could the emperor think to ſucceed in ſuch a demand againſt the lawful rights of the grandchildren of Lewis XIV, and againſt the rights of the prince of Bavaria and the duke of Orleans? This intrigue miſcarried by the taking of Barcelona.

M. de Vendome lays ſiege to Barcelona, defended by the prince of Darmſtadt, and inveſted towards the ſea by the count d'Eſtrées and the bailiff de Noailles: he defeats the count de Velaſco, viceroy of Catalonia, who attempted to relieve the town; but this did not ſlacken the operations of the ſiege: and Barcelona did not ſurrender till the 10th of Auguſt, after two and fifty days open trenches. M. de Vendome was made viceroy of Catalonia, and the count de Coigny governor of Barcelona: this conqueſt determined the king of Spain and the emperor to conſent to a peace.

REMARKABLE EVENTS under LEWIS XIV.

In Germany, the prince of Baden makes himself master of Ebernburg, the 27th of September.

The expedition of M. de Pointis, to Carthagena, where he landed the 15th of April: after making himself master of the town with all its treasure, and demolishing the fortifications, he reimbarked his troops, got clear of a fleet of four and twenty English men of war, fought a squadron of seven, and returns to Brest the 9th of August; the plunder was valued at ten millions of livres. M. de Nesmond on the 10th of August takes three English ships very richly laden. M. d'Iberville recovers fort Nelson in new France on the 5th of September, after taking two English ships, and sinking a third. On the 24th of April, M. du Gue-Trouin had taken the Dutch fleet coming from Bilboa.

M. d'Argenson is made lieutenant-general of the police; and Paris is indebted to him for its present good order and security: being of a very ancient family, and a superior genius, he would soon have figured in a higher sphere, if the government had not required his service in that station, to preserve order and tranquility in the capital; he was made keeper of the seals, and president of the council of finances in 1718; and died on the 8th of May 1721. He succeeded in the office of lieutenant of the police to M. de la Reynie, who from intendant to the late duke d'Epernon, became master of requests, and was lieutenant of the police, in the year 1667, when the duties of this office were separated from those of the civil lieutenant. M. de la Reynie died the 14th of June, 1709, upwards of ninety years old.

The death of Adrian de Vignacourt, grand master of Malta: his uncle had been raised to the same dignity in 1601, and he was succeeded by Raymond Perellos de Roccaful, an Arragonian. A regulation by which the intendants of the finances are made counsellors of state, and allowed a seat in council, from the day they enter upon their office.

On the 27th of June, Francis Lewis de Bourbon, prince of Conty, was proclaimed king of Poland, by cardinal Radzujouśky, primate of the kingdom; and two hours after Frederic Augustus, elector of Saxony, who had abjured the Lutheran religion, was also proclaimed by the bishop of Cujavia. The queen dowager
of

REMARKABLE EVENTS under LEWIS XIV.

of Poland did not underſtand her real intereſt in this important affair: being the mother of three princes, it was natural ſhe ſhould endeavour to ſecure the crown for the eldeſt; but her fondneſs for the ſecond, named Alexander, made her ſlight James her eldeſt ſon; by which means ſhe loſt all the friends of the late king; and ſhe was neither able to continue the crown in her own family, nor had ſhe any weight, or intereſt, to ſupport other competitors. It was thought in France that the abbé de Polignac, who was entruſted with this negotiation, had not concerted his meaſures right; and the abbé de Chateauneuf was ſent with freſh inſtructions. Couriers are diſpatched on both ſides to the princes elected. The elector of Saxony, being neareſt at hand, arrives in Poland, ſigns the *pacta conventa*, the 21ſt of July, and is crowned at Cracow, the 15th of September. The prince of Conty did not reach Dantzick road till the 26th, and finding his party declining, though he was the only perſon lawfully elected, he put to ſea again the 6th of November. The inteſtine broils did not ceaſe till the year following, when the parties were at length reconciled, and the elector, after ſpending immenſe ſums, was recognized by the whole kingdom.

Four treaties of peace concluded at Ryſwick. Charles XI, who acted as mediator at this congreſs, died at the age of forty-two. This deſpotic prince aboliſhed the authority of the ſenate of Sweden: his ſon, Charles XII, though a minor, continued the mediation: his father had been mediator in his minority at the peace of Oliva.

The firſt treaty was ſigned the 20th of September, at midnight, between France and Holland. The treaties of Munſter and Nimeguen were the baſis of this; and Pondichery was reſtored to the French.

The ſecond was ſigned an hour after, betwixt France and Spain; it contained a reſtitution of the towns taken in Catalonia, as alſo of Luxemburg, the county of Chiney, Charleroy, Mentz, Ath, Courtray, and all that had been reunited to the crown of France by the chambers of Metz and Doway. The town of Dinan was alſo reſtored to the biſhop of Liege, and the isle of Ponza to the duke of Parma. From the great sacrifice which Lewis XIV. made at this treaty, it was natural to impute it to the approaching death of the king of Spain.

By the third treaty made with England, his majesty engages not to disturb the king of Great Britain in the possession of the kingdoms and provinces, which he then enjoyed.

And lastly, by the fourth treaty concluded with the emperor, and signed the 30th of October, every thing was settled agreeably to the treaties of Westphalia and Nimeguen, and Friburg was restored. By this treaty the duke of Lorrain was reinstated in his dominons, in the same manner, with very little exception, as Charles his great uncle enjoyed them in 1670.

The marriage betwixt the duke of Burgundy and the princess of Savoy, is celebrated the 7th of December.

Penthievre erected into a dutchy and peerage in favour of the count of Touloufe: this dutchy was created at first in behalf of the house of Luxemburg, had passed by marriage to that of Vendome, from thence by purchase to the princess of Conty, and by her was sold to the count of Touloufe.

1698.

Mutual embassies from all the princes of Europe: the marquis d'Harcourt was appointed to Spain, M. de Bonrepos to Holland, the marquis de Puisieux to Swisserland, the count de Chamilly to Denmark, the marquis de Villars to Vienna, and M. de Tallard to London. There the first treaty of partition of the Spanish monarchy was concluded; which did not take place, because of the death of the prince of Bavaria. This same treaty of partition between Lewis XIV. on the one hand, and the king of England and the states general on the other, is signed at the Hague the 11th of October. By virtue thereof the electoral prince of Bavaria is nominated to the throne of Spain; the dauphin has for his share the kingdoms of Naples and Sicily, and the strong towns dependent on the Spanish monarchy, situated on the coast of Tuscany, or the adjacent islands, with the town and marquisate of Final, the province of Guipuscoa, particularly the towns of Fontarabia and St. Sebastian in that province, and Port Passage; Charles archduke of Austria was to have the dutchy of Milan.

The

REMARKABLE EVENTS under LEWIS XIV.

The king of Spain provoked to see his crown partitioned out in his life-time, and willing to hinder it from being dismembered after his decease, makes his first will, by which he calls the prince of Bavaria to the throne of Spain, as his next heir, in consequence of the renunciation of Mary Theresa of Austria.

The reality of this will is contested; and indeed it is not mentioned by any historian: however the following are the reasons given for taking notice of it. We find in the memoirs of the count d'Harrach, that there had been a former will of Charles II. in favour of the prince of Bavaria. Lamberty quotes (t. i. p. 96.) a letter from the minister of Lewis XIV, written in Italian to the king of Spain, where he speaks of this testament as a matter of certainty: the continuator of Mezeray makes no doubt of it: and lastly, we meet with the following account of this affair in the memoirs of D. the 16th of December, 1698. " De Guilville, major of the regiment of Normandy, arrived " from Madrid; he is one of those trusty officers, whom the " marquis d'Harcourt took with him into Spain. We find by " his account, that the Spanish monarch is much better, but that " he has nevertheless made a will, by which he institutes the elec- " toral prince of Bavaria his heir, and appoints his wife re- " gent during the minority of that prince. This testament " is not as yet made public in Spain, but his Catholic majesty " has shown it to his council of state; cardinal Portocarrero, " a member of the council, has informed the marquis d'Har- " court of the affair; and it is for this reason he has sent away " de Guilville, who is not to return to Spain. The marquis " d'Harcourt will not make a long stay in this country." We find likewise in the same memoirs the 7th of November, 1700; " That the king of Spain made a new will a month ago, " which he signed with his own hand &c." and this proves the existence of a prior will.

It remains now for us to explain the order of the heirs of Charles II, in case he died without issue (which really happened); they were, first, the children of Mary Theresa, daughter by the first venter of Philip IV, and wife of Lewis XIV: secondly, the electoral prince of Bavaria, whose mother was Margaret Theresa of Austria, daughter by the second venter of Philip IV, and first wife

wife of the emperor Leopold: thirdly, the duke of Orleans, brother of Lewis XIV, and consequently a younger son of Anne of Austria, who was the eldest daughter of Philip III, and had been married to Lewis XIII: fourthly, the archduke Charles, son of Leopold, whose right was by his grandmother, Mary Anne of Austria, second daughter of Philip III, and wife of Ferdinand III, the father of Leopold: fifthly, the duke of Savoy in right of Catharine his great grandmother, daughter of Philip II, and wife of Charles Emmanuel duke of Savoy.

The camp of Compiegne, where the duke of Burgundy arrived the 30th of August: he was generalissimo, and had under him the marshal de Boufflers, who lived there with such magnificence, that the king said to Livry, *the duke of Burgundy must not keep a table, for we cannot make a better figure than the marshal, so that the duke shall dine with him, when he goes to the camp.* This camp was intended for the entertainment of the court, and for the instruction of the king's grandson.

The duke d'Elbœuf espoused mademoiselle de Chartres at Fontainebleau the 13th of October, in the name of Leopold duke of Lorrain. This prince had obtained a patent from the emperor, granting him the title of *royal highness*, as the son of an archdutchess, who had been queen of Poland; but the French did not acknowledge that title, till he made a visit to France under the regency of the duke of Orleans.

Madam Guyon is sent to the Bastile for the affair of Quietism. The disputes betwixt the bishop of Meaux and the archbishop of Cambray, make a great noise, and the friends of the latter are dismissed from court.

Peter, Czar of Muscovy, undertakes a voyage *incognito* to Holland and England, and visits the court of Vienna on his return to his dominions: " A great many princes before him had " resigned their crowns from a disrelish to public affairs; but " none had ever laid aside their royalty, with a view of learn- " ing to reign." (*Hist. of the house of Brandenburg.*)

1699.

The treaty of Carlowitz concluded by the Porte, the emperor, Russia, Poland, and the Venetians: there were properly

four

REMARKABLE EVENTS under LEWIS XIV.

four diftinct treaties, the firft between the Porte and the emperor, contained a truce of twenty-five years; the Turks refigned Tranfylvania to his imperial majefty, but would not confent to deliver up Tekely. The fecond was between the Turks and the Poles; this was a perpetual peace: the former furrendered the fortrefs of Caminiek, which was attended with the ceffion of Podolia and the Ukraine; the latter on the other hand refigned Moldavia. By the third treaty, which was only a truce, the Ruffians kept poffeffion of Afoph, which they afterwards loft at the treaty of Pruth; but at length it was relinquifhed to them by the treaty of Belgrade. By the fourth, the Morea remained in the hands of the Venetians. The king of England and the Dutch were mediators on this occafion; they wanted to put the emperor in a capacity of afferting his claim to the crown of Spain, upon the deceafe of Charles II. which could not be at a great diftance.

The prince of Conty, by an arret of parliament of the 13th of December, 1698, attempts to difturb madam de Nemours in the poffeffion of Neufchatel, adjudged to her by the ftates of that country; but the king of England putting in his claim, as heir of the houfe of Chalons, Lewis XIV. ordered the prince of Conty to relinquifh his pretenfion: meffieurs de Matignon and de Villeroy, &c. had likewife their claims, which they defended by memorials.

The death of the electoral prince of Bavaria at Bruffels on the 6th of February, at feven years of age.

A conftitution in the form of a brief, on the 22d of March, wherein Innocent XII. condemns the book of the archbifhop of Cambray, intituled, *An explication of the maxims of the faints*. This conftitution was fent to the bifhops by the king; and upon the drawing up of the verbal proceffes in all the provincial affemblies, his majefty publifhed his declaration of the 4th of Auguft, which was verified the 14th in parliament, from the opinion of M. Dagueffau, afterwards chancellor, who died in 1751. His difcourfe on this occafion, will be a lafting monument of the found doctrine of the church of France, and reflect perpetual honour on the memory of that great magiftrate. The fubmiffion which the archbifhop of Cambray paid to the decifions of

REMARKABLE EVENTS under LEWIS XIV.

the church, answered the public opinion of the wisdom of that prelate.

The king grants an audience to the ambassador of the emperor of Morocco, on the 6th of February. M. de Monaco, his majesty's ambassador, makes his public entry into Rome, the 8th of February. The duke of Lorrain does homage the 25th of November for his dutchy of Bar.

The calendar had been reformed by pope Gregory XIII. in 1582, and the Protestants refused to accept of the alteration: yet they agreed to it this year, all but England, Sweden, and Denmark, who still kept to the ancient calculation, which makes the difference of ten days betwixt the old and new style: but these three powers have at length adopted the Gregorian reformation. M. de Pontchartrain succeeds the chancellor Boucherat, who died the 25th of September; and M. Chamillard is made comptroller-general, in the room of M. de Pontchartrain. The duke of Burgundy takes his seat in the council of dispatches, where he did not vote in the beginning: he was afterwards made a member of the council of state.

An equestrian statue is erected in the *place des conquetes*, or of *Lewis the great*, otherwise called *place de Vendome*. His Majesty had given this spot of ground to the city, in order to change it from a quadrangular figure to an octagon; at the same time, the city engaged to build an hotel for the black musketeers, viz. that which now stands in the suburb of St. Antony; there is another in the suburb of St. Germain for the grey musketeers.

M. de Torcy is made postmaster general, after the decease of M. de Pomponne his father-in-law. M. Mansart is appointed superintendant, or chief surveyor of the king's buildings, upon the resignation of M. de Villacerf.

1700.

The death of the electoral prince of Bavaria, occasions a second treaty of partition, signed at London the 13th of March, and at the Hague the 25th, by the same powers as the first. This treaty made no alteration in the former with regard to the dauphin, except that Lorrain was added to his share, and in lieu thereof duke Leopold had the dutchy of Milan, which

was

REMARKABLE EVENTS under LEWIS XIV.

was to be taken from the archduke, and the remainder of the Spanish monarchy was to be settled on this prince. The two conditions of this treaty were, that the emperor should accept of the conventions mentioned therein, in the space of three months; and that the crown of Spain and the imperial dignity should never be united in the same person. Leopold thought himself so sure of the Spanish monarchy, that he spurned at the advantages conferred upon him by this treaty, and it was too late to repent his error, when he came to hear of the will of Charles II; so that the emperor's ambition alone was the cause of the following war. He was so much the more to blame for not accepting this treaty of partition, as he had signed a like convention at Vienna, in the year 1668, between the commander de Gremonville and the count d'Aversberg.

The second will of Charles II, king of Spain, whereby he declares Philip of France, duke of Anjou, the dauphin's second son, heir to the whole Spanish monarchy; in default of him, either in case of death, or of his becoming king of France, he calls the duke of Berry upon the same conditions; in failure of him, the archduke Charles, with the same reserve of not uniting the imperial dignity to the crown of Spain; and last of all the duke of Savoy. The duke of Orleans, the king's brother, who was forgot in this testament, entered his protest against it the first of December. The marshal d'Harcourt is said to have had a hand in this second will; but this is a mistake; great men have no need of borrowed merit: the marshal departed from Madrid before there was any talk about a will; and did not return to that capital as ambassador extraordinary, till Philip V. ascended the throne.

The death of Charles II, king of Spain, at thirty-nine years of age. The king accepts of the will the 11th of the same month, and declares his mind to the Spanish ambassador the 16th. Philip V. is proclaimed king at Madrid the 24th, and sets out from Versailles on the 4th of December. Lewis XIV. granted letters patent the 3d of February following, by which he secures to the king of Spain, and to his issue male, the right of succession to the crown of France. England and Holland acknowledged the new king; the duke of Savoy and the duke of Bavaria went

further,

further, for they acted in his behalf. The emperor Leopold entered his protest, the other powers of Europe remained neuter, and all sides prepared for war. Leopold indeed might blame himself for losing so important an inheritance; he needed only to have sent the archduke to king Charles, who had invited him into Spain with a body of twelve thousand men, which he undertook to maintain at his own expence. The confidence of his imperial majesty made him neglect this offer, from the same motives which induced him to reject the treaty of partition; and when he saw the preference given to France, he exclaimed against the injustice of that proceeding; just as if Charles II. had not an equal right to reduce things to the order of nature, as Philip IV. had to pervert it by renunciations.

The cardinal de Bouillon is disgraced: he had been great almoner of France upon the decease of cardinal Barberini, and was nephew to M. de Turenne.

Augustus, king of Poland, Frederic IV, king of Denmark, and the Czar of Muscovy, commence a war in the north against Charles XII, then only eighteen years of age. The elector of Saxony wanted to enslave Poland, and to render himself more powerful by the conquest of Livonia; the king of Denmark intended to wrest Slefwick from the duke of Holstein, brother-in-law to the king of Sweden; the Czar's design was to train his subjects to war, and to strip Sweden of her possessions between the gulf of Finland and the Baltic; the king of Sweden, single against so many united powers, aimed only at preserving the conquests of his ancestors, and chastising his enemies, who despised his youth. King Augustus fell the first victim in this dispute; the Czar was very near being dethroned; and Charles XII. met with an untimely fate, when he had it in his power to be the arbiter of Europe.

The king of Sweden, at the head of 8000 men, obtains a complete victory at Narva, the 28th and 30th of October, over the Czar, who had an army of eighty thousand.

The board of trade instituted by an arret of council: there had been a commission of much the same nature, created by Henry IV, but it ceased at his death. Cardinal Richelieu resumed the like design; but it was dropped again at the decease of

REMARKABLE EVENTS under LEWIS XIV.

Lewis XIII, which happened soon after that of the cardinal. Lewis XIV, having at length restored this board in 1700, it only changed its form at his demise, and was put on the present footing.

An arret of council on the 10th of May, ordaining that the abbé de Luxemburg shall give an account of the benefices belonging to the grand mastership of the order of the Holy Ghost of Montpellier, to which he had been preferred in 1693, this being a regular order.

The death of Innocent XII, the 27th of September. Cardinal Albani succeeds him, at the age of fifty-one, and takes the name of Clement XI; he was not consecrated bishop till after his election, of which there had not been a similar instance, since Clement VIII. In the course of the ensuing war this pope acted the part of a common father.

1701.

The death of M. de Barbesieux, secretary of state for the department of war: he is succeeded by M. Chamillard, who was comptroller-general.

This year was formed the grand alliance against France. The view of the confederates in the beginning, was to dismember as much as they could of the Spanish succession; but in consequence of the advantages obtained in the prosecution of the war, they carried their pretensions so high, as to insist upon dethroning Philip V.

The duke of Bavaria, on whom Charles II. had conferred the government of the Netherlands, admits of French garrisons into Newport, Oudenard, Ath, Mons, Charleroy, Namur, and Luxemburg: there were two and twenty Dutch battalions in those towns; the king was so delicate as not to detain them prisoners; lest he should be charged with having committed the first act of hostility, (a principle no less noble than dangerous.) What M. de Puisegur says upon this subject in his treatise of the art of war, is extremely curious. " Upon the decease of Charles II, the king sent for me, and " said ..... I am very uneasy to see the Dutch troops in most " of the strong towns of the Spanish Netherlands: besides, the

" elector

"elector of Bavaria has seven or eight thousand men of his own; while the king my grandson has but a very small force. It is true, the elector of Bavaria is treating with me; but at the same time he is in treaty with the king of England. I have thought proper to send you to Brussels, that you may observe the conduct of the elector, and procure my troops admittance into such towns, as have a Dutch garrison. Tell the marquis de Bedemar, that I repose an intire confidence in him; and let him know that I am sending the marshal de Boufflers to Lille; that whatever assistance he shall want, either as to troops, ammunition, or money, he need only to mention it to you; and upon your intimating it to the marshal de Boufflers, he has orders to supply him with every thing."

An offensive and defensive alliance, entered into by Portugal, France, and Spain. The war breaks out in Italy, where the city of Mantua received a French garrison. Prince Eugene commanded the imperial army, M. de Vaudemont the king of Spain's, and M. de Catinat the French troops, which were only auxiliaries. The duke of Savoy, whose second daughter espoused the king of Spain the 11th of September, was to have been generalissimo of those two armies.

Prince Eugene penetrates into Italy through the Venetian state: the French might have opposed his passage by seizing the gorges of the bishopric of Trent; but then they must have marched through the territories of the republic, and there was a neutrality at that time, which we thought right to observe: prince Eugene however was not so circumspect. To the same delicacy it was owing, that M. de Catinat, who had orders not to commence hostilities, contented himself with defending the dutchy of Mantua and the Milanese.

The battle of Carpi the 9th of July: M. de St. Fremont, who guarded this post, was forced; prince Eugene remained master of the whole country between the Adige and the Adda; and M. de Catinat was obliged to retire behind the Oglio and the Adda, with a view to prevent the enemy from penetrating into the Milanese by the way of Brescia.

REMARKABLE EVENTS under LEWIS XIV.

The repeated checks of M. de Catinat, made him conjecture, they were not intirely owing to the abilities of prince Eugene: he acquainted the court with his fuspicions concerning the duke of Savoy. The king's fincerity not fuffering him to harbour fuch furmifes; he appointed the marfhal de Villeroy to fucceed M. de Catinat, in the command of the army.

The battle of Chiari on the firft of September, where the duke of Savoy, the marfhal de Villeroy, and the marfhal de Catinat, who had not as yet quitted the army, were repulfed with great lofs. This action was fought contrary to the opinion of M. de Catinat; it was a rafh undertaking, and even had it fucceeded, would have been attended with no utility. Never was there a general perhaps feen to expofe himfelf with fo much intrepidity, as the duke of Savoy did on this occafion, againft an enemy with whom he may be fuppofed to have already entered into a correfpondence. The league concluded by the emperor, king William, and the Dutch.

Lewis XIV. and the king of Spain grant unto the dukes, grandees of Spain, and to their ladies, the fame honours at their refpective courts.

The elector of Cologne, having in vain applied to the emperor for a neutrality, admits a French garrifon, firft into the citadel of Liege, on the 23d of November, and afterwards into all his ftrong towns. Cologne by furprize received a Dutch garrifon. The death of the duke of Orleans, the king's only brother, at St. Cloud, on the 9th of June, aged fixty-one years. The king continues to that prince's fon, the duke of Orleans, all the honours of the fons of France, fuch as guards, officers of ftate, &c.

The death of James II, king of England, aged fixty-eight years, at St. Germain en laye, on the 16th of September; a prince worthy of a better fortune, if fortune were the reward of courage, fincerity and religion: after his deceafe, the king acknowledged his fon, as king of Great Britain; and the pope did the fame.

His majefty created two directors of the revenue; one was M. d'Armenonville, the other, M. Rouillé de Coudray, who was fucceeded the next year by M. Defmarets. M. d'Armemonville

REMARKABLE EVENTS under LEWIS XIV.

monville had been made intendant of the revenue, by his connexion with M. le Pelletier, who married his sister: he was secretary of state, and keeper of the seals under the minority of Lewis XV; and M. de Morville, his son, was appointed secretary of state in his stead.

An insurrection at Naples on the 23d of September, in favour of the archduke; it was quelled by the care of the duke de Medina Celi, viceroy of that kingdom.

Upon the death of the duke of Gloucester, son of the princess of Denmark, which happened the preceding year, an act passed in the parliament of England on the 13th of March, declaring, that in case of the death of king William, or of the princess Ann of Denmark, without issue, the princess Sophia, dutchess dowager of Hanover, as the next protestant heir, should succeed to the crown, and after her the issue of her body.

Frederic, elector of Brandenburg, had been proclaimed king of Prussia at Konigsberg, the 15th of January: he died in 1713. His grandson Frederic, who is become formidable to the house of Austria by the gaining of five victories, still holds the balance of power in Germany, and is equally distinguished for the accomplishments of his mind, his love of justice, and the reputation of his arms. The king of Sweden defeats the Saxons the 18th of July, in the neighbourhood of Riga, and carries the fort of Dunemonde the 21st of December.

1702.

The death of William III, king of England, on the 19th of March, at the age of fifty-two, makes no alteration in the system of the allies: he is succeeded by his sister-in-law, queen Ann. It has been said of that prince, that he was stadtholder of England, and king of Holland: and, indeed, the English ceased to have a regard for him, as soon as they raised him to the throne; but the Dutch always loved him, and he made them a most grateful return. In England he met with continual disgusts; they even obliged him to send away his Dutch guards; which was one of the greatest mortifications he ever received in his life. Fortune exhausted herself in making him a king, and afterwards forsook him; he was unprosperous in war; but

REMARKABLE EVENTS under LEWIS XIV.

ill fuccefles only helped to difplay the fertility of his genius; for though always beaten, he was never defeated.

On the 6th of January the duke of Modena delivers up the fortrefs of Berfello to the Imperialifts, who had alfo penetrated into the Milanefe. Cremona is furprifed the 1ft of February, by prince Eugene, who was driven out again by the bravery of the French and Irifh: on this occafion the marfhal de Villeroy was taken prifoner.

The emperor, the Englifh, and the Dutch, declare war againft France, who makes the fame declaration againft thofe powers.

The king of Spain fets out from Madrid to receive the homage of his fubjects in the kingdom of Naples: paffing through Genoa he gives the title of *highnefs* to the doge, and permits that magiftrate and all the fenators to be covered, as reprefenting the body of the republic: the emperor Charles V. behaved to them in the fame manner. From thence he proceeds to the army, the command of which had been taken from the duke of Savoy, and given to M. de Vendome, after the marfhal de Villeroy was made prifoner.

The duke de Vendome defeats general Vifconti at Santa Vittoria beyond the Cruftulo on the 26th of July. Albergotti poffeffes himfelf of Reggio and Modena. Prince Eugene is obliged to raife the blockade of Mantua, the firft of Auguft. The battle of Luzara the 15th of Auguft, where the king of Spain was in perfon. Both fides claimed the victory; but M. de Vendome certainly obtained his point, which was the taking of Luzara and Guaftalla. The marquis de Crequy, fon of the marfhal, was killed at this engagement, without leaving any iffue.

In Flanders there were no tranfactions of any importance: the duke of Burgundy, having M. de Boufflers to ferve under him, pufhed the allies as far as the cannon of Nimeguen the 11th of June. The enemy carried Venlo the 23d of September; Ruremond the 7th of October, and the citadel of Liege the 23d.

In Germany, M. de Blainville furrendered Keyferwert in the electorate of Cologne the 15th of June, after fifty-nine days open trenches: the duke of Bavaria furprized Ulm the 8th of September.

REMARKABLE EVENTS under LEWIS XIV.

September. M. de Melac defended Landau near four months, and at length surrendered it the 11th of September.

The marquis de Villars having been detached from the army, under the command of the marshal de Catinat, made himself master of Newburg the 11th of October, and on the 14th obtained a victory at Fredelingen, over the imperial forces, commanded by prince Lewis of Baden: this victory procured him the staff of a marshal of France. In vain did the Imperialists, according to custom, endeavour to call our advantage in question; this at least is certain, that the enemy made no further attempt to force their way into Alsace; and that the marshal de Villars was able the next campaign to take fort Kell, and to join the duke of Bavaria, by opening a passage through the Black forest. The cavalry under M. de Magnac had a great share in the glory of that day.

Prince Frederic of Brandenburg raises the siege of Rhimberg, the 30th of October. The count de Tallard makes himself master of Treves the 25th of the same month, and of the town and castle of Traerback, the 6th of November. The French troops take possession of Nancy the 3d of December.

The English miscarry in their attempt against Cadiz, and wreak their vengeance upon our fleet.

The count de Chateau-Renaud is intirely defeated by the duke of Ormond, the 22d of October, in the harbour of Vigo, whither he had convoyed the gallions coming from Mexico; they were all taken, sunk, or burnt; but M. de Chateau-Renaud had landed the best part of the effects. Lewis XIV. transfers the sovereignty of the Spanish Netherlands, in the name of Philip V, to the duke of Bavaria.

An arret of council of the 12th of May, determining the independency of the archbishop of Rouen, on the see of Lyons; the primacy of which is however acknowledged by the archbishops of Sens, Tours, and Paris.

Charles, king of Sweden, having in the month of May made his entry into Warsaw, from whence Augustus was retired, declares he will not withdraw from Poland till his enemy is dethroned;

REMARKABLE EVENTS under LEWIS XIV.

throned; then pursuing him as far as Cliffon, in the neighbourhood of Cracow, he obtains a complete victory on the 19th of July: if Charles had not broke his thigh by a fall from his horse, king Augustus would have been utterly undone.

An arret of parliament of the 19th of December, containing a prohibition *to arreft any perfon in his own houfe for debt, without leave from the judge.*

1703.

Ten marshals of France created the 14th of January, viz. messieurs de Chamilly, d'Estrées, de Chateau-Renaud, de Vauban, de Rozen, d'Huxelles, de Tessé, de Montrevel, de Tallard, and d'Harcourt: at that time there were twenty marshals of France. The duke d'Harcourt is made captain of the guards upon the death of the marshal de Lorges.

Prince Eugene does not command this year, but is succeeded by count Staremberg.

On the 5th of January, the duke of Savoy concluded an alliance with the emperor; which defection was one of the chief causes of the misfortunes that befel the French this war. Fra-Paolo (who died in 1623), wrote these words a hundred years before: " We might receive some assistance from Sa-
" voy, if there were any dependance to be made upon a treaty
" with that prince; but he is a Proteus continually changing
" form, and his caprices might quickly exhaust the treasure of St.
" Mark." The allies retook Rhimberg, the 9th of February; but the marshal de Tallard obliged them to raise the siege of Taerbach the 25th.

Marshal de Villars, having possessed himself of the towns of Offemburg and Rastadt without resistance, as also of the redoubts of the enemy upon the Quinche, carries fort Kell, the 9th of March. The elector takes Newburg on the Danube, the 3d of February; defeats the enemy at Passau, the 11th of March; at Burglenfeldt the 28th; seizes Ratisbon the 8th of April; is joined the 12th of May, at Dutlingen, by the marshal de Villars, who directed his march through the Black forest.

The elector's scheme was to possess himself of the county of Tirol, to which he had ancient pretensions, while the duke de Vendome

REMARKABLE EVENTS under LEWIS XIV.

Vendome was entering into the bishopric of Trent, in order to open a passage from the Milanese to Bavaria, and to cut off the communication of the imperial army. With this view he makes himself master of Kuftein, the 18th of June, and of Infpruck the 26th. On the other hand, M. de Vendome forces the passage of the mountains at the entrance of the territory of Trent, on the 26th of July: but Staremberg having detached general Vaubonne to occupy the gorges and forts in that country; this step, together with the open defection of the duke of Savoy, obliged M. de Vendome to march back into Italy, while the duke of Bavaria was also compelled to retire from Infpruck, and to join once more the marshal de Villars, whom he had left in Swabia to obferve the prince of Baden. During M. de Vendome's march, M. de Vaubecourt had taken Berfello, the 27th of July.

The marshal de Villars, hearing that prince Lewis of Baden had sent a body of troops to furprize Augfburg, sends away M. de Legal to attack them; the enemy being apprized of this march, advance towards Munderkinguen; M. de Legal, though furprized, and inferior in numbers, puts them to flight the 30th of July. Notwithstanding this advantage, the city of Augfburg admits a garrifon of imperial troops, the 5th of September. The two armies, under the elector and the marshal, pass the Danube at Donawert, to prevent the junction of the count de Stirum with prince Lewis of Baden: the marquis d'Uffon's miftaking a fignal, brought on an action before the whole army was arrived; this turned out to his difadvantage; but the lofs was foon repaired, and count Stirum was intirely defeated at Hochftet; this battle was fought the 20th of December.

In the Netherlands, the marshal de Villeroy, who had recovered his liberty, carries Tongres the 10th of May: my lord Marlborough makes himself mafter of the town of Bonne the 15th, which was valiantly defended by the marquis d'Alegre; and Huy furrenders to him the 26th of June. This was the ftage on which that great captain made his firft appearance. He fucceeded king William in the command of the allied army, and was the moderator and arbiter of the grand confederacy.

REMARKABLE EVENTS under LEWIS XIV.

deracy. Concurring with prince Eugene in his hatred against France, he rendered it subservient to his own ambition, which he carried to such a length, as to make his sovereign tremble.

The battle of Ekeren the 30th of June. The baron de Spaart had, with the loss of a great number of men, forced the lines of the country of Vaas, defended by the count de la Motte; the baron d'Opdam wanted to break through those of Antwerp, where he found the marshal de Boufflers and the marquis de Bedmar. The engagement lasted long; or rather there were several engagements, occasioned by the situation of the ground, intersected with dykes and canals: the baron was repulsed with a very considerable loss, and his army retired under the cannon of Lillo. The enemy make themselves masters of Limburg the 27th of September, and of the town of Gueldres the 17th of December, after a bombardment and blockade of fourteen months.

M. de Vendome having, on the 29th of September, seized and disarmed the troops of the duke of Savoy, on the 20th of October defeats general Visconti, who was marching with a detachment of 1500 horse to the relief of that prince; but he could not prevent general Staremberg, who had stolen two marches upon him, from joining the duke of Savoy with a considerable reinforcement.

In Germany, the duke of Burgundy, having the marshal de Tallard and M. de Vauban under him, made himself master of old Brisac in fourteen days, and obliged the garrison to capitulate the 6th of September. The battle of Spire the 15th of November. The marshal de Tallard had laid siege to Landau; and the prince of Hesse (who succeeded Charles XII. in the kingdom of Sweden) being joined by the prince of Nassau, marched to the relief of that place, with an army of English, Dutch, and Germans. M. de Tallard quitted the siege, leaving M. de Laubanie to guard the trenches, and gave battle to the prince of Hesse, who was intirely defeated. The French army was weaker by one third than that of the enemy. The slow march of Pracontal, whom the marshal de Villeroy had unwillingly detached from his army in Flanders, and whom he ordered to make but short days marches, had like to have been fatal to

REMARKABLE EVENTS under LEWIS XIV.

M. de Tallard; but Pracontal being an officer of great reputation, got himself killed in that battle through despair. Follard gives a very high encomium of M. de Tallard: the morrow Landau surrendered, and Laubanie was made governor.

The king of Portugal accedes to the grand alliance the 13th of May. The emperor and prince Joseph, his son, who had been elected king of the Romans in 1690, renounce all their rights to the Spanish monarchy, in favour of the archduke Charles, by an instrument of the 12th of September. The Imperialists possess themselves of Amberg, the capital of the upper Palatinate, the 30th of November.

The king of Spain makes a declaration, by way of interpreting the will of Charles II, in favour of the duke of Orleans.

The insurrection of the Cevenes, which the marshal de Montrevel is not able to suppress, notwithstanding all his diligence in pursuing and chastising the rebels, who were called Camisars. At sea the English were repulsed by Gabaret the 18th of May off Guadaloupe. M. de Coetlogon on the 22d of May defeated five men of war, with a fleet of English and Dutch merchant men under convoy: four of the men of war were taken, and the fifth was sunk; but the merchant ships had time to escape during the engagement. Admiral Rook attempts a descent upon Belleisle the 6th of June, to no effect. M. de St. Pol on the 10th of August attacks a Dutch fleet to the north of Scotland, defeats the men of war that convoyed it, and takes several of the ships. M. Ducasse brings home three millions of livres from the Havanna. M. du Quesne causes the town of Aquila, where the enemy had a great magazine, to be burnt by M. de Beaucaire, captain of a frigate. The king of Sweden having routed five thousand Saxons the 1st of May at Pultausk, possesses himself of Thorn the 14th of October, and of Elbing the 10th of December.

1704.

This year intirely changes the face of affairs in Europe. The emperor, who lately trembled for his capital, gives laws to the empire: Spain, from a peaceful state, is upon the point of entering into a war, to defend the very heart of the monarchy: three

Italian

REMARKABLE EVENTS under LEWIS XIV.

Italian sovereigns are expelled their dominions: the king of Poland is dethroned: and France, hitherto triumphant, undergoes the greatest reverses.

In Spain, the archduke Charles having assumed the title of king, lands at Lisbon the 9th of March, with eight thousand English and Dutch troops, commanded by the duke de Schomberg. At that time a medal was struck with this inscription: *Charles III, by the grace of heretics, his Catholic majesty.* King Philip begins with obtaining considerable advantages over the Portuguese. The duke of Berwick commanded the French troops, which Lewis XIV. sent to the assistance of Spain: after taking several small places in the month of May, he makes himself master of Port Alegre on the 8th of June. The Portuguese were more successful towards the close of the year; and did not leave the king of Spain any part of his conquests. The prince of Hesse-Darmstadt, after attempting to surprize Barcelona by a correspondence in the town, which was detected, sets sail with admiral Rook for Gibraltar, of which he possessed himself the 4th of August. With a view of enabling M. de Pointis and M. de Villadarias to recover so important a place, the French fleet under the command of M. de Toulouse, seconded by the marshal de Coeuvres, came to an engagement with the enemy on the 24th of August; and though our fleet obtained some advantage, we miscarried in our main design; for Gibraltar has ever since continued in the possession of the English. This battle, which was fought within eleven leagues of Malaga, would have been as advantageous to Spain, as it proved glorious to the count de Toulouse, if we had attacked the enemy again the next day: this was the count's own opinion, in which he was backed by M. de Relingue, who happened to be mortally wounded. But we were ignorant of the bad condition of the enemy's fleet; and the loss we sustained of about fifteen hundred men, determined the council of war, to follow the opinion of M. d'O, and not to venture upon a second action.

In Italy, the duke of Modena having entered into a treaty with the emperor, the duke de Vendome seized his dutchy: the duke of Mirandola concluded an alliance with France, and

REMARKABLE EVENTS under LEWIS XIV.

met with the same treatment on the part of the Imperialists: the duke of Mantua finding his territories were to be the seat of war, removed to Paris, where he married mademoiselle d'Elbœuf; he was the last duke of this family, in whose favour that dutchy was erected by Charles V, in 1530; it has since devolved to the house of Austria. The grand prior of Vendome makes himself master of Revere the 10th of April. M. de la Feuillade, who towards the end of the preceding year had seized all Savoy, except Montmeliand, carries the castle of Susa the 12th of June, and afterwards the town of Pignerol. Verceil surrenders to M. de Vendome, the 20th of July, who, from the 17th of September to the 28th, makes himself master of the town and citadel of Yvrea. The grand prior takes Sensano, the 25th of November.

In Germany, the marshal de Villars had ceased to command, on account of some difference with the elector of Bavaria: he was succeeded by the marshal de Marsin. The elector seizes Passaw the 9th of January. The duke of Marlborough, having forced a detachment of the Bavarian army, possesses himself of Donawert the 2d of July. This conquest gave him a bridge upon the Danube, and separated the French troops on the upper Danube from those on the lower: yet the advantage of this situation only would not have much availed the enemy, who could not penetrate into Bavaria, without removing too far from the magazines of Nuremberg and Nordlingen, whence they drew their subsistence: therefore, by declining an engagement, we might have forced them to retire towards the Maine. But the generals reasoned otherwise: since the arrival of the reinforcement under marshal Tallard, the elector was grown more eager to engage; so that on Wednesday the 13th of August was fought the battle of Hochstet, in which prince Eugene and the duke of Marlborough obtained a complete victory over the armies of France and Bavaria, commanded by the elector with the marshals de Tallard and de Marsin. M. de Tallard lost his son, was wounded himself, and taken prisoner, just as he was going to withdraw his troops from the village of Plintheim. It is still unaccountable, how those troops, which

REMARKABLE EVENTS under LEWIS XIV.

amounted to twenty-seven battalions and four regiments of dragoons, consented to surrender without making the least defence. The prince of Baden was employed, at that very time, in the siege of Ingolstadt. In consequence of this defeat we were driven from the Danube, and obliged to repass the Rhine: notwithstanding the brave defence of M. de Laubanie, we could not hinder the taking of Landau, which surrendered to the king of the Romans, and to the prince of Baden, the 23d of November. Traerbach is carried by the Imperialists the 12th of November.

The marshal de Villars appeases the troubles of the Cevenes.

In Flanders, the campaign was confined to the bombarding of Namur, in the month of July, by M. d'Auverquerque, general of the Dutch troops. The duke of Marlborough, on the 29th of October, possesses himself of Triers, which we had abandoned. The marshal de Boufflers is made captain of the guards upon the death of marshal de Duras, and with concern resigns the regiment of guards, which the king wanted to bestow on the duke de Grammont. It was usual to waver between those two posts; when M. de Boufflers obtained the regiment of guards in 1692, it was said, that the duke de Noailles, captain of the guards, petitioned for that very regiment.

An arret of the council of dispatches on the 17th of February, determining, that the archbishop of Rheims, may fill the place of dean of the council, contrary to what M. de la Reynie pretended.

The disgrace of madam des Ursins in Spain, who was afterwards reinstated in the king's favour. The introducing of mint bills *.

Stanislaus Leczinsky, palatine of Posnania, aged twenty-six years, is chosen king of Poland the 12th of July. The defeat of the Saxons on the Duna, the 6th of August: another engagement, in which they were likewise beaten, on the 19th, notwithstanding the gallant stand of general Schullemburg, whose retreat was admired even by Charles XII. Narva

---

* In imitation of the paper credit of England; they could not obtain currency, but at a discount of above fifty per cent.

taken by the Muscovites on the 21st. King Augustus makes his entry into Warsaw the 5th of September, but is obliged to retire from thence, upon the arrival of Charles XII. The Saxons, after obtaining an advantage the 1st of November, are beaten the 7th by the king of Sweden, and by king Stanislaus: Augustus retires to Dresden.

A court of monies or coinages created at Lyons.

1705.

In Italy, the grand prior surprizes some of the enemy's quarters on the 2d of February. M. de la Feuillade carried Villa-franca by storm, the 7th of March, and the castle the 3d of April; the 9th he made himself master of Nice; so that the duke of Savoy lost all hopes of being succoured by sea. The taking of Verue by M. de Vendome, on the 10th of April: this siege was begun so long ago as the 22d of October in the foregoing year; and M. de Vendome did not carry the place, till he had cut off all communication between the town and the Crescentine. Mirandola taken the 11th of May; it was M. de Lapara that directed the siege. Chivas surrenders to M. de la Feuillade the 28th of July. The battle of Cassano the 16th of August: prince Eugene, who had always commanded an army much inferior to that of the two crowns, acted in the war of Italy with the utmost caution: the point in contest was to carry succours to the duke of Savoy, for which he wanted to pass the Adda, defended by M. de Vendome: the action was bloody; it began with attacking the bridge of Cassano; and the infantry only were engaged: prince Eugene was wounded, and M. de Vendome had a horse killed under him: the enemy retired with great loss; the duke of Savoy was not relieved; and we kept possession of the field of battle. The grand prior, having had some dispute with his brother, quitted the service.

Soncino surrenders to M. de Vendome the 23d of October. Montmelian capitulates the 11th of December.

In Spain, the marshal de Tessé is obliged to raise the siege of Gibraltar the 23d of April, notwithstanding all that M. de Pointis could do by sea. The Portuguese take Salvaterra, Valentia d'Alcantara, and Albuquerque, in the month of May.

REMARKABLE EVENTS under LEWIS XIV.

The king of Spain gives orders for arresting M. de Leganes, upon suspicion of treason, the 10th of June: he is carried to the citadel of Pampelona, and from thence removed to the castle of Vincennes.

Gironne declares in favour of the archduke, the 4th of October; Barcelona surrenders to that prince the 9th. The marshal de Tessé obliges the marquis de la Minas to raise the siege of Badajos on the 16th.

The marshal de Villars seizes the camp of Sirk; by which means he covers Thionville and Saarlouis, and baffles the enemy's project of penetrating into Champagne: this is one of the most brilliant campaigns of that general. A battle was expected, and the duke of Marlborough, having a much stronger army than that of the marshal, would have been glad to attack him; but restrained by the difficulty of the situation, he was obliged to decamp the 16th of June, and march back into Flanders, leaving all his magazines at Treves behind him. My lord Marlborough complained very heavily of prince Lewis of Baden, who had disappointed him, as he said, in every thing, and frustrated all the operations of this campaign: and what is very extraordinary, my lord made an apology to the marshal de Villars for not attacking him. The marshal having sent away two detachments from his army, one to the Netherlands, the other to the Rhine, forces the lines of Weissemburg the 3d of July. Hombourg surrenders to the marquis de Conflans the 26th. M. de Villars, weakened by the detachment which he had sent to the elector of Bavaria, was unable to defend the lines of Haguenau against the prince of Baden, who forced them the 28th of September, and entered that town the 5th of October. M. Pery had withdrawn the garrison, when the prince of Baden expected to make them prisoners of war.

In the Netherlands, the elector carries the town of Huy the 1st of June, and the allies retake it the 12th of July. His electoral highness having raised the siege of the citadel of Liege, was encamped at Vignamont, with the marshal de Villeroy: but his lines being too extensive, were forced the 18th of July, at the post assigned to M. de Roquelaure: M. de Caraman, assisted by
Steckemberg,

REMARKABLE EVENTS under LEWIS XIV.

Steckemberg, lieutenant-colonel of the regiment of Alsace, had the honour of conducting the retreat, by forming a square battalion, which the enemy were unable to penetrate. The army retired to Lovain, and the allies took possession of Tillemont and Lovain.

The elector made himself master of Diest the 25th of November.

The death of the emperor Leopold, on the 6th of May, had made no alteration in the state of affairs. This prince was of a virtuous disposition, but had no abilities: the ambition which directed all his movements, was rather a passion of the court of Vienna, than his own. The emperor his son inherited his ministers, together with his dominions and dignities; and the same council continued to act under his name as had acted hitherto under that of Leopold.

The bull *vineam Domini sabaoth* was registered in parliament, the 4th of September: it is a condemnation of the famous case of conscience, approved by forty doctors of Sorbonne in 1701, which renewed the distinction of fact and right, and therefore rendered the signing of the formulary altogether useless, with regard to the five propositions of Jansenius.

The Swedes defeat the Muscovites, the 26th of July, in the neighbourhood of Mittaw, and the 31st near Warsaw. Mittaw surrenders to the Russians the 16th of September.

1706.

This year France underwent the greatest vicissitudes.

In Spain, if we except the forcing of Villareal on the 8th of January, by the count de las Torres, the rest of the campaign was one continued series of disgraces. Alcantara surrenders to my lord Galway the 16th of April. The king of Spain, having under him the marshal de Tessé, raises the siege of Barcelona, the 12th of May, after it had lasted thirty-seven days. Catalonia is open to the archduke; and Ciudad Rodrigo is taken by the Portuguese. On the 13th of June, Carthagena surrenders to the English. My lord Galway possesses himself of Salamanca the 7th of June, and marches to Madrid, from whence the queen is obliged

REMARKABLE EVENTS under LEWIS XIV.

obliged to retire; the archduke is proclaimed king in that capital. Philip V, not at all difheartened, puts himfelf at the head of the troops commanded by the duke of Berwick, within four leagues of Madrid, and follows the enemy, who retire at his approach, and, for want of fubfiftence, take the road to the kingdom of Valentia, ftill purfued by the duke of Berwick. On the 8th of Auguft the allies make themfelves mafters of Alicant, which was gallantly defended by Mahony, who retook Carthagena, the 18th of November. The ifland of Ivica furrenders to the archduke the 20th of September, and Majorca the 25th. The marquis de Bay takes Alcantara from the Portuguefe, the 14th of December.

In Flanders was fought the battle of Ramillies, the 23d of May, on Whitfunday. The elector of Bavaria and the marfhal de Villeroy commanded the army of France; the duke of Marlborough, the duke of Wurtemberg, and marfhal d'Auverquerque, that of the allies. Our right wing being covered by the little river Gheet, and by the neighbouring moraffes, could neither be attacked nor attack; this made my lord Marlborough ftrengthen his left with the troops from the right, which in that fituation could be of no ufe to him; but the elector and the marfhal made no alteration in their left, fo that their right alone had to engage with the enemy's whole army, drawn up in feveral lines: this error in the difpofition of the French army was the caufe of its defeat; the troops, having no confidence in their commanders, were feized with a panic, and a general rout enfued: we had not above three or four thoufand men killed in the engagement; yet we loft Antwerp, Lovain, Mechlin, Lierres, Bruffels, Bruges, Ghent, Oudenard, Oftend, Menin, Dendermond, Ath, &c. Lewis XV. retook all thofe towns; to which he added, in Flanders, Brabant and Hainault, the towns or forts of Ipres, Furnes, Courtray, fort Knocke, Tournay, Newport, Dixmude, Grammont, Aloft, Deinfe, Ninove, Leffines, Enguien, Soignies, Plaffendal, Wilworden, &c. The marfhal de Villeroy was recalled, and the fame unlucky ftar, which purfued the French arms, was the caufe of M. de Vendome's being removed from Italy, to fucceed

M. de

M. de Villeroy, which occasioned fresh disasters, with our expulsion out of the Milanese, Piedmont, and Savoy.

The beginning of the campaign proved favourable. The duke of Berwick, who had not as yet taken upon him the command in Spain, makes himself master of the citadel of Nice, the 4th of January. The battle of Calcinato on the 19th of April, where M. de Vendome defeated C. Reventlau the Danish general. The loss of the enemy was so great, that prince Eugene, who did not arrive till the day after the battle, was not in a situation to wait for M. de Vendome, who, pursuing his victory, that very same day defeated another corps of more than two thousand men: this prince was forced to retire into the Trentine, and there to expect the succours from Germany. M. de Vendome had so well concerted his measures, that he predicted this victory to the king, when he set out from court, to command the army in Italy. It were to be wished, that in the sequel of this campaign, he had not suffered prince Eugene to pass the Adige, and the white canal; and that being the only man who could rectify his own mistakes, he had not been recalled into Flanders, after the battle of Ramillies, to succeed M. de Villeroy. He resigned the command of the army to the duke of Orleans.

M. de la Feuillade, having invested Turin the 13th of May, opened the trenches in the night the 2d of June: this siege had been proposed the preceding year, when the marshal de Vauban offered his service as a volunteer, merely to assist M. de Feuillade with his advice. The raising of the siege of Turin, the 7th of December. Prince Eugene, after a long and painful march, in which however he did not meet with the obstructions he might have expected, attacked and forced our lines: the duke of Orleans was wounded, and the marshal de Marsin lost his life. Prince Eugene's view was to relieve Turin, and he could not flatter himself at that time, with the hopes of any greater advantage: but the success that followed, from the conduct of our commanders, surpassed his most sanguine expectations: instead of retiring under the cannon of Casal, which would have preserved the Milanese, they marched back to Pignerol; so that in less than four hours we lost the dukedoms of Modena, Man-

REMARKABLE EVENTS under LEWIS XIV.

tua, and Milan, the principality of Piedmont, and lastly, the kingdom of Naples. The complete victory, which the count de Medavy obtained the 9th of the same month, in the neighbourhood of Castiglione, over the prince of Hesse (afterwards king of Sweden) proved of no manner of service. Follard throws the whole blame of this affair upon marshal de Marsin, and Albergotti; upon the former, for neglecting to obey the orders of the duke of Orleans, which were to bring all the troops that could not act in the other parts of the entrenchments, and to strengthen the post attacked by prince Eugene, which was but of a very small extent; upon the latter, for refusing to weaken his own post, where there was nothing at all to do, in order to support the troops, against whom the prince had directed his attack: besides, he does not think it would have been proper to march out of the lines. The king in vain makes offers of peace to the allies, more advantageous than the terms they had proposed to themselves upon entering into the grand alliance, or those which they obtained at last. The mistake the ministers of Lewis XIV, in 1672, ought to have been a lesson to his enemies.

In Germany, the marshal de Villars maintained the honour of our arms: he obliged the enemy to raise the blockade of fort Louis, by possessing himself of the entrenchments of Drusenheim, which had been abandoned by the prince of Baden. He had with him the marshal de Marsin, who was not yet gone to Italy. The count du Bourg, commanding the vanguard, routed a body of eight hundred of the enemy's horse, on the first of May. M. de Villars detached the marquis de Vieuxpont, who carried Drungenheim the 2d of May; and M. de Peri, who took Haguenau the 11th. The marshal encamped at Spire, from whence he laid all the Palatinate under contribution; and he finished the campaign with making himself master of the island of Marquisat, the 20th of July.

The electors of Bavaria and Cologne are put under the ban of the empire, by a decree of the 29th of April.

The union of the kingdoms of England and Scotland, *which are to be governed by the same parliament, stiled that of Great-Britain.*

Thus

Thus queen Anne effected what king William had in vain attempted to accomplish.

The Saxons are defeated again by the Swedes at the battle of Frauftadt, the 13th of February; the victory was complete: king Auguftus retired to Cracow, while Charles XII. deftroyed the remainder of the Saxon party in Lithuania. This prince advances afterwards into Saxony, and at length obliges king Auguftus to fign the treaty of Alt-Ranftadt the 24th of September, by which he abdicates the crown of Poland.

1707.

The count de Villars, brother to the marshal, retakes the ifland of Minorca the 5th of January. The French and Spanifh troops evacuate all Lombardy, by a capitulation figned the 13th of March: Modena had furrendered the 10th of February, and the caftle of Milan, the 20th of March.

General Thaun makes himfelf mafter of Capua, the 2d of July; the caftle furrenders the 5th; the city of Naples opens her gates to him the 28th, and the whole kingdom follows the example of the capital. Gaeta furrenders the 30th of September, the caftle of Sufa the 4th of October, and Orbitello the 21ft of December.

The battle of Almanza on the 25th of April: the Englifh and Portuguefe, under the command of the earl of Galway and the marquis de las Minas, were intirely defeated by the marfhal duke of Berwick: the chevalier, afterwards marfhal d'Asfeldt, and the marquis d'Avaray, had a great fhare in the fuccefs of this day. One thing, very extraordinary, was to fee an Englifhman (the duke of Berwick, a natural fon of king James II.) commanding the army of France; while the Englifh, on the other hand, were conducted by a Frenchman, my lord Galway, known hitherto by the name of Ruvigny, who quitted his country, at the time of the revocation of the edict of Nantes. The duke of Orleans, although he ufed the utmoft expedition, was not able to reach the army till the day after the action: the confequences of this victory were as rapid, as thofe of our defeats. Requena fubmits to the duke of Orleans on the 3d of May,

and

REMARKABLE EVENTS under LEWIS XIV.

and Valentia the 8th; the other towns throughout the kingdom followed the example of the capital, except a few reduced by the chevalier d'Asfeld. His royal highnefs marches immediately towards Arragon; and Sarragoffa opens her gates to him, the 25th of the fame month. The duke d'Offuna carries Serpa the 26th, and M. de Mahony takes Alcira the 18th of June; Mequinença furrenders the 7th of July, and Monçon the 7th of Auguft. The duke de Noailles poffeffing himfelf of Puicerda, and all Cerdagna, caufes a citadel to be built at Puicerda at the expence of that part of Cerdagna, which belongs to Spain.

The marquis de Bay takes Ciudad-Rodrigo the 4th of October.

The town of Lerida, which had baffled the greateft captains, is befieged by the duke of Orleans, and obliged to furrender the 13th of October, after eleven days open trenches: the caftle did not capitulate till the 12th of November.

The duke of Savoy, and prince Eugene, raife the fiege of Toulon, the 22d of Auguft: this important enterprize was unfkilfuly managed. On the 15th of Auguft the marfhal de Teffé caufed an attack to be made, againft the hill of St. Catharine, of which the enemy had taken poffeffion: whereupon they thought proper to retreat; and all this grand enterprize terminated in the throwing of a few bombs into the town by fir Cloudefly Shovel: the marquis de Goefbriand acquired great honour on this occafion. The houfe of Auftria has not been fuccefsful in her invafions of Provence: we have feen how Charles V. mifcarried in his attempt under the reign of Francis I, in 1536: and fince this affair of prince Eugene, the army of the queen of Hungary was driven from thence in 1747, by the marfhal de Belleifle, who having been created an hereditary duke in 1742, for his care in negotiating the election of the emperor Charles VII, was made a peer in 1747 for faving Provence.

Marfhal de Villars furprizes the lines of Stolophen the 22d of May; they extended from that place to the foot of the mountain of the Black foreft. Meffieurs de Vivant and de Broglio, having affembled the troops under Lauterburg, landed in good order in the ifle of Newburg, while the marfhal de Villars, advancing as far as Bihel, poffeffed himfelf of the lines which the enemy had abandoned, and fixed his quarter at Radstadt. This enterprize having opened a passage into the heart of Germany, he seized the dutchy of Wurtemberg, raised contributions as far as Ulm, and even on the other side of the Danube, made himself master of Schorendorff, defeated general Janus at the abbey of Lork, and took him prisoner, with upwards of two thousand men, and carried his incursions as far as Mariendal, &c. The margrave of Bareith commanded the Imperialists since the death of prince Lewis of Baden, which happened on the 4th of January. The elector of Hanover (afterwards king of England) succeeded the margrave, and after surprizing the marquis de Vivant in the neighbourhood of Offemburg, obliged the marshal to repass the Rhine.

Nothing happened in Flanders. The duke of Marlborough made a tour to Saxony before the opening of the campaign: it was said, that by the power of money he gained over Piper, the Swedish minister, who persuaded Charles XII. to employ his forces against the Czar, by which means he lost his reputation and his army, while he might have acquired the greatest glory, by making use of his influence to restore peace to Europe. But Charles XII. did not suffer himself to be determined by any one, and has since justified Piper, by acknowledging that resolution to have been entirely his own. The king of Sweden was a man of veracity; he loved to do justice to merit, without ever adopting an action, which he did not perform, though it would have procured him praises, to which he was an avowed enemy, even when he really deserved them. Never was there a man more mild, nor more simple in his transactions, nor of a more unbounded courage in war: he was not influenced by what appeared merely possible; he wanted to obtain success when there was not the least probability of doing it.

By sea, the chevalier de Forbin took two English men of war, and twenty merchant ships, the 13th of May: in the month of July he took another prize of forty English and Dutch ships to the northward; and having joined M. de Gué Trouin, he fought the English fleet on the 21st of October, but did not obtain any considerable advantage.

REMARKABLE EVENTS under LEWIS XIV.

The introducing of promissory notes on the gabelles *. M. le Premier is seized in the road to Versailles, on Candlemas eve' by a party belonging to the garrison of Courtray, and commanded by a colonel in the Dutch service, named Gueston: but he was rescued four leagues beyond Ham. Madam de Montespan, who had been superintendant of the queen's houshold, died at Bourbon the 28th of May, where she had been to drink the waters. The death of the dutchess de Nemours, on the 10th of June: the states of Neufchatel invest the king of Prussia with that principality, together with that of Valengin, on the 3d of November; this possession was confirmed to him at the peace of Utrecht, in prejudice to the legitimate heirs.

A conspiracy at Geneva, of which the duke of Savoy was suspected, from his old pretensions to this petty state.

1708.

If M. de Vendome committed some mistakes this campaign, we must acknowledge that the contradictions he met with, did not contribute to repair them. The correspondences we had in Ghent, which made it a sure conquest, determined the king to let the duke of Burgundy have the honour of that expedition: accordingly he possessed himself of that town the 5th of July, having M. de Vendome under him, while the count de la Mothe seized Bruges and Plassendal.

Then the siege of Oudenarde was resolved upon, as we may judge by the march of our troops to take possession of the post of Lessines; but there they perceived, that the allied army, under the command of the duke of Marlborough and prince Eugene, had already passed the Scheld: we were obliged to engage, and on the 11th of July was fought the battle of Oudenarde, where the enemy had some advantage, because we formed too late, and there was only one front of our army, which attacked successively, and in brigades, a line of infantry much

---

* The French call them *billets sur la caisse des emprunts*; the *caisse des emprunts* was an office established in the reign of Lewis XIV, at the *hotel des fermes*, for receiving money of private people, who were willing to lend it to the government at a certain interest; the farmers of the revenue gave them promissory notes for value received, which were payable to the bearer, and passed as current money, by the name of *promisse des gabelles*.

stronger

stronger and more extended than ours. M. de Vendome was for having the troops lie on the field of battle, with a view to renew the action the next day: but the opinion for decamping carried it; and with very good reason, for we should have been in a much worse situation than the day before, our army being separated by the enemy: we therefore retired towards Ghent, and the loss we sustained by our march in the night, was greater than that in the engagement.

The enemy lay siege to Lille; and the trenches are opened in the night of the 22d of August: the marshal de Boufflers defended the capital of his government. The particular of this siege, which lasted four months, would be tedious, and reflexions would carry us too far. M. de Vendome wanted to attack the allies, but could not do as he pleased: the count de la Mothe, being sent to intercept a convoy belonging to the enemy, who were distressed for provisions, was beaten * at Winnendal the 28th of September; and at length prince Eugene, against all probability, gained his point, in an enterprize, which success itself could hardly justify. Lille surrendered the 23d of October, and the citadel the 8th of December. The gallant behaviour of M. de Boufflers in the defence of this place, procured him the dignity of peer of France, and to his eldest son the reversion of the government of Flanders, which upon the death of that eldest son devolved to the next brother; this nobleman's son, only fifteen years of age, succeeded afterwards to the same government, in consideration of the services, which the duke de Boufflers, his father, had done his country, in defending the city of Genoa against the Austrians, where he died the 2d of July, 1747, the same day that the enemy raised the siege.

The duke de Vendome makes himself master of Leffingue the 25th of October; this post intercepted the communication between Ostend and the enemy's camp, and would have been of use two months sooner. The same may be said of the elector's

---

* La Mothe had 20000 men; general Webb was dispatched by the duke o Marlborough with only 6000 men to guard the convoy; the French attacked an were defeated, so that the convoy arrived safe the 30th of September. Genera Webb gained immortal honour by this victory.

scheme

REMARKABLE EVENTS under LEWIS XIV.

scheme for attacking Bruffels: the enemy were incapable of defending this city in the month of September, being too busy before Lille; but the scheme was not thought of till the 26th of November, at which time prince Eugene and the duke of Marlborough were in a condition to march to its relief: accordingly they passed the Scheld, the 27th of November; and advancing towards Bruffels, obliged the elector to decamp. M. de la Mothe surrenders the town of Ghent to the allies, the 30th of December.

Neither was the attempt of the chevalier de St. George against Scotland more successful. The count de Forbin conducted the expedition, and the troops for the embarkation were under the command of the count de Gacé, who was declared a marshal of France at sea; the squadron arrived, the 23d of March, in Edinburg Frith; but no answer being made to the signals, the fleet returned to Dunkirk the 7th of April, and the chevalier remained in Flanders, where he finished the campaign.

The English seize the island of Sardinia the 15th of August, and Port-Mahon the 29th of September. La Jonquiere, who had the command of the latter, was tried at Toulon by a court martial, and degraded.

On the side of Savoy, the marshal de Villars carried both the towns of Sezana on the 11th of August, the duke of Savoy in sight; who, on the other hand, made himself master of Fenestrelle on the 31st, after taking the forts of Exille, and Peroufe. The emperor confers the investiture of Montferrat on the duke of Savoy.

In Spain, Mahony takes Alcoi the 9th of January: the duke of Orleans obliges Tortofa to surrender the 11th of July; the chevalier d'Asfeldt possesses himself of Denia, in the kingdom of Valentia, the 12th of November, and of Alicant, the 3d of December. Count Staremberg makes an ineffectual attempt the 4th of December, to retake Tortofa. In the month of January, the Moors had retaken Oran, that famous town, the conquest of which completed the glory of cardinal Ximenes; but the count de Montemar recovered it again out of their hands in 1732.

The Russians abandon Grodno, the 8th of February, upon the approach of the king of Sweden. On the 14th of July this

REMARKABLE EVENTS under LEWIS XIV.

prince attacks 30000 Muscovites intrenched in the town of Hollosin, and puts them to flight; then passing the Borysthenes, he treats with the Cossacks, and encamps upon the banks of the Desna. The Czar in person attacks general Lewenhaupt, the 8th of October, near Lesnau, and defeats a body of about 4000 Swedes.

Alberoni, protected by M. de Vendome, obtains a pension of a thousand crowns from the king: the abbé du Bois had been presented some years before to a benefice, at the recommendation of the duke of Orleans. Who could have foreseen, that those men were one day to be prime ministers of France and Spain? they were both raised to the purple: the abbé du Bois died in 1723, and cardinal Alberoni was disgraced in 1719.

On the 27th of February, M. Chamillard resigns the place of comptroller-general of the finances to M. Desmarets.

1709.

M. Mansard, superintendant of the royal buildings, dies at Marly, the 11th of May. M. d'Antin succeeded him only as director-general; but he obtained the place of superintendant in 1716, by a new creation, at the same time that the superintendancy of the post-office was erected in favour of M. de Torcy: they were both suppressed in 1726, and M. d'Antin was once more made director-general of the royal buildings.

Pope Clement XI, being forced to acknowledge the archduke as king of Spain, makes an apology to Philip V, by saying, that such a recognition did not confer a new right: this was not the style in which Gregory VII, and Boniface VIII, used to explain themselves.

His majesty sends first the president Rouillé, and afterwards M. de Torcy, to the Hague, to try to put an end to a war, which had exhausted all Europe, and which from the scarcity of the present year was become an intolerable burden to France: but the enemy made such extravagant proposals, that we were obliged to continue the war. It has been said, that the pensionary Heinsius had been gained over by my lord Marlborough, whose ambition was not confined to the command of armies.

REMARKABLE EVENTS under LEWIS XIV.

mies. M. de Torcy's journey was a politic stroke: he reckoned he should not succeed in his negotiation; but it was a great point gained to convince all Europe of the obstinacy of the enemy, in rejecting such concessions as were almost incredible, which his majesty however submitted to, in hopes of accelerating a peace. Another advantage expected from it, was, that the French might be animated the more to resent this indignity. In consequence hereof the king wrote to all the governors of the provinces.

The marshal de Villars commanded the French army in Flanders, which was not near so strong, as that of the allies. The count d'Artagnan carries Warneton upon the Lis, the 4th of July. The encampment of marshal de Villars, his right to Couriere, and his left drawing towards Bethune, with la Bassée and le Pont-Avendin in front: this reduced the enemy to the necessity of laying siege to Tournay, instead of falling upon Doway or Arras, which would have given them a greater opening into the country.

The marquis de Surville surrenders the town of Tournay to the enemy, the 29th of July, after one and twenty days open trenches, and the citadel the 5th of September. M. de Beauvau, bishop of Tournay, refuses to sing *te deum*. Under the walls of this very town, thirty-six years afterwards, Lewis XV, accompanied by the dauphin, and having the marshal count de Saxe under him, obtained a signal victory (at Fontenoy the 11th of May, 1745) over the duke of Cumberland, who attempted to raise the siege, but could not hinder the French from becoming masters of the town in twenty-two days open trenches.

Prince Eugene and the duke of Marlborough pass the Scheld with a view to lay siege to Mons; marshal Villars assembles his army, and marches to the relief of that place. The battle of Malplaquet, the 11th of September: it has been said that M. de Villars might have attacked the allied army the 9th and the 10th to an advantage, because he was superior in number at that time; and, indeed, one would think, at first sight, that this was his intention; but, no doubt, he was loath to expose an army, the last resource of France. It is further added, but without foundation, that the marshal had been amused by some negotiations, which the confederate generals had set on foot, to the end that

REMARKABLE EVENTS under LEWIS XIV.

their troops before Tournay might have time to join the army. Be that as it may, as soon as this junction was effected, finding themselves much stronger than the marshal, they attacked him the 11th, at eight in the morning. This was the bloodiest and longest action during the whole war. The enemy kept the field of battle, and gained their point, which was the taking of Mons: still this was a glorious day to the French nation, when we reflect on the courage and alacrity of the private men; they had been three days streightened for bread, yet when a supply came, they would not stay to eat it, from an impatience to engage. Marshal de Villars was wounded: the marshal de Boufflers, who with a true Roman generosity, had desired to serve under that general, retreated in such good order, that he left neither cannon nor prisoners behind him; the chevalier de Luxemburg was in the rear, and we retired towards Quenoy. A great foraging party, in which the count de Broglio defeated prince Lobkowitz the 11th of October. Mons surrenders to the enemy the 20th.

In Germany, the count du Bourg saved the upper Alsace. The count de Mercy, having traversed the canton of Basil with his cavalry, advanced between Huningen and Brisac, where he rejoined his infantry by means of a bridge, which he had caused to be laid opposite to Neuburg, and which our troops did not defend. From thence he marched against the count du Bourg, whom the marshal d'Harcourt had detached with eighteen squadrons, six battalions, and four hundred grenadiers: on the 26th of August they met at Rumershim; and du Bourg routed the Germans, who lost very near 7000 men killed or drowned: he was rewarded with the order of the Holy Ghost, and afterwards created a marshal of France in 1724. We have beheld a more memorable piece of service done to that very same province by the marshal de Coigny, when prince Charles passed the Rhine; the marshal ventured to attack that prince at Weissemburg, and this vigorous resolution preserved the upper Alsace.

In Spain, the chevalier d'Asfeld took the castle of Alicant, the 17th of April; the marquis de Bay defeated lord Galway, the 7th of May, in the plains of Gudina, upon the frontier of

REMARKABLE EVENTS under LEWIS XIV.

Portugal: on the first of June he dispossessed the Portuguese of the castle of Alconchel. The duke de Noailles, who commanded in Catalonia, attacked on the 7th of August two regiments of the enemy, coming out of Figuieres; and they were all killed or taken: the 2d of September this same general fell upon eighteen hundred horse, who were encamped within half a cannon-shot of Gironne, and he put them to flight; the commander of the Palatine forces was taken prisoner. The marshal de Bezons was not so fortunate, for he could not hinder count Staremberg from making himself master of Balaguier.

On the side of Savoy, M. Dillon, who commanded in the neighbourhood of Briançon, obtained a complete victory on the 28th of August, over general Rebender, who had advanced to attack him in his entrenchments.

The battle of Pultowa, on the 11th of July, proved the *ne plus ultra* of Charles XII: he was defeated by the Czar, whom he had taught the art of war; the whole Swedish army were either destroyed or taken prisoners, and their king was obliged to save himself by flight: he crossed the Borysthenes, got to Oczakow, and from thence retired to Bender. This reverse of fortune brought on the ruin of his party in Poland: king Augustus returned to that kingdom, the Czar followed soon after, and the Swedes retired. Stanislaus being unable to withstand these united powers, repaired to Bender, where he joined the king of Sweden. The vicissitudes of Stanislaus are very remarkable. The Poles, being witnesses to the bravery of this prince, and charmed with the wisdom and lenity of his government, during the short period he sat upon that throne, chose him a second time after the death of Augustus (1733). This election was frustrated by the Russians, who supported his competitor: but Stanislaus still preserving, with the consent of all Europe, the title of king, which he so richly deserved, was made duke of Lorrain, and lived to see new subjects happy under his government. *See the year* 1675. I cannot forbear doing honour to Mr. Huet, for having presaged the great power of Russia, in his *history of the commerce, and navigation of the ancients*. His words are these; " if some time or
" other they should happen to have a wife prince, who seeing
" into

REMARKABLE EVENTS under LEWIS XIV.

"into the errors of the present government, would take care to redress them, and at the same time to soften their ferocity and give a new polish to their manners, this nation would become formidable to all its neighbours."

Father le Tellier is made the king's confessor, in the room of father de la Chaise, who died the 20th of January: father de la Chaise had succeeded father Ferrier in 1674, and the latter was successor to father Annat in 1670. The death of Francis Lewis de Bourbon, prince of Conty, on the 22d of February, at the age of forty-five: he was the second son of Armand, prince of Conty, who died in 1666, and of Anne Martinozzi, a princess of exemplary virtue, deceased in 1672. Notwithstanding his having signalized himself at the battles of Gran, Steinkerk, and Landen, the king could not forget his expedition to Hungary without permission: but upon being nominated to the crown of Poland, he found his majesty still retained such sentiments of affection for him, as a prince of his merit really deserved. He was the father of Lewis Armand II, prince of Conty, who died in 1727, and grandfather to the present prince of Conty, who, like the great Condé, brother of his great grandfather, was victorious, almost at the same age, over the king's enemies, the first time he commanded a French army. Henry Julius of Bourbon, prince of Condé, stiled *monsieur le prince*, died the first of April, aged sixty-six years. M. Voisin succeeded M. Chamillard the 10th of June, in the place of secretary of state for the department of war.

The dukedoms of Villars and Harcourt are erected into peerages.

A riot in Paris, occasioned by the dearness of bread.

The French ships, which came from the South sea, laden with gold and silver, were a great relief to the kingdom, exhausted by war, and desolated by famine, the consequence of a most severe winter.

1710.

The congress of Gertrudenberg, where the marshal d'Huxelles and the abbé de Polignac arrived in the month of March. The king affected with the miseries of his subjects, carried his proposals of peace so far, as to promise he would furnish the allies with money, to help to dethrone his grandson; they were not

satisfied

REMARKABLE EVENTS under LEWIS XIV.

satisfied with this concession, but insisted that he should take upon himself to dethrone him; by this single proposal one may form a judgment of all the rest: we were therefore obliged to continue the war.

In Spain, the success of the allies seemed to decline these two last years; but the battle of Saragossa, which count Staremberg gained against the marquis de Bay, the 20th of August, plunged Philip V. into fresh misfortunes; from which it was so much the more difficult for him to extricate himself, as Lewis XIV. had withdrawn his troops to defend his own dominions. Philip V. quits Madrid the 9th of September the second time, and retires to Valladolid, where he is joined by the duke de Vendome; this was all the indemnity he asked of his grandfather, for the recalling of his forces. What wonders may not be effected by one great man! Philip V. was destitute of troops and money; but this general found new resources, and was soon in a condition to pursue the allies: the army under the archduke was mouldering away in Castile for want of provisions, which the Spaniards chose rather to burn, than fell to that prince: the duke de Noailles had entered into the Lampourdan, with a body of troops raised upon his own credit; whereupon the archduke departed for Barcelona, the 11th of November.

The king of Spain returns to Madrid; then all of a sudden passing the Tagus with M. de Vendome, he carries the town of Brihuega by assault, on the 9th of December: five thousand English, under the command of general Stanhope, surrender themselves prisoners. Count Staremberg, having marched with great expedition to the relief of this place, Philip V. gives him battle the 10th of December, at Villa Viciosa: the king commanded the right wing himself, and M. de Vendome the left. Staremberg, being obliged to give way, after a very warm dispute, made a gallant retreat. This victory was followed by the reduction of several places. The king entered Saragossa in triumph, and affairs began to wear a new aspect.

The duke de Medina Celi, being convicted of high treason, is sent to the castle of Segovia, and from thence to Fontarabia, where he died.

REMARKABLE EVENTS under LEWIS XIV.

In Flanders, the town of Doway, where M. Albergotti was governor, is carried by the allies, the 25th of June, after two and fifty days open trenches. The count de Vauban, ſtiled at that time Dupuis Vauban, nephew to the marſhal, ſurrenders Bethune, after a ſiege of two and forty days, on the 29th of September. M. de Ravignan takes a convoy, which the enemy were conducting upon the Lis, and beats the eſcort. St. Venant is obliged to capitulate, the 29th of September. The marquis de Goeſbriand ſurrenders the town of Aire, the 9th of November, after the trenches had been opened two and fifty days.

By ſea, the enemy's fleet of four and twenty ſail make a deſcent in the harbour of Cette: this enterprize might have been attended with great conſequence to the country of Vivarais, and to the Cevenes, from the danger of the enemy's making a ſettlement, which it would have been eaſy for them to maintain by means of the ſea. The duke de Noailles, marching with all expedition from Rouſſillon with nine hundred horſe, a thouſand grenadiers, and ſome cannon, preſerved this place, obliged the enemy to retire from Agde, defeated ſix hundred of them in the neighbourhood of Cette, and retook the fort which had been in their poſſeſſion.

The cardinal de Bouillon quits the kingdom: the parliament by an arret of the 29th of June, at the motion of the attorney-general, orders him to be arreſted, and his revenue to be ſeized: the cauſe of his withdrawing was the irkſomeneſs of his exile.

The death of Lewis duke of Bourbon, ſtiled *monſieur le duc*, on the 3d of March, at the age of forty-two; he was father of the duke of Bourbon, who ſucceeded the duke of Orleans as chief miniſter of ſtate, and died in 1740. The marriage of the duke of Berry to mademoiſelle d'Orleans.

The king makes a regulation, that the children of the duke du Maine, a legitimated ſon of France, ſhall, as grandſons of his majeſty, enjoy the ſame rank, honour and precedency, as had been granted to the duke du Maine; and he ordains that this regulation ſhall be inſerted in the regiſter of the lord ſteward of the houſhold. On the 15th of May the duke de Vendome eſpouſes mademoiſelle d'Anguien, at Sceaux.

REMARKABLE EVENTS under LEWIS XIV.

An order for raising the tenth of all the revenues of the kingdom; this edict was registered in the chamber of vacations, the 26th of October.

The battle of Elsimburg the 10th of March, where the Swedes had a considerable advantage over the Danes. Wyburg in Finland is taken by the Muscovites, the 25th of June: Riga surrenders to them the 11th of July, fort Dunemunde the 12th of August, and Revel the 1st of November.

Warty erected into a dutchy and peerage, under the name of Fitz-James, in favour of the duke of Berwick, a natural son of king James II, and of Arabella Churchill, sister to the duke of Marlborough; to have and to enjoy for himself, and for his son by his second lady; his son by a former marriage, stiled the duke of Liria, having been made a grandee of Spain. The duke of Berwick was willing to establish a second branch of his family in France.

An academy of sciences and belles lettres instituted at Lyons.

1711.

In Spain, the most considerable expedition, during the whole campaign, was the taking of Gironne by the duke de Noailles: nothing less than the great constancy of this general could accomplish that undertaking: he had opened the trenches before Fort-rouge, the 27th of December, and his army was in some measure encompassed by the inundations, yet he carried the lower town, the 23d of January, by assault, and the upper capitulated the 25th. He was made marshal of France, in 1734, and minister of state in 1743: the marshal his father had taken the same town in 1694. The Germans abandoned Balaguier, the 23d of February. The inhabitants of the plain and district of Vic, who had given the lead to the insurrection in Catalonia, were compelled by the taking of this town, to grant quarters of refreshment to our army. The kingdom of Arragon is intirely reduced by the surrender of Venasso, of which the marquis d'Arpagon made himself master the 16th of September; and a few days after he possessed himself of Castel Leon. The count de Muret had taken the town of Cardonna, the 17th of November, but was obliged to raife the fiege of the citadel, the 24th of December.

In Flanders, the count d'Harling makes himfelf mafter of the fluices of Harlebek on the Lis the 28th of May, a little below Courtray. The allies, who feized the caftle of Arleux the 6th of July, ufed all poffible diligence in fortifying it, by reafon of the importance of the poft; and covered their workmen with ten battalions and twelve fquadrons: the count de Gaffion and the marquis de Coigny furprized and beat them, the 12th; but the poft ftill remaining in the enemy's hands, the marfhal de Montefquiou carried it the 23d of July. The marfhal de Villars, in confequence of an order from court, did not think proper to expofe his front to the duke of Marlborough, who had juft paffed the Sanzet: the fame reafon determined him, inftead of marching to Thun-l'Eveque (which would have inevitably brought on a battle) to take poft on the heights of Cambray, his right under the cannon of that place, and his left to the brook of Marquion, which he had lately croffed. This pofition difappointed the duke of Marlborough, who wanted a battle; and obliged him to pafs the Scheld in the night, (the marfhal being at fome diftance) in order to inveft Bouchain, which furrendered the 13th of September.

On the 5th of Auguft, the marquis de Coigny attacked and defeated, in the neighbourhood of Landrecy, feven fquadrons of the allies, that covered a foraging party.

Nothing of confequence was tranfacted in Germany, where the marfhals d'Harcourt and de Bezons had the direction; nor on the fide of Savoy, where the duke of Berwick commanded the two laft years againft general Thaun, and covered Provence and Dauphiné.

By fea, the fieur Saus took the greateft part of the Virginia fleet, the 16th of January. Off Vado, on the coaft of Genoa, was fought a drawn battle between an Englifh fquadron and ours. In Canada, the Englifh mifcarried on the 3d of September, in their attempt againft Quebec *.

The

---

* Sir Hoveden Walker with a fleet of men of war and tranfports, carrying feven regiments, and a battalion of marines, was fent from England to make an attempt
upon

REMARKABLE EVENTS under LEWIS XIV.

The expedition of M. du Gué-Trouin to Rio-Janeiro in the Brasils, in the months of September and October; from which the Portuguese sustained a loss of upwards of five and twenty millions of livres, and our privateers gained above seven.

The dutchy and peerage of Chaulnes. The county of Chaulnes had been erected into a dutchy and peerage in 1621, in favour of Honoré d'Albret, lord of Cadenet, and brother of the constable de Luines. Lewis Augustus d'Albret, the constable's great grandson, succeeded by intail to the estate of Honoré d'Albret, whose son died without issue; and as Lewis was not a descendant of Honoré, the king granted him a new patent.

The battle of Falczim upon the Pruth, the 20th of July, where the Czar was surrounded by the Turks, and had no possibility of escaping; but the avarice of the grand vizir saved that prince, in spite of the remonstrances of the king of Sweden, who had but just joined the army. The most important article in the treaty betwixt them, was the restitution of Asoph. The king of Denmark makes himself master of Rostock, the 19th of August.

The Czar, whom we shall have no occasion to mention again, died in 1725. The revolutions occasioned by the succession to this great empire, from the decease of that prince to the present time, are too curious to be omitted. The Czar Alexis, who departed this life in 1676, left three sons; Foedor (who died without issue in 1682) John, and Peter. Foedor reigned till the day of his death, in 1682; John and Peter reigned jointly after him; or rather Peter, who already gave strong presages of his future destiny, reigned alone. John, who was both blind and infirm, breathed his last in 1696, and left two daughters. Peter the Great died in 1725; the empress Catharine his wife, whose great accomplishments cancelled the meanness of her extraction, succeeded him in the government of that empire: she deceased in 1727; and by virtue of the power bequeathed to her by Peter the Great, she nominated her grandson Peter II. her successor. Peter II. dying in 1730, was succeeded by Anne, dutchess of Courland,

---

upon Canada. Eight of the transports, with eight hundred officers and soldiers, were cast away in the river of St. Lawrence; whereupon the rest of the fleet returned to New England.

daughter of the Czar John, and great aunt to Peter II. Anne departed this life in 1740, after having declared her succeffor, John of Brunfwick, her fifter's grandfon, only three months old, under the regency of her niece, Elizabeth of Mecklenburg, wife of the duke of Brunfwic, and mother of John. Thus the empire feemed to be perpetuated in the elder branch of Alexis: but this regency was not of long continuance; for in 1741, Elizabeth and her fon were difpoffeffed of the throne, by another Elizabeth, the reigning emprefs, fecond daughter of Peter the Great. This princefs has declared her succeffor, Charles Peter Ulric, duke of Holftein Gottorp, the fon of her eldeft fifter deceafed in 1728, whom fhe caufed to be named great duke of Ruffia in 1742. This prince had been called to the crown of Sweden, upon the death of the laft king, the landgrave of Heffe-Caffel, who died without iffue by Ulrica, the younger fifter of Charles XII, to whom he was indebted for the crown: but when the throne of Sweden became vacant, Charles had been already declared heir to the Ruffian empire in right of his mother, the Czar Peter's eldeft daughter, and had made profeffion of the Greek religion.

The dauphin dies of the fmall-pox, aged fifty years, at the caftle of Meudon, the 14th of April.

The death of the old duke of Lefdiguieres (Canaples); upon his deceafe this dutchy became extinct: it had been erected in 1611 in behalf of the conftable of that name, and at the fame time, by a particular grant, in favour of M. de Crequy, his fon-in-law.

That which neither reafon nor juftice had hitherto been able to obtain, from the obftinacy of the allies, was at length effected by a court intrigue. The queen of England opened her eyes, and faw how fhe was befet by the dutchefs of Marlborough: her faithful fervants, or thofe who envied the duke of Marlborough, laid hold of this circumftance, and demonftrated to her majefty, that to ferve the ambitious views of this general, the Englifh bore the whole burden of the war, from which they alone received no benefit. Doctor Sacheverel, a clergyman of the church of England, and a leading man among the Tories, encouraged thefe notions, and inflamed the minds of the populace,

REMARKABLE EVENTS under LEWIS XIV.

lace, with his discourses from the pulpit. The relations of my lord Marlborough were dismissed from court, and his power in the army was abridged, till an opportunity offered to divest him of his command. In the mean while negotiations of peace had been set on foot in England; and there were several conferences between Mr. Prior and monsieur Menager*, by which this great work was considerably advanced. The death of the emperor Joseph, which happened on the 17th of April, greatly forwarded the negotiations. If the dread of an uncertain event was sufficient to kindle a war, with a view of preventing the union of the French and Spanish monarchies; what could be said to the actual union of the empire and Spain under the same prince, the archduke, who had been elected emperor the 12th of October? In a word, all these considerations together, made an impression on queen Anne, who was now resolved to bring her allies into the same way of thinking as herself, or, if they should prove obstinate, to quit the confederacy. The preliminaries were signed at London in the month of October: the chief articles were that Lewis XIV. should acknowledge the queen of Great-Britain, as also the succession to the crown, according to the present establishment: that just and reasonable measures should be taken, to prevent the crowns of France and Spain from being united under the same prince: that the Dutch should have a barrier against France: that the empire and the house of Austria should also have a sure and proper barrier: that the fortifications of Dunkirk should be demolished upon the conclusion of the peace, &c.

The marquisate of Antin erected into a dutchy and peerage: it was upon this occasion, and to determine the dispute between the marshal de Luxemburg and the other dukes and peers, that the famous edict of the month of May was published; by which it is ordained that the new dukes shall have rank only from the day of their reception, and not from the date of their creation.

---

* Monsieur Menager was deputy of the council of commerce in France; he came over into England in 1711, with proposals of peace, and published afterwards his memoirs, containing an account of these negotiations.

REMARKABLE EVENTS under LEWIS XIV.

The erection of the dutchy and peerage of Rambouillet, with a very remarkable clause: Rambouillet was held of the king, on account of the tower of the Chatelet, or of the county of Paris; and although this county was the first seignory in France, that had been reunited to the crown by Hugh Capet, yet the king releases the land of Rambouillet from this dependence, so as it shall be held hereafter of the tower of the Louvre.

1712.

The opening of the congress of Utrecht, the 29th of January. This famous congress, which gave peace to all Europe, was not terminated till the year following: the plenipotentiaries of all the contending powers repaired to that city, except those of the king of Spain, because his title was not acknowledged by the allies: the emperor's ambassadors were also present, but withdrew as soon as the peace was signed; and this prince continued the war against France by himself. The king's ministers were the marshal d'Huxelles, the abbé de Polignac, and M. Menager. The sieur du Theil was secretary of the embassy: but it was the abbé Gautier that set the negotiations on foot in London.

The king of Spain transfers the sovereignty of the Spanish Netherlands to the elector of Bavaria, and to the heirs of that prince.

The death of the dauphiness, Mary Adelaid of Savoy, formerly dutchess of Burgundy, which happened at Versailles, in her six and twentieth year, on the 12th of February. The dauphin survived her but six days, and died at Marly on the 18th, at the age of thirty. The duke of Britany, the eldest of the two princes whom he left behind, followed soon after, and died at Versailles on the 8th of March, only five years old; the duke of Anjou (Lewis XV.) was likewise in great danger.

The war—afforded nothing remarkable in Spain. The enemy made an unsuccessful attempt upon Venasco; neither were they more successful before Cervera or Roses: the town of Gironne having been blockaded by the allies, the marquis

REMARKABLE EVENTS under LEWIS XIV.

quis de Brancas, governor of that place, held out eight months; and by his perseverance obliged them to retire. The king of Spain sent him the order of the Golden Fleece: he was afterwards twice ambassador to Madrid, was made a grandee of Spain in 1729, and a marshal of France in 1741.

The campaign in Flanders was the only object worthy of attention; and indeed the operations on that side contributed to forward the peace.

The duke of Marlborough is dismissed from all his employments. The vicissitudes of this man's life are very extraordinary. He had been a favourite of king James II, yet deserted him abruptly, to follow William III, by whom he was afterwards discarded. Queen Anne had been most liberal of her favours to him and his dutchess; yet she saw him connected with those, who used all their arts to defeat her pacific intentions: the elector of Hanover succeeding to queen Anne, restored the duke to all his posts: he died the 27th of June, 1722, at the age of seventy-four, and was interred in Westminster-abbey, in Henry VII's chapel.

The duke of Ormond commands in Flanders, in the room of my lord Marlborough. On the 2d of March, the earl of Albemarle burns some forage in the suburbs of Arras. The count de Broglio becomes master of the post of l'Ecluse, the 30th of March. He was made marshal of France in 1734, hereditary duke in 1742, and died in 1745.

Quesnoy surrenders to prince Eugene the 4th of July. An engagement between the cavalry of the French and allied armies, on the 7th of July; the count de Broglio, having passed the Scarpe to cover the foragers, defeated eight hundred of the enemy's horse; another foraging party of the enemy were beaten the 10th, in the neighbourhood of Valenciennes. The duke of Ormond withdraws his troops from the allied army, the 17th of July. A suspension of arms is proclaimed in the French and English camps. Dunkirk is put into the hands of the English, on the 19th of July, till the conclusion of the peace. Prince Eugene, notwithstanding this separation, lays siege to Landrecy.

REMARKABLE EVENTS under LEWIS XIV.

The succesful temerity of the preceding campaigns had rendered prince Eugene more enterprizing: if he had been attacked at Lille, perhaps he would not have been beaten at Denain.

The affair of Denain. The marshal de Villars wanted to relieve Landrecy; but finding prince Eugene too strongly entrenched, he determined to force the post of Denain, which favoured the passage of the enemy's convoys from Marchiennes to Landrecy. The business was to deceive prince Eugene, and to threaten his camp at Landrecy, to the end that he might weaken that of Denain; and in this the French general succeeded. The dispositions previous to that memorable day, which saved France from ruin, are as much to the honour of this commander, as the victory itself. Denain was forced the 24th of July; and Marchiennes, where the enemy had all their magazines, was carried the 30th of the same month. The siege of Landrecy was raised the 2d of August; and St. Amand surrendered to Albergotti. The marshal de Villars made himself master of Doway, the 8th of September; of Quenoy, the 4th of October; and of Bouchain, the 19th. The suspension of arms agreed to by France, Spain, and England, which had been proclaimed at Paris the 24th of August, was prolonged; and a like suspension was declared with regard to Portugal.

The king of Spain renounces the crown of France, for himself and his descendants, by an act of the 5th of November; and, on the other hand, the dukes of Berry and Orleans relinquish their pretensions to Spain. The king's letters patent, concerning these renunciations, were verified in parliament the 15th of March the year following: " When that political law, " which has established in the kingdom a certain order of suc- " cession, becomes destructive to the body politic, for whose " sake it was established; there is not the least room to " doubt but another political law may be made to change " this order: and so far would this law be from opposing the " former, in the mean it would be conformable to it, since " both would depend on this principle, that the SAFETY OF " THE PEOPLE IS THE SUPREME LAW. (The Spirit of Laws, book 26. chap. 23.)

The

REMARKABLE EVENTS under LEWIS XIV.

The treaty of Araw in Swifferland, concluded the 2d of Auguft, by the mediation of the count de Luc, extinguifhes the civil broils between the Proteftant and Catholic cantons: the latter fupported the abbot of St. Gal againft the inhabitants of Tockemburg.

Louifa Maria Stuart, daughter of king James II, departs this life in her twentieth year, at St. Germains, on the 18th of April.

Lewis Jofeph, duke de Vendome, fon of Lewis duke de Vendome, who was afterwards cardinal, dies at Vignaros in Spain, the 11th of June, at fifty-eight years of age: the king of Spain granted him the fame rank, as had been enjoyed by Don John of Auftria; and he was treated as a prince of his family. The eminent abilities of M. de Vendome in the art of war, together with his courage, and good nature, plainly fhewed him to be the grandfon of Henry IV.

1713.

The peace is figned at Utrecht. The different treaties are as follow: a barrier treaty between England and Holland, on the 29th of January. A treaty concerning the evacuation of Catalonia, and the neutrality of Italy, on the 14th of March. A treaty with Portugal, touching the fettlements out of Europe. A treaty between the kings of France and Pruffia; the chief articles of which are the 7th, 8th, 9th, and 10th; by the 7th and 8th his majefty in virtue of the power delegated to him by the king of Spain cedes the town of Gueldre, &c. to the king of Pruffia; by the 9th the king acknowledges him as fovereign of Neufchatel and Valengin; by the 10th the king of Pruffia renounces all his rights and pretenfions to the principality of Orange; by two other articles, the king promifes for himfelf and for the king of Spain, to grant the title of majefty to the king of Pruffia, who engages on the other hand to reftore the town of Rhimberg to the elector of Cologne. By the treaty with Savoy, the limits of France and Savoy are determined by the fummit of the Alps; and his majefty acknowledges the duke of Savoy as king of Sicily, which had been ceded to him by the king of Spain. The 4th, 9th, 10th, 12th, and 13th articles of the treaty with England, are important, and agreeable to the preliminaries figned in the month of October, 1711. By the treaty with Holland, the king engages for himself and his allies, to deliver up to their high mightinesses, in favour of the house of Austria, pursuant to the treaty of barrier to be concluded between them, whatever either he, or his allies, are possessed of in the Spanish Netherlands, &c. he likewise resigns the dutchy, town, and fortress of Luxemburg, with Namur, Charleroy, and Newport, and engages to obtain from the elector of Bavaria, a cession of all his rights to the Netherlands, on condition that this prince shall be restored to his dominions. The king likewise delivered up several other places. All these treaties were signed the 11th of April. The chevalier de St. George made his protest against them the 25th. The peace is signed the 13th of July, between Spain on the one hand, and Great-Britain and Savoy on the other: by this treaty, Gibraltar and Port-Mahon, with the island of Minorca, were ceded for ever to the English, who likewise received considerable advantages with regard to their West-India trade.

The king publishes an edict, the 18th of September, expressing, that the liberty of commerce, stipulated in the treaties of peace, shall not authorize the protestant refugees to return and settle in France without his permission, nor the new converts to remove to foreign countries.

The war with the emperor continued. The marshal de Villars having made himself master of the towns of Spire, Worms, Keyserlauter, &c. without resistance, causes Landau to be invested by the marshal de Bezons, the 22d of June, and carries it the 20th of August: he then passed the Rhine, and, intending to lay siege to Friburg, he attacked general Vaubonne (who lay between him and that town), and defeated him in his entrenchments, on the 20th of September. The trenches were opened before Friburg the 30th of September, in the night: the siege was long and painful: there were two principal attacks, one of the lunette, and the other of the covert-way. The regiment of guards distinguished themselves in the latter. The baron d'Ars, who was governor of Friburg, finding himself unable to defend the town any longer, retired in great haste with the garrison into the castles, the last of October, in the night; and the capitulation, for the castles and fort, was signed the 16th of the same month. The

REMARKABLE EVENTS under LEWIS XIV.

The marſhal de Villars and prince Eugene repair to Raſtadt, where the conferences of peace were to be held.

In Spain, the archdutcheſs ſet ſail for Italy, the 18th of March, in order to return to Germany, leaving count Staremberg to command the troops, which could not embark at the ſame time. The count himſelf withdrew from thence, the 10th of July: but this did not reſtore the tranquillity of Catalonia; for the city of Barcelona was not taken till the year following.

The duke of Bourbon marries the princeſs of Conty; and the prince of Conty eſpouſes mademoiſelle de Bourbon, the 9th of July.

The king grants the title of hiſtoriographer, and a penſion of two thouſand livres, to father Daniel: this author is more impartial, and better informed than many imagine.

The emperor Charles VI. ſells the marquiſate of Final and its dependencies to the republic of Genoa, for the ſum of ſix millions of livres, to have and enjoy it with the ſame prerogatives as had been poſſeſſed by Charles II, king of Spain, and his predeceſſors, who wreſted this place from the houſe of Caretto. Final had been taken from Philip V, in the courſe of this war, by the powers in alliance with the emperor.

The enemies of the king of Sweden obtained an order from the Porte, to oblige this prince to depart from Bender: upon his refuſal he was attacked in his houſe the 12th of February, and in a manner beſieged. Never did prince run more riſk, or diſplay greater courage. The grand ſignior diſavowed this violence; yet the king of Sweden obtained no ſuccours: nay, the Muſcovites, that ſame day, made themſelves maſters of Frederickſtadt.

An academy of ſciences and belles lettres eſtabliſhed at Bourdeaux. Letters patent confirming the inſtitution of the royal academy of inſcription, begun in 1663; and that of the academy of ſciences, begun in 1666.

1714.

The duke of Berry takes his ſeat in the council of finances:

he had been already made a member of the council of dispatches.

On the 15th of February, the parliament verifies the king's letters patent, published the 14th of the same month, concerning the constitution Unigenitus, pursuant to the arret of the same day.

The treaty of peace signed at Rastadt, the 6th of March, by prince Eugene, in the name of the emperor; and by the marshal de Villars, in behalf of the king. This treaty restored the German frontier to the terms of the peace of Ryswick; and the Netherlands were settled according to the late treaty of Utrecht. It was also agreed, that the affairs of Italy should be continued in the same posture, as they had been in, since the emperor seized the Spanish possessions in that country; but his imperial majesty promised to restore the princes of Italy, such as the dukes of Guastalla, Mirandola, &c. to the dominions, of which they had been stripped during the late war; a just regulation, but never carried properly into execution. The emperor likewise engaged not to disturb the neutrality of Italy, which had been settled by the treaty of the 14th of March, 1713. The electors of Cologne and Bavaria recovered their dominions and titles, and the king acknowledged the electoral dignity in the house of Hanover. The elector of Bavaria died in 1726; and his son, the emperor Charles VII, in 1745.

A peace is concluded with the empire at Baden in Argaw, the 7th of September. It contained nearly the same articles, as those of the treaty of Rastadt. The plenipotentiaries on the part of the emperor, to whom the princes of the empire had committed their interests, were prince Eugene, and the counts de Goes and de Seilern: for the king, were the marshal de Villars, the count de St. Luc, and M. de St. Contest. In this treaty no mention was made of Philip V, because the emperor did not own him as king of Spain; nor did the latter acknowledge Charles VI. as emperor.

The treaty of peace and commerce betwixt Spain and the United Provinces, signed at Utrecht the 26th of June.

Mary

REMARKABLE EVENTS under LEWIS XIV.

The marshal de Villars and prince Eugene repair to Rastadt, where the conferences of peace were to be held.

In Spain, the archdutchess set sail for Italy, the 18th of March, in order to return to Germany, leaving count Staremberg to command the troops, which could not embark at the same time. The count himself withdrew from thence, the 10th of July: but this did not restore the tranquillity of Catalonia; for the city of Barcelona was not taken till the year following.

The duke of Bourbon marries the princess of Conty; and the prince of Conty espouses mademoiselle de Bourbon, the 9th of July.

The king grants the title of historiographer, and a pension of two thousand livres, to father Daniel: this author is more impartial, and better informed than many imagine.

The emperor Charles VI. sells the marquisate of Final and its dependencies to the republic of Genoa, for the sum of six millions of livres, to have and enjoy it with the same prerogatives as had been possessed by Charles II, king of Spain, and his predecessors, who wrested this place from the house of Caretto. Final had been taken from Philip V, in the course of this war, by the powers in alliance with the emperor.

The enemies of the king of Sweden obtained an order from the Porte, to oblige this prince to depart from Bender: upon his refusal he was attacked in his house the 12th of February, and in a manner besieged. Never did prince run more risk, or display greater courage. The grand signior disavowed this violence; yet the king of Sweden obtained no succours: nay, the Muscovites, that same day, made themselves masters of Frederickstadt.

An academy of sciences and belles lettres established at Bourdeaux. Letters patent confirming the institution of the royal academy of inscription, begun in 1663; and that of the academy of sciences, begun in 1666.

1714.

The duke of Berry takes his seat in the council of finances:

REMARKABLE EVENTS under LEWIS XIV.

he had been already made a member of the council of difpatches.

On the 15th of February, the parliament verifies the king's letters patent, publifhed the 14th of the fame month, concerning the conſtitution Unigenitus, purfuant to the arret of the fame day.

The treaty of peace figned at Raftadt, the 6th of March, by prince Eugene, in the name of the emperor; and by the marfhal de Villars, in behalf of the king. This treaty reftored the German frontier to the terms of the peace of Ryfwick; and the Netherlands were fettled according to the late treaty of Utrecht. It was alfo agreed, that the affairs of Italy fhould be continued in the fame pofture, as they had been in, fince the emperor feized the Spanifh poffeffions in that country; but his imperial majefty promifed to reftore the princes of Italy, fuch as the dukes of Guaftalla, Mirandola, &c. to the dominions, of which they had been ftripped during the late war; a juft regulation, but never carried properly into execution. The emperor likewife engaged not to difturb the neutrality of Italy, which had been fettled by the treaty of the 14th of March, 1713. The electors of Cologne and Bavaria recovered their dominions and titles, and the king acknowledged the electoral dignity in the houfe of Hanover. The elector of Bavaria died in 1726; and his fon, the emperor Charles VII, in 1745.

A peace is concluded with the empire at Baden in Argaw, the 7th of September. It contained nearly the fame articles, as thofe of the treaty of Raftadt. The plenipotentiaries on the part of the emperor, to whom the princes of the empire had committed their interefts, were prince Eugene, and the counts de Goes and de Seilern: for the king, were the marfhal de Villars, the count de St. Luc, and M. de St. Conteft. In this treaty no mention was made of Philip V, becaufe the emperor did not own him as king of Spain; nor did the latter acknowledge Charles VI. as emperor.

The treaty of peace and commerce betwixt Spain and the United Provinces, figned at Utrecht the 26th of June.

Mary

REMARKABLE EVENTS under LEWIS XIV.

Mary Louisa of Savoy, queen of Spain, died at Madrid the 14th of February, in her 28th year; and the king of Spain married a second wife, the princess of Parma, on the 24th of December. Queen Anne breathed her last the 12th of August, and was succeeded by prince George Lewis of Brunswick, duke of Hanover. Had these two events happened a year sooner, they might have proved a great hinderance to the peace.

An edict registered in parliament the 2d of August, by which the legitimated princes, and their descendants, are called to the crown, in failure of the princes of the blood: the 23d of the ensuing May was published a declaration, which not only confirmed this edict, but rendered the legitimated princes equal in every respect to the princes of the blood. Lewis XV, by an edict of the year 1717, repealed that of 1714, as well as the declaration of 1715; reserving nevertheless to the legitimated princes, the honours settled by the edict of 1714; reserving also to a future decision, the point of rank in parliament, and of the honours of the court, as far as they related to the princes of Dombes and the count d'Eu: but on the 26th of August, 1718, his majesty published an edict, in a bed of justice at the Thuilleries, whereby he revoked not only the edict of 1714, and the declaration of 1715, but morever the edict of 1694. The same day the king issued out a declaration, by which the count de Touloufe was restored, only during life, to the state he had possessed by virtue of the edict of 1717. At length, by a declaration of 1723, his majesty restores the duke du Maine and the count de Touloufe, (and after the resignation of the peerages of the duke du Maine, he extends the same favour to his children, only during their life) to the honours which they enjoyed in parliament next to the princes of the blood, and before the peers; and this by virtue of their peerages, even tho' the latter should happen not to be of such ancient date, as those of some dukes and peers: *provided however, that when they come to take their seat, they shall not be at liberty to go across the court, a privilege we reserve only for the princes of the blood; nor to be preceded by more than one usher; nor shall their votes be taken otherwise than calling them by the name of their peerage,*

as

REMARKABLE EVENTS under LEWIS XIV.

as hath hitherto been the practice. The same year all the honours of the court were restored to the duke du Maine, and to the count de Touloufe. In 1727, the king issued out the like patents in favour of the princes of Dombes, count d'Eu, and the duke de Penthievre; and, in 1745, thefe honours were granted to the fon of the duke de Penthievre, who married the princefs of Modena.

On the 30th of Auguft the king fends his will to the parliament, with an edict, declaring, that it fhall be depofited in their rolls, and not opened till after his deceafe. By this teftamentary difpofition, dated the 2d of Auguft, he eftablifhed a council of regency, of which the duke of Orleans was to be prefident: the perfon of the young king was committed to the tutelage and direction of that council; and the duke du Maine was to have the care of his education. The day after the king's death, the parliament being affembled, together with the princes of the blood, the peers, and great officers of the realm, the title of regent was unanimoufly conferred on the duke of Orleans.

The taking of Barcellona by the duke of Berwick, reftored tranquillity to Spain: this conqueft was the work of almoft a whole year, from the obftinate refiftance of the befieged; the blockade lafted eleven months, and they reckoned fixty-one days open trenches to the 11th of September, when a general affault was given to the town, which furrendered the 12th. That place being taken, Philip V. had only to reduce the inhabitants of Majorca, who were obliged to fubmit the year following to the chevalier d'Asfeld.

The duke de Berry died at Marly on the 4th of May, in the 28th year of his age. The chancellor de Pontchartrain retired from court, and from the management of public affairs, notwithftanding the oppofition of the king, who loft with reluctance fo great a magiftrate, and fo able a minifter. The vivacity of his mind did not deprive him of that peace and ferenity, which he knew how to enjoy in folitude; and he was greater ftill from his generous retreat, than from the important offices, which he had difcharged with fuch fuperior abilities. He

died

REMARKABLE EVENTS under LEWIS XIV.

died December 28, 1727, at the age of eighty-five. M. Voifin, the prefent fecretary of ftate, fucceeded him in the office of chancellor.

A citation of the knights of Malta, upon the news of a formidable armament at Conftantinople: but either it was not the intention of the grand fignior to attack that ifland, or he was diverted from this defign, by hearing that it was in a good pofture of defence: his whole efforts therefore fell upon the Venetians.

The king of Sweden having traverfed Germany *incognito*, arrived at Stralfund the 22d of November, in the morning, attended only by three officers. This prince, whom we fhall have no more occafion to mention, was killed, in 1718, at the fiege of Frederickftadt: what happened after his death, with regard to the fucceffion, is too curious to be omitted, though it does not belong to this reign. Charles XII. left two fifters: Hedwig, the eldeft, who had been married to the duke of Holftein, was excluded from the crown, being confidered as a ftranger, by not refiding in the kingdom: her fifter Ulrica efpoufed Frederic, landgrave of Heffe-Caffel, with the confent of the nation, who called her to the fucceffion of her brother; but fhe chofe to have the crown fettled on her hufband, and accordingly he was elected, upon her renunciation; with this provifo, that if they had children, thefe fhould fucceed to the crown; otherwife, the kingdom was to become elective. After a courfe of years, when they had no iffue, nor a probability of any, the nation afferted its right, and nominated a fucceffor: this was the duke of Holftein, grandfon of Hedwig, and fon of the princefs Anne, daughter of the Czar Peter the Great. But as he had been declared grand duke of Mufcovy, in right of his mother, by the emprefs Elizabeth, who had no children, he was obliged to renounce the Swedifh election; and the Swedes caft their eyes on Adolphus Frederic, defcended from a younger branch of the dukes of Holftein; this prince had no manner of right to the crown, yet fucceeded Frederic, landgrave of Heffe-Caffel, who died in 1751. The grand fignior, having concluded a peace with Mufcovy and Poland, fell with his united force upon the Venetians, and difpoffeffed them of the Morea.

The difgrace of the princefs Orfini, who went to meet the queen fifteen leagues from Madrid, but received orders forthwith to depart the kingdom of Spain.

The barony of Frontenay created a dutchy and peerage, by the name of Rohan-Rohan: the erection of this peerage had been made already in 1626, but the letters patent were not regiftered.

The vifcounty of Joyeufe erected into a dutchy and peerage, in favour of the prince d'Epinoy: it is extinct.

The Englifh ambaffador * made loud complaints againft the works, which Lewis XIV. had ordered to be carried on at the harbour of Mardyke: he demanded a particular audience on the occafion, which was granted him, and he fpoke to the king with more warmth than decency: his majefty did not interrupt him in his harangue; but when it was ended, he faid to him, *Monfieur l'ambaffadeur, I have always been mafter at home, and fometimes abroad; do not put me in mind of this circumftance.*

1715.

The congrefs of Utretcht concluded with the treaty between Spain and Portugal, figned the 13th of February: the barrier treaty between the emperor and the Dutch, which the minifters of thofe powers were fettling at Antwerp, was not determined till the 15th of November.

The chevalier d'Asfeld landed in Majorca the 16th of June, and completed the reduction of that ifland the 2d of July, by the furrender of Palma, the capital.

The king grants an audience to the Perfian ambaffador the 19th of February. The arrival of the envoys from Tripoli.

The alliance with the Catholic cantons and the Valais, renewed by the count du Luc on the 9th of May. This treaty contains thirty-five articles, and is much the fame, as that which

---

* The earl of Stair.

REMARKABLE EVENTS under LEWIS XIV.

was signed in 1663, with all the cantons: the 5th article deserves particular notice; the king engages thereby to grant succours to the Catholic cantons, in case they should be molested by any foreign power; and even to assist the weaker against the stronger, if there should happen to be any division in Swisserland.

The marquisate of Hostun had been created a dukedom in 1712, in favour of the marshal de Tallard: this dukedom he resigned to his son Joseph, upon the occasion of that young nobleman's marriage in 1713, to the daughter of the prince de Rohan: the king grants new letters patent to the son, by which the title of Hostun is raised to a dutchy and peerage.

The council of dispatches pass a decree, that the Jesuits shall be at liberty to resume their estates, till the age of thirty-three: M. Chauvelin (afterwards keeper of the seals) was president of the council.

On the 12th of August, the people about court began to perceive that the king was out of order: he had a pain in his leg and thigh, which the physicians treated as a sciatica. From that day he did not stir out of his apartment: he intended to review the gendarms, who were drawn up in the outer court of the palace of Versailles; but his health not permitting him, he appointed the duke du Maine to make this review the 22d of August, in the *champ de Mars* near Marly. The dauphin, dressed in his uniform, came to see the troops after the review; and the duke of Orleans saluted him at the head of the gendarms of Orleans.

The death of Lewis the *great* on the first of September: he was worthy of this name independently of all his conquests.

It has been justly observed, that the reigns of Augustus and Lewis XIV. resemble each other, in the concourse of great men of all kinds, who distinguished those æras: yet we are not to imagine that this was merely the effect of chance; for if two reigns have a very great resemblance, it is because they have been attended with nearly the same circumstances. Those two princes both freed themselves from a civil war; and this happened at a time, when the people, constantly in arms, and bred in the midst of danger, with their heads full of the boldest designs, saw nothing they could not obtain; at a time when a continual succession of happy and unhappy events enlarged their ideas, strengthened the mind by putting it to the proof, increased its activity, and gave it that desire of glory, which never fails to produce great things.

In this situation Augustus and Lewis XIV. found the world. Julius Cæsar had rendered himself the master of it, and prepared the way for Augustus: Henry IV. had conquered his own kingdom, and was the grandfather of Lewis XIV. There was much the same ferment in the minds of their subjects: the people, of both the one and the other, had been for the most part soldiers; and the captains heroes. To such tempestuous times, and intestine broils, succeeded a calm, the effect of united authority: the pretensions of the republicans, and the foolish enterprizes of the seditious being defeated, the power remained in the hands of a single person; and those two princes obtained the supreme authority, though by different titles, since Augustus was no better than an usurper. They had now no other employment, but to render that ferment useful to the state, which had hitherto only contributed to the unhappiness of the public: their genius and particular character, had here a near resemblance, as well as the ages in which they lived. They were both actuated by ambition, and the love of glory; both were heroes without rashness, enterprizing without being adventurers: both had been exposed to the storms of a civil war; both had commanded their armies in person; and both knew how to conquer and to pardon. In peace they also resembled each other in a certain air of grandeur, in their magnificence, and liberality: each of them possessed that natural taste, that happy instinct, necessary to know and to distinguish those fit to be employed: their ministers thought like them; and Mecænas protected under Augustus, as Colbert did under Lewis, all the distinguished geniuses of Rome and France. In short, both happening to be born in the same month,

REMARKABLE EVENTS under LEWIS XIV.

month, they both died almoſt at the ſame age: and to add to the glory of their reigns, no other princes ever ruled ſo long.

By how many means was it neceſſary for nature to prepare two ſuch illuſtrious ages! The ſame cauſe that had produced great men in war, gave birth to ſublime geniuſes in the arts and ſciences: emulation took place of rebellion; their minds accuſtomed to independency, fought for it only in the ſalutary views of philoſophy; it was no longer the queſtion, to oppoſe their equals, but to render themſelves admired; the ſuperiority acquired by arms, was reſigned for that given by mental abilities; in a word, the ſame concurring circumſtances uſhered into the world the reigns of Auguſtus and of Lewis XIV.

PARTICULAR REMARKS.

WE shall finish this work with some remarks on the third race, as we have done on the two former.

Those who find the Greek and Roman histories more interesting than ours, do not sufficiently distrust the prejudices of infancy: this would have been pardonable before the appearance of our good historians; but at present, if they compare, for example, what M. de Thou has written of our history with that of Rome by Titus Livy; they must acknowledge, that we are neither inferior in the merit of our writers, nor in the variety and singularity of the events, in the greatness of the personages, their magnificence, their gallantry, nor even in the marvellous, in which last these two authors, and particularly M. de Thou, are least worthy of excuse. But ancient history is connected with a religion, embellished with fable, and by poetry, that has been the study of our youth. The prodigies of our times seem absurd to us, while we please ourselves with the old tales, which we no longer believe: Greece recals more agreeable ideas than Swabia or Pannonia; and Troy and Carthage seem to have greater dignity than Tolbiac and Orleans; because the Iliad and the Æneid are finer poems, than those of Clovis and the Maid of Orleans. Yet whoever reads our history with a philosophic eye, will find that it teaches as great a knowledge of the human heart, that it affords as much improvement in respect to manners, and that it exhibits as many rules of conduct as any history of the ancients: besides, France will appear so much greater, as it never had feeble enemies to contend with; as the marine of the ancients, destitute of artillery, was only children's play, when compared with our naval battles; as the progress of commerce has opened to us new worlds, of which the ancients had not the least idea; and as we ought to interest ourselves in the events of our history, in proportion as the whole globe expands itself to our view.

I say nothing of the progress of the arts and sciences which we see increase, in proportion as the authority of our kings became

PARTICULAR REMARKS.

confirmed; nor of the flourishing state of literature, which spread a lustre on our conquests, at the same time its prosperity was owing to our arms, subjects so proper for the embellishment of history. Charlemain, Francis I, and Lewis XIV, gave us ages as glorious, as every thing we repeat of the republic of Greece and Rome, and of the empire of the Cæsars. Let us then, without abandoning the study of ancient history, to which we are invited by the celebrated authors, who have transmitted it down to us, love to study our own: I shall give no other motives to this, but those of curiosity and pleasure; though I might add, the duty incumbent on all men, of being instructed in the laws, manners, and customs of their native country.

As the form of this work has not permitted me to expatiate on every particular, I shall here recollect some of those, that appeared to me the most important, and shall include them all under the general idea of the plan which our kings have formed, to put a stop to usurpations in every branch of government, with respect to justice, the army, the ecclesiastical affairs, in which the secular power is concerned, the great fiefs, &c. Let us begin with the administration of justice, an article of the highest importance, and which most demands a particular discussion.

Our kings had great difficulties to encounter in restoring the regal authority, which was almost annihilated. They were obliged to alter the prejudices and customs of a whole nation, a task more arduous perhaps than that of conquering it. *The kingdom of France*, as we have already observed, was held at that time according to the feudal law, *being governed like a great fief, rather than like a monarchy*. This abuse was owing to the usurpation of the great lords: and how extraordinary soever it may appear to us at present, yet it is easy to perceive, that such was the form of our government at the beginning of the third race; if we consider, that there were three essential points, wherein the political laws of the state were agreeable to those by which the fiefs were administered. 1°. The majority of our kings did not begin, no more than that of feudal possessions, till the age of twenty-one years complete: witness St. Lewis, who being born the 25th of April, 1215, was not declared of age till the 25th of April, 1236; though he had succeeded his father, Lewis

PARTICULAR REMARKS.

VIII, in the month of November, 1226. 2°. Our kings held fiefs of their own subjects: this abuse was abolished, as we have explained in the reign of Philip I. 3°. That the kingdom was governed, during the space of very near three hundred years, after the manner of a great fief, appears from this, that even late in the thirteenth century, the vassal, who charged *the king with denying him the judgment of his court*, that is, with refusing to let the difference between them be decided there, was entitled to maintain his right by force of arms, and even to compel his rear-vassals to join with him against their common sovereign.

It must be allowed, that these usages are not agreeable to our present notions of a monarchical government. To reduce things to the state they had been in under Charlemain, was the work of prudence and time. Nay, this prince himself would have found it very difficult to effect this change; if, upon coming to the crown, the regal authority had been dismembered in the manner it was at the accession of Hugh Capet. Hence it could not be the work of a single prince; and we may affirm, that till the reign of Philip the Fair, who instituted the parliaments, and thereby established the just authority of the sovereign, every one of his predecessors contributed to this design.

As the administration of justice is the strongest tie between the people and the sovereign, the chief point our kings had in view, was to rescue this jurisdiction out of the hands of their subjects, by whom it had been usurped.

Under our kings of the first race, and for a long time under those of the second, the dukes and counts, as governors in the provinces, were possessed of the administration throughout their respective dutchies or counties. They conferred the military benefices, when a *vacancy* happened; and they gave judgment in the last resort, upon the appeals of the *centenarii*, who were the ordinary judges appointed by the king: but this they did by the authority of the sovereign, who still held the supreme jurisdiction. They caused money to be coined in the king's name; published all sorts of regulations and grants; and raised the necessary supplies for the public service. In a word, whatever related to the royal demesne, to the administration of justice, to the police, and to

PARTICULAR REMARKS.

to the revenue, was under their direction; each person acted in his own government; and all of them under the sanction and authority of the king, as his lieutenants and officers.

When those dukes and counts, taking advantage of the weakness of the government, had appropriated their offices, and changed them into hereditary estates, they continued in possession of those privileges. Then all the marks of the royal authority were effaced in the provinces, except those which Hugh Capet possessed, as duke and count, upon his coming to the crown; and in the room of those marks of regal authority was substituted the seigniorial jurisdiction.

The first attempt our kings made to prevent the great lords from being any longer absolute masters of the lives and property of their subjects, was to send into those very provinces, as we have observed elsewhere, commissioners, called *missi dominici*, in the nature of those who were appointed under the first and second race; but with this difference, that the former were appointed by the king to inquire into the conduct of his own judges; whereas the latter were sent to examine the lords, who had usurped the royal jurisdiction. These new commissioners, at that time stiled *judges of the exempt*, were to be a check to the lords, to inspect their behaviour, and to receive the complaints of such as happened to be oppressed either by them, or by their deputies; they were also to redress those abuses in a summary manner, if possible; or else to refer the complainants to the king's great assizes. *See the reign of Lewis the Fat.*

These commissioners were too great a restraint to the independency of the lords, not to meet with opposition; in short, the latter exerted themselves in such a manner, that no more commissioners were sent into the provinces.

In the mean while the royal authority was dwindling away to nothing, and vassals succeeded in the place of subjects; for a people who might take up arms against the king in the cause of their lords, and who, to defend their property, knew no other court of jurisdiction, than that of those same lords, could no longer be deemed subjects.

The shortest way, no doubt, would have been to abolish all these seigniorial courts, and deliver them up to the king; but this could not be effected: there remained therefore two expedients; the first was to diminish the extent and authority of those jurisdictions, either by no longer suffering them to take cognizance of several sorts of causes, or by admitting of appeals to the royal jurisdiction; the second was to deprive them, at least of the exercise of the judicative power, when they could not touch the power itself. This diminished their weight and authority; for there is a wide difference between a person's ordering justice to be administered in his name, and administering it himself: the people know only their judge, and go no higher; but when the lords themselves exercise the judiciary power, that is, administer justice in person, they have every requisite to command obedience.

The first expedient therefore devised by our kings, to supply the place of the *missi dominici*, or commissioners, whom the great lords would no longer admit, was to create high-bailiffs in the towns reunited to the crown, which were only four, at the time of this establishment, *all the other towns and bailiwicks in France belonging to the dukes and counts*. These four high-bailiwicks were Vermandois, Sens, Macon, and Saint-Pierre-le-Moustier. Upon the creation of those officers, the business was to employ them in such a manner, that they might have it in their power to take cognizance of some causes in the towns subject to the jurisdiction of the lords. For this purpose were contrived the *royal cases*, that is, those in which the king was interested; for this expression did not extend as yet to what we understand at present by *royal cases*, in which the public is equally concerned. The pretension for those royal cases, of which the bailiffs were to be judges, was, that as disputes frequently arose on the lands or estates of the nobility, in which the king was interested, *it did not seem proper that he should apply to his subjects and vassals for justice*; but it was highly reasonable, that his own judges should take cognizance of them: now it is easily understood, that those royal cases were more or less extended, in proportion to the greater or lesser power of the nobility; that the greatest resumptions were made, where the lords were weakest; and when they were obstinate, the king was obliged to have patience. As soon as a town was reunited to the royal demesne, it became a royal jurisdiction.

PARTICULAR REMARKS.

jurisdiction, though it had been held before of another lord, who notwithstanding received no indemnity; and immediately a new bailiff was appointed, who, by the privilege of royal cases, drew all the causes he could from the courts of the neighbouring lords. We have an edict of the year 1190, by which Philip Augustus, being possessed of a larger territory than his predecessors, appointed bailiffs in all the principal towns. Thus by the institution of those officers, the first design was obtained, namely, that of diminishing, as much as possible, the jurisdiction of the nobility.

The method of appeal was still another more effectual way of reducing the usurped authority of the lords, since the royal cases could not extend to every point; whereas the appeal was general; and a judge, whose decisions can be amended, loses great part of his power; while the person, who has a right to amend them, is possessed of the real authority. The way this was effected, is as follows.

The first pretext was *the default of law.* If the great lords refused to do justice; the way was to apply to the royal judges, *per viam querælæ.* Again, if those lords determined contrary to the feudal law, this was another case of appeal. It is obvious, that this second case must have been very extensive, since every man who lost his cause, was sure to alledge, that judgment had been given contrary to law. But it is not to be imagined, that this was the method of proceeding in regard to all the great lords. Some were so considerable, as to determine in the last resort, and without appeal. The duke of Normandy, and the count of Toulouse, carried their prerogatives to this pitch; and a great while afterwards, when the dukes no longer administered justice in person, but had courts where causes were determined in their name, the dukes of Normandy still preserved this privilege: the court of exchequer in that province was as absolute in its decisions as the parliament of Paris. Hence it is expresly mentioned by Lewis Hutin, in the charter granted to the Normans in 1315, notwithstanding this province was then reunited to the crown, that pursuant to the ancient custom of Normandy, no cause whatever, after it has been tried in the court of ex-

PARTICULAR REMARKS.

chequer, shall be removed upon any account to the parliament of Paris, even before the king in person; nor shall the Normans be summoned before this tribunal for facts committed in that dukedom: and the reason is, the dukes of Normandy were possessed of greater power in their own territories than the king himself; since the king suffered lords in his dominions, who had subordinate courts of jurisdiction; whereas under the dukes of the Norman race, or of the house of Anjou, *no lord whatever was possessed of high jurisdiction, or of the power of determining all civil and criminal causes throughout that province:* which is the reason, that to this very day, we see so few seigniorial courts of high jurisdiction in Normandy.

It was not the same in regard to the dukes of Guienne and Burgundy. Towards the decline of the thirteenth century, it was a very common practice to appeal to parliament, from the seneschals of the dukes of Guyenne. This is fully proved by the letters patent of Philip the Hardy, in the month of June, 1283, whereby he grants to Edward, king of England, duke of Aquitaine, all the fines, forfeitures, and other penalties, which shall be decreed in parliament, with respect to that province; as also in the cases of appeal from the sentences awarded by the seneschals of the said king of England in Gascony, and in the territories of Agenois, Quercy, Perigord, Limosin, and Xaintonge. An appeal was likewise allowed from the courts of the duke of Burgundy, to a royal bailiwick, and from thence to the king. This appears sufficiently from a declaration given by Charles of France, regent of the kingdom, during the imprisonment of king John his father: there it is mentioned, that before the county of Macon was annexed to the crown, by the acquisition which St. Lewis made of it, in 1283, the count de Macon and his subjects, as also the archbishop, dean and chapter, and inhabitants of Lyons, the bishop and chapter of Macon, the bishop and chapter of Chalons, the abbots of Fontiny, (Tournus) and Cluny, the duke of Burgundy, *who is a peer of France*, the count de Forest, the lord of Beaujeu, their lands and their subjects, were all dependent on the castle and castellany of St. Jengoul: *and that in order to take cognizance of causes subject to the sovereign jurisdiction,*

PARTICULAR REMARKS.

jurifdiction, to hear and to determine them, our lords the kings of France were accuftomed, time immemorial, to have a royal bailiwick and bailiff in the faid place, who were called the bailiwick and bailiff of *Jengoul*. From whom they occafionally appealed to the parliament of Paris, and to no other court.

It appears therefore, that the jurifdiction of the lords was curtailed, either by the cafes withdrawn from their cognizance, or by appeals: we muft now examine in what manner thofe appeals were made, which will not be the leaft curious part of the prefent difquifition.

The dukes and counts growing tired of adminiftering juftice in perfon, appointed lieutenants, or deputies, to try caufes in their room, ftill indeed referving to themfelves, the privilege of holding the affizes or court of feffions: but finding it difagreeable afterwards to hold even thofe affizes, they committed the care thereof to a bailiff, who became the fuperior judge, to whom appeal might be made from the lieutenant or vifcount.

It was from the decifions of this bailiff, that appeals were made to the royal officer of that name: when the former had abfolutely deviated from the rules of juftice, or when the grievance was clear and manifeft, and the injuftice evident, recourfe was had to the royal bailiff; as afterwards to the parliament, when it became a fedentary court, and concerned itfelf only about private caufes. The complainant therefore prefented his petition, not againft the defendant, but againft the judge himfelf, to the end that he might come and give an account of his conduct, and the motives of his award. It behoved the inferior magiftrate to maintain the equity of his fentence, againft the party who had appealed, or fummoned him before the royal judge; and from thence is derived the word appeal.

As thofe appeals were not admitted, but in cafes, where the judge was charged in the petition with that fort of mifdemeanor, which is called *lata culpa quæ dolo æquiparatur*, the affair became perfonal in regard to the judge appealed. If the fact was proved, he was punifhed by the fame arret, which contained his fentence; if the appellant could not prove the fact, he was condemned in a fine, and obliged to pay cofts and charges of fuit.

PARTICULAR REMARKS.

In process of time this rigour was abated, so that they made less difficulty in receiving petitions of appeal upon the slightest facts, and sometimes upon a general charge of injustice. The judges finding themselves less interested in this sort of petitions, took less notice of them; and then the party, in whose favour they had determined, endeavoured to maintain the equity of the decision: nay, it was afterwards ordained, that the parties themselves should be summoned to support the award: and when the multiplicity of business increased to such a height, that the parliament found it necessary to sit all the year; as it was impossible for the provincial judges to be all that time attending the court, in order to account for their decisions, there were rolls made for every province, so that the respective bailiff or seneschal was obliged to attend the court upon a call of the rolls, and to assist at all the pleadings, in order to state the reasons of each award. From that time they ceased to summon the judges upon every affair; the publication of the roll, or register of the province, being a general citation. The former kind of summons still subsists, in regard to the case which originally introduced it: when there is any fact personally relating to the judge, permission is given, upon a petition presented to that effect, and according to the nature of the charge, to cite the judge in his own name, and to make him a party. But while we have still retained the custom of summoning the judges in certain cases, for the good of the public, and to bind them to their duty; we have with just reason laid aside the practice of making them assist at the pleadings, where the party, who maintains the equity of the sentence, is summoned in person, and has an interest in maintaining its validity.

We have been somewhat diffuse upon the history of these appeals; let us now return to our main point. The introduction of appeals was one of the principal means to weaken the jurisdiction of the lords, who not only suffered in their judiciary capacity, but likewise in their general authority, the prerogative of administering justice being without all manner of doubt, as Loyseau observes, the surest support of the sovereign power. By this means, the lords were indirectly abridged of the privilege of enacting laws, inasmuch as the parliament neither fol-

lowed,

lowed, nor approved of their ordinances, in the determination of causes.

The same reason which made the dukes and counts relinquish the exercise of the judiciary power, induced the royal bailiffs to follow their example. As the king did not appoint gentlemen of the law to this important office, but some of the chief lords of his court, their military employments under the crown would not permit them to discharge the office of bailiffs, and therefore they nominated others to act as their lieutenants. But when they wanted afterwards to resume that part of their office, the king perceiving that the administration of justice in the hands of those lords would render them too considerable, and might endanger their loyalty, so as to tempt them to shake off the yoke of obedience, as had been the case already in regard to the dukes and counts; the king, I say, for that reason would not permit them to resume their judiciary function, but appointed proper judges to discharge that part of their office. (*Ordinance of Philip the Fair*, 1287.)

Thus far have we given a summary illustration of some of the principal points of our public law: we shall now proceed to two other articles, which are no less curious, namely, the nature of the king's demesne, and the sale of offices.

It is a standing maxim in France, that the crown lands are inalienable; and it is a mistake to believe, that it was only since the reign of Philip the Hardy, when the custom of appanages began to be better known, (*see the year* 1283) that our sovereigns ceased to have a power of alienating their demesne.

This mistake may be owing to the following fact, that till the reign of Philip the Hardy, the kings of France did alienate or dispose of their demesnes; but this alienation for the general only regarded their children: and if we meet with some other alienations, made in favour of persons who were not of the royal family, this does not at all prove that the crown lands are alienable.

When we find that our kings granted some apportionments of land to their daughters, we must examine carefully, whether those lands constituted a part of the royal demesne; for if they were only private property, this is no argument

at

at all of the alienability in queſtion. Lewis the Debonnaire (*Thegan, Perard, collection of pieces towards a hiſtory of Burgundy*) was ſo magnificent, and of ſo generous a diſpoſition, that he gave away lands and ſegniories to ſeveral lords of his court; but they had formerly belonged to his grandfather or great grandfather. Charles the Bald (*Perard*) did the ſame; but the grants he made, were his own property, belonging to him *jure proprietario*; from whence we may conclude, that our kings of the firſt and ſecond race had a private demeſne or patrimony, of which they were maſters; and when we ſee them diſpoſing of theſe demeſnes, as well as ſome of our kings of the third race, who had alſo a private patrimony, *res juris noſtri, res proprietatis noſtræ*, we muſt not imagine, that the royal demeſne was alienable. But to underſtand this matter rightly, it ſhould be obſerved, that our kings had two ſorts of demeſnes, one of which belonged to their crown, and the other, as du Moulin phraſes it, to their perſon. The latter continued to be the private property of the prince, and were not annexed to the crown, upon his acceſſion. But by the ordinance of Moulins, in 1566, it was ordained, that the prince's demeſne, upon his coming to the crown, ſhould be annexed thereto by law at the expiration of ten years; a proof that before this time there were demeſnes, which were not reunited to the crown.

There are, ſays Pontanus in his commentary on the cuſtom of Blois: (this Pontanus lived in 1439, and wrote agreeably to the cuſtom, that had obtained in the preceding centuries, and was ſtill in force in his time:) "There are, ſays he, two ſorts of
"demeſnes, one belonging to the crown, the other to the prince;
"the former is inalienable, the king having only the ſimple admi-
"niſtration of it, as huſbands, fathers, and prelates, have the bare
"adminiſtration of the eſtates of their wives, their children, and
"their churches; they have no power to diſpoſe thereof, for
"the benefit of individuals, either in the nature of grant
"or otherwiſe; on the contrary, they are obliged to preſerve it
"intire, and tranſmit it undiminiſhed to their ſucceſſors; but
"with regard to the prince's demeſne, which he defines to be
"that ariſing from acqueſt or ſucceſſion, he is ſo far maſter
"thereof, that he may diſpoſe of it at his will and pleaſure."

Du

PARTICULAR REMARKS.

Du Moulin goes further, and says, that even if the king were to confound his private with his public patrimony, and had suffered the revenue of both to be received, and administered by the same officers, this would not however effectuate a reunion, which could not be done tacitly, but, on the contrary, must be made in a solemn manner by public instruments. It is obvious that this must have been antecedent to the ordinance of Moulins.

From what has been said, I think it has been sufficiently proved, that our kings had private demesnes, and that their power of alienating these, is no argument at all of their having the same liberty with regard to the crown lands. Yet allowing the distinction of these two patrimonies, examples, you will say, may be produced, of an alienation of the royal demesne, made in favour of private persons. But I answer, that the law does not cease to be obligatory by being violated; now it is a fundamental law of the state, that the royal demesne is inalienable; which remains for me to prove, and is the chief object of this article.

Of what use would it have been to reunite demesnes to the crown, if it were not to hinder them from being ever separated again? Thus Normandy conquered by Philip Augustus, Artois acquired by his marriage, the dukedom of Burgundy fallen by succession to king John, the county of Toulouse inherited by the descendants of St. Lewis, (in consequence of the marriage between the heiress of that county and Alphonsus brother of that king,) the county of Champagne acquired by the exchange, which Philip of Valois made with the daughter of Lewis Hutin; all those fiefs were annexed to the crown, to prevent their being ever separated from it again. It is therefore the reunion of the fiefs to the crown, that operates their inalienability, because the royal demesne is inalienable; and a strong instance thereof is the annexing of the dutchy of France to the crown, at the time of the election of Hugh Capet.

Such has been the doctrine of this kingdom time immemorial. It was customary, says Giannone, to give the name of the patrimony of the prince to the lands or estates which belonged to him in private property, and did not depend on the crown; in order to distinguish them from the patrimony of his subjects, as well as from that of the fisc or treasury, which was called *sacrum pa-*
trimonium

PARTICULAR REMARKS.

trimonium (see the code, l. 12.) But without losing time in quoting ancient authorities, let us keep to more modern proofs, which exhibit the chain and tradition of these principles.

How came the parliament of Paris so vigorously to oppose the registering of the letters patent published by Henry IVth the 13th of April, 1590, and the 13th of December, 1576, in which he declared his intention of holding his private patrimony separate and independent of the crown; if it was not from an opinion, that as soon as his patrimony was reunited, it became inalienable? The more this prince seemed to be under a necessity of selling his own demesnes, at a time when his right to the succession was disputed; the more the parliament judged it a sure way to hinder him, by reuniting them to the crown. The king indeed might have mortgaged some of those demesnes for a limited time, as our princes have sometimes done under urgent necessities; but Henry IV. wanted to sell them outright, which would have raised more money, than a simple mortgage. The parliaments of Bourdeaux and Toulouse obeyed Henry IV; but that of Paris, the bulwark of the monarchy, would never comply: and those magistrates had reason to be pleased with their opposition, when Henry IV, being made sensible of the expediency of the law of reunions, published an edict in the month of July, 1607, and united his patrimony, which was held as a fief of the crown, to the royal demesnes: this indeed was an unnecessary act, because it had been provided for already by the ordinance of Moulins.

This restriction, which renders our princes incapable of alienating their demesnes, is so far a fundamental law of the state, that the king, says Juvenal des Ursins, takes a solemn oath at his coronation, that he will never dispose of any part of his inheritance: and in the memoirs drawn up by the command of Charles VII, the same author continues, "it would be very extraordinary, "that the king should have a power of alienating part of the crown "inheritance, yet shall swear the contrary at his coronation." Bouchel, in the *Bibliotheque Françoise*, says, "Our kings never "fail to swear at the time of their coronation, that they will "maintain the rights and honour of their crown inviolate and "intire." M. le Bret asserts the same thing. It is therefore

owing,

PARTICULAR REMARKS.

owing, says M. Chopin, to a fundamental law, that the imperial, as well as royal, patrimony is reckoned sacred. Let us hear what answer M. de Selve, first president of the parliament of Paris, gave to the emperor's ambassadors, who came to demand the performance of a promise made by Francis I, which was to surrender Burgundy as a ransom for his liberty: " our lord " the king cannot alienate the said dutchy, for he is obliged " to maintain the rights of the crown, which are common to " him and his subjects." But the question, whether the king can dispose of his demesne, under so pressing a necessity as that of captivity, would afford matter for another dissertation: it is however of use in the present question, since if a captive king cannot alienate part of his demesne to procure his liberty; much less has he a right to do it, with a view of raising a sum of money.

But the argument that carries conviction with it, and with which I finish, is the declaration of Charles IX, in the preamble to his ordinance concerning the demesne, in the year 1566; an ordinance, which having been composed from the loose papers of the states of the kingdom, (as appears by the concurrence of the states and of the royal authority) and published at Moulins in the month of February, 1566, was registered in the parliament of Paris the 13th of May the same year. " Whereas at our coro- " nation, says the king, among other things we promised and " swore to keep and preserve the demesne and patrimony of our " crown, one of the chief sinews of our state, whole and intire, " . . . . and as *the rules and ancient maxims of the union and* " *preservation of our demesne,* are to some but indifferently, and " to others but very little known, we have therefore judged ne- " cessary to have them collected, &c." which shews that the king did not intend to enact a new law; and therefore, in the notes on this ordinance, it is said, " that the royal demesne is, in some " measure, the kingdom's dower, and of course inalienable, like " a woman's dower, over which her husband hath no power."

From what has been said, we may establish the following principles, relative to the royal demesne. Before the ordinance of 1566, whatever was not reunited to the crown, might have been

PARTICULAR REMARKS.

been *disposed* of by the king; but immediately after a reunion, it became *inalienable*: and since the ordinance on the demesne in 1566, the private patrimony of our kings, administered by public receivers, becomes a part of the royal demesne, after ten years possession, without the necessity of an act of reunion. Let us conclude with the following passage of Cujas: *Ea de re cum consulerer, respondi nullam esse legem specialem quæ id prohibuisset; sed hanc esse legem omnium regnorum, cum ipsis regnis natam, & quasi jus gentium.*

The question concerning the sale of offices, is more difficult to resolve, than one would imagine. The reader expects to have the matter clearly stated; and with good reason. It is well known, that public offices were not sold in former times, and that judicial employments were conferred by election; but now they are purchased: therefore some would infer, that there has been a sudden transition from the former to the present practice. They imagine, that in such a year, and on such a day, there was an edict to render all the offices saleable, which the preceding day were elective.

But the revolutions of manners, customs, and discipline, in most countries, happen in a different manner. From a previous combination of circumstances, and a variety of particular facts, in process of time there rises a general law, by which we are governed. Such is the sale of offices, of which we intend to treat at present.

There are three sorts of offices, judicial, military, and those belonging to the revenue. Here we shall treat only of the judicial, though occasionally we may happen to make mention of the others.

According to Mezeray, Varillas, father Daniel, &c. it was the Italian war under Francis I, that gave birth to the sale of judiciary employments. Now upon this subject two questions arise; the first, whether this sale is attended with greater advantages than inconveniencies to the state; concerning which the reader may see the political testament of the cardinal de Richelieu [*]: the second, whether the sale of offices was really introduced in the reign of Francis I.

[*] Part. I. c. 4. sect. 1.

I shall

PARTICULAR REMARKS.

I shall first of all give what Loyseau has written on this subject, in the chapter of the sale of offices. (Loyseau died in 1628.) The testimony of this lawyer, in the matter before us, is of much greater weight, than that of historians, who only transcribe from one another. Lewis XI, he says, rendered the offices perpetual by his ordinance of 1467; therefore they were not purchased before. Charles VIII, by his ordinance of 1493, forbad the sale of judicial offices; and so well was this law maintained before the reign of those two kings, that Pasquier mentions two arrets of the chamber of accounts in 1373 and 1404, by which those, who had paid for their places, were deposed. Lewis XII. began to put up offices to sale, but it was only those of the finances. Upon this occasion, Nicholas Gille and Gaguin observe, "that with a view of discharging the great
" debts contracted by his predecessor Charles VIII, of recovering
" the dutchy of Milan, and of easing his people, he took money
" for the sale of offices, by *which he raised considerable sums:* (Loy-
" seau, vol. 3. chap. 1. n. 86.) however, by an edict of
" 1508 he prohibited the sale of judiciary employments: but
" when once corruption has made an opening, it grows wider
" every day; and thence it came to pass that Francis I. extended
" the sale of places of the revenue to those of judicature." Not but that there had been an indirect method a great while before, of putting up offices to sale, as appears by the chronicle of Flanders, ch. 33. where it is mentioned, that Philip the Fair,
" solliciting the canonization of St. Lewis, was refused by pope
" Boniface the VIII, because it was found, that he had farmed
" his provostships and bailiwicks." For, at that time, they made use of the pretext of leasing the duties of the king's demesnes; and they farmed the office of provost, viscount, &c. because they had the management of the farm, and administration of justice, at the same time: but this was not a sale of offices, such as afterwards obtained; for it might be said, that only the land was farmed.

We must therefore date the sale of offices from the reign of Francis I; because at that time great numbers of them were sold. But is there any law by which we can fix this æra? and how shall we explain the accounts in all historians, even of ju-

PARTICULAR REMARKS.

dicial offices, which were sold long before that reign, and of the prohibition afterwards made against this sale?

In answer, first of all, to the instances of this kind prior to the reign of Francis I, it appears to me beyond all manner of doubt, that the sale of judicial offices was not so much as tolerated. This is sufficiently proved by the ordinances of Charles VII, Charles VIII, and Lewis XII, and even by edicts of a more ancient date. See the dialogue of the advocates, intitled *Pasquier*; *see* also the 7th vol. of the collection of ordinances. In the letters of the 19th of November, 1393, we read the following passage with regard to the procurators of the Chatelet at Paris, *that in consequence of the above ordinance*, the said office *of procuration* was usually *set up to sale, and some persons had obtained it by purchase*. In the collection of Quinet, we meet with complaints of the states general to Lewis XI, that some judicial employments had been exposed to sale; and Philip de Commines mentions the same thing. Examples of these purchases are very numerous; but at the same time, they afford us a strong proof, that those purchases were not authorized, because of the complaint to the sovereign. This did not hinder however the traffic from being carried on by the nobility, or by people in place, who sold their credit or influence, without giving any notice thereof to the king, or even without his seeming to be at all acquainted with the practice; and in this sense we ought, I think, to understand all those passages, which mention the sale of offices; it was an abuse, and consequently is of no authority in establishing this æra.

We must therefore fix it to the reign of Francis; yet we do not find that he published any law to that purpose: so far from it, as a salvo for the oath they were obliged to take in parliament, of not having purchased their places, this commerce was coloured over with the notion of a loan to relieve the necessities of the state, and consequently was not a purchase. Indeed Henry II. was not so nice: we find by an edict of the year 1554, which regulates the form of proceeding in the tax and sale of places, upon their escheating to the crown, that this prince makes no difference between the judi-

cial

PARTICULAR REMARKS.

cial offices and those of the revenue; and he ordains, that such as intend to be invested with an employment, either upon a vacancy, resignation, or new creation, shall be registered every week; and that the comptroller-general shall mark the name and quality of such offices as are to be taxed, &c. The people imagining, that the sale of offices was attended with that of justice, could not see this system take place, without murmuring: besides the nobility did not find their account in it, because it debarred them from preferring persons devoted to their interest: and for both these reasons, Catharine de Medicis, upon the accession of Francis II, wanted to revive the ancient form of elections.

Not but that the elections had their inconveniency; for where is the system that has not? They were attended with such cabals and intrigues, that by the edict of Francis II. the parliament was ordered to present three candidates to the king, for his majesty to chuse one of the number: but this did not mend the matter; all the vacant places were filled with persons devoted, either to the constable, or to the Guises, or to the prince of Condé, and but very few to the king; so that the several bodies of magistrates were actuated much more by the spirit of party, than by the love of their country and the public welfare; and in all probability this was one of the sources of the disorder and confusion of our civil wars.

Under the reign of Charles IX. the sale of places was become a regular system; and this perhaps is the right æra of the sale of judicial offices: not that it was expressly declared those offices should be purchased; but something like it. The king permitted all persons possessed of employments, which, without being saleable of their nature, were reputed such, because of their being purchased, to resign them upon paying the third penny; the judicial offices which came under that head, were considered in the same light as the rest of the employments, that escheat to the crown; and the traffic became public, contrary to the ancient practice; so that in case the person who resigned those places, did not live forty days after his resignation, they escheated to the crown, and were taxed like the rest;

PARTICULAR REMARKS.

rest, on which occasion discharges from the exchequer were given in the usual form.

It is obvious, that when once this traffic was authorized, the elections fell of themselves, so that there was no necessity for a law to abolish them.

Hence we may look upon the edicts of Charles IX. relative to this subject, namely, those of the years 1567 and 1568, as subversive of the ancient custom of elections, which has never been revived since; for the ordinance of Blois, of 1579, was not put into execution. These ordinances were renewed or confirmed at different times by Charles IX. himself, and afterwards by Henry III. At length the edict of 1604, which declares all employments whatever, even those of the courts of parliament, hereditary, has put the judicial offices upon the same footing with the rest; and ever since all places, without exception, have been purchased under the government.

From what has been said, we may justly conclude, that the reign of Francis I. should not be reckoned the æra, in which the sale of offices was first established: it is not indeed, if I may so express myself, the *judicial* æra; but it is the real cause of this practice, because under that prince many of those employments were to be had for money.

We have already taken notice of the offices of the revenue: with regard to military preferments, we read in the memoirs of Duplessis Mornay (Vol. I. p. 456.) that it was the Guises who exposed them to sale in the reign of Henry III; and upon this occasion we ought not to forget, that the reigning king (Lewis XV.) with a view of multiplying rewards to a profession so respectable and useful to the state, has formed a plan of suppressing the sale of those offices, by reducing the price of them at each remove; a regulation of infinite advantage to the gentlemen of the army; which, added to the edict on the noblesse and the military school, must render the reign of this monarch, and the zeal of his minister, ever dear to the French nobility.

As the dukedom of Burgundy is the last appanage, that has been annexed to the royal demesne, and by its reunion has extinguished that extravagant species of sovereignty, which, like

an

PARTICULAR REMARKS.

an extraneous body, obstructed the springs of government, it is proper to see what became of it upon the death of Charles the Bold. This dukedom might be considered in relation to three persons: Lewis XI. had a right to it by the law of appanages, in failure of the male descendants of Philip the Hardy, the first duke of that second house; upon this principle, that the dukedom having been given to Philip the Hardy, on condition of reverting to the crown in failure of male heirs, Mary of Burgundy, the daughter of Charles, was consequently excluded from the succession. This same Mary had a right to her father's inheritance, if the law of appanages were not to take place. And lastly, a male descendant of Philip the Hardy, if there were any such, ought, according to the law of appanages, to be preferred to Lewis XI, and to Mary of Burgundy. This being supposed, I want to know who was the legitimate heir of Charles the Bold? I can find none but John, count de Nevers, grandson of Philip the Hardy, who being born in 1491, was the only male issue living of that family, upon the death of Charles the Bold, which happened fourteen years before. What claim had Lewis to set up against him? The law of appanages? This was in his favour, for he was a male descendant of Philip the Hardy. What right had Mary, the daughter of Charles, in preference to this prince? That of her being the only heir to her father? This she had forfeited by the law of appanages, which excluded the females at all events: and yet, what is very surprizing, we do not find there was any notice taken of the count de Nevers upon the decease of the last duke of Burgundy. Is it because the count de Nevers was too weak to maintain his right? But at least he would have entered his protest. Or is it, on the other hand, that the law of appanages was not sufficiently clear, so as to exclude Mary of Burgundy? So far from that, it was become a fundamental law of the state. Or is it, in fine, as the abbé de Longuerue supposes, that the count de Nevers had resigned his right to Lewis XI? but there is not the least vestige of any such resignation.

In so knotty a point of history, our best way is to be determined by the conduct, which Lewis XI. observed on that occasion. We can never be persuaded, let some writers say what they will, (du Tillet, Laguesle, Dupuy) that this prince would not have asserted the right of reunion, in failure of heirs male, if he thought he had an authority to do it. But he did not take this method, as there was a descendant of Philip the Hardy living; he chose rather to manage artfully, by seizing the strong towns of the dutchy of Burgundy: after he had missed the opportunity of marrying the princess Mary, in which respect he was inexcusable, he had recourse to the feudal law, and annexed the dukedom of Burgundy to the crown for the crime of felony, which Charles the Bold had been but too guilty of all his life. As for the rest, it is obvious, that this is merely a question of curiosity; for the count de Nevers died without issue.

This same king thought his authority would be better established, if the laws of France were intirely uniform; but pretended he had no other design in a scheme of that kind, than to promote the public good. In every government, he said, there ought to be but one law, one weight, and one measure: a plausible scheme, yet extremely inconvenient in practice. I do not mean in regard to weights and measures; for if we rightly consider the matter, this is only a verbal dispute; the price of things will always follow their weight and measure. It is otherwise in regard to laws, that have been enacted, and to customs that have been introduced, in conformity to the nature of each country, and the manners of the inhabitants: people have not the same mode of life at Dunkirk, as at Toulouse; at Marseilles, as at Paris; in Normandy, as at St. Maloes; and the burghers, the noblesse, and the merchants, ought to be governed in a different manner.

A gentleman who wants to perpetuate his family, ought to transmit his estate intire to his eldest son. A merchant, whose passion is the increase of commerce and wealth, ought, on the contrary, to share his substance among his children, to the end that each of them may be in a capacity to represent him, and he may be able to extend his credit. The custom of Normandy is necessary in the former case; and both the law and custom ordain an equal division in the latter. The magistrate detained at Paris by the functions of his office, has no leisure for the improvement of lands, and therefore

PARTICULAR REMARKS.

stands in need of an easier revenue, which shall nevertheless descend to his heirs as a landed estate: for this purpose the government hath contrived to render annuities immoveable, which was not practised before the sword and gown became two different professions. The jurisdiction of consuls has also been established to try the causes of merchants in a summary manner, by reason that the latter have not time to attend to long proceedings, which would be prejudicial to trade; and besides this sort of causes does not require any nice discussion: but it is obvious, that these laws are not adapted (and therefore would be difficult to execute) to the gentlemen of the army, to magistrates, and, in a word, to any but commercial people.

The court of marshals of France takes cognizance of quarrels among the nobility: yet can they pretend to determine points of the feudal law, or civil contracts? and so on.

In order to establish an uniformity of laws, what rule ought we to pursue? what class of men are we to prefer? The nobility are the support of the state, which owes its prosperity to the merchant: now are we to protect the one in prejudice to the other? *Lex est commune præceptum*, it is true, but not for mankind in general, nor even for every profession, but for each province, which from its nature and situation has chosen, time immemorial, a peculiar manner of living, called *custom*, which is become a law by the approbation of the sovereign. Let it be observed, that the primitive laws of every country were made by the people. The government should not enact new institutions, but as emanations from the ancient; when once this consideration is laid aside, the new ordinances throw every thing into a state of violence: and, as Mr. Pope expresses it, right becomes

Still for the strong too weak, the weak too strong.

Let us remember our original; did not the nations which united under the victorious arms of our ancient kings, preserve each of them their respective laws?

Let us proceed to the military state.

PARTICULAR REMARKS.

It was a great point gained by the sovereign, to resume the administration of justice, which had been usurped by his subjects; but still they continued to have a military force; and the king depended on them and their vassals in waging war: nay, they committed hostilities against the sovereign himself, and refused to come to court; in short, their only concern was, how to appear in time of war, according to their rank, and the duty of their fief. At the conclusion of a peace, they returned to their castles, attended by their vassals, whose military disposition they encouraged, by holding assemblies or meetings on the great festivals, and by exhibiting tilts and tournaments. It is easy to perceive what authority those lords derived from this manner of life, and how greatly they were strengthened by an union with their vassals, whom they never lost sight of either in peace, or war: this was the power of the nobles, and this our kings undertook to weaken. They began with diminishing that union, by prohibiting tournaments, under pretence of untoward accidents: they called in the assistance of the pope, who forbad those combats, under pain of excommunication, and privation of christian burial: they afterwards released the nobility, under colour of indulgence, from the service due on account of their lands; with a proviso, that the levies made by the king should be maintained upon those lands by their vassals and subjects: but still as this left a kind of relation between the lords and soldiers, which it was proper to put an end to, the invention of the royal aid and tallage completed the great work; and they granted money to the king, which enabled him to keep armies on foot independent of the nobility.

The great lords, being grown idle upon their estates, began to find the time hang heavy upon their hands; this induced them the more readily to come to court, whither they were also invited by places and preferments; and endeavours were used to keep them there by a variety of amusements. The ladies were likewise introduced into the same scene of pleasure: and as there was no longer any dispute about the supreme authority; the favour of the prince, and that of the fair sex, became the object of pursuit in regard to the nobility, who were now trans-

PARTICULAR REMARKS.

formed into courtiers. Yet tilts and tournaments were still in fashion, being the diversion of the times. As they scarce knew how to read, and as little how to reason, their whole attention was turned towards bodily exercise; whereas our habit of reading, reflecting, and examining the objects around us, is the cause of our requiring diversions more suited to our ideas, and present conceptions. Hence they went to tilts and tournaments, just as we go to see a play. There were indeed a few, who had a notion of being somewhat better entertained than by military shows, which set them upon the representation of mysteries, farces, and ancient ballads, a kind of prelude to our plays, and operas. Such was the state of the court under the reign of Francis I, and especially under that of Henry II.

Upon taking a view of this military ferocity, which resembled in some measure the rudeness of the early times of our monarchy, one would imagine, that men who fought for their diversion, had not much leisure to indulge other passions: but this is far from being the case; never was there a more dissolute court than that of Henry II. The bravery of the age was seen even in their gallantry; for women were as bold in making advances towards men, as these were in encountering one another. The poets (there were a great number of them at that time, and Henry II. was a prince of taste, and some learning) the poets, I say, were infected with the corruption of the age; or rather they contributed to increase it, by debauching the minds of young women with unchaste verses, and loose, immoral, songs: in short, to give an idea of this age, the folly of soothsayers, drawers of horoscopes, and judiciary astrologers, had seized the whole court, and continued long in France, till philosophy, which perhaps has caused other inconveniencies, shewed those ridiculous impostures in their true light.

I come now to treat of a very important article, namely, the Concordate, in which we find how conducive the union of authority is to good order, and of course to the felicity of the people; when that authority is well administered, and when our princes weigh their power in the scale of the laws: for we cannot too often repeat this saying of Loyseau, " That the laws are a boun-

" dary

PARTICULAR REMARKS.

"dary to the power of the sovereign, without endangering the sovereignty."

The chancellor du Prat has been very ill treated by our historians: he is charged with being the author of the sale of offices, which perhaps is an evil, although cardinal Richelieu, after examining the arguments on both sides in his political testament, does not venture to decide the question. He is also accused of having suggested to the king, that it was in his majesty's power to augment the *tailles*, and to impose new duties; of having introduced the maxim, that there is no land or *estate without a lord*; of having prejudiced the dutchess of Angouleme against the constable de Bourbon, from private views; in fine, of having endeavoured to separate the king's interest from that of the public. But the great complaint against this magistrate, was for his having deprived the clergy and people of the right of election to benefices, and given the power of nomination to the king, by suppressing the pragmatic sanction, and establishing the Concordate. Hence his memory has not been spared; and what has contributed to render him the more odious, two of the most respectable bodies of the state, viz. the church and the law, have joined in opposing this new regulation, as the most prejudicial that possibly could be to religion, and to public order. May I be permitted, notwithstanding such strong prejudices, to offer a few reflexions upon the subject? It seems, that by the Concordate, the king only recovered a right, which his predecessors of the two first races had constantly exercised; that in those days (Plea of M. Talon) they did not apply to Rome for collations to benefices; that the bishops disposed of those, which were vacant in their diocesses; and that our kings generally nominated to bishoprics, for this reason, that the right which the faithful had originally to choose a superior to themselves, being very difficult to exercise in a collective body, and ever attended with inconveniencies, ought to be invested in the sovereign, on whom the subjects rely for the government of the realm, of which the church is the noblest part. It is equally true, that the annates are a new and unusual tax, to which the pope acquired a right, not by the Concordate, as hath been supposed, for it takes no notice of them;

PARTICULAR REMARKS.

them; but by a bull publifhed foon after, authorizing this prerogative of the fee of Rome, which had been introduced towards the year 1316: therefore the pope gave no more to our kings, by the Concordate, than what really belonged to them; whereas, by virtue of the bull, the fee of Rome acquired a power, to which it had no manner of right.

But is this the whole matter of inquiry, with regard to the Concordate? I think not. The point is to know, whether the pragmatic fanction was prejudicial to the ftate? or whether, on the other hand, the Concordate, as it now ftands, and with all its inconveniencies, is not by far more ufeful? Now I apprehend it would be eafy to prove, that the pragmatic fanction was attended with a number of inconveniencies; and that the Concordate is the propereft method of maintaining the public tranquillity.

The brevity I prefcribed to myfelf, will not permit me to expatiate upon this fubject: I fhall therefore confine my difcourfe to the following proofs. 1. That the Concordate is a juft regulation, inafmuch as it reftores our kings to the right of prefentation; for it is they that founded moft of the great benefices, and therefore the collation to thofe benefices ought to belong to their fucceffors. 2. As the king reprefents the nation, it belongs to him to exercife the rights, enjoyed by the primitive Chriftians, which they refigned to the fovereign when the church was received as a part of the ftate, in return for his granting a protection to their religion. 3. I affirm, and this was one of the reafons of the chancellor du Prat, that the elections were carried on by public fimony, fo that they who had moft money to purchafe, were raifed to the chief preferments. 4. The great fees were frequently filled with the dregs of the people, whereas fuppofing every thing elfe equal, the nobility ought to have the preference in the diftribution of ecclefiaftical benefices, for two reafons; the firft, that many of the great livings were founded by that order; the fecond, as the great livings give an authority to the bifhops in their diocefes, it is of importance, for the fecurity of the kingdom, that the king fhall chufe fuch perfons as are of known attachment to his perfon, and whofe abilities extend, not only to matters of religion,

PARTICULAR REMARKS.

religion, but to the prefervation of the public order and tranquillity: *intereſt*, ſays Gaguin, *reges noſſe, qui majores maxime eccleſias adminiſtrant, quarum ipſi tutores ſunt*. The Romans had the ſame way of thinking in regard to their augurs: *ɴɪ ars tanta*, ſays Tully, *propter tenuitatem hominum, a religionis autoritate abduceretur ad mercedem*. What ſhall we conclude? but that the Concordate is not a thing of ſuch dangerous conſequence, as was imagined at its firſt publication? The annates might give offence to the nation, and, I confeſs, it was natural they ſhould; (though the popes had enjoyed theſe profits near two centuries, which after all were but a ſmall indemnity, for the rights they had formerly uſurped, and now relinquiſhed; ſuch as mandates, reſerves, expectatory graces, foreſtallments, vacancies *in curia*, &c.) but if in the preſent ſituation of affairs, our kings could not recover the rights of collation but upon this condition, the whole queſtion is reduced to a ſingle point, whether it be a greater inconveniency to the kingdom, that a little money ſhould be paid to the court of Rome, or the king deprived of a right, which eſtabliſhes his power, and ſecures the government againſt all diſturbances and factions, that have been ſo often occaſioned by elections, and would be ſtill more frequent in a ſtate divided by different opinions in religion: now I apprehend, that every form of government being founded on particular principles, that by which monarchy ſubſiſts, is the concurrence of the whole in lodging the ſupreme power in the hands of a ſingle perſon. (See the hiſtory of the public eccleſiaſtic law of France, 1737.)

Before I conclude, I ſhall add a word or two to what has been already mentioned in the courſe of this work, concerning the cruſades: they contributed greatly to rid our kings of thoſe petty tyrants, who carried their turbulent humours abroad, and eaſed the government at home. But independently of the advantage, accruing to our ſovereigns, they are of uſe, I think, when conſidered in themſelves, as they point out the manners and opinions of thoſe times.

Far be it from me to arraign the motive of the cruſades, which cannot be too much reſpected; but the manner of carrying them

PARTICULAR REMARKS.

them into execution was ill concerted (perhaps from the impossibility of the thing) though the object itself was religious and sacred. I shall only take notice, that the crusades afford us a very good opportunity to consider the wanderings of the human understanding: nothing is more curious, and at the same time more instructive, than to observe, how mankind are actuated by passion in the pursuit of every object; and how even things the most sacred, are rendered subservient to the indulgence of irregular desires. Religion was far from being always so pure, as we find it at present: though philosophy is sometimes suspected, of not favouring that sacred cause, yet this is owing to the evil disposition of particular persons; for it must rather have a contrary tendency, when we employ it only in reasoning, from principles of undoubted evidence. This is easily perceived in ecclesiastic history: we observe, that in the times of ignorance, that is, when people did not make use of their reason, a gross superstition obtained, instead of that improvement of the mind, which we owe to philosophy. The Christian religion was become, ever since the eleventh century, a cloak for all manner of abuses and iniquity; and its professors were grown a species of idolaters, who honoured the true God, in the same manner as the heathens formerly worshipped the false deities. The reformation of manners, and the sacrifice of the passions, made no part of their worship; and they thought like pagans, that they had satisfied every obligation, after performing the external exercises of religion. It is only since we have begun to reason, that we have discovered the outward practices of piety to be of no avail, without the inward submission of the heart: and so sensible is this progress of the understanding, that, even at this very day, it is easy to distinguish among Christian nations, the difference between those that have cultivated, and such as have neglected the study of philosophy. In France, for example, there is no sort of doubt, but that religion is better understood, and superstitious practices are more exploded, than in other countries: the morals of the people are not indeed the purest; but they know when they do wrong, and they are no longer so mistaken as to believe, that external acts of religion can atone for a criminal course of life. Not but

the

PARTICULAR REMARKS.

the abuse of philosophy has done a great deal of mischief; yet I take upon me to affirm, that when once it submits to the authority of religion, the latter shines forth with greater purity and lustre. Little would it avail to preach up a crusade to the Holy Land in our time; much less would whole nations be persuaded, that the displaying of the sign of the cross upon one's sleeve, or the undertaking of voyages or wars, in order to visit the Holy Land, or to rescue it from oppression, could intitle people to indulge their irregular passions.

And yet this was the general creed at the beginning of the crusades. (*The abbé Fleury in his sixth discourse on church history.*) The monks, grown tired of a conventual life, abandoned their cells; the women, surfeited of their husbands, went in pursuit of their gallants; the nobility, involved in debt, sold or mortgaged their estates; and all flocked to the Holy Land, with a firm persuasion of receiving forgiveness of their sins. It must have been a very extraordinary spectacle, to behold the march or procession of such a multitude of people of both sexes, who notwithstanding they had been guilty of all manner of crimes, and were strangers to true Christianity and virtue, yet sincerely believed they were going to fight for the glory of God; and who upon their journey committed all manner of excess and debauchery, or amused themselves with the criminal remembrance of their absent mistresses. A poet of those days (see Fauchet, French poets, book 2. chap. 17.) has given us the history of the lord of Coucy, who went a crusading, when he was deeply in love with the wife of a neighbouring gentleman; and who with this guilty flame in his breast, died upon the voyage: in his last moments he charged a friend to embalm his heart, and present it to the lady, which was accordingly performed. Fine fruits of repentance! Thus we see how every thing may be abused, and how an undertaking, in itself holy and worthy of respect, may become an object of ridicule and scandal.

I shall mention one word more, which though foreign to the subject in hand, will serve to shew the notions of religion, entertained by military people. "La Hire, being upon his march

PARTICULAR REMARKS.

"to raise the siege of Montargis, met with a priest, whom he desired to grant him absolution immediately: and the priest told him, that he should confess his sins. La Hire made answer, that he had not time, for he was just going to engage the enemy, and that he had committed what people of his profession were accustomed to commit: upon which the priest gave him absolution in the best manner he could. La Hire then prayed to God, expressing himself thus in the Gascon dialect, with both his hands joined: O God, I beseech thee to do as much to day for la Hire, as thou wouldst be glad that la Hire should do for thee, if he were God, and thou la Hire; and he fancied, says the historian, that he made a very good prayer."

We shall finish these remarks with two curious articles, the infranchisement of the *serfs* or villains, and the establishment of the corporations, or third estate.

With regard to the villains, it appears, 1. That the Franks made no new slaves in Gaul. 2. That the slaves carried arms. 3. That they were the real property of the lords.

So far were the Franks from making new slaves in Gaul, it appears, on the contrary, that the manner of treating the villains, introduced by those conquerors, was less severe to those poor people, and more advantageous to their masters. "The Germans, says Tacitus, do not keep their slaves in their houses, after our manner, in order to make them perform a certain task; on the contrary, they assign to each his particular manour, or farm, where he lives as the father of a family: all the hardship the master imposes upon him, is to oblige him to pay an annual rent or acknowledgment, which is generally of corn, cattle, skins, &c." Hence it appears, that the condition of those poor people was more in the nature of our country farmers, than in that of slaves. Those Germans or Franks settled in Gaul, and introduced their own customs, which the Romans in that country took care not to imitate.

Among the latter the condition of villains was very different. The property of the lands was such, that every thing upon them belonged to the lords. If a male villain married a female villain of another lord, the children born of that marriage were divided

between

PARTICULAR REMARKS.

between their masters, in the same manner as they would divide their cattle. Further, how great soever their respect might be for ecclesiastic matters, a villain could enter into no engagement in the church, without the express leave of his lord. (Capit. l. 1. art. 23. 28. 80. 113.)

In France there were therefore two sorts of *serfs* or villains, those of the Franks, and those of the Gauls.

But they all served in time of war, notwithstanding the chimerical system of M. de Boulainvilliers, according to which all the villains were denied the use of arms, and consequently one half of the nation rendered useless to their prince and to the government. "When a Roman and a barbarian shall be summoned upon an ex-
" pedition, they shall be obliged to bring the tenth part of their vil-
" lains along with them, and see they be properly armed." (Law of the Visigoths.) Those same villains were also admitted to fight single combats, as appears from the letters granted for that purpose by king Lewis the Fat to the church of Chartres, and to the abbey of St. Maur des Fossés.

With regard to the infranchisements, though the reign of Lewis the Fat is the real æra of this establishment, the subsequent edict upon this subject, published by Lewis Hutin, is so beautiful, that we have thought proper to make an extract from it, in order to give an idea of this great revolution. " Lewis, by
" the grace of God, king of France and Navarre, to our trusty
" and beloved ...... as according to the law of nature, every
" man ought to be born free, ... we, considering that
" this is called the kingdom of the Franks, and being de-
" sirous that the reality should agree with the name, ... by
" the advice of our great council, have ordained, and do now
" ordain, that generally throughout our realm, ... infranchise-
" ments be granted upon good and suitable conditions ..... and
" to the end that other lords, who have villains under them,
" may follow our example, in granting them their freedom, &c.
" Given at Paris the 3d day of July, and in the year of grace
" 1315."

Such was the civil constitution of the kingdom. The king began with enfranchising his own villains, with a view of setting an

example

PARTICULAR REMARKS.

example to the other lords; but such examples become laws, when once the royal authority is established. "Some of the "inhabitants (says Bouchel, letter A. *Affranchissement*) of the "country of Charolois, or other districts of Burgundy, were sub-"ject to a lady, as villains or mainmort men: these people took "out letters of infranchisement from the king, paying a certain "sum of money: the lady, *quæ patrona erat*, opposed this step, "and insisted that, *invitâ patronâ, manumissio concedi non potuit a* "*principe*. By an arret, which the president Seguier pronounced "in his scarlet robe, on Friday the first of June 1571, it was "declared, that the infranchisement should hold good and take "effect, the said subjects paying an indemnity to the lady." But it is proper to observe, that though the villains belonging to a lord obtained their liberty, upon being infranchised by the king, and the lord was obliged to confirm this infranchisement, it was not the same in regard to a villain infranchised by his lord; in the latter case, the consent of the king or of the lord paramount was necessary, by reason that this was diminishing his feudal dependance; and in failure hereof, the villain so infranchised, came under the power of the king, or of the lord paramount. (Brussel.)

To be ingenuous, we are not to form a high idea of the advantage, which those villains derived from their infranchisement, especially in latter times: servitude then was so gentle and mild, that even some freemen chose this state of subjection to lords, when they were not wealthy enough to be their vassals, to the end that they might belong to some master, and not be considered as vagabonds. Lewis Hutin foreseeing the case might happen, in which a villain would not chuse to be infranchised, (du Cange) ordered the commissioners to exact a sum of money from him by way of subsidy.

Let us come now to the corporations, or third estate. The French writers, says Brussel, are all agreed, that Lewis the Fat is the first of our kings, who granted the privilege of corporations to towns; though it seems as if some favour of this nature had been obtained from our princes of the second race, and even that the Gauls had enjoyed the like under the Romans. He did it with a view of appeasing seditions, which at that time were very frequent; and especially of enabling the inhabitants, by a conjunction of interest, to defend themselves against the great lords: hence it is, that those corporations were established by the king only on his own demesnes, and not in the towns belonging to the great lords, except at Soissons, where the count was not powerful enough to oppose this regulation.

Those privileges were *common* charters, which empowered the towns, and sometimes the boroughs, to have a senate or assembly, composed of the principal citizens, at the nomination and choice of the members of the corporation: the business of this senate was to provide for the public security, to levy the usual taxes, to impose extraordinary duties, to administer justice to their fellow citizens, and to keep a regular militia on foot, in which all the inhabitants were to enrol.

Though by instituting these corporated societies, one would think that our princes ran some risk of making the cities too powerful, yet they removed an evil of a more urgent nature. It was necessary to reduce the power and ambition of the lords; and this the crown was not able to effect (at a time when there were no regular troops) but by opposing them singly. But as soon as the great lords were reduced, our kings turned their attention towards those towns, which they had rendered almost independent; and by degrees resumed the privileges which they had formerly granted. This appears from the famous ordinance of Moulins, published by the chancellor de l'Hopital, where the 71st article ordains, that the mayors, sheriffs, consuls, and in general the magistrates of all corporate bodies, shall no longer take cognizance of civil causes, which was depriving them of their most valuable privilege.

It was not long before the great lords, who were constant imitators of royalty, began to establish corporations in the towns belonging to their seignories, in order to defend their vassals; as the king did it to protect his subjects. We meet with a charter granted to the inhabitants of the town of Meaux, by the count of Champagne and Brie, in 1179: but we may easily judge, that if our kings resumed those privileges from the towns belonging to their own demesne; they must have paid less regard to such as were subject to private lords.

All

PARTICULAR REMARKS.

All these affairs may appear at present trifling. The face of things has been so vastly altered, that there is not now a greater difference between the kingdom of France and the empire of Germany, than there was between the two first races and the third; and there is less resemblance between the time of Hugh Capet and ours, with respect to the form of government, than there was between that of Clovis and Hugh Capet. Yet it must be confessed, that every man, who shall be so curious as to ascend to the source of our laws, or our customs, and shall endeavour to form a general idea of our history, will take pleasure in reviewing those distant times; as we love to see old tapestry, that bring to our remembrance the modes and customs of our forefathers.

F I N I S.

THE
INDEX.

THIS index refers to the years of our Lord, and not to the pages: we have not mentioned the names in the columns, as they are eafy to find without this affiftance: but when there happen to be any facts contained in the columns, we then refer to the page. Thus to the word *fcrutiny*, we have put p. 273. V. I. We likewife refer to the remarks at the *end* of every race of our kings, for the facts there contained. Thus at the word *monarchy*, we refer to p. 36. V. I; and at the word *falic lands*, to p. 94. V. I. When two figures are feparared by a bar —, the reader is then to fuppofe all the intermediate figures, as 1580—84. he muft look for 80. 81. 82. 83. 84. and when there happen to be ftops or points between the figures, ... this is to fignify that the perfons are not the fame. When the figures belong to the fame century, we do not repeat the initials; thus after faying 1600, we continue 01. 02. 03; which imports, 1601. 1602. 1603. We generally refer to the reign of each king, mentioning him by name; for inftance, *Charlemain*, we fay, *fee his reign*, otherwife had we attempted to infert all the actions of each king in an index, we fhould have been obliged to repeat the whole abridgment: but as generally fpeaking the moft memorable actions are confined to a battle, to a fiege, a treaty, an ordinance, &c. thefe will be all found under each of thofe articles.

AB.

A Bares, 787. 96.
  Abbeville, 992. 1658. V. I. p. 105.
Abderamen, 732.
Abdication, 814. 1369. 1439. 1555. 59. 1634. 54. 67. 69.
Abelard, 1140.
Abjuration, 1572. 93. 1668.
Abfolution, 751. 867. 1100. 03. 1304. 1561. 95. See *Excommunications, Cenfures*, &c.
Abufe. See *Appeal*.

AC.

Academies, 789. 1663. French, 1635. 72. of fciences, 1666. of architecture, 1671. of Nifmes, 1682. of painting and fculpture, 1692. of Soiffons, 1674. of Angers, 1686. Floral games, 1694. of Lyons, 1710. of Bourdeaux, 1703.
Acceffion, joyful, 1274.
Accompts, firft prefidents of the chamber of, Montpellier, 1477. Paris, 1686. V. I. p. 311.

Y z *Achenheim*,

INDEX.

AC.
Achenheim, 1675.
Ac nd Galatea, 1686.
Acr 1191. 1329.
Act of navigation, 1660.
Acts, public, 628. 1179. 1360. 1539. 60. 79. 1629.

AD.
Adalgifus, 776. 87.
Adaloaldus, 601.
Adelbert, 1001.
Adela, mother of Charles the Good, 1127. mother of Stephen, 1135.... V. I. p. 113.
Adrige, 1701.
Admiral, Admiralties, 1336. 80. 1570. 72. 1627. 40. 69. 95. See *Coligny*.
Administration, 1391. 1560. See *Finances, Minority, Regency*.
Adolphus of Nassau, 1296. Gustavus, 1611. 27. 30-32. 77.
Adoption, 1154.
Adrets, baron des, 1586.
Adrian I. 774-76. II. 867. VI. 1521. 22. Peter 1628.
Adristes, 794.
Adultery, 1313. V. I. p. 100.
Advocates general, 1589. 1629. 90. in council, 1643. p. 411. 437. V. I.
Advocates, 1092. 1148.

Æ.
Æneas Sylvius, 1439.
Ærarchia, p. 45. V. I.

AF.
Africa, 534. 1026. 1269. 1534. 36. 1664.

AG.
Agde, 506. 1710.
Agenois, 1258. 1638.
Agent of France, 1534.
Agincourt, 1415.
Agnani, 1242. 1303.
Agnes Sorel, 1445. p. 293. V. I.
Agousta, 1675. 76.
Agramont, 1645.

AI.
Aidie, Odet d', 1469. Riberac, 1578.
Aids, court of, 1355. 1477. 1631. tax, 1364.
Aignadel, 1509.
Aigues mortes, 1509.
Aiguillon, 1 34. 38.
Aille, d', 1534.
Ailli, d', 1567.
Aire, 1641. 76. 78. 1710.
Aix, 1501. 45. 90. 1646. la Chapelle, 796 800. 805. 814. 75. 988. 1501. 1668. 72. 77. 85.

AL.
Alain the Great, 877. Chartiers, 1436.
Alais, town, 1629. count d', 1156. 1649.
Alaric, 507. 11.
Albani, 1700.
Abergotti, 1702. 06. 10. 12.
Alberic, V. I. p. 123.
Albemarle, 1666. 1712.
Alberoni, 1708.
Albert, emperor, 1296. II. 1500. of Brandenburg, 1525. 51. archduke, 1596-98. 1600. See *Luines, Chaulnes*.
Albi, Albigenses, 562. 1206. 23. 25. 26. 58. baronness of, 1645. bishopric, 1673.
Albion, 497.
Alboinus, 568.
Albret, John d', 1512. 16. Henry, 1521. Jane, 1548. 69. 72. dukedom, 1642. 51. marshal d', 1650. 78. marquis d', 1678.
Albuquerque, 1705.
Alcantara, 1706.
Alcira, 1707.
Alcoi, 1708.
Alconchel, 1709.
Alcuinus, 789.

Alegre,

INDEX.

Alegre, d', 1703.
Alenſon, Peter, count d', 1329.
 René, duke d', 1440. 57. 74.
 .... 1523. Margaret, 1525
 Francis, duke d', 1574—76.78.
 83. 84.
Alet, biſhop of, 1673.
Alexander, the Great, 1189.1535.
 popes, III. 992. 1156. 71. IV.
 1255. V. 1408. VI. 1493-9:.
 98. 1503. VII. 1387. 1648.
 57. 62. VIII. 1662. 90-92.
 biſhop of Jeruſalem, 892.
Alexandria, 1215. della Paglia,
 1657.
Alexis. See *Comnenus*.
Algiers, Algerines, 1541. 47. 1665.
 70 82-84. 88. 89.
Alicant, 1691. 1706. 08 09.
Alienation, 1275. p. 299. V II. See
 Demeſne.
Aligre, d', 1624. 61. 67. 72.
Alincourt, 1589. 94.
Alix, 1116. 71. 86. 1226. V. I.
 p. 137.
Allegiance, or fealty, oath of, 1206.
 13. 23. 1589. 1649.
Alliance, with the north, 1542.
 with the Swifs, 1549. 82. 1602.
 63. 1715. with the Dutch,
 1627. with Sweden, 1633. tri-
 ple, 1668. againſt France, 1701.
 03.
Almanza, 1707.
Aloſt, 1667. 82. 1705.
Alpaid, 714.
Alps, 1713.
Alphonſus, king of Spain, 1206.
 73. 74. 83. 85. count of Barcelona, 1179. count of Toulouſe,
 1331. king of Portugal, 1088.
 .... 1667. king of Naples,
 1493-15. count de Poitiers,
 1226. 30. 45. 49. 70. XI.
 1516.
Alſace, 612. 1634. 43. 48. 59.
 61. 74. 75. 80. 1709. Gerard
 d', 1056. 60. Thierry d', 1127.
 p. 45. V. I.
Altena, treaty of, 1689.
Alt-Ranſtadt, 1705.
Altenheim, 1675.
Alviana, 1509.

AM.

Amadeus. See *Savoy*.
Amalaric, 531.
Amaury, 1223.
Ambaſſadors. See *Embaſſies*.
Amberg, 1703.
Amblimont, 1674.
Amboiſe, town, 1560. 1624. p. 327.
 V. I. Chaumont d', 1479 Charles
 d', 1500. George, cardinal d',
 1503. 05. 08. Buſſy, 1579.
 James, rector, 1594.
America, 1492. 1623. 28. 76.
 83.
Amfreville, d', 1684.
Amiens, 1329. 1419. 70. 75.
 1597. 1625. 46.
Amneſty, 1652.
Amſterdam, 1672.
Amyot, 1521. p. 408. 409. V. I.

AN.

Anabaptiſts, 1536.
Anaclet, pope, 1130.
Anaſtaſius, emperor, 508.
Ancre, marſhal d', 1612. 16. 17.
Andelot, d', 1562. 90.
Andolo, d', 1204.
Andouins, Coriſande d', 1587.
Andrew, king of Hungary, 1344.
 82.
Andronicus, 1324.
Anet, 1566. 1686.
Angeli, St. John d', 1588.
Angennes, 1593.
Angers, 1047. 1103. 1502. 19.
 20. 52. See *Anjou*.
Angevine kings, ſurnamed *Plan-
 tagenets*, 1485.
Anglo-Saxons, 1215.

Angoria,

INDEX.

Angoria, 1394.
Angouleme, town, 508. 1352. 1441. 1515. 34. 1619 Ifabella d', 1200. Guy de Lufignan, count d', 1302. John, count d', 1497.... 84.86. Francis I. count d', 1477. 1505. 14. Louifa, dutchefs d', 1515. 21-24. 26. 28. 29. 31. 35. 47. duke d', 1589. 1602. 27.
Angoumois, 585.
Anguien, town, 1706. Francis, count d', 1443. 44, 46. 57. Lewis, duke d', 1640. 43-46. See *Condé*, mademoifelle d', 1710.
Anian, 511.
Anjou, counts, 877. province and houfe of, 1092. 1103. 1200 25. 55. 85. 96. 1493. 94. 1576. Geoffry, great fenefchal, d', 978. ... 1116. 35. Henry, 1150. 54. Charles, 1245. 55. 70. 83. 85. 92. Lewis, 1255. 58. 1371. 78. 80-82. Lewis II. 1389. 1415. 93. René, 1431. 76. 80. Margaret, 1457. 62. 71. John, 1464 Jolande, 1476. Charles, count du Maine, 1480. Ferdinand, 1493. Francis, duke d Aumale, 1548. Henry III. 1567. 69-71. 73. Francis d'Alenfon, 1576-78. 80-84. Monfieur, brother of Lewis XIV. 1640. Philip V. 1683. 1700 Lewis XV. 1712.
Annals of St. Bertin, 879
Annales Victoriani, p. 157. V. I.
Annates, 1438. See *Benefices*, *Expectatives*, *Referves*, &c. p. 314. V. II.
Anne, wife of Henry I. 1060. See *de Boaujeau*, of Auftria, 1612. 28. 39. 43. 45. 46. 48-52. 58. 66. See *Britany*. Queen of England, 1673. 1701. 02-06. 11. 14. of Poland, 1575. Mary, 1684.
Annuities, 1441. 1638.

Annunciades, V. I. p 339.
Anfelm, the father, 840.
Anfgardis, 879.
Antin, d', 1663, 1711.
Antioch, prince of, 1150. patriarch of, 1215.
Antipopes, 1439.
Antragues, 1578. 99. 1605.
Antwerp, 1583. 1645. 1703. 06. 15.

AP.
Apoftles, lot of the, 506. 789. V. I. p. 97.
Appeal, 922. 1135. 40. 1245. 1303. 29. 1527. 85. 1623. 88
Appanage, 628. 1200. 25. 83. 1313. 01. 1466 68. 1576. V.I. 259. V.II. p. 297.
Appenzel, 1305.
Apremont, Mary Louifa d', 1675.
Apulia, 1026. 1137. 1503. 09.

AQ.
Aqueduct, 1613. 86.
Aquila, 1490,
Aquileia, 1703.
Aquilles, Onufre, 1645.
Aquitaine, 585. 628. 30. 719. 1283 85.1329. homage, 1278. 80. 85. Eudes, duke of, 731. 32. 34. 36. 39. 44. 58. 67. Pepin, 800. 14. 17. 35. 40. 42. 45. 53. Lewis, 854. Carloman, 879. William, 910. Henry, 1150. 80.

AR.
Arablay, d', 1316.
Arbacius, 996.
Arbiter, 1255.
Arbriffel, d'. See *Robert*.
Archambaud, 646. 54. 996.
Archangel, Capuchin, 1605.
Archbifhoprics, 1622. 74. 95.
Archers, free, 1480. 1532.
Archduke, Maximilian, 1486. Philip,

INDEX.

lip, 1495. 1504. Charles, 1505. Matthias, 1578. Albert, 1597. 1608 Leopold, 1642. 48. 50. 54. Charles, 1700. 01. 03. 05. 06. 09. 10.
Archdukedom, 1477.
Archdutchefs, 1713.
Architect, firſt, 1665.
Architecture, 1671.
Arc, Jane d', 1428. 30. 31. 54.
Arcos, 1647.
Arcueil, 1613.
Ardres, 1520. 96. 1657.
Aregonda, 562.
Argenlieu, d', 1663.
Argenſon, d', 1697. miniſter, 1643.
Argoia, 1273.
Arianiſm, 500, 511. 65. 85. 822.
Ariſtotle, 1206.
Arles, 508. 70. 879. 1245. 58. Conſtantia d', 1032. p. 69. V. I.
Arleux, 1645. 1711.
Armagnac, 630. counts, 1283. 1413. 15. 51. Lewis, 1369. John, 1470. 77. 84. V. I. p. 237. Charles, 1473. James, 1477. 84. Lewis, 1501. 03. Lorrain, 1550.
Armies, 1214. 1532. command, 1627. 39. 72.
Armenonville, d', 1701.
Armentieres, 1645. 47. 67. 68.
Arminians, 1619.
Armorica, 497. 591. 1230. V. I. p. 36.
Arms, ſerjeant at, 1215. fire, 1336. profeſſion of, 1600. . . . . V. II. p. 310. &c.
Arnay-le-duc, 1570.
Arnauld, 1594. biſhop of Angers, 1657. of Corbie, V. I. p. 273.
Arnheim, 1672.
Arnold, ſon of Lewis the Debonnaire, 840. baſtard of Carloman, 877. emperor, 888. 98. count of Flanders, 942. 65. archbiſhop of Rheims, 988. 96. Duke of Gelders, 1473.
Arnolphus, 996.

Arpajon, dutcheſs of, 1680. marquis d', 1711.
Arpin, 1100.
Arques, William d', 1047. battle of, 1589.
Arragon, 827. 1258. 850. Sancho, 1316. John, 1454. 62. 1516. 21. Catharine, 1529. 34. admiral, 1636. . . . . 1711.
Arras, peace of, 1435. 63. 77. 82. 83. . . . . 99. taken, 1640. the ſiege raiſed, 1654. . . . 1712. See *Artois*.
Arraw, treaty of, 1712.
Arrets, lord of Vernon, 1255. appanage, 1283. regiſters, 1313. 1594. Salic law, 1316, 1593. duke of Britany, 1371. duel, 1386. Charles VII. 1420. provoſt of Paris, 1501. Brion, 1540. Poyet, 1541. Tanquerel, 1561. St. Bartholomew's, 1572. ſigning of parties, 1579. Charles de la Trimouille, 1588. 89. 96. 98. breviary, 1602. regency, 1610. Santarel, 1626. repealed, 1632. marriage of Gaſton, 1634. Aiguillon, 1638. de Thou, 1642. regency, 1643. troubles, 1648. of council, 1692. 1700. 1704. priſoners for debt, 1704. cardinal of Bouillon, 1710. V. I. p. 177.
Ars, Lewis d', 1512. baron d', 1713.
Arſenal, 1587. 88.
Artagnan, 1709, d', 1666. Artaud, 936.
Arteville, d', 1336. 82.
Artillery, 1495. 1525. 1600. 69. 94.
Artiſan, 1626.
Artois, province, 1192. 1215. 25. county and peerage, 1296. Robert, count d', 1245. 49. Robert II. 1283. 85. Mahault, 1302. Robert, 1316. 28. 31. county, 1384. . . . . 1477. 86. 99. 1529. 1642. 59. See *Arras*, p. 225. V. I. 299. V. II.

Y 4 *Arthur*,

INDEX.

Arthur, 1200. 15.
Arts, 1180. See *Learning.*

AS.

Asfeld, d', 1688. 89. 1707-09. 14. 15.
Assemblies, parliaments, 615. 51. 767. 79. Charlemain, 806. 40. of Compiegne, 888. of Worms, 1103. of Montpellier, 1275. demesne, 1275. Salic law, 1316. benefices, 1397. of the Notables, 1558. 96. 1617. 26. Fontainebleau, 1560. 74. Sens, 1612. the four articles, 1682. See *Councils.*
Asoph, 1699. 1711.
Assizes, of Jerusalem, 1067. . . . 1135. great and general, 635.
Associations, 813. 17. 954. 1127. 1576.
Asti, 1529. 1615. 43.
Astolphus, 568. 753.
Astrology, judicial, 1159. V. I. p. 259.
Astronomy, 789. 840.
Asturias, V. I. p. 31.

AT.

Ath, 1667. 68. 97. 1701. 06.
Athanagildus, 565. 68.
Athelstan, 922.
Athens, 1567.
Attigny, 822.
Attorney, 1484. 1620. general, 1688. 89.

AU.

Avaray, d', 1707.
Avaux, d', 1644. 47. 75.
Aubenton, 1650.
Aubigny, d', 1495. 99. 1501. 02.
Aubriot, 1369.
Aubusson, 1565.
Audefleda, 500.
Audigier, 511.
Audovera, 584.

Avein, 1635.
Avenelle, 1560.
Avenes, les d', 1258. John d', 1206. . . . . 1659.
Aversberg, count d', 1700.
Augustus, title of, 508. emperor, 511. 1215. age of, 1663.1715. See *Saxony.*
Augsburg town, 1632. 46. 48. 1703. confession of,1530. league of, 1687. 88.
Augustinians, 1255.
Augustulus, 800.
Avignon, 570. 1225. 1305. 29. 48. 52. 76. 79. 89. 1617. 62. 88. 90.
Aulneau, 1687.
Aumale, town, 1592. marquis d', 1546. Francis, duke d', 1548. 89. p. 385. V. I. chevalier d', 1591. mademoiselle d', 1667.
Aumont, John d', 1509. 92. 95. Ant. 1644. 65. 67. duke, 1669.
Aunix, 1223. 1653. See *Rochelle.*
Auray, 1364.
Aurisabert, John, 1546.
Austrasia, 576. 93. 96. 98. 612. 13. 22. 25. 32. 44. 54. 56. 70. 73. 78. 88. 715. 42. 46. V. I. p. 45.
Astregilda, 593.
Austria, country, 796. 1657. first house of, 1226. second house, 1273. 96. 1305. 1477. 1536. 55. 98. 1617. 20. 27. 33. 87. . . . . 94. 98. 1711. duke of, 1475. Leopold, 1191. 93. Rodolphus, 1226. 73. 82. Albert I. 1282. 96. 1305. Frederic, duke of, 1322. Frederic III. 1477. See *Maximilian.* Charles V. 1505. See *Charles.* Margaret, daughter of Maximilian, 1508. 29. 30. 56. Mary, 1552. 56. Margaret, natural daughter of Charles V. 1565.

INDEX.

1565. Elizabeth, 1570. John, 1571. 78. See *Anne.* Eleonora Maria. 1675. John. 1647. 56. 58. 71. 79. 1712. Mary Theresa, 1656. 59. 60. 65. 67. 83. 98. V. II. p. 91.
Autun, 511. 613. 68. 936.
Auverquerque, 1704. 06.

Auvergne, 534. 1215. 30. 1355. 1665. William, 910. dauphin of, 1589. county of, 1602. 05. 16.
Auxerre, 1358. 1410. 23. 28.
Ayetonne, 1634.
Azores, 1582.

B.

BACON, 1336. 1509.
Badajos, 1658. 1705.
Baden, prince Lewis of, 1678. 88. 91. 93. 97. 1702-05. 07. treaty of, 1714.
Babus, 1678.
Bajazet I. 1394. II. 1495.
Bailiwick, Bailiffs, 912. 92. 1135. 1498. 1563. 1684. p. 303 V. II.
Bailliol, John, 1292. town, 1678.
Balagnier, 1644. 45. 50. 1707. 11.
Balagny, 1594. 95.
Balderic, 520.
Baldwin, a crusader, 1092. count of Flanders, 861. .... 1031. 56. 6. 62. 67. 1103. 1204. count d' Hainaut, 1180. emperor of Constantinople, 867. 1204. 99. impostor, 1213.
Ballet, 1391.
Ballue, la, 1469. 80. V. I. p. 311.
Baltic, sea, 1676.
Balzac, d'Antragues, 1578. 1602.
Ban of the empire, 1706.
Bards, 1532.
Banier, 1636. 37. 41.
Banishment, 1331. 1661.
Bapaume, 1641.
Baptism, 496. 780. 1056.
Bar, count of, 1296. Catharine, 1599. 1604. dukedom, 1419. 1632. 33. 41. 61. 99.
Baradas, 1626.

Barbarism, 1390.
Barbarossa, 1536. 37. 43. 47.
Barbasan, 1404. 31.
Barbeaux, abbey, V. II. p. 309.
Barberini family, 1644-46. cardinal, 1625. .... 1700.
Barbesieux, 1701.
Barbets, 1691.
Barbette, street, 1407.
Barcelona, 800. 1156. 1245. 58. 1529. 1649. 51. 52. 55. 91. 97. 1704-06. 10. 14.
Bareith, 1707.
Barfleur, 1120.
Barillon, 1648.
Barnabites, 1532.
Barnwelt, 1616. 19.
Baronius, 1605.
Barons, 1226. 55. 69.
Barricades, 1588. 1629. 48.
Barrier, towns, 1711. 13. treaty, 1715. John de la, 1587. Peter, 1593.
Bart, 1694. 96.
Bartholomew St. massacre, 1572. church, V. I. p. 104.
Bascara, 1675.
Base alliances, p. 121. V. I.
Basil, St. V. I. p. 39.
Basil, town, 1387. 1431. 32. 35. 38. 39. 43. 1676.
Basée, la, 1641. 42. 47.
Bassompierre, 1621. 27. 29. 31. 43. 47.
Bastards, 1321. See *Legitimated.*
Bastide,

INDEX.

Bastide, the battle of, 1511.
Bastile, 1369. 1574. 75. 87-89. 1611. 52.
Batavia, 1619.
Batilde, 656.
Batteville, 1661.
Battle, of the herrings, 1428, of the spurs, 1513. of corn, 1591.
Battori, 1575.
Bavaria, country, 743. 87. 875. Tassillo, 593. 768. 87. Lewis, 817. 35. 40-42. 53. 58. 75. Lewis IV. 912. Lewis V. 1322. 28. Isabella, 1389. 1408. 15. 22. Joan, 1424. Robert, 1474. Sabina, 1558. Maximilian I. 1617. 20. 31. 32. 45. 46-48. Maximilian II. 1680. 85. 87. 88. 90. 92. 93. 98. 1700-12. 14. Mary Anne Victoria, 1680. 90. prince of, 1698. 99.
Bavay, 1678.
Bauché, 1593.
Baune, Semblansay, 1522.
Baux, Mary of, 1349.
Bay, marquis de, 1706. 07. 09. 10.
Bayard, chevalier, 1510-12. 24.
Bayle, 1650. 80.
Bays, 1628.

BE.

Beard, 1521.
Bearn, 1620. 82. prince of, 1569.
Beatrix, 956. .... 1245.
Beaucaire, 1743.
Beaufort, duke de, 1643. 48. 50. 52. 64. 66. 69. dukedom, 1557. 98. 1688.
Beaugé, 1421.
Beaujeu, Edward de, 1682. Anne, 1483-85. 88. Peter, 1484. Quiqueran de, p. 91. V. II.
Beaulieu, 1426.
Beamanoir, Landes de, 1364.
Beaumont, William de, 1223. le Roger, 1331.
Beaune, Renaud de, 1593.
Beauté, madam de, 1445.
Beauvais, town, 1472. bishop of, 1643.

Beauveau, de, 1709. p. 311. V. I.
Beauvilliers, 1663. 89. 91.
Beauviré, 1672.
Beauvoisin, bridge of, 1575.
Bec, general, 1646.
Becquet, Thomas, 1161. 69. 79.
Bed of justice, 1331. 1420. 1598. 1643. 51.
Bede, 743.
Bedford, duke of, 1422. 24. 35.
Bees of gold, origin of the flowers de luce, 1655.
Beffort, 1636. 54.
Beggars, or *Gueuses*, 1566.
Beguine, 1275.
Belgrade, 1688.
Belin, count de, 1594.
Belisarius, 534.
Belleisle, 1674. 1703. marshal de, 1707.
Bellay, du, 1428. 1543.
Bellfons, 1638. 67. 68. 72. 75. 84. 92.
Bellegarde, town, 1675. Roger de, 1574. master of the horse, 1602. 31. gentleman of the bedchamber, 1612.
Bellesme, 1226.
Bellievre, Pomponne de, 1588. 98. first president, 1657. p. 7. V. II.
Bender, 1709. 13.
Benefices, 1230. 1397. 1415. 39. 97. 1521. 50. 53. 61. V. II. military, V. I. p. 94. V. II. p. 296.
Benevento, 850. 75. 1255.
Benedict, Saint, p. 39. V. I. 1215. X. 1304. antipope, 1401. 08.
Benfeld, 1675.
Benoise, 1589.
Bentivoglio, 1546.
Beranger, in Italy, 1047. 56.
Bergen-op-zoom, 1588.
Bergues, Saint-Vinox, 1646. 51. 58. 67. prince de, 1691.
Beringhen, 1602. 45.
Bernard, Saint, 1130. 45. 48. king of Italy, 807. 18. 22.

count

INDEX.

count of Barcelona, 830. bishop, 1303. Van-Galen, 1666.
Berne, 1549.
Berry, province, 1576. John, duke de, 1380. 86. 91. 1415. Charles, 1464. 68. 72. Charles, 1686. 1700. 10. 12. 14.
Bersello, 1702. 03.
Bertairé, 688.
Bertha, 996. ... 1092. p. 45. V.I.
Berthilda, 636.
Bertrade Montfort, 1092. 1103.
Bertrand, 630. William, p. 211. V.I. de Got, 1305. bishop, 1329. de la Cueva, 1504.
Bertrandy, 1559.
Bertruda, 628.
Berulle, 612.
Berwick, duke of, 1688. 89. 1704. 06. 07. 10. 11. 14.
Besan, 1219.
Besançon, 1568. 74.
Besil, 1306.
Besine, 1572.
Besila, 1580.
Bethencourt, 1492.
Bethune, town, 1645, 1710. Robert de, 1304. 22. Lewis, 1322. marquis de, 1624. See *Rosny*.
Beuf, le, 593.
Beze, 1561.
Beziers, 1156. 1258.
Bezons, 1709. 11. 13.

BI.

Bicestre, 1410.
Bichy, 1644.
Bicoque, 1521.
Bideux, 1544.
Birz, de, 1545.
Bignon, 1624. 67. 90. p. 43. V.I.
Bilbao, 1697.
Bilichildis, 612.
Bilihildis, 673.
Bills, 1704. 07.
Billettes, miracle of, 1285.
Binck, town, 1668. 75. admiral, 1677.
Binghen, 1639. 40. 44.
Biorn III. p. 59. V. I.

Birague, 1574. 1672.
Biron, Armand de, 1570. 83. 89. 92. 1660. Charles de, 1590. 95. 1602.
Bishoprics, Pamiers, 1292. 1303. Paris, 1622. 92. Bulls, 1693. V. I. p. 39.
Bishops, 511, 657. revenue, 794. 1385. ordination, 796. Lewis the Debonnaire, 822. 40. Robert, 996. 1022. rank, 1092. 1103. 48. 1225. 26. oath, 1223. excluded from parliament, 1319. judges of hereticks, 1560. 1633. 39. 99. V. I. p. 38, 39. V. II. 313.

BL.

Black prince, 1376.
Blake, admiral, 1653.
Blainville, 1702.
Blamont, 1638.
Blanche, wife of Lewis V. 986. of Castile, 1215. 25. 26. 45. 52.
Bloncménil, Poitier de, 1648.
Blasphemers, 1258.
Blavet, 1625.
Blaye, 630.
Bleneau, 1652.
Blois, count, 1226. town, 1560. 76. 79. 88. 89. 1617. 19. 22. 52. Charles, 1341. 64. 79. John, 1419. mademoiselle de, 1692.
Blomberg, Barbara, 1556.

BO.

Bobigny, 1562.
Bodegrave, 1672.
Bodillon, 673.
Borgis, 630. 731.
Bohemia, kingdom, 1526. 1617-20. 34. *Ottocaris*, 1282. John, 1336. Frederic, 1613. 19. 20. 32. Anne Jagellon, 1526. king of, 1684.
Bohemond, 1026. 92.
Boileau, Stephen, 1269. Nicholas, 1677.
Boine, the, 1690.
Bois-Baillet, du, 1682.

Boisbourdon

INDEX.

Boisbourdon, 1415.
Bois-Dauphin, 1594.
Boisi. Gouffier de, 1514. 21.
Bois-Jourdan, 1675.
Boiselleau, 1690.
Bologna, a city in Italy, 1510-12. 15 29.
Bombardment, 1682. 85. 88. 91. 94. 96. 1703. 1704.
Bombs, 1588. 1634.
Bomel, 1672.
Bonaventure, St. 992.
Boniface, St. 751. VIII. 557. 992. 1202. 99. 1303. 05. 21. p. 303. V. II. de Montferrat, 1204.
Bonivet, 1521. 23-25.
Bon-Mouflier, 612.
Bonne de Luxembourg, 1336. See *Lesdiguieres*.
Bonrepos, 1698.
Books, scarcity of, 1067. impression of, 1626.
Borgia, Cesar, 1498. 1504.
Boristhenes, 1708.
Boson, 875. 77. 79 88 1245.
Bossuet, 1661. 68. 90.
Bossut, countess de, 1641.
Bothwel, 1587.
Bouchage. See *Joyeuse*.
Bouchain, 1676. 78. 1711. 12.
Bouchard, 992. See *Montmorency*.
Bouchel, p. 300. V. II.
Boucherat, Lewis, 1667. 85. 99.
Bouchers, called Cabochians, 1410.
Boucicaut, 1394. 1401.
Boufflers, 1674. 81. 08. 85. 88. 93. 95. 98. 1702-04. 09.
Bouillon, town, 1652. 76. Godfrey, 1067 92. 1443. la Marck, 1521. marshal, p. 385. V. I. marshal de, 1591. 96. 1602. 04. 06. 11. 13-15. 20. 23. duke de, 1591. 1636. 41. 42. 48. 50. 51. . . . . 61. madam de, 1680. cardinal de, 1700. 10. M. de, 1612.
Boullainvilliers, de, p. 43.

Boulogne, 807. 1492. 1544. 46. 49. 50. Stephen, 1135. 48. Philip, 1214. 26. Magdalen, 1517.
Boulonnois, 1376.
Boundaries of Paris, 1550.
Bondman, 196. 1135. 1225. 1316.
Bourbon, dutchy and peerage, 1324. 29 James, 1361. Jane, 1349. Lewis II. 1355. 80. 1682. Peter, 1355. Charles, 1440 John II. 1464. 66. 84. 86. constable, 1484. 86. Peter de Beaujeu. 1484. Charles, constable, 1509.15. 21. 23. 24. 26. 27. 51. Antony. 1548. 59. 60. 62. p. 550. Jane d'Albret, 1548. 72. cardinal, 1559. 84 85. 88-90. branch royal, 1588. p. 181. V I 2. V. II. the young cardinal, 1591. Soissons, 1612. 41. Blanche, 1366. Gabrielle, 1488. Louisa-Benedicta, 1692. Louisa, 1713. See *Anguien*, *Condé*, *Conti*.
Bourbourg, 1645.
Bourdeaux, city, 511. 1223. 1355. 78. 1451. 62. 1589. 94. 1615. 38. 41. 50. 53 79. parliament, 1462. assassin. 1587. ambassador, 1655. academy, 1713.
Bourdeille, Andrew de, 1573.
Bourdillon, 1562.
Bourg, in Guyenne, 1653. Robert du, 1126. Anne du, 1559. marshal du, 1706. 09.
Bourges, viscounty, 1100. city, 1438. 1594. 1650. archbishopric, 1142. 1593. 1676. university, 1463. professorship of law, 1665. See *Berry*.
Bourignon, 1680.
Bournonville, 1674. 75. 84.
Bouthillier, 1603. 17. 43.
Boutteroue, 539.
Boutteville, 1627. 54. 95.
Bouvard, 1634.
Bouvines, 1114. 1474.

Brabant,

INDEX.

BR.

Brabant, province, 1543. 54. Jacquelina, 1424. Francis, duke d'Alençon, d'Anjou & de, 1575. 78. 8o. 84.
Braganza, duke de, 1580.
Braga, archbishopric of, 1641.
Brahe, de, 1661.
Brancas, Villars, 1591. 94. 95. dutchy and peerage, 1652. marshal de, 1712.
Brandenbourg, Albert, 1551. marquis de, 1609. John Sigismond, 1610. 14. Frederic III. 1672-75. 77-79. 87. 89. 1701. Frederic IV. 1701. 02. Frederic V. the reigning king, his character, 1701.
Brantôme, 1482. 1574.
Brasil, 1624. 57. 61. 63. 1711.
Bread, dearness of, 1709.
Breauté, 1640.
Breda, 1590. 1624. 25. 37. 67. 70.
Bremen, a city, 1638. 48.
Bremerfurt, 1675.
Brenneville, 1116.
Bresse, 1037. 1512. 1600. 01.
Brest, 1371. 1681. 94.
Bret, le, p. 300. V. II.
Bretagne, *Bretons*, province, 1497. 929. 1516. Alain, 560. Waroc, 591. 94. counts, 636. 780. 818. 40. 1509. subjects of France, 845. Nomenoe, 845. Herispoé, 845. dukes, 877. holds of Normandy, 912. 92. devolves to the house of France, 1116. 67. Conan, 1116. Peter de Dreux, 1116. 1226. 30. Geoffrey, 1200. Peter Mauclerc, 1230. dutchy and peerage, 1296. John II. 1296. John III. 1341. John de Montfort, 1341. 64. 79. succession, 1341. 44. 64. Charles de Blois, 1364. John V. 1371. 79. 81. 87. 91. 97. confiscated, 1379.

Clisson, 1419. John VI. 1419. 23. 24. Francis II. 1445. 64. 66. 68. 70. 72. 74. 75. 85. 86. 88. Peter II. 1448. Anne, 1488. 90. 92. 99. 1505. 11. 13. 15. union, 1532. parliament, 1553. league, 1590. 92. 96. subdued, 1598. 1604. count de Toulouse, 1695. government, 1661. duke de, 1712.
Bretesche, la, 1678.
Bretigny, 1360.
Brevet de retenue, 1692.
Breviary, 1602.
Brezé, admiral de, 1488. Urban, marshal de, 1635. 40. 43. 46.
Brianson, 1709.
Briare, 1604.
Briconnet, William, 1494.
Bridieu, 1643.
Bridge, 1309. 1578. 1604. 14.
Brie, 1233. 1331. 1468. 69. p. 221. V. I.
Brief, 1682-90. 99. See *Bulls*.
Brienne, John de, 1092. Henry, 1620. 43. 61.
Briffe, la, 1689.
Brigadier, 1633. 67.
Brignais, battle of, 1361.
Brihuega, 1710.
Brille, the, 1616.
Brinvilliers, 1676.
Brion, admiral, 1535. 40.
Brionne, 1689.
Brios, 875.
Briqueras, 1630.
Brisgaw, 1675.
Brisac, 1638, 48. 80. 1703.
Brissac, Charles, marshal de, 1553-55. 57. p. 99. V. I. Charles de Cossé, 1594. dutchy and peerage, 1611.
Brisson, 1589. 91.
Britain, Great, 800-29. 1603. 1706.
Britany. See *Bretagne*.
Brieve-la Gaillarde, 585.
Broglio, 1707. 09. 12.

Brosse,

INDEX.

Brosse, Peter la, 1275. James de, 1615. Guy de la, 1634.
Brouage, 1653.
Broussel, 1648.
Bruges, 1127. 1360. 1430. 1706. 08.
Brun, Antony, 1647. John le, 1383. first painter to the king, 1664. 65. 90.
Brunehaut, or *Brunechild*, 565. 68. 75-77. 84. 88. 96-99. 605. 12. 13.
Brunswick, Henry, surnamed the Lion, 1180. George, 1675. George William, 1714. Christian, 1620. 1711.
Brusol, treaty of, 1610.
Brussels, 1555. 1631. 41. 95-97. 1706. 08.

BU.

Bucelin, 539.
Buch, captal of, 1364. 71. 97.
Buckingham, duke of, 1624-28. 60.
Buda, 1684. 86.
Budeus, 1305. 1547.
Budes, Louisa de, 1602. Guébriant, 1643.
Bueil, Sancerre, 1560.
Bugey, 888. 1037. 1601.
Bulgarians, 807. 929.
Bullegneville, 1431.
Bullen, Anne, 1534-47.
Buildings, 1661. 91. 1709.
Bulls, unam sanctam, 1305. 16. Clementines, 1321. golden, 1355. 1556. on the benefices of cardinals, 1521. for the indult, 1538. prohibited, 1551. in cœna Domini, 1568. against the king of Navarre, 1585. against Jansenius, 1657. on the franchises, 1687. 88. refused, 1692, 93. vineam Domini, 1705.
Bullion, 1624. 32. 36.
Bulonde, 1691.
Buquoy, 1618.
Burgaw, marquis de, 1609.
Burglenfeld, 1703.
Burgundy, kingdom, 493. 500. 08. 11. 23. end, 534. 68. Childebert II. 593. Clotaire II. 613. mayors, 646. duke, 695. Childeric III. 742. Charles the Bald, 835. Boson, 879. kingdom, 888. annexed to the empire, 1037. dutchy and county, 695. 830. 77. 79. 88. 956. first royal branch, 1001. 31. 37. count, 1285. Eudes, 1316. Philip de Rouvre, 1361. 64. 65. ambassadors, 1432. 51. 70. 77. 83. 1526. Rodolph, 888. Godefile, 500. Childebert, 593. Pepin, 695. Charles the Bald, 836. Henry 1001. Robert, 1001. Margaret, 1313. Philip the Hardy, 1371. 80. 82. 84. 85. 91. 1401. 04. John the Fearless, 1404. 07. 08. 10. 15. 19. 24. Philip the Good, 1419 22. 24. 30-32. 35. 36. 40. 56. 63. 65. 67. Charles the Bold, 1468-74. 77. p. 307. V. II. &c. parliament of, 1477. Mary, 1477. 82. 1508. p. 307 V. II. &c. duke of, father of Lewis XV. 1682. 97-99. 1702. 03. 08. 12. deputies of, 1:26. Mary Adelaïd, mother of Lewis XV. 1696. 1712. comedians of the hotel of, 1609. 73. p. 299. V. II.
Burgundians, 1410. p. 37. V. I.
Burial of the kings, 879. 1448. p. 37. V. I.
Buricb, 1672.
Busancy, 593.
Bussi, d'Amboise, 1579. 95. le Clerc, 1588. 89. Rabutin, 1665. Lamet, 1637. 78.
Bust on coins, 1450. p. 327. V. I.
Butler, p. 38. V. I.

INDEX.

C.

Cabinet, secretary of the, 1589.
Caboche, chief of the Cabochians, 1410.
Cabrieres, 1545.
Cadets, 1682.
Cadix, 1596. 1626. 86. 1702.
Caen, 1067.
Cahors, 1258. 1580.
Cajetan, cardinal, 1590. 92.
Caillavel, 1686.
Cailus, 1578.
Calabria, kingdom of, 978. 1026. 1503. dutchy of, 1503. duke of, 1474.
Calais, 1347. 60. 1451. 62. 1518. 58. 59. 96. 1658. 96.
Calcinato, 1706.
Calendar, 1582. 1699.
Calignon, 1598. 1603.
Calixtus, 1120. 71.
Callieres, 1697.
Calmar, 1391.
Calvin, Calvinism, 1529. 34. 53. 59. 60. 76. 93. 1621. 28. 82.
Calvo, 1676. 79.
Camaldulenses, 1001.
Cambray, 481. 510. league of, 1508. treaty, 1529. 34. 35. ... 54. 81. 83. 94. 95. 1649. 57. 77. 78. archbishopric, 1695. archbishopric, 1698. 99.
Caminiek, 1676. 99.
Camisards, 1703.
Camp, of cloth of gold, 1520. of Compiegne, 1698.
Campaign of l'Isle, 1667. (of 1745.) 1672.
Campobasso, 1477.
Campredon, 1689.
Camus, le, 1426.
Canada, 1604. 96. 1711.
Canal, 789. 1604. 64. 81.
Canaple, 1711.
Canary, islands, 1492.

Canart, John, 1379.
Candale, duke de, 1620. 53.
Candia, 1572. 1660. 69.
Canonisation, 992. p. 181. V. I.
Canons, 1150.
Cantecroix, 1637. 41. 57. 75.
Cantelme, 1645.
Cantons, 1305. 1712. 15. See Swiss.
Canterbury, kingdom, 597. Thomas of, 1161. 69. 79...... 1206. Cranmer, 1547. William Laud, 1637. 45.
Canus, Melchior, 1269.
Canut, 1197.
Canutson, 1542.
Cape de Quiers, 1655.
Capelle, 1594. 1636. 37. 50. 56.
Capet, Hugh, 863. 956. 87. 88. See his reign.
Capitation, 1695.
Capitouls, 1415.
Capitularies, 511. 615. 779. 800. 805. 807. 40. 922. p. 97. V. I.
Capitulation, of the empire, 1519. 1658. of Strasburg, 1681.
Caprara, 1654.
Captain of the guard, 1669. 71. 76. 86. 91. 95. 1703. 04.
Captal. See Buch.
Captives, redemption of, 1195.
Captivity of the king, p. 301. V. II.
Capua, 539. 1707.
Capucins, 1592. 99. 1604. p. 432. V. I.
Carabiniers, 1693.
Caracéna, 1647. 48. 53. 55.
Caraffa, 1555. 56.
Caraman, 1705.
Cara Mustapha, 1683.
Cararic, 510.
Carcassonne, 585. 1156. 1258.
Cardinals, 1092. 1156. 1245. 1313. 16. 79. 1465. 1595. Henry king of Portugal, 1578. 80.

benefices

INDEX.

benefices of the, 1521. rank of, 1614. 24. 30. 51. 86. 96.
Francis, duke de Lorrain, 1634. infant, 1634. 36. 38. 40. 41.
Cardonne, town, 1711. Hugh de, 1503.
Caretto, 1713.
Caribbee iflands, 1628.
Caribert, 566. 68. 767. p. 45. V. I.
Carloman, 741-43. 46. ..... 68. 71. 74. .... 875. 77. 79. 80. 82 81. p. 45. V. I.
Carlos, Don, 1568.
Carlowitz, 1699.
Carmagnola, 1639. 91.
Carmelite nuns, p. 93. V. II.
Carmelites, 1252.
Carnavalet, de, p. 432. V. I.
Caroufal, 1662. 85.
Carpentras, 1313. 1641.
Carpi, 1701.
Carrouge, 1386. 1588.
Carthagena, 1697. 1706.
Carthufians, 1097. p.
Cafe, of confcience, 1705. royal, 1135. p. 292, &c. V. II.
Cafal, 1629. 30. 39. 40. 52. 81. 93. 95. 1706.
Cafilin, 539.
Cafimir, Mary, 1645. John, 1660. 69.
Caffano, 1705.
Caffel, Robert de, 1323. .... 28. 1645. 77. 78.
Caffin, mount, p. 39. V. I.
Caffini, 1680.
Caffovia, 1685.
Caftanaga, 1695.
Caftelfollit, 1694.
Caftellamare, 1654.
Caftellane, Philip de, p. 433. V. I.
Caftel-Leon, 1711.
Caftelnau, marquis de, 1655.
Caftelnaudary, 1632.
Caftiglione, 1706.
Caftile, Alphonfo, 1088. Conftantia, 1154. See *Blanche.* Alphonfo, 1274. Don Sancho,

1285. .... 1366. 67. 71. 1432. John, 1462. 72. See *Ifabella.* Philip, 1505. Ferdinand, 1516. .... 1710. conftable of, 1366. 1647.
Caftillon, 1451. 1655.
Caftruccio Caftracani, 1354.
Caftres, 1541. 44.
Catalagirone, 1601.
Catalans, 1641. 45.
Catalonians, acts, 1179. rights of France, 1258. war, 1474. revolts, 1640-43. marfhal de la Mothe, 1645. Marfin, 1650. Cervers, 1651. Schomberg, 1675. M. de Vendome, 1696. 97. archduke, 1706. duke de Noailles, 1709. infurrection, 1711. war, 1713.
Catania, 1675.
Cateau-Cambrefis, 1559. 1639.
Catelet, 1636. 38. 50. 55.
Catherine, wife of Henry V. 1420. 85. de Foix, 1712. de Medicis, 1517. p. 305. V. II. See *Medicis,* of Arragon, 1529. 34. 47. fifter of Henry IV. 1593. 99. 1604. of Sienna, 1376. Czarina, 1711.
Catholicon, 1593.
Catinat, 1681. 90-93. 96. 97. 1701. 02.
Calvary, 767. 1532. 1667. 92.
Cavallerini, 1696.
Caudebec, 1592.
Cauffin, father, 1639.
Cayenne, 1676.
Cayet, 1604.

CE.

Cé, 1620.
Cecilia, cardinal faint of, 1646.
Celeftins, convent of, 1299.
Cenfures, 996. 1303. See *Excommunication, Interdict.*
Centenarii, p. 290. V. II.
Cerda, la, 1274. 85. 1352.
Cerdaigne, 1462. 93. 1707.
Ceremonial, Ceremonies, 1579. 1684-86.

INDEX.

86. 96. p. 44. 409. V. I. See *Rank, Science, Presence,* &c.
Cérignoles, 630. 1503.
Cerisolles, 1544.
Cervera, 1712.
Cervers, 1651.
Cæsar, 1532. 1674. 1715. monsieur, 1598. 1614. 26.
Cession, 1526. 35.
Cette, 1666. 1710.
Cevennes, 1703. 04.

CH.

Chabannes, 1461. 1512. 21.
Chabot, 1648. 49.
Chacrise, 593.
Chaise, father la, 1709.
Chalais, 1626. 45. 63.
Chalard, 1635.
Challenge, 1528. 1674.
Chalons, 593. 612. 1428. 1589-91. house, 1584.
Chalus, 1193.
Chamberlain, p.38. 177. V. I.
Chambers, jurisdictions, of moneys, 1551. bi-partite, 1576. of Chalons, 1589. of Spire, 1633. of justice, 1661, of the edict, 1669. 79. of accounts, 1686. of Metz, 1680. 97.
Chamier, 1598.
Chamillart, 1699. 1701. 08. 09.
Chamilly, 1672. 74. 76. 81. 98. 1703.
Champagne, duke, 695. Eudes, 1031. 37. Thibaut, 1040. .... 1137. 42. 44. 80. 91. 1204. Alix, 1226. Thibaut VI. 1204. 25. 26. 30. 52. VII. 1270. Henry, 1283. John, 1283. 96. .... 1331. Reunion of the county, 1296. province, 1361. 64. 65. 1468. 69. 1639. 42. 1705. John de Conflans, marshal de, 1358. count de, p.221. V. I. 299. V. II.
Chancellor, lord keeper, the nature of his office, 1309. p. 177. V. I.

Vol. II.

Latilly, 1315. grand consul, 1497. indult, 1538. Poyet, 1540. Biragué, 1574. the seals, 1590. Seguier, 1639. 50. authority, 1678. Pontchartrain, 1699. Voisin, 1714. archbishop of Rheims, p.129. V. I. double, p. 293. V. I. turned out of his office, p.311. V. I. Mary of Burgundy, 1477. de Navarre, 1598. p. 38. 273. 277. V. I.
Chandos, 1364. 69.
Chantelonbe, 1631.
Chantilly, 1539. 1686.
Chanvalon, 1594.
Chapel, holy, 1269. 83. 1316, royal, 1324.
Chapelles, des, 1627.
Chapelon, 1358.
Chapter, 1561.
Charenton, 1647. 49. 82.
Charibert, 628. 30. 731.
Charité, town of, 1577.
Charity, brothers of, 1602. Christian, 1605.
Charlemont, 1558. 1678.
Charleroy, 1667. 68. 72. 77. 90. 92. 93. 97. 1701. 13.
Charles, St. Borromeus, 1576. Martel, 688. 714. 15. 19. 25. 32-34. 36. 37. 39-41. 47. Charlemain, his character, 813. 1150. p. 45. V. I. See his reign; his son's, 807. the Bald, 830. 36. 75. p.97. V. I. See his reign; the Fat, 877. 80. 82. 84. 85. 88. See his reign; the Simple, 877. 79. 84. king of Provence, 855. duke of the lower Lorrain, 954. 74. 87. 88. 92. the Good, 1127. IV. the Fair, 1316. See his reign; V. also the *dauphin,* 1355. 57-60. See his reign; his character, 1380. VI. See his reign; character of his reign, 1422. his death, p. 271. V. I. VII. 1415. 19. 20. See his reign; his character,

Z

INDEX.

character, 1457. p. 300. V. II. VIII. See his reign; his character, 1497. p. 303. V. II. IX. See his reign, his character, 1574. p. 301. V. II. &c. count d'Anjou, 1245. 55. 70. 83. the Lame, 1255. 75. 83. 85: de Duras, 1255. 1382. de Valois, 1283. 85. 92. 96. 99. 1305. 15. 24. d'Anjou, 1331. de Blois, 1364. 69. duke de Berry, 1464. 66. 68-72. duke of Burgundy, 1467-78. father of Lewis XII. 1407. 10. 15. X. pretended king of France, 1590. 91. Charles IV. emperor, 1245. 1355. the fifth emperor and king of Spain, 1500. 03-05. 14-16. 18-23. 25-30. 32. 34. 36-39. 41. 44. 47. 48. 53-56. 1661. p. 385. V. I. VI. emperor, 1713. 14. VII. 1707. II. king of Spain, 1667. 70. 79. 80. 84. 85. 89. 98. 1700. p. 91. V. II. I. king of England, 1625-29. 37. 39-43. 45-49. 53. II. 1649. 50. 54. 58. 59-62. 68. 70. 74. 77. 78. 85. 87. king of Navarre, surnamed the Bad, 1352. 55. 57-58. 60. 64. 65. 78. 80. 87. X. king of Sweden, 1654. 57. 59. XI. 1660. 67. 68. 71. 75-78. 97. XII. 1700-04. 06. 08. 09. 11. 13. 14. his character, 1707. duke of Lorrain, 1585. IV. See *Lorrain*; duke of Burgundy, surnamed the Bold, 1464-68. 70-77. p. 307. &c. V. II. count of Flanders, surnamed the Good, 1127.

Charlotte de la Trimouille, 1588. 96. de la Marck, 1591.
Charmes, 1633.
Charnacé, 1631.
Charny, 1572.
Charolois, 1672. 73.
Charpentier, 1628.

Charters, 875. 922. 1067. 1103. 1215. 75.
Chartres, town, 1359. 1408. 1588. 91. 94. Thibaut, 1226. bishop of, 1622. mademoiselle de, 1698. duke de, 1661. 83. 92. dutchess of, 1680.
Chasteaubriand, countess de, 1521. edict de, 1551.
Chasteaudun, 1226.
Chasteauneuf, l'Aubespine de, 1611. 32. 43. 50. 52. .... 89. the abbé de, 1697.
Chasteaurenaud, 1688-91. 1702. 03.
Chasteau-Saint-Ange, 1527.
Chasteau-Thierri, 1575. 83. 91. 1642. 51.
Chasteau-Trompette, 1451. 1653.
Chasteauvieux, 1611.
Chasteignerate, la, 1547.
Chastel, Tanequi du, 1419. John, 1594.
Chastelart, 1524.
Chastelet, 1684. Ferri du, p. 277. V. I.
Chastillon, count de, 1226. Gaucher, 1245. 1318. Hugh, 1245. marshal de, 1521. Gaspard, marshal de, 1635-41. duke de, 1648. 49. dutchess de, 1651. 55. dutchy, 1688.
Chastre, la, 1594. 1610. 43.
Chatté, 1651. 70.
Chattes, Aimar de, 1589.
Chavigny, 1410.
Chaulnes, marshal de, 1639. 40. duke de, 1665. 90. dutchy and peerage, 1711.
Chaumont, 1032. marshal de, 1509-11. chevalier de, 1684. 86.
Chauvel, 1675.
Chelles, 584. 656. 70.
Chemeras, 1628.
Chemeraut, 1639.
Cherbourg, 1692.
Cheverny, 1588. 90. 95. 1672.
Chevreuse, madame de, 1626. 43. 50. 51. 61.

Chi-

INDEX.

Chiari, 1701.
Chiavene, 1625.
Chierasco, 1631. 39.
Chievres, 1505.
Ghigi, 1648. 62.
Childebert I. 511. 58. II. 575-96. III. furnamed the Juſt, 695 711.
Childeric I. 481. II. 654. 56. 70. 73. III. 742. 50. his tomb, 1655.
Children, natural, p. 51. V. I.
Chilperic, king of the Burgundians, 493. I. 562-84. II. 715. 19. 20. ſon of Charibert, 628. p. 38. V. I.
Chinei, 1681. 92. 97.
Chinon, 1431.
Chivas, 1562. 1639. 41. 1705.
Choiſeuil, p. 137. V. I. Dupleſſis Praſlin, 1643. Claude, 1693. dutchy and peerage, 1665.
Choiſi, 711. 1695. abbé de, 1684.
Chonſene, 562.
Choppin, p. 301. V. I.
Chramne, 556. 60.
Chriſtian, Chriſtianity, 496. 597. 725. title of moſt Chriſtian king, 875. p. 303. V. I.
Chriſtmas holidays, 767. p. 97. V. I.
Chriſtiandſtat, 1678.
Chriſtiern IV. See Denmark.
Chriſtina, 1632. 36. 46. 47. 53. 54. 57.
Chronicles of St. Denis, 1150.
Chronology, 1604.
Church, 814. 1328. 1415. See Eccleſiaſtics.
Churchill, 1688. 1712. See Marlborough.

CI.

Cinq-Mars, 1639. 42.
Cipierre, 1574. p. 408. V. I.
Circles of the empire, 1500.
Ciſtercians, 1092.
Ciudad, 1705. 07.

Cixilane, 818.

CL.

Clairvaux, 1113.
Clara-Eugenia, 1598.
Clarence, 1421. 57. 70. 71.
Clarendon, 1628. 62. 73.
Claude, wife of Francis I. 1503. 05. 14. 34. de Lorrain, 1634.
Clauſſe, 1575.
Clemence of Hungary, 1316.
Clement, St. 1242. IV. 1255. 58. 75. p. 181. V. I. V. 1305. 09. 13. VI. 1348. p. 239. V. I. VII. anti-pope, 1379. 82. 83. 89. VII. 1521. 23. 25-27. 29. VIII. 1593. 98. 99. 1604. IX. 1662. 69. XI. 1700. 09. James, 1589. family, 1214. p. 433. V. I.
Clementines, 1321.
Clerk, chancellor, 1420. of the diſpatches in the court of Rome, 1594.
Clerks, Clergy, 822. 27. 40. 992. 1001. 1189. 1206. 23. 1316. 29. 1447. 1561. 1633. 34. 82. 93. p. 39. V. I.
Clermont, council, 1092 ... 1584. town, 1632. 50. 54. Simon, 1269. Raoul, 1292. Bourbon, 1329. Robert, 1358. college, 1574. 1618. county, 1661. count, 1692.
Cleves, country, 1610. 14. 79. duke of, 1543. Anne, 1547. Mary, 1573. Henrietta, 1574. John, 1609.
Clichi, 625.
Clientela, 1567.
Cliſſon, town, 1702. Oliver de, 1344. 80. 87. 91. Margaret, 1419.
Cliton, William, 1116. 20. 27.
Clock, 988.
Clodion, 481.
Clodoald, 533.
Clodoberga, 577.

Clodomir,

INDEX.

Clodomir, 511. 23. 33.
Clodoric, 510.
Clotaire, or Clotharius, I. 511-62. II. 613-28. III. 656-70. IV. 719. 67.
Cloth of gold, camp of, 1520.
Cotilda, 493. 511. 23. 31. 43. daughter of Gontram, 577. 90. 93.
Cloud, St. 533.
Clovis, 822. p. 36. &c. V. I. 47. 116. See his reign; son of Chilperic I. 570. 81. son of Chilperic II. 636. 44. III. 692. 95.
Cluni, foundation of, 910. church, 1180. Hugh, 1321. Peter of, 1140. p. 39. V. I.

CO.

Coach, 1607.
Coadjutor, 892. of Paris. See Retz.
Coats of arms, 1149. 1380. 1483. 1655.
Coblentz, 1688.
Cocherel, 1364.
Cochiliac, 539.
Coconas, 1574. 76.
Code, 511. 1137. 1629.
Coetlogon, 1674. 1703.
Coeverden, 1672.
Cœur, James, 1445. 51. 61.
Cœuvres, 1623. 24. dutchy and peerage, 1648. marshal de, 1704.
Cognac, 1302. 1651.
Coborn, 1588. 1692.
Coigneux, 1631.
Coigny, 1643. 97. 1709. 1 F.
Coiflin, 1640. 43. 63.
Cokersberg, 1677.
Colbert, 1380. 1422. 1661. 63. 65. 67. 79. his elogium, 1683. See Croissi.
Coligny, admiral de, 1534. 57. 60. 69. 70. 72. 75. d'Andelot, 1590. .... 1643. 64.

Colour, 1642.
Collation of benefices, 1397. 1415. 1553. p. 39. V. I. 313. V. II.
College, 1179. 1215. 1302. 1499. 1531. 74. 1618. 63. 73. p.211. V. I.
Colloquy, 1561.
Colloredo, 1635. 36.
Colmar, 1636. 75.
Cologne, 510. 612. 1474. 1642. 54. 70. 73. electorate, 1688. electors, 1637. 71. 74. 79. 1701. 06. 13. 14.
Colomba, 1492.
Colonna, Sciarra, 1303. constable, 1661.
Colonel, of the guards, 1661. 72. general of the infantry, 1544. 1661. of the cavalry, 1567. of the Swiss, 1589. 1643. 47. 61. 94. of dragoons, 1670.
Colonels, 1661.
Colours, white, 1639.
Combalet, 1620. 38.
Combats, private, or duels, 1040. 1404. 1547. 78. 79. p.98. V. I. tilts, 1559.
Comedians, 1609. 73.
Comet, 840. 1680.
Comines, town, 1645. 47. ......
Philip, 1472. 86. p. 311. V. I.
Command, 1397. letters of, 1527.
Command of the troops, 1627. chancelor Seguier, 1639.
Commerce, St. Eloi, 628. value of gold and silver, 840. Cluni, 992. Maritime, 1380. isle of Rhodes, 1522. Dutch, 1604. superintendant, 1627. difference between that of the east and the west, 1628. Morocco, 1635. edict, 1670. treaty of, 1714. council de, 1700.
Comminges, count, 1443. Odet d'Aidie, count de, 1469. .... 85. .... 1650.
Commissaries, Commissions, missi dominici,

INDEX.

minici, 1135. p. 29. V. II. Brion, 1540. Biron, 1602. masters of the requests, delegates, honours, 1631-34. la Valette, 1638. Fouquet, 1661. marshals of France, p. 357. V. I. seals, 287. V. I.
Committimus, 1566.
Commons, 992. 1135. parliament of England, 1255. what is understood by that word, p. 317. V. II.
Communicants, 1269.
Communication of the ocean and the Euxine sea, 789.
Communities, 1269.
Commutation of punishment, 1474. 1661.
Comnenus, Isaac, 1189. Alexis, 1148. 1204.
Como, lake of, 1636.
Compact Breton, 1553.
Companies, great, 1361, 66. of the Indies, 1665. of the Scotch gendarmes, 1690.
Comper, 1595.
Compiegne, 562- 756. 888. 987. 1026. 1428. 30. treaty, 1624. review, 1666. 98. p. 78. V. I. forest of, 1324.
Comptroller-general, 1611. 61. 83. 89. 99. 1708. p. 99. V. II.
Conan, 1116. 67.
Conception, immaculate, 1387.
Concini. See *Ancre*.
Conclave, 1242. 1590.
Concordate, 973. 1447. 61. 1515. 17. 53. 60. 84. 1695. p. 312. &c. V. II.
Concubinage, 1001. p. 51. V. I.
Condé, town, 1649. 55. 56. 78. Francis, count d'Anguien, 1546. John, duke d'Anguien, 1557. Lewis I. 1560. 62. 67-69. Henry I. 1569. 70. 72. 74. 76. 84. 85. 88. cardinal de Bourbon, 1591. Catherine de la Trimouille, 1596. Montmorency, 1600. Henry II. 1588. 1609. 14-16.

19. 28. 36. 38. 39. 41. 46. Lewis II. 1598. 1643-59. 68. 69. 72. 74. 75. his character, 1686. Clare-Clemence, 1671. Henry Julius, 1675. 1709. Lewis III. surnamed M. le Duc, 1685. 88. 92. 1710. Lewis-Henry, 1710. 13. Louisa-Elizabeth, 1713. princess de, 1671. 85. p. 90. V. II.
Conference, of Peronne, 1468. Lyons, 1500. Troyes, 1563. Nerac, 1579. Suresne, 1593. Fontainebleau, 1600. 46. gate de la, 1653.
Confession, granted to criminals, 1397. of Augsburg, 1530.
Confessors of kings, 1103. 1269. 1603. 1709.
Confirmation of popes, 774. 817. 23. 27. 40. 1067.
Confiscation, 1040. 1203. 23. 92. 1321. 31. 69. 79. 1470.
Conflans, treaty of, 1465. 66. 68. le, 1659. Stephen de, 1316. John de, 1358. marquis de, 1678. 1705.
Confraternities, 1269. 1401. 1576.
Congregation of Saint-Maur, 1621.
Congress of peace, Westphalia, 1644. 47. 74. Nimeguen, 1675. Courtray, 1680. Riswick, 1697. Gertrudemberg, 1710. Utrecht, 1712. 15. abolished, 1677.
Coni, 1641. 91.
Conimbra, 1149.
Conjuration, de Fieschi, 1547. de Solfede, 1582. See their names.
Connestaggio, 1578.
Conobre, 560.
Conrad, emperor, 912. II. 1037. p. 95. V. I. III. 1103. 45. 48. 50. IV. 1189. 1255. 73. marquis of Montferrat, 1191.
Conradin, 1255.
Conrart, 1635.
Consarbrick, 1675.

Z 3 *Conscience,*

INDEX.

Conscience, liberty of, 1532. case of, 1705.
Consecration of popes, 827. 45.
Constable, 807. office, 1223. Du Guesclin, 1366. 69. 80. Douglas, 1421. Bourbon, 1523. rank, 1624. office, 1627. p. 123. V. I. 33. V. II. 587. of Castile, 1366. of Portugal, 1580. p. 39. V. I.
Constance, council of, 1415. 38. 1553. wife of Robert, 996. 1026. 31. wife of Lewis the Young, 1154. of Britany, 1116. 67. heiress of the two Sicilies, 1026. 1189. 1226. 55. minister, 1688.
Constantine, town, 1641. anti-pope, 767. the Great, 511. 753. 54. 1001. p. 39. V. I. Copronymus, 756. 96. his son, 796.
Constantinople, city, 539. council, 867. taken, 1204. patriarch, 1215. Baldwin, 1223. II. 1238. 99. taken, 1451. resigned to Charles VIII. 1494. ambassadors, 1683. armament, 1714.
Constellation, 1660.
Constitution, of Childebert, 593. of Constantine, 753. of the emperor Frederic, 1315. of Charlemain, p. 97. V. I. concerning Quietism, 1699. Unigenitus, 1714. Henry VI. 1345.
Consuls, dignity, 508. 740. 1056. jurisdictions, 1564. p. 309. V. II.
Contade, 1617.
Contagion, 1503. 56. See *Pestilence*.
Contarini, 1648.
Conti, Francis, 1589. 92. 1614. Louisa of Lorrain, 1631. Armand, 1648. 50. 51. 54. 55. 57. 66. Lewis-Armand, 1685. Francis-Lewis, 1685. 88. 91. 92. 94. 97. 99. his elogium, 1709. Anne-Martinozzi, 1709. Lewis-Armand II. 1709. 13. Mary-Anne, 1667. 85. 93. 97. Louisa-Elizabeth, 1713. Mary-Anne, 1713. Lewis-Francis, 1691. his elogium, 1709.
Contreras, 1595.
Contribution, of monasteries, 840. of curates, 840. bull against, 1568.
Contumacy, 1631.
Convent, 787. 830. 31.
Convention, assembly in England, 1689.
Cop, 1547.
Copernicus, 1633.
Coprogli, 1675. 83.
Corbeil, town, 1590. count de, 1108.
Corbie, town, 1636. monastery, 656.
Corbieres, 1328.
Cordeliers, 1387.
Cordemoi, 1661.
Cordova, Gonsalo, 1495. 1501.
Cornaro, 1189.
Cornwall, Richard, 1273.
Cornuel, madam, 1675.
Coronation, 1179. 1314. 71. 80. 1431. 1594. 1654.
Corsairs, 1665.
Corsica, isle, 1153. 54.
Corsican guards at Rome, 1662.
Cortez Fernand, 1521.
Cosmo, duke of Tuscany, 1614.
Cossacks, 1708.
Cossa, John, 1480.
Cossa, Arthur de, 1570. 74. 75.
Cotton, father, 1603.
Couci, lords of, 1108. Enguerrand, 1226. 52. 1394. John 1380.
Covenant, 1639.
Coulanges, M. de, 1689.
Coulon, 1479.
Council, the king's, 1380. 1401. 84. 1617. 24. 39. 89. 90. 97. 1704. 14. of state, 1590. 91. of the union, 1589. of the regency, 1643. 1714. president of the, 1667. 89. of Brisac, 1680.

INDEX.

1680. of Tournay, 1668. arret of, 1704. grand, 1497. of commerce, 1700. of difpatches, 1682. 99. of finances, 1688. 1714.

Councils, right of convoking, p.96. V. I. of Agde, 506. of Orleans, 511. of Paris, 615. of Leftine, 743. of Rome, 775. of Francfort, 794. of Nice, 794. of Aix-la-Chapelle, 814. of Toulouſe, 840. of Conſtantinople, 867. of Florence, 867. 1438. 39. of Savonnieres, 875. of Troyes, 877. of Treves, 945. of Ingelheim, 945. of Rheims, 988. of St. Baſle, 988. of Rome, 996. 1056. of Toledo, 1001. of Clermont, 1092. of Poitiers, 1100. of Troyes, 1103. p.137. V. I. of Rheims, 1120. of Eſtampes, 1130. of Sens, 1140. of Rheims, 1148. of Tarragona, 1179. of Lateran, 1179. 1215. of Lombez, 1206. of Paris, 1206. of Tours, 1223. of Aix-la-Chapelle, 1223. of Lyons, 1245. 74. of Vienna, 1309. of Senlis, 1315. of Piſa, 1408. of Conſtance, 1415. 38. 1553. of Baſil, 1387. 1431.32. 35. 38. 39. transferred to Florence, 1439. of Tours, 1510. of Piſa, 1510. 11. 14. transferred to Milan, 1511. of Lyons, 1512. of Lateran, 1179. 1511. 12. 14. 15. 53. of Trent. See Trent; appeals to, 1303. 1585. 1688.

Counſellors, judges, 1344. creation, 1522. 1690. of ſtate, 1687.

Count of Paris, 992.

Count of the palace, p. 38. V. I.

Counts, ancient, 800. 1225. 73. p. 94. V. I.

Court, of peers, 1200. plenary, 767. of aids, 1355. 1631. of juſtice, 1419. of Normandy, 1499. of moneys, 1551. the king writes to the court, 1643.

Courci, Hugh de, p. 211. V. I.
Courland, 1714.
Cours, the, 1615.
Courtanvaux, 1692.
Courtenay, princes, 1603.
Courtin, 1667. 79.
Courtray, 1302. 16. 1646-48. 67. 68. 80. 83. 97. 1706.
Couſin, title, p. 287. V. I.
Couſſay, 1617.
Coutras, 1587.

CR.

Cranmer, 1547.
Cramoiſy, 1642.
Craon, town, 1591. Peter, 1391. 97.
Crato, 1580. 82. 95.
Creations of offices, 1522. 1690.
Crecy, plenipotentiary, 1697. battle of, 1344.
Cremieu, 1536.
Cremona, 1512. 1648. 1702.
Crenant, 1695.
Crepi, town, 1544.
Crequy, Charles, marſhal de, 1611. 25. 29. 30. 35-38. duke de, 1659. 62. Francis, marſhal de, 1667. 68. 70. 72. 75-79. 83. 84. 87. marquis de, 1702. dutchy, extinct, 1711.
Creſcent, order, 1269.
Creſcentin, 1705.
Creſcentius, 996.
Creſſels, 1628.
Crevant, 1423.
Crevecœur, fort of, 1672.
Creutznac, 1644. 88.
Crimes, 566.
Croiſades, firſt, 1092. 1108. ſecond, 1145. 48. 49. third, 1189. empire of the Latins, 1204. Albigenſes, 1206. particular, 1230. fifth, 1245. ſixth, 1269. 1303. 09. 13. 20. 24. 29. 1465. p. 314. V. II.

Croiſaders,

INDEX.

Croisaders, p. 129. V. I.
Croissi, 1668. 75. 79. 84. 89. 96.
Cromwell, 1642. 44. 45. 48-50. 53-55. 57. 58. 62.
Cross, true, 1230. judgment of the, 803. of St. Lo, 1483.
Cross-bow men, 1600.
Crosse, 1120. 1215. 58.
Crostollo, 1702.
Croui, 1505.
Crown, of thorns, 1230. imperial, 818. 912. 1022. 1355. of Rome, 973. of France, 954. 88. 92. 1215. 1316. 36. 60. 1420. 68. 1548. 84. 85. 88. 90. 1607. 1714. duty of the, 1584. 1607. reunion, p. 259. V. I. 298. V. II.
Cry of Haro, 912.

CU.

Cuba, 1492.
Cueva, Bertrand de la, 1504.

Cugnieres, 1329.
Cujas, 1137.
Cujavia, bishop of, 1697.
Cuirasses, p. 98. V. I.
Cuirassiers, 1672.
Cuise, forest of, 1324.
Cumberland, duke of, beaten by Lewis XV. 1588. 1709.
Curates, 840. 1594. presence necessary, 1682.
Customs, 992. 1067. 1316. 1580. p. 308. V. II.

CY.

Cycle, 743.
Cydnus, 1189.
Cypher, or *Figure*, Arabic, 988.
Cyprus, 1189. 91. Alix of, 1226.

CZ.

Czar, 1479. 1611. 42. 98. 1700. 09. 11.

D.

D*Achtein*, 1675.
Dagobert I. 622-44. p. 38. V. I. II. 654. 56. 70. 73. 78. III. 711-15. son of Childeric II. 673. 88.
Daguesseau, 1690. his elogium, 1699.
Daim, Oliver le, p. 311. V. I.
Damascus, 1148.
Damietta, 1249.
Dampierre, Will. de. 1245. Guy, 1245. les, 1258.
Damville, Charles, 1559. 74.
Damvilliers, 1637.
Dandelot, 1590.
Danès, p. 435. V. I.
Danes, 539. 807. 23. 1632. 76-78. 1796. 10.
Daniel, son of Childeric II. 673. 715. Jesuit, 875. 1713. p. 36. V. I.

Dante, 1299.
Danube, junction to the Rhine, 789.
Darnley, 1587.
Darmstadt, of, 1695. 97. 1704.
Dates, short, 1550. incertitude of, 1560. See *Christian*.
David, 789. I. king of Scotland, 1369.
Dauphin, Philip Humbert, 1349. p. 237. V. I. Charles, 1355. 57. 58. 64. 80. Lewis, 1410. 15. John, 1415. Charles III. 1415. 19. 21. 36. 40. 45. 56. 75. Francis, 1536. 51. Henry, 1542. 44. Francis, 1558. Montpensier, 1589. monsieur, 1661. 74. 88. 93. 94. 98. 1700. 11. the king's father, 1712. son of Lewis XV. 1709.

Dauphiness,

INDEX.

Dauphiness, Margaret of Scotland, 1436. p. 309. V. I. Margaret of Auſtria, 1482. 1556. p. 327. V.I. Mary Stuart, 1558. Mary Anne of Bavaria, 1680. 90. Mary Adelaïd, 1696. 97.1712.
Dauphin, 879. 1037. 1349. 1445. 80. 1548. 75. of Auvergne, 1589. 1692.
Dauvet, John, 1465.

DE.

Dean of the council, 1704.
Debonnaire, explication of this word, 840.
Debts of the nation, 1560. excommunicated for debt, 1355. priſoner for debt, 1702.
Declarations, concerning the homage, which the king paid to his ſubjects, 1100. concerning the Jews, 1315. offices of parliament, 1387. againſt the aſſaſſins of John the Fearleſs, 1420. againſt the duke of Burgundy, 1470. for the *mercuriales*, 1551. of Chartres, 1560. of eſtates, 1561. concerning dutchies and peerages, 1566. 76. concerning printing, 1626. ſuppreſſion of offices, 1631. interdicting the parliament of Rouen, 1639. concerning marriage, 1640. for the regency, 1643. to reſtrain any but members from being admitted into the privy-council, 1651. concerning the formulary, 1657. againſt fortunetellers and poiſoners, 1680. touching eccleſiaſtical power, 1682. 93. concerning the principality of Dombes, 1682. in regard to perſons legitimated,1694. 1714. in relation to Quietiſm, 1699. See *Edicts, Ordinances*, and *Arrets*.
Declination, line of, 1493.
Decree, of Gratian, 1150. of the ſenate of Venice, 1515. of the Sorbonne, 1590. of the univerſity, 1594.
Decretals, 1150.
Deinſe, 1695. 1706.
Delft, 1584.
Demeſnes, given in portion, 567. diſmembered, 877. the king's, 922. 92. dowry, 1103. made permanent, 1108. interdicted, 1142. 1255. inalienable, 1275. 1349. 1607. alienated, 1364. 1552. ordinance, 1556. reunion, 1680. p. 297. &c. V. II.
Demetrius, impoſtor, 1605.
Demeville, firſt preſident, p. 261. V. I.
Demin, 1631. 39.
Denain, 1712.
Dendermond, 1706.
Denia, 1708.
Denis, St. 657. 1242. the little, 743. p. 89.
Denmark, 1391. 1660. V. I. interregnum, p. 309.V.I. Waldemar, 1542. Chriſtiern IV. 1626. 27. 29. Frederic III. 1659. 60. 66. 67. Chriſtiern V. 1675-78. 99. Frederic IV. 1710. 11.
Dependance of a fief, 922. 1056.
Depoſition, of Charles the Fat,888. Arnold, 988. 96. of Frederic, 1230. 45. Adolphus, 1296. of Edward II. 1324. of Gregory XII. and of Benedict XIII. 1408. of Eugene IV. 1439. of James II. 1689.
Deputation, 1576.
Deſcartes, 1650.
Deſcent, in Britany, 1230. in England, 1545. in Provence, 1635. at Belleiſle, 1674. in Martinico, 1693. at Breſt, 1694. at Belleiſle,1703. at the port of Cette, 1710.
Deſcentiers, 1587.
Deſiderius, general of Chilperic, 577. king of the Lombards,

INDEX.

756. 68. 74.
Desmarets, academician, 1635. minister, 1701. 08.
Des-Novers, 1641. 43. 44.
Despreaux, 1677.
Dessau, 1626.
Deventer, 1672.
Devices, 1350. 1505. p. 338. 354. 384. 408. V. I.
Devolution, 1667.
Deuteria, 534.
Deux-Ponts, duke of, 1609. 35.

DH.
Dhona, 1668.

DI.
Diana of Poitiers, 1544. p. 309. V.I. See *Valentinois*.
Dictatus, 1067.
Dieppe, 1443. 1589. 1690. 94.
Diest, 1705.
Diet, 831. 1206. 1529.
Digest, 511.
Dignities, 1559.
Dijon, 1477. 1513. 1650.
Dike, 1627. 28.
Dillon, 1709.
Dinan, 1674. 75. 97.
Diois, 1445.
Directors of the finances, 1611. 1701.
Discipline of the church, 1415, 1579.
Discovery, de Thou, 1642.
Dismembering, 1468.
Dispatches, council of the, 1682.
Dispensations, 1632.
Dissolution of marriage, divorce, 1499. 1529. 34. 99.
Distaff, 798.
Divon, 1331.
Dixmude, 1647. 58. 83. 95. 1706.

DO.
Doctrine, fathers of the, 1592.
Docsbourg, 1672.
Doëteckum, 1672.
Doignon, of, 1653.

Doge, 1685. 1702.
Dole, 1480. 1636. 68. 74.
Dole, 1594.
Dombes, Henry, prince of, 1592. declaration concerning the sovereignty, 1682. prince of, 1714.
Domfront, 1574.
Dominicans. See *Jacobins*.
Dominick, St. 1206. 30. order, 1349.
Domremi, 1428.
Donawert, 1704.
Donations, to the holy see, 753. 74. 817. of the empire of Constantinople to Charles VIII. 1494.
Doncheri, 1641.
Dordrecht, 1619.
Doria, Andrew, 1528. general, 1630.
Dormans, Renaud de, p. 313. V.I.
Dorstein, 1641.
Doway, 1562. 1667. 68. 1710. 12.
Dower, 567. 1103. 1313. p. 39. 100. V. I.
Douglas, 1421. 24.
Dourlens, 1595.
Downs, valley of, 1047. battle of the, 1658.

DR.
Drach, du, 1336.
Dragoons, 1667. 92.
Dream of the orchard, 1371.
Dreux, battle of, 1562. siege of, 1590. Robert, 1149. 79. Peter, 1116. 1226. 30.
Drogon, son of Carloman, 746. ... 1026.
Drossi, 593.
Druids, 992.
Drusenheim, 1706.

DU.
Dubois, cardinal, 1708.
Dubos, p. 36. V. I.
Ducange, 802.

Ducas,

INDEX.

Ducas, Alexis, 1204.
Ducaſſe, 1703.
Duels, law of combat, 511. repreſentation, 973. religious of St. Maur, 1116. reſtriction, 1167. prohibition, 1258. 1305. Carouge, 1386. Jarnac, 1547. edict, 1602. 13. des Chapelles, 1627. duke de Guiſe, 1643. duke de Nemours, 1652. la Frette, 1663. Brionnes, 1689. 95. p. 98. V. I. See *Combats*.
Dufay, 1676.
Duſerrier, 1563.
Dugaſt, 1542.
Dumoulin, p. 299. V. II.
Duna, the, 1704.
Dunbar, 1650.
Dunemond, 1701. 10.
Dukes, of Venice, 803. of France, 737. 863. ancient, 1135. 1498. 1581, 1607. 88. 1701. p. 299. &c. V. II. See *Rank*, *Seat*, *Prerogatives*, *Peers*.
Dunkirk, 1558. 1646. 52. 58. 62. 94. 1711. 12.
Dunois, John count de, 1407. 26. 28. 51. 62. 64. Francis, 1484. 85. 1525.
Dupes, day of, 1630.
Duprat, 1514. p. 312. &c. V. II.
Duqueſne, 1675. 76. 81-84. 1703.
Durance, the, 562.
Duras, Charles de, ſurnamed the Peaceable, 1382. lord of, 1579. marſhal de, 1675. 88. 1704. duke de, 1672.
Duret, advocate, 1594.
Durfort, James de, 1579.
Dutchy, 992. p. 237. V. I. Auſtria, 1382. Borgia, 1498. 1566. Seguier, 1650. Luxemburg, 1688. edict, 1711. of Lorrain, 1431. See *Peerage*.
Dutillet, 1559. 60.
Dutlingen, 1703.

E.

Earthen-ware, manufacture of, 1603.
Eaſter, feaſt of, 767. 79. veſpers, 1282. battle of Ravenna, 1512.

EB.
Ebernbourg, 1692. 97.
Ebroin, 656. 70. 73. 78. 88.

EC.
Ecbert, 827.
Eccleſiaſtics, perſons and affairs, government, p. 39. V. I. depoſition, 988. canoniſations, 992. marriage, 996. 1061. Bertrade, 1103. inveſtiture, 1120. ſchiſm, 1130. Abelard, 1140. domain, 1142. council of Rheims, 1148. regale, 1161. 1673. Albigenſes, 1206. council of Lyons, 1245. Boniface VIII. 1303. of the two powers, 1329. council of Baſil, 1439. juriſdiction, 1539. 1695. ordinance of Orleans, 1560. chancellor de l'Hopital, 1568. Bearn, 1620. edict, 1695. See *Councils*, *Edicts*, *Regale*, *Annates*, &c.

ED.
Edeſſa, 1145.
Edifices, 1547.
Edicts, concerning the coin, 840. againſt heretics, 1226. bailiffs and ſeneſchal, 1498. court of aids, 1355. of Cremieu, 1536. againſt the abuſes of the Roman chancery, 1550. forbidding money to be ſent to Rome,

INDEX.

Rome, 1551. againſt the Lutherans, 1551. d'Eſcouan, 1559. touching clandeſtine marriages, 1556. againſt young women that deſtroy the fruit of their womb, 1556. againſt the wearing of fire-arms, 1559. on the king's domains, 1559. concerning offices of judicature, 1559. touching the hour of ſitting in parliament, 1559. de Romorantin, 1560. on religion, 1560. on ſecond nuptials, 1560. of January in favour of the Huguenots, 1562. of pacification, 1563. 76. 91. of Rouſſillon, 1564. juriſdiction of conſuls, 1564. of the mothers, 1567. reformation of the calendar, 1582. of reunion, 1588. of Nantes, 1598. 1622. 85. of the nobility, 1600. of duels, 1602. 43. on the tailles, 1600. touching the coin, 1602. for the reunion of Bearn, 1620. of pacification, 1629. refuſed to regiſter, 1631. 48. touching the parliament, 1641. of Lewis XI. 1642. againſt Gaſton, 1643. pecuniary, 1648. touching ſtamped paper, 1655. ſuppreſſion of the chambers of the edict, 1669. commerce does not derogate from nobility, 1670. perpetual againſt the houſe of Orange, 1672. concerning the regale, 1673. 82. the lectures on civil law reſtored, 1680. concerning eccleſiaſtical juriſdiction, 1695. concerning the tenths, 1710. on dutchies and peerages, 1711. againſt the proteſtants, 1713. calling the legimated princes to the crown, 1714. ſale of offices, p. 306. V. II. See *Ordinances, Declarations, Arrets*, &c.

Edward, the elder, king of England, 929. St. 1047. 62. 1215. I. 1285. 92. 96. 1703. 05. II. 1296. 1324. III. 1324. 28. 23. 31. 36. 40. 41. 44. 47. 49. 55. 59. 60. 67. 69. 76. IV. 1457. 70. 71. 74. 75. 77. 83. 85. V. 1483. VI. 1547. 48. prince Palatine, 1684.

EF.

Effiat, d', 1639.

EG.

Ega, 644. 46.
Egmond, count d', 1558. 65-67.
Egra, 1634.
Egypt, 1249. 1517.

EK.

Ekeren, 1703.

EL.

Elbene, d', 1591, 1634.
Elbing, 1703.
Elbœuf, branch of, 1550. duke d', 1631. madam d', 1631. duke d', 1671. 88. dutcheſs of Mantua, 1704. See *Lorrain*.
Electors, fixed to ſeven, 1206. 73. 1305. golden bull, 1355. rank, 1432. capitulation, 1519. title, 1630. eighth electorate, 1648. league of the Rhine, 1658. Hanover, 1714. See their names.
Elections, to benefices, 827. 40. conteſt, 1142. 1206. 1397. pragmatic, 1438. Germany, 1447. indult, 1695. p. 313. V. II. of popes, 775. 823. 1056. 1120. 56. 1242. 1313. 16. 79. 1560. of emperors and kings, 634. 912. 1001. 56. 1226. 1305. 55. 1657. of officers. p. 305. V. II.
Electorate, 1547. 1620. 48. 92.
Eleonor, wife of Lewis the Young, 1137.

INDEX.

1137. 45. 50. 89. queen of Portugal and France, 1523. 29. 56. de Roye, 1569.
Elizabeth, of France, 1558. 59. .... 68. 98. .... 1612. of Austria, 1570. of England, 1558. 68. 71. 75. 80. 81. 87. 1603. 13. 20. 93.
Elne, 1641.
Eloi, St. 628. 36.
Eloisa, 1140.
Elsimbourg, 1677. 78. 1710.
Elvas, 1645. 58.

EM.

Embassies, ambassadors, envoys, 1432. 35. 1534. 42. 58. 63. 75. 98. 1602. 24. 61. 62. 83-85. 87. 89. 98. 99. 1715. ambassadress, 1645.
Emanuel II. duke of Savoy, 1660. See *Savoy*.
Embrun, 1692.
Emeric, 1672.
Emetic, 1658.
Eminence, 1630.
Emma, 956. 86.
Emperors, of the east, 803. 1451. of the west, 800. 03. 23. 912. 1001. 22. 56. 1140. 1206. 26. 73. 96. 1336. 55. 1519. Greek, 1451. p. 49. V. I. See their names.
Empire, 796. 877. 912. 73. 1037. lower, 803. of the Latins, 1204. eastern, 1451. western, 800. 1120. 50. 1226. 73. 1305. 1451. 1500. 1648. 79. of the Czar, 1479.

EN.

England, *English*, isle of Albion, 497. northern nation, 807. William the Conqueror, 1062. 67. Robert, 1092. Henry I. 1100. 13. 16. 20. 48. 49. Henry II. 1156. 61. 67. 69. 71. 79. 80. 86. 89. John Lackland, 1200. 06. 14. 15. Henry III. 1223. 26. 52. 58. Edward I. 1292. Edward II. 1305. 24. Edward III. 1336. 41. 44. 47. 50. 55. 58-60. 71. 76. 96. Richard II. 1380. 83. 86. 94. 97. Henry IV. 1410. Henry V. 1415. 19. Henry VI. 1420. 22. 23. 28. 30. 35. 36. 41. 48. 51. 57. Edward IV. 1470. 75. 77. Henry VII. 1485. Henry VIII. 1513. 18. 34. 41. 44-48. Mary, 1450. 53. 54. Elizabeth, 1458. 63. 64. 81. 88. 96. James I. 1603. 25. change of religion, 1603. Charles I. 1626. 27. 29. 33. 39. 44. 53. 54. Cromwell, 1657. 58. 60. Charles II. 1660-62. 64. 66-68. 70. 72-74. 77. 78. 84. James II. 1688. William III. 1688-90. 92. 93. 96. 97. 99. 1700. Anne, 1703. 13. See the names of the several kings.
Enguerrand, de Couci, 1226. 52. de Marigni, 1309. 15. 24.
Ennoblement, 84. 1270. 1313. 1579. 1600. 94. See *Nobility, Plebeians, Bondmen, Infranchisement*.
Ensheim, 1674.
Ensisheim, 1681.

EO.

Eon, 1148.

EP.

Epernai, 1592.
Epernon, 1581. 84. 87. 89. 92. 95. 96. 1607. 10. 19. 42. 49. .... 53. 61.
Epinal, 1641. 70.
Epinoi, 1714.
Episcopacy, 1637.
Epocha. See *Year*, *Calender*, *Era*.

ER.

Era, Christian, 743. 74. 1171.
Erasmus, 1547.

INDEX.

Erchinoald, 1646.
Erections. See *Peerages.* Bishop-rics, 1292. 1622.
Erfurt, 1636.
Erlac, 1639.
Ernest, bastard of Mansfeld, 1618. Ferdinand, king of Hungary, 1636.

ES.

Escale, chevalier de l', 1404.
Escalonne, 1694.
Escarpe, fort, 1667. 68.
Escouan, 1559.
Espieres, pont d', 1694.
Espinao, Peter d', 1590.
Espinosa, cardinal, 1661.
Essex, earl of, 1596. 1601. 42. 44.
Este, Anne d', 1593. cardinal d', 1560. 1648. Mary, 1673.
Establishments of St. Louis, 1200. 69.
Estampes, domain, 1108. council, 1130. combat, 1652. dutchess d', 1540. 41. 44. 47. count, 1360.
Estival, 612.
Estrades, marshal d', 1643. 52. 61. 62. 67. 75-77. 82. 83. count d', 1670.
Estramadura, 1556.
Estrées, 1600. Francis-Hannibal, 1639. dutchy and peerage, 1648. John, 1672. 73. 76. 77. 83. 85-88. 90. 91. 93. 97. 1703. cardinal d', 1690. 93. duke d', 1685. 87. Gabrielle, 1598. 99. marshal, 1683. count, 1692.

ET.

Etaire, 1645.

Ethelwolf, 855.

EU.

Eu, Raoul, count d', 1350. ... 94. ... 1714.
Evangelic, the, 1620.
Eucharist, 1097. 1285. 1600.
Eudes, duke of Aquitaine, 731. 32. 34. 67. duke of Burgundy, 956. ... 1316. son of Robert, 1040. of France, 888. 92. 98. of Champagne, 1031. 37.
Eugene II. 825. III. 1145. 48. IV. 1339. 1538. 53. prince, 1661. 91. 1701. 02. 04-09. 12-14.
Eugenia, Clara, 1598.
Evreux, Charles, count d', 1512. Philip, p. 221. V. I. king of Navarre, 1328. 31. 65. Bouillon, 1642.
Eutropius, 875.
Euxine sea, 789.

EX.

Exarchate, 568. 753. 978.
Excester, 1644.
Exchange, Sedan, 1642. 51. Meudon, 1695.
Excommunication, Robert, 996. Philip I. 1092. 1103. Henry III. emperor, 1120. Albigenses, 1206. John Lackland, 1215. Gregory IX. 1226. Frederic II. 1245. Conradin, 1255. Peter de Bourbon, 1355. bull in cæna Domini, 1568. Henry IV. 1585. 90. Lavardin, 1687. 88.
Exemption, 657. 1283. 1316. p. 39. 40. V. I.
Exile, fort, 1708.
Expectatives, 1438. p. 314. V. II.
Exposition of the faith, 1668.

Fabert,

INDEX.

F.

Abert, marshal, 1642. 54. 60. 62.
Fagel, 1684.
Faileube, 596.
Fair of Landi, 875.
Fairfax, 1645.
Falcfim, 1711.
Famine, 1336.
Fanaticifm, 1680.
Farces, p. 311. V. II.
Farines, action of, 1591.
Farnese, 1547. 55-57.
Fauchet, 1643.
Favourites of kings, 1574.
Fauftus, John, 1457.
Fay, du, 1676.
Fayette, marshal de la, 1421. mademoifelle de la, 1639.

FE.

Fealty and homage, 1324.
Frederic, king of Pruffia, 1701.
Felix V. 1439. de Valois, St. p. 131. V. I.
Felony, 1040. 1230. 92. 1379.
Fenelon, archbishop of Cambray, 1689. 95. 99.
Fenestrelle, 1708.
Fer, ifle of, 1634.
Ferdinand, emperor, I. 1522. 26. 29. 55. 56. 1617. II. 1617-20. 30. 31. 35-37. III. 1636. 57. IV. king of Caftile, 1309. the Catholic, 1472. 93. 95. 1500-05. 08-10. 12-14. of Naples, 1493. 96. duke of Mantua, 1629.
Fere, la, 1596.
Feria, 1593. 94. 1625.
Feronnerie, rue de la, 1610.
Ferrara, duke of, 1510. daughter of the duke of, 1548. dutchefs of, 1560.

Ferrete, count de, 1475.
Ferri, 1476.
Ferrier, du, 1575.
Ferté, Henry de la, marshal of France, 1643. 50. 54-58. 63.
Feafts, 1252. of the church, 1255. p. 97. V. I. 140. at court, 1661. 85.
Feuillade, Francis de la, marshal of France, 1664. 74-76. 78. 91. 92. duke de la, 1704-06.
Feuillans, 1587.
Feuquieres, marquis de, 1633. 39. .... 91. 92.

FI.

Fidelity, or fealty, oath of, 1206. 13. 23. 1589. 1649.
Fiefs, law, 511. p. 95. V. I. 293. 307. V. II. Bretagne, 845. eftablifhment, 923. Lorrain, 978. peerage, 992. vaffals of the king, 1108. fenefchal, 1116. Britany, 1230. liberty, 1316. freeholds, 1328. held by foccage, 1531. 79. 1600. 29. dependent on the crown, p. 103. V. I. 289. 299. V. II.
Field, of Mars, 768. 1715. of lies, 813.
Fiennes, de, 1369.
Fiefchi, 1547. .... 1652.
Figuier, fort, 1638.
Figuieres, 1675.
Final, 1447. 1698. 1713.
Finances, Financiers, 1322. 28. 91. 1603. 1701. fecretaries of the, 1341. 1410.
Fire, of the palace, 1618. of London, 1666.
Firft, gentleman, 1669. painter to the king, 1690.
Fift, or hand, cut off, 1383.
Fiftula, 1586.

INDEX.

Fitz-James. See *Berwick.*

FL.

Flag, 1680. 85. 88. fuperiority of, 1667.
Flagellants, 1348.
Flamarens, 1663.
Flanders, Baldwin, 1067. Charles the Good, 1127. Philip, 1179. impoftor, 1223. Guy, 1299. 1331. 1471. Arteville, 1336. Lewis, 1484. 1529. Mary of Auftria, 1556. duke d'Anjou, 1583. 1634. 41. peace of Breda, 1667. 75. 80. ftates of, 1477. 1505. counts of, 863. 965. 72. 1031. 1127. 1204. 06. 14. 26. 58. 1304. 09. 16. 20. 22. 28. 84. p. 225. V. I. Margaret, 1258. Flemings, 1149. 1223. 1303. 04. 28. 36. 82. 85. 1536.
Flaochat, 646.
Fleece. See *Order.*
Fleet, Caftilian, 1371. of Charles V. 1541. of Philip II. 1588. Englifh, 1627. 28. Spanifh, 1628. 38. 39. 43. 55. 75. 76. Swedifh, 1677. French, 1689. 92. 1704. Englifh and Dutch, 1690. of Smyrna, 1693. Dutch, 1697. 1703. Englifh, 1703. 07. of Virginia, 1711. See *Marine.*
Fleta, le, 1275.
Fleury, abbé, 1689.
Fleurus, 1690.
Fleury, monaftery. 695.
Flix, 1650.
Florence, council, 867. 1438. 39. city, 1494. 1502. 12. cardinal of, 1598.
Florent Chrétien, 1593.
Florentines, 1376. 1522. 30.
Flower de Luces, 1380. 1527. 1655.
Flushing, 1616.

FO.

Fæderowitz, Michael, Czar, 1611.
Foix, count, 1255. 70. 75. 1397. count de, 1451. Germain, 1505. Gafton, 1505. 11. 12. Catherine, 1512. Andrew, 1521. Paul, 1574. l'abbé de, 1631. count de Flex, 1663.
Folard, 1675.
Fontaine, count de, 1643.
Fontainebleau, 1600.
Fontaine-Françoife, battle of, 1595.
Fontaines, Petèr de, p. 183. V. I.
Fontange, dutchefs of, 1681.
Fontarabia, 1470. 1521. 1638. 98.
Fontenai, 841. 1590.
Fontenelle, chronicle, 742. monaftery, 750.
Fontenoi, 1709.
Fontevrault, 1103.
Fontrailles, 1642.
Forbin, Palamede de, 1480. chevalier de, 1707. 08.
Forcalquier, 1258.
Force, James de la, marfhal of France, 1589. 1610. 21. 22. 30. 34-36. 38. dutchy, 1637.
Formofa, pope, 892.
Formulary, 1657. 69. 73. 1705.
Formula, 1419. 20.
Formulas of the civilians, 511.
Fornova, 1495.
Fort de Cohorn, 1692.
Fort-Louis, 1622. 25. 1706.
Fort-Royal, 1674.
Fortune-tellers, 1680.
Forty, 1245. council of union, 1589.
Fotheringal, 1587.
Foucault, Lewis, 1653.
Foulks, 892. Nerra, 1135. count d'Anjou, 1099. 1135. high fteward, 1309.
Foundations, 612. 46.
Fouquet, Nicholas, 1661. Francis, 1661. p. 95. V. II.
Fourmigny, 1448.

Fracaftor,

INDEX.

FR.
Fracaſtor, p. 287. V. I.
France, dutchy, 992. p. 299. V. II. crown, 1711. union, 1532.
Frankfort, council, 794. diet, 1206. .... 1631.
Franche-Comté, 842. 79. 1479. 1639. 68. 74. 78.
Franchiſes, 1687. 88.
Franciſcans, 1387.
Francis, of Aſſiſi, St. p. 177. V. I.
Francis I. 1505. 14. 15. 25. 35. 47. his death, p. 355. V. I. See his reign; his eldeſt ſon, 1518. 36. 51. II. 1558-60. p. 306. V. II.
Franconia, 1632.
Franecker, 1680.
Frankendal, 1688.
Fraternity, 1542.
Frawſtadt, 1706.
Fredegonda, 568. 70. 75. 78. 81. 84. 85. 90. 94. 97.
Fredlingen, 1702.
Fredelon, 1449.
Frederic, duke of lower Lorrain, 956. seneſchal, 995. I. emperor, 1092. 1150. 56. 80. 86. 89. 90. 1269. 82. II. emperor, 1206. 14. 23. 26. 30. 42. 45. 55. 1315. 1516. duke of Auſtria, 1321. 22. III. emperor, 1447. 65. 93. king of Sicily, 1298. king of Naples, 1496. 1501. III. king of Denmark, 1660. V. elector Palatine and king of Bohemia, 1613. 19-21. 32. Henry, prince of Orange.

See *Orange*. King of Pruſſia, 1701.
Frederune, 929.
Freeholds, 817. 1328.
Free-archers, 1480.
Fregoſa, 1447. John, 1512. ambaſſador at Venice, 1542.
French, or *Francs*, 481. 536. 39. ... 58. p. 36. V. I.
French language, 1360. 1539.
Frenc, Trichet du, 1642.
Freret, p. 40. V. I.
Frette, la, 1663.
Friburg, 1516. 1638. 44. 77. 78. 97. 1713.
Friday, ſuperſtition, 1503.
Friderickſtadt, 1713.
Friuli, duke of, 776.
Friſeland, 1296. 1424.
Friſons, 733.
Froiſſart, John, p. 261. V. I.
Frondeurs, 1648. 51.
Frontenac, de, 1696.
Frontenai, dutchy of Rohan-Rohan, 1714.
Froullai de Teſſé, Réné, 1696. 1706. 07.

FU.
Fuenſaldagna, 1654.
Fuentes, count de, 1596. ambaſſador, 1661.
Funerals, 1643.
Furnes, 1646. 48. 58. 67. 68. 93. 1706.
Furſtemberg, William of, 1671. 74. duke of, 1689. Francis Egon, 1681.

G.

Gabaret, 1689. 93. 1703.
Gabelle, 1344. 1548.
Gabrielle d'Eſtrées, 1599.
Gacé, marſhal de Matignon, 1708.
Gaëta, 1707.
Gaimar, 1026.
Galas, 1635. 36. 45.
Galeas, John, 1494. 98.
Galeran, count de Meulan, 1040. 41.

Gallies, general of the, 1544.
Galileo, 1633. p. 287. V. I.
Galiguai, Eleonor, 1612. 17.
Gallati, 1616.
Gallicans, 1645.
Galloons, 1702.
Galway, 1706. 07. 09.
Games, edict concerning them, 1369. Floral, 1324. 1694.

INDEX.

Garden, 1547. 1603. 34.
Garter, 1349. 1564. 96.
Gap, 1692.
Garai, 1649.
Garde, baron de la, 1544. 45.
Gardie, la, 1646.
Gariglian, 1503.
Garlande, the brothers, 1116. 35. William, senefchal, 1116.
Garlangues, 1628.
Garonne, the, 593. 732.
Gafcons, Gafcony, 593. 601. 03. 25. 35. 767. 78. 818. 1001. 62. 1562.
Gaffendi, 1559.
Gaffion, marshal of France, 1631. 35. 39. 40. 43-47. 1711.
Gafton, see *Foix*; brother of Lewis XIII. 1617. 26. 31-34. 36. 42-45. 48. 49. 51. 52. his character, 1660. de Foix, 1663.
Gatari, 1638.
Gaucourt, 1652.
Gaul, Gauls, 481. 511. 1532. p. 36. &c. 40. 94.
Gaunt, 1678. 1706. 08. John of, 1485. inhabitants, 1488. sack of, 1044.
Gauric, Luc, 1559.
Gautier, archbishop, 888. l'abbé, 1712.
Gayan, 1648.
Gazette, 1631.

GE.

Gegembak, 1678.
Gelders, 1478. 1638. 1703. 13. province, 1672.
Gendarmery, 1690. 91. 93.
Gendarms, 1643.
General, of dragoons, 1692. of the gallies, 1544.
Geneva, 888. 1553. 79. 1602. 38. 1707.
Genialis, duke of Gafcony, 601.
Gennaro, 1647.
Genoa, Genoefe, Jacobus de Voragine, 1269. expedition, 1390. Boucicaut, 1401. furrenders herfelf into the arms of France, 1447. project, 1497. fubdued, 1499. 1513. revolts again, 1505. 12. furrenders to Lautrec, 1527. to the emperor, 1528. confpiracy, 1547. expedition, 1625. declares for the king, 1515. league, 1522. bombarded, 1684. fubmits to the king, 1685. doge takes the title of highnefs, 1702. Final fold, 1713.
Gentil, 1522.
Gentleman, firft, 1612. 89. ordinary, 1690.
Gentlemen, 1478. 1600.
Geoffry, Grifegonelle, 978. d'Harcourt, 1344. count d'Anjou, 1116. Plantagenet, 1135. fon of Henry II. 1167. of Britany, 1200. abbé of St. Alban's, 1179.
Gerard d'Alface, 1056. 60.
Gerard, a Spanish emiffary, 1584.
Gerberga, 936. 54.
Gerbert, 928. 96.
Germany, Germans, Tolbiac, 496. .... 595. ... 743. ... 835. 42. 912. 1022. p. 45. V. I. 1149. Charlemain, 778. Frederic, 1189. independency of the imperial crown, 1336. clergy, 1447. printing, 1547. Lanfquenets, 1497. in Champagne, 1523. battle of Mulberg, 1547. 52. 70. calendar, 1582. 87. project of Henry IV. 1610. pacification of Ulm, 1620. 21. peace of Lubeck, 1629. Guftavus Adolphus, 1631. 33. Walftein, 1634. 36. 41. 42. 44-46. league of the Rhine, 1658. 74. Lewis XIV. 1689. Hanover, 1692. 93. 1711.
Gertrudemberg, 1710.
Gefvres, de, 1640. dutchy and peerage, 1648. governor of Paris, 1687.
Gevaudan, 534.

Giac,

INDEX.

GI.
Giac, minister, 1426.
Giannone, p. 299. V. II.
Gibelines, 1140. 1285. 1354.
Gibraltar, 1704. 05. 13.
Gie, marshal de, 1505.
Gien, 1215. 23.
Gigeri, 1664.
Gilbert, duke of Lorrain, 936. de la Porée, 1148.
Gillot, 1593.
Girardin, 1689.
Girardon, 1642.
Gironne, 1684. 94. 1705. 11.
Giselles, daughter of Charles the Simple, 912. 29. p. 45. V. I.
Gisors, 1032. 1113.
Givri, 1589.

GL.
Glass manufacture, 1603.
Glesne, 1645.
Glocester, 1424..... 1658......
1701.

GO.
Godfrey, of Bouillon, 1067. 92. of Bologne, 1095.
Godegisilus, 500.
Godfathers, p.156.V. I. 90.V.II.
Godmothers, the king's, 1180. p. 90. V. II.
Goes, 1714.
Goesbriand, de, 1707. 10.
Gœutz, 1638.
Goüaric, 511.
Gold, value of, 840. golden bull, 1355.
Goldsmith, 1270. 72.
Golsonda, 568. 84.
Gomarists, 1619.
Gomatrude, 636.
Gombaud, 830.
Gomberville, 1643.
Gombett law, 511.
Gondebaud, king of Burgundy, 500. 11. 23. duke, 576. pretended son of Clotaire, 585.
Gondemar, 523. 34.
Condi, cardinal, 1592. house, 1589.

Gondiucque, 533. 62.
Gonsalvo of Cordova, 1495. 1501. 03. 04.
Gontaut de Biron, Armand de, 1592. Charles, 1602.
Gontran, 562-93.
Gonzaga, of Mantua, 1598. 1629. 41. 45. Charles, 1629. Mary, 1645. Francis, general of the Cordeliers, 1598.
Good, league of the public, 1466.
Gorde, de, 1572.
Gordon, 1634.
Gorges, 635.
Gorlitz, 1641.
Goslin, 888.
Got, Bertrand de, 1305.
Gothia, 758.
Goths, 493. 634. 715.
Gouffier, de Boisy, 1514. 21. Arthur de, 1667. Claude and Louis, 1667.
Goulas, 1652.
Governess of the children of France, 1661.
Governors, of provinces, 845. of Havre, 1665. of Paris, 1669. 87. p. 7. V. II. of Bretagne, 1695. of Gaston, 1617. of Charles IX. p. 408. V. I. of Henry III. p. 432. V. I. of Lewis XIV. p. 90. V. II. of the dauphin, 1668. of the sons of France, 1663. 89. of the duke of Chartres, 1683. of the Netherlands, 1701.

GR.
Graces, the great almoner, ought to say grace before the parliament, p. 409.V. I.
Graduates, 1498.
Grai, town, 1668. 74. Jane, 1553.
Grailly, Archambault de, 1397.
Gramont, town, 1706. count de, 1562. 93. Antony de, marshal of France, 1644-46. 48. 57. 58. 61. 67. 72. 1704. order, p. 39. V. I.

INDEX.

Gran, 1683. 85.
Grancei, counts de, 1639. 41. marſhal de, 1653.
Grand-Almoner, 1645. 1700. p. 409. V. I.
Grand-Bailiffs, p. 292. V. II.
Grand-Companies, 1361. 66.
Grand-Council, 1497. 1631. 90.
Grand-Duke, 1598.
Grand-Foreſter, 863.
Grand-Huntſman, 1669.
Grand-Maſter, or lord ſteward, p. 313. 357. V. I. of the croſs-bow men, 1600. of the wardrobe, 1669. of the artillery, 1600. 69. 94. of the waters and foreſts, 1575.
Grand-Maſters, of Malta, 1309. 1522. 65. 1630. 97. of the order of the Holy Ghoſt of Montpellier, 1700.
Grand-Officers, 1103. 1577. 1607. p. 177. V. I.
Grand-Provoſt, p. 39. V. I.
Grand-Referendary, p. 38. V. I.
Grand-Seſſions, 1579. 1634. 65.
Grand-Signior, 1559. 1714. See *Turks.*
Grandee, title, 1521.
Grandee of Spain, 1701.
Grandier, Urban, 1634.
Grandpré, 1654.
Grandſon, 1476.
Granvelle, Antony, 1539. 65. cardinal, 1661.
Gratian, 1150.
Gratifications, 1663.
Grave, 1672. 74.
Gravelines, 1558. 1644. 52. 58.
Graville, admiral de, 1494.
Greece, 1067.
Greeks, 787. empire, 802. 67. 1026. 1148. 1204. 74. 1439. 51. 1547. p. 49. V. I.
Gregory II. 740. III. 740. IV. 827. 33. V. 996. VII. 1067. IX. 1226. 30. X. 1274. 1348. XI. 1376. 79. XII. 1408. XIII. 1067. 1585. calendar, 1699.

XIV. 1590. XV. 1387. 1622. of Tours, 845.
Greipſwalde, 1678.
Gremonville, 1700.
Grenada, king of, 1320. city of, 1492. 1516.
Grenoble, 1451. 1590. 1639. 44.
Grignaux, 1514.
Grimoald, mayor, 644. 46. 54. 56. p. 38. V. I.
Grippon, 747. 58.
Gris, le, 1386.
Griſegonelle, Geoffry, 978.
Griſons, 1305. 1621. 25. 30. 31. 37.
Grodno, 1708.
Groenland, 1634.
Groningen, 1674.
Grool, 1672.
Groſglogau, 1642.
Grotius, Hugo, 1619. 36.

GU.

Guadaloupe, 1635. 1703.
Guaſtalla, town, 1702. duke of, 1714.
Guard, of the king's perſon, 1380. of our kings, 1215. of the high roads, 1255.
Guards, regiment of, 1644. 53. 72. 91. 92. 1703. 13. colonel of the, 1661.
Guard-du-corps, 1626. 71. 95.
Guardian of Henry VI. 1422.
Gudina, 1709.
Guebriant, J. B. Budes de, 1638. 43. marſhal de, 1645.
Guelfs, 1140. 1285. 1354.
Guenegaud, Dupleſſis, 1661.
Guerande, 1364.
Guercheville, madam de, 1600.
Guerin, biſhop of Senlis, 1214. 1309. p. 159. 177. V. I. advocate-general, 1545.
Gueſchlin, conſtable du, 1364. 66. 69. 80.
Gueſle, la, p. 7. V. I.
Gueſton, 1707.

Guſt,

INDEX.

Guet, chevalier du, 1350.
Gue-Trouin, du, 1697. 1707. 11.
Guette, la, 1322.
Geufes, the, 1566.
Guy, 912. count de Thouars, 1116. count of Flanders, 1292. 99. de Luſignan, 1302. 4.
Guiche, Coriſande de, 1593. duke de, 1640. marſhal de, 1642. count de, 1665. 78. peerage, 1648.
Guienne, Eleonor, 1150. John Lackland, 200. Henry III. 1258. confiſcated, 1292. war, 1296. reſtored, 1303. Charles de Valois, 1324. homage, 1329. renunciation, 1360. Peter the Cruel, 1367. conquered, 1378. duke de, 992. .... 1469. 70-72. troubles, 1548-51. 78. 80. dutchy, 1292. p. 294. V. II.
Guilére, 577.
Guillard du Mortier, 1560.
Guillerague, de, 1685.
Guinea, 1664.
Guinegate, 1479. 1513.
Guines, count de, 1350. town, 1558.
Guipuſcoa, 1698.

Guiſcard, Robert, 1025. 56. count de, 1695.
Guiſe, town, 1650. dutchy, 1527. Claude de, 1542. 50. p. 384. V.I. their poſterity, 1550. Francis de, 1347. .... 1523. 47. 48. 50. 53-55. 57-60. 62. 63. 1559. 60. 74. 82. 85. 98. Henry de, 1550. 69. 72. 74-76. 78. 82. 84-88. cardinal de, 1582. 88. p. 432. V.I. Charles, 1550. 89. 91. 94-96. 1614-16. 22. chevalier de, 1613. Henry II. 1550. 1641. 43. 47. 48. 54. .... 84. Lewis-Joſeph, 1660. 69. mademoiſelle de, 1688. 95. madam de, 1694.
Guitaut, 1650.
Guitry, marquis de, 1669.
Gunpowder, 1336. gunpowder-treaſon, 1605.
Gurce, cardinal de, 1494. 1510. 12.
Guſtavus, king of Sweden, (Vaſa) 1542. See *Adolphus*; Charles, 1654. 59.
Guttemberg, John, 1457.
Guyon, madam, 1698.

H.

HA, 1451. 1653.
Habſbourg, 1273. 82. p. 199. V. I.
Hachette, Jane, 1472.
Hacquin, king of Norway, 1391.
Hadwiſe, 1200.
Hague, 1709.
Haguenau, 1675. 1705. 06.
Hailbrun, 1645. 88. 93.
Hainaut, 1296. 1324. 36. 40. 1424. 83. 1554. See *Flanders*, *Brabant*.
Hair, 654. 1191. 1523. p. 39. 104. V. I.
Halberſtadt, adminiſtrator, 1626.
Haltetrude, 628.

Hall, treaty of, 1610. .... 42. Notre-Dame, 1691.
Halley, 1660.
Hallier, du, 1624. 38. 41.
Halluin, Anne d', 1620. duke d', 1637.
Ham, 1595. 1655.
Hamburg, 1238. 1641. 44.
Hamilton, 1685.
Hanau, 1636.
Hanover, 1692. 1701. 07. 14. madam, 1684. duke, 1672.
Hanſe towns, 1238.
Haraucourt, d', 1625.
Harcourt, Geoffry d', 1344. branch of, 1550. count d', 1637. 39-

INDEX.

43. 45. 46. 49-51. 53. 54. 60. M. d', 1692. 96. 1703. 09. 11. dutchy and peerage, 1709. marquis, 1689. marshal, 1698. 1700.
Hardouin, counts, 879.
Harfleur, 1415.
Harlay, first president, Achilles de, 1588. 94. ... 1689. archbishop, 1674. 95. M. de, 1697. 1709.
Harlebec, 1711.
Harling, 1711.
Haro, cry, 912. Lewis de, 1658. 59. 61. 77.
Harrach, 1697.
Hat, cardinals, 1245.
Havannah, la, 1703.
Haubert, 1140.
Havre, 1563. 1665. 94.
Haute Bruyere, 1103.
Hautefort, madam de, 1639. 43. M. de, 1689,
Hauteville, 1026,

HE,

Hearts of kings and queens, p. 409. V. I. 3. 91. V. II.
Hedge-hog, 1498. 1515.
Hegira, 622.
Heidelberg, 1622. 88. 93.
Hein, Peter, 1628.
Heinsius, 1709.
Heirs, 1245. male, 1313. 1566,
Helena, St. 1230.
Helgaud, 1022.
Helmets, p. 98. V. I,
Helvetians, 794.
Hennebont, 1590.
Henry, emperor I. 920. II. the Lame, 1001. 22. III. 1056. IV. 1056. 1103. V. 1103. 16. 20. 35. VI. 1026. 1186. 93. 1206. of Luxemburg, 1305. heretic, 1206. kings of France, I. 1026. See his reign; II. 1532. 46. 1641. See his reign; surnamed the Lion, 1180. p. 304. V. II. III. 1573. See his reign, *Poland*, *Anjou*; his character, 1589.
IV. 1564. 69. 70. 72. 74. 76. 77. 87. 89. 90. 1672. his character, 1610. See his reign; funeral oration, p. 3. ... 301. V. II. duke of Burgundy, 956. 1001. king of Spain, IV. 1472. 1505. See *Spain*; king of Portugal, 1088. 1578. 80. kings of England, I. 1067. 1100. 13. 16. 20. 35. II. 1135. 50. 54. 56. 61. 67. 69. 79. 80. 86. 89. 1331. 1541. III. 1215. 23. 26. 30. 42. 52. 58. IV. 1397. 1410. V. 1415. 20. 22. VI. 1422. 31. 35. 57. 70. 71. VII. 1420. 75. 95. 1502. his history, 1485. 92. 1509. 10. VIII. 1510. 12-15. 20. 22. 25-27. 29. 34. 41. 43. 44. 46. 47. Clement, marshal of France, 1214. kings of Navarre, 1521. 89. See *Navarre*; war of the three Henries, 1586. *Henrietta*, wife of Charles I. 1625. 44. first wife of monsieur, 1661. 70.
Heptarchy, 827.
Herald, 734. 36.
Herbert, converts Sweden, p. 59. V, I, de Vermandois, 922. 28, de Troyes, 929. vice-admiral, 1689.
Heresies, 7409. 4. 1022. 47. 1517. 34,
Heretics, 1022. 1226. 1553.
Heriold, 823.
Herispoe, 845. 58.
Heristal, 779.
Heristel, 688.
Hermandfrid, 520. 31.
Hermenigild, 575.
Hermenstein, 1637.
Hermit, the, 1624.
Hermits, 1255.
Herrings, battle of, 1428.
Hervè, abbot of St. Victor, p. 156. V. I.
Hesdin, 1521. 53. 1639. 57.
Hesse, 778. landgrave of, 1547. 52. 1636. 40. 92. troops of, 1641.

INDEX.

1641. prince of, 1703. 06.

HI.
Hidde, mademoiselle, 1673.
Hieres, abbey, 1161.
Highness, title, 1644. 98. 1702.
Hire, la, 1451. 57.
Hispaniola, 1492.
History, p. 101. V. I. of France, p. 288. V. II.
Historiographer, 1713.

HO.
Hobbes, 1650.
Hocquincourt, Ch. de Monchi, 1647. 52. 54. 55.
Hockstet, 1703 04.
Holland, Hollanders, William, 1273, John, 1296. John d'Avesnes, 1296. Jacquelina of Bavaria, 1424. 79. troubles, 1565-67. 78. revolt, 1581. 84. 96. 98. 1603. 04. 08. truce, 1609. war of Cleves, 1614. Batavia, 1619. 20. America, 1623. 24. league, alliance, marine, 1626. 28. treaty against Spain, 1634-36. war with Portugal, 1657. 59. 61. treaty, 1662. war with England, 1664. 66-68. war of Holland, 1670-78. 88-90. 93-94. 96. 97. acknowledge Philip V. 1700-07. 13. 14. See the *Netherlands, Flanders*.
Holoffin, 1708.
Holstein, duke of, 1675.
Holy Ghost, procession, 1274. institution of the order, 1579. 98. promotions, 1662. bridge, 1309.
Holy-See, 714. 1206. 42. 1305. 13. 76. 1644.
Homburg, 1705.
Homelies, 1067.
Homer, 789.
Homicide, 593.
Homage, Charlemain, 778. 96. Britany, 845. 1116. 1341. 64. 81. Bourges, 1190. 98. Nor-

mandy, 1120. league, 1135. 1258. Bar, 1296. 1641. 99. Montpellier, 1320. Guienne, 1324. 29. dispensation, 1499.
Honnecourt, 1642.
Honours, 1559.
Honorius III. 1225. 1680.
Hopital, Michael de l', 1371. 1560. 65. 74. his character, 1568. marshal de l', 1624. 43.
Horn, marshal de, 1634. counts de, 1566. 67.
Horoscopes, p. 311. V. II.
Hospitallers, 1092.
Horse, light, 1643. 65.
Hostel-Dieu, 1324.
Host, 1269. 85.
Hostage, 1526.
Hostun. See *Tallard*.
Hotenwiel, 1642.
Hotman, Antony, 1667. p. 94. V. I.
Houdancourt. See *la Mothe*.
Houge, la, 1692.
Houshold, the king's officers of the, 1380.....91. 92. 1670.
Howard, Catherine, 1547.

HU.
Huet, 1709.
Hugh, Capet, 861. 956. 87. V. his reign, p. 299. V. II. le grand, l'abbé, le Blanc, 923. 36. 45. 54. 56. son of Robert, 1026. son of Henry, and count de Vermandois, 1092. archbishop of Lyons, 1092. abbot of St. Germains, 1180. d'Abbeville, 992. de Lusignan, 1226. IV. duke of Burgundy, 1245. abbot of Cluni, 1321.
Hugonet, 1477.
Huguenots, 1545. 60-65. 67. 69-76. 80. 86. 96. 97. 1612. 15. 16. 20. 21. 25. 29. 82. See *Protestants*.
Hui, 1674. 75. 93. 94. 1703. 05.
Huillier, l', 1594.

Hults,

INDEX.

Hults, 1645.
Humbert, with the white hands, 1056. dauphin, 1349.
Humieres, marshal de, 1589. 95. marshal d', 1668. 72. 75-79. 83. 89. 94.
Hungary, Hungarians, Charlemain, 796. Lewis the Debonnaire, 818. Raoul, 924. 29. Ferdinand I. 1526. 29. Anne, 1526. John, 1529. Soliman, 1529. 41. Mary, 1552. 56. Ferdinand II. 1617. 18. Leopold, 1671. hereditary, 1687. Lewis, p. 259. V. I. Clemence, 1316. Andrew, 1347. Sigismond, 1394. Ferdinand, 1634.
Huningen, 1678. 80.
Huns, 563. 787. 96. 803.
Hunsdon, lord, 1564.
Husse, John, 1415.
Hutin, Lewis, 1314.
Huxelles, Nicholas du Blé d', 1686. 88. 89. 1703. 10. 12.

HY.

Hymns, 1026.

I.

Jacobins, or *Dominicans*, 1215. 30. 1387. James Clement, 1589. Seraphin Bauché, 1593.
Jacquerie, 1358.
James I. king of England, 1603. 16. 20. 22. 24. 25. 53. II. 1672. 73. 85. 88-90. 92. 96. 1701. his son, 1673. 1701. 08. 13. king of Sicily, 1283. 85. 92. king of Scotland, 1483. 1502.
Jagellon, Anne, 1526. 73. 1617.
Jamaica, 1655.
Jametz, 1632. 50. 61.
Janissaries, 1648.
Jansenius, 1657. 69.
Jansenism, 1641.
Janson, Toussaints de Forbin, 1693.
January, 1564.
Janus, 1707.
Jaraslaus, p. 121. V. I.
Jarnac, 1547. 69.
Jasamergot, 1156.
Java, 1619.

IB.
Iberville, d', 1697.
Ibinalarabi, 778.
Ibrahim, 1648.

IC.
Iconoclasts, 740. 51. 94.

ID.
Idol, 772.

IE.
Jeannin, 1591. 98. 1608. 11. 20. 22.
Jengoul, p. 295. V. II.
Jerome of Prague, 1415. p. 277. V. I.
Jerusalem, kingdom, 1092. 1226. city, 1186. 89. 91. Godfrey, 1067. 92. assizes, 1067. p. 141. V. I.
Jesuits, 1521. 34. 74. 94. 1603. 18. 57.
Jews, 875. 99. 1180. 1206. 69. 1313. 1420. 60. 71. 91. p. 273. 275. V. I.

IG.
Ignatius, patriarch of, 867. of Loyola, 1521. 34.
Ignorance, age of, 992.

IM.
Imbercourt, 1497.
Immunities, ecclesiastical, 1161.
Immichilde, 654.
Imperiali, Francesco Maria, 1585.
Importants, party, 1643.

Impes-

INDEX.

Impostors, 1223. 1605. p. 3. 31. V.II.
Imposts, 562. 1269. 1315. 16. 67. 80. 1416. p. 312.V.II.

IN.
Indies, 1628. 65. 80. 1713.
Indulgences, 1299. 1517.
Indult, 1538. 1695.
Infantry, 511. 1480. 97. 1532. 44. 84. 1643. 67.
Information of the life and behaviour, 1567.
Infranchisement, 1135. 1225. 70. 1316.
Ingelger, 877.
Ingelheim, 945.
Ingelram, 1103.
Ingerburga, 1193. p. 157.V.I.
Ingoberga, 566.
Ingolstat, 1704.
Ingomer, 511.
Ingonda, 562.
Inigo, 827.
Innocents, feast, 1483. p. 97.V.I. church-yard, p. 273. V.I.
Innocent II. 1130. 42. III. 1206. 15. p. 157.V.I. IV. 1226. 42. 45. X. 1644-46. 57. XI. 1662. 82. 85. 87. 89. XII. 1692. 93. 1700.
Inundation, 1608.
Inquisition, 1230. 1560. 66. 1633.
Inspector, 1689.
Inspruck, 1552. 1703.
Institution of the Eucharist, book of, 1600.
Intendants, of provinces, 1629.82. 89. of finances, 1697.
Interdict, Interdiction, 1142.1206. 1303. 22. 1512. 1606. 07. 31. 32. 39. 87.
Interim, 1548.
Interregnum, 742. 1273.
Invalids, 1605. 70. 71.
Investiture, quarrel about, 1103. 20. p. 97. V.I. right of, 1156. of the two Sicilies, 1130. of Anjou, 1135. of Poitou, 1230. of Arragon, 1283. of Milan, 1494. 98. 1504. 39. 55.

JO.
John, St. p. 97. V. I. of God, St. 1602. popes, VIII. 877. p. 68. V. I. XII. p. 91. V. I. XV. 938. XVIII. anti-pope, 996. XXII. 1292. 1313. 22. 24. 28. 29. John de Matha, 1193. p. 121. V. I. king of France, who lived but eight days, 1316. p. 221. V. I. son of Philip de Valois, 1331. king of France; see his reign; son of king John, 1415. son of St. Lewis, surnamed Tristan, 1270. son of Charles V. 1415. See *count de Montfort*; son of Charles VI. 1415. 24. Infant of Spain, 1508. 30. of Portugal, 1580. Lackland, king of England, 1200. 06. 15. count de Hainaut, 1324. Fearless, 1404. 07. 08. 10. 19. 20. 24. count de Nevers, p. 307.V.II. dukes of Britany, 1296. 1371. Waywod, 1526. 29. of Anjou, 1464. See *de Wert*; of Portugal, 1641. See *Austria*. Joan, pope, 875. p. 67. V. I. wife of Philip the Fair, 1283. 96. 1302. daughter of Lewis Hutin, heiress of Navarre, 1316. 28. p. 230. V. I. wife of Philip the Long, 1313. 16. 31. daughter of Philip the Long, 1331. d'Evreux, wife of Charles the Fair, p. 231. V. I. wife of Philip de Valois, p. 237. V. I. de Boulogne, p. 249. V. I. de Bourbon, p. 259. V. I. wife of Lewis XII. 1499. p. 339. V. I. d'Albret, 1569. countess of Flanders, 1226. the Lame, 1341. 64. daughter of Ferdinand, 1477.

INDEX.

1477. 82. daughter of Henry IV. king of Caſtile, 1472. 1504. the Fooliſh, 1504. of Naples, 1255. 1341. 44. 48. 82. . . . . 1493. wife of the count de Montfort, 1341.
Joinville, 802. 1269.
Jonquiere, la, 1708.
Joſeph, father, 1636. emperor, 1703. 11.
Jovius, Paul, 1536.
Jourdain de l'Iſle, 1322.
Journal, 1665.
Journey of the court, 1625. 46.
Joux, fort, 1639.
Joyeuſe, dutchy and peerage, 1581. 96. 1714. Anne de, 1587. Antony, 1592. father Angel, 1592. 96. 99. marſhal de, 1693. cardinal de, 992. 1607. p. 30. V. II. the duke, 1642.

IP.

Ipres, 1648. 49. 58. 78. 1706.

IR.

Ireland, 651. 54. 70. 1189. 1541. 1649. 89-91.
Irene, 794. 96. 803.
Irminſula, 772.
Iron, 1638.
Iroquois, 1696. 97.
Irſon, 1650.

IS.

Iſaac, Angelus, 1204.
Iſabella, wife of Philip Auguſtus, 1192. of Arragon, 1255. queens of England, 1200. 1324. daughter of Philip the Fair, 1296. 1324. 28. daughter of Philip the Long, p. 225. V. I. wife of Charles VI. 1389. 94. 1415. 19. 22. p. 271. V. I. wife of Philip II. 1565. 68. queen of Caſtile, 1472. 77. 92. 1504. 16. daughter of Charles IV. duke of Lorrain, 1580. of Arragon, 1472. 1501. 04. of Hungary, 1526. . . . p. 227. V. I.
Iſidore, 1150.
Iſle, Jourdain de l', 1322. marchineſs d', 1573. marquiſate d', 1665. de Fer, 1634. Adam-John de Villiers de l', 1415. Philip de Villiers de l', 1522. 65.
Iſſoire, 1577.

IT.

Italy, Lombards, 568. 87. 753. 74. 80. Bernard, 807. Normans, 1026. kingdom, 493. 818. 35. Lotharius, 842. popes, 912. exarchate, 978. king of the Romans, 1056. Guelfs, 1140. Gregory IX. 1226. wars, 1510. 15. 51. 1629. 31. 39. neutrality, 1713. fiefs, p. 95. V. I.
Italians, 1322.

JU.

Jubilee, 1299.
Judicature, office of, 1316.
Judicial, 636.
Judith, wife of Lewis the Debonnaire, 818. 30. 31. 33. 35. p. 71. V. I. daughter of Charles the Bald, p. 83. V.I.
Judges of the exempt, 1135. p. 291. V. II.
Judges, counſellors, 1344.
Ivica, 1706.
Julian, emperor, 481. count, 715.
Juliers, 1610. 14. 59.
Julius II. 1503. 08-11. 13. 19.
Ivri, 1590.
Juriſdiction, eccleſiaſtical, 657. 1329. 1539. 1695. ſecular, 1560. 64. Guienne, 1360. Montpellier, 1365. dutchy of Angouleme, 1515. 27.
Juſſel, 1682.

Juſtice,

INDEX.

Juſtice, capitularies, 800. ordinance, 1321. hand of, p. 104. V. I. ſeigniorial, 1135. p. 94. 98. V. I. ordinary, 992. 1539. 60. p. 289. V. II. &c.

Juſtin, emperor I. 511. II. 568.
Juſtinian I. 511. 34. 35. 39. 1137.
Juvenal des Urſins, p. 275. 308. V. I.

K.

KEinſton, 1642.
Keiſerlauter, 1635. 88. 1713.
Keiſerwert, 1671. 89. 1702.
Kell, 1678. 1703.
Kemnits, 1639.

KI.
Kilconnel, 1691.
Kimpen, 1642.
King of the Romans, 973. 1056. 1555. Ferdinand Erneſt, 1636. Prince Joſeph, 1703. 34. 1593.
Kingdom, Rodolph, 888. duke of Burgundy, 1473. interdicted, 1512. Ireland, 1541.

KN.
Knights, Templars, 992. coats of arms, 1149. of St. John of Jeruſalem, 1309. of the Star, 1350. created by the emperor, 1415. of St. Michael, 1469. of St. John of Jeruſalem, 1522. of Malta, 1530. tournaments, 1559. of the Holy Ghoſt, 1579. 1620. 33. 52. 89. of honour, 1680. See *Order*.
Knock, 1647. 1706.

KO.
Kocheim, 1689.
Konigſberg, 1701.
Konigſmarc, 1618. 45. 48. 78.
Koribut, 1669.

KU.
Kuſtein, 1703.
Kuniſfeld, 1638.

L.

LAboureur, le, 1559.
Labourers, 1315.
Ladiſlaus, king of Naples, 1255. IV. king of Poland, 1645.
Lady, of honour, 1600. 19. 63. 65. 80. of attire, 1680. of the palace, 1673.
Laffin, 1602.
Lagni, 1590.
La Hire, 1451. 57.
Lambale, 1591.
Lambert, 912. biſhop of Arras, 1103. marſhal de camp, 1644.

Lamboi, 1640-42. 46.
Lamoignon, 1614. 67.
Lampourdan, 1677.
Lancaſter, duke of, 1397. red roſe and white roſe, 1457. 85. p. 99. V. I.
Land, ſalic, p. 94. V. I. Holy, 1204. p. 316. V. II. Lack, original of this word, 1200. St. Lewis, 1242.
Landau, 1644. 1702-04. 13.
Landeric, 651.
Landes de Beaumanoir, 1364.

Landgrave

INDEX.

Landgrave, of Hesse, 1547. 52. 1640. 92. of Thuringia, 1226.
Landi, 875.
Landois, 1485.
Landrecy, 1543. 1637. 47. 55. 1712.
Landri, 584. 93. 603. ..., 1001.
Landriane, 1529.
Langlade, 1688.
Language, 511. 1067. 1147. 80. 1360. 1539. p. 100. V. I.
Languedoc, Saracens, 736. Amaulry de Montfort, 1223. treaty of St. Lewis, 1258. D. Vaissette, 1275. servitude abolished, 1296. subsidy, 1359. imposition, 1415. government, 1614. estates, 1629. canal of, 1664. 81.
Lanoi, viceroy of Naples, 1525, 26. lady of honour, 1619.
Lanoue, 1567. 91.
Lansquenets, 1497.
Laon, 892. 928. 45. 57. 88, 1594. count, p. 45. V. I.
Lapara, 1705.
Laquay, 1636.
Larcher, 1591.
Las Minas, 1705. 07.
Las Torres, 1706.
Late comers, 1361.
Lateran. See *Council.*
Latilli, 1315.
Latins, empire, 1204.
Laval, Peter de, p. 326. V. I. count de, 1712.
Lavardin, M. de, 1610. ambassador at Rome, 1687. 88. 90.
Laubanie, 1703. 04.
Laubardemont, 1642.
Laubespine, Chateauneuf, 1632.
Laud, 1637. 45.
Laufeld, 1588.
Lausun, 1669-71. 88. 89. 93.
Lauterburg, 1676.
Lautrec, 1512. 21. 22. 27. 28.
Law, Flavian, 511. of the emperors in council, 794. elections, 817. 23. 27. bishops, 822. 1633. monasteries, 840. presents, 817. dictates, 1067. absolution, 1100. 03. interdict, 1142. canons of Eugenius, 1148. regale, 1161. repudiation, 1193. John Lackland, 1206. Boniface VIII. 1303. joyful accession, 1274. of the two powers, 1329. English, 1275. the Roman chancery, 1550. 61. breviary, 1602. Santarel, 1626. assembly, 1682. French, 1665. 80. canon, 1680. civil, 1680. franchises, 1687. 88. 92. jurisdiction, 1695. quietism, 1699. bull, 1705. public, civil, peerages, 912. 1200. ordinance, 922. demesne, 1103. pragmatic, 1269. coronation, 1314. Sigismund, 1415. States-General, 1614. 1700. of war and peace, 1619. professorship, 1680. laws seigniorial, of procuration, &c. 992. p. 40. V. I. 290. V. II.
Law, salic, 511. 1316. 1593. 1633. p. 40. 98. V. I. mundana, 511. Gombette, 511. of the Romans, 511. private wars, 803. sumptuary, 813. of England, 1067. spirit of laws, 1670. history of our laws, 1568. 74. p. 97. V. I. 308. 309. V. II.
Lazy kings, 688.

LE.

League, against Lewis XI. 1464. 74. concluded at Venice, 1495. of Cambray, 1508. 10. in Italy, 1522. 25. holy, 1526. of Smalcald, 1532. for the Germanic liberty, 1551. protestant, 1552. of Henry II. with the pope, 1555. the, 1571. 76. 79. 84. 86. 88-94. 1602. between France and the republic of Venice, 1623. against the emperor, 1626. 31. 33. 35. 37. with

INDEX.

with Sweden, 1633. 39. 40. of the Rhine, 1658. between the king and Holland, 1662. of Augsburg, 1687. 89. of the emperor and the Dutch, 1701. with Savoy, 1703.
Learned, presents to the, 1663.
Learning, in Gaul, 511. See *Letters*.
Lectemberg, 1678.
Leczinski, Stanislaus, 1675. 1704. 09.
Leek, 1632.
Leffingue, 1708.
Legal, 1703.
Leganes, 1636. 38-40. 46. 1705.
Legate, Legation, 1026. 1303. 1435. 1556. 90. 93. 96. 1625. p. 96. V. I.
Legend, on coins, 1490. golden, 1269.
Leger, 670.
Legions, 1532.
Legitimation, Legitimated, 1321. 1576. 1602. 94. 1710. 14. p. 157. V. I.
Leicester, 1258.
Leictoure, 1470. 73.
Leipsick, 1631. 42.
Lemberg, 1642.
Lendeskroon, 1677.
Lens, 1641. 42. 45. 47. 48.
Leo III. 796. 800. 805. IV. 850. VIII. 973. 1215. IX. 753. p. 121. V. I. X. 1513-15. 17. 21. 34. emperors, Isaac, 740. 41. IV. 796. p. 45. V. I.
Leonine, Rome, 845.
Leopold, marquis of Austria, 1193. archduke, 1610. 41. 42. 45. 47. 48. emperor, 1657. 58. 64. 71. 82. 87. 88. 99. 1700. 05. of Lorrain, Charles, 1664.
Lepanto, 1571. 1692.
Lerida, 1642. 44. 46. 1707.
Lerma, duke de, 1621. 61.
Lesbos, 803.
Lescun, 1521.
Lesdiguieres, 1575. 90. 92. 97. 1617. 21. 22. 24. 25. 27. 60. Canaple, 1711. madam de, 1631.
Lesparre, 1521.
Lessines, 1706. 08.
Lestine, 743.
Lestre, de, p. 7. V. II.
Lesno, 1708.
Letters, belles, 789. 813. 992. 1067. 1380. 1522. 47. 74. 1683. p. 101. 201. 261. V. I. royal, 1357. 80. p. 41. warrants, 1418. 1560. patents, 1561. 67. 74. 1700. of cachet, 1629. 62. monitory, 1589. 91. ennoblement, 1600. of legitimation, 1602.
Leucate, 1637.
Leudegisilus, 585.
Leva, Antonio di, 1503. 29.
Levies, Impositions, 1309. 55. 1636.
Leuve, 1678. 1705.
Leuvigildus, 575.
Lewenhaupt, 1708.
Lewis, the Debonnaire, 813. 14. See his reign. See *Bavaria*; the Germanic, 835. 67. 75. 84. II. emperor, 855. 58. 67. 75. the Stammerer, 877. III. 879. 80. 82. IV. 898. 912. Transmarine, 922. 29. 36. 54. V. 986. 87. the Fat, 1103. See his reign, 1135. VII. 1130. 37. 80. VIII. 1214. 15. See his reign; IX. 800. 1225. establishments, 1200. p. 303. V. II. See his reign and character, 1270. his grandson, 1324. X. 1309. See his reign. XI. 875. 1436. See his reign and character, 1483. p. 303. 04. V. II. XII. 1484. 85. 88. 90. 95. 97. See his reign, and character, 1515. p. 303. V. II. XIII. 1601. 43. 72. his campaign, 1620. 22. 28-30. 33. 36. 42. his character, 1643. XIV. 1638. court, 1660. polite

INDEX.

lite age, 1663. 89. letter, 1701. his campaigns, 1646. 52. 55. 58. 63. 67. 68. 72-74. 76. 78. 80. 81. 84. 90. 91. 93. his anfwer to lord Stairs, 1714. parallel between him and Auguftus, 1715. XV. 1600. his grandmother, 1684. his birth, p. 91. V. II. has the furname of *the Beloved*, 1643. beautiful paffages, 1643. 61. 91. takes Ipres (in 1744.) 1678. takes Friburg (in 1744.) 1677. retakes (in 1745.) the towns loft after the battle of Ramillies, and adds new conquefts, 1706. campaign (of 1745.) compared to that (of 1672.) 1672. wins the battle of Fontenoy, and takes Tournay (in 1745.) 1709. takes Mons (in 1746.) 1691. takes Namur (in 1746.) 1692. takes Bergen-op-zoom (in 1746.) after gaining the battle of Lawfeld, 1588. (acquires the fovereignty of Lorrain, 1662. 75. becomes mafter of Maeftricht (in 1748.) 1673. gives peace to Europe, 1673. 85. changes the form of the grand council (in 1738.) 1497. drives the enemy out of Provence (in 1747.) 1707. takes Philipfburg, (in 1736.) 1688. Genoa preferved (in 1746.) 1685. king of Hungary, 1526. duke of Anjou, 1382. See *Anjou*; duke of Orleans, 1389. 1407. 08. See *Orleans*; fon of Charles VI. 1410. 15.

Leuze, 1691.
Leyden, Jack of, 1536.
Lezeau, 1667.

LI.

Liancourt, 1599. 1610.
Libertat, 1696.
Liberties, of the Gallican church, 1067. 1269. 1305. in fief, 1316. diftinction of the two powers, 1329. 1561. 63. 94. of confcience, 1532. Germany, 1551.
Library, 380. 1622. 61. 63. p. 411. V. I. tower of the, 1380.
Lie, field, 833.
Liege, Liegeois, 1465. 67. 68. 1675. 76. 91. 93. 97. 1701. 02. 05.
Liege, 1135. 1258. 1329. See *Homage*.
Lieres, 1706.
Lieutenants, of the bailiffs, 1560. p. 297. V. II. general, 1547. 1633. general of the ftate, 1357. of the Milanefe, 1515. of the kingdom, 1558. 60. 67. 89. 1652. of the league, 1585. 90. of the army, 1636. of the king a minor, 1643. civil, 992. of policy, 1697.
Ligne, prince de, 1658. 67.
Life, information, 1567.
Ligneville, count de, 1499.
Liguria, 568.
Lilers, 1645.
Lillo, 1703.
Lima, 1624.
Limburg, 1675. 1703.
Limerick, 1690. 91.
Limeul, mademoifelle de, 1569.
Limits, of Paris, 1550. of the empire of the eaft and weft, 803.
Limoufin, 628. 1223. 58. 1355. 1441.
Lines, Retrenchments, 1328. 1654. 1703. 05-07.
Link, 1645.
Lionne, 1644. 56-58. 61. 71. 79.
Liorens, 1645.
Lipftad, 1679.
Liria, 1710.
Lifbon, 1149. 1704.
Lifle, campaign of, 1667. fiege of, 1708.
Lifle, John de, 1605.
Lifle-Adam, John de Villiers de l', 1415.

INDEX.

1415. Philip de Villiers de l', 1522. 65.
Liſlebonne, princeſs of, 1675.
Lithuania, 1573. 1706.
Liturgy, 1659.
Livarot, 1578.
Liverdun, 1632.
Livri, foreſt of, 673.

LO.

Loans, 1560. 1701.
Lobkowitz, 1709.
Loches, 1469. 1500.
Lockhart, 1662.
Loewendahl, 1588. 1673.
Loire, the, 1350. 1608.
Loiſel, 1594. p. 435. V. I.
Lombardy, 780. 1707.
Lombards, law of, 511. kingdom, 568. war, 587. Adaloald, 601. Gregory II. 740. Zachary, 751. Aſtolphus, 753. 56. Didier, 768. extinction of the kingdom, 774. weſt, 800. kingdom of Italy, 818. 1026. concubinage, 1001. financiers, 1322. p. 45. 49. 95. V. I.
Lombez, 1206.
Lomenie, 1590. ... 1643.
Lonchamp, p. 175. V. I.
London, 1215. 1364. 1462. 1601. 42. 61. 66. 88. 98.
Londonderry, 1689.
Lougin, 568.
Longjumeau, peace of, 1568.
Longueval, d'Haraucourt, 1625.
Longuetille, 1621.
Longueville, count de Dunois, 1407. 28. Lewis, duke de, 1514. ... 69. Henry I. 1589. Henry II. 1614. 37-40. 42. 47. 48. 50. 54. Anne of Bourbon, 1645. 48. 54. 70. 79. Charles Paris, 1672. chevalier de, 1688. John Lewis, abbé de, 1694.
Longwi, 1670.
Lorck, 1707.

Lord, *Lordſhips*, 845. 992. truce 1040. ought to preſerve the ſecurity of the public roads, 1255. introduction, 1269. 70. 73. excluſion, 1135. 1252. 55. 1315.
Lorges, captain de, 1521. 74. marſhal de, 1675. 76. 90-93. 1703.
Lorrain, province, 612. 855. kingdom, 867. 75. 80. 936. 74. 78. dutchy, 1419. 31. 1584. 95. 1634. 37. 63. 75. 76. 78. 80. 1700. Lewis, 880. 1585. Otho, 978. Charles, duke of the lower, 987. 88. 92. Gothelo, duke of the upper, 1037. Gerard d'Alface, 1056. René, 1443. 74. 76. 77. 1550. dutchy and peerage, 1527. 84. Iſabella, daughter of Charles II. 1431. 76. Charles III. 1585. 88. 90. 91. 95. See *Guiſe*; Charles IV. 1624. 28. 31-34. 36-41. 43. 46. 48. 49. 52. 54. 55. 57. 59. 61-63. 70. 74. his character, 1675. Charles V. 1634. 64. 69. 74-78. 83-86. 89. 90. Francis, 1634. 55. Margaret, 1631. 33. 43. 60. 72. Leopold, 1675. 97-99. Francis II. grand duke of Tuſcany, emperor, 1675. cardinal of, 1540. 47. 48. 55. 59. 61. 63. 74. 76. chevalier de, 1677. branches eſtabliſhed in France, 1550. Elizabeth Charlotte, 1671.
Lothaire, emperor, 814. 17. 23. 30. 31. 33. 35. 40-42. 45. 55. king of Italy, 986. king of Lorrain, 855. 58. 63. 67. king of France, 954. 57. 61. 86.
Loudun, treaty of, 1616. ſynod of, 1659.
Loup, 778.
Louvain, 1635. 1706.
Louveſtein, 1619.
Louvet, the preſident, 1424.

Louvois,

INDEX.

Louvois, 1661. 67. 68. 71. 78. 79. 81. 88. 89. his character, 1691. madam de, 1695.
Louvre, tower of the, 1380..... 1564. 1607. 17. 73. front of the, 1665.
Loyola, St. Ignatius of, 1521. 34.
Loyseau, p. 296. V. II.

LU.

Lubeck, 1328. 1629.
Luc, count du, 1712. 14. 15.
Luciana, p. 137. V. I.
Luçon, bishop of. See *Richelieu*.
Lucquois, country of the, 612.
Lude, count du, 1617. 69. duke, 1694.
Ludovic, See *Sforce*.
Ludovisio, pope, Gregory XV. 1622.... 46.
Ludres, madam de, 1675.
Luines, constable de, 1617. 19-21. 40. 72..... 1711.
Lulli, 1661. 73. 86.
Lunden, 1676.
Luneburg, duke de, 1640. 41. prince de, 1675.
Luneville, 1633. 34. 38.
Lupus, 771.
Lusace, 1620.
Lusignan, Guy de, king of Jerusalem, 1092. 1189. 91. Hugh, 1226. Guy, count d'Angouleme, 1302. town, 1574.

Luther, Lutheranism, 1517. 22. 34. 46. 48. 49. 51. 52. 59. See *Protestants*.
Lutter, battle of, 1629.
Lutzen, battle of, 1632.
Luxemburg, country, 1543. 1614. 39. 47. 78. 82-84. 96. 97. 1701. 13. house, 1697. Henry, emperor, 1305. Charles, emperor, 1478. Mary, 1475. Lewis, count de Ligni, 1499. Charles, afterwards Charles V. 1503. duke de, 1581. 90. 96. 1614. marshal de, 1581. 1655. 68. 72. 75-78. 80. 88. 90-95. Lewis de Brienne, 1643. chevalier de, 1709. l'abbé de, 1700. palace of, 1615. 94. See *Montmorenci, Laval,* &c.
Luxeuil, abbey, 612.
Luxury, 628. 1292. 1313. 64. laws sumptuary, 813.
Luz, baron de, 1613. St. John de, 1660.
Luzara, 1702.

LY.

Lyons, Lyonnois, 842. 79. 1037. councils of, 1245. 74. 1512. county of, 1309. city, 1490. 1557. 93. 94. 1630. 58. treaty of, 1503. 1601. primacy, 1702. court of monies, 1704.
Lyon-le-Saunier, 1637.

M.

MAboul, p. 91. V. II.
Machault, 1667.
Machiavel, p. 338. V. I.
Machine, of Marli, 1682. infernal, 1693.
Mâcon, 1238. 45.
Maçon, R. le, p. 273. V. I.
Madam, 1670.

Madellonnettes, 1618.
Mademoiselle, 1653. her character, 1693.
Madrid, 1525. 26. 1621. 25. 42. 1706. 10.
Magdeburg, 1636.
Magic, 1634.
Magistracy, 1558.

INDEX.

Magnac, 1702.
Maguellonne, 1536, p. 411. V. I.
Mahomet I. 622. 867. II. 867. 1451. IV. 1664. kings of Morocco, 1578.
Mahoni, 1706-08.
Majesty, title of, 1578. 1713.
Maids of honour, 1497. 1534. 1673.
Maid of Orleans, 1428. 30. 31.54.
Major, Majority, 1200. 70. 1371. 80. 91. 1407. 1559. 63. 1614. 51. p. 261. V. I.
Maillard, John, 1358.
Maillé, 1619.
Maillotins, 1383.
Maine, le, 1200. 15. 25. 58. 85. 1576. count du, 1480. Lewis-Auguſtus, duke du, 1598.1682. 88. 90. 92-95. 1710. 14. 15.
Mainfroi, 1255. 1516.
Maintenon, madam de, 1680. 86. 90. camp de, 1686.
Majority, treatiſe of, 1559. See *Major*.
Majorca, 799. 1349. Sancho, king of, 1316. 1706. 14. 15.
Maitre, John le, 1589. 93. 94.
Malachy, St. 1590.
Malady, p. 355. V. I.
Malaga, 1704.
Malandrins, 1361.
Mallaſſiſe, peace, 1570.
Malecontents, the war is carried on againſt them, 1617.
Mallum Imperatoris, 1135.
Malplaquet, 1709.
Malta, 1522. 30. 65. 1630. 97. 1714.
Maminot, Gilbert, p. 129. V. I.
Mammeluke, 1517.
Mancini, Olimpia, 1651. Laura, 1661. Hortenſia, 1661.
Mandelot, 1572.
Manheim, 1688.
Manicheans, 1022. 1206.
Manifeſto, 1585.
Vol. II.

Mans, king of, 510. biſhop, 1593. town, 1189.
Manſard, Francis, 1645. Harduin, 1691. 99. 1705.
Mansfeld, 1618. 21. 26. 42.
Mante, Philip, count de, 1108. town, 1223. 1365
Mantua, 1684. Francis II. marquis of, 1495. 1503. Francis III. 1543. dutcheſs of, 1600. Charles, 1629-31. Francis IV. 1629. Ferdinand,1629. Vincent, 1629. Charles III. 1652. 58. Charles IV.1081. 95.1704. dutchy of, 1629-31. 1701. 02. 06.
Manuſcripts, 1067.
Manufactures, 1603. 65.
Maraboduus, p. 40. V. I.
Marais, comedians of, 1609. quarter of, 1673.
Marcatrude, 593.
Mark of ſilver, p. 208. V. I.
Marcel, provoſt of the merchants, 1358.
Marche, Hugh de la, 1200. 26. 30. 42. 45. James, 1362.
Marchienne, 1645. 1712.
Marcian, battle of, 1554.
Marcigni, 1321.
Marck, Robert de la, 1521. Henrietta, 1559. Charlotte, 1591. Bouillon, p. 385. V. I.
Marcoueſe, 566.
Marcouſſi, 1650.
Mardyke,1645.46.57. 62.75.1715.
Marechal general, 1621. 60. 72.
Marechals of France, 1191. 1214. 1559. 94. 1643. 60. 67. 75. 93. 1703. 09. p. 239. 357. 287. V. I. tribunal, p. 309. V. II. of Normandy, 1358. de Champagne, 1358. de camp, 1547.
Marfée, la, 1641.
Margaret, wife of St. Lewis, 1245. p. 181. V. I. counteſs of Flanders, 1258. wife of Lewis Hutin, 1313. of Lewis XI. 1436.

B b   daughter

INDEX.

daughter of Lewis the Young, 1169. of Philip the Hardy, 1292. of Evreux, p. 249. V. I. of Valois, natural daughter of Charles VI. p. 271. V. I. of Scotland, 1436. daughter of Francis I. 1559. daughter of Maximilian, contracted to Charles VIII. 1482. 90. 1508. 29. 30. p. 327. V. I. of Flanders, 1384. Waldemar, 1391. of Scotland, 1445. of Austria, natural daughter of Charles the fifth, 1565. queen of Navarre, and sister of Francis I. 1525. 34. 49. first wife of Henry IV. 1571. 72. 74. 79. 99. of Anjou, 1471. of Lorrain, 1631. 33. 43.

Marguerie, de la, 1667.

Marriages, 1200. formerly subject to be annulled, 992. 96. of priests, 1103. 48. 1576. dissolution, 1156. 1313. 1499. 1529. 99. 1667. p. 100. 327. 339. V. I. 3. V. II. of Philip the Hardy, 1283. of Francis I. 1529. clandestine, 1556. 1629. 40. promise, 1604. of Gaston, 1631. 34. 36. of Charles IV. duke of Lorrain, 1633. 34. 43. 75. of Nicole, 1657. 75. of Lewis XIV. 1658. of Huguenots, 1682. of Monsieur, 1661. 71. duke of Burgundy, 1697. of Berry, 1710.

Mariendal, 1645. 1707.

Marignan, battle of, 1515.

Marigni, Enguerrand, 1309. 15. 24. p. 211. V. I.

Marillac, Michael de, 1624. 30. code, 1629. marshal de, 1632. 61.

Marin, master of the requests, 1667.

Marine, its antiquity, 539. Charlemain, 807. Philip-Augustus, 1206. St. Lewis, 1269. Philip de Valois, 1336. Coulon, 1479. Charles V. 1541. decline, 1589. admiral, 1627. Rochelle, 1628. Spain, 1638. 40. 41. 43. 46. 88. England, 1654. 55. 90. 92. 97. act of navigation, 1660. Dutch, 1666. 72. 74. 76. Indies, Brest, 1680-82. Genoese, 1684. 85. prizes, 1703. 07. 09-11. count de Touloufe, 1704. commission, 1661. p. 288. V. II.

Marlborough, 1688. 1703-09. 11. 12.

Marle, Henry de, p. 273. V. I.

Marli, 1682.

Marot, 1560. p. 261. V. I.

Marquisate, isle, 1706.

Marsaille, la, 1693.

Marsal, 1632. 62. 63.

Marsan, 1550.

Marseilles, 539. 1255. 1524. 34. 76. 96. 1660.

Marsillac, prince de, 1648. 50.

Marshal, Marshals. See Marechal, &c.

Marsin, count de, 1649. 50. 52. 67. marshal de, 1704. 06.

Martel, Charles, 715. 19. 25. 32. 34. 36. 37. 40. 41. marquis de, 1670.

Martene, 613.

Martin, St. 1226. p. 97. V. I. IV. 1283. p. 183. V. I. V. 1415. 31. mayor of the palace, 678.

Martinico, 1674. 93.

Martinozzi, Anne, 1654. Laura, 1655. 73. See Mazarin.

Martinuzzi, cardinal, 1526.

Mary, queen of Hungary, 1552. 56. wife of Philip the Hardy, 1275. p. 199. V. I. of Lewis XII. 1514. 15. Therefa, 1656. 59. 60. 65. 67. 83. 98. p. 91. V. II. Louisa, 1679. 89. queen of England, 1547. 53. 55. Stuart, 1558. 61. 68. 87. wife of

INDEX.

of the prince of Orange, 1673. 77. 95. Burgundy, 1477. 82. 1508. See *Medicis*; de Montpellier, 157. V. I.
Maseic, 1672.
Massillon, p. 91. V. I.
Massoure, battle of, 1249.
Master, in parliament, p. 211. V. I. of requests, 1269. 1497. 1629. 31. 48. of the wardrobe, 1671.
Masters de camp, 1661.
Mastricht, 1673. 76. 78.
Matha, John de, 1193. p. 121. V. I.
Matthias, emperor, 1617. 18. archduke, 1578.
Mathieu, abbot of St. Denis, 1269.
Mathilda, countess, 1067. betrothed to Henry, I. p.121. V. I. daughter of Henry, 1116. wife of Geoffry Plantagenet, 1135.
Mathurins, p. 121. V. I.
Matignon, 1589..... 1641. 99. Grace, 1708.
Matthew Paris, 1242. 52.
Maubeuge, 1678.
Maubuisson, 1252. 1349. p. 231. V. I.
Mauclerc, Peter de Dreux, count de Bretagne, 1226. 30. p. 137. V. I. John, 1383.
Maud, daughter of Henry, 1116. 1302. 16. 31.
Maugiron, 1578.
Maupertuis, 1355.
Maurevert, 1572.
Maurice, emperor, 587. elector of Saxony, 1547. 51. 52. prince of Orange, 1584. 90. 1604. 19-21. 25. bishop, 1223.
Maurienne, Humbert, count de, 1056.
Mausoleum, 1642.
Maxims of the Saints, 1699.
Maximilian I. emperor, 1477. 79. 80. 85. 88. 90. 93-95. 98. 1501.

08. 09. 11-13. 15. 16. 19. II. 1574. p. 408. V. I. See *Bavaria*.
Mayenne, branch of, 1550. duke de, 1587-91. 93-96. his death, 1611. Henry, duke de, 1614. 21.
Mayors of the palace, 613. 36. 44. 46. 56. 73. 88. 90. 714. 19. list of the, 41. V. I. their origin, p. 48. V. I.
Mazaniella, ringleader of the Neapolitans, 1647.
Mazarin, Julius, 1630. stands godfather at St. Germain en Laye, p. 90. V. II. cardinal, 1641-43. 45-49. 51-54. 56. 58. 59. 61. duke de, 1661. 63. 69..... 81. college, 1661. 73.

ME.

Measures and weights, 1321.
Meaux, the queen retires to, 1567. governor to, 1594. bishop of, 1622. 68. 98.
Mecca, la, 622.
Mechlin, 1706.
Mecklemburg, dukes of, 1631.
Medal, struck for Charles III. 1704.
Medavi, count de, 1706.
Medicis, Louis XI. honoured their arms with the scutcheon of France, 1483. Peter de, 1502. the, 1512. John, cardinal de, 1513. Laurence, 1517. cardinal de, 1523. Alexander, 1530. 31. 47. 55. 96. Catharine, 1517. 32. 59. 60. 64. 65. 68. 74. 75. 82. 84. 88. p. 385. V. I. Mary, 1600. 02. 10. 11. 13-17. 19. 20. 22. 24. 29-31. 34. 42.
Medina, descendants of Cerda, 1285. duke de, 1701. 10.
Mediterranean, advantages obtained in the, 1642.

INDEX.

Meilleraie, marshal de la, 1639-42. 44. 46. 61. dutchy and peerage, 1663.
Melac, M. de, 1702.
Melander, general, 1648.
Melun, town, 1590. Charles de, p. 313. V. I.
Memoir, of Enguerrand de Marigni, 1324. of the maid of Orleans, 1454. 55.
Menager, M. 1711. 12.
Menardeau, 1667.
Menars, 1682.
Mendoza, ambassador, 1590.
Menesses, Don Francisco de, 1656.
Menin, taken, 1658. 78. 1706.
Menton, de, 1496.
Mentz, regulations, 803. elector of, 1570. elector, 1632. town, 1631. 35. 36. 44. 88. 89.
Mequinença, taken, 1707.
Merchants, 1269. 1528.
Merci, general, 1642-45. count de, 1709.
Mercia, king of, 855.
Mercœur, duke de, 1590-92. 95. 96. 98. . . . 1656. 60.
Mercuriales, 1551. 59.
Meridian, first, 1634.
Merindol, execution of, 1545.
Merinville, marquis de, 1655.
Meroveus, king of France, 481. son of Chilperic I. 576. 77. son of Clotaire, 603. 84. p. 40. V. I.
Merovingians, end of the race, 750.
Merville, taken, 1645.
Mesmes, M. de, 1570. first president, p. 409. V. I.
Messina, siege of, 1283. revolt, 1674-76.
Mestezeau, Lewis de, 1627.
Metropolitan, p. 39. V. I.
Metz, Thierri reigns at, 511. siege, 1443. taken, 1552. siege raised, 1553. . . . 59. 1633. 48. 61.

80. 97.
Meudon, exchange of, 1695.
Meulan, Galeran, count de, 1040. town, 1365.
Mezeray, p. 36. 103. 113. V. I.
Mexico, Peter Arian sets out for, 1628.

MI.

Michaut, code, 1629.
Michael, king of Poland, 1676.
Micislaus, p. 90. V. I.
Mignard, first painter to the king, 1690.
Milan, Milanese, 568. Lewis II. 875. Valentine de, 1387. 1408. 98. domination of the viscounts, 1447. Ludovic Sforza, 1494. Lewis XII. 1498. conquest, 1499. 1500. investiture, 1504. council of Pisa transferred, 1511. . . . . 12. 15. 21. 22. 24. 26. 28. 29. 34. 35. 55. 76. 1609. 98. 1700. 06. 07.
Militia, French, 1690.
Millefleurs, treaty of, 1631.
Minard, president, 1559.
Minas, Las, 1705. 07.
Minden, 1679.
Mines, 1602.
Minions, the dauphin's, 1680.
Ministers, foreign, 1660. of state, 1689.
Minority, of emperors, 1056. 1206. of John Lackland, 1200. under the third race, p. 180. V. I. St. Lewis, 1226. of Charles VI. 1380. ordinance, 1401. 1613. See *Majority, Regency*.
Minorca, the island taken, 799. 1707. 13.
Minutes signed by the parties, 1560. 69.
Mioffans, 1650.
Mirabels, 1628.
Miracle of the sacred host, 1285.
Miramolin, 1206.

Mirandola,

INDEX.

Mirandola, taken, 1511. 1702. 04. 05.
Mirebeau, M. de, 1610.
Mirefleur, 566.
Misnia, la, 1636.
Miſſi Dominici, 800. 1135. p. 292. 293. V. II.
Miſſion, prieſts of the, 1632.
Mitilene, iſle of Leſbos, 803.
Mittau, city, 1705.

MO.

Mode, or faſhion of wearing ſhort hair, in the reign of Francis I. 1521. See *Uſages*.
Modena, army of the duke, 1637. 46. 48. 49. 55-58. death of the, 1658. .... 73. 1702. 04. 06. 07.
Mohacs, battle of, 1526.
Moine, cardinal of, 1215.
Moldavia, 1699.
Mole, of Gatari in Biſcay, 1638. la, 1574. 76.
Mole, 1589. 94. 1632.
Moleſme, 1092.
Moliere, 1673.
Molſeim, 1675.
Monaco, Honorius, prince of, 1641. Anthony, 1641. 99.
Monaldeſchi, 1657.
Monarchy, reunited in the reign of Clotaire I. and II. 560. 613. 28. opinion in regard to our, p. 36. V. I. Monarchy of Sicily, 1605.
Monaſteries, 840.
Monaſtic, order, p. 39. V. I.
Moncallier, 1639.
Monceaux, 1567. marquis de, 1598.
Monclar, 1677. 81. 88.
Monçon, treaty of, 1625. taken, 1642. 43. 50. 1707.
Monitories, 1560. 89.
Monk, general, 1653. 60. 66.
Monks, 1576. 90. See *Religious*, p. 39. V. I. inherit the eſtates of their relations, p. 98. V. I.

Money, gold of Theodebert, 539. 774. right of coining, 992. ordinances, 840. 1258. 68. alteration, 1309. 13. 15. 44. 64. 1445. p. 208. V. I. the firſt with a buſt, 1490. ..... p. 327. V. I. chamber of, 1551. Lewis I. prince of Condé, 1567. ediƈt of, 1602. Francis II. p. 400. V. I. .... 1689. bills of, 1704. court of, 1704. p. 290. V. I.
Mons en Puelle, battle of, 1304.
Monſeigneur, ſon of Lewis XIV. birth of, 1661. ... 74. marriage of, 1679. 80. .... 82. 86. 88. 90. 91. 93-95. 1711.
Monſieur, brother of Lewis XIV. his marriage, 1661. .... 70. marries a ſecond time, 1671. ... 72. 76. 77. 79. 92. 1700. death of, 1701.
Monſigot, maſter of accounts, 1631.
Montaigu, John de, p. 273. V. I. chapel of, 1499. college, p. 211. V. I.
Montal, de, 1653. 72. 76. 77. 95.
Montargis, is reunited to the crown, 1215. ſiege, 1426. treaty of, 1485.
Montauban, revolt of, 1573..... 1621. 29.
Montauſier, duke de, 1661. 68. madam de, 1661. 65.
Montbazon, erection of the dutchy and peerage of, 1588. M. de, 1610. madam de, 1643.
Montbelliard, 1676.
Montbrun, chief of the Huguenots, 1575.
Montcontour, battle of, 1569.
Montdejeu, 1654.
Montdidier, taken, 1470.
Montecuculli, general, 1648. 64. 73. 75.
Montemar, 1708.

B b 3 *Monteran*,

INDEX.

Monteran, bridge of, 1419.
Monterei, count de, 1674. 77.
Montespan, madam de, 1680. 1707.
Montesquieu, 840. 1270. 1670.
Montesquiou, 1569, marshal de, 1711.
Montfaucon, 1315. 1572. p. 211. V. I.
Montferrat, count de, 1092. Conrad, marquis of, 1191. Boniface, 1204. N. marquis of, 1401. conquest of, 1544. 1613. 15. 30. 1708.
Montfort, Bertrade de, 1092. p. 127. V. I. count de, 1108. Simon, 1296. 58. 69. Amauri, 1223. 24. John, 1341. 64. 79. 81.
Montgommeri, de Lorges, sieur de, 1521. 47. 74. p. 385. V. I. ... 1688.
Months, division of the, 1553.
Montholon, Francis de, 1541. 88. lord keeper, 1590. 1670. 72.
Montigni, marshal de, 1616.
Montlberi, count of, 1108. battle of, 1465.
Montluc, John de, 1313. 1554. 67. John de, bishop of Valence, 1573. 94.
Montmartre, abbey, p. 137. V. I. treaty of, 1663.
Montmædi, taken, 1657.
Montmelian, taken, 1691. 1705.
Montmirail, taken, 1169. 70.
Montmorenci, Matthew II. 1214. 23. p. 123. 159. V. I. Anne, constable de, 1527. 39. 47. 96. 1614. 25. baron of, 1451. 1551. duke de, 1555. 57. 59. 60. 67. 74. 77. Francis, marshal de, 1575. Charles, p. 270. V. I. Margaret, 1609. Henry, 1614. the constable de Montmorenci's lady, 1619. duke de, 1627. 28. 30. 32. Beaufort erected into a dutchy under this name, 1688.

Montmouth, 1685.
Montpellier, count, 1156. Mary de, p. 157. V. I. barony de, 1258. assembly, 1275. university, 1283. court of aids, 1477. town, 1316. 49. 65. 78. 1621. 28. first bishop, p. 411. V. I.
Montpensier, count de, 1496. duke de, 1541. 57. 74. 83. 89. 91. 92. p. 384. V. I. madam de, 1589. mademoiselle, 1626. 52. 60. 71. 82. 93. p. 90. V. II, castle, p. 175. V. I.
Montpesat, 1324.
Montresor, 1636.
Montreuel, marshal of France, 703.
Montreüil, Edward, 1329. John de, p. 275. V. I.
Montrond, 1652.
Montross, 1650.
Montsoreau, the lady of, 1472. the lord of, 1579.
Moor, sir Thomas, 1534.
Moors, 715. 827. 50. 1206. 1492. 1516. 78.
Mora, river, 1645. Christopher de, 1598.
Morangis, 1667.
Morat, siege of, 1476.
Morea, 1699. grand signior, 1714.
Moret, count of, 1631. 32.
Moriscos, 1610.
Mornai du Plessis, 1600.
Morocco, 1578. 1635. 99.
Mortara, town, 1658.
Mortemar, 1650. 69.
Mortmain, 1275. 1328.
Morville, 1701.
Mosarabic, 715.
Mothe, la, 1634. 45. aux Bois, 1645. Houdancourt, 1639. 41. 45. 48. 52. ... 1703. 08. St. Herai, 1587. the marshal's lady, 1661.
Mothers, edict concerning them, 1567.
Motte, bridge, 1589.

Moulins,

INDEX.

Moulins, ordinance of, 1566.
Mountain, the old man of the, 1230.
Mourning, 1514.
Mouzon, 1521. 1639. 53.
Moyen-Mouſtier, 612.
Moyenvic, 1631. 48. 61.
MU.
Mulberg, battle of, 1547.
Mulhauſen, 1305. 1674.
Mummol, 568. 77.
Mundana lex, 511.
Munderkinghen, 1703.
Munſter, 1689. peace of, 1644. 47. 48. 97. biſhop of, 1665. 66. 71. 72. 74.
Murder. See *Aſſaſſination*.

Muret, count de, 1711..... p. 409. V. I.
Murtzulphus, emperor, 1204.
Muſcovy, *Muſcovites*, their power fixed by Alexander duke of Ruſſia, p. 209. V. I. falſe Demetrius, 1605.... 1611. 99. 1704. 05. 08-10. 13. la, 1711. 14.
Muſic, 1661.
Muſqueteers, 1622. 66. 77. 99.
Muſtapha, Cara, 1683.
Mutzig, 1675.
Muyden, 1672.
MY.
Myſteries, repreſentation of the, 1179. 1401. p. 311. V. II.

N.

N*Aſeby*, battle of, 1645.
Naerden, taken, 1672. 1673.
Nails, 1191.
Namur, count, p. 157. V. I. ſiege of, 1678. 92. 95. 1701. 04. 13.
Nancy, taken, 1475 - 77. town, 1633. 61. 1702.
Nantes, 591. ſiege of, 1486. edict of, 1598. 1622. 69. 85..... 1652. 61. mademoiſelle de, 1685.
Nanterre, Matthew de, 1465.
Nanteuil, village, 593.
Nantilde, 636. 44.
Nantouillet, chevalier de, 1677.
Naples, *Neapolitans*, kingdom, 1026. 1326. 55. 93. 1495. Frederic II. 1292. maſſacre, 1282. 83. ſeparation of, 1292. Joan, 1341. 44. 82. Lewis duke of Anjou, 1389. René, 1431. 43. 73. 80. Ferdinand, 1493. 94. Alphonſo, 1493..... 94. 95. Ferdinand, 1495. 96. Lewis XII, 1498. 1500-03. 05..... 25. ſiege of, 1528. league, 1555. revolt, 1647-48.... 98. ...

1701.... 06... 07.
Narbonne, province, 1156. 1258. 83. metropolis, 1252. city, 1642. cardinal de, 1505.
Nargonne, Francis de, 1589.
Narſes, 539. 68.
Narva, the czar, 1700. taken, 1704.
Naſſau, 1296. William, 1565. Maurice, 1600. 10. count de, 1636. William, 1638. See *Orange*, prince of, 1703.
Navailles, 1658. 65. 69. 74-78. 83.
Navarre, college, 1302. Jane, 1302. Peter, 1512. Calignon, chancellor, 1598. Navarrois, 827. the crown, 1252. 70. 1548. Philip IV. 1283. Lewis Hutin, 1314. Philip the Long, 1316. 28. p. 230. V. I. count d'Evreux, p. 199. 221. V. I. Charles the Bad, 1352. 55. 57. 58-60. 64. 65. 78. 87. John, king of Arragon, 1454. 62. Ferdinand, 1512. Charles

B b 4   V.

INDEX.

V. 1516. Henry d'Albret, 1521. Margaret, 1525. 34. 49. Antony, 1559. 60. 62. 69. Jane d'Albret, 1548. 69. 72. Henry IV. 1569. 72. 74. 76. 77. 79. 80. 84. 87. 89. reunion of, 1607.

Naude, p. 273. V. I.

Navigation, 1627. 60. See *Marine*.

NE.

Nelson, fort, 1697.
Nemours, dutchy, 1331. James d'Armagnac, duke de, 630. 1477. Lewis, 1501. 03. Gaston de Foix, 1505. 11. 12. Philip of Savoy, 1528. James of Savoy, 1596. 1640. 48. 51. 52. Henry of Savoy, 1654. madam de, 1694. 99. 1707.
Nerac, conference of, 1579.
Nereftan, 1608.
Nerwind, battle of, 1693.
Nefle, Simon, count de, 1269.
Nefmond, 1695-97.
Neftorius, doctrine of, 794.
Netherlands, Philip, son of Maximilian, 1499. Margaret, 1508. 30. Mary of Austria, 1552. .... 55. 65-67. 78. 80. 81. 84. Albert, 1596. 98..... 1621. 39. 42. 62. 68. 75. 1701. 02. 12. 13.
Nevers, *Nivernois*, Renaud, p. 105. 113. V. I. Landry, count de, 1001. 02. Philip the Hardy, 1394. count de, 1505. duke de, 1558. 74. 91. 93. 95. 1614. 29. 66. p. 384. V. I. madam de, 1574. Mancini, 1661. John count de, p. 307. V. II.
Neufchatel, 1514. 1694. 99. states of, 1707. 13.
Neuhaufel, 1685.
Neus, 1642.
Neuftad, taken, 1688.
Neuftria, afterwards called *Nor-mandy*, 622. 46. 742. 841. 42. 58. 79. 912. p. 45. V. I.
Neutrality, treaty of, 1633.
Neuville, Nic. de, 1547.
Newburg, duke of, 1609. 10. 14. 69. 87. town, 1639. 1702. 03. 07.
Newbury, battle of, 1643.
Newport, 1600. 1701. 06. 13.

NI.

Nice, 1538. siege of, 1543..... 1647. taken, 1691. 1705. 06.
Nice, second council, 794. 1215. 1562.
Nicephorus, 803. 07.
Nicolai, de, 1686.
Nicholas I. 861. II. 1056.
Nicole, dutchess, 1624. 33. 34. 37. 57. 75.
Nicopolis, battle of, 1394. 96.
Nicot, p. 9. V. II.
Niefter, 1694.
Nieudam, the taking of fort, 1647.
Nights, the French reckon by, p. 40. V. I.
Nimeguen, diet, 830.. : .. 1672. congress, 1675. peace, 1678. 79. 83. 97... 1702.
Ninove, 1706.
Niort, taken, 1223.
Nifmes, 1258. 63. 82.

NO.

Noailles, Francis, 1558. 72. 84. dutchy and peerage, 1663. duke de, 1689. 91. marshal de, 1643. 94. 95. cardinal, 1695. bailiff de, 1697. duke de, 1704. 07. 09-11.
Nobility, Fiefs, 840. 1149. 1200. 70. 73. 13.13. 28. 58. 71. 1579. 1600. Venetians, 1515..... p. 95. V. I. 309. V. II.
Nogaret, 1303. 04.

Nogent,

INDEX.

Nogent, le Rotrou, p. 237. V. I. le Roi, p. 237. V. I. fur Seine, 533.
Nointel, 1683. 85.
Noirmontier, 1663.
Nomeni, treaty of, 1663.
Nomenoe, duke of the Bretons, 845.
Nomination, right of, p. 312. V. I.
Nominals, p. 129. V. I.
Noradin, 1145. 47.
Norbert, St. 1120.
Normandy, *Normans*, people, 807. 40. 50. 53. 80. 82. 92. 912. 24. 92. fiege of Paris, 885. 88. Rollo, 929. William, 942. Richard, 945. Lothaire, 961. peerage, 992. in Italy, 1026. towns refigned, 1032. difputes, 1047. Richard, p. 113. V. I. reunion with England, 1100. Englifh, 1113. 16. 20. 27. 79. 1331. Roger, 1130. 50. Philip Auguftus, 1192. 1200. reunion with the crown, 1215. Henry, 1223. 58. Charles, 1355. exchequer, 1285. 1499. p. 299. V. II. Edward, 1344. 60. 61. king John, 1362. Charles VI. 1415. Charles VII. 1448. ....
66. 68. 72. 99. 1549. 92. 1620. 50. 74. 92. duke of, p. 299. V. II.
North, kings of, 823. 1542. war of the, 1700.
Northumberland, duke of, 1553.
Nortlingen, battle of, 1634. 45.
Norway, 1391.
Noferai, taken, 1639.
Notables, affembly, 1558. 96. 1617. 26.
Notaries, 1309. 12. 1410. 14. 1579. See *Secretaries*.
Notre-Dame, church, 1180. 1304. 76. 1431. 1547. 1643.
Novarre, fiege of, 1495. 1512. battle of, 1513. .... 21.
Noue, la, 1567. 91.
Novempopulani, 593.
Novion, de, 1689.
Noyers, Sublet des, 1641-43.
Noyon, treaty de, 1516.

NU.

Nuits, Peter de, 1628. fiege of, 1474. .... 1671. 79.
Nuncio, the pope's, 1639. 62. 86. 88.
Nuptials, edict concerning, 1560.
Nuremberg, golden bull, 1355. diet, 1500. treaty of, 1532.

O.

O d', 1704. p. 7. V. II.
, *Oak*, the royal, 1660.
Oath, relicks, 1022. of allegiance, 1223.

OB.

Obdam, admiral, 1665. baron d', 1703.
Obedience to Benedict XIII. 1401.
Oblats, 1671.
Obfequies, p. 409. V. I.

Obfervatory, 1665.

OC.

Ocean, 789.

OD.

Oder, 1648.
Odet, d'Aidie, 1469.
Odoacer, king of Italy, 493.

Offem

INDEX.

OF.

Offembourg, taken, 1703. 07.
Office, 1316. 87. 1467. 1567. 1600. 31. p. 302. &c. V. II.
Offices, creation of, 1690. of the crown, 1600. sale of, 1515. public, 1567. p. 38. V. I. 302. &c. V. II.

OG.

Ogier, the Dane, a romance, p. 199. V. I.
Ogine, 929.

OL.

Oleron, isles of, 1653.
Olim, 1313.
Oliva, treaty of, 1660. peace, 1697.
Olivares, duke d', 1621. 25. 40. 42. 61.
Olivença, 1657.
Olivier, murder, 1344. 80. chancellor, 1559. 60.
Olmutz, 1642.
Olonne, bombarded, 1696.
Onfroi, 1026.
Onufres, 1645.

OP.

Oppede, 1545.
Oppenheim, 1644. 88.
Opra Pitracha, 1688.

OR.

Oran, 1708.
Orange, city, 1713. history of this house, 1584. 1654. 1703. William, 1565. 66. 69. 71. 78. 81-84. Maurice, 1584. 1619-21. 25. Frederic - Henry, 1584. 1625. 34. 35. 37. 38. 44-46. William II. 1584. 1660. 72. William III. 1660. 66. 78. 87-97. 99. his character, 1702. Mary his wife, 1673. 77. 95. university, 1365.

Oration, funeral, p. 409. V. I. 3. 91. V. II.
Oratory, foundation of, 1612.
Orbitello, siege of, 1646. 1707.
Orçai, Boucher d', 1590.
Orchies, taken, 1645.
Ordinances, 1574. of Philip-Augustus, 922. in favour of the Jews, 1206. called Quarantaine, 1245. of St. Gilles, 1252. on the coin, 1258. 1344. blasphemers, 1258. of camp de Roncal, 1269. majority, 1270. mortmain, 1275. on luxury, 1292. private wars, 1296. 1371. reformation of the kingdom, 1302. usury, 1313. excludes the bishops from parliament, 1319. of Philip the Long, 1321. free fiefs, 1328. to incorporate counsellors, judges, and reporters, 1344. on gaming, 1369. majority of the kings, and the regency, 1371. goods of the bishops, 1385. concerning the tutelage of the children of France, and the regency, 1391. election of presidents, 1397. majority, 1401. 07. concerning annuities, 1441. permitting suits by proxy, 1484. of Villiers-Cotterets, 1539. d'Orleans, 1355. 1560. 64. 1680. of Roussillon, 1564. of Moulins, stiled of the Domain, 1355. 1532. 66. p. 298. 301. V. II. of Moulins for the reformation of the law, 1566. of Blois, 1579. 80. 1600. of the police touching the comedians, 1609. civil, 1667. criminal, 1670.
Ordinary, 1397.
Ordination, 796.
Ordonnance, company of, 1600.
Order, wives of the second, p. 51. V. I.
Orders, Hospitallers, Templars, and Teuto-

INDEX.

Teutonics, 1092. of Malta, 1522. of the redemption of captives, 1193. of friars preachers, 1215. of the ship and crescent, 1269. abolition of the Templars, 1309. of the Garter, 1349. 1564. of the Star, 1350. 51. of the Girdle of Hope, 1389. of St. Michael, 1469. 1516. 23. 27. 59. of the Golden Fleece, 1430. 83. 1516. 29. 55. of the Porcupine, 1515. of the Holy Ghost, 1579. 1620. 33. 62. 89. of St. Lazare, 1608. of Mountcarmel, 1608. of Montpellier, 1700. of St. Lewis, 1693.
Organ, 756.
Oriflamme, 1135. 1415.
Oriftan, taken, 1637.
Orleans, council, 511. kingdom, 533. 93. ... 1022. university, 1305. Lewis, duke d', 1397. 1401. 07. 08. Charles, 1410. 15. 40. Lewis XII. 1484. Lewis, 1498. Charles, 1545. faction, 1410. 14. siege, 1428. 29. city, 1652. Henrietta, 1670. states, 1560. 62. 63. 67. 94. Philip, 1671. 1703. 06-08. 12. Berri, 1686. 1700. 10. 12. 14. bishopric, 1622. See *Monsieur*; maid of, 1428. 30. 54. Lewis d', advocate, 1589. palais d', 1694. duke d', 1653. 1701. school of law, 1680. ordinance, 1355. 60. 64. 1680.
Ormesson, d', 1661.
Ormond, marquis d', 1649. duke d', 1702. 12.
Ornano, marshal d', 1594 . . . . .
1626. madam d', 1631.
Orsoi, count d', 1672.
Ortes, count d', 1572.
Orvietto, canonization of St. Lewis at, p. 181. V. I.

OS.

Osnabrug, conference, 1647. treaty of, 1648.
Ossa, James d', 1313.
Ossat, Arnauld d', 1593. 95. 98.
Osson, duke d', 1618. 94. 1707.
Ostalric, 1694.
Ostend, taken, 1604. 1706.
Ostrogoths, Theodoric, king of 500. 08. . . . 35. 36. 68.
Othelin, 1285.
Otho, duke of Burgundy, 956. the great, emperor, 912. 36. 40. 41. 45. 47. 73. II. 974. 78. III. 996. 1001. IV. 1206. 14. of Brunswic, 1382. See *Lorrain*.
Ottoboni, 1689.
Ottocare, 1282.
Ottoman empire, 1296. 98.

OU.

Oudenard, 1658. 67. 68. 74. 1701. 06. 08.
Overissel, the province taken, 1672.
Ouin, 1597.
Owen Tudor, 1420.

OX.

Oxenstiern, chancellor, 1633. 34. 47. 78.

INDEX.

P.

P*Acification*, of Paſſau, 1552. edict of, 1563. 76. 91. of Ulm, 1620.... 29.
Pacta conventa, 1697.
Paderborn, 772. 76.
Padille, Mary, 1366.
Padua, 1509.
Pajot, Marianne, 1675.
Painting, academy of, 1663.
Peers, Peerage, beginning of the peerages of France, divers opinions concerning their original, they depend on the crown, eccleſiaſtic peers, 922..... 1451. p. 225. 259. V. I. dukedom of Burgundy, 1001. rank of the peers at the coronation, 1179. rank at trial, p. 177. V. I. court of peers to which John Lackland is ſummoned, 1200. ſummons to the court of peers, 1292. firſt letters of erection of Britany into a dutchy and peerage, after the county and peerage of Champagne had been reunited to the crown, 912. 1296. letters of the ſame kind for the counties of Anjou and Artois, 1296. erection of the barony of Bourbon, 1324. peerage of Orleans, p. 237. V. I. trial of the count d'Artois, 1331. erection of Beaumont-le-Roger into a county and peerage, 1331. John, the eldeſt ſon of Philip de Valois, is emancipated and made a peer, to the end that there be a ſufficient number of peers at the trial of the count d'Artois, 1331. peerage of Flanders, 1361. Philip the Hardy is made duke of Burgundy, and firſt peer of France, 1361. p. 270. V. I. he aſſiſts ſingly at the coronation of Charles VI. p. 270. V. I. difference in the peerages, 1451. trial of the peers, 1457. they guaranty the treaties of peace, 1482. the county of Nevers is the firſt peerage created in favour of a foreign prince, 1505. the county of Nemours erected into a dutchy and peerage, 1505. erection of the county of Angouleme into a dutchy and peerage, 1515. peerage of Dunois, 1525. the eſtate of Guiſe erected into a dutchy and peerage, 1527. juriſdiction, 1527. Nemours, 1528. the emperor Charles V. cited before the court of peers, 1537. the duke de Montpenſier, as prince of the blood, precedes the duke de Nevers, a more ancient peer than himſelf, at the ceremony of the coronation, 1541. p. 384. V. I. the barony of Montmorency created a dutchy and peerage, 1451. 1551. the peers begin to ſit in parliament with their ſwords on, 1551. ordinance touching the dutchies and peerages, 1566. peerages of wives, 1572. declaration publiſhed at Blois, in regard to the precedency of dukes and peers, 1576. erection of the county of Joyeuſe and the barony of Epernon into a dutchy and peerage, 1581. erection of the dutchy and peerage of Luxemburg, hiſtory of that dutchy, 1581. erection of the dutchy and peerage of Montbazon, remarks on this ſubject, 1588. arret, 1591. the dutchy of Thouars erected into

INDEX.

into a peerage, 1595. the privileged precedency of the dukes de Joyeuse and d'Epernon abolished, 1596. dutchy and peerage of Beaufort and Vendome, its privileges, 1598. Biron, after having been erected into a dutchy and peerage, becomes a barony again, and is once more created a peerage, 1602. Rohan, 1603. Tully erected into a dutchy and peerage, 1606. Brissac erected into a dutchy and peerage, 1611. the ecclesiastic peers yield the precedency to the cardinals, 1614. dutchy and peerage of Luines, 1619. dutchy and peerage of Halluin, anecdote, 1620. dutchy and peerage of Rochefoucaut, 1622. Richelieu erected into a dutchy and peerage, 1631. dutchy and peerage of St. Simon, 1635. la Force, 1637. erection of the dutchy and peerage of Aiguillon, history of that dutchy, 1638. dutchy of Valentinois, history of that dutchy, 1641. dutchies and peerages of Rohan Chabot, Estrées, Grammont and Tresmes, 1648. suppression of the house of peers in England, 1649. Mortemart, dutchy and peerage, 1650. Albret, Chateau-Thierry and Villeroy, created dutchies and peerages, 1651. Villars-Brancas, 1652. Nevers, anecdote, 1661. of Rendan, 1663. la Meilleray, Mazarin, St. Aignan, Noailles, Coislin, created dutchies and peerages, 1663. Aumont, 1665. la Valliere, 1667. Charost, 1673. archbishopric of Paris, 1674. ranks above the peers, 1694. of Penthievre, 1697. Boufflers, 1708. Villars and Harcourt, 1709. Warti,

1710. famous edict concerning the dutchies and peerages, Chaulnes and Antin, erected into dutchies and peerages, 1711. of Rambouillet, 1711. Rohan-Rohan, 1714. Joyeuse, 1714. Hostun, 1715. See *Commissioners*, *Rank*, &c.

Palace, fired, 1618. royal, 1642. 92. re-establishment of bailiwicks, 1684.

Paladins, 1026.

Palamos, taken, 1694. . . . 95.

Palatine, *Palatinate*, Frederic V. elector, 1619. 20. 32. 39. 48. . . . . 59. 74. 75. 81. 84. 89. 93. 1703. . . . . c6. . . . 09. princess, 1651. 84. Charlotte, 1671.

Paleologus, Michael, emperor, 867. 1204. Andrew, 1494. Constantine, 1494.

Palestine, 1067.

Palermo, Ant. of, p. 311. V. I.

Palice, la, 1512.

Palma, taken, 1715.

Palsey, p. 145. V. I.

Palauu, 1647. 48. 52.

Palmiers, made a bishopric, 1292. 1303. taken, 1628. bishop of, 1673.

Pampelona, 1521.

Pamphilio, 1644.

Pannonia, 803.

Papachim, 1688.

Paper, stamped, 1655.

Papinian, 1408.

Pappenheim, 1631.

Par, Catharine, 1547.

Paraclet, 1140.

Paramount, 922.

Parck, Thomas, 1635.

Paré, Ambrose, 1572.

Paris, capital of the kingdom, 508. enlarged, 1550. Childebert I. 1558. Chilperic, 562. possessed jointly, 566. Childebert II. 584. part reunited, 593. council,

INDEX.

council, 615. 1206. bishop, 657. siege, 885. count, 888. archbishopric, 1622. dutchy and peerage, 1674. Hugh Capet, 987.˙ dutchy of France, 1108. church,1161. Notre-Dame,1180. St. Lewis, 1352. states, 1355. police, 1269. 1697. troubles, 1358. 59. 83. 1404. 07. 10.14. 36. 64. 1587-90. 92. 93. 1648. 49. 1709. Bastile, 1369. emperor, 1378. impression, 1470. provostship,1560. barrier, 1550. chapter, 1561. St. Bartholomew, 1572. custom, 1580. the sixteen, 1585. contraction,1594. contagion, 1596. comedians, 1609. assembly, 1612. governor, 1687. 95. p. 7. V. II.

Parish, chapel, of St. Roch, erected, 1633.

Parliaments, ancient, 616. Aix-la-Chapelle,796. the king's assizes, 1135. of All-Saints, 1296. origin of, 1305. of Paris, 1319. 22. 29. Montfort, 1341. counsellors, 1344. 69. 71. assembly, 1359. p. 98. V. I. captal de Buch, 1397. Poitiers, 1415. Amiens, 1419. 36. 1522. continual, 1422. appeals, 1527. indult, 1538. 40. legate, 1547. swords, 1551. constitutes a fourth order, 1558-60. register, Rouen, 1562-64. arret, 1567. 68. St. Bartholomew, 1572. 76. 85. Harlay, 1588. in the Bastile, 1589. Tours and Chalons, 1591. president le Maitre, returned, 1593. 94. 96. breviary, 1602. regency, 1610. bed of justice, 1614. 15. rank, 1627. arret annulled, 1632. troubles, 1648-53. registers,1668. chamber of the edict, 1669. 74. congress abolished, 1677. appeal to the council, 1688-90. bull vineam, 1705. constitution, 1714. great almoner ought to say grace, p. 409. V. I. 301. 305. V. II. of Grenoble, 1451. 1644. of Aix, 1501. 90. of Bourdeaux, 1462. 1594. 1679. p. 300. V. II. of Pau, 1620. of Tournay, 1668. of Besançon, 1674. of Burgundy,1477. of Bretagne, 1553. of Metz, 1633. of Rouen, 1499. 1563. 1639. of Toulouse,1305. 1594. 1679. p. 300. V. II. of Milan, 1515. of England,1258. 1628. 39-41. 48. 1706.

Parma, dutchy, 1551. duke of, 1555. 81. 88. 90. 92. 1635. 37. 41. 44. 97. dutchess of, 1565. princess of, 1714.

Partition of the crown, 805. 17. 30. 36. 55. 75. 954. 1283. p. 39. 43. V. I. treaty of, 1698-1700.

Party, 1707.

Pas, du, 1673.

Pascal, Blaise, 840. pope I. 823. II. 1103. III. 1171.

Pasquier, 840. p. 304. V. II.

Pasquin, 1691.

Passage, 1638. 98. of the Rhine, 1672.

Passau, pacification, 1552..... 1703. 04.

Passerat, 1593.

Passion, brothers of the, 1401.

Pastors, 1067.

Patay, 1428.

Patriarch of Constantinople, 867. 1215. Ignatius, 867. Latin,867. p. 39. V. I.

Patrician, Clovis, 508. Charlemain, 774.

Patrimony of the prince, p. 299. V. II.

Pavia, 568. battle of, 1525. treaty of, 1617. siege of, 1655.

Paul I. 767. II. 1465. III. 1555. IV. 1555. 56. V. 1465. Jovius, 1536.

Paula, Francis of, p. 309. V. I.

Paulette,

INDEX.

Paulette, 1604.
Payen, counsellor, 1631.

PE.

Peace, Clovis, 508. Lewis the Fat, 1120. Montmirail, 1169. Flanders, 1320. king of Navarre, 1359. Biceſtre, 1410. England, 1419. Arras, 1435. Conflans, 1465. Charles VIII. 1493. Noyon, 1516. Creſpy, 1544. Henry VIII. 1546. Edward VI. 1560. 58. Cateau-Cambreſis, 1559. Charles IX. 1563. 64. Longjumeau, 1568. lame peace, 1570. Turks, 1572. 73. Henry III. 1576. 77. 80. of Nemours, 1585. Rouen, 1588. duke de Mayenne, 1595-98. Lubeck, 1629. Queraſque, 1631. of Weſtphalia, 1648. of the Pyrenees, 1659. of Vincennes, 1661. of Breda, 1667. Aix-la-Chapelle, 1668. of Clement IX. 1669. plenipotentiaries, 1673. of Nimeguen, 1678. 79. Savoy, 1696. Riſwick, 1697. d'Oliva, 1697. Carlowitz, 1699. Utrecht, 1711. 13. Raſtad, Baden, 1714.
Peaſants, 1358.
Pedro, don, 1667.
Peliſſier, p. 411. V. I.
Peliſſon, 1661.
Pelletier, 1683. 89.
Pellevé, 1593.
Pence, St. Peter's, 855.
Penance, of Lewis the Debonnaire, 822.
Penſions, 1643. 63. 77.
Pentecoſt, Henry III. 1579.
Penthievre, Jane the Lame, 1341. 64....1419. 24. count de, 1451. duke de Mercœur, 1590. 98.
Pepin, 644..... 78. 88. 90. 92. 95. 714. 15. 31-47. 51. 53. 56. 58. 67. ... 814. 17. 30. 35. .... 40. 41. 45. 75. 1150. his tomb, p. 45. V. I.

Perefixe, p. 90. V. II.
Perellos de Roccafull, 1697.
Pery, 1705. 06.
Perigny, de, 1661.
Perigord, 585. 1223. 25. 58. 1369. 1592.
Perkins, 1492.
Perlis, baron de, 1694.
Permiſſion of the judge to arreſt for debt, 1702.
Peronne, 922. 29. 1468. 1536. 76. 1655.
Perpignan, 1473. 1542. 1642. 59. 74.
Perrault, Charles, 1665.
Perron, du, 1591. 95. 1600. 17.
Perſia, 800. 1715.
Peru, 1624.
Perugia, 1574. 1708.
Peſcaire, 1525.
Peſtilence, 823. 1269. 1348. 1496. 1576.
Peter, of Piſa, 789. the Cruel, king of Arragon, 1206. 82. 83. 1516. p. 157. V. I. king of Spain, 1366. 67. de Dreux, 1226. the Venerable, 1140. Charlot, p. 157. V. I.
Petit, John, 1408. William, 1547.
Peyrere, la, 1634.

PF.

Pflug, 1548.

PH.

Phalſbourg, princeſs of, 1631...61.
Pharo, 807.
Pheaſants, iſle of, 1659.
Philibert II. duke of Savoy, 1508. 30.
Philip I. 1056. 60. 1101. an infant, 1127. 30. II. ſurnamed Auguſtus, 1180. 1215. III. ſurnamed the Hardy, 1255. 70. 83. 1348. IV. ſurnamed the Fair, 1283. 85. 92. 1304. p. 303. V. I. V. ſurnamed the Long, 1285. 1316. VI. of Valois, 1328. de Rouvre, 1361.

count

INDEX.

count of Flanders, 1179. 80. count de Boulogne, 1226. emperor of the west, 1206. 14. I. king of Spain, surnamed the Handsome, 1482. league, 1495. 99. treaty, 1503-05. II. marriage, 1548. 54. 55. St. Quentin, 1557. espoused Elizabeth, 1558. 59. John of Austria, 1571. Netherlands, 1578. revolution of Portugal, divested of the sovereignty of the Netherlands, suspected of poisoning the prince of Orange, 1580-82. fleet, 1588. league, 1590. 91. 98. treaty of Brusol, 1610. 61. III. 1598. p. 31. V. I. Moriscos, 1610. 17. 21. 61. IV. 1621. treaty against, 1635. war, 1640. 44. peace, 1659. 61. 65. V. his birth, 1683. 85. king of Spain, 1700-10. 12. 14. king of Castile, Henry IV. 1504. 05. the Hardy, duke of Burgundy, 1200. 1361. Charles VI. 1380. Rosebecq, 1382. Flanders, 1384. 85. 91. 1401. 04. the Good, 1419. joins the English, 1422. 24. 28. the golden fleece, 1430. 31. peace of Arras, 1435. 36. is reconciled to the duke of Orleans, 1440. 56. 63. 67. count de Bresse, 1200. de Comines 1472. bishop of Evreux, 1269.

Philippide, p. 157. V. I.
Philipsburgh, 1634. 35. 44. 48. 54. 76-78. 88.
Phocenses, 539.
Phortzeim, 1692.
Photius, 867.
Physic garden, 1634.
Physician, Charles the Bald is poisoned by his, 875.

PI.

Pibrac, 1579.

Picardy, 1463. 72. 77. 1512. 23. 36. 43. 44. 52. 96.
Picolomini, 1439. ... 1503 ..... 1639. 41. 46.
Picpus, 1601.
Picquigny, 1475. 1567.
Piedmont, 1451. 1535. 38. 42-44. 53. 55. 57. 74. 1630. 36. 39. 1706.
Pienne, mademoiselle de, 1556.
Pierre-Encise, 1644.
Pignerol, 1574. 1630. 31. 48. 61. 71. 91. 93. 95. 1704. 06.
Pilgrimage, 1026. of St. James, 1159. St. Thomas of Canterbury, 1180.
Pimentel, 1646. 58.
Piney, 1581. 96.
Piombino, 1646.
Piper, 1707.
Pisani, 1592.
Pisa, 1408. 94. 1510. 11. 1662.
Pisseleu. See *Estampes*.
Pithou, 506. 1593. 94. p. 7. V. II.
Pius II. 1439. 65. III. 1503. V. 1568. 1602.
Pizighitonne, 1521.

PL.

Place, 1639. 86. 99.
Placentia, 1551. 57.
Placita, 616.
Plantagenet, 1135. 89. 1485.
Plassendal, 1706. 08.
Plate, 1689.
Pleadings, 616.
Plebeians, ennobling, 923. 1200. 70. 1313. 15. 28. 1579. 1629.
Plessis, du Mornai, 1600. Praslin, 1643. 45-48. 50. 53. 72. Guenegaud, 1661.
Plintheim, 1704.

PO.

Podestas, 1056.
Podolia, 1699.

Poets,

INDEX.

Poets, 1302. 1465. p. 311. V. II.
Pointis, 1697. 1704. 05.
Poison, Charles the Bald, 875. Lothaire, 986. Lewis V. 987. Charles V. 1380. dauphin, 1415. duke de Guienne, 1472. Sforza, furnamed the Moor, 1498. dauphin, 1536. Henry I. prince de Condé, 1588. Brinvilliers, 1676. la Voifin, 1680. queen of Spain, 1689.
Poisoners, 1315. 1680.
Poitiers, council, 1100. univerfity, 1431. Alphonfo, count de, 1283. 1313. 55. 1415. Diana of, 1544. 60. 79. 1650. p. 309. V. I. city, 570. 732. 1534. 69. 1634.
Poitou, 1150. 1214. 15. 25. Alphonfe, count de, 1230. 70.... 1369. 1441.
Poland, Poles, p. 90. 259. V. I. Henry III. king of, 1573. 74. Battori, 1575. Sigifmund, 1604. 27. Ladiflaus IV. 1645. ... 60. Wiefnowifki, 1669. 76. duke de Longueville, 1672. Sobiefki, 1676. 83. 94. prince de Conti, 1697. ... 99. 1702. Staniflaus, 1704. Auguftus, 1706. 09. 14. See *Saxony, Cafimir*; queen of, 1684.
Police, 1269. 1609. 97.
Polignac, 1697. 1710. 12.
Poligny, 1638.
Politicians, 1574. 92.
Poltrot, 1563.
Pomerania, 1631. 42. 48. 75.
Pomereu, 1689.
Pompey, 1562.
Pomponne, 1670-72. 79. 91. 96. 99.
Poncet, 1667.
Poncher, 1547.
Pondicheri, 1680. 93. 97.
Pont-à-Mouffon, 1632.
Pontanus, p. 298. V. II.
Pontarlier, 1639.
Pont-Avendin, 1645.

Pontchartrain, 1689. 90. 99. his elogium, 1714.
Point-du-Chafteau, 1634.
Pont-Courlay, 1638.
Ponthieu, original of the counts of, 992. Hugh I. p. 105. V. I. John, count de, 1269. Charles VII. p. 290. V. I. the counts de, 1226. Edward de, 1329.....69.
Pont-major, 1684.
Pontoife, 1032. 1441. 1560. 89. 94. 1652.
Pont, des deux, 1609. ; ...37.
Ponza, ifle, 1697.
Popes, convoke councils, p. 96. V. I. temporalities, 740. 53. confecration, 827. name of, 1092. Conftantine, 767. Leo III. 796. Stephen, V. 817. Eugene, 823. Gregory IV. 827. ....40. St. Peter's Pence, 855. 75. 92. power, 875. 912. 45. 92. authority, 996. 1145. 1336. confirmation, 1067. Nicholas II. 1056. Alexander II. 1067. Urban III. 1092. inveftitures, 1103. Calixtus II. 1120. Guelfs, 1140. Eugene III. 1145. Alexander III. 1156. Innocent III. 1206. 15. Honorius III. 1223. 26. 1680. Gregory IX. 1230. Innocent IV. 1242. Martin IV. 1283. Boniface VIII. 1292. 99. 1303. Clement V. 1305. 09. John XXII. 1313. 16. 29. Clement VI. 1348. p. 237. V. I. Gregory XI. 1379. Urban and Clement VII. 1376. 83. 1404. Gregory XII. and Benedict XIII. 1408. Martin V. 1435. 38. Eugene IV. 1439. ... 69. ... 95. .... 1511. 12. 21. Clement VII. 1527. ..... 53. 55. Clement VIII. 1598. ..... 1605. Urban VIII. 1626. 33. 34. 43. 44. 1700. See their names.
Poperingue, 1678.

INDEX.

Porée, father, p. 91. V. II.
Porentru, 1635.
Porrée, Gilbert da la, 1148.
Port paſſage, 1698.
Port-Alegre, 1704.
Port, or gate, 1591. 1631. 53.
Port, Ottoman, 1542. 1699.
Porte, de la, See *la Meilleraie*, 1617.
Portier, du, 1315.
Port-Louis, 1625.
Port-Mahon, 1708. 13.
Portolongone, 1646. 50.
Portſmouth, 1670.
Portugal, Portugueſe, crown of, 1582. Henry, count de, 1088. 1149. Elizabeth, 1430. John II. 1493. Eleonora, 1493. 1529. Don Sebaſtian, king, 1578.... 80. falſe, 1601. Henry IV. 1595.... 1640. 41. 44. 45. 57-59. 61. 63. 65. Alphonſo, 1667.... 1701. 03-07. 09. 11. 13. 15.
Poſts, 1477. 1691. 1709.
Potier, 1643. 48.
Pouillet, 1328.
Poulain, 1587.
Pouſin, le, 1626. 28.
Power, eccleſiaſtic, 753. 822. 1329. 1612 82.
Pox, p. 355. V. I.
Poyet, 1540. 41.
Pozzuolo, 1496.

PR.

Pracontal, 1703.
Pragmatic Sanction, 1269. 1438. 61. 1548. 53. 60. 84. p. 313. V. II.
Prague, Jerome of, 1415 p. 277. V. I. battle of, 1620.... 31. 43.
Praguerie, 1440.
Praſlin, 1639. 53. 65.
Prat, du, 1514. p. 312. V. II.
Preadamites, 1634.
Precedency, Seat, Rank, 1092. 1361. 1553. 63. 1624. 61. 94. See *Rank*.

Preceptors of the kings, 1103. 1689. of the dauphin, 1661. p. 90. V. II.
Pregent de Bidoux, 1544.
Prelates, 1319. 1639.
Premier, M. le, 1636. 1707.
Premontrés, 1120.
Preſage, p. 432. V. I.
Preſbyterians, 1639.
Preſent, law, 817.
Preſidents, firſt, 1324. 1497. 1515. 89. 1689-91. p. 211. V. I. creation of, 1690. preſident of the council, 1667.
Preſidials, 1551.
Preſle, Raoul de, 1371.
Pretextat, 577. 90.
Prie, Aymar de, 1600.
Prieſts, marriage of, 1103. 48. 1576.
Primacy, Primates, 1092. 1120. 1215. 1676. 1702. p. 39. V. I.
Princes of the blood, 1482. 84. 1541. 76. 81. p. 384. V. I. Courtenai, 1603. legitimacy, 1714. foreign, 1581. M. le prince, 1654. madam la princeſſe, 1684.
Prior, 1711.
Priſcillian, 1226.
Priſoner, Charles the Simple, 922. Lewis VII. 1149. Richard, 1193. count of Flanders, 1214. Saint Lewis, 1249. Iſabella, wife of Edward II. 1324. king John, 1355. du Gueſclin, 1364. Captal de Buch, 1371. cardinal de la Balue, 1469 the duke d'Alençon, 1474. Francis I. 1525. John Frederic, 1547. Mary Stuart, 1587. Grotius, 1619. for debt, 1702.
Privas, 1629.
Proceſs, or trial, of the count d'Artois, 1331. of the duke d'Alençon, 1457. cardinal de la Balue, 1469. chancellor Poyet, 1540. Henry de Montmorenci, 1632.

Pro-

INDEX.

Procession, of the Holy Ghost, 1274. confraternities, 1576. of the league, 1590.
Procopius, 539.
Professors, nineteen, 1663.
Professorship, of divinity, 1230. of law, 1665. 80.
Profession of faith, 557.
Promise, Henry IV. 1599. 1603. 05.
Promotion, 1559. 1620.
Prophecies, 1590.
Propositions of the assembly of the clergy, 1682.
Protectorship, 1648. Richard, 1658.
Protestants, 1529. 47. 62. 79. 1668. 85. 91. 1713.
Protests, against the council of Trent, 1563. of the chancellor de Cheverny, 1595. of the clergy, 1633. of the duke of Orleans, 1700.
Provence, see *Toulon, Marseilles*, 539. 62. 736. 39. 1707. Childeric III. 742. Lothaire, 842. Charles, 855. counts, 877. 1156. Boson, 879. . . . . 1037. Beatrix, 1245. the king of Arragon, 1258. Charles d'Anjou, 1331. Lewis XI. 1480. Charles V. 1536. plague, 1576. of the duke of Savoy, 1590. Charles, duke of Guise, 1595. the grand duke, 1598. . . . . 1635. 49. 60. 1707.
Provinces, intendants, 1653.
Provosts, Provostship, farmers, 992. 1269. of Paris, 992. 1501. p. 39. V. I. of seigniories, 992. of merchants, 1371. 1594. p. 275. V. I.
Prum. 833. 55.
Prussia, 1525. Frederic, king of, 1701. 07. 13. Frederic, 1701.
Pruth, 1711.

PT.

Ptolemais, 1191.
Puffendorf, 1678.
Puicerda, 1654. 78. 1707.
Puilaurens, 1631. 32. 34.
Puiset, du, 1108.
Puisieux, 1619. 22. 24. 98.
Pultausk, 1703.
Pultowa, 1709.
Purple, 1465.
Pussort, 1667.
Puysegur, 1650. 1701.

PY.

Pyramid, 1662.
Pyrenees, 588. 93. 178. 1659.

Q.

Q*Uarrel*, 1292.
Quarters, 1585. 1687.

QUE.

Quebeck, 1674. 96. 1711.
Querasque, 1631. 39.
Querci, 562. 85. Henry III. 1255.
Quesne, du, 1675. 76. 81-84. 1703.

Quesnoy, 1654-56. 93. 1712.

QUI.

Quiers, 1639. 55.
Quietism, 1698. 99.
Quillebœuf, 1674.
Quincbe, 1703.
Quit-rent, 992.

INDEX.

R.

Rabutin, de Buffi, 1665.
Racine, 1677. 90.
Radegonde, 562.
Ragnetrude, 636.
Raimbert, p. 129. V. I.
Raimond, count de Toulouse, 1092. 1245. 49. 1365.
Rainfroi, 714. 15. 19.
Rambouillet, 1711.
Ramée, la, 1596.
Ramekens, 1616.
Rameru, 1581.
Ramilies, 1706.
Ramire, 1516.
Ranacaire, 510.
Randan, 1663.
Rank, 1701. in the court of peers, p. 438 V. I. among the princes of the blood, 1570. 76. of the duke of Burgundy, 1361.1432. messieurs de Montmorenci, 1551. states, 1558. in council, 1563. messieurs de Joyeuse and Epernon, 1581. 96. messieurs de Vendome in 1598. duke of Vendome in Spain, 1712. cardinals, 1614. 17. 24. 96. siege of Lisle, 1667. the marshal de Guebriant's lady, 1645. ambassadors, 1661. at the king's mass, 1669. the duke du Maine, 1694. among the marshals of France, 1675. in council, 1689. patriarch of Constantinople, 1215. intendants of the finances, 1697. grandees of Spain and dukes, 1701. legitimated princes, 1710. 14.
Rangabè, 807.
Rantzau, 1636. 43. 45. 47. 48.
Ranuzzi, nuncio, 1686.
Raoul, duke of Burgundy and king, 922. 24. 28. 29. 36. count de Vermandois, 1145.
goldsmith, 1270. count de Clermont, 1292. constable, 1350.
Rape, ordinance, 1579. 1640.
Rapin, 1593.
Rastadt, 1677. 1703. 13. 14.
Ratabon, 1661.
Ratisbon, 1630. 41. 84. 89. 1703.
Ratziejouski, 1697.
Ravaillac, 1610. p. 3. V. II.
Raucourt, 1642.
Ravenna, 568. 753. 978. 1512.
Ravignan, 1710.
Rawenhaup, 1674.

RE.

Realists, p. 129. V. I.
Realmont, 1628.
Rebec, 1524.
Rebellion, see Revolt; private lords, 1108. John, surnamed Lackland, 1203. count d'Armagnac, 1470. constable of Bourbon, 1523.27. Gaston and the prince of Condé, 1649. king of Navarre, 1357.
Rebender, 1709.
Recaredus, 585. p. 38. V. I.
Rechin, 1092. 1103.
Recollects, 1584.
Rector, university, 1371.
Redemption, order, 1193.
Reduction of Paris, 1594.
Rees, 1672.
Referendaries, p. 38. 41. V. I.
Reform, state, 1465. custom of Paris, 1580. Gregory's calendar, 1582. abbeys of St. Genevieve, 1624.
Reformed, 1576.
Refuge, 1639.
Regale, prerogative, 511. 992. 1161. 89. 1673. 82. 95.
Regency, Irene, Constantinople, 798. kingdom of France, Baldwin,

INDEX.

win, 1103. the abbé Suger, 1145. queen Blanche, mother of St. Lewis, 1225. 26. 45. the abbé de St. Denis and Simon de Clermont de Nesles, 1269. Robert d'Artois, 1283. Philip the Long, 1316. Charles V. 1357. 58. abuse of regencies, 1371. ordinance, 1371. duke d'Anjou, 1380. ordinance, 1391. John the Fearless, 1404. the dauphin, 1415. Henry V. 1420. duke de Bedford, 1422. 35. Anne de France, 1483. 84. the mother of Francis I. 1515. Catharine de Medicis, 1560. 63. 74. Charles of Sudermania, 1604. Mary de Medicis, 1610. Anne of Austria, 1629. 43. Gaston, 1643. duke of Orleans, 1714.

Regesberg, 1619.
Reggio, 1655. 1702.
Regiment of guards, 1692. 1704. of carabineers, 1693.
Reginon, 859.
Registering, 1371. 1562. 1710. 12. 14.
Registers, parliament, 1313. 1594. 1668.
Relics, cause of superstition, 1022. 1483. of St. Lewis, 1230. chapel royal, 1324.
Religion, preached in Sweden p. 59 V. I. in Denmark, p. 87. V. I. troubles, 1517. Protestants, 1529. diet of Augsburg, 1530. schism of England, 1534. massacre at Cabrieres, 1415. punishments, 1547. Cranmer changes it in England, 1547. *interim*, 1548. edict, 1551. pacification of Passau, 1552. Mary restores it in England, 1553. edict, 1559. Huguenots, 1560. edicts, 1560. 64. troubles in the Netherlands, 1566. the judges are to be Chatholics, 1567. civil war, 1568. peace, 1570. pretended reformed, 1576. peace, 1577. Netherlands, 1578. calendar, 1582. endeavours to make the king of Navarre change, 1584. war, 1585. 1620. the English change theirs, 1603. Grisons, 1621. league against the emperor, 1626. 27. 31. edicts, 1669. 82. 85. 1713. See *Arianism, Calvinism, Lutheranism.*

Religious, men and women, rule, 814. 1148. 1321. right of being exempted from preserts, 817.
Relingue, 1684. 1704.
Remi, 1328.
Remiremont, 612.
Remonstrances, parliament, 1563. 1602. 15.
Renaudie, 1560.
Renaudot, 1631.
Rendon, castle, 1380.
René, duke d'Alençon, 1474. duke of Lorrain, 1419. 76. See *Anjou.*
Renée, Lewis XII. 1514. 15.
Rennes, 591.
Renomer, king of Mans, 510.
Rentes, 1441. 1638.
Renti, 1554. 1638.
Renunciation, king John, 1630. the infanta Mary Theresa, 1659. the emperor, 1703. the king of Spain, 1712. 13.
Representation, 973. 1200. 1302. 22.
Reporters, 1344.
Republic, Swiss, 1305. Florence, 1502. Henry IV. 1610. Catalans, 1641.
Repudiation, p. 157. V. I. Himiltrude, p. 49. V. I. Ansgarde, p. 79. V. I. Dagobert, 638. Bertha, 1092. Eleonora, 1150. Agnes of Merania, p. 157. V. I. Ingerburga, 1193. p. 157. V. I. Blanche of Burgundy, p. 231. V. I.

Cc 3 *Requena,*

INDEX.

Requena, 1707.
Requesens, 1578.
Retaliation, 1215.
Rethel, 1384. 1650. 52. 53.
Rethelois, duke, 1629.
Retreat, Rebec, 1324. duke of Parma, 1592. of Vaudemont, 1695.
Retz, Gondi de, 1567. 74. cardinal de, 1621. ...48. 51. 52. 54. 55. his character, 1679.
Revel, 1672. fort de, 1710.
Reventlau, 1706.
Revenue, the king's, 992.
Reverse, 1704.
Reversion, 1692.
Reunion, Frifeland, 746. dutchy of Aquitaine, 767. Septimania, 751. dutchy of Bavaria, 787. kingdom of Italy, 818. of the eastern and western churches, 867. dutchy of France, 992. dutchy of Burgundy, 1001. Vermandois, 1180. Artois, 1192. Philip Augustus reunites several provinces, 1215. king John, 1361. the king reunites Britany, 1379. Normandy, 1448. marquisate of Saluces, 1548. domain, edict, 1588. Navarre, 1607. edict, 1620. Bearn, 1620. dutchy of Bar, 1633. Alsace, 1680. p. 259. V. I. .....900. &c.
Revel, 1588.
Revolt, count de Sancerre, 1180. impostor, surnamed Baldwin, 1223. the barons of England, 1255. the dauphin, 1457. England, 1640. 88. Catalonia, 1640. Portugal, 1580. 1640.
Reynie, la, 1697. 1704.

RH.

Rhe, isle, 1625. 27. 53. 96.
Rheims, the people submit to Clovis, 493. taken and retaken, 563. Carloman, 771. Lewis Transmarine, 954. Lothaire, 986. coronation of Philip, 1056. dignity of chancellor, p. 129. V. I. schism, 1108. council, 1120. prerogative of crowning the king, 1179. Charles VII. 1428. le Tellier, archbishop of, 1704. university, 1548.
Rhetia, 830.
Rhimberg, 1671. 72. 74. 1702. 3. 13.
Rhine, project of Charlemain, 789. league, 1658. courts, 1644. passage, 1672. elector of Brandenburg, 1673. ... 75. marshal de Villars, 1707. 13.
Rhinfelds, 1638. 78. 93.
Rhodes, isle, 1309. 1522. 65. 88.

RI.

Riberac, 1578.
Richard, 1542. duke of Normandy, 942. 56. king of England, 1171. 86. 89. 91-93. II. 1376. 94. 97. duke of York, 1435. 57. III. 1483. son of Cromwell, 1658.
Richardot, treaty of Vervins, 1598.
Richelieu, 1380. 1592. 1616. 17. 19. 20. 22. 24. 26-42. 92. duke de, 1647. 80. dutchess de, 1680. marshal, 1685.
Richmond, Edmund, earl of, 1420. 24. constable of, 1426. 28. 31. 39. earl of, 1475. 85. duke of, 1470.
Richenaw, 888.
Richer, doctor of Sorbonne, 1612.
Richilde, 877.
Rienzi, 1352.
Ries, isle, 1622.
Rieux, Renée de, p. 433. V. I.
Riga, 1701. 10.
Rinçon, ambassador at Venice, 1542.
Ring, 1120.
Rio-Janeiro, 1711.

Ripaille,

INDEX.

Ripaille, Amadeus, duke of Savoy, 1439.
Riquet, 1664.
Ritual, Vannes and Clermont, 1584.
Riviere, l'abbé de la, 1648. 50. 57.
Rivoli, league, 1635.

RO.

Robe, separated from the sword, 1560.
Robert, king, 988. 95. see his reign; I. duke of Burgundy, 1001. 31. p. 113. V. I. son of Baldwin, 1067. the Frison, 1127. child of France, 922. .... 1139. See *Artois* and *Dreux*; le Fort, 851. the Devil, 1031. 47. son of William the Conqueror, 1067. 92. 1100. 13. 16. d'Arbrissel, 1103. count of Flanders, 1304. Guiscard, 1026. 56. the Sage, king of Naples, 1341. prince, son of the king of Bohemia, 1644. 65. 66. 73.
Robertet, Florimond, p. 329. V. I.
Rocca, 1645.
Roche, chevalier de la, 1565.
Rochefort, 1108. Guy, 1499. p. 137. V. I. William, p. 311. V. I. marshal de, 1672. 73. 75. 76. 80. marquis de, 1669.
Rochefoucauld, 1569. 1612. dutchy and peerage, 1622 cardinal de la, 1617. 24. duke de la, 1643. 51. Marsillac, 1679.
Rocheguyon, la, 1546.
Roche la-Belle, la, 1569.
Roche!, *Rochellois*, 1223. Francis I. 1542. .... 73. 74. Lewis XIII. 1622. 27. 28.
Rochester, 1688.
Roche-sur-Yon, prince de la, 1559. ... 1685. p. 408. V. I.
Rocroy, 1643. 53.
Roderic, king of the Goths, 714.

Rodolph, son of Conrard, 888. III. 1037. count d'Habsbourg, 1245. 73. emperor, 1282.
Rodolphine, league, 1648.
Rodrigo, 1706.
Roger, Norman prince, 1130. king of Sicily, 1026. 1130. 49. 50. Peter, nominated to the archbishopric of Sens, 1329.
Rogier, chancellor, 1348. p. 239. V. I.
Rohan, house of, 1588. John, 1562. duke de, 1603. 12. 14. 21. 22. 27-29. 35-38. 52. chevalier de, 1669. 74 dutchy and peerage, 1714. Catharine, 1603. Margaret, 1648.
Rollans, 1380.
Rollo, first duke of Normandy, 912. 29.
Rolls, p. 295. V. II.
Romain, cardinal, 1226.
Romania, Paleologus, 1494.
Romances, origin of, p. 101. V. I.
Romaric, 612.
Rome, *Romans*, 536. 68. 715. 67. 842. 45. 1001. 26. 1532. p. 36. 95. V. I. &c. 113. See *Popes*, Spain, 714. Astolphus, 751. Lothaire, 842. Leo IV. 845. council, 996. 1056. consuls, 1056. clergy, 1120. Lewis the Young, 1142. broils, 1193. holy see, 1376. Charles VIII. 1494. 95. constable of Bourbon, 1527. abuse, 1550. differences, 1662. 90. M. de Monaco, 1699. king of the, 1556.
Romorantin, edict, 1560.
Romuald, St. 1001.
Romulphus, 612.
Roncevaux, defeat, 778.

RO.

Rook, admiral, 1693. 1703. 04.
Roquelaure, 1610. 1705.
Roquette, la, 1653.
Rosieux, 1602.

Rose,

INDEX.

Rose, red and white, 1557. 71.
Rose, bishop of Senlis, 1593. 98.
Rosebecq, battle, 1382.
Rosen, marshal, 1645. 1703.
Roses, battle of, 1541.
Roses, town, 1645. 93. 1712.
Rosmadec, 1627.
Rosni. 1589. 1600. 03. 06. 07. 11. de Bethune, 1610. p. 7. V. I.
Rostock, 1631. 1711.
Rothelin, 1514.
Rothwil, taken, 1643.
Rouanes, 1631. dutchy and peerages, 1667. 69.
Rouen, Charles, son of king John, 1355. taken, 1419. maid of Orleans, 1431. Huguenots, 1562. parliaments, 1563. 1639. siege, 1591. 92. admiral de Villars, 1594. assembly, 1596. 1617. archbishop, 1702.
Rovere, cardinal de la, 1480. 1503.
Rouergue, le, 534. du Guesclin, 1369.
Rouillé, 1691. creation of an office, 1701. president, 1709.

Roussillon, 1642. king of Arragon, 1258. Lewis XI. 1462. king of Arragon, 1493. ordinance, 1564. conquest, 1642. 59. 74. marshal de Schomberg, 1674. 75.
Rouvre, duke of Burgundy, 1361. 84.
Rowland, 1778.
Royalists, 1585. 90. 92.
Royan, siege, 1622.
Roye, town, 1470. 1653. Eleonor de, 1569.

RU.

Rubempre, bastard, 1464.
Rugen, 1630. 48. 78.
Rule, of canons, 814. of St. Austin, 1255. of Mentz, 803. of Passy, 1309. brothers of the Passion, 1401.
Ruremond, 1702.
Russ, 888.
Ruyter, admiral, 1666. 72-74. 76.
Ruzé de Beaulieu, 1588.
Ryswick, peace, treaty, 1697.

S.

Sabine, cardinal de, 1179.
Sacheverel, 1711.
Sacrament, blessed, heresy, 1047.
Sadolet, 1587.
Sague, la, 1560.
Sailors, 1687.
Saint-Abre, 1657.
Saint-Aignan, dutchy and peerage, 1663. 65.
St. Amand, Albergotti, 1712.
St. Amour, castle, 1637.
St. André, marshal de, 1547. 57. 60. 62. 69.
St. Angel, castle, 1527.
St. Antoine, battle, 1652. port, 1660.

St. Arnoul of Metz, p. 59. V. I.
St. Aubin, battle, 1481.
St. Aunais, 1645.
St. Bartholomew, church, p. 104. V. I. massacre, 1572.
St. Benoit on the Loire, p. 309. V. I.
St. Bertin, 750. 879.
St. Chamond, 1633.
St. Christopher, isle, 1666. 90.
St. Cir, foundation, 1686.
St. Clare, 912.
St. Cloud, 1674.
St. Contest, 1714.
St. Corneille, 756.
St. Denis in France, Dagobert, 635. 36.

INDEX.

36. Clovis II. 651. Lewis the Debonnaire, 833. Charles Martel, 741. Landit, 875. Lewis III. 882. Carloman, 884. Lewis the Fat, 1150. apoftlefhip, 1242. du Guefclin, 1380. battles, 1567. 1678. chevalier d'Aumale, 1591. Henry IV. 1593. Turenne, 1675. reunion of St. Cir, 1686.

St. Die, abbey, 612.
St. Efprit, 1409.
St. Evremond, 1659.
St. Fremond, 1701.
St. Gal, 1305. abbey, 712.
St. George, legate, 1547.
St. Germain en Laye, peace, 1570. 71. ... 1638. 41. 43. 49. 62. 77. 89. p. 90. V. II. des Prés, Childebert, 558. Clotaire II. 628. Childeric, 670. Hugh, abbot, p. 156. V. I. Cafimir, 1669.
St. Godard, battle, 1664.
St. Guiflain, taken, 1655. 56. 77.
St. Heran, 1572.
St. Honcrat, ifles, 1637.
St. Honorè, gate, 1591. 1651.
St. Ibal, 1636.
St. John, knights, 1309. 1522. Charles V. 1530. d'Angeli, 1223. 1569. 88. 1612. de Lofne, 1636. de Luz, 1636. 60.
St. Lazare, foundation, 1632.
St. Leger, 1636.
St. Lo, Crofs, 1483.
St. Lewis, inftitution of the order, 1693.
St. Malo, bombardment, 1693. cardinal de, 1494.
St. Marcel, 593.
St. Martin, of Autun, 612. fort, 1627.
St. Matthias, Charles V. 1500. 25.
St. Maur, 992. Lewis the Fat, 1116. the emperor, 1378. peace, 1465. edict, 1567. congregation, 1621.
St. Medard, Clotaire, 562. 75. the emperor, 833. Charles the Bald, 850. Raoul, 923.
St. Megrin, 1578.
St. Michael, order, 1527. inftitution, 1469. promotion, 1559.
St. Mibel, town, 1632. 33. 35.
St. Olon, 1684.
St. Omer, town, 1067. 1638. 77. 78.
St. Paul, hotel, 1380. p. 271. V. I. count de, 1401. 10. Vendome, 1529. conftable of, 1466. 70. 71. 74. 75. church, 511. 628. 40.
St. Peter, church, 511. tribute, 855.
St. Pol, 1703.
St. Preuil, 1641.
St. Quintin, 1470. 74. 75. 1557. battle, 1557.
St. Remi, Clovis, 493. church, 1130. mademoifelle de, 1675.
St. Riquier, 992. 80. 1180.
St. Roch, parifh, 1633.
St. Ruth, 1690. 91.
St. Saturnin, 1309.
St. Sebaftian, 1698.
St. Simon, 1626. 36. dutchy and peerage, 1635. 43. 45.
St. Venant, 1645. 49. 57. 1710.
St. Victor, abbey, 1135.
St. Vincent, church, 558.
St. Vinox, 1558. 1667.
St. Waft d'Arras, 690.
St. Bridget, duke of Savoy, 1693.
St. Catharine, church, 1215. marfhal de Teffé, 1707.
St. Cecil, archbifhop of Aix, 1646.
St. Genevieve, abbey, 511. 43. Clovis, 511. church, 1180. reform, 1624. proceffion, 1693.
St. Margaret, ifles, 1637.
St. Menehould, treaty, 1614. 52. 53.
Saintot, 1603.

Saintrailles,

INDEX.

Saintrailles, 1451.
Saints, lot of, 789.
Saissetti Bernard, 1303.
Saladin, 1150. 86.
Salamander, Francis I. 1515.
Salamanca, 1706.
Salankemen, 1691.
Salces, 1639. 40. 42.
Sale of offices, 1515. 22. p. 302. &c. V. II.
Salerno, siege, 1026.
Salignac, de, 1579.
Salins, 1668. 57.
Salic, law, 511. 58. 1316. p. 99. V.I. 118. lands, 1593. p. 94. V.I.
Salo, journal des Sçavans, 1665.
Salomon, 845.
Salsbac, 1675.
Salsede, conspiracy, 1582.
Salt, impost, 1344.
Salvaterra, 1705.
Saluces, 1503. 36. 48. 88. 99. 1600. 01. 30. 90.
Salvius, 1647.
Salvation, difficulty, 1653.
Samon, 632.
Samoucy, 771.
Sancerre, homage, 1100. 80. county, 1226. revolt, 1180. king of Navarre, 1205. 52.
Sancho, king of Arragon, 1316. 1516. III. 1285.
Sanci, 1589.
Sansalvador, 1624.
Santarel, 1626.
Santa-Vittoria, 1702.
Santen, treaty, 1614.
Santia, town, 1644.
Saracens, in the reign of Dagobert III. 715. in the reign of Thierri IV. 732. 36. interregnum, 739. 58. treaty, 773. Lewis the Debonnaire, 800. 14. Inigo, 827. Lothaire, 850. battle in Calabria, 978. reign in Africa, 1026. in the reign of Lewis the Young, 1148. Lisbon, 1149. treaty, 1226. Provence, 1245.

Roussillon, 1258.
Sarbourg, 1661.
Sardinia, 1226. Philip of Valois, 1349. isle, 1226. 1637. 1708.
Sarlat, 1653. 80.
Sar-Lewis, 1680.
Saragossa, 543. Ybinalarabi, 778. 1670. 1707. 10.
Sas de Gand, 1644.
Sassenage, de, 1566.
Satyr, Menippè, 1593.
Saveli, 1638.
Savern, 1635. 36. 40. 75.
Savillan, 1574. 1639.
Saulx, 1711.
Savona, interview, 1505. revolution, 1528.
Savonieres, council, 875.
Savoy, 878. 88. count, 1037. house, 1056. rights, 1189. dutchy, 1415. Peter, 1309. Amadeus, 1439. Lewis, 1445. Philibert II. 1508. 30. dukes, 1515. bastard, 1522. Philip, 1528. Louisa, 1531. See *Angouleme,* duke of, 1535. Amadeus VIII. p. 249. V. I. Honorat, 1572. Emanuel Philibert, 1553. 57. 62. 74. 79. 88. 90. 96. 97. ambassadors, 1598. negociation, 1599. 1600. 01. enterprise, 1602. 13. treaty, 1610. 17. league, 1623. enterprizes, 1625. 29. 30. ... 35. Charles-Emanuel, 1630. Charles, 1189. Victor-Amadeus, 1189. 1635-37. prince Thomas, 1635. 37. 39. 55. 56. war, 1640. 42. .... 43. the young duke, 1645. 52. 53. Spaniards, 1646. the cardinal, 1637. 41. archbishop of Rheims, 1653. dutchess Margaret, 1658. Charles-Emanuel, 1660. 67. Victor, 1684. 90-93. 95. 96. peace, 1697. .... 1700. ... 01. 08. 13. Mary-Adelaid, 1697. 1712. 13. Mary-Louisa, 1714. Henry, 1654.

INDEX.

1654. character of the dukes of Savoy, 1703.
Saus, 1711.
Saufoy, du, 1658.
Sauvebœuf, 1653.
Saxony, Saxons, 555. 739. 43. 53. Charlemain, 772. 75. 76. 78. ... 94. children, 803. ... 14. 35. Guſtavus, 1632...1701. the king of Sweden, 1703. 04. 06. duke Otho, 912. Otho, 1206. duke Weimar, 1626. 31. 32. 34. emperor, 1635. elector, John-Frederic, 1547. Maurice, 1551. 52. pretenſions, 1609. .... 20. 31. 36. 41. John-George, 1631. 60. Luxemburg, 1632. Eiſenach, 1677. Frederic-Auguſtus, 1697. 1700-04. 06. 09. marſhal, count de, 1673. 1709.

SC.

Scalette, 1676.
Scarred, duke, 1575.
Sceau, feaſt, 1685.
Scheld, 1521.
Scheleſtad, 1675.
Schenck, 1625. 36. 72.
Schiſm, of the Greeks, 867. church, 1103. Rheims, 1108. Innocent II. and Anaclet, 1130. Alexander III. Victor IV. 1171. proceſſion of the Holy Ghoſt, 1274. Gregory XI. 1379. 82. 83. war, 1383. 94. 1404. council, 1408. 15. death of Eugene IV. 1439. England, 1534.
Schoeffer, 1457.
Schomberg, 1578. 98. 1614. 20. 21. 27. 30. 32. 37. 42. 43. 47. 48. 56. 58. 63. 74-76. 78. 88. 90. 91. duke de, 1704.
Schonen, 1676.
Schorendorf, taken, 1707.
Schools, public, 989. 1179. of canon law, 1680. military, 1600.

p. 306. V. II.
Scholars, 1648.
Schovel, 1707.
Schullembourg, general, 1704.
Schwarts, Berthod, 1336.
Schweidnitz, imperialiſts, 1642.
Sciara Colonna, 1303.
Sciences in Gaul, 511. See *Letters*.
Scoti, nuncio, 1639.
Scotland, John Bailliol, 1292. Edward, 1340. 69. 1421. James III. 1483. 1548. Mary Stuart, 1558. 87. James Stuart, 1567. 87. James I. 1603. epiſcopacy, 1637. Charles I. 1647. Cromwell, 1650. Orange 1689. union, 1706. Margaret, 1436. See the names of the reſpective kings.
Scrutiny, p. 273. V. I.
Sculpture, academy, 1663.

SE.

Seals, 1541. 74. 90. p. 223. V. I. 1590. Luines, 1621. Seguier, 1650. the king holds the, 1672.
Seat. See *Rank*.
Sebaſtian, Don, king of Portugal, 1578. falſe, 1601.
Secret, clerks, 1341.
Secretary, 1309. 1589. of the finances, 1341. 1410. of ſtate, 1309. 1574. 1639. 43. 61. 89. 90. 1701. 09. of the cabinet, 1589. the king's, p. 287. V. I. of the queen's orders, 1661.
Sedan, ceſſion, 1606. battle, 1641. duke de Bouillon, 1642. exchange, 1651.
Sedition, faction, troubles, Lewis the Groſs, 1103. Jacquerie, 1358. Burgundians, Armagnacs, 1410. Britany, 1419. 1604. Rouen, 1639. Naples, 1701.
Segovia, caſtle, 1710.
Seguier, dean of Notre-Dame, 1593.

INDEX.

1593. bishop of Meaux, p. 90. V.
II. chancellor, 1639. 43. 50. 67.
72. minister, 1689.
Seignelay, 1380. 1684. seals, 1685.
88. death, 1690.
Seilern, 1714.
Selim II. 1189. ... 1517.
Selve, John de, 1515. Don Philip de, 1644. p. 301. V. II.
Semblance, 1522.
Seminara, battle, 1495. 1503.
Senator, dignity, 1145. 1255.
Seneschals, 1214. count d'Anjou, 978. 1116. functions, 978. p. 38. V. I. judges, 1498. 1560.
Senef, battle, 1674.
Senlis, town, 853. council, 1315. chancellor, 1309.
Sennecy, marchioness de, 1663.
Senneterre, ambassador, 1637.
Senone, abbey, 612.
Sens, 936. count de, 840. council, 1140. primate, 1092. assembly, 1612.
Senfano, 1704.
Septimania, 508. 751.
Seraphin, auditor of the rota, 1592.
Serbelloni, 1635. 37.
Sergeants at arms, 1215.
Serizay, academy, 1635.
Serpa, 1707.
Servetus, Michael, 1553.
Service, military, 817. king of England, 1376. Henry VIII. 1547. marshal de Guebriant, 1643.
Servien, plenipotentiary, 1644. 47. 61.
Servitude, 1296. p. 36. V. I.
Seu, la, 1691.
Seve, de, 1657.
Sevigné, de, 1673.
Seurne, 1650.
Sexte, Boniface VIII. 1321.
Seymour, Jane, 1547. Thomas, 1547.
Sezanne, 1708.

SF.

Sfifer, Lewis, 1557.
Sforza, Francis, 1447. 98. Ludovico, 1494. 95. 98. 1500. Maximilian, 1512. 13. 15. Francis, 1521. 22. 25-27. 29. 34.

SH.

Shaved, kings, p. 39. V. I.
Sheriffs, 1371. 1594.
Ship, order of, 1269.

SI.

Siagrius, general of the Romans, 486.
Siam, envoys, 1684. 86. revolution, 1688.
Sichilde, 628.
Sicily, 1026. 56. dependance, 1060. foundation, 1026. 1130. Charles of Anjou, 1130. 86. 1226. 75. 1522. Manfred, 1255. 83. duke of Anjou, 1292. separation. 1292. Charles, 1480. James, 1283. 85. Lewis II. 1415. Lewis III. 1428. 31. Philip, 1555. monarchy, 1605. ... 78. duke of Savoy, 1713.
Sienna, St. Catharine, 1376. town, 1493. 94. 1554. 57.
Sigebert, king of Cologne, 510. king of Austrasia, 663. 65. 75. II. or III. 632. 36. 44. 46. 54. 70. p. 38. V. I.
Sigismund, king of Burgundy, 523. 34. emperor, 1394. 1415. duke of Austria, 1443. king of Hungary, 1394. king of Poland, 1604. 27.
Signing of the minutes, 1560. 79.
Sillery, negociator, 1598. Henry IV. 1622. chancellor, 1614. 22. 24. commander of, 1623. 24.
Silva, John de, 1493.
Silver, and gold, 628. 57. 840. 1321. 1521. 1689.
Silvester II. Gerbert, 988.

Simon,

INDEX.

Simon, 1682: count de Montfort, 1206.
Simony, 1022. p. 343. V.II.
Sinibald, 1242.
Sintal, 780.
Sintzim, 1674.
Sion, cardinal, 1521.
Sirk, 1643. 61. 1705.
Sirmond, the king's confessor, 875. 1643.
Sisenand, king of the Goths, 634.
Sithieu, St. Bertin, 750.
Sixteen, council, 1585. faction, 1587. duke de Guise, 1588. 91. division, 1592.
Sixtus-Quintus, 992. the king of Navarre, 1585. 88-90.

SL.
Sluys, battle of, 1336. town, 1645. 47. 1712.

SM.
Small-pox, Lewis XIV. 1647. the dauphin, 1711.
Smalcalde, league, 1532.
Smyrna, fleet, 1693.

SO.
Sobieski, king of Poland, 1676. 83. 96.
Society, of Jesus, 1534. royal of London, 1660.
Soignies, 1706.
Soissons, battle, 486. seat of the monarchy, 486. 593. 628. Childebert II. 596. kingdom, 628. council, 1140. Charles VII. 1428. count de, 1593. Charles de Bourbon, 1612 Lewis, 1626. 36. 41. Savoy, 1651. countess de, 1665. 80. chevalier de, 1694. academy, 1674.
Soliman II. 1522. 29. 32. 41.
Solis, Fernando, 1644.
Soldan of Babylon, 1329.
Solsonne, 1655.
Solms, prince of, 1684.
Somme, river, 1344.

Somerset, Margaret of, 1485.
Soncino, 1705.
Song, Gregorian, 789.
Sopha, 1683. 85.
Sophia, Hanover, 1701.
Sorbonne, 1269. arret, 1587. decree, 1589. ... 90. 1642. 82.
Sorcery, maid of Orleans, 1431. Urban Grandier, 1634.
Sorel, Agnes, 1445.
Soubize, 1621. 22. 25. prince, 1677.
Souche, count de, 1674.
Southwold-bay, sea fight, 1672.
Sourdis, archbishop of, 1641. marquis, 1679.
Soveraign, Sovereignty, vassals, 1108. king of Arragon, 1255. Charles VIII. 1495. Holland, 1609.
Silkworm, 1511. manufactures, 1603.
Soyecourt, 1669.

SP.
Spain, 543. 88. 1658. Saracens, 715. Inigo, 827. crusade, 1149. Henry IV. 1472. Columbus, 1492. Ferdinand, 1493. 1503. the league, 1513. 93. Vervins, 1598. 1603. Baronius, 1605. the truce, 1609. II. marriages, 1612. Savoy, 1617. Valteline, 1621. James I. 1622. 24. 25. war of Mantua, 1629. 32. war, 1634-42. 48. 50. 52. peace, 1659. Batteville, 1661. 65. war of the Netherlands, 1667. peace, 1668. madam, 1670. war, 1673-76. peace of Nimeguen, 1678. flag, 1680. 81. truce of Ratisbon, 1684. 86. war, 1694. 97. 98. will, 1700. 01. 03. 06. 11. 15. succession to the crown, 1687 .... 94. See the names of the respective kings.
Spart, baron de, 1703.
Spenser, 1324.

Spezzia,

INDEX.

Spezzia, port of, 1495.
Spinola, 1588. 1614. 20. 21. 24. 25. 30.
Spinosa, 1674.
Spire, diet, 1529. imperial chamber, 1633. Francis, 1634. 44. 88. battle, 1703. 06. marshal de Villars, 1713.
Spoleto, duke, 875. 77.
Sporck, 1674.
Spurs, battle of, 1513.

ST.

Staffarde, duke of Savoy, 1690.
Standons, John, 1499.
Stanhope, the king of Spain, 1710.
Stanislaus, king of Poland, 1675. 1704. 09.
Star, order of, 1350. 1469.
Staremberg, 1688. 1703. 08-10. 13.
States, assembly, general, 1252. 1355. p. 301. V. II. third estate, 1255. Philip the Fair, 1303. king John, 1350. 55. 59. Lewis XI. 1468. Charles VIII. 1484. of Flanders, 1505. the parliament makes a fourth order, 1558. Francis II. 1560. Henry III. 1576. of Blois, 1588. of Paris, 1593. their authority, 1614. of the long robe and the sword, 1560. of Holland, 1644. 77.
Statholder, prince of Orange, 1672. 77.
Statue, of Philip the Fair, 1304. Cailus and Maugiron, 1578. Henry the Great, 1614. Lewis XIII. 1639. Lewis XIV. 1686. 89.
Statutes, 1269.
Steckemberg, 1705.
Steinkirk, 1692.
Stenai, 1591. duke of Lorrain, 1632. 50. 54. 61.
Stephen III. 753. 56. IV. 767. V. p. 58. V. I. king of England, 1135. 54. of Hungary,

1526. of Champagne, 1040.
Stetin, Gustavus Adolphus, 1631. 48. elector of Brandenburg, 1677.
Stile, old and new, 1699.
Stirum, Hochstet, 1703.
Stockholm, Descartes, 1650.
Stolophen, 1707.
Stone, philosopher's, p. 273. V. I.
Storm, 1359.
Strafford, lord lieutenant of Ireland, 1641.
Stralsund, king of Sweden, 1630. elector of Brandenburg, 1678. king of Sweden, 1714.
Strangers, 1651.
Strasburg, 636. 1673-75. 78. 81.
Strozzi, 1534. 54. 58. 82.
Stuart, crown of Scotland, 1369. John, constable, 1424. Mary, 1558. 61. 68. 71. 87. prince of Wales, 1712. James, 1502. 59. ... 67. Louisa-Mary,1712. house, 1649. 90. Mary, 1690. comp. of Scotch, 1690.
Stures, bridge, 1643.

SU.

Suavegotte, 534.
Sublet, king's printing-house,1672.
Subsidy, states-general, 1355. Languedoc, 1359.
Substitution, 1560. 66.
Succession, Saxon children of, 803. 14. of monks, p. 98. V. I. contested, 1316. 28. 55. 1567. of the Netherlands, 1667. to the crown of France, 954. 1700. p. 43. V. I. the king's children, p. 39. V. I.
Sudermania, Charles, 1604. 27.
Suffolk, duke de, 1553.
Suger, abbot of St. Denis, 1120. 45. 49. 50.
Sulli, bishop of Paris, 1180. Rosni, 1600. 03. 06. 07. 11.
Summerhausen, 1648.

Sum-

INDEX.

Summons, to the council, 1511. of the knights of Malta, 1714.
Sumptuary, laws, 813.
Sundgaw, 1648.
Superintendant, of the king's houshold, 1380. of the queen's houshold, 1619. 80. 1707. of the seas, the cardinal, 1627. 46. the duke de Vendome. 1650. of the mines, Roger de Bellegarde, 1602. of the buildings, Sublet, 1642. . . . . 91. 99. Manſart, 1709. of the poſt office, 1699. 1709. of the finances, 1589. 1603. p. 357. V. I. of muſic 1661. office ſuppreſſed, 1661. p. 95. V. II. of education, 1643. 1714.
Superſtition, relicks, 1022. Lewis XI. 1483. epocha, 1503.
Supremacy, 1534. oath, 1649.
Surenne, conference, 1593.
Surname, 1643. 80.
Surville, 1709.
Suſa, paſſage, 1629. 39. 90. treaty of, 1629.
Suſa, 1635. 36. . . . 1704. 07.

SW.

Swabia, houſe of, 1026. 1255.
Swammerdam, 1672.
Sweden, Swedes, 1391. 1542. 1604. 1127. 30. 31. 33-36. 39. 41. 42. 46-48. 54. 60. 67. 68. 69. 71. 75-78. 89. 97. 99. 1700-07. 09-11. 14. p. 59. V.I.
Swiſs, 888. 1305. 1443. 51. 64. 75-77. 80. 96. 97. 1500. 10-13. 15-17. 21. 24. 32. 49. 67. 82. 89. 1602. 16. 43. 47. 61. 63. 71. 73. 81. 1712. 15.
Switz, canton, 1305.
Swordmen, ſeparate from the gentlemen of the long robe, 1560.

SY.

Synod, Dordrecht, 1619. Loudun, 1659.
Syria, 1522.

T.

Tabago, count d'Eſtrées, 1677. *Tables*, the XII. 511.
Tabor, 1645.
Taille, perpetual, 1445. change of the coin, 1364. 1445. raiſing, 1483. 1547. 81. edict, 1600. p. 310. 312. 320. V. II.
Taillebour, 1242.
Talbot, the brave, 1428. 43. 51.
Tallard, 1693. 98. 1702-04. dutchy and peerage, 1715.
Talon, 1667. 74.
Tamerlane, Bajazet, 1394.
Tancred, de Hauteville, 1026. de Rohan, 1649.
Tannegui, du Châtel, 1419. le Veneur, 1572. 88.
Tannes, 1654.
Tanquerel, arret, 1561.
Tapeſtry, manufactures, 1603.
Taraſcon, cardinal de Richelieu, 1642.
Tardieu, 1665.
Tardif, 1591.
Targon, Pompey, 1628.
Tarn, 1592.
Tarragona, 1179. 1641. 44.
Taſſo, p. 9. V. II.
Taſſillon. See *Bavaria*.
Tavannes, Charles IX. 1567. prince de Condé, 1568.
Tax, clergy, 1223. the king's council, 1688.
Taxis, treaty of Vervins, 1598.

Te

INDEX.

TE.

Te Deum, *M. de Beauveau*, 1709.
Teios, king of Italy, 568.
Teil, du, 1712.
Tekely, 1683. 85. 99.
Telescope, p. 287. V. I.
Tellier, 1643. 44. 61. 85. the king's confessor 1709.
Temeswar, truce, 1664.
Temple, Saxon, 772. Sir William, 1619. 68. 78.
Templars, order, 992. 1092. 1309.
Tendes, count de, 1572.
Tenths, tithes, 1179. 89. 1303. 16. 24.
Ter, passage, 1694.
Termes, 1553. 54. 58.
Terouenne, 577. 1479. 1515. 53.
Terracuse, 1645.
Tesin, 1636.
Tessè, 1692. 96. 1703. 05-07.
Testament, Charlemain, 805. Philip-Augustus, 1189. Lewis VIII. 1225. Ferdinand, 1617. Charles, II. 1685. 98. 99. 1700. 03. interpretations, 1703. Lewis XIV. 1714. cardinal de Richelieu, 1344. p. 302. V. II. Longueville, 1694.
Testoons, Francis II. p. 400. V. I.
Teutonic, 1092.
Texel, Holland, 1694.

TH.

Thanes, 1638.
Thaun, general, 1707. 11.
Theatins, 1644.
Theatre, first representations of the, 1179... 1609.
Themines, 1616.
Theodat, king of Italy, 535. 36.
Theodebald, king of Italy, 548. 55. mayor of the palace, 714. 15.
Theodebert, king of Metz, 534. son of Chilperic, 573. 75. king of Austrasia, 596-612.
Theodechildes, 511. 34.

Theodon, Charlemain, 787.
Theodoric, king of Italy, 493. king of the Ostrogoths, 500. 08. 20.
Theodosian, code, 511.
Theology, professorship, 1230. decree, 1594.
Theophania, 978.
Theresa, Mary of Austria, 1683. 98.
Thesis, or proposition, Tanquerel, 1561.
Theudegilde, 566.
Theudichilde, 612.
Thiarre, 1331.
Thibaut, king of Navarre, 1252. 70. See *Champagne*.
Thierri I. 511. 20. 31. 33. 34. II. king of Burgundy, 596-613. III. 656. 70. 73. 78. lazy kings, 688. 90. 92. IV. surnamed de Chelles, 715. 20. 37. son of Childeric III. 750. d'Alsace, 1127.
Thionville, 1558. 1639. 43.
Third-Estate, 1255. 1303. 1558.
Tholuis, passage of the Rhine, 1672.
Thomas, St. of Canterbury, 1161. 69. 79. prince of Savoy, 1635. 37-41. 43-46. 55. 56. du Louvre, 1179.
Thorn, 1703.
Thou, de, first president, 1576. 98. 1611. p. 409. V. I. de, 1559. 60... 1642. Nic. p. 2. V. II.
Thouars, Guy, count de, 1116. dutchy and peerage, 1595.
Three hundred, hospital, 1258. 1309.
Thuilleries, palace, 1547. assembly, 1626. 62.
Thuis, Roussillon, 1674.
Thun-l'Eveque, 1336.
Thuringia, 520. 31. landgrave of, 1226. empire of the west, 1273.

Tibe-

INDEX.

TI.
Tiberiad, battle, 1092. 1189.
Tilladet, 1692.
Tillemont, fack, 1635. taken, 1705.
Tillet, du, 1559. 60.
Tilli, count de, 1623. 26. 27. 31. 32. 93.
Tillieres, James de, 1588.
Tilts, 1148. 1559. p. 310. V. II.
Tinchebrai, battle, 1100.
Tinmouth, count d'Eſtrées, 1690.
Tircomel, Ireland, 1689.
Tire-woman, 1680.
Tiriot, dike, 1627.
Tirol, 1703.
Title, 1644.
Titles, eccleſiaſtic; p. 39. V. I.

TO.
Tobacco, p. 9. V. II.
Toiras, 1627. 36.
Tokay, 1526.
Tokembourg, 1712.
Tolbiac, battle, 496.
Toledo, 1001. 1654.
Tolet, cardinal, 1593. p. 9. V. II.
Toll, 1255.
Tomb of Childeric, 1655.
Tongres, town, 491. 1703.
Tontine, 1689.
Torbay, 1688.
Torci, 1689. 96. 99. 1709.
Torf, 1690.
Toris, 1711.
Torres, Las, 1706.
Tortenſon, general of the Swedes, 1642. 45.
Tortona, 833. 1642. 43.
Tortoſa, council, 1171...1648. 50. 1708.
Touchard, cardinal de Bourbon, 1591.
Touchet, Mary, 1566.
Toul, 1552. 85. 1648.
Toulon, 1681. 1707.
Toulouſe, 508. 11. Charibert, 628. 30. kingdom of Aquitaine, 800. council, 840. count, 1156.

Vol. II.

71. count de Montfort, 1215. king John, 1362. arrets, 1589. 94. duke de Montmorenci, 1632. edict, 1679. count of, war, 1156. Raimond, VI. 1206. 15. 26. VII. 1249. count, 1226. 70. Alphonſo, 1270. 1304. 31. floral games, 1324. reunited, 1451. precedence, 1694. Britany, 1695. 1704. Lewis-Alexander, count de, 1598. 1704. 14. count de, 1697. p. 299. V. II. diocese, 1292. univerſity, 1215. parliament, 1305.
Tour, la; ſee *Bouillon* and *Turenne*; Henry 1591.
Touraine, 594. Philip-Auguſtus, 1400. 15. duke d'Alençon, 1576.
Tournaments, 1148. 1547. 59. p. 310. &c. V. II.
Tournay, 575. 76. 1340. 1513. 18. 21. 1667. 68. 1706. 09.
Tournelles, Lewis XII. 1515. Catharine de Medicis, 1564. dutcheſs, d'Angouleme, 1547.
Tournon, cardinal, 1539. 41. 55. 61. 62.
Tours, 543. 70. 732. archbiſhop, 996. ſtates, 1468. 84. 1505. Frederic, 1501. council, 1510. parliament, 1589. 91. 94. duke de Guiſe, 1591.
Tourville, 1683. 85. 88, 90. 92-94.

TR.
Trade, 1200.
Traerbac, caſtle, 1702-04.
Tragedies, 1179.
Tranſactions, philoſophical, 1666.
Tranſjurana, kingdom of Burgundy, 888.
Tranſlation, 892. of the holy ſee, 1305. of the parliament, 1589.
Tranſtamare, Henry, 1366. 67. 71. 1516.
Tranſylvania, 1326. 75. 1699.
Treaſon of Campobaſs, 1477. M. de Leganes, 1705. duke de Medina Cœli, 1710.

D d

Trea-

INDEX.

Treasures, the king's, 992. of the charters, p. 177. V. I.
Treaties, of St. Clair, 912. between St. Lewis and James I. king of Arragon, 1255. Bretigni, 1360. Landes de Beaumanoir, 1364. Guerande, 1364. 65. Troyes, 1420. Swiss, 1453. Conflans, St. Maur, 1465. Bouvines, 1474. Piquigni, 1475. truce of a hundred years, 1477. Arras, 1482. Montargis, 1485. Lyons, 1503. 14. with Charles V. 1515. Noyon, 1516. Fribourg, 1516. with Leo X. 1517. Madrid, 1525. 26. Cambray, 1529. Barcelona, 1529. Nuremberg, 1532. Chateau-Cambresis, 1559. Peronne, 1576. in favour of the league, 1585. league offensive and defensive, 1596. Vervins, 1598. Lyons, 1601. Brusol, 1610. St. Menehoud, 1614. Santen, 1614. Asti, 1615. Loudun, 1616. Pavia, 1617. Angouleme, 1619. Catholics and Evangelics, 1620. Madrid, 1621. Compiegne, 1624. Monçon, 1615. Susa, 1629. Ratisbon, 1630. St. Germain, 1671. Querasque, Millefleurs, 1631. Vic, 1631. Liverdun, 1632. Charmes, 1633. Sweden, 1634. France and Holland, 1634. Gaston with Spain, 1634. Paris, 1635. Weimar, 1635. of commerce, 1635. Wismar, 1636. Landgrave of Hesse, 1636. 40. St. Germain, 1641. Spain, 1642. of exchange, 1642. Savoy, 1642. with the States-general, 1644. with Portugal, 1644. Munster, 1648. between Cromwell and Holland, 1655. Westphalia, 1657. Pyrenees, 1659. Oliva, 1660. Vincennes, 1661. Montmartre, 1662. Pisa, 1662. of Breda, 1667. of the triple alliance, 1668. of Aix-la-Chapelle, 1668. of neutrality, 1673. Nimeguen, 1678. with England and Holland, 1687. with Savoy, 1696. Ryswick, 1697. Utrecht, 1713. Vienna, (1738.) 1688. Altena, 1689. Carlowits, 1699. Pruth, 1699. Belgrade, 1699. Vienna, 1700. Arraw, 1712. enumeration of treaties signed at Utrecht, 1713. 15. Radstadt, 1714. Baden, 1714. of commerce, 1714. of barrier, 1715.

Trebisond, empire, 1204.
Trent, Trentin, council, 1387. protest, 1551. inclosure, 1563. 79. passage of the mountains, 1703.
Tresmes, dutchy and peerage, 1648. duke de, 1669.
Treves, 511.
Trevoux, 1642.
Trials, 831.
Triboulet, fool, 1539.
Tribunal, N. Rienzi, 1352.
Tribur, 1056.
Tribute, Chilperic, 562. Salomon, 851. St. Peter's pence, 855. kingdom of England, 1206.
Trichet, king's printing-house, 1642.
Trimouille, la, 1428. 31. 88. 98. 1500. 01. 03. 09. 13. 21. 23. Charlotte, 1588. duke de la, 1596. 1614.
Trin, 1639. 43. 58.
Trinity, 1141.
Tripoli, 1681. 85.
Triumvirate, 1560.
Trivulce, 1499. 1509. 11. 15.
Tromp, 1639. 53. 65. 66. 73. 74. 76.
Trompette, Chateau, 1451.
Troops, regular, 1214.
Troubadours, 1324.
Trouin, du Gué, 1697.
Troyes, council, 877. 1103. p. 137.

INDEX:

V. I. treaty, 1420. 28. conference, 1563.
Truce of the lord, 1040. betwixt France and England, 1230. betwixt England and the emperor, 1340. between Lewis XI. and the duke of Burgundy, 1475. between Lewis XII. and Ferdinand, 1513. 14. with the leaguers, 1593. between Holland and Spain, 1609. between Holland and Portugal, 1641. between Leopold and the Turk, 1664. of Ratisbon, 1684.
Trucciacum, 593.

TU.

Tubingen, 1647.
Tudelingen, battle, 1643.
Tudesque, language, p. 101. V. I.
Tudert, John, 1457.
Tudor, Owen, 1420. 85.
Tunis, St. Lewis, 1269....1320. 90. 1536. 1685.
Turks, Turky, Ottomans, 1204. 96. 1394. 1451. 1508. 22. 51. 65. 71. 72. 88. 1664. 69. treaty, 1676. 82-86. 88. 91. 92. 94. 99. 1711. 14.
Turenne, de la Tour, 1579. 91. viscount de, 1636. 38. 40. 43-48. 50-58. 60. 63. 67. 68. 70. 72-75. prince de, 1685.
Turin, duke of Savoy, 1662. the princes, 1639... 40. the young duke, 1645....93. prince Eugene, 1706.
Turkheim, battle, 1675.
Tuscany, marquis of, 877. dukes of, 1555. Alexander de Medicis, 1530. Philip II. 1557... 98. equestrian statue, 1614. Cosmo III. 1660. house of Lorrain, 1675.
Tuscans, 1494.
Tutelage, Clovis, 644. Theobald, 714. Philip, 1056. 60. Frederic, 1206. Lewis IX. 1226.... p. 230. V. I. ordinances, 1371, 80. 91. Charles of Austria, 1505. Mary de Medicis, 1610. Amadeus of Savoy, 1637. Anne of Austria, 1643.

TY.

Tycho, 1660.

V.

VAcancy, of the holy see, 1242. 1313. in curia, p. 314. V. II.
Vacquerie, p. 311. V. I.
Vado, sea fight, 1711.
Vagne, count de la, 1242.
Vair, du, 1621.
Val de Grace, 1645. p. 91. V. II.
Val, des Dunes, 1047. des Ecoliers, 1215.
Valais, 888. 1305.
Valangin, the king of Prussia, 1707. 13.
Valavoir, marquis de, 1675.
Valbelle, chevalier de, 1674.
Valcourt, marshal d'Humieres, 1689.
Valençai, commander, 1628.
Valence, 1656. 96. 1707.
Valencia, d'Alcantara, 1705.
Valenciennes, 1656. 77. 78.
Valentina, of Milan, 1387, 1408 98.
Valentinois, count, 1445.... 53. 98. dutchess of, 1547. 53. 58. 59. 66. dutchy, 1641.
Valeri, 1569.
Valette, grand-master, 1565. cardinal de la, 1630. 35-37. 39 42. duke de la, 1638.

Valladolid,

INDEX.

Valladolia, king of Spain, 1710.
Valliere, la, dutchy and peerage, 1667. Choify, 1695. dutchefs of, p. 91. V. II.
Vallot, 1658.
Valois, branch, 1328. 1589. princes, 1515. peerage, p. 259. V. I. John, 1340. duke de, 1505. marriage, 1599. Henry, 1145. Charles, 1283. 85. 92. 96. 99. 1302. 05. 14. 15. 24. 28. 31. St. Felix de, p.121.V.I.
Vals, battle, 1642.
Valteline, treaty, 1621. war, 1624. 25. 35. 37.
Vanbuningen, 1672.
Vance, Sebaftian, p. 435. V. I.
Vandals, 534.
Vanden-Ende, 1674.
Vannes, rituals, 1584.
Vardes, 1665.
Varnes, 595.
Vaffals, 922. 92. 1108. 16. 20. 1206. 30. 69. p. 95. V. I. 291. V. II. &c. Edward, 1369.
Vaffi, maffacre, 1562.
Vatican, 1585.
Vauban, 1688. 92. 93. 1703. 06. Dupuis, 1710.
Vaubecourt, 1703.
Vaubonnes, 1703. 13.
Vaubrun, 1675.
Vaucelles, truce, 1556.
Vaucouleurs, maid of Orleans, 1428.
Vaudemont, 1431. 76. 1674. 75. 95. 1701.
Vaudrevange, defeat, 1635.
Vaudreuil, 585.
Vaugelas, 1650.
Vaujour, 1657.
Vautier, the queen's phyfician, 1631.

VE.

Vau, le, 1665.
Veil, religious, 1321.
Veillane, 1630. 91.

Velafco, Ferdinand, 1595. count de, 1697.
Vellei, le, 534.
Velleius Paterculus, 1663.
Venaiffin, count, 1274. 1348.
Venafque, 1711. 12.
Vence, baron de, 1245.
Vendome, Francis de, 1475. the duke, 1523. Cæfar Monfieur, 1598. legitimation, 1602. 14. 26. 43. 48. 50. 53. 55. 61. Alexander, 1614. 43. duke de, 1675. 86. 92-97. 1702-06. 08. 10. 12. grand prior, 1704. 05. cardinal, 1590.
Venerable, Peter, 1140.
Venerande, 593.
Venerie, 1693.
Veneur, Tannegui le, 1572. 88.
Venice, Venetians, dukes, 803. Cyprus, 1189. IV. crufade, 1204. crown of thorns, 1230. fhips, 1269. war in Italy, 1494. 1501. league of Cambray, 1508. 09. 11-13. Francis I. 1515. 16. 22. league, 1525. peace with the Turks, 1572. Henry III. 1574. Henry IV. 1589. interdict, 1606. 07. Mantua, 1613. 30. confpiracy, 1618. league, 1623. duke de Rohan, 1629. 38. mediators, 1646. Jefuits, 1657. Candia, 1660. precedency of France, 1661. league of Augfburg, 1687. Lepanto, 1692. Chio, 1694. Carlowitz, 1699. Turks, 1714.
Venlo, bombs, 1588.... 1702.
Ventadour, madam de, 1661.
Verberie, Pepin, 830.
Verceil, 1638. 1704.
Verden, 1648.
Verdun, 1552. 59. 85. 1648. firft prefident, p. 33. V. II.
Verification, parliament, 1563.
Vermandois, Herbert, 928. count de, 992. Raoul, 1145. reunion, 1180....... 1215. Lewis of Bourbon,

INDEX.

Bourbon, p. 93. V. I. admiral, 1669. 83.
Verneuil, marquis de, 1566. 1605.
Vernon, arret, 1255.
Verona, 1516.
Verreikens, negociator, 1508.
Versailles, 655. 1630. 82. 85. 87.
Vertaman, 1690.
Vertot, 1230.
Vertus, Philip, count de, 1407.
Verue, 1625. 1705.
Vervins, truce, 1475. .... 1544. treaty, 1598.
Vesc, de, 1394.
Veserouce, 523.
Vesoul, 1674.
Vespers, Sicilian, 1282. 83.
Vespucius, America, 1492.
Vexin, duke of Normandy, 1032. 1186.

VI.

Vianne, prince de, 1454. 62.
Vic, de, 1594. 1621. treaty, 1631.
Viceroy, of Naples, 1526. Catalonia, 1642. 97.
Victoire, abbey, 1214. p. 159. V. I. place des, 1686.
Victor IV. pope, 1171.
Vidame, 818.
Vienna, siege, 1529. Henry III. 1574. siege, 1683. court, 1689. 94.
Vienne, town, 500. archbishopric, 1120. John de, 1380. council, 1309.
Viennois, count, 1037. .... 1349.
Vieuville, la, 1624. 83.
Vieux-Pont, 1706.
Vigevano, 1645.
Vignacourt, Adrian de, 1697.
Vignamont, 1694. lines, 1705.
Vignaros, M. de Vendome, 1712.
Vignerod, marriage, 1620. Aiguillon, 1638.
Vigo, port of, 1702.
Viguerie, 1711.

Villacerf, 1691. 99.
Villadarias, 1704.
Villane, 1523.
Villareal, count de Las-Torres, 1706.
Villaret, 1309.
Villars, Honorat de Savoy, 1572. marquis de, 1671. marshal de, 1660. 77. 1702-09. 11-14. count de, 1707. marchioness, 1689. marquis, 1698.
Villaviciosa, 1658. battle 1665. ... 1710.
Ville, marquis de, 1658.
Villefranche, battle, 1642. ... 54. 91. 1705.
Villemor, 1650.
Villemur, battle, 1592.
Villeneuve, baron de Vence, 1245.
Villequier, madam de, 1445. .... 1474. 87.
Villeroy, Charles IX. 1574. Henry III. 1588. .... 91. marquis de, 1643. p. 45. dutchy and peerage, 1651. marshal of France, 1667. 76. 93. 95. 97. 99. 1701-03. 05. 06.
Villiers, de l'Isle-Adam, 1415. Philip, 1522. 65. George, 1628. madam de, 1674.
Villiers-Cotterets, ordinance, 1539.
Vimery, in Gatinois, 1587.
Vincennes, 1324. 1422. 1643. 50. 52. 61.
Virgil, 789. 1546.
Virgin, blessed, protection, 1638.
Virginia, fleet, 1711.
Virton, 1654.
Viscounts, 818.
Viscounty, 1447. 98. general, 1702. 03.
Visigoths, peace, 508. 31. 34. 65. 85. p. 37. V. I.
Visir, Cara-Mustapha, 1683.
Viterbo, city, 1522.
Vitiges, king of Italy, 536.

INDEX.

Vitri, town, Lewis the young, 1142....1589. Meaux, 1594. l'Hopital, 1617. 35. 43.
Vivant, de, 1707.
Vivarès, 562.
Viviers, 1603.
Vivonne, duke de, 1675. 76. 78.

UK.
Ukraine, the Turks, 1699.

UL.
Ulm, pacification, 1620. duke of Bavaria, 1702. marshal de Villars, 1707.
Ulnits, Imperialists, 1639.
Ultrogote, 558.

UN.
Underwal, Swiss canton, 1305.
Union, Reunion, county of Lyons, 1309. Dauphiny, county of Viennois, 1349. county of Valentinois, 1445. Britany, 1532. council of, 1589.
University, history of, 1215.1663. troubles, 1230. rector, 1371. process, 1594. of Toulouse, 1215. of Montpellier, 1283. of Orleans, 1305. of Orange, 1365. of Poitiers, 1431. of Bourges, 1463. of Rheims, 1548. of Doway, 1562.

VO.
Voerden, 1672.

Voges, 612.
Voisin, secretary of state, 1667. 1709. 14. la, 1680.
Voiture, 1660.
Voragine, Jacobus de, 1269.
Vortigern, 1215.
Vossius, 1663.
Vouglé, battle, 507.
Vow, St. Lewis, 1242. of religion, 1321. 1579. the emperor Charles, 1378.

UR.
Urban II. 1092. IV. 1255. VI. 1379. 82. 83. VIII. 992. 1622. 24. 25. 28. 33. 41. 44.
Urgel, 1650. 57. 91.
Uri, Swiss canton, 1305.
Vrilliere, la, 1639. 43.
Urseline nuns, 1611.
Ursins, madam des, 1703. 14.

US.
Usages, 1514. 15. 21. 47. 59. 1643. 44. 74. p. 409. V. I.
Usson, marquis, 1703.
Usury, 1313.

UT.
Utrecht, 1672. congress, 1712. peace, 1713.

UZ.
Uxés, 1572. 98.

W.

WAAS, 1638. 1703.
Waddon, p. 38. V. I.
Waifre, 767.
Waldeck, prince, 1674. 89-91.
Waldemar, Margaret of, 1391. 1542.

Waldred, 562.
Wales, country, 1305. prince of, 1344. 55. 67. 71. 76. 1688.
Yvain, 1371.

Walstein,

INDEX.

Waiftein, the Imperial general, 1626. 27. 31. 32. 34.
Waldrada, concubine, 863.
War, private, 1803. 1296. intestine, 901. civil, 1258. 1562. 68. 73. 1648. holy, 1390. of thirty years, 1618.
Waradin, 1692.
Warneton, 1645. 78. 1709.
Warnston, 767.
Waroc, 591. 94.
Warty, 1710.
Warsaw, king of Sweden, 1702. of Poland, 1704. battle, 1705.
Warwick, earl of, 1457. 70. 71. treaty, 1678.
Watch, knights of the, 1350.
Waywod, of Transylvania, elected king of Hungary, 1526. 29.
Waters and forests, 1575.

WE.

Weimar, duke, 1626. 34. 39.
Weissemburg, lines, 1703.
Weights, 813. 1321. p. 308. V. II.
Wells, 1320.
Wenceslaus, son of the emperor Charles, 1378.
Wert, John de, 1635. 38.
Wessel, 1672.
Weser, the, 555.
Wessex, 877.
Westminster, houses of parliament, 1646.
Westphalia, advantages, 1623. treaties, 1641.

WH.
Whitehall, Charles I. 1649.

WI.
Wich, 1647. 48.
Wiclef, 1415. p. 275. V. I.

Wild boar, Carloman, 884.
William, duke of Normandy, 942. duke of Aquitaine, 910. the Conqueror, the bastard, 1047. 48. 62. 67. Long-sword, 929. d'Arques, 1047. count of Holland, 1226. 73. Rufus, 1100. See Orange, *bras de fer*, 1026. king of Sicily, 1026. 1186. the Breton, p. 157. V. I. count of Provence, 1245.
Wilworden, 1706.
Wimphen, 1645.
Winnendal, M. la Motte, 1708.
Winter, 1544. 1608. 1709.
Wismar, 1631. treaty, 1636. 48. 75.
Wirtenwal, battle, 1638.
Wirtemberg, prince of, 1692. duke of, 1706. dutchy, 1707.
Wisigarde, 534.
Wistoc, elector of Saxony, 1636.
Witt, John de, 1665. 66. 68. .... 72. Cornelius, 1672.
Wilfegonde, 636.
Wittekind, 780.

WO.

Wolfembuttle, battle, 1641.
Wolgast, 1677.
Wolsey, cardinal, 1515. Francis I. 1518. 22. 25. 34.
Worms, 888. 1103. 1644. 88. 1713.

WR.
Wrangel, 1648. 75. 86.

WU.
Wurtzburg, 1631.

WY.
Wyburg, 1710.

X A.

INDEX.

X.

XAintes, 1242.
Xaintonge, 1369.

du Guefclin,

XI.
Ximenes, 1708.

Y.

YEar, epocha, 743. 1560. 64.

of. See *Wolsey*.

YO.

Yolande, 1226. daughter of Charles VII. 1451.
York, houfe of, 1457. 85. Richard, duke of, 1435. Perkins, 1492. battle, 1644. duke of, 1665. 72. 73. 85. 90. religion, 1673. marriage, 1677. cardinal

YP.
Ypres, knight of, p. 237. V. I.

YV.
Yvain, of Wales, 1371.
Yvetot, 534.
Yvoi, 1022. 1637. 39.
Yvrée, 1554. 1639. cardinal of Savoy, 1641. 1704.

Z.

Z*Achary*, pope, 751.
Zapol, 1526.

ZE.
Zealand, 1424. 1645.
Zedechias, phyfician, 875.
Zell, duke of, 1675.

ZI.
Zizime, 1495.

ZU.
Zuentibold, 898.
Zuric, 1549.
Zutphen, 1672.

ZW.
Zwol, 1672.

FINIS.

The following columns belong to the reign of Hugh Capet, and ought to have been in the 107th page of Vol. I.

The THIRD RACE. 107

MINISTERS.	WARRIORS.	MAGISTRATES.	EMINENT and LEARNED MEN.	
Senefchals. Geoffrey, surnamed *Grifegonelle*, count of Anjou. 987. The office of seneschal was the first of all, and became extinct in the person of Thibaud, who died at the siege of Acre, 1191. Bouchard, count de Melun.	Foulk Nerra, count d'Anjou, 1040. Adelbert, count de la Marche. Joffelin, viscount de Melun. 998. Bouchard, sire de Montmorency, was living in the year 1005. Thibaud File-e-toupe, stem of the lords of Montlheri, was living in the year 1015.	*Chancellors.* Adalberon. 988. Renaud. Gerbert. 1003.	Adalberon. Adson. Folcuin. S. Maieul.	988. 992. 999. 994.

ERRATA.

Besides a few others of less consequence, the reader will be pleased to correct the following mistakes.

VOL. I.

Page 39. l. 15. for *of the kings* r. *of the Franks.* p. 105. col. 2. l. 17. after *Hugh I.* insert *count de Ponthieu.* p. 150. l. 10. from the bottom, after *incapable* insert *conducting.* p. 284. l. 11. from the last, for *Macine* r. *Maine.* p. 317. l. 14. for *John* r. *Joan.* p. 377. l. 10. instead of *for* r. *and.* p. 416. l. 9. from the bottom, for *werex.* *was.*

VOL. II.

Page 89. l. 9. from the bottom, for *a fit of a violent* r. *a violent fit of.* p. 91. col. 1. l. 25. for 1666. r. 1660. p. 106. l. 4. for *Segne* r. *Segre.* p. 124. l. 18. and in the note, for *surannation* r. *renewal.* p. 212. L 4. from the bottom, for *this* r. *his.* p. 228. l. 7. for *returns* r. *returned.* p. 295. l. 4. from the bottom, for *contained* r. *annulled.* p. 304. l. 10. from the bottom, after *Francis* insert *I.*

www.ingramcontent.com/pod-product-compliance
Lightning Source LLC
Chambersburg PA
CBHW022112290426
44112CB00008B/651